2

2

Theory and Practice of Error Control Codes

Richard E. Blahut

▲▼ **ADDISON-WESLEY PUBLISHING COMPANY**

Reading, Massachusetts
Menlo Park, California • London
Amsterdam • Don Mills, Ontario
Sydney

"WORDS ALONE ARE NOTHING"

—motto of the Royal Society

Richard E. Blahut
IBM Corporation
Owego, NY 13827

Library of Congress Cataloging in Publication Data

Blahut, Richard E.
  Theory and practice of error control codes.

  Includes index.
  1. Error-correcting codes (Information theory)
I. Title.
QA268.B54   1983   001.53'9   82-11441
ISBN 0-201-10102-5

ISBN 0-201-10102-5
ABCDEFGHIJ-MA-89876543

Contents

Preface

The topic of error-control codes now fills an important page in the handbook of the practicing design engineer. The current interest contrasts sharply with the early days of the subject, when it was considered impractical for all but the most expensive communication systems. Now the need for error control is far greater, and the capability of electronic circuits is so much improved that the subject has enjoyed a growth in interest. A working knowledge of the topic has become an important asset to anyone involved in the design of modern communication systems or of large digital systems, and this engineering importance shows every sign of continuing to grow. Excellent books on the subject are available, but with emphasis primarily on the mathematical and research aspects of the subject. The traditional emphasis is on finding the best code. Although this is important to the future of the subject, the designer is principally concerned with what he can build.

This book is written for the student or the engineer who is interested in error-control codes because his goal is to use them in applications. Having said this, however, we must also say that it is not possible to divorce practice from theory. Although it is not necessary for the designer to master the subject in all the areas that are important to the researchers of the field, he cannot function satisfactorily with only a superficial knowledge of the subject or without the necessary mathematical background.

The book began as class notes for a course on error-control codes that the author taught many times, both at Cornell University and for IBM. It was never possible to assume any background in abstract algebra in these classes. Therefore one challenge was to shape the required basic algebra to be rigorous and sufficient, yet to fit it within a few weeks of class time. Because of this constraint, I have tried to include in the book all of the algebra necessary for an introduction to error-control codes and to supply proofs or plausibility arguments throughout. Without at least this, the engineer cannot be sure of his pilings.

During the years that this course was given, it shifted from a graduate course to one containing a mixture of graduates and undergraduates, and thus care was taken to keep explanations simple and, as far as possible, in engineering terms. Mathematical sophistication was kept at the lowest level possible, but many will still find the level to be quite high in some areas.

A theorem-proof format is used rather than the more discursive format common to most engineering texts. The theorem-proof format enables the reader to skip the proofs when it is expedient and to find the main facts when they are needed. Also, for one who is serious about rigor, the theory must be broken down into digestible fragments.

I have tried to emphasize the finite field Fourier transform because it is so quickly grasped by one with an engineering background, and because to the engineer it is rich in intuitive insight. The use of the Fourier transform also makes it clear that error-control coding is a branch of the subject of digital signal processing. Although the Mattson-Solomon polynomial has priority as a similar way of presenting the same ideas, it forces the engineering student to learn a new language when he already knows one just as applicable.

The close relationship between the subject of error-control codes and the subject of digital signal processing is stressed whenever possible. Most treatments obscure this relationship because the two subjects had very different historical origins: one subject was developed largely by algebraists, and the other was developed largely by engineers. Aside from the use of different number systems—Galois fields as opposed to the field of complex numbers—the techniques used are similar. The two subjects both are strongly based on Fourier transforms, FIR filters, cyclic convolutions, and the interplay between the time-domain and frequency-domain properties of sequences.

The emphasis throughout is on the design of shift-register circuits to implement the encoders and decoders. As far as possible, the engineering terminology of filter theory is used. The shift-register circuits are designed to illustrate the ideas as clearly as possible. Often, modifications that reduce the number of components will be apparent. Of course the encoders and decoders are often implemented in software, but even then, some thinking about a shift-register implementation will help simplify the program. My view is always that the final test of a code or of an algorithm is in the cost of the encoder/decoder. Codes with superior minimum distance are of little interest to the engineer if no good algorithm is known for decoding them. Good codes need good decoders, and good decoding algorithms have been difficult to find. In the end, it may be just as fruitful for theoreticians to search out new codes to fit known decoders as it is to search out new decoders to fit known codes.

In selecting notation and terminology, there is always a clash between precedent and internal consistency. Precedent was carefully considered in choosing notation. In some cases, however, I felt that it was more important to achieve pedagogical clarity and consistency. For example, in the discussions of convolutional codes, I choose notation that emphasizes the similarities with block codes, even though it sometimes differs from the notation found in much of the literature of convolutional codes.

Richard E. Blahut

ACKNOWLEDGMENTS

It is impossible to sort all of life's conversations and readings into those that had a major influence on this book and those that had none; every such partition is a distortion. At best I can mention those influences of which I am most aware. Professor Toby Berger was a friend and consultant throughout the years of writing; he always gave the right advice. Professor D. L. Sarwate carefully read through most of the manuscript and saved me from many errors and clumsy passages. Valuable advice and criticism also came from C. L. Chen, A. ElGamal, M. R. Best, N. M. Blachman, T. Hashimoto, K. Kobayashi, M. Shimada, G. Ungerboeck, W. Vanderkulk, S. Winograd, and S. C. West. The books and papers that had a large influence on this book, either directly or indirectly, are listed in the references. Many other papers had a lesser influence; the list would be endless.

I am indebted to the International Business Machines Corporation for supporting the preparation of this book, and to Cornell University for providing the classroom settings where the book could be tested. The book also matured during classes I taught at the South China Institute of Technology.

The most important participant in the preparation of this book was Barbara, my wife. She helped in many ways, physical and psychological, quietly absorbing some of my deflected frustrations, but sharing the days that went right. And finally, this book is dedicated to Edward J. Blahut, Andrew S. Chamer, and Carl A. Krachenfels. A little of them lives here.

REB

CHAPTER 1
Introduction

Digital signal processing is an engineering subject with many branches. Among them is the theory of error-control codes, a special topic with its own goals and its own arithmetic systems. Within these arithmetic systems, however, the most fruitful techniques are the familiar operations of signal processing—operations that involve convolutions, Fourier transforms, filters, and shift registers. Error-control coding is a topic with its own history and charm and has faces that touch many other subjects.

The engineering problem treated by the subject of error-control codes is that of protecting digital data against the errors that occur during transmission through a communication channel. Many ingenious error-protection techniques have been developed based on a rich mathematical theory, and they have matured into an important engineering subject with frequent applications.

1

The need for error control arises from the large volume of data now communicated or stored, much of which is very sensitive to error. A mature theory of good codes and good coding algorithms is available to meet this need. In addition, the rapid advances in digital integrated circuitry have made possible the implementation of these algorithms.

1.1 THE DISCRETE COMMUNICATION CHANNEL

A communication system connects a data source to a data user through a channel. Microwave links, coaxial cables, telephone circuits, and even magnetic tapes are examples of channels. The designer of the communication system develops devices that prepare the input and process the output of the channel. It is traditional to partition the major functions of a digital communication system as in the block diagram of Fig. 1.1. Data, which enters the communication system from the data source, is first processed by a source encoder designed to represent the source data more compactly. This interim representation is a sequence of symbols called the *source codeword*. Then, the data is processed by the channel encoder, which transforms a sequence of source codeword symbols into another sequence called the *channel codeword*. The channel codeword is a new, longer sequence that has more redundancy than the source codeword. Each symbol in the channel codeword might be represented by a bit or, perhaps, by a group of bits. Next, the modulator converts each symbol of the channel codeword into a corresponding analog symbol from a finite set of possible analog symbols. The sequence of analog

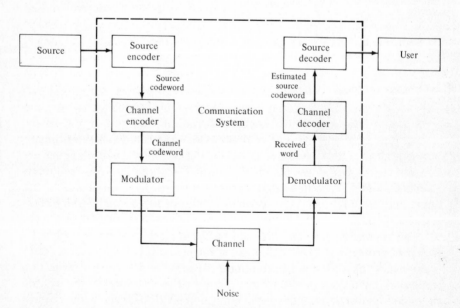

Figure 1.1   Block diagram of a digital communication system.

symbols is transmitted through the channel. Because the channel is subject to various types of noise, distortion, and interference, the channel output differs from the channel input. The demodulator converts each received channel output signal in the sequence into one of the channel codeword symbols. Each demodulated symbol is a best estimate of the transmitted symbol, but the demodulator makes some errors because of channel noise. The demodulated sequence of symbols is called the *received word*. Because of error, the symbols of the received word do not always match those of the channel codeword.

The channel decoder uses the redundancy in a channel codeword to correct the errors in the received word and then produces an estimate of the source codeword. If all errors are corrected, the estimated source codeword matches the original source codeword. The source decoder performs the inverse operation of the source encoder and delivers its output to the user.

This book deals only with the design of the channel encoder and decoder, a subject known as *error-control coding*. The data compression or data compaction functions performed by the source encoder and source decoder are not discussed here, nor are the modulator and the demodulator. The channel encoder and decoder will be referred to herein simply as the encoder and the decoder, respectively.

1.2 THE HISTORY OF ERROR-CONTROL CODING

The history of error-control coding began in 1948 with the publication of a famous paper by Claude Shannon. Shannon showed that associated with any communication channel is a number C (measured in bits per second), called the capacity of the channel, which has the following significance. Whenever the transmission rate R (in bits per second) required of a communication system is less than C, it is possible to design for the channel a communication system using error-control codes, whose probability of output error is as small as desired. In fact, an important footnote to Shannon's theory of information tells us that it is wasteful to build a channel that is too good; it is more economical to make use of a code. Shannon did not, however, tell us how to find suitable codes; his achievement was to prove that they exist. Throughout the 1950s much effort was devoted to finding explicit constructions for classes of codes that would produce the promised arbitrarily small probability of error, but progress was meager. In the 1960s, for the most part, there was less obsession with this ambitious goal; rather, coding research began to settle down to a prolonged attack along two main avenues.

The first avenue has a strong algebraic flavor and is concerned primarily with *block codes*. The first block codes were introduced in 1950, when Hamming described a class of single-error-correcting block codes. The Hamming codes were disappointingly weak compared with the far stronger codes promised by Shannon. Despite diligent research, no better class of codes was found until the end of the decade. During this period many codes of short blocklength were found, without any general theory. The major advance came when Bose and Ray-Chaudhuri (1960) and Hocquenghem (1959) found a large class of multiple-error-correcting codes (the BCH codes), and Reed and Solomon (1960) found a related class of codes for nonbinary channels. Although these remain among the most important classes of codes, the theory of the subject since has been greatly strengthened, and new codes are discovered periodically.

The discovery of BCH codes led to a search for practical methods of designing the hardware or software for implementing the encoder and decoder. The first good algorithm was found by Peterson. Later, a powerful algorithm for doing the calculations of Peterson was discovered by Berlekamp and Massey, and its implementation became practical as new digital technology became available.

The second avenue of coding research has a more probabilistic flavor. Early research was concerned with estimating the error probability for the best family of block codes, despite the fact that the best codes were not known. Associated with these studies were attempts to understand encoding and decoding from a probabilistic point of view, and these attempts led to the notion of sequential decoding. Sequential decoding required the introduction of a class of nonblock codes of indefinite length, which can be represented by a tree and can be decoded by algorithms for searching the tree. The most useful tree codes are highly structured codes called *convolutional codes*. These codes can be generated by a linear shift-register circuit that performs a con-volution operation on the information sequence. Convolutional codes were successfully decoded by sequential decoding algorithms in the late 1950s. It is intriguing that a much simpler algorithm—the Viterbi algorithm—for decoding them was not developed until 1967. The Viterbi algorithm gained widespread popularity for convolutional codes of modest complexity, but it is impractical for stronger convolutional codes.

During the decade of the 1970s, these two avenues of research began to combine again. The theory of convolutional codes was studied by the algebraists, who brought new insights to the subject. In the theory of block codes, advances were also made at this time toward the codes promised by Shannon when two different schemes were proposed, one by Justesen and one by Goppa, for designing families of codes that simultaneously can have very large blocklength and very good performance. Both schemes, however, have practical limitations, and further advances are awaited. Meanwhile, as the decade of the 1980s opened, encoders and decoders began to appear frequently in newly designed digital communication systems and digital storage systems.

1.3 APPLICATIONS

Because the development of error-control codes was motivated primarily by problems in communications, the terminology of error-control coding has been drawn from the subject of communications theory. These codes, how-ever, have many other applications. Codes are used to protect data in com-puter memories and on digital tapes and disks, and to protect against circuit malfunction or noise in digital logic circuits. Codes have also been used for the compression of data, and coding theory is closely related to the theory of the design of statistical experiments.

Applications to communications problems are diversified. Binary data commonly is transmitted between computer terminals, between aircraft, and from spacecraft. Codes can be used to achieve reliable communication even when the received signal power is close to the thermal noise power. And, as the electromagnetic spectrum becomes ever more crowded with man-made signals, error-control coding becomes an even more important subject because it permits communication links to function reliably in the presence of interference. In military applications it often is essential to employ an error-control code to protect against intentional enemy interference.

Many communication systems have limitations on transmitted power. For example, power is very expensive in communication relay satellites. Error-control codes are an excellent way to reduce power needs, because messages received weakly at their destinations can be recovered correctly with the aid of the code.

Transmissions within computer systems usually are intolerant of even very low error rates, because a single error can destroy a computer program. Error-control coding is becoming important in these applications. Bits can be packed more tightly into some kinds of computer memories (magnetic tapes, for example) by using an error-control code.

Another kind of communication system structure is a time-division multiple-access system, in which each of a number of users is assigned some predetermined time slots (intervals) during which he is permitted to transmit. A long binary message is divided into packets, and one packet is transmitted during an assigned time slot. Occasional packets may be lost because of synchronization or routing problems. A suitable error-control code protects against this loss, because missing packets can be deduced from known packets.

Communication is also important within a system. In today's complex digital systems, a large data flow may exist between subsystems. Digital autopilots, digital process-control systems, digital switching systems, and digital radar signal-processing all are systems that involve large amounts of digital data that must be shared by multiple interconnected subsystems. This data might be transferred either by dedicated lines or by a more sophisticated time-shared data bus system. In either case, error-control techniques are becoming important to ensure proper performance.

Eventually, error-control codes and the circuits for encoding and decod-ing will reach the point where they can handle massive amounts of data. One may anticipate that error-control techniques will play a central role in all communication systems of the future. It seems likely that the phonograph records, tapes, and television waveforms of the future will employ digital messages protected by error-control codes. Scratches in a record or interference in a received signal will be completely suppressed by the coding as long as the errors are less serious than the capability designed into the error-control code.

1.4 ELEMENTARY CONCEPTS

The subject of error-control coding is at once simple and difficult. It is simple in the sense that the problem is easily explained to any technically trained person. It is difficult in the sense that the development of a solution—and only a partial solution at that—occupies the length of this book and requires a digression into topics of modern algebra before it can be studied.

Suppose that all data of interest can be represented as binary (coded) information; that is, as a sequence of zeros and ones. This binary information is to be transmitted through a channel that causes occasional errors. The purpose of a code is to add extra symbols to the information symbols so that errors may be found and corrected at the receiver. That is, a sequence of data symbols is represented by some longer sequence of symbols with enough redundancy to protect the data.

A binary code of size M and blocklength n is a set of M binary words of length n called codewords. Usually, $M = 2^k$ for an integer k, and the code is referred to as an (n, k) binary code.

For example, we can make up the following code.

$$\mathscr{C} = \begin{cases} 1\ 0\ 1\ 0\ 1 \\ 1\ 0\ 0\ 1\ 0 \\ 0\ 1\ 1\ 1\ 0 \\ 1\ 1\ 1\ 1\ 1 \end{cases}$$

This is a very poor (and very small) code with $M = 4$, and $n = 5$, but it satisfies the requirements of the definition. We can use this code to represent 2-bit binary numbers by using the following (arbitrary) correspondence:

$$0\ 0 \leftrightarrow 1\ 0\ 1\ 0\ 1$$

$$0\ 1 \leftrightarrow 1\ 0\ 0\ 1\ 0$$

$$1\ 0 \leftrightarrow 0\ 1\ 1\ 1\ 0$$

$$1\ 1 \leftrightarrow 1\ 1\ 1\ 1\ 1$$

If one of the four 5-bit codewords is received, we then suppose that the corresponding two bits is the correct information. If an error is made, we receive a different 5-bit word. We then attempt to find the most likely transmitted word to serve as our estimate of the original two information bits. For example, if we receive 01100, then we presume that 01110 was the transmitted codeword, and, hence, 10 is the information word.

The code of the example is not a good code because it is not able to correct many patterns of errors. We wish to pick codes so that every codeword is as different as possible from every other codeword, and we wish to do this especially when the blocklength is long.

The first purpose of this book is to find good codes. Although superficially this may seem like a simple task, it is in fact exceedingly difficult, and many good codes are as yet undiscovered.

To the inexperienced it may seem that it should suffice to define the requirements of a good code and then let a computer search through the set of all possible codes. But how many codes exist for a given (n, k)? Each codeword is a sequence of n binary symbols, and there are 2^k such codewords. Therefore a code is described by $n \cdot 2^k$ binary symbols. Altogether there are $2^{n \cdot 2^k}$ ways of picking these binary symbols. Hence, the number of different (n, k) codes is $2^{n \cdot 2^k}$. Of course a great many of these codes are of little value (as when two codewords are equal), but either the search must check these, or some theory must be developed for excluding them.

For example, take $(n, k) = (40, 20)$, which is a very modest code by today's standards. Then the number of such codes is larger than $10^{10,000,000}$, an inconceivably large number. Hence, undisciplined search procedures are worthless.

In general, we define block codes over an arbitrary finite alphabet, say the alphabet with q symbols $\{0, 1, 2, \ldots, q - 1\}$. At first sight, it might seem an unnecessary generalization to introduce alphabets other than the binary alphabet. For reasons of efficiency, however, many channels today are nonbinary, and codes for these channels must be nonbinary. In fact, error-control codes for nonbinary channels are often quite good and thus can reinforce the reasons for using a nonbinary channel. It is a trivial matter to represent binary source data in terms of a q-ary alphabet, especially if q is a power of 2; as it usually is in practice.

□ **Definition 1.4.1** A *block code* of size M over an alphabet with q symbols is a set of M q-ary sequences of length n called *codewords*. □

If $q = 2$, the symbols are called *bits*. Usually, $M = q^k$ for some integer k, and we shall only be interested in this case, calling the code an (n, k) code. Each sequence of k q-ary information symbols can be associated with a sequence of n q-ary symbols comprising a codeword.

There are two basic classes of codes: block codes and tree codes. These are illustrated in Fig. 1.2. A block code represents a block of k information symbols by an n-symbol codeword. The *rate R* of a block code* is defined by

---

*This rate is dimensionless, or perhaps measured in units of bits/bit or symbols/symbol. It should be distinguished from another use of the term *rate* measured in bits/second through a channel. Yet another definition, $R = (k/n) \log_e q$, which has the units of nats/symbol, with a nat equaling $\log_2 e$ bits is in use. The definition $R = (k/n) \log_2 q$, which has the units of bits/symbol, is also popular.

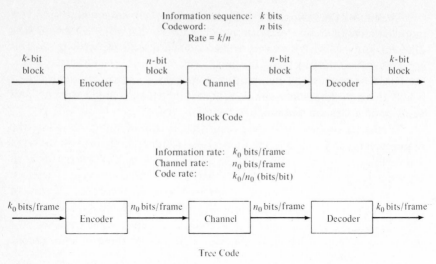

Figure 1.2   Basic classes of codes.

$$R = \frac{k}{n}.$$

A tree code is more complex. It takes a nonending sequence of information symbols at a rate of k_0 symbols per time interval and puts out a continuous sequence of codeword symbols at a rate of n_0 symbols per time interval. We shall defer the study of tree codes until Chapter 12. Initially, we will restrict our attention to block codes.

Whenever a message consists of a large number of bits, it is better in principle to use a single block code of large blocklength than to use a succession of codewords from a shorter block code. The nature of statistical fluctuations is such that a random pattern of errors usually exhibits some clustering of errors. Some segments of the random pattern contain more than the average number of errors, and some segments contain less. Hence, long codewords are considerably less sensitive to random errors than are shorter codewords of the same rate; but, of course, the encoder and decoder may be more complex. As an example, suppose that 1000 information bits are transmitted with a (fictitious) 2000-bit binary codeword that can correct 100 bit errors. Compare this with a scheme for transmitting 100 bits at a time with a 200-bit binary codeword that can correct 10 bit errors per block. Ten such blocks are needed to transmit 1000 bits. This latter scheme can also correct a total of 100 errors, but only if they are properly distributed—10 errors to a 200-bit block. The first scheme can correct 100 errors no matter how they are distributed within the 2000-bit codeword. It is far more powerful.

This heuristic argument can be given a sound theoretical footing, but that is not our purpose here. We only wish to make plausible the fact that good codes are of long blocklength, and that very good codes are of very long blocklength. Such codes can be very hard to find and when found may require complex devices to implement the encoding and decoding operations.

Block codes are judged by three parameters: the blocklength n, the information length k, and the minimum distance d^*. The minimum distance is a measure of the amount of difference between the two most similar codewords. The minimum distance is given by the following two definitions.

□ **Definition 1.4.2** The *Hamming distance* $d(\mathbf{x}, \mathbf{y})$ between two q-ary sequences $\mathbf{x}$ and $\mathbf{y}$ of length n is the number of places in which they differ. □

For an example, take $\mathbf{x} = 10101$, $\mathbf{y} = 01100$, then $d(10101, 01100) = 3$. For another example, take $\mathbf{x} = 30102$, $\mathbf{y} = 21103$, then $d(30102, 21103) = 3$.

□ **Definition 1.4.3** Let $\mathscr{C} = \{\mathbf{c}_i, i = 0, \ldots, M - 1\}$ be a code. Then the *minimum distance* of $\mathscr{C}$ is the Hamming distance of the pair of codewords with smallest Hamming distance. That is,

$$d^* = \min_{\substack{c_i, c_j \in \mathscr{C} \\ i \neq j}} d(\mathbf{c}_i, \mathbf{c}_j)$$

□

An (n, k) block code with minimum distance d^* is also described as an (n, k, d^*) block code.

In the code $\mathscr{C}$ in the first example of this section,

$$d(10101, 10010) = 3$$
$$d(10101, 01110) = 4$$
$$d(10101, 11111) = 2$$
$$d(10010, 01110) = 3$$
$$d(10010, 11111) = 3$$
$$d(01110, 11111) = 2$$

Hence, $d^* = 2$ for this code.

Suppose that a codeword is transmitted, and a single error is made by the channel. Then the received word is at a Hamming distance of 1 from the transmitted codeword. If the distance to every other codeword is larger than 1, then the decoder will properly correct the error if it presumes that the closest codeword to the received word was actually transmitted.

More generally, if t errors occur and if the distance from the received word to every other codeword is larger than t, then the decoder will properly correct the errors if it presumes that the closest codeword to the received word was actually transmitted. This always occurs if

$$d^* \geqslant 2t + 1.$$

It may be possible sometimes to correct certain error patterns with t errors even when this inequality is not satisfied. However, t-error correction cannot be guaranteed if $d^* < 2t + 1$, because it then depends on which codeword is transmitted and on the actual pattern of the t errors within the block.

Figure 1.3 illustrates the geometric situation. Within the space of all q-ary n-tuples, a set of n-tuples is selected and the elements are designated as codewords. If d^* is the minimum distance of this code and t is the largest integer satisfying

$$d^* \geq 2t + 1,$$

then nonintersecting spheres of radius t can be drawn about each of the codewords. A received word in a sphere is decoded as the codeword at the center of that sphere. If t or fewer errors occur, then the received word is always in the proper sphere, and the decoding is correct.

Some received words that have more than t errors will be in a decoding sphere about another codeword and hence will be decoded incorrectly. Other received words that have more than t errors will lie in the interstitial space between decoding spheres. Depending on the requirements of the application, these can be treated in either of two ways.

An *incomplete decoder* decodes only those received words lying in a decoding sphere about a codeword. Other received words have more than the allowable number of errors and are declared by the decoder to be unrecognizable. Such error patterns in an incomplete decoder are called *uncorrectable error patterns*. Most decoders in use are incomplete decoders.

A *complete decoder* decodes every received word as a closest codeword. In geometrical terms, the complete decoder carves up the interstices and

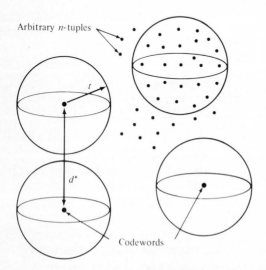

Figure 1.3 Decoding spheres.

attaches portions to each of the spheres so that each point is attached to a closest sphere. Usually, some points are equidistant from several spheres. These are arbitrarily assigned to one of the closest spheres. When more than t errors occur, the complete decoder will often decode incorrectly but occasionally will find the correct codeword. A complete decoder is used when it is better to have a best guess of the message than to have no estimate of the message at all.

We will also deal with channels that make erasures as well as errors. That is, a receiver may be designed to declare a symbol erased when it is received ambiguously, or when the receiver recognizes the presence of interference or a transient malfunction. Such a channel has an input alphabet of size q and an output alphabet of size $q + 1$, and the extra symbol is called an *erasure*. For example, an erasure of 3 from the message 12345 gives 12—45. This should not be confused with another notion known as a *deletion*, which would give 1245.

An error-control code can be used with such a channel. If the code has minimum distance d^*, then any pattern of ρ erasures can be filled if $d^* \geqslant \rho + 1$. Further, any pattern of v errors and ρ erasures can be decoded provided

$$d^* \geqslant 2v + 1 + \rho$$

is satisfied. To prove this, delete from all codewords the ρ components where the receiver has specified erasures. This is a new code whose minimum distance is not smaller than $d^* - \rho$; hence, v errors can be corrected provided the above inequality is satisfied. Thus we can recover the shortened codeword with ρ components erased. Finally, because $d^* \geqslant \rho + 1$, there is only one codeword that agrees with the unerased components; thus the entire codeword can be recovered.

1.5 ELEMENTARY CODES

Some codes are simple enough to be described at the outset.

Simple Parity-Check Codes   These are high-rate codes with poor error performance. Given k bits of information, add a $(k + 1)$th bit so that the total number of ones in a codeword is even. Thus, for example, with $k = 4$,

    0 0 0 0 ↔ 0 0 0 0 0

    0 0 0 1 ↔ 0 0 0 1 1

    0 0 1 0 ↔ 0 0 1 0 1

    0 0 1 1 ↔ 0 0 1 1 0

and so forth. This is a $(k + 1, k)$ or an $(n, n - 1)$ code. The minimum distance is 2, and hence no errors can be corrected. A simple parity-check code is used to detect (but not correct) a single error.

Simple Repetition Codes These are low-rate codes with good error performance. Given a single information bit, repeat it n times. Usually, n is odd.

$$0 \leftrightarrow 0\ 0\ 0\ 0\ 0$$

$$1 \leftrightarrow 1\ 1\ 1\ 1\ 1$$

This is an $(n, 1)$ code. The minimum distance is n, and $\frac{1}{2}(n-1)$ errors can be corrected by assuming that the majority of received bits agree with the correct information bit.

Hamming Codes These are codes that can correct a single error. At this time, we will introduce these codes via a direct descriptive approach. For each m, there is a $(2^m - 1, 2^m - 1 - m)$ Hamming code. When m is large, the rate is close to 1, but the fraction of the total number of bits that can be in error is very small. The (7, 4) Hamming code can be described by the implementation in Fig. 1.4(a). Given four information bits (i_1, i_2, i_3, i_4), let the first four bits of the codeword equal the four information bits. Append three *parity bits* (p_1, p_2, p_3), defined by

$$p_1 = i_1 + i_2 + i_3$$
$$p_2 = i_2 + i_3 + i_4$$
$$p_3 = i_1 + i_2 + i_4.$$

Table 1.1 Hamming (7, 4) code.

0	0	0	0	0	0	0
0	0	0	1	0	1	1
0	0	1	0	1	1	0
0	0	1	1	1	0	1
0	1	0	0	1	1	1
0	1	0	1	1	0	0
0	1	1	0	0	0	1
0	1	1	1	0	1	0
1	0	0	0	1	0	1
1	0	0	1	1	1	0
1	0	1	0	0	1	1
1	0	1	1	0	0	0
1	1	0	0	0	1	0
1	1	0	1	0	0	1
1	1	1	0	1	0	0
1	1	1	1	1	1	1

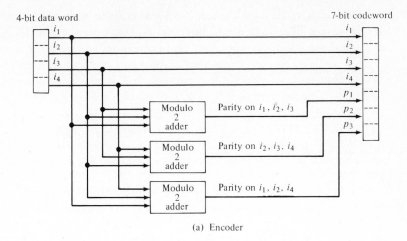

(a) Encoder

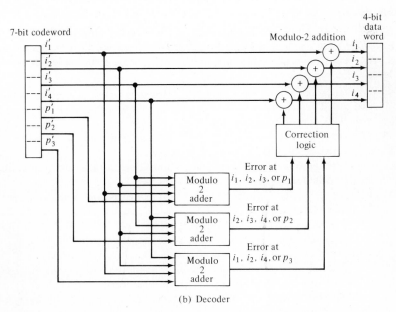

(b) Decoder

Figure 1.4 A simple Hamming (7, 4) encoder/decoder.

Here $+$ denotes modulo-2 addition $(0+0=0,\ 0+1=1,\ 1+0=1,\ 1+1=0)$. The 16 codewords of the Hamming (7, 4) code are shown in Table 1.1. The decoder receives a 7-bit word $\mathbf{v}=(i_1',\ i_2',\ i_3',\ i_4',\ p_1',\ p_2',\ p_3')$. This corresponds to a transmitted codeword with at most one error. The decoder, shown in Fig. 1.4(b), computes

$$s_1 = p_1' + i_1' + i_2' + i_3'$$

$$s_2 = p_2' + i_2' + i_3' + i_4'$$

$$s_3 = p_3' + i_1' + i_2' + i_4'.$$

The 3-bit pattern (s_1, s_2, s_3) is called the *syndrome*. It does not depend on the actual information bits, but only on the error pattern. There are eight possible syndromes: one that corresponds to no error, and one for each of the seven possible single-error patterns. Inspection shows that each of these error patterns has a unique syndrome. Hence, it is a simple matter to design digital logic that will complement the bit location indicated by the syndrome. After correction is complete, the parity bits can be discarded. If two or more errors occur, then the design specification of the code is exceeded, and the code will fail. That is, it will make a wrong correction and put out false information bits.

Of course, the idea of the code is not changed if the bit positions are permuted. All of these variations are called the Hamming (7, 4) code.

PROBLEMS

1.1. A single-error-correcting Hamming code has $2^m - 1$ bits of which m bits are parity bits.

  a. Write (n, k) for the first five nontrivial Hamming codes (starting at $m = 3$).

  b. Calculate their rates.

  c. Write an expression for the probability of decoding error, p_e, when the code is used with a binary channel that makes errors with probability q. How does the probability of error behave with n?

1.2. Design an encoder/decoder for a Hamming (15, 11) code by reasoning as in Fig. 1.4. Omit repetitive details (that is, show the principle).

1.3. a. Find by trial and error a set of four binary words of length 3 such that each word is at least a distance of 2 from every other word.

  b. Find a set of 16 binary words of length 7 such that each word is at least a distance of 3 from every other word.

1.4. a. Describe how to cut 88 circles of 1-inch diameter out of a sheet of paper of width 8.5 inches and length 11 inches. Prove it is not possible to cut out more than 119 circles of 1-inch diameter.

  b. Prove that it is not possible to find 32 binary words, each of length 8 bits, such that every word differs from every other word in at least three places.

1.5. For any (n, k) block code with minimum distance $2t + 1$ or greater, the number of information symbols satisfies

$$n - k \geqslant \log_q \left[1 + \binom{n}{1}(q-1) + \binom{n}{2}(q-1)^2 + \cdots + \binom{n}{t}(q-1)^t \right].$$

Prove this statement, which is known as the Hamming bound.

1.6. The simplest example of a kind of code known as a product code is of the form:

				┌──── Parity on rows
i_{11}	i_{12}	$\cdots$	i_{1k_1}	p_{1,k_1+1}
i_{21}				
$\vdots$		$\vdots$		$\vdots$
i_{k_21}		$\cdots$	$i_{k_2k_1}$	p_{k_2,k_1+1}
Parity on columns → $p_{k_2+1,1}$		$\cdots$	p_{k_2+1,k_1}	p_{k_2+1,k_1+1}

where the $k_1 k_2$ symbols in the upper left block are binary information symbols. This gives a $((k_1 + 1)(k_2 + 1), k_1 k_2)$ code.

a. Show that $p_{k_2 + 1, k_1 + 1}$ is a parity check on both its column and its row.
b. Show that this is a single-error-correcting code.
c. Show that this code is double-error detecting. Give two double-error patterns that cannot be distinguished from one another when using this code.
d. What is the minimum distance of the code?

1.7. Show that Hamming distance has the following three properties:

  (i) $d(\mathbf{x}, \mathbf{y}) \geqslant 0$, with equality if and only if $\mathbf{x} = \mathbf{y}$.
 (ii) $d(\mathbf{x}, \mathbf{y}) = d(\mathbf{y}, \mathbf{x})$.
(iii) Triangle Inequality
     $d(\mathbf{x}, \mathbf{y}) \leqslant d(\mathbf{y}, \mathbf{z}) + d(\mathbf{x}, \mathbf{z})$.

A distance function with these three properties is called a *metric*.

1.8. a. Show that a code $\mathscr{C}$ is capable of detecting any pattern of d or fewer errors if and only if the minimum distance of the code $\mathscr{C}$ is greater than d.
b. Show that a code is capable of correcting any pattern of t or fewer errors if the minimum distance of the code is at least $2t + 1$.
c. Show that a code can be used to correct all patterns of t or fewer errors and simultaneously detect all patterns of d or fewer errors $(d \geqslant t)$ if the minimum distance of the code is at least $t + d + 1$.
d. Show that a code can be used to fill ρ erasures if the minimum distance of the code is at least $\rho + 1$.

1.9. a. Show that if the binary Hamming (15, 11) code is used on a channel that makes two errors, the decoder output is always wrong.
b. By using an overall parity-check bit, show how to extend the Hamming (15, 11) code to a (16, 11) code that corrects all single errors and detects all double errors. What is the minimum distance of this code?

CHAPTER 2
Introduction to Algebra

The search for good error-control codes has relied to a large extent on the powerful and beautiful structures of modern algebra. A variety of important codes based on the structures of polynomial rings and Galois fields have been discovered. Further, this algebraic framework provides the tools necessary to design encoders and decoders. This chapter and Chapter 4 are devoted to developing those topics in algebra that are significant to the theory of error-control codes. The treatment is rigorous, but it is limited in scope to material that will be useful in later chapters.

2.1 THE BINARY FIELD AND THE HEXADECIMAL FIELD

The real numbers form a familiar set of mathematical objects that can be added, subtracted, multiplied, and divided. Similarly, the complex numbers

16

form a set of objects that can be added, subtracted, multiplied, and divided. Both of these arithmetic systems are of fundamental importance in engineering disciplines. We will need to develop other less familiar arithmetic systems that are useful in the study of error-control codes. These new arithmetic systems consist of sets together with operations on the elements. Although we will call the operations "addition," "subtraction," "multiplication," and "division," they need not be the same operations as those of elementary arithmetic.

Modern algebraic theory classifies the many arithmetic systems it studies according to their mathematical strength. These classifications will be defined formally later in this chapter. For now, we have the following loose definitions:

1. *Abelian Group** A set of mathematical objects that can be "added" and "subtracted."
2. *Ring* A set of mathematical objects that can be "added," "subtracted," and "multiplied."
3. *Field* A set of mathematical objects that can be "added," "subtracted," "multiplied," and "divided."

Note that the names of these operations are enclosed in quotation marks because, in general, they are not the conventional operations of arithmetic; these names are used because the operations resemble the conventional operations.

Before we study these concepts formally, we will do some sample calculations in the simplest of all possible fields, namely, the field with only two elements. (The real field has an infinite number of elements.) Let the symbols 0 and 1 denote the two elements in the field. Define the operations of addition and multiplication by

$$0 + 0 = 0 \qquad 0 \cdot 0 = 0$$
$$0 + 1 = 1 \qquad 0 \cdot 1 = 0$$
$$1 + 0 = 1 \qquad 1 \cdot 0 = 0$$
$$1 + 1 = 0 \qquad 1 \cdot 1 = 1.$$

The addition and multiplication defined here are called *modulo-2 addition* and *modulo-2 multiplication*. Note that $1 + 1 = 0$ implies that $-1 = 1$, and $1 \cdot 1 = 1$ implies that $1^{-1} = 1$. With these observations, it is easy to verify that subtraction and division are always defined, except for division by zero. The alphabet of two symbols, 0 and 1, together with modulo-2 addition and modulo-2 multiplication is called the field of two elements and, for reasons given in Chapter 4, is denoted by the label $GF(2)$.

---

*An abelian group is a special case of a group. The arithmetic operation in a general group is too weak to be called addition.

The familiar ideas of algebra can be used with the above arithmetic. The following set of equations in $GF(2)$ provides an example.

$$X + Y + Z = 1$$
$$X + Y \quad\ = 0$$
$$X \quad\ + Z = 1$$

This set can be solved by subtracting the third equation from the first to get $Y = 0$. Then from the second equation $X = 0$, and from the first equation $Z = 1$. Substitution of this solution into the original set of equations verifies that it is correct.

For an alternative solution, we assume that all the usual techniques of linear algebra can be proved to hold in $GF(2)$. The determinant is computed as follows:

$$D = \det \begin{bmatrix} 1 & 1 & 1 \\ 1 & 1 & 0 \\ 1 & 0 & 1 \end{bmatrix} = 1 \cdot \begin{bmatrix} 1 & 0 \\ 0 & 1 \end{bmatrix} - 1 \cdot \begin{bmatrix} 1 & 0 \\ 1 & 1 \end{bmatrix} + 1 \cdot \begin{bmatrix} 1 & 1 \\ 1 & 0 \end{bmatrix}$$
$$= 1 \cdot 1 - 1 \cdot 1 - 1 \cdot 1 = -1 = 1.$$

We can solve the set of equations by Cramer's rule:

$$X = D^{-1} \begin{bmatrix} 1 & 1 & 1 \\ 0 & 1 & 0 \\ 1 & 0 & 1 \end{bmatrix} = 0 \qquad Y = D^{-1} \begin{bmatrix} 1 & 1 & 1 \\ 1 & 0 & 0 \\ 1 & 1 & 1 \end{bmatrix} = 0$$

$$Z = D^{-1} \begin{bmatrix} 1 & 1 & 1 \\ 1 & 1 & 0 \\ 1 & 0 & 1 \end{bmatrix} = 1$$

A second example of a field is a hexadecimal field. This field has exactly 16 elements, which can be denoted by the symbols 0, 1, 2, 3, 4, 5, 6, 7, 8, 9, A, B, C, D, E, and F. The addition and multiplication tables for this field are shown in Fig. 2.1. Notice that addition and multiplication are quite different from that which is familiar from the real numbers. The tables are internally consistent, however, and allow subtraction and division. For division, $x \div y = x \cdot (y^{-1})$, where y^{-1} is that element of the field satisfying $y \cdot y^{-1} = 1$. Inspection of the multiplication table shows that every nonzero element has an inverse, and, hence, division is always defined except for division by zero.

Most of the techniques of linear algebra, such as matrix operations, can be justified for an arbitrary field. Because of this, fields with a finite number of elements will prove very useful. We shall study these fields and find a method of constructing the addition and multiplication tables that will produce a field even when the number of elements is large. In time we shall see that finite fields with q elements can be constructed when, and only when,

+	0	1	2	3	4	5	6	7	8	9	A	B	C	D	E	F
0	0	1	2	3	4	5	6	7	8	9	A	B	C	D	E	F
1	1	0	3	2	5	4	7	6	9	8	B	A	D	C	F	E
2	2	3	0	1	6	7	4	5	A	B	8	9	E	F	C	D
3	3	2	1	0	7	6	5	4	B	A	9	8	F	E	D	C
4	4	5	6	7	0	1	2	3	C	D	E	F	8	9	A	B
5	5	4	7	6	1	0	3	2	D	C	F	E	9	8	B	A
6	6	7	4	5	2	3	0	1	E	F	C	D	A	B	8	9
7	7	6	5	4	3	2	1	0	F	E	D	C	B	A	9	8
8	8	9	A	B	C	D	E	F	0	1	2	3	4	5	6	7
9	9	8	B	A	D	C	F	E	1	0	3	2	5	4	7	6
A	A	B	8	9	E	F	C	D	2	3	0	1	6	7	4	5
B	B	A	9	8	F	E	D	C	3	2	1	0	7	6	5	4
C	C	D	E	F	8	9	A	B	4	5	6	7	0	1	2	3
D	D	C	F	E	9	8	B	A	5	4	7	6	1	0	3	2
E	E	F	C	D	A	B	8	9	6	7	4	5	2	3	0	1
F	F	E	D	C	B	A	9	8	7	6	5	4	3	2	1	0

(a) Addition Table

×	0	1	2	3	4	5	6	7	8	9	A	B	C	D	E	F
0	0	0	0	0	0	0	0	0	0	0	0	0	0	0	0	0
1	0	1	2	3	4	5	6	7	8	9	A	B	C	D	E	F
2	0	2	4	6	8	A	C	E	3	1	7	5	B	9	F	D
3	0	3	6	5	C	F	A	9	B	8	D	E	7	4	1	2
4	0	4	8	C	3	7	B	F	6	2	E	A	5	1	D	9
5	0	5	A	F	7	2	D	8	E	B	4	1	9	C	3	6
6	0	6	C	A	B	D	7	1	5	3	9	F	E	8	2	4
7	0	7	E	9	F	8	1	6	D	A	3	4	2	5	C	B
8	0	8	3	B	6	E	5	D	C	4	F	7	A	2	9	1
9	0	9	1	8	2	B	3	A	4	D	5	C	6	F	7	E
A	0	A	7	D	E	4	9	3	F	5	8	2	1	B	6	C
B	0	B	5	E	A	1	F	4	7	C	2	9	D	6	8	3
C	0	C	B	7	5	9	E	2	A	6	1	D	F	3	4	8
D	0	D	9	4	1	C	8	5	2	F	B	6	3	E	A	7
E	0	E	F	1	D	3	2	C	9	7	6	8	4	A	B	5
F	0	F	D	2	9	6	4	B	1	E	C	3	8	7	5	A

(b) Multiplication Table

Figure 2.1   The Hexadecimal field.

q is equal to p^m, where p is a prime number and m is an arbitrary positive integer. But first we must develop the concepts of groups and rings.

2.2 GROUPS

A group is a mathematical abstraction of an algebraic structure. Although there are many concrete examples of interesting groups, the abstract idea is introduced into mathematics because it is easier to study all mathematical systems with a common structure at once rather than to study them one by one.

    ☐ **Definition 2.2.1** A *group* G is a set together with an operation on pairs of elements in the set (denoted by *) satisfying four properties:
1. *Closure* For every a, b in the set, $c = a * b$ is in the set.
2. *Associativity* For every a, b, c in the set,

$$a * (b * c) = (a * b) * c.$$

3. *Identity* There is an element e called the *identity element* that satisfies

$$a * e = e * a = a.$$

for every a in the set.
4. *Inverses* If a is in the set, then there is some element b in the set called an *inverse* of a such that

$$a * b = b * a = e. \qquad\qquad ☐$$

    If G has a finite number of elements then it is called a *finite group*, and the number of elements in G is called the *order* of G.

    Some groups satisfy the additional property that for all a, b in the group,

$$a * b = b * a.$$

This is called the *commutative property*. Groups with this additional property are called *commutative groups*, or *abelian groups*. With the exception of some of the material in this section, we shall always deal with abelian groups.

    In the case of an abelian group, the symbol for the group operation is written + and is called "addition" (even though it might not be the usual arithmetic addition). In this case, the identity element e is called "zero" and written 0, and the inverse element of a is written $-a$, so that

$$a + (-a) = (-a) + a = 0.$$

Sometimes the symbol for the group operation is written · and called "multiplication" (even though it might not be the usual arithmetic multiplication). In this case, the identity element e is called "one" and written 1, and the inverse element of a is written a^{-1}, so that

$$a \cdot a^{-1} = a^{-1} \cdot a = 1.$$

☐ **Theorem 2.2.2** In every group, the identity element is unique. Also, the inverse of each group element is unique, and $(a^{-1})^{-1} = a$.

Proof Suppose e and e' are identity elements. Then $e = e * e' = e'$. Next, suppose that b and b' are inverses for element a. Then

$$b = b * (a * b') = (b * a) * b' = b'.$$

Finally, $a^{-1}a = aa^{-1} = 1$, so a is an inverse for a^{-1}. But because inverses are unique, $(a^{-1})^{-1} = a$. ☐

There is a limitless supply of examples of groups. Many groups have an infinite number of elements. Examples are: the integers under addition; the positive rationals under multiplication†; the set of two-by-two real-valued matrices under matrix addition. Many other groups have only a finite number of elements. Examples are: the two-element set $\{0, 1\}$ under the exclusive-or operation (modulo-2 addition); the set $\{0, 1, \ldots, 8, 9\}$ under modulo-10 addition; and so forth.

For a more difficult example, we shall construct a finite nonabelian group that is not a familiar structure. One way to construct groups with interesting algebraic structures is to study transformations of simple geometrical shapes and mimic these with the algebra. For example, an equilateral triangle with vertices A, B, and C (labeled clockwise) can be rotated or reflected into itself in exactly six different ways, and each of these has a rotation or reflection inverse. By making use of some obvious facts in this geometrical situation, we can quickly construct an algebraic group. Let the six transformations be denoted by the labels 1, a, b, c, d, and e as follows:

$$
\begin{aligned}
1 &= (ABC \to ABC) & &\text{(no change)} \\
a &= (ABC \to BCA) & &\text{(counterclockwise rotation)} \\
b &= (ABC \to CAB) & &\text{(clockwise rotation)} \\
c &= (ABC \to ACB) & &\text{(reflection about bisector of angle } A) \\
d &= (ABC \to CBA) & &\text{(reflection about bisector of angle } B) \\
e &= (ABC \to BAC) & &\text{(reflection about bisector of angle } C),
\end{aligned}
$$

where the transformation $(ABC \to BCA)$ means that vertex A goes into vertex B, vertex B goes into vertex C, and vertex C goes into vertex A. That is, the triangle is rotated by $120°$. Let the group $(G, *)$ be defined by

$$G = \{1, a, b, c, d, e\},$$

†This example is a good place for a word of caution about terminology. In a general abelian group, the group operation is usually called addition but is not necessarily ordinary addition. In this example, it is ordinary multiplication.

and $y * x$ is that group element that denotes the transformation one obtains by performing sequentially first the transformation denoted by x and then the transformation denoted by y. Thus, for example,

$$a * d = (ABC \to BCA) * (ABC \to CBA)$$
$$= (ABC \to ACB) = e.$$

In this way, one can construct a table for $x * y$.

x \ y	1	a	b	c	d	e
1	1	a	b	c	d	e
a	a	b	1	d	e	c
b	b	1	a	e	c	d
c	c	e	d	1	b	a
d	d	c	e	a	1	b
e	e	d	c	b	a	1

Once the table is constructed, we can discard the geometrical scaffolding. The table alone defines the group. Notice that this example is a nonabelian group, because $a * c \neq c * a$. Notice also that every element appears once in each column and once in each row. This must always happen in a finite group.

Our final example of a group is the group of permutations on n letters. Let X be the set $\{1, 2, 3, \ldots, n\}$. A one-to-one map of this set onto itself is called a permutation. There are $n!$ such permutations, and we can define a group called the symmetric group and denoted by the label S_n, whose elements are the permutations of X. (This may be a little confusing at first because the elements of the group are operators—the permutation operators on X. In fact, the example obtained from the transformations of an equilateral triangle is a permutation group.) If we take a permutation of the integers and permute it, we just end up with another permutation of the integers. The group operation $*$ is taken to be this composition of permutations. For example, take $n = 4$. There are $4! = 24$ permutations in S_4. A typical element of S_4 is

$$a = [(1\ 2\ 3\ 4) \to (3\ 1\ 4\ 2)],$$

which is the permutation that replaces 1 by 3, 2 by 1, 3 by 4, and 4 by 2. Another such permutation is

$$b = [(1\ 2\ 3\ 4) \to (4\ 1\ 3\ 2)].$$

Then in S_4 the product $b * a$ is the permutation obtained by applying first a, then b. That is,

$$b * a = [(1\ 2\ 3\ 4) \to (2\ 3\ 4\ 1)]$$

which is an element of S_4. With this definition of multiplication, the permutation group S_4 is a nonabelian group with 24 elements.

Let G be a group and let H be a subset of G. Then H is called a *subgroup* of G if H is a group with respect to the restriction of $*$ to H. To prove that a nonempty set H is a subgroup of G, it is only necessary to check that $a * b$ is in H whenever a and b are in H (closure), and that the inverse of each a in H is also in H. The other properties required of a group will then be inherited from the group G. If the group is finite, then even the inverse property is satisfied automatically if the closure property is, as we will see shortly in the discussion of cyclic subgroups.

As an example, in the set of integers (positive, negative, and zero) under addition, the set of even integers is a subgroup, as is the set of multiples of 3.

One way to get a subgroup H of a finite group G is to take any element h from G and let H be the set of elements obtained by multiplying h by itself an arbitrary number of times. That is, form the sequence of elements

$$h, h * h, h * h * h, h * h * h * h, \ldots,$$

denoting these elements more simply by h, h^2, h^3, $h^4, \ldots$. Because G is a finite group, only a finite number of these elements can be distinct, so the sequence must eventually repeat. The first element repeated must be h itself, because if two other elements h^i and h^j are equal, they can be multiplied by the inverse of h, and thus h^{i-1} and h^{j-1} are also equal. Next, notice that if $h^j = h$, then $h^{j-1} = 1$, the group identity element. The set H is called the subgroup generated by h. The number c of elements in H is called the *order* of the element h. The set of elements $h, h^2, h^3, \ldots, h^c = 1$ is called a *cycle*. A cycle is a subgroup because a product of two such elements is another of the same form, and the inverse of h^i is h^{c-i} and, hence, is one of the elements of the cycle. A group that consists of all the powers of one of its elements is called a *cyclic group*.

Given a finite group G and a subgroup H, there is an important construction known as the *coset decomposition* of G, which illustrates certain relationships between H and G. Let the elements of H be denoted by $h_1, h_2, h_3, \ldots$, and choose h_1 to be the identity element. Construct the array as follows: The first row consists of the elements of H, with the identity at the left and every other element of H appearing once and only once. Choose any element of G not appearing in the first row. Call it g_2 and use it as the first element of the second row. The rest of the elements of the second row are obtained by multiplying each subgroup element by this first element on the left. Similarly, construct a third, fourth, and fifth row, each time choosing a previously unused group element for the element in the first column. Stop when, after some step, all the group elements appear somewhere in the array. The process must stop because G is finite. The array is:

$$h_1 = 1 \qquad h_2 \qquad h_3 \qquad h_4 \quad \cdots \qquad h_n$$

$$g_2 * h_1 = g_2 \quad g_2 * h_2 \quad g_2 * h_3 \quad g_2 * h_4 \quad \cdots \quad g_2 * h_n$$

$$g_3 * h_1 = g_3 \quad g_3 * h_2 \quad g_3 * h_3 \quad g_3 * h_4 \quad \cdots \quad g_3 * h_n$$

$$\vdots \qquad\quad \vdots \qquad\quad \vdots \qquad\quad \vdots \qquad \vdots$$

$$g_m * h_1 = g_m \quad g_m * h_2 \quad g_m * h_3 \quad g_m * h_4 \quad \cdots \quad g_m * h_n.$$

The first element on the left of each row is known as a *coset leader*. Each row in the array is known as a *left coset*, or simply as a *coset* when the group is abelian. If the coset decomposition is defined instead with the elements of G multiplied on the right, the rows are known as *right cosets*. The coset decomposition is always rectangular with all rows completed because it is constructed that way. We will now prove that we always obtain an array in which every element of G appears exactly once.

□ **Theorem 2.2.3** Every element of G appears once and only once in a coset decomposition of G.

Proof Every element appears at least once, because otherwise the construction is not halted. We will now prove that an element cannot appear twice in the same row and then prove than an element cannot appear in two different rows.

Suppose that two elements in the same row, $g_i * h_j$ and $g_i * h_k$, are equal. Then multiplying each by g_i^{-1} gives $h_j = h_k$. This is a contradiction, because each subgroup element appears only once in the first row.

Suppose that two elements in different rows, $g_i * h_j$ and $g_k * h_l$, are equal and that $k < i$. Multiplying on the right by h_j^{-1} gives $g_i = g_k * h_l * h_j^{-1}$. Then g_i is the kth coset because $h_l * h_j^{-1}$ is in the subgroup. This contradicts the rule of construction that coset leaders must be previously unused. □

□ **Corollary 2.2.4** If H is a subgroup of G, then the number of elements in H divides the number of elements in G. That is,

(Order of H)(Number of cosets of G with respect to H) = (Order of G)

Proof This follows immediately from the rectangular structure of the coset decomposition. □

□ **Theorem 2.2.5** The order of a finite group is divisible by the order of any of its elements.

Proof The group contains the cyclic subgroup generated by any element, and thus Corollary 2.2.4 proves the theorem. □

2.3 RINGS

The next algebraic structure we will need is that of a ring. A ring is an abstract set that is an abelian group and also has an additional structure.

□ **Definition 2.3.1**   A *ring R* is a set with two operations defined: the first is called *addition* (denoted by $+$); the second is called *multiplication* (denoted by juxtaposition); and the following axioms are satisfied:

1. R is an abelian group under addition ($+$).
2. *Closure*   For any a, b in R, the product ab is in R.
3. *Associative Law*

    $a(bc) = (ab)c.$

4. *Distributive Law*

    $a(b + c) = ab + ac,$

    $(b + c)a = ba + ca.$ □

The addition operation is always commutative in a ring, but the multiplication operation need not be commutative. A *commutative ring* is one in which multiplication is commutative; that is, $ab = ba$ for all a, b in R.

The distributive law in the definition of a ring links the addition and multiplication operations. This law has several immediate consequences, as follows.

□ **Theorem 2.3.2**   For any elements a, b in a ring R,

(i) $a0 = 0a = 0,$
(ii) $a(-b) = (-a)b = -(ab).$

Proof

(i) $a0 = a(0 + 0) = a0 + a0.$

   Hence, subtracting $a0$ from both sides gives $0 = a0$.
   The second half of (i) is proved the same way.

(ii) $0 = a0 = a(b - b) = ab + a(-b).$

   Hence,

   $a(-b) = -(ab).$

   The second half of (ii) is proved the same way. □

The addition operation in a ring has an identity called "zero." The multiplicative operation need not have an identity, but if there is an identity, it is unique. A ring that has an identity under multiplication is called a *ring with identity*. The identity is called "one" and is denoted by 1. Then

$$1a = a1 = a$$

for all a in R.

Every element in a ring has an inverse under the addition operation. Under the multiplication operation there need not be any inverses, but in a ring with identity inverses may exist. That is, given an element a, there may exist an element b with $ab = 1$. If so, b is called a *right inverse* for a. Similarly, if there is an element c such that $ca = 1$, then c is called a *left inverse* for a.

☐ **Theorem 2.3.3**   In a ring with identity,

  (i) The identity is unique.
 (ii) If an element a has both a right inverse b and a left inverse c, then $b = c$. In this case, the element a is said to have an inverse (denoted by a^{-1}). The inverse is unique.
(iii) $(a^{-1})^{-1} = a$.

Proof   The argument is similar to that used in Theorem 2.2.2. ☐

An element that has an inverse is called a *unit*. The set of all units is closed under multiplication, because if a and b are units, then $c = ab$ has inverse $c^{-1} = b^{-1}a^{-1}$.

☐ **Theorem 2.3.4**

  (i) Under ring multiplication, the set of units of a ring forms a group.
 (ii) If $c = ab$ and c is a unit, then a has a right inverse and b has a left inverse.

Proof   Straightforward. ☐

There are many familiar examples of rings. Some of them follow. It will be instructive to review Theorems 2.3.3 and 2.3.4 in terms of these examples.

1. The set of all real numbers under the usual addition and multiplication is a commutative ring with identity. Every nonzero element is a unit.
2. The set of all integers (positive, negative, and zero) under the usual addition and multiplication is a commutative ring with identity. This ring is conventionally denoted by the label **Z**. The only units are ± 1.
3. The set of all n by n matrices with real-valued elements under matrix addition and matrix multiplication is a noncommutative ring with identity. The identity is the n by n identity matrix. The units are the nonsingular matrices.
4. The set of all n by n matrices with integer-valued elements under matrix addition and multiplication is a noncommutative ring with identity.

5. The set of all polynomials in x with real-valued coefficients under polynomial addition and multiplication is a commutative ring with identity. The identity is the zero-degree polynomial $p(x) = 1$.

2.4 FIELDS

Loosely speaking, an abelian group is a set in which one can add and subtract, and a ring is a set in which one can add, subtract, and multiply. A more powerful algebraic structure, known as a field, is a set in which one can add, subtract, multiply, and divide.

□ **Definition 2.4.1** A *field F* is a set that has two operations defined on it: *addition* and *multiplication*, such that the following axioms are satisfied.

1. The set is an abelian group under addition.
2. The field is closed under multiplication, and the set of nonzero elements is an abelian group under multiplication.
3. The distributive law

   $(a + b)c = ac + bc$

   holds for all a, b, c in the field. □

It is conventional to denote the identity element under addition by 0 and to call it "zero"; to denote the additive inverse of a by $-a$; to denote the identity element under multiplication by 1 and to call it "one"; and to denote the multiplicative inverse of a by a^{-1}. By subtraction $(a - b)$, we mean $a + (-b)$; by division (a/b), we mean $b^{-1}a$.

The following examples of fields are well known.

1. **R**: the set of real numbers.
2. **C**: the set of complex numbers.
3. **Q**: the set of rational numbers.

These fields all have an infinite number of elements. We are interested in fields with a finite number of elements. A field with q elements, if it exists, is called a *finite field*, or a *Galois field*, and is denoted by the label $GF(q)$.

What is the smallest field? It must have an element zero and an element one. In fact, these suffice with the addition and multiplication tables.

+	0 1		·	0 1
0	0 1		0	0 0
1	1 0		1	0 1

This is the field $GF(2)$, which we have already seen in Section 2.1. Inspection shows that no other field with two elements exists.

In Chapter 4, we shall study finite fields in great detail. For now we will be content with two more simple examples. These are described by their addition and multiplication tables. Subtraction and division are defined implicitly by the addition and multiplication tables.

The field $GF(3) = \{0, 1, 2\}$ with the operations:

+	0 1 2	·	0 1 2
0	0 1 2	0	0 0 0
1	1 2 0	1	0 1 2
2	2 0 1	2	0 2 1

The field $GF(4) = \{0, 1, 2, 3\}$ with the operations:

+	0 1 2 3	·	0 1 2 3
0	0 1 2 3	0	0 0 0 0
1	1 0 3 2	1	0 1 2 3
2	2 3 0 1	2	0 2 3 1
3	3 2 1 0	3	0 3 1 2

Notice that multiplication in $GF(4)$ is *not* modulo-4 multiplication, and addition is *not* modulo-4 addition.

Many other Galois fields exist. Even though these examples are very small fields, it is not easy by inspection to see what is promised by the structure. An understanding of the structure of these and larger fields will be developed in Chapter 4.

Before leaving these examples, notice that $GF(2)$ is contained in $GF(4)$, because in $GF(4)$ the two elements 0, 1 add and multiply just as they do in $GF(2)$. However, $GF(2)$ is not contained in $GF(3)$.

☐ **Definition 2.4.2** Let F be a field. A subset of F is called a *subfield* if it is a field under the inherited addition and multiplication. The original field F is then called an *extension field* of the subfield. ☐

To prove that a subset of a finite field is a subfield, it is only necessary to prove that it contains a nonzero element, and that it is closed under addition and multiplication. All other necessary properties are inherited from F. Inverses under addition or multiplication of an element β are contained in the cyclic group generated by β under the operation of addition or multiplication.

A field has all the properties of a ring. It also has an additional important property—it is always possible to cancel. Cancellation is a weak form of division that states that if $ab = ac$, then $b = c$.

☐ **Theorem 2.4.3** In any field, if $ab = ac$ and $a \neq 0$, then $b = c$.

Proof Multiply by a^{-1}. ☐

Some rings may also satisfy this cancellation law and yet not be fields. The ring of integers is a simple example. Cancellation is possible in this ring but cannot be proved as in Theorem 2.4.3, because a^{-1} does not exist in this ring. There is a special name for rings in which cancellation is always possible.

☐ **Definition 2.4.4** An *integral domain* is a commutative ring in which $b = c$ whenever $ab = ac$ and a is nonzero. ☐

2.5 VECTOR SPACES

A familiar example of a vector space is the three-dimensional Euclidean space that arises in problems of physics. This can be extended mathematically to an n-dimensional vector space over the real numbers. The concept of an n-dimensional vector space is closely related to the ideas of linear algebra and matrix theory and is important in many applications.

Vector spaces also can be defined abstractly with respect to any field.

☐ **Definition 2.5.1** Let F be a field. The elements of F will be called *scalars*. A set V is called a *vector space* and its elements are called *vectors* if there is defined an operation called *vector addition* (denoted by $+$) on pairs of elements from V, and an operation called *scalar multiplication* (denoted by juxtaposition) on an element from F and an element from V to produce an element from V, provided the following axioms are satisfied.

1. V is an abelian group under vector addition.
2. *Distributive Law* For any vectors $\mathbf{v}_1, \mathbf{v}_2$ and any scalar c,

    $c(\mathbf{v}_1 + \mathbf{v}_2) = c\mathbf{v}_1 + c\mathbf{v}_2$.

3. *Distributive Law* For any vector $\mathbf{v}$, and any scalars c_1, c_2, $1\mathbf{v} = \mathbf{v}$ and

    $(c_1 + c_2)\mathbf{v} = c_1\mathbf{v} + c_2\mathbf{v}$.

4. *Associative Law* For any vector $\mathbf{v}$, and any scalars c_1, c_2,

    $(c_1 c_2)\mathbf{v} = c_1(c_2\mathbf{v})$.

The zero element of V is called the *origin* of V and is denoted by **0**. $\square$

Notice that we have two different uses for the symbol $+$: vector addition and addition within the field. Also notice that the symbol **0** is used for the origin of the vector space and the symbol 0 for the field. In practice, these ambiguities cause no confusion.

As a less familiar example of a vector space, take V to be the set of polynomials in x with coefficients in $GF(q)$, and take $F = GF(q)$. In this space, the vectors are polynomials. Vector addition is polnomial addition, and scalar multiplication is multiplication of a polynomial by a field element.

In a vector space V, a sum of the form

$$\mathbf{u} = a_1\mathbf{v}_1 + a_2\mathbf{v}_2 + \cdots + a_k\mathbf{v}_k,$$

where the a_i are scalars, is called a *linear combination* of the vectors $\mathbf{v}_1, \ldots, \mathbf{v}_k$. A set of vectors $\{\mathbf{v}_1, \ldots, \mathbf{v}_k\}$ is called *linearly dependent* if there is a set of scalars $\{a_1, \ldots, a_k\}$, not all zero, such that

$$a_1\mathbf{v}_1 + a_2\mathbf{v}_2 + \cdots + \mathbf{a}_k\mathbf{v}_k = \mathbf{0}.$$

A set of vectors that is not linearly dependent is called *linearly independent*. No vector in a linearly independent set can be expressed as a linear combination of the others. Note that the all-zero vector **0** cannot belong to a linearly independent set; every set containing **0** is linearly dependent.

A set of vectors is said to *span* a vector space if every vector in the space equals at least one linear combination of the vectors in the set. A vector space that is spanned by a finite set of vectors is called a *finite-dimensional vector space*. We are interested primarily in finite-dimensional vector spaces.

$\square$ **Theorem 2.5.2**   If a vector space V is spanned by a finite set of k vectors $A = \{\mathbf{v}_1, \ldots, \mathbf{v}_k\}$ and V contains a set of m linearly independent vectors $B = \{\mathbf{u}_1, \ldots, \mathbf{u}_m\}$, then $k \geqslant m$.

Proof   We will describe how to construct a sequence of sets A_0, A_1, $A_2, \ldots, A_m$ in such a way that each set spans V; each set has k elements chosen from A and B; and the set A_r contains $\mathbf{u}_1, \ldots, \mathbf{u}_r$. Consequently, A_m contains $\mathbf{u}_1, \ldots, \mathbf{u}_m$ among its k elements, and thus $k \geqslant m$.

Because no nonzero linear combination of vectors of B is equal to zero, no element of B can be expressed as a linear combination of the other elements of B. If the set A_{r-1} does not contain $\mathbf{u}_r$, and it spans V, then it must be possible to express $\mathbf{u}_r$ as a linear combination of elements of A_{r-1}, including at least one vector of A (say $\mathbf{v}_j$) not in B. The equation describing the linear combination can be solved to express $\mathbf{v}_j$ as a linear combination of $\mathbf{u}_r$ and the other elements of A_{r-1}.

The construction is as follows. Let $A_0 = A$. If A_{r-1} contains $\mathbf{u}_r$, then let $A_r = A_{r-1}$. Otherwise, $\mathbf{u}_r$ does not appear in A_{r-1} but can be expressed as a linear combination of the elements of A_{r-1} involving some element $\mathbf{v}_j$ of A not in B. Form A_r from A_{r-1} by replacing $\mathbf{v}_j$ by $\mathbf{u}_r$.

Any vector $\mathbf{v}$ is a linear combination of the elements of A_{r-1} and so too of A_r if $\mathbf{v}_j$ is eliminated by using the linear equation that relates $\mathbf{v}_j$ to $\mathbf{u}_r$ and the other elements of A_{r-1}. Therefore the set A_r spans V; from A_{r-1} we have constructed A_r with the desired properties. Hence, we can construct A_m, and the proof is complete. $\square$

☐ **Theorem 2.5.3**   Two linearly independent sets of vectors that span the same finite-dimensional vector space have the same number of vectors.

Proof   If one set has m vectors and the other has k, then by Theorem 2.5.2 $m \geqslant k$ and $k \geqslant m$, and thus $m = k$. $\square$

The number of linearly independent vectors in a set that spans a finite-dimensional vector space V is called the *dimension* of V. A set of k linearly independent vectors that spans a k-dimensional vector space is called a *basis* of the space. From Theorem 2.5.3, every set of more than k vectors in a k-dimensional vector space is linearly dependent.

☐ **Theorem 2.5.4**   In a k-dimensional vector space V, any set of k linearly independent vectors is a basis for V.

Proof   Let $\{\mathbf{v}_1, \mathbf{v}_2, \ldots, \mathbf{v}_k\}$ be any set of k linearly independent vectors in V. If they do not span V, then one can find a vector $\mathbf{v}$ in V that is not a linear combination of $\mathbf{v}_1, \mathbf{v}_2, \ldots, \mathbf{v}_k$. The set $\{\mathbf{v}, \mathbf{v}_1, \mathbf{v}_2, \ldots, \mathbf{v}_k\}$ is linearly independent and contains $k + 1$ vectors in V, which contradicts Theorem 2.5.3. Therefore $\{\mathbf{v}_1, \mathbf{v}_2, \ldots, \mathbf{v}_k\}$ spans V and is a basis. $\square$

If a linearly independent set of vectors in a k-dimensional vector space is not a basis, then it must have less than k vectors. To append vectors to such a set in order to make it into a basis is called *completion* of the basis.

☐ **Theorem 2.5.5**   Given a set of linearly independent vectors in a finite-dimensional vector space, it is always possible to complete the set to form a basis.

Proof   If the set is not a basis, then some vector in the space is not a linear combination of vectors in the set. Choose any such vector and append it to the set, making the size of the set larger by one. If it is still not a basis repeat the process. The process must eventually stop because the number of linearly independent vectors in a set is not larger than the dimension of the space. The final set of vectors satisfies the requirements of the theorem. $\square$

A nonempty subset of a vector space is called a *vector subspace* if it is also a vector space under the original vector addition and scalar multiplication. Under the operation of vector addition, a vector space is a group, and a vector subspace is a subgroup. In order to check whether a nonempty subset of a vector space is a subspace, it is only necessary to check for closure under vector addition and under scalar multiplication. Closure under scalar multiplication ensures that the zero vector is in the subset. All other required properties are always inherited from the original space.

□ **Theorem 2.5.6**   In any vector space V, the set of all linear combinations of a set of vectors $\{v_1, \ldots, v_k\}$ is a subspace of V.

Proof   Every linear combination of $v_1, \ldots, v_k$ is a vector in V, and thus W, the set of all linear combinations, is a subset. Because $\mathbf{0}$ is in W, it is not empty. We must show that W is a subspace. If $w = b_1 v_1 + \cdots + b_k v_k$ and $u = c_1 v_1 + \cdots + c_k v_k$ are any two elements of W, then $w + u = (b_1 + c_1)v_1 + \cdots + (b_k + c_k)v_k$ is also in W. Next, for any w, any scalar multiple of w, $aw = ab_1 v_1 + \cdots + ab_k v_k$, is in W. Because W is closed under vector addition and scalar multiplication, it is a vector subspace of V. □

□ **Theorem 2.5.7**   If W, a vector subspace of a finite-dimensional vector space V, has the same dimension as V, then $W = V$.

Proof   Let k be the dimension of the two spaces. Choose a basis for W. This is a set of k linearly independent vectors in V, and thus it is a basis for V. Therefore every vector in V is also in W. □

Given a field F, the quantity $(a_1, a_2, \ldots, a_n)$, composed of field elements, is called an *n-tuple* of elements from the field F. Under the operations of componentwise addition and componentwise scalar multiplication, the set of n-tuples of elements from a field F is a vector space and is denoted by the label F^n. Any finite-dimensional vector space can be represented as an n-tuple space by choosing a basis $\{v_1, \ldots, v_n\}$ and representing a vector $v = a_1 v_1 + \cdots + a_n v_n$ by the n-tuple of coefficients $(a_1, \ldots, a_n)$. Hence, we need consider only vector spaces of n-tuples.

The *inner product* of two n-tuples of F^n

$$u = (a_1, \ldots, a_n)$$

$$v = (b_1, \ldots, b_n)$$

is a scalar defined as

$$u \cdot v = (a_1, \ldots, a_n) \cdot (b_1, \ldots, b_n) = a_1 b_1 + \cdots + a_n b_n.$$

We can immediately verify that $\mathbf{u} \cdot \mathbf{v} = \mathbf{v} \cdot \mathbf{u}$, $(c\mathbf{u}) \cdot \mathbf{v} = c(\mathbf{u} \cdot \mathbf{v})$, and also that $\mathbf{w} \cdot (\mathbf{u} + \mathbf{v}) = (\mathbf{w} \cdot \mathbf{u}) + (\mathbf{w} \cdot \mathbf{v})$. If the inner product of two vectors is zero, they are said to be *orthogonal*. It is possible for a nonzero vector over $GF(q)$ to be orthogonal to itself. A vector orthogonal to every vector in a set is said to be orthogonal to the set.

□ **Theorem 2.5.8**   Let V be the vector space of n-tuples over a field F, and let W be a subspace. The set of vectors orthogonal to W is itself a subspace.

Proof   Let U be the set of all vectors orthogonal to W. Because $\mathbf{0}$ is in U, U is not empty. Let $\mathbf{w}$ be any vector in W, and let $\mathbf{u}_1$ and $\mathbf{u}_2$ be any vectors in U. Then $\mathbf{w} \cdot \mathbf{u}_1 = \mathbf{w} \cdot \mathbf{u}_2 = 0$, and $\mathbf{w} \cdot \mathbf{u}_1 + \mathbf{w} \cdot \mathbf{u}_2 = 0 = \mathbf{w} \cdot (\mathbf{u}_1 + \mathbf{u}_2)$; thus $\mathbf{u}_1 + \mathbf{u}_2$ is in U. Also, $\mathbf{w} \cdot (c\mathbf{u}_1) = c(\mathbf{w} \cdot \mathbf{u}_1) = \mathbf{0}$, and thus $c\mathbf{u}_1$ is in U. Therefore U is a subspace. □

The set of vectors orthogonal to W is called the *orthogonal complement* of W and is denoted by $W^\perp$. In a finite-dimensional vector space over the real numbers, the intersection of W and $W^\perp$ contains only the all-zero vector, but in a vector space over $GF(q)$, $W^\perp$ may have a nontrivial intersection with W or may even lie within W or contain W. In fact, one can construct examples of subspaces that are their own orthogonal complements. For example, in $GF(2)^2$, the subspace $\{00, 11\}$ is its own orthogonal complement.

□ **Theorem 2.5.9**   A vector orthogonal to every vector of a set that spans W is in the orthogonal complement of W.

Proof   Suppose the set $\{\mathbf{w}_1, \ldots, \mathbf{w}_n\}$ spans W. A vector $\mathbf{w}$ in W can be written in the form $\mathbf{w} = c_1 \mathbf{w}_1 + \cdots + c_n \mathbf{w}_n$. Then

$$\mathbf{w} \cdot \mathbf{u} = (c_1 \mathbf{w}_1 + \cdots + c_n \mathbf{w}_n) \cdot \mathbf{u} = c_1 \mathbf{w}_1 \cdot \mathbf{u} + \cdots + c_n \mathbf{w}_n \cdot \mathbf{u}$$

If $\mathbf{u}$ is orthogonal to every $\mathbf{w}_i$, it is orthogonal to every $\mathbf{w}$ in W. □

If a vector space of n-tuples has a subspace W of dimension k, then the orthogonal complement $W^\perp$ has dimension $n - k$. This fact will be used frequently in later chapters, and it will be proved as Theorem 2.6.9 at the end of the next section. We refer to this fact in proving the following theorem.

□ **Theorem 2.5.10**   Let W be a subspace of the space of n-tuples, and let $W^\perp$ be the orthogonal complement of W. Then W is the orthogonal complement of $W^\perp$.

Proof   Let k be the dimension of W. Then by Theorem 2.6.9, $W^\perp$ has dimension $n - k$ and the orthogonal complement of $W^\perp$ has dimension k. But every vector of W is orthogonal to $W^\perp$. Therefore W is contained in the orthogonal complement of $W^\perp$ and has the same dimension. Hence, they are equal. □

2.6 LINEAR ALGEBRA

The topic of linear algebra, particularly matrix theory, is a much-used topic in applied mathematics but usually is studied only for the field of real numbers and the field of complex numbers. Most of the familiar operations of linear algebra are also valid in an arbitrary field. We will outline the development of this subject partly for review and partly to prove that the techniques remain valid over an arbitrary field (sometimes even over an arbitrary ring).

□ **Definition 2.6.1** An n by m matrix $\mathbf{A}$ over a ring R consists of nm elements from R arranged in a rectangular array of n rows and m columns.

$$\mathbf{A} = \begin{bmatrix} a_{11} & a_{12} & \cdots & a_{1m} \\ a_{21} & a_{22} & \cdots & a_{2m} \\ \vdots & \vdots & & \vdots \\ a_{n1} & a_{n2} & \cdots & a_{nm} \end{bmatrix} = [a_{ij}]$$

In most applications the ring R is actually a field, and we restrict attention to this case. We are mostly concerned with matrices over a finite field $GF(q)$. □

The set of elements a_{ii} for which the column number and row number are equal is called the *main diagonal*. If n equals m, the matrix is called a *square matrix*. An n by n matrix with the field element one in every entry of the main diagonal and the field element zero in every other matrix entry is called an *n by n identity matrix*. An identity matrix is denoted by $\mathbf{I}$. Examples of identity matrices are

$$\begin{bmatrix} 1 & 0 \\ 0 & 1 \end{bmatrix} \quad \text{and} \quad \begin{bmatrix} 1 & 0 & 0 \\ 0 & 1 & 0 \\ 0 & 0 & 1 \end{bmatrix}.$$

Two n by m matrices $\mathbf{A}$ and $\mathbf{B}$ over $GF(q)$ can be added by the rule

$$\mathbf{A} + \mathbf{B} = \begin{bmatrix} a_{11} + b_{11} & a_{12} + b_{12} & \cdots & a_{1m} + b_{1m} \\ \vdots & & & \vdots \\ a_{n1} + b_{n1} & a_{n2} + b_{n2} & \cdots & a_{nm} + b_{nm} \end{bmatrix}.$$

An n by m matrix $\mathbf{A}$ can be multiplied by a field element β by the rule

$$\beta \mathbf{A} = \begin{bmatrix} \beta a_{11} & \beta a_{12} & \cdots & \beta a_{1m} \\ \vdots & & & \vdots \\ \beta a_{n1} & \beta a_{n2} & \cdots & \beta a_{nm} \end{bmatrix}.$$

An l by n matrix **A** and an n by m matrix **B** can be multiplied to produce an l by m matrix **C** by using the following rule:

$$c_{ij} = \sum_{k=1}^{n} a_{ik}b_{kj} \qquad \begin{aligned} i &= 1, \ldots, l \\ j &= 1, \ldots, m. \end{aligned}$$

This matrix product is denoted as

$$C = AB.$$

With this definition of matrix multiplication, and the earlier definition of matrix addition, the set of n by n square matrices over any field F forms a ring, as can be easily verified. It is a noncommutative ring, but it does have an identity, namely the n by n identity matrix.

A matrix can be broken into pieces as follows:

$$\mathbf{A} = \left[\begin{array}{c|c} \mathbf{A}_{11} & \mathbf{A}_{12} \\ \hline \mathbf{A}_{21} & \mathbf{A}_{22} \end{array} \right],$$

where $\mathbf{A}_{11}$, $\mathbf{A}_{12}$, $\mathbf{A}_{21}$, and $\mathbf{A}_{22}$ are smaller matrices whose dimensions add up to the dimensions of **A** in the obvious way. That is, the number of rows of $\mathbf{A}_{11}$ (or $\mathbf{A}_{12}$) plus the number of rows of $\mathbf{A}_{21}$ (or $\mathbf{A}_{22}$) equals the number of rows of **A**, and a similar statement holds for columns. Matrices may be multiplied in blocks. That is, if

$$\mathbf{A} = \left[\begin{array}{c|c} \mathbf{A}_{11} & \mathbf{A}_{12} \\ \hline \mathbf{A}_{21} & \mathbf{A}_{22} \end{array} \right] \quad \text{and} \quad \mathbf{B} = \left[\begin{array}{c|c} \mathbf{B}_{11} & \mathbf{B}_{12} \\ \hline \mathbf{B}_{21} & \mathbf{B}_{22} \end{array} \right]$$

and $C = AB$, then

$$\mathbf{C} = \left[\begin{array}{c|c} \mathbf{A}_{11}\mathbf{B}_{11} + \mathbf{A}_{12}\mathbf{B}_{21} & \mathbf{A}_{11}\mathbf{B}_{12} + \mathbf{A}_{12}\mathbf{B}_{22} \\ \hline \mathbf{A}_{21}\mathbf{B}_{11} + \mathbf{A}_{22}\mathbf{B}_{21} & \mathbf{A}_{21}\mathbf{B}_{12} + \mathbf{A}_{22}\mathbf{B}_{22} \end{array} \right],$$

provided the dimensions of the blocks are compatible in the sense that all matrix products and additions are defined. This decomposition can be readily verified as a simple consequence of the associativity and distributivity axioms of the underlying field.

The *transpose* of an n by m matrix **A** is an m by n matrix, denoted $\mathbf{A}^T$, such that $a_{ij}^T = a_{ji}$. That is, the rows of $\mathbf{A}^T$ are the columns of **A**, and the columns of $\mathbf{A}^T$ are the rows of **A**. The *inverse* of the square matrix **A** is the square matrix $\mathbf{A}^{-1}$, if it exists, such that $\mathbf{A}^{-1}\mathbf{A} = \mathbf{A}\mathbf{A}^{-1} = \mathbf{I}$. The set of all square n by n matrices for which an inverse exists is a group under matrix multiplication, as can be immediately checked. Therefore, whenever a matrix has an inverse it is unique, because we have seen in Theorem 2.2.2 that this property holds in any group. A matrix that has an inverse is called *nonsingular*; otherwise, it is called *singular*. If $C = AB$, then $\mathbf{C}^{-1} = \mathbf{B}^{-1}\mathbf{A}^{-1}$ provided the inverses of **A** and **B** exist, because $(\mathbf{B}^{-1}\mathbf{A}^{-1})\mathbf{C} = \mathbf{I} = \mathbf{C}(\mathbf{B}^{-1}\mathbf{A}^{-1})$.

We will see later that if the inverse of either **A** or **B** does not exist, then neither does the inverse of **C**.

□ **Definition 2.6.2** Let the field F be given. For each n, the *determinant* of a square n by n matrix **A** is the value assumed by det(**A**), a function from the set of n by n matrices over F into the field F. The function det(**A**) is given by

$$\det(\mathbf{A}) = \sum \xi_{i_1 \ldots i_n} a_{1 i_1} a_{2 i_2} a_{3 i_3} \ldots a_{n i_n},$$

where $i_1, i_2, \ldots, i_n$ is a permutation of the integers $1, 2, \ldots, n$; $\xi_{i_1 \ldots i_n}$ is ± 1 according to whether the permutation is an even or odd permutation; and the sum is over all possible permutations. □

An odd permutation is one that can be obtained as a product of an odd number of transpositions. An even permutation is one that cannot be obtained by an odd number of transpositions. A transposition is an interchange of two terms.

One way to visualize the definition is to take the set of all matrices that can be obtained by permuting the rows of **A**. Then for each such matrix, take the product of terms down the main diagonal. Reverse the sign if the permutation is odd, and add all such product terms together. Of course, one should not actually compute the determinant this way, but it is a good way to establish properties.

The following theorem contains properties of the determinant that follow easily from the definition.

□ **Theorem 2.6.3**

(i) If all elements of any row of a square matrix are zero, the determinant of the matrix is zero.

(ii) The determinant of a matrix equals the determinant of its transpose.

(iii) If two rows of a square matrix are interchanged, the determinant is replaced by its negative.

(iv) If two rows are equal, then the determinant is zero.

(v) If all elements of one row of a square matrix are multiplied by a field element c, the value of the determinant is multiplied by c.

(vi) If two matrices **A** and **B** differ only in row i, the sum of their determinants equals the determinant of a matrix **C** whose ith row is the sum of the ith rows of **A** and **B** and whose other rows equal the corresponding rows of **A** or **B**.

(vii) If k times the elements of any row are added to the corresponding elements of any other row, the determinant is unchanged. *Proof:* Combine properties (iv), (v), and (vi).

(viii) The determinant of a square matrix is nonzero if and only if its rows (or columns) are linearly independent.

Proof   Exercise. *Note:* In general, line (iv) cannot be proved by interchanging the two equal rows and using line (iii). Why? □

If the row and column containing an element a_{ij} in a square matrix are deleted, then the determinant of the remaining $(n-1)$ by $(n-1)$ square array, is called the *minor* of a_{ij} and denoted M_{ij}. The *cofactor* of a_{ij}, denoted here by C_{ij}, is defined by

$$C_{ij} = (-1)^{i+j} M_{ij}.$$

By examination of the definition of the determinant, we see that the cofactor of a_{ij} is the coefficient of a_{ij} in the expansion of $\det(\mathbf{A})$:

$$\det(\mathbf{A}) = \sum_{k=1}^{n} a_{ik} C_{ik}.$$

This is known as the Laplace expansion formula for determinants. It gives the determinant of an n by n matrix in terms of n determinants of $(n-1)$ by $(n-1)$ matrices. The Laplace expansion formula is used as a recursive method of computing the determinant.

If a_{ik} is replaced by a_{jk}, then $\sum_{k=1}^{n} a_{jk} C_{ik}$ is the determinant of a new matrix in which the elements of the ith row are replaced by the elements of the jth row, and hence it is zero if $j \neq i$. Thus,

$$\sum_{k=1}^{n} a_{jk} C_{ik} = \begin{cases} \det(\mathbf{A}) & i=j \\ 0 & i \neq j. \end{cases}$$

Therefore the matrix $\mathbf{A} = [a_{ij}]$ has inverse

$$\mathbf{A}^{-1} = \left[\frac{C_{ji}}{\det(\mathbf{A})} \right],$$

provided that $\det(\mathbf{A}) \neq 0$. When $\det(\mathbf{A}) = 0$, an inverse does not exist.

The rows of an n by m matrix $\mathbf{A}$ over $GF(q)$ may be thought of as a set of vectors in $GF(q)^m$ of length m. The *row space* of $\mathbf{A}$ is the set of all linear combinations of row vectors of $\mathbf{A}$. The row space is a subspace of $GF(q)^m$. The dimension of the row space is called the *row rank*. Similarly, the columns of $\mathbf{A}$ may be thought of as a set of vectors in $GF(q)^n$ of length n. The *column space* of $\mathbf{A}$ is the set of all linear combinations of column vectors of $\mathbf{A}$, and the dimension of the column space is called the *column rank*. The set of vectors $\mathbf{v}$ such that $\mathbf{A}\mathbf{v}^T = \mathbf{0}$ is called the *null space* of the matrix $\mathbf{A}$. It is clear that the null space is a vector subspace of $GF(q)^n$. In particular, the null space of $\mathbf{A}$ is the orthogonal complement of the row space of $\mathbf{A}$, because the null space can be described as the set of all vectors orthogonal to all vectors of the row space.

The *elementary row operations* on a matrix are as follows:

1. Interchange of any two rows.
2. Multiplication of any row by a nonzero field element.
3. Replacement of any row by the sum of itself and a multiple of any other row.

Each elementary row operation is inverted by an elementary row operation of the same kind. Each elementary row operation on an n by m matrix $\mathbf{A}$ can be effected by multiplying the matrix $\mathbf{A}$ from the left by an appropriate n by n matrix $\mathbf{F}$ called an *elementary matrix*. The elementary matrices are of the form of the following modifications of an identity matrix:

$$
\begin{bmatrix} 1 \\ & \ddots \\ & & 0 & 1 \\ & & & \ddots \\ & & 1 & & 0 \\ & & & & & \ddots \\ & & & & & & 1 \end{bmatrix}, \quad
\begin{bmatrix} 1 \\ & \ddots \\ & & & a \\ & & & & \ddots \\ & & & & & & 1 \end{bmatrix}, \quad \text{or} \quad
\begin{bmatrix} 1 \\ & \ddots \\ & & 1 \\ & & & \ddots \\ & & a & & 1 \\ & & & & & \ddots \\ & & & & & & 1 \end{bmatrix}.
$$

Elementary row operations are used to put a matrix in a standard form called the *row-echelon form*, which is as follows:

1. The leading nonzero term of every nonzero row is a one.
2. Every column containing such a leading term has a zero as all its other entries.
3. The leading term of any row is to the right of the leading term in every higher row. All-zero rows are below all nonzero rows.

An example of a matrix in row-echelon form is the matrix

$$
\mathbf{A} = \begin{bmatrix} 1 & 1 & 0 & 1 & 3 & 0 \\ 0 & 0 & 1 & 1 & 0 & 0 \\ 0 & 0 & 0 & 0 & 0 & 1 \\ 0 & 0 & 0 & 0 & 0 & 0 \end{bmatrix}.
$$

Notice the all-zero row at the bottom. Also, notice that if the last row is deleted, then all columns of a 3 by 3 identity matrix appear as columns but are scattered about the matrix. In general, if there are k rows, none of them all zero, and at least this many columns, then all columns of a k by k identity matrix will appear scattered about a row-echelon matrix. A special case of a matrix in row-echelon form is a matrix of the form

$$
\mathbf{A} = [\mathbf{I} : \mathbf{P}],
$$

where $\mathbf{I}$ is an identity matrix. Every matrix with at least as many columns as rows can be put in row-echelon form, but not every such matrix can be put in this special form by elementary row operations.

☐**Theorem 2.6.4**　If two matrices **A** and **A'** are related by a succession of elementary operations, both matrices have the same row space.

Proof　Each row of **A'** is a linear combination of rows of **A**. Therefore any linear combination of rows of **A'** is a linear combination of rows of **A** also, and thus the row space of **A** contains the row space of **A'**. But **A** can be obtained from **A'** by the inverse operation, and thus the row space of **A'** contains the row space of **A**. Therefore **A** and **A'** have equal row spaces. ☐

☐ **Theorem 2.6.5**　If two matrices **A** and **A'** are related by a succession of elementary row operations, any set of columns that is linearly independent in **A** is also linearly independent in **A'**.

Proof　It suffices to prove the theorem for a single elementary row operation, and the theorem is obvious if it is the first or second kind of elementary row operation. Hence, suppose **A'** is formed from **A** by adding a multiple of row α to row β. In any linearly dependent combination of columns of **A'**, the elements in row α must combine to give zero and thus can have no effect in row β. That is, this set of columns is also linearly dependent in **A**. ☐

☐ **Theorem 2.6.6**　A k by n matrix **A** whose k rows are linearly independent has k linearly independent columns.

Proof　Put **A** in row-echelon form **A'**. Because the rows are linearly independent, no row has all zeros. Hence each row has a column where it is equal to one, and every other row is equal to zero. This set of k columns of **A'** is linearly independent, and thus by Theorem 2.6.5, this same set of columns of **A** is linearly independent. ☐

☐**Theorem 2.6.7**　The row rank of a matrix **A** equals its column rank, and both are equal to the dimension of any largest square submatrix with determinant not equal to zero. (Hence, this value is simply called the *rank* of the matrix.)

Proof　It is only necessary to show that the row rank of **A** is equal to the dimension of a largest square submatrix with a nonzero determinant. The same proof applied to the transpose of **A** then proves the same for the column rank of **A** and thus proves that the row rank equals the column rank.

　　A submatrix of **A** is a matrix obtained by deleting any number of rows and columns from **A**. Let **M** be a nonsingular square submatrix of **A** of largest dimension. The rows of **M** are linearly independent by Theorem 2.6.3(viii), and thus the rows of **A** that give rise to these rows of

M must be linearly independent. Therefore the row rank of **A** is at least as large as the dimension of **M**.

On the other hand, choose any set of k linearly independent rows. A matrix of these rows, by Theorem 2.6.7, has k linearly independent columns. Hence, choosing these k columns from these k rows gives a matrix with a nonzero determinant. Therefore the dimension of a largest nonsingular submatrix of **A** is at least as large as the row rank of **A**. This completes the proof. □

Let **A** be a square n by n matrix with a nonzero determinant. Then the row-echelon form is an n by n matrix with no all-zero rows by Theorems 2.6.4 and 2.6.7. Hence it is the identity matrix. Because **A** can be obtained from **I** by the inverse of the sequence of elementary row operations, **A** can be written in terms of elementary matrices as

$$\mathbf{A} = \mathbf{F}_1 \mathbf{F}_2 \dots \mathbf{F}_r.$$

□ **Theorem 2.6.8** In the ring of n by n matrices over a field F, let $\mathbf{C} = \mathbf{AB}$. Then

$$\det(\mathbf{C}) = \det(\mathbf{A}) \det(\mathbf{B}).$$

Proof *Step 1* First we show that det(**C**) equals zero if either det(**A**) or det(**B**) equals zero. Suppose det(**B**) equals zero; then by Theorem 2.6.3(viii), the rows of **B** are linearly dependent. But the rows of **C** are linear combinations of the rows of **B**. Hence, the rows of **C** are linearly dependent, and det(**C**) equals zero. A similar argument is followed if det(**A**) equals zero.

Step 2 Suppose det(**A**) is not zero. Then it is possible to write **A** as a product of elementary matrices:

$$\mathbf{A} = \mathbf{F}_1 \mathbf{F}_2 \dots \mathbf{F}_r.$$

Each of the $\mathbf{F}_i$ corresponds to an elementary row operation, and thus by Theorem 2.6.3(iii), (v), and (vii)

$$\det(\mathbf{AB}) = \det[(\mathbf{F}_1 \mathbf{F}_2 \dots \mathbf{F}_r)\mathbf{B}] = \det[\mathbf{F}_1(\mathbf{F}_2 \dots \mathbf{F}_r\mathbf{B})]$$
$$= (\det \mathbf{F}_1) \det(\mathbf{F}_2 \dots \mathbf{F}_r\mathbf{B})$$
$$= (\det \mathbf{F}_1)(\det \mathbf{F}_2) \dots (\det \mathbf{F}_r)(\det \mathbf{B}).$$

When $\mathbf{B} = \mathbf{I}$, this gives

$$\det(\mathbf{A}) = (\det \mathbf{F}_1)(\det \mathbf{F}_2) \dots (\det \mathbf{F}_r).$$

Substituting this into the formula for a general **B** gives det(**AB**) = det(**A**)det(**B**), as was to be proved. □

One consequence of this theorem is that if $C = AB$, then C has an inverse if and only if both A and B do, because a square matrix has an inverse if and only if its determinant is nonzero.

To end this section, we will finish up a piece of work left over from the last section.

☐ **Theorem 2.6.9**   If W, a subspace of a vector space of n-tuples, has dimension k, then $W^\perp$, the orthogonal complement of W, has dimension $n - k$.

Proof   Let $\{g_1, \ldots, g_k\}$ be a basis for the subspace W, and define the matrix G by

$$G = \begin{bmatrix} g_1 \\ \vdots \\ g_k \end{bmatrix},$$

where the basis vectors appear as rows. This matrix has rank k, and the column space of G has dimension k. A vector v is in $W^\perp$ if

$$Gv^T = 0,$$

because it is then orthogonal to every basis vector. Let $\{h_1, \ldots, h_r\}$ be a basis for $W^\perp$. Extend this to a basis for the whole space, $\{h_1, \ldots, h_r, f_1, \ldots, f_{n-r}\}$. Now every vector v in the column space of G is expressible as $v = Gb^T$ in terms of some vector b that is a linear combination of the basis vectors. Hence, every vector in the column space of G must be expressible as a linear combination of $\{Gh_1^T, Gh_2^T, \ldots, Gh_r^T, Gf_1^T, \ldots, Gf_{n-r}^T\}$.

Now show that $\{Gf_1^T, \ldots, Gf_{n-r}^T\}$ is a basis for the column space of G. Because $Gh_i^T = 0$, this set spans the column space of G. Further, these are independent, because if

$$a_1(Gf_1^T) + \cdots + a_{n-r}(Gf_{n-r}^T) = 0,$$

then

$$G(a_1 f_1^T + \cdots + a_{n-r} f_{n-r}^T) = 0,$$

and hence $a_1 = a_2 = \cdots = a_{n-r} = 0$, because 0 is the only linear combination of $f_1, \ldots, f_{n-r}$ in the null space of G. Therefore $\{Gf_1^T, \ldots, Gf_{n-r}^T\}$ is a basis for the column space of G. Hence $n - r = k$, which proves the theorem. ☐

PROBLEMS

2.1. A group can be constructed by using the rotations and reflections of a pentagon into itself.

 a. How many elements are in this group?

 b. Is it an abelian group?

    c. Construct the group.

    d. Find a subgroup with five elements and a subgroup with two elements.

    e. Are there any subgroups with four elements? Why?

2.2. **a.** Show that only one group exists with three elements. Construct it and show it is abelian.

    b. Show that only two groups exist with four elements. Construct them and show they are abelian. Show that one of the two groups with four elements has no element of order four. This group is called the Klein four-group.

2.3. Let the group operation in the groups in Problem 2 be called addition.

    a. Define multiplication to make the three-element group a ring. Is it unique?

    b. For each of the two four-element groups, define multiplication to make it a ring. Are they unique?

2.4. Which of the three rings in Problem 2.3 are also fields? Can multiplication be defined differently to get a field?

2.5. Show that the set of all integers (positive, negative, and zero) is not a group under the operation of subtraction.

2.6. Give an example of a ring without identity.

2.7. Consider the set $S = \{0, 1, 2, 3\}$ with the operations

+	0 1 2 3
0	0 1 2 3
1	1 2 3 0
2	2 3 0 1
3	3 0 1 2

·	0 1 2 3
0	0 0 0 0
1	0 1 2 3
2	0 2 3 1
3	0 3 1 2

Is this a field?

2.8. Let G be an arbitrary group (not necessarily finite). For convenience, call the group operation multiplication and the identity one. Let g be any element, and suppose that v is the smallest integer, if there is one, such that $g^v = 1$, where g^v means $g \cdot g \ldots \cdot g$, v times. Then v is called the order of g. Prove that the subset $\{g, g^2, g^3, \ldots, g^{v-1}, g^v\}$ is a subgroup of G. Prove that the subgroup is abelian even when G is not.

2.9. Prove Theorems 2.3.3 and 2.3.4.

2.10. Given a ring with identity 1, and given $a \cdot b = 1$, prove that the following are equivalent:

    (i) b is a left inverse for a.

    (ii) $ax = 0$ implies $x = 0$.

    (iii) $yb = 0$ implies $y = 0$.

Note: In some rings condition (ii) is not true. In such a ring an element may have a right inverse or a left inverse that only works on one side.

2.11. The field with four elements, $GF(4)$, is given by the arithmetic tables

+	0 1 2 3
0	0 1 2 3
1	1 0 3 2
2	2 3 0 1
3	3 2 1 0

·	0 1 2 3
0	0 0 0 0
1	0 1 2 3
2	0 2 3 1
3	0 3 1 2

In $GF(4)$, solve:

$$2x + y = 3,$$
$$x + 2y = 3.$$

2.12. The field with three elements, $GF(3)$, is given by the arithmetic tables

+	0 1 2		·	0 1 2
0	0 1 2		0	0 0 0
1	1 2 0		1	0 1 2 .
2	2 0 1		2	0 2 1

Calculate the determinant of the following matrix and show that its rank is 3.

$$\begin{bmatrix} 2 & 1 & 2 \\ 1 & 1 & 2 \\ 1 & 0 & 1 \end{bmatrix}$$

2.13. Put the matrix

$$A = \begin{bmatrix} 1 & 1 & 0 & 1 \\ 1 & 0 & 1 & 1 \\ 0 & 1 & 1 & 0 \\ 0 & 1 & 0 & 1 \end{bmatrix}$$

into row-echelon form. Can the problem be solved without specifying the field? Why?

2.14. How many vectors are there in the vector space $GF(2)^n$?

2.15. Is it true that if $\mathbf{x}$, $\mathbf{y}$, and $\mathbf{z}$ are linearly independent vectors over $GF(q)$, then so also are $\mathbf{x} + \mathbf{y}$, $\mathbf{y} + \mathbf{z}$, and $\mathbf{z} + \mathbf{x}$?

2.16. Does there exist a vector space with 24 elements and dimension greater than 1 over some field $GF(q)$?

2.17. Given that S and T are distinct two-dimensional subspaces of a three-dimensional vector space, show that their intersection is a one-dimensional subspace.

2.18. Let S be any finite set. Let G be the set of subsets of S. If A and B are two subsets, let $A \cup B$ denote the set of elements in either A or B, let $A \cap B$ denote the set of elements in both A and B, and let $A - B$ denote the set of elements in A but not in B.
  a. Show that G with the operation $*$ as set union $\cup$ is not a group.
  b. The set operation of symmetric difference Δ is given by

$$A \Delta B = (A - B) \cup (B - A).$$

Show that G with $*$ as the operation of symmetric difference does give a group. Is it abelian?
  c. Show that G with the operations Δ and $\cap$ gives a ring. Is it a commutative ring? Is there an identity?

2.19. A field with an infinite number of elements that contains a finite field is also called a Galois field. Let F be the set of formal expressions

$$F = \left\{ \frac{\sum\limits_{i=0}^{I-1} a_i x^i}{\sum\limits_{j=0}^{J-1} b_j x^j} \right\},$$

where I and J are any positive integers; and a_i and b_j are elements of $GF(3)$. Provide your own definitions of addition and multiplication in this set so that F is a Galois field with an infinite number of elements.

NOTES

This chapter deals with standard topics in modern algebra. Many textbooks can be found that cover the material more thoroughly. The book by Birkhoff and MacLane (1953) is intended as an introductory text and is easily understood at the level of this book. The book by Van der Waerden (1949, 1953) is a more advanced work, addressed primarily to mathematicians, and goes more deeply into many topics. The material on linear algebra and matrix theory can also be found in textbooks written specifically for these topics. The book by Thrall and Tornheim (1957) is especially suitable because it does not presuppose any underlying field.

The Galois fields are named for Evariste Galois (1811–1832). Abelian groups are named for Niels Henrik Abel (1802–1829).

CHAPTER 3
Linear Block Codes

Most of the known good codes belong to a class of codes called *linear codes*. This class of codes is defined by imposing a strong structural property on the codes. The structure provides guidance in the search for good codes and also helps to make the encoders and decoders practical.

It should be emphasized that we do not study linear codes because the best codes are linear, but rather because at present we have few clues about how to search out good nonlinear codes. There are good linear codes, however, and some are known. Most of the strongest theoretical techniques are useful only for linear codes, and thus attempts to find new codes are usually restricted to the class of linear codes.

3.1 STRUCTURE OF LINEAR BLOCK CODES

Recall that under componentwise vector addition and componentwise scalar multiplication the set of n-tuples of elements from $GF(q)$ is a vector space called $GF(q)^n$. A special case of major importance is $GF(2)^n$, the vector space of all binary words of length n with two such vectors added by modulo-2 addition in each component.

☐ **Definition 3.1.1** A *linear code* is a subspace of $GF(q)^n$. ☐

That is, a linear code is a nonempty set of n-tuples over $GF(q)$ called codewords such that the sum of two codewords is a codeword, and the product of any codeword by a field element is a codeword. In any linear code, the all-zero word, as the vector-space origin, is always a codeword. More directly, if $\mathbf{c}$ is a codeword, then $(-\mathbf{c})$ is a codeword, and hence $\mathbf{c} + (-\mathbf{c})$ is a codeword.

Every codeword in a linear code bears a relationship to the rest of the code that is completely equivalent to the relationship any other codeword bears to the rest of the code. The arrangement of neighboring codewords about the all-zero codeword is typical of the arrangement of the neighboring codewords about any other codeword. For example, suppose that $\mathbf{c}$ is any codeword, and $\mathbf{c}_1, \ldots, \mathbf{c}_r$ are all the codewords at some distance d from $\mathbf{c}$; then $\mathbf{c} - \mathbf{c}$ is the all-zero codeword, and $\mathbf{c}_1 - \mathbf{c}, \mathbf{c}_2 - \mathbf{c}, \ldots, \mathbf{c}_r - \mathbf{c}$ are all the codewords at distance d from the all-zero codeword. Hence, to determine the minimum distance of a linear code, it suffices to determine the distance between the all-zero codeword and the codeword closest to it.

☐ **Definition 3.1.2** The *Hamming weight* $w(\mathbf{c})$ of a codeword $\mathbf{c}$ is equal to the number of nonzero components in the codeword. The *minimum weight* w^* of a code is the smallest weight of any nonzero codeword. ☐

☐ **Theorem 3.1.3** For a linear code, the minimum distance d^* satisfies

$$d^* = \min_{\mathbf{c} \neq 0} w(\mathbf{c}) = w^*,$$

where the minimum is over all codewords except the all-zero codeword.

Proof

$$d^* = \min_{\substack{\mathbf{c}_i, \mathbf{c}_j \in \mathscr{C} \\ i \neq j}} d(\mathbf{c}_i, \mathbf{c}_j) = \min_{\substack{\mathbf{c}_i, \mathbf{c}_j \in \mathscr{C} \\ i \neq j}} d(\mathbf{0}, \mathbf{c}_i - \mathbf{c}_j) = \min_{\substack{\mathbf{c} \in \mathscr{C} \\ \mathbf{c} \neq 0}} w(\mathbf{c}). \qquad \Box$$

Hence, to find a linear code that can correct t errors, one must find a linear code with minimum weight satisfying

$$w^* \geqslant 2t + 1.$$

The study of the distance structure of a linear code is much easier than that of nonlinear codes.

3.2 MATRIX DESCRIPTION OF LINEAR BLOCK CODES

A linear code $\mathscr{C}$ is a subspace of $GF(q)^n$. The theory of vector spaces can be used to study these codes. Any set of basis vectors for the subspace can be used as rows to form a k by n matrix $\mathbf{G}$ called the *generator matrix* of the code. The row space of $\mathbf{G}$ is the linear code $\mathscr{C}$; any codeword is a linear combination of the rows of $\mathbf{G}$. The set of q^k codewords is called an (n, k) linear code.

The rows of $\mathbf{G}$ are linearly independent, and the number of rows k is the dimension of the subspace. (The dimension of the whole space $GF(q)^n$ is n.) There are q^k codewords, and the q^k distinct k-tuples over $GF(q)$ can be mapped onto the set of codewords.

Any one-to-one pairing of k-tuples and codewords can be used as an encoding procedure, but the most natural approach is to use the following:

$$\mathbf{c} = \mathbf{iG},$$

where $\mathbf{i}$, the information word, is a k-tuple of information symbols to be encoded and $\mathbf{c}$ is the codeword n-tuple. With this expression defining the encoder, the pairing between information words and codewords depends on the choice of basis vectors appearing as rows of $\mathbf{G}$; but, of course, the total set of codewords is unaffected.

For a simple example of a binary linear code, take the generator matrix

$$\mathbf{G} = \begin{bmatrix} 1 & 0 & 0 & 1 & 0 \\ 0 & 1 & 0 & 0 & 1 \\ 0 & 0 & 1 & 1 & 1 \end{bmatrix}.$$

The information vector

$$\mathbf{i} = \begin{bmatrix} 0 & 1 & 1 \end{bmatrix}$$

is encoded into the codeword

$$\mathbf{c} = \begin{bmatrix} 0 & 1 & 1 \end{bmatrix} \begin{bmatrix} 1 & 0 & 0 & 1 & 0 \\ 0 & 1 & 0 & 0 & 1 \\ 0 & 0 & 1 & 1 & 1 \end{bmatrix} = \begin{bmatrix} 0 & 1 & 1 & 1 & 0 \end{bmatrix}.$$

The generator matrix is a concise way to describe a linear code. Compare a binary (100, 50) linear code, which is described by $100 \times 50 = 5000$ bits as elements of **G**, with an arbitrary (100, 50) code, which has 2^{50} codewords requiring approximately 10^{17} bits to list.

Because $\mathscr{C}$ is a subspace, it has an orthogonal complement $\mathscr{C}^{\perp}$, which is the set of all vectors orthogonal to $\mathscr{C}$. The orthogonal complement is also a subspace and thus can be used as a code. Whenever $\mathscr{C}^{\perp}$ itself is thought of as a code, it is called the *dual code* of $\mathscr{C}$.

The orthogonal complement $\mathscr{C}^{\perp}$ has dimension $n - k$ and $n - k$ vectors in any basis. Let **H** be a matrix with these basis vectors as rows. Then an n-tuple **c** is a codeword if and only if it is orthogonal to every row vector of **H**. That is,

$$\mathbf{c}\mathbf{H}^T = \mathbf{0}.$$

This gives a way for testing whether a word is a codeword. The matrix **H** is called a *parity-check matrix* of the code. It is an $(n - k)$ by n matrix. Because $\mathbf{c}\mathbf{H}^T = \mathbf{0}$ holds when **c** is equal to any row of **G**, we have

$$\mathbf{G}\mathbf{H}^T = \mathbf{0}.$$

Using the same example of a generator matrix **G** as before, we have

$$\mathbf{H} = \begin{bmatrix} 1 & 0 & 1 & 1 & 0 \\ 0 & 1 & 1 & 0 & 1 \end{bmatrix}$$

as one choice for **H**. Notice that just as there is more than one choice for **G**, there is more than one choice for **H**.

□ **Theorem 3.2.1** A generator matrix for $\mathscr{C}$ is a parity-check matrix for the dual code $\mathscr{C}^{\perp}$.

Proof The proof is immediate. □

The minimum weight of a code is related to the parity-check matrix by the following theorem.

□ **Theorem 3.2.2** The code $\mathscr{C}$ contains a nonzero codeword of Hamming weight w or less if and only if a linearly dependent set of w columns of **H** exists.

Proof For any codeword **c**, $\mathbf{c}\mathbf{H}^T = \mathbf{0}$. Let **c** have weight w. Drop the components of **c** that are zero. This is a linear-dependence relation in w columns of **H**. Hence, **H** has a linearly dependent set of w columns.

Conversely, if **H** has a linearly dependent set of w columns, then a linear combination of at most w columns is equal to zero. These w nonzero coefficients define a vector of weight w or less for which $\mathbf{c}\mathbf{H}^T = \mathbf{0}$. □

□ **Corollary 3.2.3** A code has minimum weight not smaller than w if and only if every set of $w - 1$ columns of **H** is linearly independent. □

Hence, to find an (n, k) code that can correct t errors, it suffices to find an $(n - k)$ by n matrix $\mathbf{H}$ with every set of $2t$ columns linearly independent.

Given an (n, k) code with minimum distance d^*, a new code with the same parameters can be obtained by choosing two components and transposing the symbols in these two components of every codeword. This, however, gives a code that is only trivially different from the original code; it is said to be *equivalent* to the original code. In general, two linear codes that are the same except for a permutation of components are called equivalent codes.

The generator matrices $\mathbf{G}$ and $\mathbf{G}'$ of equivalent codes can be simply related. The code itself is the row space of $\mathbf{G}$ and thus is unchanged under elementary row operations. Permutation of the components of the code corresponds to permutation of the columns of $\mathbf{G}$. Hence, two codes are equivalent if and only if their $\mathbf{G}$ matrices are related by

1. Column permutations

and

2. Elementary row operations.

Every generator matrix $\mathbf{G}$ is equivalent to one in row-echelon form, and because the rows are linearly independent, no row will contain all zeros. Hence, by column permutations, every generator matrix is equivalent to one with a k by k identity in the first k columns. That is,

$$\mathbf{G} = [\mathbf{I} \vdots \mathbf{P}],$$

and $\mathbf{P}$ is a k by $(n - k)$ matrix. Every generator matrix can be reduced to this special form by a sequence of elementary row operations followed by a sequence of column permutations. We call this the *systematic form* of the generator matrix.

Suppose that $\mathbf{G} = [\mathbf{I} \vdots \mathbf{P}]$. Then clearly, the appropriate definition of a systematic parity-check matrix is $\mathbf{H} = [-\mathbf{P}^T \vdots \mathbf{I}]$, because

$$\mathbf{G}\mathbf{H}^T = [\mathbf{I} \vdots \mathbf{P}] \begin{bmatrix} -\mathbf{P} \\ \cdots \\ \mathbf{I} \end{bmatrix} = -\mathbf{P} + \mathbf{P} = \mathbf{0}.$$

□ **Definition 3.2.4** A *systematic** code is one that starts each codeword with the information symbols unmodified. The remaining symbols are called *parity symbols*. □

It is common practice here to speak of a systematic code, although what is always meant is a systematic encoding of an appropriate code.

---

*When dealing with cyclic codes in Chapter 5, it will be convenient and conventional to think of a codeword as beginning with the high-index component c_{n-1} and ending with c_0. Then we should use the equivalent matrices of the form $\mathbf{G} = [\mathbf{P} \vdots \mathbf{I}]$ and $\mathbf{H} = [\mathbf{I} \vdots -\mathbf{P}^T]$ for some new $\mathbf{P}$. These are obtained by reversing all rows and reversing all columns of the earlier form. They also are called systematic matrices.

☐ **Theorem 3.2.5** Every linear code is equivalent to a systematic linear code.

Proof A systematic linear code is encoded by multiplying the information vector by a generator matrix in systematic form, and every **G** is equivalent to one in systematic form. ☐

For an example, choose

$$\mathbf{G} = \begin{bmatrix} 1 & 0 & 0 & 1 & 0 \\ 0 & 1 & 0 & 0 & 1 \\ 0 & 0 & 1 & 1 & 1 \end{bmatrix}, \qquad \mathbf{H} = \begin{bmatrix} 1 & 0 & 1 & 1 & 0 \\ 0 & 1 & 1 & 0 & 1 \end{bmatrix},$$

then $\mathbf{i} = \begin{bmatrix} 0 & 1 & 1 \end{bmatrix}$ is systematically encoded as $\mathbf{c} = \begin{bmatrix} 0 & 1 & 1 & 1 & 0 \end{bmatrix}$.

By looking at a code in its systematic form, it is possible to obtain a simple inequality relating the parameters of a code. This bound is very loose in that most good codes have a minimum distance well below the bound, but it is sometimes useful. Consider an arbitrary systematic linear (n, k) code with minimum distance d^*. The possible values of (n, k, d^*) are limited by the following theorem.

☐ **Theorem 3.2.6 (Singleton Bound)** The minimum distance (minimum weight) of any linear (n, k) code satisfies

$$d^* \leqslant 1 + n - k.$$

Proof The smallest-weight nonzero codeword has weight d^*. Systematic codewords exist with only one nonzero information symbol and $(n - k)$ parity symbols. Such a codeword cannot have weight larger than $1 + (n - k)$. Hence the minimum weight of the code cannot be larger than $1 + n - k$. ☐

☐ **Definition 3.2.7** Any code whose minimum distance satisfies

$$d^* = 1 + n - k$$

is called a *maximum-distance code*. ☐

The Singleton bound tells us that in order to correct t errors, a code must have at least $2t$ parity symbols—2 parity symbols per error to be corrected. Most codes, even optimum codes, have considerably more parity symbols than required by the Singleton bound, but some meet it with equality. A maximum-distance code has exactly $2t$ parity symbols.

3.3 THE STANDARD ARRAY

Because the difference of two codewords in a linear code is a codeword, the all-zero word is always a codeword. For a linear code, if we know which set of received words lies closest to the all-zero codeword, then we know which received words lie closest to any other codeword simply by translating the origin.

Thus, suppose d^* is odd and $d^* = 2t + 1$. The sphere of radius t about the all-zero word is

$$S_0 = \{\mathbf{v} \mid d(\mathbf{0}, \mathbf{v}) \leqslant t\}.$$

The sphere contains all received words that will be decoded into the all-zero codeword. The sphere of radius t about codeword $\mathbf{c}$ is

$$S_{\mathbf{c}} = \{\mathbf{v} \mid d(\mathbf{c}, \mathbf{v}) \leqslant t\}.$$

Then we have

$$S_{\mathbf{c}} = S_0 + \mathbf{c} = \{\mathbf{v} + \mathbf{c} \mid \mathbf{v} \in S_0\}.$$

Hence we can either record the members of every decoding sphere or, more efficiently, record the members of the decoding sphere about the all-zero codeword, and compute the others as needed by a simple translation.

The standard array is a way of tabulating all of the spheres. Let $\mathbf{0}, \mathbf{c}_2, \mathbf{c}_3, \ldots, \mathbf{c}_{q^k}$ be the q^k codewords in an (n, k) code. Form the table of Fig. 3.1 as follows. Write all the codewords in the first row. Of the unused words in $GF(q)^n$ lying at a distance of 1 from the all-zero codeword, choose

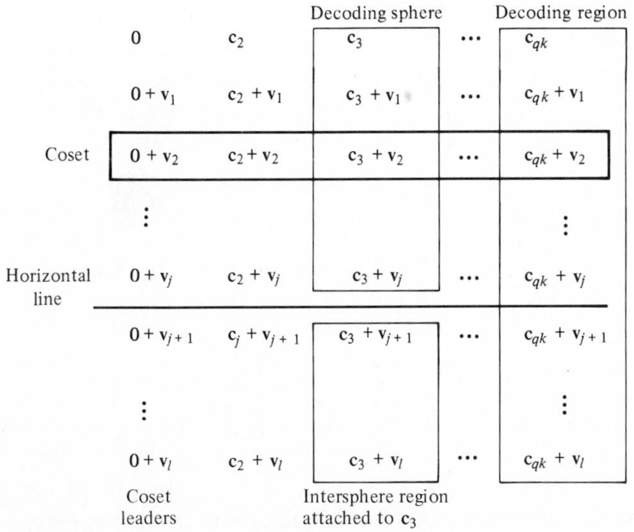

Figure 3.1   The standard array.

any word and call it $\mathbf{v}_1$. Write $\mathbf{0} + \mathbf{v}_1, \mathbf{c}_2 + \mathbf{v}_1, \mathbf{c}_3 + \mathbf{v}_1, \ldots, \mathbf{c}_{qk} + \mathbf{v}_1$ in the second row. Continue in this way to form additional rows. At the jth step, choose $\mathbf{v}_j$, a previously unused word that is as close as possible to the all-zero word, and write $\mathbf{0} + \mathbf{v}_j, \mathbf{c}_2 + \mathbf{v}_j, \mathbf{c}_3 + \mathbf{v}_j, \ldots, \mathbf{c}_{qk} + \mathbf{v}_j$ for the jth row. Stop when, after some step, no unused words remain.

Now the code is a subgroup, and this process generates cosets. Hence, it halts with each word used exactly once. By Corollary 2.2.4, there will be q^{n-k} rows. The words in the first column are called *coset leaders*.

Because the rows are constructed like the shells of an onion by starting at the all-zero word, the first column must include all words in the decoding sphere about the all-zero codeword; that is, all words within distance t of it. When the shells of radius t are complete, draw a horizontal line across the standard array. There may be points still unused at this point, and the construction of the standard array then goes on to attach these to a nearby codeword, but this is partly arbitrary.

There are two basic classes of decoders that can be described in terms of the standard array: complete decoders and incomplete decoders. A complete decoder is one that assigns every received word to a nearby codeword. When a word is received, find it in the standard array and decode it into the codeword at the top of its column.

An incomplete decoder is one that assigns every received word to a codeword within distance t, if there is one, and otherwise refuses to decode. When a word is received, find it in the standard array. If it lies above the horizontal line, decode it into the word at the top of its column. If it is below the line, flag the received word as uncorrectable. It has more than t errors.

For an example, consider the (5, 2) code with

$$\mathbf{G} = \begin{bmatrix} 1 & 0 & 1 & 1 & 1 \\ 0 & 1 & 1 & 0 & 1 \end{bmatrix}.$$

This code corrects one error. The standard array is

0 0 0 0 0	1 0 1 1 1	0 1 1 0 1	1 1 0 1 0
0 0 0 0 1	1 0 1 1 0	0 1 1 0 0	1 1 0 1 1
0 0 0 1 0	1 0 1 0 1	0 1 1 1 1	1 1 0 0 0
0 0 1 0 0	1 0 0 1 1	0 1 0 0 1	1 1 1 1 0
0 1 0 0 0	1 1 1 1 1	0 0 1 0 1	1 0 0 1 0
1 0 0 0 0	0 0 1 1 1	1 1 1 0 1	0 1 0 1 0
0 0 0 1 1	1 0 1 0 0	0 1 1 1 0	1 1 0 0 1
0 0 1 1 0	1 0 0 0 1	0 1 0 1 1	1 1 1 0 0

Spheres of radius 1 are disjoint. There are four spheres, six points per sphere, and eight points outside of any sphere.

It is obvious that the standard array is of value only conceptually. For large n and k such a table would be impractical to list.

The table can be simplified if we can store only the first column and compute the remaining columns as needed. This we do by introducing the concept of the syndrome of the error pattern.

For any received word **v**, define the *syndrome* of **v** by

$$\mathbf{s} = \mathbf{v}\mathbf{H}^T$$

☐ **Theorem 3.3.1** All vectors in the same coset have the same syndrome unique to that coset.

Proof If **v** and **v′** are in the same coset, then $\mathbf{v} = \mathbf{c}_i + \mathbf{y}$, $\mathbf{v}' = \mathbf{c}_j + \mathbf{y}$ for some **y** and for some codewords $\mathbf{c}_i$ and $\mathbf{c}_j$. For any codeword **c**, $\mathbf{c}\mathbf{H}^T = \mathbf{0}$. Hence

$$\mathbf{s} = \mathbf{v}\mathbf{H}^T = \mathbf{y}\mathbf{H}^T$$

$$\mathbf{s}' = \mathbf{v}'\mathbf{H}^T = \mathbf{y}\mathbf{H}^T$$

and $\mathbf{s} = \mathbf{s}'$. Conversely, suppose $\mathbf{s} = \mathbf{s}'$; then $(\mathbf{v} - \mathbf{v}')\mathbf{H}^T = \mathbf{0}$, and thus $\mathbf{v} - \mathbf{v}'$ is a codeword. Hence, **v** and **v′** are in the same coset. ☐

Any two vectors in the same coset have the same syndrome. Hence, we need only tabulate syndromes and coset leaders. We can then decode as follows. Given a received word **v**, compute the syndrome and look up its associated coset leader. This coset leader is the difference between the received word and the center of its decoding sphere. Hence, subtract the coset leader from **v** to correct the error.

For the example introduced above, the parity-check matrix is

$$\mathbf{H} = \begin{bmatrix} 1 & 1 & 1 & 0 & 0 \\ 1 & 0 & 0 & 1 & 0 \\ 1 & 1 & 0 & 0 & 1 \end{bmatrix}.$$

The new table is

Coset leader	Syndrome
0 0 0 0 0	0 0 0
0 0 0 0 1	0 0 1
0 0 0 1 0	0 1 0
0 0 1 0 0	1 0 0
0 1 0 0 0	1 0 1
1 0 0 0 0	1 1 1
0 0 0 1 1	0 1 1
0 0 1 1 0	1 1 0

This is a simpler table than the standard array. Suppose $\mathbf{v} = 10010$ is received. Then $\mathbf{s} = \mathbf{v}\mathbf{H}^T = 101$. The coset leader is 01000. Therefore the transmitted word is $10010 - 01000 = 11010$, and the information word is 11.

3.4 HAMMING CODES

· A code whose minimum distance is at least 3 must, by Corollary 3.2.3, have a parity-check matrix all of whose columns are distinct and nonzero. If a parity-check matrix for a binary code has m rows, then each column is an m-bit binary number. There are $2^m - 1$ possible columns. Hence if the $\mathbf{H}$ matrix of a binary code with d^* at least 3 has m rows, then it can have $2^m - 1$ columns, but no more. This defines a $(2^m - 1, 2^m - 1 - m)$ code. The simplest nontrivial example is $m = 3$. Then in systematic form,

$$\mathbf{H} = \begin{bmatrix} 1 & 1 & 0 & 1 & 1 & 0 & 0 \\ 1 & 0 & 1 & 1 & 0 & 1 & 0 \\ 0 & 1 & 1 & 1 & 0 & 0 & 1 \end{bmatrix}$$

and

$$\mathbf{G} = \begin{bmatrix} 1 & 0 & 0 & 0 & 1 & 1 & 0 \\ 0 & 1 & 0 & 0 & 1 & 0 & 1 \\ 0 & 0 & 1 & 0 & 0 & 1 & 1 \\ 0 & 0 & 0 & 1 & 1 & 1 & 1 \end{bmatrix}.$$

These $(2^m - 1, 2^m - 1 - m)$ codes are the Hamming codes.

Clearly, every pair of columns of $\mathbf{H}$ is independent (because no pair of distinct binary vectors can sum to zero), and some sets of three columns are dependent. Hence, by Theorem 3.2.2, the minimum weight is 3, and the code can correct a single error.

Hamming codes can be easily defined for larger alphabet sizes. One merely notes that the main idea is to define an $\mathbf{H}$ with every pair of columns linearly independent. Over $GF(q)$, $q \neq 2$, one cannot use all nonzero m-tuples because some pairs will be linearly dependent. To force linear independence, choose all nonzero m-tuples that have a one in the first nonzero component. Then two columns can never be linearly dependent but three columns can, and the code has minimum weight equal to 3.

There are $(q^m - 1)/(q - 1)$ such distinct columns. Hence the code is a $((q^m - 1)/(q - 1), (q^m - 1)/(q - 1) - m)$ code. A single-error-correcting Hamming code with these parameters exists for each q for which a field $GF(q)$ exists and for each m. Some sample parameters are shown in Table 3.1.

For example, a $(13, 10)$ Hamming code over $GF(3)$ is given by the parity-check matrix

$$\mathbf{H} = \begin{bmatrix} 1 & 1 & 1 & 1 & 1 & 1 & 1 & 1 & 1 & 0 & 0 & 1 & 0 & 0 \\ 0 & 0 & 1 & 1 & 1 & 2 & 2 & 2 & 1 & 1 & 0 & 1 & 0 \\ 1 & 2 & 0 & 1 & 2 & 0 & 1 & 2 & 1 & 2 & 0 & 0 & 1 \end{bmatrix}$$

and the generator matrix

$$
\mathbf{G} = \begin{bmatrix}
1 & 0 & 0 & 0 & 0 & 0 & 0 & 0 & 0 & 0 & 1 & 0 & 1 \\
0 & 1 & 0 & 0 & 0 & 0 & 0 & 0 & 0 & 0 & 1 & 0 & 2 \\
0 & 0 & 1 & 0 & 0 & 0 & 0 & 0 & 0 & 0 & 1 & 1 & 0 \\
0 & 0 & 0 & 1 & 0 & 0 & 0 & 0 & 0 & 0 & 1 & 1 & 1 \\
0 & 0 & 0 & 0 & 1 & 0 & 0 & 0 & 0 & 0 & 1 & 1 & 2 \\
0 & 0 & 0 & 0 & 0 & 1 & 0 & 0 & 0 & 0 & 1 & 2 & 0 \\
0 & 0 & 0 & 0 & 0 & 0 & 1 & 0 & 0 & 0 & 1 & 2 & 1 \\
0 & 0 & 0 & 0 & 0 & 0 & 0 & 1 & 0 & 0 & 1 & 2 & 2 \\
0 & 0 & 0 & 0 & 0 & 0 & 0 & 0 & 1 & 0 & 0 & 1 & 1 \\
0 & 0 & 0 & 0 & 0 & 0 & 0 & 0 & 0 & 1 & 0 & 1 & 2
\end{bmatrix} .
$$

The second example is more practical. Suppose that a four-bit-wide data path exists between a computer and a remote peripheral. Across this path, a 4-bit byte is transmitted in parallel. The four bits are viewed as a single hexadecimal symbol, and a sequence of such information symbols is transmitted. We wish to block the symbols and protect against one symbol error per block. Taking $q = 16$ and $m = 2$, we see that we can have a (17, 15) hexadecimal Hamming code provided that $GF(16)$ exists. But we have already exhibited $GF(16)$ in Fig. 2.1 (although we have not yet verified that it satisfies the field axioms). Using this field, we can construct the generator matrix for the Hamming (17, 15) code over $GF(16)$. From the matrix, we could read off the following equations for the parity symbols:

$$p_1 = i_1 + i_2 + i_3 + \cdots + i_{14} + i_{15},$$

$$p_2 = i_1 + 2i_2 + 3i_3 + \cdots + Ei_{14} + Fi_{15}.$$

After every block of 15 information symbols, these 2 parity symbols are inserted. Using these, the decoder can correct a single symbol error in the block of 17 symbols. Of course, this only makes sense if we accept that the field $GF(16)$ exists and is given by Fig. 2.1. Before we can use the above construction in any field $GF(q)$, we must prove that $GF(q)$ exists and find how to add and multiply in this field.

Table 3.1 Parameters (n, k) for some Hamming codes.

$GF(2)$	$GF(4)$	$GF(8)$	$GF(16)$	$GF(27)$
(7, 4)	(5, 3)	(9, 7)	(17, 15)	(28, 26)
(15, 11)	(21, 18)	(73, 70)	(273, 270)	(757, 754)
(31, 26)	(85, 81)	(585, 581)		
(63, 57)	(341, 336)			
(127, 120)				

3.5 PERFECT AND QUASI-PERFECT CODES

Visualize a small sphere about each of the codewords of a code, each sphere with the same radius (an integer). Allow these spheres to increase in radius by integer amounts until they cannot be made larger without causing some spheres to intersect. That value of the radius is equal to the number of errors that can be corrected by the code. It is called the *packing radius* of the code. Now allow the radii to continue to increase by integer amounts, until every point in the space is contained in at least one sphere. That radius is called the *covering radius* of the code.

The packing radius and the covering radius may be equal; if so, then the construction of the standard array stops just when the spheres of radius t are completed. All points of the space are used in these spheres; none are left over.

☐ **Definition 3.5.1** A *perfect code* is one for which there are equal-radius spheres about the codewords that are disjoint and that completely fill the space. ☐

A perfect code satisfies the Hamming bound of Problem 1.5 with equality. A Hamming code with blocklength $n = (q^m - 1)/(q - 1)$ is perfect. This is because there are $1 + n(q - 1) = q^m$ points in each sphere of radius 1, and the number of points in the space divided by the number of spheres is $q^n/q^k = q^m$ because $n - k = m$. Perfect codes, when they exist, have nice properties and are aesthetically pleasant, but they are so rare that they are not often important in practical applications.

☐ **Definition 3.5.2** A *quasi-perfect code* is one in which spheres of radius t about each codeword are disjoint and all words not in such a sphere are at a distance of $t + 1$ from at least one codeword. ☐

Quasi-perfect codes are more common than perfect codes. When one exists for a given n and k (and no such perfect code exists), then for this n and k no other code can have larger d^*. We must again remark, however, that these are rare and do not seem to be of any special importance in practical applications.

3.6 SIMPLE MODIFICATIONS TO A LINEAR CODE

There are a number of simple things that one might do to make slight changes to a linear code to get a new code. If the new code is also linear, these changes correspond to simple changes that can be made to the generator matrix **G**: namely, one can add a column or a row; delete a column or a row; add both a column and a row; or delete both a column and a row. These change the code in ways that are simply described, although it might not be a simple matter to find such modifications that are worthwhile.

The blocklength n can be increased by increasing k or by increasing $n - k$. We call these *lengthening* and *expanding* and subsume both notions under the more general term *extending*. By extending we mean increasing the blocklength either by expanding or by lengthening. The six basic changes are as follows:

Expanding a Code   Increasing the length by adding more parity-check symbols. This corresponds to increasing the larger dimension of the generator matrix.

Lengthening a Code   Increasing the length by adding more information symbols. This corresponds to increasing both dimensions of the generator matrix by the same amount.

Puncturing a Code   Reducing the length by dropping parity-check symbols. This corresponds to decreasing the larger dimension of the generator matrix.

Shortening a Code   Reducing the length by dropping information symbols. This corresponds to decreasing both dimensions of the generator matrix by the same amount.

Augmenting a Code   Increasing the number of information symbols without changing the length. This corresponds to increasing the smaller dimension of the generator matrix.

Expurgating a Code   Decreasing the number of information symbols without changing the length. This corresponds to decreasing the smaller dimension of the generator matrix.

These modifications can be used to remodel a known code to fit a specific application. They might also be used to devise new classes of good codes.

Any binary (n, k, d^*) code whose minimum distance is odd can be expanded to an $(n + 1, k, d^* + 1)$ code by appending the sum of all other codeword components as an overall parity check. This is because if the original codeword has odd weight, the new bit will be a one. Hence, all codewords of weight d^* become codewords of weight $d^* + 1$. If $\mathbf{H}$ is the parity-check matrix of the original code, then the expanded code has parity-check matrix

$$\mathbf{H}' = \begin{bmatrix} 1 & 1 & \dots & 1 \\ 0 & & & \\ \vdots & & \mathbf{H} & \\ 0 & & & \end{bmatrix}.$$

Specifically, every $(2^m - 1, 2^m - 1 - m)$ Hamming code can be expanded into a $(2^m, 2^m - m)$ single-error-correcting, double-error-detecting code, usually also called a Hamming code.

One can also reduce a code over one field to another code over a smaller field. Start with a code over a field $GF(q^m)$, and gather up all those codewords that have only components in the subfield $GF(q)$. This code over $GF(q)$ is called a *subfield-subcode* of the original code. If the original code is linear, then the subfield-subcode is linear. It is not, however, a subspace of the original code. This is because a subspace must contain all multiples of code-words by elements of $GF(q^m)$. The subfield-subcode is linear because over the subfield $GF(q)$ all linear combinations of codewords must be in the subfield-subcode. Any set of basis vectors for the subfield-subcode is also linearly independent, even over $GF(q^m)$, and thus the dimension of the original code is at least as large as the dimension of the subfield-subcode. In general, however, the original code has a larger dimension; a subfield-subcode usually has a smaller rate than the original code.

3.7 REED-MULLER CODES

Reed-Muller codes are a class of linear codes over $GF(2)$ that are easy to describe and can be decoded by a simple voting technique. For these reasons, the Reed-Muller codes are important even though with some exceptions, their minimum distances are not noteworthy.† For each integer m, and for each integer r less than m there is a Reed-Muller code of blocklength 2^m called the rth-order Reed-Muller code of blocklength 2^m.

A Reed-Muller code is a linear code. It will be defined by a procedure for constructing a generator matrix; we will construct a nonsystematic generator matrix that will prove convenient for decoding. First, define the *product* of two vectors **a** and **b** by a componentwise multiplication. That is, let

$$\mathbf{a} = (\mathbf{a}_0, \mathbf{a}_1, \ldots, \mathbf{a}_{n-1}),$$

$$\mathbf{b} = (\mathbf{b}_0, \mathbf{b}_1, \ldots, \mathbf{b}_{n-1}).$$

Then the product is the vector

$$\mathbf{ab} = (\mathbf{a}_0\mathbf{b}_0, \mathbf{a}_1\mathbf{b}_1, \ldots, \mathbf{a}_{n-1}\mathbf{b}_{n-1}).$$

The generator matrix for the rth-order Reed-Muller code of blocklength 2^m is defined as an array of blocks:

$$\mathbf{G} = \begin{bmatrix} \mathbf{G}_0 \\ \mathbf{G}_1 \\ \vdots \\ \mathbf{G}_r \end{bmatrix},$$

where $\mathbf{G}_0$ is the vector of length $n = 2^m$ containing all ones; $\mathbf{G}_1$, an m by 2^m matrix, has each binary m-tuple appearing once as a column; and $\mathbf{G}_l$ is constructed from $\mathbf{G}_1$ by taking its rows to be all possible products of rows of $\mathbf{G}_1$, l rows of $\mathbf{G}_1$ to a product. For definiteness, we take the leftmost column

---

†A Reed-Muller code was used to transmit the Mariner photographs of Mars in 1972. Today, a more powerful code would be preferred.

of $\mathbf{G}_1$ to be all zeros, the rightmost to be all ones, and the others to be the binary m-tuples in increasing order, with the low-order bit in the bottom row.

Because there are $\binom{m}{l}$ ways to choose the l rows in a product, G_l is an $\binom{m}{l}$ by 2^m matrix. Clearly, for any Reed-Muller code,

$$k = 1 + \binom{m}{1} + \cdots + \binom{m}{r},$$

$$n - k = 1 + \binom{m}{1} + \cdots + \binom{m}{m-r-1},$$

provided the rows of $\mathbf{G}$ are linearly independent. The 0th-order Reed-Muller code is an $(n, 1)$ code. It is a simple repetition code and is decoded trivially by a majority vote. It has a minimum distance of 2^m.

As an example, let $m = 4$, $n = 16$, and $r = 3$. Then

$$\mathbf{G}_0 = [1\ 1\ 1\ 1\ 1\ 1\ 1\ 1\ 1\ 1\ 1\ 1\ 1\ 1\ 1\ 1] = [\mathbf{a}_0],$$

$$\mathbf{G}_1 = \begin{bmatrix} 0\ 0\ 0\ 0\ 0\ 0\ 0\ 0\ 1\ 1\ 1\ 1\ 1\ 1\ 1\ 1 \\ 0\ 0\ 0\ 0\ 1\ 1\ 1\ 1\ 0\ 0\ 0\ 0\ 1\ 1\ 1\ 1 \\ 0\ 0\ 1\ 1\ 0\ 0\ 1\ 1\ 0\ 0\ 1\ 1\ 0\ 0\ 1\ 1 \\ 0\ 1\ 0\ 1\ 0\ 1\ 0\ 1\ 0\ 1\ 0\ 1\ 0\ 1\ 0\ 1 \end{bmatrix} = \begin{bmatrix} \mathbf{a}_1 \\ \mathbf{a}_2 \\ \mathbf{a}_3 \\ \mathbf{a}_4 \end{bmatrix}.$$

Because $\mathbf{G}_1$ has four rows, $\mathbf{G}_2$ has $\binom{4}{2}$ rows,

$$\mathbf{G}_2 = \begin{bmatrix} 0\ 0\ 0\ 0\ 0\ 0\ 0\ 0\ 0\ 0\ 0\ 0\ 1\ 1\ 1\ 1 \\ 0\ 0\ 0\ 0\ 0\ 0\ 0\ 0\ 0\ 0\ 1\ 1\ 0\ 0\ 1\ 1 \\ 0\ 0\ 0\ 0\ 0\ 0\ 0\ 0\ 1\ 0\ 1\ 0\ 1\ 0\ 1 \\ 0\ 0\ 0\ 0\ 0\ 0\ 1\ 1\ 0\ 0\ 0\ 0\ 0\ 0\ 1\ 1 \\ 0\ 0\ 0\ 0\ 0\ 1\ 0\ 1\ 0\ 0\ 0\ 0\ 0\ 1\ 0\ 1 \\ 0\ 0\ 0\ 1\ 0\ 0\ 0\ 1\ 0\ 0\ 0\ 1\ 0\ 0\ 0\ 1 \end{bmatrix} = \begin{bmatrix} \mathbf{a}_1\mathbf{a}_2 \\ \mathbf{a}_1\mathbf{a}_3 \\ \mathbf{a}_1\mathbf{a}_4 \\ \mathbf{a}_2\mathbf{a}_3 \\ \mathbf{a}_2\mathbf{a}_4 \\ \mathbf{a}_3\mathbf{a}_4 \end{bmatrix},$$

and $\mathbf{G}_3$ has $\binom{4}{3}$ rows,

$$\mathbf{G}_3 = \begin{bmatrix} 0\ 0\ 0\ 0\ 0\ 0\ 0\ 0\ 0\ 0\ 0\ 0\ 0\ 0\ 1\ 1 \\ 0\ 0\ 0\ 0\ 0\ 0\ 0\ 0\ 0\ 0\ 0\ 0\ 0\ 1\ 0\ 1 \\ 0\ 0\ 0\ 0\ 0\ 0\ 0\ 0\ 0\ 0\ 1\ 0\ 0\ 0\ 1 \\ 0\ 0\ 0\ 0\ 0\ 0\ 1\ 0\ 0\ 0\ 0\ 0\ 0\ 0\ 1 \end{bmatrix} = \begin{bmatrix} \mathbf{a}_1\mathbf{a}_2\mathbf{a}_3 \\ \mathbf{a}_1\mathbf{a}_2\mathbf{a}_4 \\ \mathbf{a}_1\mathbf{a}_3\mathbf{a}_4 \\ \mathbf{a}_2\mathbf{a}_3\mathbf{a}_4 \end{bmatrix}.$$

Then the generator matrix for the third-order Reed-Muller code of blocklength 16 is the 15 by 16 matrix:

$$\mathbf{G} = \begin{bmatrix} \mathbf{G}_0 \\ \mathbf{G}_1 \\ \mathbf{G}_2 \\ \mathbf{G}_3 \end{bmatrix}.$$

This generator matrix gives a $(16, 15)$ code over $GF(2)$. (In fact, it is a simple parity-check code.) Another Reed-Muller code obtained from these same matrices is obtained by choosing r equal to 2. This generator matrix is

$$G = \begin{bmatrix} G_0 \\ G_1 \\ G_2 \end{bmatrix}.$$

It gives a $(16, 11)$ code over $GF(2)$. (In fact, it is the $(15, 11)$ Hamming code expanded by an extra parity check.)

From the definition of their generator matrices, it is clear that an rth-order Reed-Muller code can be obtained by augmenting an $(r-1)$th-order Reed-Muller code, and an $(r-1)$th-order Reed-Muller code can be obtained by expurgating an rth-order Reed-Muller code. Clearly, because the rth-order Reed-Muller code contains the $(r-1)$th-order Reed-Muller code, its minimum distance cannot be larger. We will prove later that $d^* = 2^{m-r}$ for an rth-order Reed-Muller code.

Every row of G_l has weight 2^{m-l}. Hence, every row of G has even weight, and the sum of two binary vectors of even weight must have an even weight (see Problem 3.11). Hence, all linear combinations of rows of G have even weight; that is, all codewords have even weight. The matrix G_r has rows of weight 2^{m-r}, and thus the minimum weight is not larger than 2^{m-r}.

We must show that the rows of G are linearly independent, and we must find the minimum weight of the code. We shall show that the code must have minimum weight of 2^{m-r} and that the rows of G must be linearly independent by developing a decoding algorithm—the Reed algorithm—that corrects $(\frac{1}{2} \cdot 2^{m-r} - 1)$ errors and recovers the k information bits. This will imply that the minimum distance is at least $2^{m-r} - 1$ and, because it is even, that it is at least 2^{m-r}.

The Reed algorithm is designed specifically for Reed-Muller codes. Of course, the general syndrome techniques of Section 3.3 could be used but would not be as simple to implement. The Reed algorithm is unusual as compared to most algorithms for most codes in that it recovers the information directly from the received word and does not explicitly compute the error. Intermediate variables such as syndromes are not used.

Suppose that we have a decoder for an $(r-1)$th-order Reed-Muller code in the presence of $(\frac{1}{2} \cdot 2^{m-(r-1)} - 1)$ errors. We will construct a decoder for an rth-order Reed-Muller code in the presence of $(\frac{1}{2} \cdot 2^{m-r} - 1)$ errors by reducing it to the earlier case. Because we already know that the 0th-order Reed-Muller code can be decoded by majority vote, we have a decoding algorithm by induction.

It is convenient to break the information vector into $r+1$ segments, written $i = [I_0, I_1, \ldots, I_r]$ where segment I_l contains $\binom{m}{l}$ information bits. Each segment multiplies one block of G. The encoding can be represented as a block vector-matrix product.

$$c = [I_0, I_1, \ldots, I_r] \begin{bmatrix} G_0 \\ G_1 \\ \vdots \\ G_r \end{bmatrix} = iG$$

Consider the information sequence broken into such sections: each section corresponds to one of the r blocks of the generator matrix and is multiplied by this section of $\mathbf{G}$ during encoding. If we can recover the information bits in the rth section, then we can compute their contribution to the received word and subtract this contribution. This reduces the problem to that of decoding a smaller code, an $(r-1)$th-order Reed-Muller code. The decoding procedure is a succession of majority votes, starting with majority votes to determine the information bits in the rth section.

The received word is

$$\mathbf{v} = [\mathbf{I}_0, \mathbf{I}_1, \ldots, \mathbf{I}_r] \begin{bmatrix} \mathbf{G}_0 \\ \mathbf{G}_1 \\ \vdots \\ \mathbf{G}_r \end{bmatrix} + \mathbf{e}.$$

The decoding algorithm will first recover $\mathbf{I}_r$ from $\mathbf{v}$. Then it computes

$$\mathbf{v}' = \mathbf{v} - \mathbf{I}_r \mathbf{G}_r$$

$$= [\mathbf{I}_0, \mathbf{I}_1, \ldots, \mathbf{I}_{r-1}] \begin{bmatrix} \mathbf{G}_0 \\ \mathbf{G}_1 \\ \vdots \\ \mathbf{G}_{r-1} \end{bmatrix} + \mathbf{e},$$

which is a noisy codeword of an $(r-1)$th-order Reed-Muller code.

First, consider decoding the information bit i_{k-1}, which multiplies the last row of $\mathbf{G}_r$. This is decoded by setting up 2^{m-r} linear check sums in the 2^m received bits; each such check sum involves 2^r bits of the received word, and each received bit is used in only one check sum. The check sums will be formed so that i_{k-1} contributes to only one bit of each check sum, and every other information bit contributes to an even number of bits in each check sum. Hence, each check sum is equal to i_{k-1} in the absence of errors. But if there are at most $(\frac{1}{2} \cdot 2^{m-r} - 1)$ errors, the majority of the check sums will still equal i_{k-1}.

The first check sum is the modulo-2 sum of the first 2^r bits of the received word; the second is the modulo-2 sum of the second 2^r bits, and so forth. There are 2^{m-r} such check sums and by assumption $(\frac{1}{2} \cdot 2^{m-r} - 1)$ errors, and hence a majority vote of the check sums gives i_{k-1}. For the (16, 11) Reed-Muller code constructed earlier, these four estimates are:

$$\hat{i}_{10}^{(1)} = v_0 + v_1 + v_2 + v_3$$

$$\hat{i}_{10}^{(2)} = v_4 + v_5 + v_6 + v_7$$

$$\hat{i}_{10}^{(3)} = v_8 + v_9 + v_{10} + v_{11}$$

$$\hat{i}_{10}^{(4)} = v_{12} + v_{13} + v_{14} + v_{15}.$$

If only one error occurs, only one of these estimates is wrong; a majority decision gives i_{10}. If there are two errors, there will be no majority, and a double-error pattern is detected.

In the same way, each information bit multiplying a row in $\mathbf{G}_r$ can be decoded. This is because each row of $\mathbf{G}_r$ has an equivalent role; no row of $\mathbf{G}_r$ is preferred. By a permutation of columns each row of $\mathbf{G}_r$ can be made to look like the last row. Hence, the same check sums can be used if the indices are permuted. Each bit is decoded by setting up 2^{m-r} linear check sums in the 2^m received bits, followed by a majority vote.

After these information bits are known, their contribution to the codeword is subtracted from the received word. This results in the equivalent of a codeword from an $(r-1)$th-order Reed-Muller code. It in turn can have the last section of its information bits recovered by the same procedure.

The process is repeated until all information bits are recovered.

PROBLEMS

3.1. The generator matrix for a code over $GF(2)$ is given by

$$\mathbf{G} = \begin{bmatrix} 1 & 0 & 1 & 0 & 1 & 1 \\ 0 & 1 & 1 & 1 & 0 & 1 \\ 0 & 1 & 1 & 0 & 1 & 0 \end{bmatrix}.$$

 a. Find the generator matrix and the parity-check matrix for an equivalent systematic code.
 b. List the vectors in the orthogonal complement of the code.
 c. Form the standard array for this code.
 d. How many codewords are there of weight $0, \ldots, 6$?
 e. Find the codeword with 101 as information symbols. Decode the received word 111001.

3.2. Given a code with parity-check matrix $\mathbf{H}$, show that the coset with syndrome $\mathbf{s}$ contains a vector of weight w if and only if some linear combination of w columns of $\mathbf{H}$ equals $\mathbf{s}$.

3.3. This problem will show you that a good decoder must have some nonlinear operations (even though the code itself may be linear).
 a. Show that the operation of forming the syndrome is a linear function of the error pattern. That if $\mathbf{s} = F(\mathbf{e})$, then

$$F(a\mathbf{e}_1 + b\mathbf{e}_2) = aF(\mathbf{e}_1) + bF(\mathbf{e}_2).$$

 b. A linear decoder is a decoder for which the decoder estimate of the error pattern from the syndromes $\hat{\mathbf{e}} = f(\mathbf{s})$ satisfies

$$f(a\mathbf{s}_1 + b\mathbf{s}_2) = af(\mathbf{s}_1) + bf(\mathbf{s}_2).$$

Show that a linear decoder can correct at most $(n-k)(q-1)$ of the $n(q-1)$ possible single-error patterns.
 c. Show that the decoder estimate of the error pattern $\hat{\mathbf{e}} = f(\mathbf{s})$ must be nonlinear if the decoder is to correct all possible single-error patterns.

3.4. Show that if a linear binary code has a minimum distance that is odd, extending the code by appending an overall parity-check symbol increases the minimum distance by 1.

3.5. Define a linear (5, 3) code over $GF(4)$ by the generator matrix

$$\mathbf{G} = \begin{bmatrix} 1 & 0 & 0 & 1 & 1 \\ 0 & 1 & 0 & 1 & 2 \\ 0 & 0 & 1 & 1 & 3 \end{bmatrix}.$$

    a. Find the parity-check matrix.
    b. Prove that this is a single-error-correcting code.
    c. Prove that it is a double-erasure-correcting code.
    d. Prove that it is a perfect code.

3.6. What is the rate of the (maximal) binary subfield-subcode of the $GF(4)$-ary code given in Problem 3.5? Give a systematic generator matrix for this subfield-subcode.

3.7. By a counting argument, show that one should suspect the possible existence of a perfect (11, 6) double-error-correcting code over $GF(3)$. (Golay found such a code in 1949.)

3.8. By a counting argument, show that one should suspect the possible existence of a perfect $(q + 1, q - 1)$ single-error-correcting code over $GF(q)$. (These codes are extended Reed-Solomon codes. They are equivalent to Hamming codes.)

3.9. Find a procedure for restoring double erasures for the Hamming (7, 4) binary code. (An erasure is a position in which the transmitted symbol is lost. It differs from an error in that the position where the erasure occurs is known.)

3.10. Find a parity-check matrix and a generator matrix for the (21, 18) Hamming code over $GF(4)$. Design an encoder and decoder using a syndrome look-up technique by sketching circuits that will implement the decoder. It is not necessary to fill in all details of the decoder. Is the look-up table too large to be practical?

3.11. Prove that the sum of two binary m-vectors of even weight has even weight.

3.12. *Ball weighing*   You are given a pan balance and 12 pool balls, of which one may be either too light or too heavy.
    a. Use the parity-check matrix of a shortened Hamming (12, 9) code over $GF(3)$ to devise a procedure for determining with three uses of the balance which ball, if any, is faulty and whether it is too light or too heavy.
    b. Can the problem be solved in this way for 13 pool balls? Can it be solved for 13 pool balls if a fourteenth ball, known to be good, is made available?
    c. By sphere-packing arguments, show that the problem cannot be solved if there are 14 balls, any one of which may be too heavy or too light.

3.13. A code that is equal to its dual code is called a *self-dual code*.
    a. Show that a linear code with parity-check matrix $[(-\mathbf{P}) : \mathbf{I}]$ is a self-dual code if and only if $\mathbf{P}$ is a square matrix satisfying $\mathbf{PP}^T = \mathbf{I}$.
    b. Construct binary self-dual codes of blocklengths 4 and 8.

3.14. Develop an algorithm for decoding a Reed-Muller codeword in the presence of $2^{m-r} - 1$ erasures.

3.15. Can every nonbinary (n, k, d^*) Hamming code be expanded by a simple parity check to obtain an $(n + 1, k, d^* + 1)$ code? Give a proof or a counterexample.

3.16. Prove that the Singleton bound also holds for nonlinear codes.

3.17. Construct the Hamming (7, 4) binary code from a Venn diagram as follows. Intersect three circles to form seven regions, assigning information bits to four regions, and parity bits to three regions. Discuss error correction and erasure correction using this picture.

NOTES

The study of linear codes begins with the early papers of Hamming (1950) and Golay (1949). Most of the formal setting now used to study linear codes is from Slepian (1956, 1960). The first three sections depend heavily on his work. Earlier, Kiyasu (1953) had noticed the relationship between linear codes and subspaces of vector spaces. The maximum distance codes were first studied by Singleton (1964).

The binary Hamming codes as error-correcting codes are from Hamming, although the combinatorial structure appeared earlier in problems of statistics. Nonbinary Hamming codes were developed by Golay (1958) and Cocke (1959).

The notion of a perfect code is from Golay, although he did not use this name. Early on there was much excitement about the search for perfect codes, but few were found. In a series of difficult papers, Tietäväinen and Van Lint (concluding in 1974 and 1975, respectively) proved that there exist no linear (nontrivial) perfect codes other than the Hamming codes and the Golay codes, and no nonlinear (nontrivial) perfect codes other than the codes of Vasil'yev (1962) and Schönheim (1968).

The Reed-Muller codes were discovered by Muller (1954), and in the same year (1954) Reed discovered the decoding algorithm for them. The decoding algorithm of Reed is unusual in that it makes decisions by majority logic. Those codes are fore-runners of more extensive families of majority-decodable codes, which are treated in a later chapter.

CHAPTER 4

The Arithmetic of Galois Fields

T he most powerful and important ideas of coding theory are based on the arithmetic systems of the Galois fields. These arithmetic systems are unfamiliar to most of us, and we must develop a background in this branch of mathematics before we can proceed with the study of coding theory.

In this chapter we return to the development of the structure of Galois fields begun in Chapter 2. There we introduced the definition of a field but did not develop procedures for actually constructing Galois fields in terms of their addition and multiplication tables. In this chapter we will develop such procedures. Galois fields will be studied by means of two constructions: one based on the integer ring and one based on polynomial rings. Later, after these constructions are studied, we shall prove that all Galois fields can be constructed in this way.

4.1 THE INTEGER RING

The set of integers (positive, negative, and zero) forms a ring under the usual operations of addition and multiplication. This ring is conventionally denoted by the label **Z**. We will study the structure of the integer ring in this section.

We say that the integer s is *divisible* by the integer r, or that r *divides* s (or that r is a *factor* of s), if $ra = s$ for some integer a. Whenever r both divides s and is divisible by s, then $r = \pm s$. This is because $r = sa$ and $s = rb$ for some a and b. Therefore $r = rab$, and ab must equal 1. Because a and b are integers, a and b must both be either 1 or -1.

A positive integer p greater than 1 that is divisible only by $\pm p$ or ± 1 is called a *prime integer*. A positive integer greater than 1 that is not prime is called *composite*. The *greatest common divisor* of two integers r and s, denoted by GCD(r, s) is the largest positive integer that divides both of them. The *least common multiple* of two integers r and s, denoted by LCM(r, s), is the smallest positive integer that is divisible by both of them. Two integers are said to be *relatively prime* if their greatest common divisor is 1.

Within the ring of integers, division is not possible in general. We do, however, have the two next-best things: cancellation and division with remainder. Because cancellation is possible, the integer ring is an integral domain. Division with remainder (known as the division algorithm) is usually proved by a constructive procedure. We state it as a self-evident theorem.

□ **Theorem 4.1.1 (Division Algorithm)** For every pair of integers c and d with d nonzero, there is a unique pair of integers Q (the quotient) and s (the remainder) such that $c = dQ + s$, where $0 \leqslant s < |d|$. □

Usually, we will be more interested in the remainder than in the quotient. The remainder can also be written

$$s = R_d[c],$$

which is read as "s is the remainder or residue of c when divided by d." Another closely related notation is

$$s \equiv c \,(\mathrm{mod}\ d).$$

In this form, the expression is called a *congruence* and is read as "s is congruent to c modulo d." It means that s and c have the same remainder when divided by d, but s is not necessarily smaller than d.

The computation of the remainder of a complicated expression involving addition and multiplication is facilitated by noting that the process of computing a remainder can be interchanged with addition and multiplication. That is,

□ **Theorem 4.1.2**

(i) $R_d[a+b] = R_d\{R_d[a] + R_d[b]\}$.

(ii) $R_d[a \cdot b] = R_d\{R_d[a] \cdot R_d[b]\}$.

Proof Exercise. □

Using the division algorithm, we can find the greatest common divisor of two integers. As an example, GCD(814, 187) is found as follows:

$$814 = 4 \times 187 + 66$$

$$187 = 2 \times 66 + 55$$

$$66 = 1 \times 55 + 11$$

$$55 = 5 \times 11 + 0.$$

Because GCD(814, 187) divides 814 and 187, it must divide the remainder 66. Because it divides 187 and 66, it divides 55. Because it divides 66 and 55, it divides 11. On the other hand, 11 divides 55, and therefore 66, and therefore 187, and finally also 814. Therefore GCD(814, 187) must be 11.

We can now express 11 as a linear combination of 814 and 187 by starting at the bottom of the above sequence of equations and working as follows:

$$11 = 66 - 1 \times 55$$

$$= 66 - 1 \times (187 - 2 \times 66) = 3 \times 66 - 1 \times 187$$

$$= 3 \times (814 - 4 \times 187) - 1 \times 187$$

$$= 3 \times 814 - 13 \times 187.$$

Hence, we have found that GCD(814, 187) can be expressed as a linear combination of 814 and 187 with coefficients from the integer ring. That is,

$$\text{GCD}(814, 187) = 3 \times 814 - 13 \times 187.$$

The argument can be restated in general terms for arbitrary integers r and s to prove the following theorem and corollary.

□**Theorem 4.1.3 (Euclidean Algorithm)** Given two distinct non-zero integers r and s, their greatest common divisor can be computed by an iterative application of the division algorithm. Suppose that $r < s$ and that both are positive; the algorithm is

$$s \quad = Q_1 r + r_1$$

$$r \quad = Q_2 r_1 + r_2$$

$$r_1 \quad = Q_3 r_2 + r_3$$

$$\vdots$$

$$r_{n-1} = Q_{n+1} r_n,$$

where the process stops when a remainder of zero is obtained. The last nonzero remainder, r_n, is the greatest common divisor. $\square$

Finally, we come to an important and unintuitive result of number theory.

□**Corollary 4.1.4** For any integers r and s, there exist integers a and b such that

$$GCD(r, s) = ar + bs.$$

Proof The last remainder in Theorem 4.1.3 is $GCD(r, s)$. Use the set of equations to successively eliminate all other remainders. This gives r_n as a linear combination of r and s with integer coefficients. $\square$

4.2 FINITE FIELDS BASED ON THE INTEGER RING

A very important construction exists by which a new ring, called a *quotient ring*, can be constructed from a given ring. For an arbitrary ring, the quotient ring is defined in a somewhat technical way that involves the construction of cosets. In the ring of integers, however, the construction of the quotient ring is easy. This construction will also yield fields in some cases (when the ring is an integral domain).

□**Definition 4.2.1** Let q be a positive integer. The quotient ring, called the ring of integers modulo q and denoted by $\mathbf{Z}/(q)$, is the set $\{0, \ldots, q-1\}$ with addition and multiplication defined by

$$a + b = R_q[a + b],$$
$$a \cdot b = R_q[ab]. \qquad\qquad\qquad \square$$

Elements called $0, \ldots, q-1$ appear in both $\mathbf{Z}$ and $\mathbf{Z}/(q)$. It is probably best to think of the elements of $\mathbf{Z}/(q)$ not as the same objects as the first q elements of $\mathbf{Z}$ but as some other objects with the same names. Any element a of $\mathbf{Z}$ can be mapped into $\mathbf{Z}/(q)$ by $a' = R_q[a]$.

Two elements a and b of $\mathbf{Z}$ that map into the same element of $\mathbf{Z}/(q)$ are congruent modulo q, and $a = b + mq$ for some integer m.

□**Theorem 4.2.2** The quotient ring $\mathbf{Z}/(q)$ is a ring.

Proof Exercise. $\square$

We can see in the examples of Section 2.4 that the arithmetic of $GF(2)$ and $GF(3)$ can be described as addition and multiplication modulo 2 and 3, respectively, but the arithmetic of $GF(4)$ cannot be so described. That is, in symbols, $GF(2) = \mathbf{Z}/(2)$, $GF(3) = \mathbf{Z}/(3)$, $GF(4) \neq \mathbf{Z}/(4)$. The general fact is given by the following theorem.

☐ **Theorem 4.2.3** The quotient ring $\mathbf{Z}/(q)$ is a field if and only if q is a prime integer.

Proof Suppose that q is a prime. To prove that the ring is a field we must show that every nonzero element has a multiplicative inverse. Let s be a nonzero element of the ring. Then

$$1 \leqslant s \leqslant q - 1.$$

Because q is prime, $\text{GCD}(s, q) = 1$. Hence by Corollary 4.1.4,

$$1 = aq + bs$$

for some integers a and b. Therefore $= 0, q$ is prime

$$\begin{aligned}
1 = R_q[1] = R_q[aq + bs] &= R_q\{R_q[aq] + R_q[bs]\} \\
&= R_q[bs] = R_q\{R_q[b]R_q[s]\} \\
&= R_q\{R_q[b]s\}.
\end{aligned}$$

Hence $R_q[b]$ is a multiplicative inverse for s under modulo-q multiplication.

Now suppose that q is composite. Then $q = rs$. If the ring is a field, then r has an inverse r^{-1}. Hence

$$s = R_q[s] = R_q[r^{-1}rs] = R_q[r^{-1}q] = 0.$$

But $s \neq 0$, and thus we have a contradiction. Hence the ring is not a field. ☐

Whenever the quotient ring $\mathbf{Z}/(q)$ is a field, it is also called by the name $GF(q)$, which emphasizes that it is a field.

4.3 POLYNOMIAL RINGS

A *polynomial* over a field $GF(q)$ is a mathematical expression

$$f(x) = f_{n-1}x^{n-1} + f_{n-2}x^{n-2} + \cdots + f_1 x + f_0,$$

where the symbol x is an *indeterminate*, the coefficients $f_{n-1}, \ldots, f_0$ are elements of $GF(q)$, and the indices and exponents are integers. The *zero polynomial* is

$$f(x) = 0.$$

A *monic polynomial* is a polynomial with leading coefficient f_{n-1} equal to 1. Two polynomials are equal if coefficients f_i are equal for each i.

The *degree* of a nonzero polynomial $f(x)$, denoted deg $f(x)$, is the index of the leading coefficient f_{n-1}. The degree of a nonzero polynomial is always finite. By convention, the degree of the zero polynomial is negative infinity $(-\infty)$.

The set of all polynomials over $GF(q)$ forms a ring if addition and multiplication are defined as the usual addition and multiplication of polynomials. We define such a polynomial ring for each Galois field $GF(q)$. This ring is denoted by the label $GF(q)[x]$. In discussions about the ring $GF(q)[x]$, the elements of the field $GF(q)$ are sometimes called *scalars*.

The sum of two polynomials $f(x)$ and $g(x)$ in $GF(q)[x]$ is another polynomial in $GF(q)[x]$ defined by

$$f(x) + g(x) = \sum_{i=0}^{\infty} (f_i + g_i)x^i,$$

where, of course, terms with index larger than the larger of the degrees of $f(x)$ and $g(x)$ are all zero. The degree of the sum is not greater than the larger of these two degrees. As an example, over $GF(2)$,

$$(x^3 + x^2 + 1) + (x^2 + x + 1) = x^3 + (1+1)x^2 + x + (1+1) = x^3 + x.$$

The product of two polynomials in $GF(q)[x]$ is another polynomial in $GF(q)[x]$, defined by

$$f(x)g(x) = \sum_{i}\left(\sum_{j=0}^{i} f_j g_{i-j}\right)x^i.$$

As an example, over $GF(2)$,

$$(x^3 + x^2 + 1)(x^2 + x + 1) = x^5 + x + 1.$$

The degree of a product is equal to the sum of the degrees of the two factors.

A polynomial ring is analogous in many ways to the ring of integers. To make this evident, this section will closely follow Section 4.1. We say that the polynomial $s(x)$ is *divisible* by the polynomial $r(x)$, or that $r(x)$ is a *factor* of $s(x)$, if there is a polynomial $a(x)$ such that $r(x)a(x) = s(x)$. A polynomial $p(x)$ that is divisible only by $\alpha p(x)$ or α, where α is an arbitrary field element in $GF(q)$, is called an *irreducible polynomial*. A monic irreducible polynomial of degree of at least 1 is called a *prime polynomial*.

The *greatest common divisor* of two polynomials $r(x)$ and $s(x)$, denoted by $GCD[r(x), s(x)]$, is the monic polynomial of largest degree that divides both of them. The *least common multiple* of two polynomials $r(x)$ and $s(x)$, denoted by $LCM[r(x), s(x)]$ is the monic polynomial of smallest degree divisible by both of them. We shall see that the greatest common divisor and the least common multiple of $r(x)$ and $s(x)$ are unique, and thus our wording is appropriate. If the greatest common divisor of two polynomials is 1, then they are said to be *relatively prime*.

Whenever $r(x)$ both divides $s(x)$ and is divisible by $s(x)$, then $r(x) = \alpha s(x)$, where α is a field element of $GF(q)$. This is proved as follows. There must exist polynomials $a(x)$ and $b(x)$ such that $r(x) = s(x)a(x)$ and $s(x) = r(x)b(x)$. Therefore $r(x) = r(x)b(x)a(x)$. But the degree of the right side is the sum of the degrees of $r(x)$, $b(x)$, and $a(x)$. Because this must equal the degree of the left side, $a(x)$ and $b(x)$ must have zero degree; that is, they are scalars.

For polynomials over the real field, the notion of differentiation is elementary and very useful. It is not possible to so define differentiation of polynomials over a finite field in the sense of a limiting operation. Nevertheless it is convenient to simply define an operation on polynomials that behaves the way we expect derivatives to behave. This is called the *formal derivative* of a polynomial.

□ **Definition 4.3.1**   Let $r(x) = r_{n-1}x^{n-1} + r_{n-2}x^{n-2} + \cdots + r_1 x + r_0$ be a polynomial over $GF(q)$. The formal derivative of $r(x)$ is a polynomial $r'(x)$ given by

$$r'(x) = ((n-1))r_{n-1}x^{n-2} + ((n-2))r_{n-2}x^{n-3} + \cdots + r_1,$$

where the coefficients $((i))$ are called *integers of the field* $GF(q)$, and are given by

$$((i)) = 1 + 1 + \cdots + 1,$$

a sum in $GF(q)$ of i terms. □

It is easy to verify many of the usual properties of derivatives; namely, that

$$[r(x)s(x)]' = r'(x)s(x) + r(x)s'(x),$$

and that if $a(x)^2$ divides $r(x)$, then $a(x)$ divides $r'(x)$.

Within a polynomial ring, as in the integer ring, division is not possible in general. For polynomials over a field, however, we again have the two next best things: cancellation and division with remainder. The latter is expressed as the division algorithm for polynomials.

□ **Theorem 4.3.2 (Division Algorithm for Polynomials)**   For every pair of polynomials $c(x)$ and $d(x)$ with $d(x)$ not equal to zero, there is a unique pair of polynomials $Q(x)$, the quotient polynomial, and $s(x)$, the remainder polynomial, such that

$$c(x) = d(x)Q(x) + s(x)$$

and

$$\deg s(x) < \deg d(x).$$

Proof   A quotient polynomial and remainder polynomial can be found by elementary long division of polynomials. They are unique because if

$$c(x) = d(x)Q_1(x) + s_1(x) = d(x)Q_2(x) + s_2(x),$$

then

$$d(x)[Q_1(x) - Q_2(x)] = s_1(x) - s_2(x).$$

If the right side is nonzero, it has degree less than deg $d(x)$, whereas if the left side is nonzero, it has degree at least as large as deg $d(x)$. Hence, both are zero and the representation is unique. $\square$

In practice, one can compute the quotient polynomial and the remainder polynomial by simple long division of polynomials. Usually, we will be more interested in the remainder than in the quotient. The remainder will also be written

$$s(x) = R_{d(x)}[c(x)].$$

The remainder $s(x)$ is also called the *residue* of $c(x)$ when divided by $d(x)$. A slightly different concept is the congruence

$$s(x) \equiv c(x) \pmod{d(x)},$$

which means that $s(x)$ and $c(x)$ have the same remainder under division by $d(x)$, but the degree of $s(x)$ is not necessarily smaller than that of $d(x)$.

Computation of a remainder is sometimes made more convenient if the division can be broken down into steps. We can do this with the aid of the following theorem.

$\square$ **Theorem 4.3.3**   Let $d(x)$ be a multiple of $g(x)$. Then for any $a(x)$,

$$R_{g(x)}[a(x)] = R_{g(x)}[R_{d(x)}[a(x)]].$$

Proof   Let $d(x) = g(x)h(x)$ for some $h(x)$. Expanding the meaning of the right side gives

$$a(x) = Q_1(x)d(x) + R_{d(x)}[a(x)]$$
$$= Q_1(x)h(x)g(x) + Q_2(x)g(x) + R_{g(x)}[R_{d(x)}[a(x)]],$$

where the remainder has degree less than deg $g(x)$. Expanding the meaning of the left side gives

$$a(x) = Q(x)g(x) + R_{g(x)}[a(x)],$$

and the division algorithm says there is only one such expansion where the remainder has degree less than deg $g(x)$. The theorem follows by identifying like terms in the two expansions. $\square$

$\square$ **Theorem 4.3.4**

(i) $R_{d(x)}[a(x) + b(x)] = R_{d(x)}[a(x)] + R_{d(x)}[b(x)].$
(ii) $R_{d(x)}[a(x) \cdot b(x)] = R_{d(x)}\{R_{d(x)}[a(x)] \cdot R_{d(x)}[b(x)]\}.$

Proof Exercise: Use the division algorithm on both sides of the equation, and equate the remainders. ☐

Just as it is often useful to express positive integers as products of primes, it is often useful to express monic polynomials as products of prime polynomials.

☐ **Theorem 4.3.5 (Unique Factorization Theorem)** A nonzero polynomial $p(x)$ over a field has a unique factorization (up to the order of the factors) into a field element times a product of prime polynomials over the field.

Proof Clearly the field element must be the coefficient p_{n-1}, where $n - 1$ is the degree of the polynomial $p(x)$. We can factor this field element out and prove the theorem for monic polynomials.

Suppose the theorem is false. Let $p(x)$ be a monic polynomial of the lowest degree for which the theorem is false. Then there are two factorizations:

$$p(x) = a_1(x)a_2(x) \ldots a_K(x) = b_1(x)b_2(x) \ldots b_J(x),$$

where the $a_k(x)$ and $b_j(x)$ are prime polynomials.

All of the $a_k(x)$ must be different from all of the $b_j(x)$ because otherwise, the common terms could be canceled to give a lower-degree polynomial that could be factored in two different ways.

Without loss of generality, suppose that $b_1(x)$ has degree not larger than that of $a_1(x)$. Then

$$a_1(x) = b_1(x)h(x) + s(x),$$

where $\deg s(x) < \deg b_1(x) \leqslant \deg a_1(x)$. Then

$$s(x)a_2(x)a_3(x) \ldots a_k(x) = b_1(x)[b_2(x) \ldots b_j(x) - h(x)a_2(x) \ldots a_k(x)].$$

Factor both $s(x)$ and the bracketed term into their prime factors, and if necessary divide by a field element to make all factors monic. Because $b_1(x)$ does not appear on the left side, we have two different factorizations of a monic polynomial whose degree is smaller than the degree of $p(x)$. The contradiction proves the theorem. ☐

Now, from the unique factorization theorem it is clear that for any polynomials $r(x)$ and $s(x)$, GCD$[r(x), s(x)]$ and LCM$[r(x), s(x)]$ are unique, because the greatest common divisor is the product of all prime factors common to both $r(x)$ and $s(x)$, each factor raised to the smallest power with which it appears in either $r(x)$ or $s(x)$, and because the least common multiple is the product of all prime factors that appear in either $r(x)$ or $s(x)$, each factor raised to the largest power that appears in either $r(x)$ or $s(x)$. Further, any polynomial that divides both $r(x)$ and $s(x)$ divides $\text{GCD}[r(x), s(x)]$, and any polynomial that both $r(x)$ and $s(x)$ divide is divided by $\text{LCM}[r(x), s(x)]$.

The division algorithm for polynomials has an important consequence known as the Euclidean algorithm for polynomials.

□ **Theorem 4.3.6 (Euclidean Algorithm for Polynomials)** Given two polynomials $r(x)$ and $s(x)$ over $GF(q)$, their greatest common divisor can be computed by an iterative application of the division algorithm. If $\deg s(x) \geqslant \deg r(x) \geqslant 0$, this computation is

$$s(x) = Q_1(x)r(x) + r_1(x)$$
$$r(x) = Q_2(x)r_1(x) + r_2(x)$$
$$r_1(x) = Q_3(x)r_2(x) + r_3(x)$$
$$\vdots$$
$$r_{n-1}(x) = Q_{n+1}(x)r_n(x),$$

where the process stops when a remainder of zero is obtained. Then $r_n(x) = \alpha \text{GCD}[r(x), s(x)]$, where α is a scalar.

Proof Starting with the top equation, $\text{GCD}[r(x), s(x)]$ divides both dividend and divisor and thus divides the remainder. Push this observation down through the equations to see that $\text{GCD}[r(x), s(x)]$ divides $r_n(x)$. Starting with the bottom equation, $r_n(x)$ divides the divisor and remainder and thus divides the dividend. Push this observation up through the equations to see that $r_n(x)$ divides $\text{GCD}[r(x), s(x)]$. Because $r_n(x)$ both divides and is divided by $\text{GCD}[r(x), s(x)]$, the theorem follows. □

□ **Corollary 4.3.7**

$$\text{GCD}[r(x), s(x)] = a(x)r(x) + b(x)s(x),$$

where $a(x)$ and $b(x)$ are polynomials over $GF(q)$.

Proof In the statement of the theorem, the last equation with a nonzero remainder expresses $r_n(x)$ in terms of $r_{n-1}(x)$ and $r_{n-2}(x)$. By working the list of equations from the bottom up, eliminate $r_{n-1}(x)$, then $r_{n-2}(x)$, and so on, until only $r(x)$ and $s(x)$ remain in the expression for $r_n(x)$. □

A polynomial over $GF(q)$ can be evaluated at any element β of $GF(q)$. This is done by substituting the field element β for the indeterminate x. For example, over $GF(3)$, let

$$p(x) = 2x^5 + x^4 + x^2 + 2.$$

Then, using Fig. 4.1,

$$p(0) = 2 \cdot 0^5 + 0^4 + 0^2 + 2 = 2$$
$$p(1) = 2 \cdot 1^5 + 1^4 + 1^2 + 2 = 0$$
$$p(2) = 2 \cdot 2^5 + 2^4 + 2^2 + 2 = 2.$$

In the case of the real field, evaluation of a polynomial in an extension field is a familiar concept; polynomials with real coefficients are commonly evaluated over the complex field. Similarly, a polynomial over $GF(q)$ can be evaluated in an extension of $GF(q)$. This is done by substituting the element of the extension field for the indeterminate x and performing the computations in the extension field. For example, over $GF(2)$, let

$$p(x) = x^3 + x + 1.$$

Then for elements in $GF(4)$, using Fig. 4.1,

$$p(0) = 0^3 + 0 + 1 = 1$$
$$p(1) = 1^3 + 1 + 1 = 1$$
$$p(2) = 2^3 + 2 + 1 = 2$$
$$p(3) = 3^3 + 3 + 1 = 3,$$

If $p(\beta) = 0$, the field element β is called a *zero* of the polynomial $p(x)$, or a *root* of the equation $p(x) = 0$. A polynomial does not necessarily have zeros

GF(2)

+	0 1	·	0 1
0	0 1	0	0 0
1	1 0	1	0 1

GF(3)

+	0 1 2	·	0 1 2
0	0 1 2	0	0 0 0
1	1 2 0	1	0 1 2
2	2 0 1	2	0 2 1

GF(4)

+	0 1 2 3	·	0 1 2 3
0	0 1 2 3	0	0 0 0 0
1	1 0 3 2	1	0 1 2 3
2	2 3 0 1	2	0 2 3 1
3	3 2 1 0	3	0 3 1 2

Figure 4.1 Examples of finite fields.

in its own field. The polynomial $x^3 + x + 1$ has no zeros in $GF(2)$ and also has no zeros in $GF(4)$.

□ **Theorem 4.3.8**   A polynomial $p(x)$ has field element β as a zero if and only if $(x - \beta)$ is a factor of $p(x)$. Furthermore, at most n field elements are zeros of a polynomial $p(x)$ of degree n.

Proof   From the division algorithm,

$$p(x) = (x - \beta)Q(x) + s(x),$$

where the degree of $s(x)$ is less than 1. That is, $s(x)$ is a field element, s_0. Hence

$$0 = p(\beta) = (\beta - \beta)Q(\beta) + s_0,$$

and thus $s(x) = s_0 = 0$. Conversely, if $(x - \beta)$ is a factor, then

$$p(x) = (x - \beta)Q(x)$$

and $p(\beta) = (\beta - \beta)Q(\beta) = 0$, and thus β is a zero of $p(x)$.

Next, factor $p(x)$ into a field element times a product of prime polynomials. The degree of $p(x)$ equals the sum of the degrees of the prime factors, and one such prime factor exists for each zero. Hence, there are at most n zeros. □

4.4 FINITE FIELDS BASED ON POLYNOMIAL RINGS

Finite fields can be obtained from polynomial rings by using constructions similar to those used to obtain finite fields from the integer ring. Suppose that we have $F[x]$, the ring of polynomials over the field F. Just as we constructed quotient rings in the ring $\mathbf{Z}$, so can we construct quotient rings in $F[x]$. Choosing any polynomial $p(x)$ from $F[x]$, we can define the quotient ring by using $p(x)$ as a modulus for polynomial arithmetic. We will restrict the discussion to monic polynomials because this restriction eliminates needless ambiguity in the constructions.

□ **Definition 4.4.1**   For any monic polynomial $p(x)$ with nonzero degree over the field F, the *ring of polynomials modulo $p(x)$* is the set of all polynomials with degree smaller than that of $p(x)$, together with polynomial addition and polynomial multiplication modulo $p(x)$. This ring is conventionally denoted by $F[x]/(p(x))$. □

Any element $r(x)$ of $F[x]$ can be mapped into $F[x]/(p(x))$ by $r(x) \rightarrow R_{p(x)}[r(x)]$. Two elements $a(x)$ and $b(x)$ of $F[x]$ that map into the same element of $F[x]/(p(x))$ are congruent:

$$a(x) \equiv b(x) \qquad (\text{mod } p(x))$$

Then $b(x) = a(x) + Q(x)p(x)$ for some polynomial $Q(x)$.

☐ **Theorem 4.4.2** $F[x]/(p(x))$ is a ring.

Proof   Exercise. ☐

As an example, in the ring of polynomials over $GF(2)$, choose $p(x) = x^3 + 1$. Then the ring of polynomials modulo $p(x)$ is $GF(2)[x]/(x^3 + 1)$. It consists of the set $\{0, 1, x, x + 1, x^2, x^2 + 1, x^2 + x, x^2 + x + 1\}$. In this ring, an example of multiplication is as follows:

$$(x^2 + 1) \cdot (x^2) = R_{x^3 + 1}[(x^2 + 1) \cdot x^2]$$
$$= R_{x^3 + 1}[x(x^3 + 1) + x^2 + x] = x^2 + x,$$

where we have used the reduction $x^4 = x(x^3 + 1) + x$.

☐ **Theorem 4.4.3**   The ring of polynomials modulo a monic polynomial $p(x)$ is a field if and only if $p(x)$ is a prime polynomial.*

Proof   Suppose that $p(x)$ is prime. To prove that the ring is a field, we must show that every nonzero element has a multiplicative inverse. Let $s(x)$ be a nonzero element of the ring. Then

$$\deg s(x) < \deg p(x).$$

Because $p(x)$ is a prime polynomial, $\text{GCD}[s(x), p(x)] = 1$. By Corollary 4.3.7,

$$1 = a(x)p(x) + b(x)s(x)$$

for some polynomials $a(x)$ and $b(x)$. Hence,

$$1 = R_{p(x)}[1] = R_{p(x)}[a(x)p(x) + b(x)s(x)]$$
$$= R_{p(x)}\{R_{p(x)}[b(x)] \cdot R_{p(x)}[s(x)]\}$$
$$= R_{p(x)}\{R_{p(x)}[b(x)] \cdot s(x)\}.$$

Hence $R_{p(x)}[b(x)]$ is a multiplicative inverse for $s(x)$ in the ring of polynomials modulo $p(x)$.

Now suppose that $p(x)$ whose degree is at least 2 is not prime. Then $p(x) = r(x)s(x)$ for some $r(x)$ and $s(x)$, each of degree at least 1. If the ring is a field, then $r(x)$ has an inverse polynomial $r^{-1}(x)$. Hence

$$s(x) = R_{p(x)}[s(x)] = R_{p(x)}[r^{-1}(x)r(x)s(x)] = R_{p(x)}[r^{-1}(x)p(x)] = 0.$$

*Recall that a prime polynomial is both monic and irreducible. It is enough for $p(x)$ to be irreducible in order to get a field, but we insist on the convention of using a polynomial that is monic as well, so that later results are less arbitrary.

But $s(x) \neq 0$, and thus we have a contradiction. Hence, the ring is not a field. $\square$

Using the theory of this section, whenever we can find a prime polynomial of degree n over $GF(q)$, then we can construct a Galois field with q^n elements. In this construction, the elements are represented by polynomials over $GF(q)$ of degree less than n. There are q^n such polynomials and hence this many elements in the field.

As an example, we will construct $GF(4)$ from $GF(2)$ using the prime polynomial $p(x) = x^2 + x + 1$. This is easily verified as irreducible by testing all possible factorizations. The field elements are represented by the set of polynomials $\{0, 1, x, x+1\}$. The addition and multiplication tables shown in Fig. 4.2 are readily constructed. Of course once the arithmetic tables have been constructed, one can replace the polynomial notation by an integer notation or any other desired notation.

Table 4.1 gives a list of prime polynomials over $GF(2)$. One way to verify that these are prime is by trial and error, testing all possible factorizations—although this will require a computer for the polynomials of large degree. The particular prime polynomials selected for Table 4.1 are a special kind of prime polynomials known as primitive polynomials. These give an especially nice representation of the extension field, as will be described in the next section.

Polynomial Notation	Binary Notation	Integer Notation	Exponential Notation
0	00	0	0
1	01	1	x^0
x	10	2	x^1
$x+1$	11	3	x^2

Representations of $GF(4)$

+	0	1	x	$x+1$		$\cdot$	0	1	x	$x+1$
0	0	1	x	$x+1$		0	0	0	0	0
1	1	0	$x+1$	x		1	0	1	x	$x+1$
x	x	$x+1$	0	1		x	0	x	$x+1$	1
$x+1$	$x+1$	x	1	0		$x+1$	0	$x+1$	1	x

Arithmetic Tables

Figure 4.2   Structure of $GF(4)$.

Table 4.1   Prime polynomials over *GF*(2).

Degree	Primitive Polynomials
2	$x^2 + x + 1$
3	$x^3 + x + 1$
4	$x^4 + x + 1$
5	$x^5 + x^2 + 1$
6	$x^6 + x + 1$
7	$x^7 + x^3 + 1$
8	$x^8 + x^4 + x^3 + x^2 + 1$
9	$x^9 + x^4 + 1$
10	$x^{10} + x^3 + 1$
11	$x^{11} + x^2 + 1$
12	$x^{12} + x^6 + x^4 + x + 1$
13	$x^{13} + x^4 + x^3 + x + 1$
14	$x^{14} + x^{10} + x^6 + x + 1$
15	$x^{15} + x + 1$
16	$x^{16} + x^{12} + x^3 + x + 1$
17	$x^{17} + x^3 + 1$
18	$x^{18} + x^7 + 1$
19	$x^{19} + x^5 + x^2 + x + 1$
20	$x^{20} + x^3 + 1$
21	$x^{21} + x^2 + 1$
22	$x^{22} + x + 1$
23	$x^{23} + x^5 + 1$
24	$x^{24} + x^7 + x^2 + x + 1$
25	$x^{25} + x^3 + 1$
26	$x^{26} + x^6 + x^2 + x + 1$
27	$x^{27} + x^5 + x^2 + x + 1$
28	$x^{28} + x^3 + 1$

Note: All entries are primitive polynomials.

To conclude this section, we will summarize where we are. We have developed the constructions needed to obtain the fields that will be used later, but additional topics are still necessary for a full understanding of the subject. In particular we need to establish the following facts: (1) Prime polynomials of every degree exist over every Galois field; (2) The constructions we have are sufficient to construct all Galois fields—there are no others†; and (3) Certain preferred field elements, called primitive elements, exist in every field.

†Mathematical precision requires a more formal statement here. The technically correct phrase is that there are no others up to isomorphism. Informally, this means that any two Galois fields with the same number of elements are the same field but expressed in different notation. Possibly the notation is a permutation of the same symbols and so creates the illusion of a different structure.

1. In any Galois field, the number of elements is a power of a prime.
2. If p is prime and m is a positive integer, the smallest subfield of $GF(p^m)$ is $GF(p)$. The elements of $GF(p)$ are called the *integers of* $GF(p^m)$, and p is called its *characteristic*.
3. In a Galois field of characteristic 2, $-\beta = \beta$ for every β in the field.
4. If p is a prime and m is an integer, then there is a Galois field with p^m elements.
5. Every Galois field $GF(q)$ has at least one primitive element.
6. Every Galois field $GF(q)$ has at least one primitive polynomial over it of every positive degree.
7. Every primitive element has over any subfield a minimal polynomial that is a prime polynomial.
8. Two Galois fields with the same number of elements are isomorphic.
9. For any prime power q and positive integer m, $GF(q)$ is a subfield of $GF(q^m)$, and $GF(q^m)$ is an extension field of $GF(q)$.
10. $GF(q^n)$ is *not* a subfield of $GF(q^m)$ if n does not divide m.
11. The degree of the minimal polynomial over $GF(q)$ of any element of $GF(q^m)$ is a divisor of m.

Figure 4.3   Some basic properties of Galois fields.

Figure 4.3 summarizes the principal facts about Galois fields. The remainder of the chapter will be spent establishing most of these facts and introducing new terms. The existence of primitive polynomials will not be proved until the end of Section 5.3.

4.5   PRIMITIVE ELEMENTS

In the previous section, we constructed $GF(4)$. By inspection of Fig. 4.2, we see that the field element represented by the polynomial x can be used as a kind of logarithm base. All field elements, except zero, can be expressed as a power of x.

□ **Definition 4.5.1**   A *primitive field element* of $GF(q)$ is an element α such that every field element except zero can be expressed as a power of α. □

For example, in the field $GF(5)$ we have

$$2^1 = 2, 2^2 = 4, 2^3 = 3, 2^4 = 1,$$

and thus 2 is a primitive element of $GF(5)$. Primitive elements are useful for constructing fields, because if we can find one, we can construct a multiplication table by multiplying powers of the primitive element. We shall prove in this section that every finite field contains a primitive element.

A field forms an abelian group in two ways. The set of field elements forms an abelian group under the addition operation, and the set of field elements excluding the zero element forms an abelian group under the multiplication operation. We will work with the group under multiplication. By Theorem 2.2.5 the order of this group is divisible by the order of any of its elements,

☐ **Theorem 4.5.2**   Let $\beta_1, \beta_2, \ldots, \beta_{q-1}$ denote the nonzero field elements of $GF(q)$. Then

$$x^{q-1} - 1 = (x - \beta_1)(x - \beta_2) \ldots (x - \beta_{q-1}).$$

Proof   The set of nonzero elements of $GF(q)$ is a finite group under the operation of multiplication. Let β be any nonzero element of $GF(q)$, and let h be its order under the operation of multiplication. Then by Theorem 2.2.5, h divides $q - 1$. Hence

$$\beta^{q-1} = (\beta^h)^{(q-1)/h} = 1^{(q-1)/h} = 1,$$

and thus β is a zero of $x^{q-1} - 1$. ☐

☐ **Theorem 4.5.3**   The group of nonzero elements of $GF(q)$ under multiplication is a cyclic group.

Proof   If $q - 1$ is a prime, the theorem is trivial, because then every element except 0 and 1 has order $q - 1$, and thus every element is primitive. We need to prove the theorem only for composite $q - 1$. Consider the prime factorization of $q - 1$:

$$q - 1 = \prod_{i=1}^{s} p_i^{v_i}.$$

Because $GF(q)$ is a field, of the $q - 1$ nonzero elements of $GF(q)$ there must be at least one that is not a zero of $x^{(q-1)/p_i} - 1$, because this polynomial has at most $(q-1)/p_i$ zeros. Hence for each i, a nonzero element a_i of $GF(q)$ can be found for which $a_i^{(q-1)/p_i} \neq 1$. Let $b_i = a_i^{(q-1)/p_i^{v_i}}$ and let $b = \prod_{i=1}^{s} b_i$. We will prove that b has order $q - 1$ and therefore the group is cyclic.

Step 1   The element b_i has order $p_i^{v_i}$. *Proof:* Clearly, $b_i^{p_i^{v_i}} = 1$, so the order of b_i divides $p_i^{v_i}$. It is of the form $p_i^{n_i}$. If n_i is less than v_i, then $b_i^{p_i^{v_i-1}} = 1$. But $b_i^{p_i^{v_i-1}} = a_i^{(q-1)/p_i} \neq 1$. Therefore b_i has order $p_i^{v_i}$.

Step 2   The element b has order $q - 1$. *Proof:* Suppose $b^n = 1$. We first show that this implies $n = 0 \pmod{p_i^{v_i}}$ for $i = 1, \ldots, s$. For each i we can write

$$b^{\left(n \prod_{j \neq i} p_j^{y_j}\right)} = 1.$$

Replacing b by $\prod_{i=1}^s b_i$ and using $b_j^{p_j^{y_j}} = 1$, we find

$$b_i^{\left(n \prod_{j \neq i} p_j^{y_j}\right)} = 1.$$

Therefore

$$n \prod_{j \neq i} p_j^{y_j} = 0 \,(\text{mod } p_i^{y_i}).$$

Because the p_i are distinct primes, it follows that $n = 0 \,(\text{mod } p_i^{y_i})$ for each i. Hence $n = \prod_{i=1}^s p_i^{y_i}$. The proof is complete. $\square$

This theorem provides an important key to the understanding of the structure of Galois fields, as follows.

$\square$ **Theorem 4.5.4** Every Galois field has a primitive element.

Proof As a cyclic group, the nonzero elements of $GF(q)$ include an element of order $q - 1$. This is a primitive element. $\square$

The use of a primitive element for multiplication is shown by the following examples.

In $GF(8)$, every nonzero element has order that divides 7. Because 7 is prime, every element except 0 and 1 has order 7 and thus is primitive. We can construct $GF(8)$ with the polynomial $p(z) = z^3 + z + 1$. Based on the primitive element $\alpha = z$, we have

$$
\begin{aligned}
\alpha &= z \\
\alpha^2 &= z^2 \\
\alpha^3 &= z + 1 \\
\alpha^4 &= z^2 + z \\
\alpha^5 &= z^2 + z + 1 \\
\alpha^6 &= z^2 + 1 \\
\alpha^7 &= 1 = \alpha^0.
\end{aligned}
$$

With this representation, multiplication is easy. For example,

$$\alpha^4 \cdot \alpha^5 = \alpha^7 \cdot \alpha^2 = \alpha^2.$$

In $GF(16)$, every nonzero element has order that divides 15. An element may have order 1, 3, 5, or 15. An element with order 15 is primitive. We can construct $GF(16)$ with the polynomial $p(z) = z^4 + z + 1$, and the element $\alpha = z$ is primitive. We have

$$\alpha \quad = \quad\quad\quad\quad z$$

$$\alpha^2 \quad = \quad\quad\quad z^2$$

$$\alpha^3 \quad = z^3$$

$$\alpha^4 \quad = \quad\quad\quad\quad z + 1$$

$$\alpha^5 \quad = \quad\quad\quad z^2 + z$$

$$\alpha^6 \quad = z^3 + z^2$$

$$\alpha^7 \quad = z^3 \quad\quad + z + 1$$

$$\alpha^8 \quad = \quad\quad\quad z^2 \quad + 1$$

$$\alpha^9 \quad = z^3 \quad\quad + z$$

$$\alpha^{10} = \quad\quad\quad z^2 + z + 1$$

$$\alpha^{11} = z^3 + z^2 + z$$

$$\alpha^{12} = z^3 + z^2 + z + 1$$

$$\alpha^{13} = z^3 + z^2 \quad + 1$$

$$\alpha^{14} = z^3 \quad\quad\quad + 1$$

$$\alpha^{15} = \quad\quad\quad\quad\quad 1.$$

Again, with this representation multiplication is easy. For example,

$$\alpha^{11} \cdot \alpha^{13} = \alpha^{15} \cdot \alpha^9 = \alpha^9.$$

When constructing an extension field as a set of polynomials, it is usually convenient if the polynomial x corresponds to a primitive element of the field. Then one can use x as a logarithm base to construct a multiplication table, and this is the simplest possible base to expect. This can be done by choosing a special prime polynomial, called a primitive polynomial, to construct the field.

☐ **Definition 4.5.5** A *primitive polynomial* $p(x)$ over $GF(q)$ is a prime polynomial over $GF(q)$ with the property that in the extension field constructed modulo $p(x)$, the field element represented by x is primitive.☐

Primitive polynomials of every degree exist over every Galois field, but we will not prove this until the end of the next section. Anticipating this result, we can say that a primitive polynomial is a prime polynomial having a primitive element as a zero.

4.6 THE STRUCTURE OF FINITE FIELDS

Earlier in this chapter, we studied how to construct fields. Assuming that we can find a prime polynomial of degree n over $GF(p)$, then we know how to construct a finite field with p^n elements.

We will now reverse the point of view. Rather than construct our own field, we will suppose that we are given a finite field. We will prove that wherever this field came from, we may as well presume that it was constructed according to the ideas of the earlier sections. No other fields can be constructed.

As we work through this section, we will gain further understanding of the structure of finite fields. The structural properties will be useful in various applications. We will also prove that prime polynomials of every degree exist over every Galois field.

☐ **Definition 4.6.1**   The number of elements in the smallest subfield of $GF(q)$ is called the *characteristic* of $GF(q)$. ☐

☐ **Theorem 4.6.2**   Each Galois field contains a unique smallest subfield, which has a prime number of elements. Hence the characteristic of every Galois field is a prime number.

Proof   The field contains the elements 0 and 1. To define the subfield, consider the subset $G = \{0, 1, 1+1, 1+1+1, \ldots\}$ denoting these by $\{0, 1, 2, 3, \ldots\}$. This subset is a cyclic subgroup under addition. It must contain a finite number, p, of elements. We will show that p is a prime and $G = GF(p)$. In G, addition is modulo p because it is a cyclic group under addition. Because of the distributive law, multiplication must also be modulo p because

$$\alpha \cdot \beta = (1 + \cdots + 1) \cdot \beta$$

$$= \beta + \cdots + \beta,$$

where there are α copies of β in the sum, and the addition is modulo p. Hence multiplication is also modulo p. Each element β has an inverse under multiplication, because the sequence

$$\beta, 2\beta, 3\beta, \ldots$$

is a cyclic subgroup of G. It contains 1, so that $\alpha\beta = 1$ for some α in G.

Thus the subset G contains the identity element, is closed under addition and multiplication, and contains all inverses under addition and multiplication. Hence it is a subfield, and it has modulo p arithmetic. But this is just a field defined by Theorem 4.2.3, and hence p must be a prime. ☐

In the Galois field $GF(q)$, we have found the subfield $GF(p)$ with p as a prime. In particular, if q is a prime to start with, then we see it can be interpreted as the field of integers modulo q. Hence for a given prime, there is really only one field with that number of elements, although of course it may be represented by many different notations. Two fields differing only in notation are said to be *isomorphic*.

We have found that the original field $GF(q)$ is an extension field of the subfield $GF(p)$. We will now study polynomials over $GF(p)$ that have selected elements of $GF(q)$ as zeros. More generally, we have the following definition.

□ **Definition 4.6.3**   Let $GF(q)$ be a field and let $GF(Q)$ be an extension field of $GF(q)$. Let β be in $GF(Q)$. The prime polynomial $f(x)$ of smallest degree over $GF(q)$ with $f(\beta) = 0$ is called the *minimal polynomial* of β over $GF(q)$. □

We must prove that the minimal polynomial always exists and is unique.

□ **Theorem 4.6.4**   Every element β of $GF(Q)$ has a unique minimal polynomial over $GF(q)$. Further, if β has the minimal polynomial $f(x)$ and a polynomial $g(x)$ has β as a zero, then $f(x)$ divides $g(x)$.

Proof   First of all, β is always a zero of $x^Q - x$, which is a polynomial over $GF(q)$. Now use the unique factorization theorem:

$$x^Q - x = f_1(x)f_2(x)\ldots f_k(x),$$

where the factors on the right side are all prime polynomials over $GF(q)$. If β is a zero of the left side, then it must be a zero of some term on the right side. It can only be the zero of one term on the right side because over the extension field $GF(Q)$, the prime terms can be further factored into linear and constant terms, and β is a zero of only one of them.

To prove the second part of the theorem, write

$$g(x) = f(x)h(x) + s(x),$$

where $s(x)$ has a smaller degree than $f(x)$ and hence cannot have β as a zero. But

$$0 = g(\beta) = f(\beta)h(\beta) + s(\beta) = s(\beta).$$

Hence $s(x)$ must be zero, and the theorem is proved. □

□ **Corollary 4.6.5**   If $f_1(x), \ldots, f_k(x)$ are the distinct polynomials that are minimal polynomials over $GF(q)$ for one or more elements in $GF(Q)$, then

$$x^Q - x = f_1(x)f_2(x)\ldots f_k(x).$$

Proof This follows from the theorem because every β is a zero of $x^Q - x$. $\square$

When Q is equal to q, this reduces to

$$x^q - x = x(x - \beta_1)(x - \beta_2)\ldots(x - \beta_{q-1}),$$

which we have already seen in Theorem 4.5.2. The minimal polynomial over $GF(q)$ of an element β of $GF(q)$ is the first-degree polynomial $f(x) = x - \beta$.

☐**Theorem 4.6.6** Let $g(x)$ be any polynomial over $GF(q)$. Then there exists an extension field $GF(Q)$ in which $g(x)$ can be expressed as the product of linear factors.

Proof Without loss of generality, suppose that $g(x)$ is monic. Construct a sequence of extension fields

$$GF(q) \subset GF(Q_1) \subset GF(Q_2) \subset \cdots \subset GF(Q)$$

as follows. At each step, write $g(x)$ as a product of prime polynomials over $GF(Q_j)$. If some factors are not linear, then choose any factor $g_i(x)$ with degree greater than 1 and construct an extension of $GF(Q_j)$ using $g_i(y)$ as the prime polynomial. In this extension field $g_i(x)$ can be further factored, because the new element $\beta = y$ is a zero of $g_i(x)$. Continue in this way (redefining unique notation for the polynomials as necessary) until all factors are linear. The process must halt in a finite number of steps because $g(x)$ has finite degree. $\square$

☐**Definition 4.6.7** Any extension field of $GF(q)$ in which $g(x)$, a polynomial over $GF(q)$, factors into linear and constant terms is called a *splitting field* of $g(x)$. $\square$

We now have developed all the tools necessary to dissect the structure of an arbitrary Galois field.

☐**Theorem 4.6.8** Let α be a primitive element in a Galois field $GF(Q)$, an extension field of $GF(q)$. Let m be the degree of $f(x)$, the minimal polynomial of α over $GF(q)$. Then the number of elements in the field is $Q = q^m$, and each element β can be written

$$\beta = a_{m-1}\alpha^{m-1} + a_{m-2}\alpha^{m-2} + \cdots + a_1\alpha + a_0,$$

where $a_{m-1}, \ldots, a_0$ are elements of $GF(q)$.

Proof Clearly, any element β written in the form

$$\beta = a_{m-1}\alpha^{m-1} + a_{m-2}\alpha^{m-2} + \cdots + a_1\alpha + a_0$$

is an element of $GF(Q)$. Each is unique because if

$$\beta = b_{m-1}\alpha^{m-1} + b_{m-2}\alpha^{m-2} + \cdots + b_1\alpha + b_0$$

is another representation of element β, then

$$0 = (a_{m-1} - b_{m-1})\alpha^{m-1} + \cdots + (a_1 - b_1)\alpha + (a_0 - b_0),$$

and thus α is a zero of a polynomial of degree $m-1$, contrary to the definition of m. There are q^m such β, and therefore Q is at least as large as q^m.

On the other hand, every nonzero field element can be expressed as a power of α. But if $f(x)$ is the minimal polynomial of α, then $f(\alpha) = 0$. Hence,

$$\alpha^m + f_{m-1}\alpha^{m-1} + \cdots + f_1\alpha + f_0 = 0.$$

This can be used to express α^m in terms of lower powers of α:

$$\alpha^m = -f_{m-1}\alpha^{m-1} - \cdots - f_1\alpha - f_0.$$

This relationship can be used repeatedly to reduce any power of α to a linear combination of $(\alpha^{m-1}, \ldots, \alpha^1, \alpha^0)$. That is,

$$\alpha^{m+1} = -f_{m-1}(-f_{m-1}\alpha^{m-1} - \cdots - f_1\alpha - f_0)$$
$$-f_{m-2}\alpha^{m-1} - \cdots - f_1\alpha^2 - f_0\alpha,$$

and so forth. Hence, every element of $GF(Q)$ can be expressed as a distinct linear combination of $\alpha^{m-1}, \alpha^{m-2}, \ldots, \alpha^0$. Consequently, Q is not larger than q^m, and the theorem is proved. $\square$

□ **Corollary 4.6.9** Every Galois field has p^m elements for some positive integer m and prime p.

Proof Every Galois field has a subfield with p elements to which Theorem 4.6.8 applies. $\square$

Notice that we can use the theorem to associate with each field element a polynomial of degree of at most $m-1$ simply by replacing α by the indeterminate x. These polynomials may be regarded as the field elements. They are added and multiplied modulo $f(x)$, the minimal polynomial of α. This is just the field we would obtain from the construction of Theorem 4.4.3, using $f(x)$ as the prime polynomial. Hence, the number of elements in each Galois field is a prime power, and each Galois field can be constructed by polynomial arithmetic modulo a prime polynomial.

Finally, we must show the converse—that for every prime p and positive integer m, there is such a field. We will proceed through a series of preliminary theorems.

□ **Theorem 4.6.10** Let $GF(q)$ have characteristic p. Then for any positive integer m and for any elements α and β in $GF(q)$,

$$(\alpha \pm \beta)^{p^m} = \alpha^{p^m} \pm \beta^{p^m}.$$

Proof Suppose the theorem is true for $m = 1$. Then

$$(\alpha \pm \beta)^p = \alpha^p \pm \beta^p.$$

This can be raised to the pth power,

$$((\alpha \pm \beta)^p)^p = (\alpha^p \pm \beta^p)^p,$$

and using the theorem for $m = 1$ again,

$$(\alpha \pm \beta)^{p^2} = \alpha^{p^2} \pm \beta^{p^2}.$$

This can be repeated $m - 1$ times to get

$$(\alpha \pm \beta)^{p^m} = \alpha^{p^m} \pm \beta^{p^m}.$$

Hence, it is only necessary to prove the theorem for $m = 1$. But by the binomial theorem

$$(\alpha \pm \beta)^p = \sum_{i=0}^{p} \binom{p}{i} \alpha^i (\pm \beta)^{p-i},$$

and it suffices to show that in $GF(q)$,

$$\binom{p}{i} = 0 \qquad i = 1, \ldots, p - 1.$$

But, for such i

$$\binom{p}{i} = \frac{p!}{i!(p-i)!} = \frac{p(p-1)!}{i!(p-i)!}$$

is an integer, and p is a prime. Hence the denominator divides $(p-1)!$, and $\binom{p}{i}$ is a multiple of p. That is, $\binom{p}{i} = 0 \pmod{p}$, and because all integer arithmetic is modulo p in $GF(q)$, we have $\binom{p}{i} = 0$ in $GF(q)$. Finally, if $p = 2$, $(\pm \beta)^2 = \pm \beta^2$, and if p is odd $(\pm \beta)^p = \pm \beta^p$. This completes the proof of the theorem. □

□ **Theorem 4.6.11** Let m be a positive integer and p a prime. Then the smallest splitting field of the polynomial $g(x) = x^{p^m} - x$ regarded as a polynomial over $GF(p)$ has p^m elements.

Proof Every polynomial over $GF(p)$ has a smallest splitting field. Let $GF(Q)$ be the smallest splitting field of $g(x) = x^{p^m} - x$. Then in $GF(Q)$, $g(x)$ has p^m zeros, some possibly repeated. We will show that the p^m zeros are distinct and form a field. Consequently, $GF(Q)$ has p^m elements.

To prove that the set of zeros is a field, it suffices to prove that the subset is closed under addition and multiplication and contains inverses of all nonzero elements. Suppose α and β are zeros. Then by Theorem 4.6.10,

$$(\alpha \pm \beta)^{p^m} = \alpha^{p^m} \pm \beta^{p^m} = \alpha \pm \beta,$$

and thus $(\alpha \pm \beta)$ is a zero and the set is closed under addition. Next,

$$(\alpha\beta)^{p^m} = \alpha^{p^m}\beta^{p^m} = \alpha\beta,$$

and thus $\alpha\beta$ is a zero and the set is closed under multiplication. Next, note that $-\alpha$ is the additive inverse of α, and thus every element has an additive inverse. Similarly, α^{-1} is easily checked to be a zero whenever α is a zero.

Finally, we check that the p^m zeros of $x^{p^m} - x$ are distinct. This follows by examining the formal derivative:

$$\frac{d}{dx}[x^{p^m} - x] = ((p^m))x^{p^m - 1} - 1 = -1$$

because $((p)) = 0$ in $GF(Q)$. Hence $x^{p^m} - x$ can have no multiple zeros. $\Box$

We now have a converse to Theorem 4.6.9.

$\Box$ **Corollary 4.6.12**   For every prime p and positive integer m, there is a Galois field with p^m elements. $\Box$

Finally, we will show that even if q is not a prime but is a prime power, then $GF(q^m)$ can be constructed as an extension field of $GF(q)$. To do this, it suffices to show that prime polynomials of degree m exist over $GF(q)$.

$\Box$ **Theorem 4.6.13**   For every finite field $GF(q)$ and positive integer m, there exists at least one prime polynomial over $GF(q)$ of degree m.

Proof   Because q is a prime power, then so is q^m. By Corollary 4.6.12 there exists a field with q^m elements. This field has a primitive element α, and by Theorem 4.6.8 the minimal polynomial of α over $GF(q)$ is a prime polynomial of degree m. $\Box$

$\Box$ **Corollary 4.6.14**   For every finite field $GF(q)$ and positive integer m, there exists at least one primitive polynomial over $GF(q)$ of degree m.

Proof   Let α be a primitive element in $GF(q^m)$. Let $f(x)$ be the minimal polynomial of α over $GF(q)$. Then in the field of polynomials modulo $f(x)$, the primitive element $\alpha = x$ is a zero of $f(x)$, and thus the polynomial x represents a primitive element of the field. $\Box$

To close the chapter, we will examine the existence of square roots in a Galois field.

☐ **Theorem 4.6.15** Every element of the Galois field $GF(2^m)$ has a square root in $GF(2^m)$. Half of the nonzero elements of $GF(p^m)$—p an odd prime—have a square root in $GF(p^m)$. Half of the nonzero elements in $GF(p^m)$ have a square root in the extension field $GF(p^{2m})$ but not in $GF(p^m)$.

Proof The zero element is its own square root in any field, so we need only consider nonzero elements. First consider a field $GF(2^m)$ of characteristic 2 and with primitive element α. Then α has odd order n, and any element β can be written as α^i for some i. Then $\sqrt{\beta} = \alpha^{i/2}$ if i is even, and $\sqrt{\beta} = \alpha^{(i+n)/2}$ if i is odd. In either case $\sqrt{\beta}$ is an element of $GF(2^m)$.

Next, consider a field $GF(q)$ whose characteristic p is an odd prime and with primitive element $\alpha = \gamma^{q+1}$, where γ is a primitive element of the extension field $GF(q^2)$ [of order $q^2 - 1 = (q+1)(q-1)$] and $q+1$ is even, because q is a power of an odd prime. Any element β can be written as α^i or as $\gamma^{(q+1)i}$ for some i. Then if i is even, $\sqrt{\beta} = \alpha^{i/2}$, which is an element of $GF(q)$. If i is odd, $\sqrt{\beta} = \gamma^{i(q+1)/2}$, which is an element of $GF(q^2)$ but not $GF(q)$, because $i(q+1)/2$ then is not a multiple of $q+1$. ☐

PROBLEMS

4.1. Over $GF(2)$, let $p_1(x) = x^3 + 1$, and let $p_2(x) = x^4 + x^3 + x^2 + 1$.
   a. Find $\text{GCD}[p_1(x), p_2(x)]$.
   b. Find $A(x)$ and $B(x)$ that satisfy

$$\text{GCD}[p_1(x), p_2(x)] = A(x)p_1(x) + B(x)p_2(x).$$

4.2. **a.** How many distinct second-degree monic polynomials of the form

$$x^2 + ax + b \qquad b \neq 0$$

are there over $GF(16)$?
   b. How many distinct polynomials of the form

$$(x - \beta)(x - \gamma) \qquad \gamma, \beta \neq 0$$

are there over $GF(16)$?
   c. Does this prove that irreducible second-degree polynomials exist? How many second-degree prime polynomials are there over $GF(16)$?

4.3. Prove Theorem 4.1.2 by relating both sides to the division algorithm. Prove Theorem 4.3.4 in the same way.

4.4. **a.** Use the Euclidean algorithm to find $\text{GCD}(1573, 308)$.
   b. Find integers A and B that satisfy

$$\text{GCD}(1573, 308) = 1573A + 308B.$$

4.5. Over $\mathbf{Z}/(15)$, the ring of integers modulo 15, show that the polynomial $p(x) = x^2 - 1$ has more than two zeros. Such a polynomial over a field can only have two zeros. Where does the proof of the theorem fail for a ring?

4.6. How many distinct monic polynomials over $GF(2)$ divide $x^6 - 1$?

4.7. Construct $GF(5)$ by constructing an addition table and a multiplication table.

4.8. Construct addition and multiplication tables for $GF(8)$ and $GF(9)$.

4.9. **a.** Prove that $p(x) = x^3 + x^2 + 2$ is irreducible over $GF(3)$.

    b. What are the possible (multiplicative) orders of elements in $GF(27)$?

    c. What is the order of the element represented by x if $p(x)$ above is used to construct $GF(27)$?

    d. In the field $GF(27)$, find $(2x + 1)(x^2 + 2)$, assuming that $p(x)$ above was used to construct the field.

4.10. Find $3^{100} \pmod 5$.

4.11. Prove that the quotient rings $\mathbf{Z}/(q)$ and $GF(q)[x]/(p(x))$ are rings.

4.12. The polynomial $p(x) = x^4 + x^3 + x^2 + x + 1$ is irreducible over $GF(2)$. Therefore the ring of polynomials modulo $p(x)$ is $GF(16)$.

    a. Show that the field element represented by x in this construction is not a primitive element.

    b. Show that the field element represented by $x + 1$ is primitive.

    c. Find the minimal polynomial of the field element $x + 1$.

4.13. **a.** Construct addition and multiplication tables for $GF(2^3)$ using the irreducible polynomial $x^3 + x^2 + 1$ over $GF(2)$.

    b. Repeat (a) with polynomial $x^3 + x + 1$, and show that the two fields are isomorphic. That is, by relabeling the elements of the first field, show that the second field is obtained.

4.14. Addition and multiplication tables for $GF(2^4)$ can be constructed in at least two different ways:

    (i) using an irreducible polynomial of degree 4 over $GF(2)$.

    (ii) using an irreducible polynomial of degree 2 over $GF(4)$.

    Construct these tables using approach (ii).

4.15. The polynomial $p(x) = x^{20} + x^3 + 1$ is a primitive polynomial over $GF(2)$ and can be used to construct $GF(1,048,576)$, and the element represented by the element represented by polynomial x will be a primitive element α.

    a. What are the subfields of this field?

    b. How many of these subfields have no proper subfields of their own other than $GF(2)$?

    c. In this field, evaluate the expression

$$ab^2 - 1,$$

    where

$$a = x^{12} + x^7 + 1,$$

$$b = x^{13} + x^5 + x^2.$$

4.16. For the formal derivative of polynomials, prove that

$$[r(x)s(x)]' = r'(x)s(x) + r(x)s'(x)$$

and that if $a(x)^2$ divides $r(x)$, then $a(x)$ divides $r'(x)$.

4.17. Prove that in any field of characteristic 2, for any element β, $-\beta = \beta$.

NOTES

The subject of this chapter is a standard in the mathematical literature. The properties of Galois fields are developed in any book on abstract algebra, as for example Birkhoff and MacLane (1953) or Van der Waerden (1949, 1953). The standard treatments however, are formal, primarily concerned with abstract properties, and little concerned with examples or applications. Berlekamp (1968) concentrates on the more immediately useful properties of Galois fields.

CHAPTER 5
Cyclic Codes

*T*he class of cyclic codes is a subclass of the class of linear codes obtained by imposing an additional strong structural requirement on the codes. Because of this structure, the search for good error-control codes has been most successful within the class of cyclic codes. Here the theory of Galois fields has been used as a mathematical searchlight to spot the good codes. Outside the class of cyclic codes, the theory of Galois fields casts a dimmer light. Most of what has been accomplished builds on the ideas developed for cyclic codes.

Cyclic codes are also important because their underlying Galois-field description leads to encoding and decoding procedures that are algorithmic and computationally efficient. Algorithmic techniques have important practical applications, in contrast to the tabular decoding techniques that are necessary for arbitrary linear codes.

5.1 VIEWING A CODE FROM AN EXTENSION FIELD

The cyclic codes over $GF(q)$ are a class of linear codes that can be looked at in a way that will prove to be quite powerful. Although these codes are in the field $GF(q)$, we will often see them more clearly if we step up into an extension field $GF(q^m)$. Just as one uses the theory of functions of a complex variable to learn more about functions of a real variable, so one can learn about functions over $GF(q)$ by studying them in $GF(q^m)$. Therefore one should not view the introduction of the extension field as artificial, but rather one should be patient; the rewards will come in time.

We have seen that a linear code over $GF(q)$ can be described in terms of a matrix with elements from $GF(q)$ called the parity-check matrix. A vector $\mathbf{c}$ over $GF(q)$ is a codeword if and only if $\mathbf{c}\mathbf{H}^T = \mathbf{0}$. For example, choose the following parity-check matrix for the Hamming $(7, 4)$ code:

$$\mathbf{H} = \begin{bmatrix} 1 & 0 & 0 & 1 & 0 & 1 & 1 \\ 0 & 1 & 0 & 1 & 1 & 1 & 0 \\ 0 & 0 & 1 & 0 & 1 & 1 & 1 \end{bmatrix}.$$

The parity-check matrix can be written more compactly by working in an extension field. The columns of $\mathbf{H}$ can be identified with elements of $GF(8)$. Use the top element as the coefficient of z^0 in the polynomial representation of a field element, the next as the coefficient of z^1, and the bottom element as the coefficient of z^2. Then, using the polynomial $p(z) = z^3 + z + 1$ to construct $GF(8)$ and α the primitive element represented by z, $\mathbf{H}$ becomes

$$\mathbf{H} = \begin{bmatrix} \alpha^0 & \alpha^1 & \alpha^2 & \alpha^3 & \alpha^4 & \alpha^5 & \alpha^6 \end{bmatrix}.$$

Now the parity-check matrix is a 1 by 7 matrix over the extension field $GF(8)$. Using this matrix, a codeword is defined as any vector over $GF(2)$ such that in the extension field $GF(8)$ the product with $\mathbf{H}^T$ is zero:

$$\mathbf{c}\mathbf{H}^T = 0.$$

But this product is

$$\sum_{i=0}^{6} c_i \alpha^i = 0.$$

Now we come to the idea of representing codewords by polynomials. The codeword $\mathbf{c}$ is represented by the polynomial

$$c(x) = \sum_{i=0}^{n-1} c_i x^i.$$

The operation of multiplying the codeword by the parity-check matrix becomes the operation of evaluating the polynomial $c(x)$ at $x = \alpha$. The condition for $c(x)$ to represent a codeword becomes $c(\alpha) = 0$. That is, a binary polynomial $c(x)$ is a codeword polynomial if and only if α is a zero of $c(x)$. The Hamming $(7, 4)$ code represented as a set of polynomials is the set of all polynomials over $GF(2)$ of degree at most 6 that have α as a zero in $GF(8)$.

In the same way that we have reexpressed the Hamming code as a set of polynomials, a large class of linear codes exists for which this is possible. Suppose that the parity-check matrix $\mathbf{H}$ of a linear code has n columns, and that $n - k$, the number of rows, is divisible by m. Each group of m rows can be reexpressed as a single row of elements from $GF(q^m)$. That is, the first m rows become a single row $(\beta_{11} \ldots \beta_{1n})$, and the $\mathbf{H}$ matrix becomes

$$\mathbf{H} = \begin{bmatrix} \beta_{11} & \cdots & \beta_{1n} \\ \vdots & & \\ \beta_{r1} & \cdots & \beta_{rn} \end{bmatrix},$$

with $r = (n - k)/m$. This is now an r by n matrix over $GF(q^m)$, rather than an $(n - k)$ by n matrix over $GF(q)$. Of course, we have not really changed anything by this reinterpretation; we have just made the representation more compact.

In this chapter, we will study the special case in which the parity-check matrix can be written in the form

$$\mathbf{H} = \begin{bmatrix} \gamma_1^0 & \gamma_1^1 & \cdots & \gamma_1^{n-2} & \gamma_1^{n-1} \\ \gamma_2^0 & \gamma_2^1 & \cdots & \gamma_2^{n-2} & \gamma_2^{n-1} \\ \vdots & & & & \vdots \\ \gamma_r^0 & \gamma_r^1 & \cdots & \gamma_r^{n-2} & \gamma_r^{n-1} \end{bmatrix},$$

where $\gamma_j \in GF(q^m)$ for $j = 1, \ldots, r$, and $n = q^m - 1$.

This can also be written as a parity-check matrix over $GF(q)$ with $n = q^m - 1$ columns and mr rows by replacing each field element from $GF(q^m)$ by its coefficients when expressed as a polynomial over $GF(q)$. We prefer to work in the larger field, however.

Each codeword $\mathbf{c}$ is a vector over $GF(q)$ such that in the extension field $GF(q^m)$ the following matrix equation holds:

$$\mathbf{c}\mathbf{H}^T = \mathbf{0}.$$

Because of the special form of $\mathbf{H}$, this can be written as

$$\sum_{i=0}^{n-1} c_i \gamma_j^i = 0 \qquad j = 1, \ldots, r.$$

This is just the statement that the codeword polynomial $c(x)$ has zeros at $\gamma_1, \ldots, \gamma_r$. The code is defined as the set of polynomials $c(x) = \sum_{i=0}^{n-1} c_i x^i$ of degree of at most $n - 1$ that satisfy $c(\gamma_j) = 0$ for $j = 1, \ldots, r$.

We now have made a transition from a matrix formulation of linear codes to a polynomial formulation for a special subclass of the linear codes. The reason for restricting attention to this subclass is that the polynomial formulation makes it easier to discover good codes and to develop encoders and decoders. For reasons that will become clear in the next section, such codes are known as *cyclic codes*.

For example, take any primitive element α of the extension field $GF(16)$, and choose the blocklength equal to 15. We can form a parity-check matrix for a code over $GF(2)$ by choosing $\gamma_1 = \alpha$ and $\gamma_2 = \alpha^3$ and writing

$$\mathbf{H} = \begin{bmatrix} \alpha^0 & \alpha^1 & \alpha^2 & \alpha^3 & \alpha^4 & \alpha^5 & \alpha^6 & \alpha^7 & \alpha^8 & \alpha^9 & \alpha^{10} & \alpha^{11} & \alpha^{12} & \alpha^{13} & \alpha^{14} \\ \alpha^0 & \alpha^3 & \alpha^6 & \alpha^9 & \alpha^{12} & \alpha^{15} & \alpha^{18} & \alpha^{21} & \alpha^{24} & \alpha^{27} & \alpha^{30} & \alpha^{33} & \alpha^{36} & \alpha^{39} & \alpha^{42} \end{bmatrix}.$$

Other choices for γ_1 and γ_2 will give other parity-check matrices, some good and some bad. This choice happens to give a good parity-check matrix, but it is too soon to explain why.

If desired, by using the representation of $GF(16)$ on page 83, we can change this to a parity-check matrix over $GF(2)$. Replace each power of α by a 4-bit column with the top element given by the coefficient of z^0 in the polynomial representation of that field element, the second element given by the coefficient of z^1, and so on. The result is

$$\mathbf{H} = \begin{bmatrix} 1 & 0 & 0 & 0 & 1 & 0 & 0 & 1 & 1 & 0 & 1 & 0 & 1 & 1 & 1 \\ 0 & 1 & 0 & 0 & 1 & 1 & 0 & 1 & 0 & 1 & 1 & 1 & 1 & 0 & 0 \\ 0 & 0 & 1 & 0 & 0 & 1 & 1 & 0 & 1 & 0 & 1 & 1 & 1 & 1 & 0 \\ 0 & 0 & 0 & 1 & 0 & 0 & 1 & 1 & 0 & 1 & 0 & 1 & 1 & 1 & 1 \\ \hline 1 & 0 & 0 & 0 & 1 & 1 & 0 & 0 & 0 & 1 & 1 & 0 & 0 & 0 & 1 \\ 0 & 0 & 0 & 1 & 1 & 0 & 0 & 0 & 1 & 1 & 0 & 0 & 0 & 1 & 1 \\ 0 & 0 & 1 & 0 & 1 & 0 & 0 & 1 & 0 & 1 & 0 & 0 & 1 & 0 & 1 \\ 0 & 1 & 1 & 1 & 1 & 0 & 1 & 1 & 1 & 1 & 0 & 1 & 1 & 1 & 1 \end{bmatrix}.$$

Although it is not obvious by inspection, these rows are linearly independent, and therefore the parity-check matrix defines a (15, 7) binary code. Nor is it obvious, but the minimum distance of this code is 5. This code can also be represented as the set of polynomials over $GF(2)$ of degree of 14 or less such that each such polynomial $c(x)$ satisfies $c(\alpha) = 0$ and $c(\alpha^3) = 0$ in the extension field $GF(16)$. In other words, codewords are polynomials with zeros at α and α^3.

The matrix over the extension field will prove to be much easier to deal with, and thus we will come to work mostly in the larger field. Of course by restricting ourselves to parity-check matrices with such special forms, we eliminate many codes from further study.

5.2 POLYNOMIAL DESCRIPTION OF CYCLIC CODES

Let us begin anew; later we will refer to the previous section. A linear code $\mathscr{C}$ over $GF(q)$ is called a *cyclic code* if whenever $\mathbf{c} = (c_0, c_1, \ldots, c_{n-1})$ is in $\mathscr{C}$, then $\mathbf{c}' = (c_{n-1}, c_0, \ldots, c_{n-2})$ is also in $\mathscr{C}$. The codeword $\mathbf{c}'$ is obtained by cyclically shifting the components of the codeword $\mathbf{c}$ one place to the right. The Hamming code of Table 1.1 is an example of a cyclic code. Every linear code over $GF(q)$ of length n is a subspace of $GF(q)^n$, and a cyclic code is a very special kind of subspace because it has this cyclic property.

Each vector in $GF(q)^n$ can be represented as a polynomial in x of degree of less than or equal to $n-1$. The components of the vector are identified with the coefficients of the polynomial. The set of polynomials has a vector-space structure identical to that of $GF(q)^n$. This set of polynomials also has a ring structure, defined in Section 4.2, called $GF(q)[x]/(x^n-1)$. As a ring, the set has a product

$$p_1(x) \cdot p_2(x) = R_{x^n-1}[p_1(x)p_2(x)].$$

Notice that there are two different kinds of multiplication in the above expression. The product on the left is a product in $GF(q)[x]/(x^n-1)$ defined in terms of the product in $GF(q)[x]$ on the right.

A cyclic shift can be written as a multiplication within this ring:

$$x \cdot p(x) = R_{x^n-1}[xp(x)].$$

Hence, if the codewords of a code are denoted by polynomials, the code is a subset of $GF(q)[x]/(x^n-1)$. The code is a cyclic code if $x \cdot c(x)$ is a codeword polynomial whenever $c(x)$ is a codeword polynomial.

□ **Theorem 5.2.1** In the ring $GF(q)[x]/(x^n-1)$, a subset is a cyclic code if and only if it satisfies the following two properties*:

1. $\mathscr{C}$ is a subgroup of $GF(q)[x]/(x^n-1)$ under addition.
2. If $c(x) \in \mathscr{C}$, and $a(x) \in GF(q)[x]/(x^n-1)$, then $R_{x^n-1}[a(x)c(x)] \in \mathscr{C}$.

Proof Suppose the subset satisfies the two properties. Then it is closed under addition and closed under multiplication by a scalar. Hence it is a subspace. It is also closed under multiplication by any ring element, in particular under multiplication by x. Hence it is a cyclic code.

Now suppose that it is a cyclic code. Then it is closed under addition and under multiplication by x. But then it is closed under multiplication by powers of x and linear combinations of powers of x. That is, it is closed under multiplication by an arbitrary polynomial. Hence it satisfies the two properties, and the theorem is proved. □

Now choose a nonzero codeword polynomial of smallest degree from $\mathscr{C}$ and denote its degree by $n-k$ (it must be less than n). Multiply by a field element to make it a monic polynomial. This must also be in the code $\mathscr{C}$, because the code is linear. No other monic polynomial of this degree is in the code, because otherwise the difference of the two monic polynomials would be in the code and have degree smaller than $n-k$, contrary to the choice of the original polynomial.

The unique nonzero monic polynomial of smallest degree is called the *generator polynomial* of $\mathscr{C}$ and is denoted by $g(x)$.

---

*This subset is known as an *ideal* of the ring. In general, a subset I of a ring R is called an ideal of R if (1) I is a subgroup of the additive group of R, and (2) if $r \in R$ and $a \in I$, then $ar \in I$.

☐ **Theorem 5.2.2**   A cyclic code consists of all multiples of the generator polynomial $g(x)$ by polynomials of degree $k - 1$ or less.

Proof   All such polynomials must be in the code by Theorem 5.2.1 because $g(x)$ is in the code. But if any polynomial $c(x)$ is in the code, then by the division algorithm

$$c(x) = Q(x)g(x) + s(x),$$

where

$$\deg s(x) < \deg g(x),$$

and

$$s(x) = c(x) - Q(x)g(x)$$

is a codeword polynomial, because both terms on the right are codeword polynomials and the code is linear. But $s(x)$ has degree smaller than $n - k$, which is the smallest degree of any nonzero polynomial in the code. Hence $s(x) = 0$, and $c(x) = Q(x)g(x)$. ☐

☐ **Theorem 5.2.3**   There is a cyclic code of blocklength n with generator polynomial $g(x)$ if and only if $g(x)$ divides $x^n - 1$.

Proof   The division algorithm states that

$$x^n - 1 = Q(x)g(x) + s(x),$$

with $s(x)$ having degree less than that of $g(x)$. Then

$$0 = R_{x^n - 1}(x^n - 1) = R_{n^n - 1}[Q(x)g(x)] + R_{x^n - 1}[s(x)].$$

Therefore

$$0 = R_{x^n - 1}[Q(x)g(x)] + s(x).$$

The first term on the right is a codeword polynomial as a consequence of Theorem 5.2.1. Then $s(x)$ is a codeword polynomial with degree less than that of $g(x)$. The only such codeword polynomial is $s(x) = 0$. Thus $g(x)$ divides $x^n - 1$. Further, every polynomial that divides $x^n - 1$ can be used as a generator polynomial to define a cyclic code. This completes the proof. ☐

By Theorem 5.2.3, for any cyclic code with generator polynomial $g(x)$,

$$x^n - 1 = g(x)h(x)$$

for some polynomial $h(x)$. The polynomial $h(x)$ is called the *parity-check polynomial*. Every codeword $c(x)$ satisfies

$$R_{x^n - 1}[h(x)c(x)] = 0$$

because for some $a(x)$,

$$h(x)c(x) = h(x)g(x)a(x) = (x^n - 1)a(x).$$

Let $c(x)$ denote a transmitted codeword polynomial of a cyclic code. That is, the coefficients of the polynomial $c(x)$ are the symbols of the transmitted vector. Let the polynomial $v(x)$ denote the received word, and let $e(x) = v(x) - c(x)$. The polynomial $e(x)$ is called the *error polynomial*. It has nonzero coefficients in those locations where channel errors occurred.

The information sequence is represented by a polynomial $i(x)$ of degree of $k - 1$.† The set of information polynomials may be mapped into the set of codeword polynomials in any convenient way. A simple encoding rule is

$$c(x) = i(x)g(x).$$

This encoder is nonsystematic because the polynomial $i(x)$ is not immediately visible in $c(x)$. A systematic encoding rule is somewhat more complicated. The idea is to insert the information into the high-order coefficients of the codeword, and then choose the parity bits so as to get a legitimate codeword. That is, the codeword is of the form

$$c(x) = x^{n-k}i(x) + t(x),$$

where $t(x)$ is chosen so that

$$R_{g(x)}[c(x)] = 0.$$

This requires that

$$R_{g(x)}[x^{n-k}i(x)] + R_{g(x)}[t(x)] = 0,$$

and the degree of $t(x)$ is less than $n - k$, the degree of $g(x)$. Hence

$$t(x) = -R_{g(x)}[x^{n-k}i(x)],$$

and the rule is a one-to-one map, because the high-order k coefficients of the polynomial are unique. The systematic encoding rule and the nonsystematic rule produce the same set of codewords, but the association between the $i(x)$ and the $c(x)$ is different.

We define the *syndrome polynomial* $s(x)$, which will be used for decoding, as the remainder of $v(x)$ under division by $g(x)$:

$$s(x) = R_{g(x)}[v(x)]$$
$$= R_{g(x)}[c(x) + e(x)]$$
$$= R_{g(x)}[e(x)].$$

The syndrome polynomial depends only on $e(x)$ and not on $c(x)$ or on $i(x)$.

---

†Actually, we should say that $i(x)$ has degree of *less than or equal to* $k - 1$, but in cases such as this where $i(x)$ is one of a set of polynomials, it is more convenient, though imprecise, to refer to the maximum degree in the set.

A summary of the polynomials is as follows:

Generator polynomial:	$g(x)$	deg $g(x) = n - k$.
Parity-check polynomial:	$h(x)$	deg $h(x) = k$.
Information polynomial:	$i(x)$	deg $i(x) = k - 1$.
Codeword polynomial:	$c(x)$	deg $c(x) = n - 1$.
Error polynomial:	$e(x)$	deg $e(x) = n - 1$.
Received polynomial:	$v(x)$	deg $v(x) = n - 1$.
Syndrome polynomial:	$s(x)$	deg $s(x) = n - k - 1$.

☐ **Theorem 5.2.4**   Let d^* be the minimum distance of a cyclic code $\mathscr{C}$. Every error polynomial of weight less than $\frac{1}{2}d^*$ has a unique syndrome polynomial.

Proof   Suppose $e_1(x)$ and $e_2(x)$ each have weight less than $\frac{1}{2}d^*$ and the same syndrome polynomial. Then

$$e_1(x) = Q_1(x)g(x) + s(x),$$

$$e_2(x) = Q_2(x)g(x) + s(x),$$

and

$$e_1(x) - e_2(x) = [Q_1(x) - Q_2(x)]g(x).$$

By assumption, $e_1(x)$ and $e_2(x)$ each have weight less than $\frac{1}{2}d^*$, and thus the difference has weight less than d^*. The right side is a codeword. If it is nonzero, it has weight of at least d^*, the minimum weight of the code. Hence, the right side is zero, and $e_1(x)$ equals $e_2(x)$. This proves the theorem. ☐

The error-correction problem then is to find the unique $e(x)$ with the least number of nonzero coefficients satisfying

$$s(x) = R_{g(x)}[e(x)].$$

This can be done by constructing a table if the number of entries is not too large. For each correctable $e(x)$, compute and tabulate $s(x)$ as shown in Fig. 5.1. The table is called the syndrome evaluator table. A decoder finds the error polynomial $e(x)$ by computing $s(x)$ from $v(x)$ and then finding $s(x)$ in the syndrome evaluator table, thereby finding the corresponding $e(x)$. In practice the syndrome evaluator table, if it is not too big, can be realized in a memory or in a combinatorial logic circuit.

For the moment, we will be satisfied with this simple decoding scheme. In later chapters we will develop more efficient algorithms for computing $e(x)$ from $s(x)$ rather than storing a precomputed table.

$e(x)$	$s(x)$
1	$R_{g(x)}[1]$
x	$R_{g(x)}[x]$
x^2	$R_{g(x)}[x^2]$
$\vdots$	$\vdots$
$1 + x$	$R_{g(x)}[1 + x]$
$1 + x^2$	$R_{g(x)}[1 + x^2]$
$\vdots$	$\vdots$

Figure 5.1   Syndrome evaluator table.

5.3 MINIMAL POLYNOMIALS AND CONJUGATES

We have seen that a cyclic code of blocklength n over $GF(q)$ exists for each polynomial $g(x)$ over $GF(q)$ that divides $x^n - 1$. We now wish to study such generator polynomials explicitly. First we wish to find the possible generator polynomials for a cyclic code of blocklength n. The most direct approach is to find divisors of $x^n - 1$. This can be done by writing $x^n - 1$ in terms of its prime factors;

$$x^n - 1 = f_1(x)f_2(x) \ldots f_s(x),$$

where s is the number of prime factors. Any subset of these factors can be multiplied together to produce a generator polynomial $g(x)$. If the prime factors of $x^n - 1$ are distinct, then there are $2^s - 2$ different nontrivial cyclic codes of length n (excluding the trivial cases $g(x) = 1$ and $g(x) = x^n - 1$). Which of these, if any, gives a code with a large minimum distance is a question that we will answer only gradually.

Suppose that $g(x)$ is a generator polynomial. It divides $x^n - 1$, and thus $g(x) = \prod f_i(x)$, where the product is over some subset of the s prime polynomials. The cyclic code generated by $g(x)$ consists of all polynomials that are divisible by each of these $f_i(x)$. We can find $g(x)$ by finding all of the prime polynomials that divide it.

In this section we will look at the relationship between the prime polynomials and their zeros in an extension field. In particular, we will learn how to find prime polynomials, and hence generator polynomials, that have specified zeros. Eventually, we will design codes by choosing desirable zeros in an extension field. In Chapter 7 we will see how the zeros should be specified so as to ensure a good code.

We will start with certain preferred values of n called primitive blocklengths.

□ **Definition 5.3.1** A blocklength n of the form $n = q^m - 1$ is called a *primitive blocklength* for a code over $GF(q)$. A cyclic code over $GF(q)$ of primitive blocklength is called a *primitive cyclic code*. □

The field $GF(q^m)$ is an extension field of $GF(q)$. By the unique factorization theorem, the factorization

$$x^{q^m - 1} - 1 = f_1(x) \cdots f_s(x)$$

is unique over the field $GF(q)$. Because $g(x)$ divides $x^{q^m - 1} - 1$, it must be a product of some of these polynomials. On the other hand, every nonzero element of $GF(q^m)$ is a zero of $x^{q^m - 1} - 1$. Hence, we can also factor $x^{q^m} - 1$ in the extension field $GF(q^m)$ to get

$$x^{q^m - 1} - 1 = \prod_j (x - \beta_j),$$

where β_j ranges over all nonzero elements of $GF(q^m)$. It follows that each $f_l(x)$ can be factored in $GF(q^m)$ into a product of some of these linear terms, and that each β_j is a zero of exactly one of the $f_l(x)$. This $f_l(x)$ is the *minimal polynomial* of β_j, and we call it $f_j(x)$, also‡. It is the smallest-degree polynomial with coefficients in the base field $GF(q)$ that has β_j as a zero in the extension field.

We now can relate the definition of cyclic codes to the earlier treatment in Section 5.1.

□ **Theorem 5.3.2** Let $g(x)$, the generator polynomial of a primitive code, have zeros $\beta_1, \ldots, \beta_r$ in $GF(q^m)$. A polynomial $c(x)$ over $GF(q)$ is a codeword polynomial if and only if

$$c(\beta_1) = c(\beta_2) = \cdots = c(\beta_r) = 0,$$

where $c(\beta_j)$ is evaluated in $GF(q^m)$.

Proof If $c(x) = a(x)g(x)$, then $c(\beta_j) = a(\beta_j)g(\beta_j) = 0$. Conversely, suppose that $c(\beta_j) = 0$ and write

$$c(x) = Q(x)f_j(x) + s(x),$$

where $\deg s(x) < \deg f_j(x)$ and $f_j(x)$ is the minimal polynomial of β_j. But then

$$0 = c(\beta_j) = Q(\beta_j)\, f_j(\beta_j) + s(\beta_j) = s(\beta_j)$$

requires that $s(x) = 0$. Then $c(x)$ must be divisible by the minimal polynomial $f_j(x)$, for $j = 1, \ldots, r$. Hence, $c(x)$ is divisible by $\mathrm{LCM}[f_1(x), f_2(x), \ldots, f_r(x)] = g(x)$. □

---

‡We apologize for the ambiguity in using $f_l(x)$ for $l = 1, \ldots, s$ to denote the distinct minimal polynomials and $f_j(x)$ for $j = 1, \ldots, q^m - 1$ to denote the minimal polynomial of β_j. The context will convey the usage.

As an example of these ideas, take $n = 15$. All cyclic codes of blocklength 15 can be found by factoring $x^{15} - 1$ into prime polynomials:

$$x^{15} - 1 = (x + 1)(x^2 + x + 1)(x^4 + x + 1)(x^4 + x^3 + 1)(x^4 + x^3 + x^2 + x + 1).$$

We can verify this factorization by multiplication and verify by trial and error that every factor is a prime polynomial. There are $2^5 = 32$ subsets of these prime polynomials and hence 32 generator polynomials for cyclic codes of blocklength 15. Of these, 2 are trivial ($g(x) = x^{15} - 1$ with $k = 0$ and $g(x) = 1$ with $k = n$) and 30 are nontrivial cyclic codes. For example, to see one of these, take

$$g(x) = (x^4 + x^3 + 1)(x^4 + x^3 + x^2 + x + 1)$$
$$= x^8 + x^4 + x^2 + x + 1.$$

Because $g(x)$ has degree of 8, $n - k = 8$ and $k = 7$. Because $g(x)$ has weight 5, the minimum distance is not larger than 5. In Chapter 7, we will see that the minimum distance equals 5. Hence, this is a (15, 7, 5) code, and it can correct two errors. The parity-check operation can be represented by the following:

$$c(\alpha^i) = 0 \qquad c(\alpha^j) = 0,$$

where in the extension field $GF(16)$ α^i is any zero of $x^4 + x^3 + 1$ and α^j is any zero of $x^4 + x^3 + x^2 + x + 1$. In particular, $c(\alpha) = 0$ and $c(\alpha^3) = 0$, and hence this is the example seen earlier, in Section 5.1. ($g(x)$ has other zeros as well, but these two zeros suffice to specify $g(x)$. There is no need to check the others.)

Now suppose that we wish to construct a $g(x)$ that has $\beta_1, \beta_2, \ldots, \beta_r$ as zeros. Find the minimal polynomials of these field elements, denoting them as $f_1(x), f_2(x), \ldots, f_r(x)$. Then

$$g(x) = \text{LCM}[f_1(x), f_2(x), \ldots, f_r(x)].$$

Thus our task reduces to the problem of finding, for any element β, its minimal polynomial $f(x)$.

Let $f(x)$, the minimal polynomial of β, have degree m'. Then it must have m' zeros in $GF(q^m)$. Therefore $f(x)$ is also the minimal polynomial for all of these zeros. We can identify these additional zeros with the aid of the following two theorems.

☐ **Theorem 5.3.3** Let p be the characteristic of the field $GF(q)$. Then for any polynomial $s(x)$ over $GF(q)$ and any integer m,

$$\left[\sum_{i=0}^{I} s_i x^i \right]^{p^m} = \sum_{i=0}^{I} s_i^{p^m} x^{i p^m},$$

and hence also if p is replaced by any power of p.

Proof We start with $m = 1$ and use the same reasoning as was used in the proof of Theorem 4.6.10. To proceed in small steps, define $s'(x)$

by $s(x) = s'(x)x + s_0$. Then

$$[s(x)]^p = \sum_{i=0}^{I} \binom{p}{i} [s'(x)x]^i s_0^{p-i}.$$

But

$$\binom{p}{i} = \frac{p!}{i!(p-i)!} = \frac{p(p-1)!}{i!(p-i)!},$$

and p is a prime that does not appear in the denominator unless $i=0$ or $i=p$. Hence, except for $i=0$ or p, $\binom{p}{i}$ is a multiple of p and equals zero modulo p. Then

$$[s(x)]^p = [s'(x)]^p x^p + s_0^p.$$

Now apply the same reasoning to $s'(x)$, and continue in this way. This gives

$$[s(x)]^p = \sum_{i=0}^{I} s_i^p x^{ip},$$

as was to be proved for $m=1$. Further,

$$[s(x)]^{p^2} = [[s(x)]^p]^p = \left[\sum_{i=0}^{I} s_i^p x^{ip} \right]^p$$

$$= \sum_{i=0}^{I} s_i^{p^2} x^{ip^2}.$$

This can be repeated any number of times, and thus the theorem is true with p replaced by any power of p. $\square$

□ **Theorem 5.3.4** Suppose that $f(x)$ is the minimal polynomial over $GF(q)$ of β, an element of $GF(q^m)$. Then $f(x)$ is also the minimal polynomial of β^q.

Proof Because q is a power of the field characteristic p, Theorem 5.3.3 gives

$$[f(x)]^q = \sum_{i=0}^{\deg f(x)} f_i^q (x^q)^i.$$

But the coefficients f_i are elements of $GF(q)$, and all elements of $GF(q)$ satisfy $\gamma^q = \gamma$. Therefore

$$[f(x)]^q = \sum_{i=0}^{\deg f(x)} f_i(x^q)^i = f(x^q),$$

and because $f(\beta) = 0$, we have

$$0 = [f(\beta)]^q = f(\beta^q),$$

and hence β^q is a zero of $f(x)$. Because $f(x)$ is a prime polynomial, $f(x)$ is the minimal polynomial of β^q, as was to be proved. $\square$

$\square$ **Definition 5.3.5**   Two elements of $GF(q^m)$ that share the same minimal polynomial over $GF(q)$ are called *conjugates* (with respect to $GF(q)$). $\square$

Generally, a single element can have more than one conjugate—in fact, as many as m. We should also mention that the conjugacy relationship between two elements depends on the base field. Two elements of $GF(16)$ might be conjugates with respect to $GF(2)$ but yet not be conjugates with respect to $GF(4)$.

The conjugates of an element β are easily found using Theorem 5.3.4. If $f(x)$ is the minimal polynomial of β, then it is also that of β^q, and in turn β^{q^2}, and so forth. Hence, the elements in the set

$$\{\beta, \beta^q, \beta^{q^2}, \beta^{q^3}, \ldots, \beta^{q^{r-1}}\},$$

are all conjugates, where r is the smallest integer such that $\beta^{q^r} = \beta$. Note that because $\beta^{q^m} = \beta, r \leqslant m$. This set is called a *set of conjugates*. The conjugates are all zeros of $f(x)$, and the following theorem shows that no others exist.

$\square$ **Theorem 5.3.6**   The minimal polynomial of β is

$$f(x) = (x - \beta)(x - \beta^q) \ldots (x - \beta^{q^{r-1}}).$$

Proof   Certainly the minimal polynomial of β must have all of these zeros, as stated by Theorem 5.3.4, and thus the minimal polynomial cannot have a smaller degree. All we need to show is that $f(x)$ thus constructed has coefficients only in $GF(q)$. We will use the fact that in the field $GF(q^m)$, the set of elements that are zeros of $x^q - x$ forms the subfield $GF(q)$. First, find $[f(x)]^q$:

$$[f(x)]^q = (x - \beta)^q(x - \beta^q)^q(x - \beta^{q^2})^q \ldots (x - \beta^{q^{r-1}})^q$$

$$= (x^q - \beta^q)(x^q - \beta^{q^2})(x^q - \beta^{q^3}) \ldots (x^q - \beta),$$

where the last line follows from Theorem 5.3.3 and from the fact that $\beta^{q^r} = \beta$. Therefore

$$[f(x)]^q = f(x^q) = \sum_i f_i x^{iq},$$

whereas Theorem 5.3.3 asserts that

$$[f(x)]^q = \left[\sum_i f_i x^i\right]^q = \sum_i f_i^q x^{iq}.$$

Therefore $f_i^q = f_i$ for each i, and hence every f_i is in the subfield $GF(q)$, as was to be proved. $\square$

For example, take α as a primitive element in $GF(256)$. Then

$$\{\alpha, \alpha^2, \alpha^4, \alpha^8, \alpha^{16}, \alpha^{32}, \alpha^{64}, \alpha^{128}\}$$

is a set of conjugates. It terminates with α^{128} because $\alpha^{255} = 1$, and hence $\alpha^{256} = \alpha$, which already appears. The minimal polynomial of α is

$$f(x) = (x - \alpha)(x - \alpha^2)(x - \alpha^4) \ldots (x - \alpha^{64})(x - \alpha^{128}),$$

which, when multiplied out, must only have coefficients in $GF(2)$. Similarly, the set of conjugates that includes α^7 is

$$\{\alpha^7, \alpha^{14}, \alpha^{28}, \alpha^{56}, \alpha^{112}, \alpha^{224}, \alpha^{193}, \alpha^{131}\},$$

and the minimal polynomial of α^7 is

$$f(x) = (x - \alpha^7)(x - \alpha^{14})(x - \alpha^{28}) \ldots (x - \alpha^{193})(x - \alpha^{131}),$$

which, when multiplied out, must only have coefficients in $GF(2)$.

If instead of $GF(2)$ we now take $GF(4)$ as the base field—it also is a subfield of $GF(256)$—then the set of conjugates of α^7 is

$$\{\alpha^7, \alpha^{28}, \alpha^{112}, \alpha^{193}\},$$

and over $GF(4)$ the minimal polynomial of α^7 is

$$f(x) = (x - \alpha^7)(x - \alpha^{28})(x - \alpha^{112})(x - \alpha^{193}),$$

which, when multiplied out, must only have coefficients in $GF(4)$. In order to recognize these coefficients as elements of $GF(4)$, however, one must identify the field elements of $GF(4)$ among those of $GF(256)$. In the terminology of $GF(256)$, the subfield $GF(4)$ is given by $\{0, 1, \alpha^{85}, \alpha^{170}\}$, because α^{85} and α^{170} are the only elements of order 3.

Let us now turn to cyclic codes that are not primitive cyclic codes. We have seen that for primitive cyclic codes there is a close relationship between $g(x)$ and the field $GF(q^m)$, as described by the zeros of $g(x)$. Now we will consider codes of blocklength n other than $q^m - 1$. The following theorem is the basis for relating these codes to the earlier discussion.

☐ **Theorem 5.3.7** Suppose $GF(q)$ is a finite field. If n and q are relatively prime, then $x^n - 1$ divides $x^{q^m - 1} - 1$ for some m, and $x^n - 1$ has n distinct zeros in the extension field $GF(q^m)$.

Proof It is only necessary to prove that n divides $q^m - 1$ for some m, because once this is proved we use the general factorization

$$(x^r - 1) = (x - 1)(x^{r-1} + x^{r-2} + x^{r-3} + \cdots + x + 1)$$

together with $q^m - 1 = nb$ for some b to show that

$$x^{q^m - 1} - 1 = (x^n)^b - 1$$

$$= (x^n - 1)(x^{n(b-1)} + x^{n(b-2)} + \cdots + x^n + 1).$$

Therefore $x^n - 1$ divides $x^{q^{m-1}} - 1$ and consequently has n distinct zeros in $GF(q^m)$, because $x^{q^{m-1}} - 1$ has $q^m - 1$ distinct zeros.

To prove that n divides $q^m - 1$ for some m, use the division algorithm to write the following set of $n + 1$ equations:

$$q = Q_1 n + s_1$$
$$q^2 = Q_2 n + s_2$$
$$q^3 = Q_3 n + s_3$$
$$\vdots \quad \vdots \quad \vdots$$
$$q^n = Q_n n + s_n$$
$$q^{n+1} = Q_{n+1} n + s_{n+1}.$$

All remainders are between 0 and $n - 1$. Because there are $n + 1$ of them, two must be the same, say s_i and s_j with i smaller than j. Then

$$q^j - q^i = Q_j n + s_j - Q_i n - s_i,$$

or

$$q^i(q^{j-i} - 1) = (Q_j - Q_i)n.$$

Because n is relatively prime to q, n must divide $q^{j-i} - 1$. Setting $m = j - i$ completes the proof. $\square$

Using this theorem, we can describe any cyclic code in a suitable extension field provided that n and q are relatively prime. For a cyclic code of blocklength n, $g(x)$ divides $x^n - 1$ and $x^n - 1$ divides $x^{q^{m-1}} - 1$, and thus $g(x)$ also divides $x^{q^{m-1}} - 1$. We will always use the smallest m for which this is true. Let α be primitive in $GF(q^m)$, let $q^m - 1 = nb$, and let $\beta = \alpha^b$. Then all the zeros of $x^n - 1$, and thus of $g(x)$, are restricted to powers of β. The prime factors of $x^n - 1$ have only these zeros.

In summary, if we use $\beta = \alpha^b$ in place of α and restrict zeros to powers of β, then we obtain a cyclic code of blocklength $n = (q^m - 1)/b$.

5.4 MATRIX DESCRIPTION OF CYCLIC CODES

We began this chapter with a brief discussion that related a parity-check matrix to zeros of polynomials in an extension field. Later sections developed the idea of a cyclic code with little mention of parity-check matrices. It is now time to relate the cyclic codes to their generator and parity-check matrices.

There are a number of ways to write out these matrices. First of all, we can write out a parity-check matrix by working in the extension field, as we did in Section 5.1. If $\gamma_j \in GF(q^m)$ for $j = 1, \ldots, r$ are the zeros of $g(x)$, then

$$\sum_{i=0}^{n-1} c_i \gamma_j^i = 0 \qquad j = 1, \ldots, r,$$

which can be written in matrix form as

$$\mathbf{H} = \begin{bmatrix} \gamma_1^0 & \gamma_1^1 & \cdots & \gamma_1^{n-1} \\ \gamma_2^0 & \gamma_2^1 & \cdots & \gamma_2^{n-1} \\ \vdots & & & \\ \gamma_r^0 & \gamma_r^1 & \cdots & \gamma_r^{n-1} \end{bmatrix}.$$

Now change this r by n matrix over $GF(q^m)$ into an rm by n matrix over $GF(q)$ by replacing each matrix element β by a column vector based on the coefficients of β expressed as a polynomial over $GF(q)$. This gives a parity-check matrix over $GF(q)$, but some of the rows may be linearly dependent and thus represent excess baggage in the matrix. Delete the least number of rows necessary to obtain a matrix with linearly independent rows. This gives a parity-check matrix for the code.

While the above procedure makes clear the relationship between zeros in the extension field and the parity-check matrix, it is somewhat cumbersome to follow through. One can find the desired matrices from the generator polynomial without ever entering the extension field. One way is to construct the generator matrix from the generator polynomial by inspection. Because codewords are of the form $c(x) = i(x)g(x)$, it is simple to translate this into matrix form:

$$\mathbf{G} = \begin{bmatrix} 0 & \cdots & 0 & g_{n-k} & g_{n-k-1} & \cdots & g_2 & g_1 & g_0 \\ 0 & & g_{n-k} & g_{n-k-1} & g_{n-k-2} & \cdots & g_1 & g_0 & 0 \\ 0 & & g_{n-k-1} & g_{n-k-2} & g_{n-k-3} & \cdots & g_0 & 0 & 0 \\ \vdots & & & & & & & & \vdots \\ g_{n-k} & \cdots & & & & & & 0 & 0 \end{bmatrix}.$$

A parity-check matrix is:

$$\mathbf{H} = \begin{bmatrix} 0 & 0 & 0 & \cdots & & & h_{k-1} & h_k \\ \vdots & & & & & & & \vdots \\ 0 & h_0 & h_1 & & h_{k-1} & h_k & 0 & 0 & 0 \\ h_0 & h_1 & h_2 & \cdots & h_k & 0 & 0 & \cdots & 0 & 0 \end{bmatrix},$$

where $h(x)$ is the parity-check polynomial of the cyclic code. To verify that

$$\mathbf{G}\mathbf{H}^T = \mathbf{0},$$

let

$$u_r = \sum_{i=0}^{r} g_{r-i} h_i,$$

which is zero for $0 < r < n$ because $h(x)g(x) = x^n - 1$. But then we have

$$\mathbf{G}\mathbf{H}^T = \begin{bmatrix} u_{n-1} & u_{n-2} & \cdots & u_k \\ u_{n-2} & u_{n-3} & \cdots & u_{k-1} \\ \vdots & & & \\ u_{n-k} & u_{n-k-1} & \cdots & u_1 \end{bmatrix} = \mathbf{0},$$

and thus $\mathbf{H}$ as defined is indeed a parity-check matrix. We now can see that the dual code $\mathscr{C}^\perp$ for the code generated by $g(x)$ is also a cyclic code, because $\mathbf{H}$ is its generator matrix and it has the form of a generator matrix for a cyclic code. The generator polynomial for the dual code is $\tilde{h}(x) = x^k h(x^{-1})$, which is the reciprocal polynomial of $h(x)$. Sometimes in discussions of cyclic codes, the code generated by $h(x)$ is also called the dual code, but to be precise one should only say it is equivalent to the dual code.

One can also easily get a generator matrix in systematic form. Use the division algorithm to write for each i corresponding to an information place

$$x^{n-i} = Q_i(x)g(x) + s_i(x) \qquad i = 1, \dots, k,$$

where

$$s_i(x) = \sum_{j=0}^{n-k-1} s_{ji} x^j.$$

Thus $x^{n-i} - s_i(x)$ is a codeword, because

$$x^{n-i} - s_i(x) = Q_i(x)g(x).$$

Using the coefficients of the left-hand side as elements of the generator matrix gives

$$\mathbf{G} = \begin{bmatrix} -s_{0,k} & \cdots & -s_{(n-k-1),k} & 1 & 0 & \cdots & 0 \\ -s_{0,k-1} & & -s_{(n-k-1),k-1} & 0 & 1 & & 0 \\ \vdots & & \vdots & \vdots & & & \vdots \\ -s_{0,1} & \cdots & -s_{(n-k-1),1} & 0 & 0 & \cdots & 1 \end{bmatrix}.$$

This is a systematic generator matrix with the indices of the information places running from $n-k$ to $n-1$. To write down this matrix, it is only necessary to carry out the computation of the $s_i(x)$ as remainders of x^i divided by $g(x)$. The parity-check matrix can then be written down using the principles of Section 3.2. This is

$$\mathbf{H} = \begin{bmatrix} 1 & 0 & \cdots & 0 & s_{0,k} & \cdots & s_{0,1} \\ 0 & 1 & & 0 & s_{1,k} & & s_{1,1} \\ \vdots & & & \vdots & \vdots & & \vdots \\ 0 & & \cdots & 1 & s_{(n-k-1),k} & \cdots & s_{(n-k-1),1} \end{bmatrix}.$$

5.5 HAMMING CODES AS CYCLIC CODES

The code used to start the chapter, the Hamming (7, 4) code, has generator polynomial

$$g(x) = x^3 + x + 1.$$

This polynomial has a zero in $GF(8)$ at the primitive element α, and thus all codewords satisfy $c(\alpha) = 0$. Similarly, to get a Hamming code for any primitive blocklength $n = 2^m - 1$, take $g(x)$ with a zero at primitive element α in

$GF(2^m)$. This is $p(x)$, the minimal polynomial of α, which is the primitive polynomial used to construct $GF(2^m)$. Then $c(x) = a(x)g(x)$, and $c(\alpha) = 0$ for every codeword. That is, $\mathbf{c}\mathbf{H}^T = 0$, where

$$\mathbf{H} = [\alpha^0 \quad \alpha^1 \quad \dots \quad \alpha^{n-1}].$$

There are also Hamming codes over larger alphabets. In Section 3.4 we saw that for every m, there is a Hamming code over $GF(q)$ with $n = (q^m - 1)/(q - 1)$ and $k = [(q^m - 1)/(q - 1)] - m$. In this section we will show that many, but not all, of these are cyclic codes by finding the generator polynomials.

Let α be primitive in $GF(q^m)$, and let $\beta = \alpha^{q-1}$. Then $\beta^{(q^m-1)/(q-1)} = 1$, and thus β is a zero of $x^{(q^m-1)/(q-1)} - 1$. Hence, the minimal polynomial of β divides $x^{(q^m-1)/(q-1)} - 1$ and serves as a generator polynomial for some cyclic code of blocklength $n = (q^m - 1)/(q - 1)$. The parity-check matrix is $\mathbf{H} = [\beta^0 \quad \beta^1 \quad \dots \quad \beta^{n-1}]$.

For $q = 2$, $\beta = \alpha$, and it is easy to prove that the code is a single-error-correcting code by giving a simple procedure for decoding single errors. The received word is a polynomial of degree $n - 1$ given by

$$v(x) = a(x)g(x) + e(x),$$

where $e(x)$ has at most one nonzero coefficient. That is,

$$e(x) = 0 \text{ or } x^i.$$

The integer i indexes the location in which an error occurs. We also use the elements of $GF(2^m)$ to index the error locations. The field element α^i is assigned to index component i. Because $g(\alpha) = 0$, we have $v(\alpha) = \alpha^i$, and all powers of α from 0 to $2^m - 2$ are distinct. The error location i is immediately determined from α^i unless $v(\alpha) = 0$, in which case there is no error. Therefore the code is a single-error-correcting code over $GF(2)$ with $n = 2^m - 1$ and $k = n - m$; in fact, it is a Hamming code over $GF(2)$.

We have proved the following theorem for the special case of $q = 2$. The general case is more difficult because all terms of the form $\gamma\beta^i$ must be distinct, where γ is an arbitrary element of $GF(q)$. We shall now prove the theorem formally for arbitrary q.

□ **Theorem 5.5.1** The code with parity-check matrix $\mathbf{H} = [\beta^0 \quad \beta^1 \quad \dots \quad \beta^{n-1}]$, where $\beta = \alpha^{q-1}$ and $n = (q^m - 1)/(q - 1)$, has minimum distance at least 3 if and only if n and $q - 1$ are relatively prime, and this occurs if and only if m and $q - 1$ are relatively prime.

Proof Suppose two columns of $\mathbf{H}$ are linearly dependent:

$$\beta^i = \gamma\beta^j,$$

where γ is an element of $GF(q)$. Then β^{i-j} is an element of $GF(q)$, and thus is a zero of $x^{q-1} - 1 = 0$. But the nonzero elements of $GF(q)$ can be expressed in terms of α, the primitive element of $GF(q^m)$, as the first $q-1$ powers of $\alpha^{(q^m-1)/(q-1)}$, because these powers are distinct and $((\alpha^{(q^m-1)/(q-1)})^k)^{q-1} = 1$. Then

$$\beta^{i-j} = (\alpha^{(q^m-1)/(q-1)})^k = \alpha^{nk}$$

for some k less than $q-1$. Further, because $\beta = \alpha^{q-1}$,

$$(q-1)(i-j) = nk.$$

Because $(i-j)$ is less than n, this has a solution for $(i-j)$ if and only if n and $q-1$ are not relatively prime; that is, **H** can have two linearly dependent columns if and only if n and $q-1$ are not relatively prime.

Now we will show that m and $q-1$ are relatively prime if and only if n and $q-1$ are relatively prime, also. But

$$n = \frac{q^m - 1}{q-1} = q^{m-1} + q^{m-2} + \cdots + 1,$$

and

$$q^{m-j} = (q-1)s_j + 1$$

for some s_j because $q^{m-j} - 1$ is divisible by $q-1$. Therefore by summing over j, we obtain

$$n = m + (q-1) \sum_{j=1}^{m} s_j,$$

and thus n and $q-1$ are relatively prime if and only if m and $q-1$ are relatively prime. $\square$

The previous theorem has established that the Hamming codes of block-length $n = (q^m - 1)/(q-1)$ over $GF(q)$ are cyclic if m and $q-1$ are relatively prime. We saw some Hamming codes in Section 3.4, however, for which m and $q-1$ are not relatively prime. For these the cyclic construction does not work. The smallest such example is the (21, 18) Hamming code over $GF(4)$. This code cannot be expressed in terms of a generator polynomial. Most Hamming codes of interest, however, are cyclic.

As an example of a cyclic Hamming code, we will find the generator polynomial for an (85, 81) Hamming code over $GF(4)$. This construction takes place in $GF(256)$ and consists of finding the minimal polynomial over $GF(4)$ of $\beta = \alpha^3$. In $GF(256)$, the elements α^{85} and α^{170} are the only two elements of order 3, so we see that

$$GF(4) = \{0, 1, \alpha^{85}, \alpha^{170}\}$$

when expressed in the terminology of $GF(256)$. The conjugates of β with respect to $GF(2)$ are

$$\{\beta, \beta^2, \beta^4, \beta^8, \beta^{16}, \beta^{32}, \beta^{64}, \beta^{128}\}.$$

We need the conjugates with respect to $GF(4)$. These are

$$\{\beta, \beta^4, \beta^{16}, \beta^{64}\}.$$

Hence, the desired generator polynomial is

$$g(x) = (x - \beta)(x - \beta^4)(x - \beta^{16})(x - \beta^{64})$$
$$= (x - \alpha^3)(x - \alpha^{12})(x - \alpha^{48})(x - \alpha^{192}).$$

When multiplied out, this polynomial must have coefficients only in $GF(4)$. Thus far we have not needed to make use of the structure of $GF(256)$. Now we do. Using the primitive polynomial $p(x) = x^8 + x^4 + x^3 + x^2 + 1$, we have $\alpha^8 = \alpha^4 + \alpha^3 + \alpha^2 + 1$. We can make this substitution repeatedly to reduce $g(x)$ or alternatively write out a log table for multiplication in $GF(256)$. In either case, within an hour's worth of computation, we find that

$$g(x) = x^4 + x^3 + \alpha^{170}x + 1.$$

Finally, we change notation to something suitable for the subfield $GF(4)$ because we are finished with the big field $GF(256)$. That is,

$$g(x) = x^4 + x^3 + 3x + 1.$$

This is the desired generator polynomial of the (85, 81) Hamming code over $GF(4)$.

5.6 CYCLIC CODES FOR CORRECTING DOUBLE ERRORS

The Hamming codes were described in the previous section as cyclic codes whose generator polynomials have a zero at a suitable element of the appropriate extension field. These codes correct a single error. Now we turn to double-error-correcting codes over the field $GF(2)$. Let the blocklength n be $2^m - 1$ for some m, and let α be a primitive element of $GF(2^m)$. We will consider those binary codes having α and α^3 as zeros of the generator polynomial and show that the resulting code corrects double errors.

Let $g(x)$ be the polynomial of smallest degree with α and α^3 as zeros in $GF(2^m)$. By exhibiting a decoding procedure that corrects all single and double errors, we will prove that this code has minimum distance of at least 5.

The received word is a polynomial of degree $n - 1$ given by

$$v(x) = a(x)g(x) + e(x),$$

where $e(x)$ has at most two nonzero coefficients, because we are considering at most two errors. That is,

$$e(x) = 0 \quad \text{or} \quad x^i \quad \text{or} \quad x^i + x^{i'}.$$

The integers i and i' index the locations in which errors occur. We will also use the elements of $GF(2^m)$ to index the error locations. The field element

α^i is assigned to index component i. In this role, the field elements are called the *location numbers*. Define the field elements $X_1 = \alpha^i$ and $X_2 = \alpha^{i'}$. The error-location numbers X_1 and X_2 must be unique because n, the order of α, is also the blocklength. If only one error occurs, then let $X_2 = 0$. If no errors occur, then $X_1 = X_2 = 0$.

Let $S_1 = v(\alpha)$ and $S_3 = v(\alpha^3)$. These field elements, also known as syndromes, can be evaluated immediately from $v(x)$. Because $g(x)$ has zeros at α and α^3, $S_1 = e(\alpha)$ and $S_3 = e(\alpha^3)$. Suppose two errors occur:

$$S_1 = \alpha^i + \alpha^{i'},$$

$$S_3 = \alpha^{3i} + \alpha^{3i'}.$$

But this is just a pair of equations in $GF(2^m)$ involving the two unknowns, X_1 and X_2:

$$S_1 = X_1 + X_2,$$

$$S_3 = X_1^3 + X_2^3.$$

Given that at most two errors occur, S_1 equals zero if and only if no errors occur. The decoder needs to proceed only if S_1 is not zero. If the above pair of nonlinear equations can be solved uniquely for X_1 and X_2, the two errors can be corrected, and the code has a minimum distance of at least 5.

It is not directly apparent how to solve this pair of equations. One way is to introduce a new polynomial defined to have the error-location numbers as zeros:

$$(x - X_1)(x - X_2) = x^2 + (X_1 + X_2)x + X_1 X_2.$$

If we can find the coefficients of the polynomial on the right, then we can factor the polynomial to find X_1 and X_2. But over extensions of $GF(2)$,

$$S_1^3 + S_3 = X_1^2 X_2 + X_2^2 X_1 = S_1 X_1 X_2.$$

Thus

$$(x + X_1)(x + X_2) = x^2 + S_1 x + \frac{S_1^3 + S_3}{S_1},$$

and $S_1 \neq 0$ if one or two errors occur. We know the polynomial on the right because we know S_1 and S_3. The error-location numbers are the pair of zeros of the polynomial. The zeros of any polynomial over a field are unique. Therefore the code is a double-error-correcting code.

We have established that this $g(x)$ gives a double-error-correcting code by describing a decoding procedure. In practice, one can actually use any convenient procedure for decoding, but one such procedure is finding the zeros of the above quadratic in $GF(2^m)$. This is often done by trial and error, because there are only 2^m possibilities. Other decoding schemes will be studied in later chapters.

The double-error-correcting codes of this section illustrate how cyclic codes in one field can be constructed by working with zeros in a larger field. The general principle will be discussed in Chapter 7 for an arbitrary symbol field $GF(q)$ and an arbitrary number of correctable errors.

5.7 CYCLIC CODES FOR CORRECTING BURST ERRORS

Most codes are designed to correct any random pattern of t errors. Some channels, however, are susceptible mostly to burst errors. If one only needs to correct t errors occurring during a brief time interval but not an arbitrary pattern of t errors, then one may use this relaxed requirement to obtain a more efficient code — that is, one of higher rate. In this section we will briefly touch upon this topic to give some cyclic codes for correcting burst errors. Because of the cyclic nature of the codes, we get a little extra performance that we don't normally need—the codes correct not just burst errors, but cyclic burst errors as well. Cyclic bursts are defined as follows.

☐ **Definition 5.7.1** A *cyclic burst* of length t is a vector whose non-zero components are among t (cyclically) successive components, the first and the last of which are nonzero. ☐

We can describe a burst-error pattern as $e(x) = x^i b(x) (\mod x^n - 1)$, where $b(x)$ is a polynomial of degree at most $t - 1$ with b_0 nonzero. Thus $b(x)$ describes the burst pattern, and x^i describes the starting location of the burst.

A cyclic code for correcting burst errors must have syndrome polynomials $s(x)$ that are distinct. That is, if

$$s(x) = R_{g(x)}[e(x)]$$

is different for each polynomial $e(x)$ representing a cyclic burst of length t, then the code is capable of correcting all burst errors of length t. For example, the polynomial

$$g(x) = x^6 + x^3 + x^2 + x + 1$$

is the generator polynomial for a binary code of length 15. The cyclic error bursts of length 3 or less can be enumerated. They are

$$e(x) = x^i \qquad\qquad\qquad\qquad\qquad\quad i = 0, \ldots, 14$$
$$e(x) = x^i(1 + x) \qquad\quad (\mod x^{15} - 1) \qquad i = 0, \ldots, 14$$
$$e(x) = x^i(1 + x^2) \qquad\ \ (\mod x^{15} - 1) \qquad i = 0, \ldots, 14$$
$$e(x) = x^i(1 + x + x^2) \quad (\mod x^{15} - 1) \qquad i = 0, \ldots, 14.$$

By direct enumeration, it is straightforward to verify that each syndrome of each of these 56 patterns is distinct, and thus the cyclic code generated by $g(x)$ can correct burst errors of length 3.

Notice that a codeword plus a correctable burst error cannot be equal to another codeword plus a correctable burst error. In particular, no burst of length 6 can be a codeword. In general, a linear code that can correct all bursts of length t or less cannot have a burst of length $2t$ or less as a codeword.

The following theorem is similar to the Singleton bound for random-error-correcting codes but is proved differently. It is not restricted to cyclic codes.

☐ **Theorem 5.7.2 (Rieger Bound)**   A linear block code that corrects all bursts of length t or less must have at least $2t$ parity symbols.

Proof   Suppose the code corrects all bursts of length t or less. Then there is no codeword that is a burst of length $2t$. Now if two vectors are in the same coset, then their difference is a codeword. Choose any two vectors that are zero except in their first $2t$ components. If these are in the same coset of a standard array, then their difference is a codeword; it is a burst of length $2t$, and we have seen there are no such codewords. Therefore two such vectors must be in different cosets, and the number of cosets is at least as large as the number of such vectors. There are q^{2t} vectors that are zero except in their first $2t$ components; hence there are at least q^{2t} cosets; hence at least $2t$ parity symbols. ☐

Notice that the previous example of a cyclic burst-correcting code satisfies the Rieger bound with equality.

The best-understood burst-correcting codes are cyclic, and we shall only study this class. For small t and moderate blocklength, a number of good cyclic codes over $GF(2)$ have been found by computer search. Some of these are listed in Table 5.1.

Table 5.1   Some binary burst-correcting cyclic codes.

Generator Polynomial	Parameters	Burst-Correction Ability (Error Length)
$x^4 + x^3 + x^2 + 1$	(7, 3)	2
$x^5 + x^4 + x^2 + 1$	(15, 10)	2
$x^6 + x^5 + x^4 + x^3 + 1$	(15, 9)	3
$x^6 + x^5 + x^4 + 1$	(31, 25)	2
$x^7 + x^6 + x^5 + x^3 + x^2 + 1$	(63, 56)	2
$x^8 + x^7 + x^6 + x^3 + 1$	(63, 55)	3
$x^{12} + x^8 + x^5 + x^3 + 1$	(511, 499)	4
$x^{13} + x^{10} + x^7 + x^6 + x^5 + x^4 + x^2 + 1$	(1023, 1010)	4

Longer codes can be constructed from the codes of Table 5.1 by the technique of interleaving. To get a (jn, jk) code from an (n, k) code, take any j codewords from the original code and merge the codewords by alternating the symbols. If the original code can correct any burst error of length t, it is apparent that the interleaved code can correct any burst error of length jt. For example, by taking four copies of the (31, 25) code and interleaving the bits, one obtains a (124, 100) code. Because each of the individual codes can correct a burst error of length 2, the new code can correct any burst error of length 8.

The technique of interleaving creates a cyclic code from a cyclic code. Suppose that $g(x)$ is the generator polynomial of the original code. Then $g(x^j)$ is the generator polynomial of the interleaved code. To see this, notice that interleaving the symbols of several information polynomials and then multiplying by $g(x^j)$ gives the same codeword as multiplying each information polynomial by $g(x)$ and then interleaving these (n, k) codewords. Specifically, let

$$c_1(x) = i_1(x)g(x)$$
$$c_2(x) = i_2(x)g(x)$$
$$\vdots$$
$$c_j(x) = i_j(x)g(x)$$

be the individual codewords. To form the interleaved codeword, the symbols in each of these codewords are spread out, with $j - 1$ zeros inserted after every symbol. Then the codewords are delayed and added to give the interleaved codeword

$$
\begin{aligned}
c(x) &= c_1(x^j) + xc_2(x^j) + \cdots + x^{j-1}c_j(x^j) \\
&= i_1(x^j)g(x^j) + xi_2(x)g(x^j) + \cdots + x^{j-1}i_j(x^j)g(x^j) \\
&= [i_1(x^j) + xi_2(x^j) + \cdots + x^{j-1}i_j(x^j)]g(x^j).
\end{aligned}
$$

The bracketed term that has been factored out is just an interleaved information word. It can just as well be replaced by any information word $i(x)$. Hence,

$$c(x) = i(x)g(x^j).$$

Replacing $g(x)$ by $g(x^j)$ is equivalent to interleaving j copies of the code generated by $g(x)$.

Besides the codes obtained by computer search, and interleaved extensions of them, there are also codes constructed analytically. The Fire codes are a class of such codes. Table 5.2 shows parameters of some Fire codes.

☐ **Definition 5.7.3**   A *Fire code* is a cyclic burst-correcting code over $GF(q)$ with generator polynomial

$$g(x) = (x^{2t-1} - 1)p(x),$$

Table 5.2 Parameters of some binary Fire codes.

(n, k)	$t = m$
$(9, 4)$	2
$(35, 27)$	3
$(105, 94)$	4
$(279, 265)$	5
$(693, 676)$	6
$(1651, 1631)$	7
$(3825, 3802)$	8
$(8687, 8661)$	9
$(19437, 19408)$	10

where $p(x)$ is a prime polynomial over $GF(q)$ whose degree m is not smaller than t and $p(x)$ does not divide $x^{2t-1} - 1$. The blocklength of the Fire code is the smallest integer n such that $g(x)$ divides $x^n - 1$. □

□ **Theorem 5.7.4** A Fire code has blocklength $n = e(2t - 1)$, where e is the smallest integer such that $p(x)$ divides $x^e - 1$. Consequently, if $p(x)$ is primitive, the code is a $((q^m - 1)(2t - 1), (q^m - 1)(2t - 1) - m - 2t + 1)$ code. □

Proof With $n = e(2t - 1)$, we have several factorizations of $x^n - 1$.

$$x^n - 1 = x^{e(2t-1)} - 1 = (x^e - 1) \sum_{k=0}^{2t-2} x^{ek}$$

$$x^n - 1 = x^{e(2t-1)} - 1 = (x^{2t-1} - 1) \sum_{k=0}^{e-1} x^{(2t-1)k}.$$

Because $p(x)$ divides $x^e - 1$, it divides $x^n - 1$. Because it does not divide $x^{2t-1} - 1$, it must divide $\sum_{k=0}^{e-1} x^{(2t-1)k}$. Then

$$x^n - 1 = (x^{2t-1} - 1)p(x)a(x)$$

for some $a(x)$, and because no smaller n suffices for such a factorization, this is the blocklength.

In particular, if $p(x)$ is primitive of degree m, then $p(x)$ divides $x^e - 1$ for $e = q^m - 1$, but for no e smaller than $q^m - 1$. □

□ **Theorem 5.7.5** A Fire code can correct all burst errors of length t or less.

Proof The code is capable of correcting all bursts of length t or less if no two such bursts $x^i b_1(x)$ and $x^j b_2(x)$ appear in the same coset.

Because the code is a cyclic code, without loss of generality we can take i equal to zero. Suppose that two bursts of length t or less, $b_1(x)$ and $x^j b_2(x)$, are in the same coset of a standard array for the code. Then their difference is a codeword, and for some $a(x)$,

$$b_1(x) + x^j b_2(x) = a(x)(x^{2t-1} - 1)p(x) \qquad (\text{mod } x^n - 1).$$

But $x^{2t-1} - 1$ divides $x^{v(2t-1)} - 1$ for all positive v. Therefore we can write

$$(x^{v(2t-1)} - 1)b_1(x) = Q(x)(x^{2t-1} - 1) \qquad (\text{mod } x^n - 1).$$

Adding the two equations gives

$$x^{v(2t-1)}[b_1(x) + x^{j - v(2t-1)}b_2(x)] = a'(x)(x^{2t-1} - 1) \qquad (\text{mod } x^n - 1),$$

or equivalently

$$x^{v(2t-1)-(t-1)}[x^{(t-1)}b_1(x) + x^{j+(t-1)-v(2t-1)}b_2(x)]$$
$$= a''(x)(x^{2t-1} - 1) \qquad (\text{mod } x^n - 1)$$

for some $a'(x)$ and $a''(x)$. But now in one or the other of the last two equations we can choose a nonnegative integer v less than e such that $b_2(x)$ is multiplied by x^k, with $0 \leqslant k < t$. That is, by choice of v, either

$$x^{v(2t-1)}[b_1(x) + x^k b_2(x)] = a'(x)(x^{2t-1} - 1) \qquad (\text{mod } x^n - 1)$$

or

$$x^{v(2t-1)-(t-1)}[x^{t-1}b_1(x) + x^k b_2(x)]$$
$$= a''(x)(x^{2t-1} - 1) \qquad (\text{mod } x^n - 1),$$

where $\deg b_1(x) < t$, $\deg b_2(x) < t$, and $k < t$; thus the bracketed term has a degree at most $2t - 2$. But $x^{2t-1} - 1$ must divide the bracketed term. Therefore either

$$b_1(x) + x^k b_2(x) = 0$$

or

$$x^{t-1}b_1(x) + x^k b_2(x) = 0.$$

By definition of a burst, b_{10} and b_{20} are both nonzero. Therefore $k = 0$ or $t - 1$, respectively. In either case, $j = v(2t - 1)$, and $b_2(x) = -b_1(x) = b(x)$.

The last step is to show that $b(x)$ must be zero. But the original expression

$$b_1(x) + x^j b_2(x) = a(x)(x^{2t-1} - 1)p(x)$$

now becomes

$$(x^{v(2t-1)} - 1)b(x) = a(x)(x^{2t-1} - 1)p(x).$$

Now $p(x)$ cannot divide $x^{v(2t-1)} - 1$ unless v equals zero, because v is a nonnegative integer less than e, and $p(x)$ divides $x^{v(2t-1)} - 1$ for no positive v smaller than e. Then $p(x)$ cannot divide anything on the left-hand side except $b(x)$. Because $b(x)$ has degree less than $p(x)$, $b(x)$ must equal zero unless v equals zero. If v equals zero and $GF(q)$ has characteristic 2, then j equals zero and $b_1(x) = b_2(x)$, and the two bursts are the same. If v equals zero and $GF(q)$ has an odd characteristic, then $b(x)$ and $-b(x)$ each have a syndrome equal to itself, and these syndromes are equal because the bursts are in the same coset. That is, $b(x) = -b(x)$, and thus it must equal zero.

Thus if $b_1(x)$ and $x^j b_2(x)$ are any distinct nonzero bursts of length t or less, they are not in the same coset, and thus the code can correct bursts of length t. $\square$

As an example of a Fire code, choose $m = t = 10$, and choose $p(x)$ as a primitive polynomial of degree of 10. Then $e = 2^m - 1$, and we have a (19437, 19408) code for correcting a single burst of length 10.

The Fire codes are of very high rate, and the redundancy $n - k$ is the least when m equals t. Then the redundancy is $3t - 1$, which exceeds the Reiger bound by $t - 1$. By interleaving Fire codes, longer codes for correcting longer burst errors can be constructed. These are the best burst-correcting codes known of high rate. In the next chapter we shall see that decoders for such codes are easy to construct.

5.8 THE BINARY GOLAY CODE

Anyone disposed to study a table of binomial coefficients might notice that

$$[\binom{23}{0} + \binom{23}{1} + \binom{23}{2} + \binom{23}{3}]2^{12} = 2^{23}.$$

This is a necessary (but not sufficient) condition for the existence of a perfect (23, 12) triple-error-correcting code over $GF(2)$ because: (1) the number of points in a decoding sphere is given by the number in brackets, (2) there are 2^{12} such spheres, and (3) there are 2^{23} points in the space. Therefore one might suspect the existence of a (23, 12, 7) code. Such a code, called the Golay code, does exist. It satisfies the Hamming bound of Problem 1.5 with equality.

The Golay code occupies a unique and important position in the subject of error-control codes. Because the spheres are so neatly packed, it is not surprising that the Golay code has close ties to many mathematical topics, and one can use it as a doorway to pass from the subject of error-control coding to deep topics in group theory and other areas of mathematics. From a practical point of view, however, it is probably fair to say that because of its short blocklength, the Golay code will soon be left far behind in most new applications.

We will define the Golay code as a binary cyclic code in terms of its generator polynomial.

Let $g(x)$ and $\tilde{g}(x)$ be the following reciprocal polynomials:

$$g(x) = x^{11} + x^{10} + x^6 + x^5 + x^4 + x^2 + 1,$$

$$\tilde{g}(x) = x^{11} + x^9 + x^7 + x^6 + x^5 + x + 1.$$

It is a simple computation to verify that over $GF(2)$

$$(x - 1)g(x)\tilde{g}(x) = x^{23} - 1.$$

Hence, either $g(x)$ or $\tilde{g}(x)$ can be used as the generator polynomial of a $(23, 12)$ cyclic code. We shall use $g(x)$. By the foregoing combinatoric counting argument, the minimum distance of this code cannot be greater than 7. We now must prove that it is at least 7, but there does not seem to be a proof that is both elementary and brief. One method of proof is to write out the **H** matrix and verify that no six columns are linearly dependent, but the **H** matrix is too large to do this conveniently. We will follow a long but straightforward proof. The length of the proof does show how difficult it can be to find the minimum weight of a code.

The proof will consist of three steps that together show that the minimum weight is not less than 7. The three steps prove in turn that:

1. There is no nonzero codeword of weight 4 or less.
2. There is no codeword of weight 2, 6, 10, 14, 18, or 22.
3. There is no codeword of weight 1, 5, 9, 13, 17, or 21.

Combining these shows that the minimum weight is at least 7. Because we already know that it is not greater than 7, we will conclude that it equals 7.

We will start out by describing the zeros of $g(x)$ and $\tilde{g}(x)$ in a suitable extension field of $GF(2)$. We will do this indirectly by constructing minimal polynomials for certain elements in $GF(2048)$, and these will turn out to be $g(x)$ and $\tilde{g}(x)$. Now $2047 = 23 \times 89$, and thus if α is primitive in this field, then $\beta = \alpha^{89}$ has order 23, as does β^{-1}. Let $f(x)$ and $\tilde{f}(x)$ denote the minimal polynomials of β and β^{-1}, respectively.

According to Theorem 5.3.6, the minimal polynomial of β is

$$f(x) = (x - \beta)(x - \beta^2)(x - \beta^4)\dots(x - \beta^{2^{r-1}}),$$

where the exponents are modulo 23, and $2 \cdot 2^{r-1} = 1 \pmod{23}$. The conjugates are the elements of the set

$$B = \{\beta, \beta^2, \beta^4, \beta^8, \beta^{16}, \beta^9, \beta^{18}, \beta^{13}, \beta^3, \beta^6, \beta^{12}\},$$

which has 11 members, and thus the degree of $f(x)$ is 11. Similarly, the minimal polynomial of β^{-1} is

$$\tilde{f}(x) = (x - \beta^{-1})(x - \beta^{-2})(x - \beta^{-4})\dots(x - \beta^{-2^{r-1}}),$$

and the conjugates are the elements of the set

$$\tilde{B} = \{\beta^{-1}, \beta^{-2}, \beta^{-4}, \beta^{-8}, \beta^{-16}, \beta^{-9}, \beta^{-18}, \beta^{-13}, \beta^{-3}, \beta^{-6}, \beta^{-12}\}.$$

Now B and $\tilde{B}$ contain 22 field elements between them, and the twenty-third power of each element equals one; thus we have

$$(x-1)f(x)\tilde{f}(x) = x^{23} - 1,$$

which, by the unique factorization theorem, is unique. But we have already seen that this is satisfied by $g(x)$ and $\tilde{g}(x)$, the generator polynomials of the Golay code. Hence, these generator polynomials are the minimal polynomials of α^{89} and α^{-89} in $GF(2048)$.

□ **Lemma 5.8.1** The Golay code has no nonzero codeword of weight 4 or less.

Proof Because B contains β, β^2, β^3, and β^4, these are zeros of every codeword. Hence every codeword satisfies $\mathbf{c}\mathbf{H}^T = \mathbf{0}$, where

$$\mathbf{H} = \begin{bmatrix} 1 & \beta & \beta^2 & \cdots & \beta^{22} \\ 1 & \beta^2 & \beta^4 & & \beta^{21} \\ 1 & \beta^3 & \beta^6 & & \beta^{20} \\ 1 & \beta^4 & \beta^8 & \cdots & \beta^{19} \end{bmatrix},$$

and thus $\mathbf{c}$ is also in the code for which this $\mathbf{H}$ is a parity-check matrix. But any four columns of $\mathbf{H}$ form a nonzero multiple of a matrix known as a Vandermonde matrix, which is well known to have nonzero determinant if the elements of the first row are distinct (this will be proved in Section 7.2). Therefore by Corollary 3.2.3, $\mathbf{H}$ is the parity-check matrix of a code whose minimum weight is at least 5. □

The next lemma says no codewords have weight 2, 6, 10, 14, 18 or 22.

□ **Lemma 5.8.2** Every codeword in the Golay code whose weight is even has weight divisible by 4.

Proof Let $c(x) = a(x)g(x)$ be a codeword whose weight w is even:

$$c(x) = \sum_{i=0}^{22} c_i x^i,$$

where an even number of c_i are equal to one. Then $c(1) = 0$, and thus $x - 1$ divides $c(x)$. But $x - 1$ does not divide $g(x)$. That is,

$$c(x) = b(x)(x-1)g(x)$$

for some $b(x)$. Now define the reciprocal polynomial:

$$\tilde{c}(x) = \sum_{i=0}^{22} c_{22-i} x^i = x^{22} \sum_{i=0}^{22} c_i x^{-i}.$$

Because $\tilde{c}(\beta^{-1}) = 0$, we have that for some $\tilde{a}(x)$,

$$\tilde{c}(x) = \tilde{a}(x)\tilde{g}(x).$$

Therefore

$$c(x)\tilde{c}(x) = b(x)\tilde{a}(x)(x - 1)g(x)\tilde{g}(x) = b(x)\tilde{a}(x)(x^{23} - 1).$$

We will use this below. Now compute $c(x)\tilde{c}(x)$ by noting that polynomial multiplication can be expressed as a convolution:

$$c(x)\tilde{c}(x) = \sum_{j=0}^{44} \sum_{i=0}^{22} c_i \tilde{c}_{j-i} x^j = \sum_{j=0}^{44} \sum_{i=0}^{22} c_i c_{22+i-j} x^j,$$

where the coefficients are understood to be zero for indices less than zero or greater than 22, and thus it does no harm to replace the sum on i by a sum from $-\infty$ to ∞. This avoids later fussing with the limits of summation. The equation can be broken as follows:

$$c(x)\tilde{c}(x) = \sum_{j=0}^{21} \sum_{i=-\infty}^{\infty} c_i c_{22+i-j} x^j + \sum_{i=-\infty}^{\infty} c_i^2 x^{22} + \sum_{j=23}^{44} \sum_{i=-\infty}^{\infty} c_i c_{22+i-j} x^i.$$

The second term is zero because $c_i^2 = c_i$ in $GF(2)$ and by assumption an even number of the c_i are equal to one. In the last term make the substitution $i' = i + 22 - j$, and change j to j' in both terms. Then

$$c(x)\tilde{c}(x) = \sum_{j'=0}^{21} \sum_{i=-\infty}^{\infty} c_i c_{22+i-j'} x^{j'} + \sum_{j'=23}^{44} \sum_{i'=-\infty}^{\infty} c_{i'+j'-22} c_{i'} x^{j'}.$$

Next, replace i' by i in the second term. Set $j' = j - 1$ in the first term and $j' = j + 22$ in the second term. This becomes

$$c(x)\tilde{c}(x) = \sum_{j=1}^{22} \sum_{i=-\infty}^{\infty} c_i c_{23+i-j} x^{j-1} + \sum_{j=1}^{22} \sum_{i=-\infty}^{\infty} c_i c_{i+j} x^{j-1} x^{23}$$

$$= \sum_{j=1}^{22} \left[\sum_{i=0}^{22} c_i c_{23+i-j} + c_i c_{i+j} \right] x^{j-1} + \left[\sum_{j=1}^{22} \sum_{i=-\infty}^{\infty} c_i c_{i+j} x^{j-1} \right] (x^{23} - 1).$$

But $c(x)\tilde{c}(x)$ is a multiple of $x^{23} - 1$, and hence

$$\sum_{i=0}^{22} c_i(c_{23+i-j} + c_{i+j}) = 0 \qquad j = 1, \ldots, 22.$$

This equation holds under modulo-2 addition. Hence, evaluating the left-hand side for each j under integer addition must give an even number:

$$\sum_{i=0}^{22} c_i(c_{23+i-j} + c_{i+j}) = 2a_j \qquad j = 1, \ldots, 22,$$

for some integers a_j. The left side does not change if j is replaced by $23 - j$. Hence, $a_j = a_{23-j}$.

Therefore summing over j gives

$$\sum_{j=1}^{22} \sum_{i=-0}^{22} c_i(c_{23+i-j} + c_{i+j}) = 2 \sum_{j=1}^{22} a_j = 4 \sum_{j=1}^{11} a_j = 4a$$

for some a. Finally, the left side can be rearranged. Let $j' = 23 - j$ in the first term and $i = i' - j$ in the second. Then

$$\sum_{j'=1}^{22} \sum_{i=0}^{22} c_i c_{i+j'} + \sum_{j=1}^{22} \sum_{i'=0}^{22} c_{i'} c_{i'-j} = 4a,$$

which collapses into

$$\sum_{i=0}^{22} \sum_{j \neq i} c_i c_j = 4a.$$

Because the binary component c_i is nonzero in w places, this becomes

$$w(w - 1) = 4a.$$

Because w is even, w is a multiple of 4, which proves the lemma. $\square$

We are finally ready to prove the theorem.

$\square$ **Theorem 5.8.3** The Golay code is a perfect triple-error-correcting code.

Proof By the introductory remarks of the section, it only is necessary to prove that the minimum weight is at least 7. By Lemma 5.8.1 it is at least 5, and by Lemma 5.8.2 it is not 6. Thus we only need to show that there are no codewords of weight 5.

Now $g(x)\tilde{g}(x)$ is a codeword; in fact, $g(x)\tilde{g}(x) = \sum_{k=0}^{n-1} x^k$, because $(x-1)g(x)\tilde{g}(x) = x^n - 1 = (x-1)\sum_{k=0}^{n-1} x^k$. Thus the vector with all ones is a codeword. The all-one codeword can be added to any codeword of weight w to get a codeword of weight $23 - w$. Then by Lemma 5.8.2, there can be no codewords of weight 21, 17, 13, 9, 5, or 1; and in particular there can be none of weight 5. Thus the theorem is proved. $\square$

Notice that the proof of the theorem also tells us that the Golay codewords can only have weights of 0, 7, 8, 11, 12, 15, 16, and 23. The number of codewords of each weight, evaluated by computer, is given by Table 5.3.

Besides the binary Golay code, there is also a perfect ternary $(11, 6, 5)$ Golay code. These two codes are the only nontrivial examples of perfect codes that correct more than one error.

5.9 QUADRATIC RESIDUE CODES

The class of quadratic residue codes is a special subclass of the class of cyclic codes that has been widely studied because some of the codes are quite

Table 5.3   Weight of Golay codewords.

Weight	Number of Words	
	(23, 12) Code	Extended (24, 12) Code
0	1	1
7	253	0
8	506	759
11	1288	0
12	1288	2576
15	506	0
16	253	759
23	1	0
24	—	1
	4096	4096

n	k	d^*
7	4	3†
17	9	5†
23	12	7†
31	16	7†
41	21	9†
47	24	11†
71	36	11
73	37	13
79	40	15†
89	45	17†
97	49	15
103	52	19†
127	64	19
151	76	19

†As good as the best code known
of this n and k.

Figure 5.2   Parameters of some
binary quadratic residue codes.

good, and thus one hopes there are other good codes in the class. Figure
5.2 gives a list of the parameters of some quadratic residue codes for which
the minimum distance is known. The most notable entry is the Golay code.
Most of the codes on this list have the largest minimum distance of any code

known with the same n and k, and this is what makes quadratic residue codes attractive. Not all the codes are good, however, and it is not known whether there are good quadratic residue codes with large blocklength. Also, quadratic residue codes are difficult to decode. Thus it is still uncertain how useful quadratic residue codes will be in practical applications.

We will discuss only binary quadratic residue codes. The name of these codes comes from their relationship to those elements in a prime field $GF(p)$ that have a square root. As shown in Theorem 4.6.15, in fields of characteristic 2, every element has a unique square root. In the prime field $GF(p)$, $p \neq 2$, exactly half of the nonzero field elements have square roots in $GF(p)$—those $(p-1)/2$ field elements that are an even power of a primitive element. These elements are conventionally called the *quadratic residues* (because they are the squares of their square roots modulo p). We emphasize that although the codes are over $GF(2)$, the quadratic residues used in their definition are in $GF(p)$, $p \neq 2$. The locator field $GF(2^m)$ should not be confused with $GF(p)$, which is not a subfield of the locator field.

□ **Definition 5.9.1**   A *quadratic residue code* is a cyclic code over $GF(2)$ whose blocklength is a prime p that divides $2^m - 1$ for some m, and whose generator polynomial has zeros at all α^j in $GF(2^m)$ such that in $GF(p)$, j is a quadratic residue. □

It follows from the definition that

$$g(x) = \prod_{j \in QR} (x - \alpha^j),$$

where the product is over the set QR containing all quadratic residues of p, and provided that $g(x)$ is a polynomial over $GF(2)$. If the polynomial is not over $GF(2)$, then a quadratic residue code does not exist for this p.

From the definition of $g(x)$, we can see that

$$x^p - 1 = (x - 1)g(x)\tilde{g}(x),$$

where $\tilde{g}(x)$ has as its $(p-1)/2$ zeros all α^j such that in $GF(p)$, j is nonzero and is not a quadratic residue. The polynomial $\tilde{g}(x)$ is the reciprocal polynomial of $g(x)$ and is the generator polynomial for an equivalent code.

The polynomial

$$g'(x) = (x - 1) \prod_{j \in QR} (x - \alpha^j)$$

is the generator polynomial for another code. This polynomial has one more zero than $g(x)$, and thus the code is a subcode of the quadratic residue code. It is also called a quadratic residue code, but is not as interesting as the first given. We will not discuss it further.

The quadratic residue code over $GF(2)$ exists only if $g(x)$ has all its coefficients in $GF(2)$. We will see shortly that a quadratic residue code of blocklength p exists whenever p is a prime of the form $p = 8k \pm 1$. But to evaluate one of these codes, we must also know its minimum distance. It is usually quite difficult to find the minimum distance of a quadratic residue code. Each code requires individual study. We saw a sample of this in the study of the Golay (23, 12) code in the previous section. The quadratic residue codes listed in Fig. 5.2 are those for which the minimum distance is known. Many other quadratic residue codes exist, but their minimum distances are unknown.

We will give one bound on the minimum distance of any quadratic residue code. This bound is not very good, but it is easy to prove.

☐ **Theorem 5.9.2 (The Square-Root Bound)** The minimum distance of any quadratic residue code of blocklength p satisfies $d^* \geqslant \sqrt{p}$.

Proof Let s be a fixed nonzero element of $GF(p)$ that is not a quadratic residue. Every element of $GF(p)$ can be written as js for some j (because $GF(p)$ is a field). If j is a quadratic residue, then js clearly is not a quadratic residue. Therefore if j is not a quadratic residue, then js must be a quadratic residue.

Let $c(x)$ be a code polynomial of minimum weight d^*. Then $c(x) = a(x)g(x)$ for some $a(x)$. Define $\tilde{c}(x) = c(x^s) \pmod{x^p - 1}$. Then $\tilde{c}(x) = a(x^s)g(x^s) \pmod{x^p - 1}$, and $\tilde{c}(x)$ has weight at most d^*. But if j is a quadratic residue, then $g(\alpha^{js}) \neq 0$, and if j is not a quadratic residue, then $g(\alpha^{js}) = 0$. That is, $g(x^s) = \tilde{g}(x)$. Hence $c(x)\tilde{c}(x) \pmod{x^p - 1}$ is divisible by both $g(x)$ and by $\tilde{g}(x)$. It is a multiple of $x^{p-1} + x^{p-2} + \cdots + x + 1$ and is of degree of at most $p - 1$. That is,

$$c(x)\tilde{c}(x) = x^{p-1} + x^{p-2} + \cdots + x + 1 \qquad (\bmod \ x^p - 1).$$

Now the right side has weight p, and because $c(x)$ has weight d^*, the left side cannot possibly have weight greater than $(d^*)^2$. That is, $d^* \geqslant \sqrt{p}$, as was to be proved. ☐

Now we will determine when $g(x)$, defined as above, has only binary coefficients. If 2 is a quadratic residue, then all powers of 2 are also quadratic residues. Further, if j is another quadratic residue, then so too are $2j, 4j, 8j, \ldots$. Thus α^j and all conjugates over $GF(2)$ of α^j are zeros of the generator polynomial. Then the polynomials $g(x)$ and $\tilde{g}(x)$ are polynomials over $GF(2)$. Therefore the quadratic residue codes exist for each p for which 2 is a quadratic residue in $GF(p)$. We will see that the p for which 2 is a quadratic residue of $GF(p)$ are primes of the form $p = 8k \pm 1$ for any integer k. This is a rather difficult theorem of number theory, and we will introduce several lemmas to facilitate its proof.

☐ **Lemma 5.9.3** If p is a prime of the form $p = 8k \pm 1$, then in the field $GF(p)$, $2^{(p-1)/2} = 1$. If p is a prime of the form $p = 8k \pm 3$, then in $GF(p)$, $2^{(p-1)/2} = -1$.

Proof First notice that in $GF(p)$, $2a = -(p - 2a)$, and thus

$$\prod_{a=A_0}^{A_1} 2a = \prod_{a=A_0}^{A_1} [-(p - 2a)] = (-1)^{A_1 - (A_0 - 1)} \prod_{a=A_0}^{A_1} (p - 2a).$$

Let $\lfloor x \rfloor$ denote the greatest integer less than or equal to x. We now have the following string of equations:

$$2^{(p-1)/2} \prod_{a=1}^{(p-1)/2} a = \prod_{a=1}^{(p-1)/2} (2a)$$

$$= \prod_{a=1}^{\lfloor (p-1)/4 \rfloor} (2a) \prod_{a=\lfloor (p-1)/4 \rfloor + 1}^{(p-1)/2} (2a)$$

$$= \left[\prod_{a=1}^{\lfloor (p-1)/4 \rfloor} (2a) \right] (-1)^{\lfloor (p-1)/2 - \lfloor (p-1)/4 \rfloor \rfloor} \left[\prod_{a=\lfloor (p-1)/4 \rfloor + 1}^{(p-1)/2} (p - 2a) \right].$$

Now in the first product, $(2a)$ ranges over all even integers from 2 up to $(p-1)/2$, and in the second product, $(p - 2a)$ ranges over all odd integers from 1 up to $\frac{1}{2}(p - 1) - 1$. This should be verified by checking the case where $\frac{1}{2}(p-1)$ is even and the case where it is odd. Hence, the two product terms can be combined into one product, and thus

$$2^{(p-1)/2} \prod_{a=1}^{(p-1)/2} a = (-1)^{\lfloor (p-1)/2 - \lfloor (p-1)/4 \rfloor \rfloor} \prod_{a=1}^{(p-1)/2} a.$$

Now in $GF(p)$, all terms in the product are nonzero and can be cancelled. Then

$$2^{(p-1)/2} = (-1)^{\lfloor (p-1)/2 - \lfloor (p-1)/4 \rfloor \rfloor}.$$

If $p = 8k \pm 1$, the exponent of -1 is even, and

$$2^{(p-1)/2} = 1.$$

If $p = 8k \pm 3$, the exponent of -1 is odd, and

$$2^{(p-1)/2} = -1,$$

which completes the proof of the lemma. ☐

☐ **Lemma 5.9.4** In $GF(p)$, r is a quadratic residue if and only if

$$r^{(p-1)/2} = 1.$$

Proof Suppose that $r^{(p-1)/2} \neq 1$. Then $\sqrt{r}$ cannot exist because if it did, $(\sqrt{r})^{p-1}$ would equal 1, and it does not.

Suppose that $r^{(p-1)/2} = 1$, and let α be primitive in $GF(p)$. Obviously, all even powers of α are quadratic residues, and because half of the non-zero elements are not quadratic residues, it follows that all odd powers of α are not quadratic residues. All we need to prove is that r is an even power of α. Suppose, on the contrary, that it is odd. Then $r = \alpha^{2i+1}$, and

$$r^{(p-1)/2} = (\alpha^{2i+1})^{(p-1)/2}$$

$$= \alpha^{i(p-1)}\alpha^{(p-1)/2}$$

$$= \alpha^{(p-1)/2}$$

$$\neq 1$$

because α has order $p-1$. Thus $r^{(p-1)/2} = 1$ implies that r is an even power of α and hence is a quadratic residue. $\square$

$\square$ **Theorem 5.9.5**   In the prime field $GF(p)$, the element 2 is a quadratic residue if $p = 8k \pm 1$ for some integer k, and it is not a quadratic residue if $p = 8k \pm 3$.

Proof   The proof follows immediately from Lemmas 5.9.3 and 5.9.4. $\square$

PROBLEMS

5.1. The polynomial

$$g(x) = x^8 + x^7 + x^6 + x^4 + 1$$

is the generator polynomial for a cyclic code over $GF(2)$ with blocklength $n = 15$.
  a. Find the parity-check polynomial.
  b. How many errors can this code correct?
  c. How many erasures can this code correct?
  d. Find a generator matrix in systematic form.

5.2. Find the minimal polynomial for each element of $GF(16)$.

5.3. Find the generator polynomial for a binary (31, 21) double-error-correcting code.

5.4. Find the generator polynomial for a binary (21, 12) double-error-correcting cyclic code.

5.5. The polynomial

$$g(x) = x^6 + 3x^5 + x^4 + x^3 + 2x^2 + 2x + 1$$

is the generator polynomial for a double-error-correcting code of blocklength 15 over $GF(4)$.
  a. Find a generator matrix in systematic form.
  b. Show that every codeword in the code of Problem 5.1 is also a codeword in this code.

5.6. Let $g(x)$ be the generator polynomial of a cyclic code over $GF(q)$ of blocklength n. Prove that if q and n are relatively prime, then the all-one word is a codeword if and only if one is not a zero of $g(x)$.

5.7. Suppose that $g(x) = g_{n-k}x^{n-k} + \cdots + g_0$ is the generator polynomial for a cyclic code. Prove that g_0 is not zero. Prove that the reciprocal polynomial $g(x) = g_0 x^{n-k} + g_1 x^{n-k-1} + \cdots + g_{n-k}$ is the generator polynomial for an equivalent cyclic code.

5.8. Suppose a binary code has the property that whenever $c(x)$ is a codeword, then so is its reciprocal polynomial $\bar{c}(x)$. Prove that $g(x) = \bar{g}(x)$. What is the corresponding statement for nonbinary codes?

5.9. Find the generator polynomial of the (9, 7) Hamming code over $GF(8)$.

5.10. Expand Table 5.2 to include all Fire codes based on primitive $p(x)$ for $12 \geqslant m \geqslant t$.

5.11. Suppose that $g_1(x)$ and $g_2(x)$ are generator polynomials for two codes $\mathscr{C}_1$ and $\mathscr{C}_2$ of the same blocklength over $GF(q)$. Prove that if all the zeros of $g_1(x)$ are also zeros of $g_2(x)$ (that is $g_1(x)$ divides $g_2(x)$), then $\mathscr{C}_2$ is a subcode of $\mathscr{C}_1$.

5.12. The polynomial over $GF(4)$

$$g(x) = x^6 + 3x^5 + x^4 + x^3 + 2x^2 + 2x + 1$$

is known to be the generator polynomial for a (15, 9) double-error-correcting code over $GF(4)$.

a. Is $v(x) = x^{10} + 3x^2 + x + 2$ a codeword in this code?

b. What is the syndrome polynomial of $v(x)$?

c. How many syndrome polynomials must be tabulated to cover all correctable error patterns?

5.13. Factor $x^8 - 1$ over $GF(3)$. How many cyclic codes over $GF(3)$ of blocklength 8 are there?

5.14. Prove that all conjugates of a primitive element are also primitive elements.

5.15. Construct the generator polynomial for a Fire code of blocklength $n = 4845$ over $GF(256)$ that will correct all bursts of length 10 symbols or less.

NOTES

The major thread running through this chapter is based on the far-ranging ideas of Prange (1957, 1958). Prange introduced the notion of a cyclic code, and the relationship to the ideals of algebra was studied independently by him and by Peterson (1960) and Kasami (1960). This work occurred at the end of the decade of the 1950s and was a foundation for the major jolts that came with the 1960s. This is when it was realized that cyclic codes could be embedded in an extension field, and the ideas of Chapter 7 quickly followed. Much of the present chapter was written using the machinery of the extension field.

The study of burst-error-correcting codes was begun by Abramson (1959). Most of the codes used in practice have been found by computer search, many by Kasami (1963). The first table in Section 5.7 is based on the compilations of Peterson and Weldon (1968). The Fire codes were published by Fire in 1959.

The Golay (23, 12, 7) binary code and the Golay (11, 6, 5) ternary code were published by Golay in 1949. Our proof of the minimum distance of the Golay code follows McEliece (1977). The cyclic structure of Hamming codes was studied independently by Abramson (1960) and Elspas (1960). The quadratic residue codes were introduced by Prange (1958) and widely studied. A summary of this work is given in Assmus and Mattson (1974).

CHAPTER 6

Circuits for Implementation of Cyclic Codes

This chapter interrupts our search for cyclic codes with large minimum distance. We shall return to that search in the next chapter. In this chapter, we shall turn our attention to the design of encoders and decoders, principally those based on shift-register circuits.

Digital logic circuits can be easily organized into shift-register circuits that mimic the cyclic shifts and polynomial arithmetic used in the description of cyclic codes. Consequently, the structure of cyclic codes is closely related to the structure of shift-register circuits. These circuits are particularly well suited to the implementation of many encoding and decoding procedures and often take the form of filters. In fact, many algorithms can be described most easily using the symbolism of shift-register circuits. Many of the details are more easily understood from the circuit than from a formula. We shall study shift-register encoders and decoders in this chapter.

6.1 LOGIC CIRCUITS FOR FINITE FIELD ARITHMETIC

The arithmetic of Galois fields is done easily by logic circuits, especially if q is a power of 2. We shall need circuit elements for the storage of field elements, called *shift-register stages*, and circuit elements for the arithmetic operations in the finite field. We will define these elements for the general field $GF(q)$, but they will normally be constructed out of binary circuit elements.

A shift register, as shown in Fig. 6.1, is a string of storage devices called *stages*. Each stage contains one element of $GF(q)$. The symbol contained in each stage is displayed on an output line leaving that stage. Each stage also has an input line that carries an element from $GF(q)$. When it is not otherwise designated, this input symbol is taken to be the zero element of the field. At discrete time instants known as *clock times*, the field element in the storage device is replaced by the field element on the input line. Modern electronic shift registers can be clocked at speeds in excess of 10 million times per second.

In addition to shift-register stages, we will use three other circuit elements, as shown in Fig. 6.2. These are: a scaler, an adder, and a multiplier. The scaler is a function of a single input variable; it multiplies the input variable by a fixed field element from $GF(q)$. The adder and multiplier are functions of two inputs from $GF(q)$. In the binary case, the adder is also known as an *exclusive-or gate* and the multiplier is also known as an *and gate*.

All of these circuit elements can be built up from binary circuit elements for any $GF(q)$. We shall describe this for the case where q is a power of 2. A field element from $GF(2^m)$ can be represented by m bits and can be transferred within a circuit either serially (one bit at a time on a single wire) or in parallel (one bit on each of m parallel wires).

Figure 6.3 shows the arrangement of binary shift-register stages for use with $GF(2^m)$. The special case of $GF(16)$ is illustrated. Each field element is represented by four bits, and a sequence of field elements is represented by a sequence of 4-bit numbers. Field elements can be transferred either serially or in parallel; that is, either through one wire or through four. In the serial case, the shift register for $GF(16)$ is actually a binary shift register four times as long. It takes four actual clocks to shift a field element to the next stage.

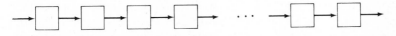

Figure 6.1   *n*-stage shift register.

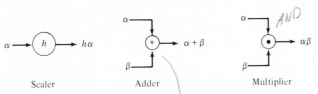

Scaler   Adder   Multiplier

Figure 6.2   Circuit elements.

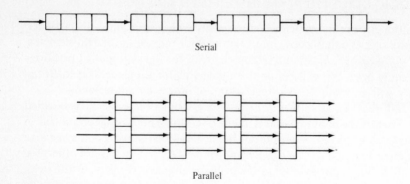

Serial

Parallel

Figure 6.3 Hexadecimal shift registers made from binary components.

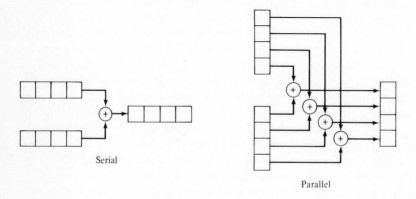

Serial

Parallel

Figure 6.4 Addition of two field elements.

Figure 6.4 shows a circuit for addition in $GF(16)$ for each of the two cases: serial and parallel data flow. In each case, the addends are in shift registers to start with, and the sum is in a third shift register at the conclusion of the addition. The circuit for serial addition requires four clock times to complete the addition; the circuit for parallel addition requires only one clock time but has more wires and modulo-2 adders. If desired, the addends could be fed back to the inputs of their own registers so that at the end of the addition the addends could again be found in their registers for other purposes.

Figure 6.5 shows the multiplication of a field element by a fixed field element $\beta = z^3$ in $GF(16)$. To explain this, we need a specific representation of $GF(16)$. Suppose the one constructed with the primitive polynomial $p(z) = z^4 + z + 1$. Let $\gamma = \gamma_3 z^3 + \gamma_2 z^2 + \gamma_1 z + \gamma_0$ be an arbitrary field element. Then

$$\beta\gamma = \gamma_3 z^6 + \gamma_2 z^5 + \gamma_1 z^4 + \gamma_0 z^3$$

$$= (\gamma_3 + \gamma_0)z^3 + (\gamma_3 + \gamma_2)z^2 + (\gamma_2 + \gamma_1)z + \gamma_1.$$

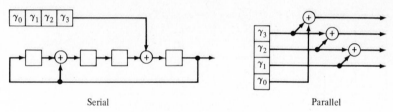

Serial   Parallel

Figure 6.5   Multiplication by a constant field element $\beta = z^3$.

Figure 6.6   Circuit for cyclically shifting a polynomial.

From this equation the parallel multiplication circuit can be sketched immediately. The serial circuit is a little less obvious. It does the two lines of the above equation, first finding $\gamma_3 z^6 + \gamma_2 z^5 + \gamma_1 z^4 + \gamma_0 z^3$, then reducing modulo $z^4 + z + 1$. This is a circuit for dividing by the fixed polynomial $z^4 + z + 1$. This circuit takes four clock times to complete the multiplication by β.

6.2 DIGITAL FILTERS

Shift-register circuits can be used for the multiplication and division of polynomials over $GF(q)$. Consequently, they are used frequently in the design and construction of encoders and decoders. Shift registers also can be useful in developing the theory, because they can play a role as a kind of quasi-mathematical notation that is an easily understood representation of some kinds of polynomial manipulation. These same shift-register circuits are known also as *filters*.

The n symbols contained in a shift register of length n may be interpreted as the coefficients of a polynomial of degree $n-1$. Our usual convention will be that the shift-register circuits are shifted from left to right. Sometimes this requires the polynomial coefficients to appear in the shift register in descending order from right to left. Unfortunately, this is opposite to the most common convention used in writing polynomials.

A shift register connected in a ring can be used to cyclically shift a polynomial. Figure 6.6 shows an n-stage shift register used to cyclically shift a polynomial of degree $n-1$. It computes $xv(x) \pmod{x^n - 1}$. This is the simplest example of a linear-feedback shift register.

A general linear-feedback shift register is shown in Fig. 6.7. This circuit implements the recurrence

$$p_j = -\sum_{i=1}^{L} h_i p_{j-i} \qquad j \geq L.$$

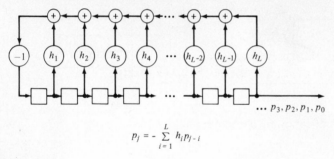

$$p_j = - \sum_{i=1}^{L} h_i p_{j-i}$$

Figure 6.7   A linear-feedback shift register.

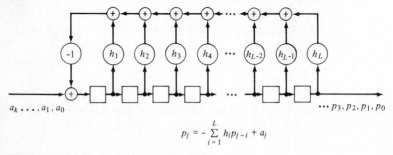

$$p_j = - \sum_{i=1}^{L} h_i p_{j-i} + a_j$$

Figure 6.8   An autoregressive filter.

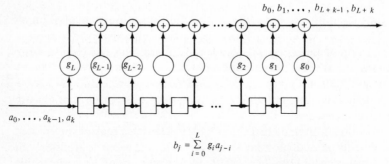

$$b_j = \sum_{i=0}^{L} g_i a_{j-i}$$

Figure 6.9   A linear-feedforward shift register.

When initially loaded with L symbols $(p_0, \ldots, p_{L-1})$, the shift-register output will be an unending sequence of symbols starting at p_0 and satisfying the above recurrence. This circuit is also called an *autoregressive filter* when used as in Fig. 6.8. Because of the feedback, it is a member of a large class of filters known as *recursive filters*.

Instead of feeding back the shift-register output, one can use an externally generated sequence as input to the shift register. This linear-feedforward shift register is shown in Fig. 6.9. It is also called a *finite-impulse-response* (*FIR*) *filter*, or a *nonrecursive filter*.

Let the coefficients of the polynomial

$$g(x) = g_L x^L + \cdots + g_1 x + g_0$$

be equal to the tap weights of a feedforward shift register, and let the input and output sequences be represented by the polynomials

$$a(x) = a_k x^k + \cdots + a_1 x + a_0,$$
$$b(x) = b_{k+L} x^{k+L} + \cdots + b_1 x + b_0.$$

Then the polynomial product

$$b(x) = g(x)a(x)$$

is a representation of the operation of the shift register of Fig. 6.9 with the understanding that the shift register initially contains zeros, and input a_0 is followed by L zeros. The coefficients of $a(x)$ and $g(x)$ are said to be convolved by the shift register because

$$b_j = \sum_{i=0}^{L} g_i a_{j-i}.$$

In terms of polynomials, the FIR filter may be viewed as a device to multiply an arbitrary polynomial $a(x)$ by the fixed polynomial $g(x)$. We will also call it a *multiply-by-g(x) circuit*.

In Fig. 6.10(a) we give an example of a multiply-by-$g(x)$ circuit for the polynomial $g(x) = x^8 + x^7 + x^4 + x^2 + x + 1$. It is a FIR filter. Notice that the internal stages of the shift register are read but not modified. It is possible to give an alternative arrangement in which the internal stages are modified, but this alternative is usually a more expensive circuit. In Fig. 6.10(b) we show this alternative multiply-by-$g(x)$ circuit. It is an unconventional form of a FIR filter.

A shift-register circuit also can be used to divide an arbitrary polynomial by a fixed polynomial. The circuit to do this very closely matches the usual procedure for polynomial division. Suppose the divisor is a monic poly-

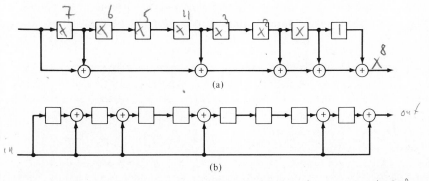

(a)

(b)

Figure 6.10 Two circuits for multiplication by $x^8 + x^7 + x^4 + x^2 + x + 1$.

nomial. If not, a scalar can be factored out and handled separately. Long division proceeds as follows:

$$
\begin{array}{r}
a_{n-1}x^{k-1}+(a_{n-2}-a_{n-1}g_{n-k-1})x^{k-2}+\cdots \\
x^{n-k}+g_{n-k-1}x^{n-k-1}+\cdots+g_0 \overline{\smash{\big)}\, a_{n-1}x^{n-1}+ \qquad\qquad a_{n-2}x^{n-2}+\cdots+a_1x+a_0} \\
a_{n-1}x^{n-1}+ \qquad\qquad a_{n-1}g_{n-k-1}x^{n-2}+\cdots \\
\overline{\qquad\qquad (a_{n-2}-a_{n-1}g_{n-k-1})x^{n-2}+\cdots} \\
(a_{n-2}-a_{n-1}g_{n-k-1})x^{n-2}+\cdots \\
\overline{\qquad\qquad\qquad\qquad\qquad \cdots}
\end{array}
$$

The procedure can be expressed as a pair of recursive equations. Let $Q^{(r)}(x)$ and $R^{(r)}(x)$ be, respectively, the trial quotient polynomial and the trial remainder polynomial at the rth recursion, with initial conditions $Q^{(0)}(x)=0$ and $R^{(0)}(x)=a(x)$. The recursive equations are:

$$Q^{(r)}(x)=Q^{(r-1)}(x)+R_{n-r}^{(r-1)}x^{k-r},$$

$$R^{(r)}(x)=R^{(r-1)}(x)-R_{n-r}^{(r-1)}x^{k-r}g(x).$$

The quotient and remainder are obtained after k iterations as $Q^{(k)}(x)$ and $R^{(k)}(x)$.

The circuit of Fig. 6.11 is a circuit for dividing an arbitrary polynomial by the fixed polynomial $g(x)$. It may be understood by referring to either of the above two descriptions of the long division process. The only thing left out of the circuit is the subtraction of the term $R_{n-r}x^{n-r}$ from itself, which is unnecessary to compute because it is always zero. After n shifts, the quotient has been passed out of the shift register, and the remainder is found in the shift register.

In Fig. 6.12(a), we give an example in $GF(2)$ of a divide-by-$g(x)$ circuit for the polynomial $g(x)=x^8+x^7+x^4+x^2+x+1$.

Notice that the divide circuit requires additions to internal stages of the shift register. This is often an inconvenient circuit operation. It is possible to use instead a circuit that only reads the internal shift-register stages but does not modify them. To develop this circuit, we organize the work of polynomial division in another way. Refer to the longhand example previously written out. The idea is to leave pending the subtractions until all of the subtractions in the same column can be done at the same time. To

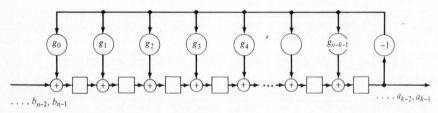

Figure 6.11 A circuit for dividing by $g(x)$.

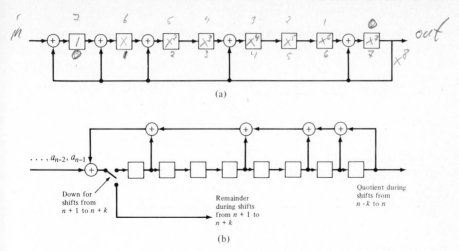

Figure 6.12 Two circuits for division by $x^8 + x^7 + x^4 + x^2 + x + 1$.

see how to do this, notice that we can write

$$R^{(r)}(x) = a(x) - Q^{(r)}(x)g(x),$$

and thus

$$R_{n-r}^{(r-1)} = a_{n-r} - \sum_{i=1}^{n-1} g_{n-r-i} Q_i^{(r-1)}$$

and

$$Q^{(r)}(x) = Q^{(r-1)}(x) + R_{n-r}^{(r-1)} x^{k-r}.$$

These equations can be implemented by a modification of a multiply-by-$g(x)$ circuit. Figure 6.12(b) shows such a circuit for dividing by the polynomial $g(x) = x^8 + x^7 + x^4 + x^2 + x + 1$.

6.3 SHIFT REGISTER ENCODERS AND DECODERS

The structure of cyclic codes makes it attractive to use shift-register circuits for constructing encoders and decoders. Cyclic codes can be encoded non-systematically by multiplication of the variable information polynomial $i(x)$ with the fixed polynomial $g(x)$ to get the codeword $c(x)$. This can be implemented with a FIR filter over $GF(q)$. A shift-register encoder for the Hamming $(15, 11)$ code is shown in Fig. 6.13. To encode a long stream of information bits into a sequence of Hamming $(15, 11)$ codewords, simply break the information sequence into 11-bit blocks, insert a pad of four zeros after every block, and pass the padded stream through the FIR filter. This provides a sequence of

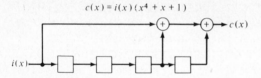

Figure 6.13 Nonsystematic (15, 11) encoder.

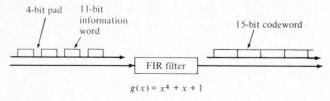

Figure 6.14 Encoding a long bit stream.

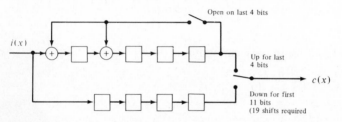

Figure 6.15 A systematic encoder for a Hamming (15, 11) code.

noninteracting 15-bit Hamming codewords. The encoder, shown in Fig. 6.14, is very simple; the codewords, however, are not systematic.

If one wants a systematic codeword, a different encoder must be used. Insert the information into the high-order bits of the codeword, and choose the parity bits so as to get a legitimate codeword. The codeword is of the form

$$c(x) = x^{n-k}i(x) + t(x),$$

where

$$t(x) = -R_{g(x)}[x^{n-k}i(x)],$$

and thus

$$R_{g(x)}[c(x)] = 0.$$

The systematic encoder is implemented by using a divide-by-$g(x)$ circuit. For the Hamming (15, 11) code,

$$t(x) = R_{g(x)}[x^4 i(x)].$$

An implementation is shown in Fig. 6.15. Eleven information bits, high-order bit first, are shifted into the divide-by-$x^4 + x + 1$ circuit from the left.

Multiplication by x^4 is implicit in the timing of the circuit. The first bit in is thought of as the coefficient of x^{15}. The division does not begin until after four timing shifts are completed, in order to position the first four bits in the register. Because of this, a four-stage buffer is included below the divide circuit so that the first bit is sent to the channel just when the first step of the division occurs. After 11 steps of the division, all information bits have been sent to the channel, the division is complete, and the remainder is ready to shift into the channel as parity. During these last four shifts, the feedback path in the divide-by-$g(x)$ circuit is opened. Altogether it takes 19 clocks to complete the encoding.

It is possible to go a little faster by a slight change in the circuit, and hence the initial four timing shifts can be deleted. This is shown in Fig. 6.16. To understand this circuit, one should notice that the incoming information bits do not immediately enter the divide-by-$g(x)$ circuit but are entered at the right time to form the feedback signal. Thus the feedback is the same as in Fig. 6.15. Further, because the last bits of $x^4 i(x)$ are zero anyway, it will not matter if we fail to add them into the remainder. Thus Fig. 6.16 computes the same remainder as does Fig. 6.15, but it does so in only 15 clock times and thus is much more convenient to use.

Now we will turn to the decoder. The channel transmits the coefficients of the polynomial $c(x)$. To this is added the error polynomial $e(x)$. The channel output is the received polynomial

$$v(x) = c(x) + e(x).$$

In Section 5.2 we described a table-lookup decoding procedure that is conceptually simple. The received sequence is divided by $g(x)$, and the remainder is the syndrome polynomial. The syndrome polynomial is used to retrieve the estimated error pattern from the syndrome evaluator table. For a binary code, the coefficients of the syndrome polynomial can be used directly as a memory address; the corresponding error pattern $e(x)$ is stored at that memory location.

Figure 6.17 shows a decoder for the nonsystematic Hamming (15, 11) code. There are 4 syndrome bits and hence a memory with a 4-bit address by 15-bit wordlength is required. Such an approach may be practical for syndromes of length $(n - k)$ of up to 12 or 14 bits, but we will see in the next section that other techniques can also be used. After the correct codeword

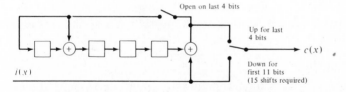

Figure 6.16 Another systematic encoder for a Hamming (15, 11) code.

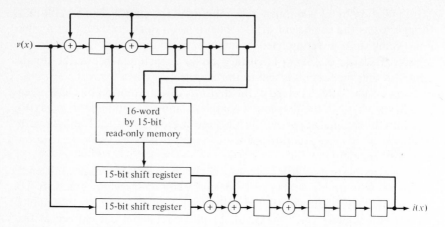

Figure 6.17 Syndrome decoder for a nonsystematic Hamming (15, 11) code.

$c(x)$ is recovered, the information bits are computed by using a divide-by-$g(x)$ circuit implementing the equation

$$i(x) = R_{g(x)}[c(x)],$$

and this completes the decoder.

6.4 THE MEGGITT DECODER

The most complicated part of the shift-register decoder described in the preceding section is the tabulation of the precomputed syndrome polynomials and their associated error polynomials. This lookup decoder can be greatly simplified by using the strong algebraic structure of the code to find relationships between the syndromes. By relying on such relationships, it is only necessary to store the error polynomials associated with a few typical syndrome polynomials. Simple computational procedures are then used to compute other entries as required.

The simplest decoder of this type, known as a *Meggitt decoder*, tests the syndrome only for those patterns that have an error in the high-order component. Errors in other positions are decoded later, using the cyclic structure of the code. Consequently, the syndrome evaluator table contains only those syndromes corresponding to an error pattern for which e_{n-1} is nonzero. If the measured syndrome is recognized by the syndrome evaluator, e_{n-1} is corrected. Next, the received word is cyclically shifted and the process repeated to test for a possible error in the next to high-order place ($e_{n-2} \neq 0$). This process repeats component by component; each component is tested in turn for error and is corrected whenever an error is found.

It is not necessary to actually recompute the syndrome for each cyclic shift of the received word. The new syndrome can be easily computed from the original syndrome. The basic relationship is given by the following theorem.

☐ **Theorem 6.4.1 (Meggitt)** Suppose $g(x)h(x) = x^n - 1$, and

$$R_{g(x)}[v(x)] = s(x).$$

Then

$$R_{g(x)}[xv(x) \pmod{x^n - 1}] = R_{g(x)}[xs(x)].$$

Proof The proof consists of the combination of three simple statements.

(i) By definition:

$$v(x) = g(x)Q_1(x) + s(x),$$

$$xv(x) = xg(x)Q_1(x) + xs(x).$$

(ii) $xv(x) \pmod{x^n - 1} = xv(x) - (x^n - 1)v_{n-1}.$

(iii) By the division algorithm:

$$xs(x) = g(x)Q_2(x) + t(x)$$

uniquely, where $\deg t(x) < \deg g(x)$.

Combining lines (i), (ii), and (iii),

$$xv(x) \pmod{x^n - 1} = [xQ_1(x) + Q_2(x) + v_{n-1}h(x)]g(x) + t(x)$$
$$= Q_3(x)g(x) + t(x).$$

Then because

$$\deg t(x) < \deg g(x),$$

by the division algorithm $t(x)$ is unique, and

$$t(x) = R_{g(x)}[xv(x) \pmod{x^n - 1}] = R_{g(x)}[xs(x)],$$

as was to be proved. ☐

In particular, the theorem states that error polynomials and their syndrome polynomials satisfy

$$R_{g(x)}[xe(x) \pmod{x^n - 1}] = R_{g(x)}[xs(x)].$$

If $e(x)$ is a correctable error pattern, then

$$e'(x) = xe(x) \pmod{x^n - 1}$$

is a cyclic shift of $e(x)$. Hence $e'(x)$ is a correctable error pattern with syndrome

$$s'(x) = R_{g(x)}[e'(x)] = R_{g(x)}[xs(x)].$$

This relationship shows how to compute syndromes of any cyclic shift of an error pattern whose syndrome is known. The computation can be achieved by a simple shift-register circuit, which often is much simpler than a syndrome lookup table.

Suppose that $s(x)$ and $e(x)$ are the measured syndrome polynomial and true error polynomial, respectively, and that we have precomputed that $\bar{s}(x)$ is the syndrome for the error polynomial $\bar{e}(x)$. We check whether $s(x) = \bar{s}(x)$, and if so, we know that $e(x) = \bar{e}(x)$. If not, we compute $R_{g(x)}[xs(x)]$ and compare this to $\bar{s}(x)$. If it agrees, then

$$\bar{e}(x) = xe(x) \,(\mathrm{mod}\ x^n - 1),$$

which is a cyclic shift of $e(x)$; thus we know $e(x)$. Continue in this way. If $R_{g(x)}[xR_{g(x)}[xs(x)]]$ is equal to $\bar{s}(x)$, then $\bar{e}(x)$ is equal to $x^2 e(x)\,(\mathrm{mod}\ x^n - 1)$, and so on.

Choose enough test error patterns $\bar{e}(x)$ so that every correctable error pattern is a cyclic shift of one (or more) of the test error patterns. These $\bar{e}(x)$ and the corresponding test syndromes $\bar{s}(x)$ are all that need be stored. The true syndrome $s(x)$ is compared to all test syndromes. Then $R_{g(x)}[xs(x)]$ is computed and compared to all test syndromes. Repeating the process n times will find any correctable error pattern.

Usually, when using shift-register circuits one chooses to correct only the error at the end of the shift register. This allows one to eliminate wires and to use shift registers whose internal stages are not directly accessible. This implementation is as shown in Fig. 6.18.

The test syndromes chosen are all those corresponding to correctable error patterns with an error in the high-order component. The decoder starts with all shift-register stages set to zero. The first step in the shift-register decoder is to divide by $g(x)$. After this is completed, the divide-by-$g(x)$ shift register contains $s(x)$, and the buffer contains the received word. The syndrome is compared to each test syndrome. If any agreement is found, the high-order symbol is corrected in the buffer. The syndrome generator and

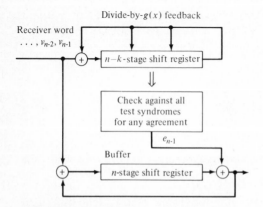

Figure 6.18   Meggitt decoder.

the buffer are then shifted once. This implements the operations of multiplication of the syndrome by x and division by $g(x)$. The content of the syndrome register has now been replaced by $R_{g(x)}[xs(x)]$, which is the syndrome of $xe(x)$ (mod $x^n - 1$). If this new syndrome is on the list of test syndromes, then there is actually an error in the next-to-high-order place, which now appears at the end of the buffer. This bit is corrected, and the syndrome generator is shifted again; it is ready to test for an error in the place second from the high-order place. The process is repeated n times, at which time all bits have been corrected.

The feedback of the corrected symbols to the buffer shown in Fig. 6.18 is unnecessary; the symbols may be passed off to a user as they are computed. We show it for conceptual clarity—the correct codeword is found in the buffer after the last shift—and also to provide a starting point for some circuit variations that will be described shortly.

The use of the Meggitt theorem is easier to understand in terms of specific examples. Consider the Hamming (15, 11) code as defined by the generator polynomial $g(x) = x^4 + x + 1$. Because this is a single-error-correcting code, there is only one pattern with an error in the high-order bit. This error is

$$e(x) = x^{14},$$

and the associated syndrome is

$$s(x) = x^3 + 1.$$

The Meggitt decoder is shown in Fig. 6.19. The syndrome is contained in the shift register after 15 shifts. Of these, the first 4 shifts are used only to position the data in the register so that the division process can begin. If the syndrome is (1001), then $e(x) = x^{14}$, and this bit is corrected. If after 1 shift the syndrome is (1001), then $e(x) = x^{13}$, and this bit is corrected. In this way, each of the 15 bits in turn is available for correction. After 15 such shifts the error correction process is complete. Hence, 30 shifts are required to complete the correction process.

The Meggitt decoder is usually drawn in a slightly different form, as shown in Fig. 6.20. The purpose of this variation is to add the path labeled

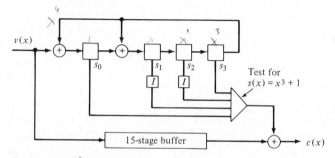

Figure 6.19 Meggitt decoder for a (15, 11) Hamming code.

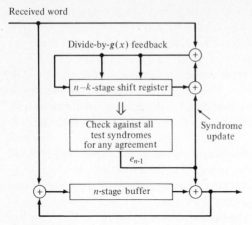

Figure 6.20 Another Meggitt decoder.

"syndrome update." Even though this path is completely unnecessary in the circuit as shown, it will be necessary in some variations that will be described later. For now, the syndrome update is used only to add a kind of neatness to the circuit with no significant cost in complexity.

To understand the use of the syndrome update path, suppose that once an error is corrected we prefer to remove all traces of that error from the circuit and pretend that it never existed. Then we must remove the effect of this error from the syndrome. Because of the Meggitt theorem, we need only treat the case where the error is in the high-order symbol. All other error components will be taken care of automatically at the right time.

Let

$$e'(x) = e_{n-1}x^{n-1}.$$

Then the contribution to the syndrome from this single error component is

$$s'(x) = R_{g(x)}[e_{n-1}x^{n-1}].$$

When e_{n-1} is corrected, this must be subtracted from the actual syndrome in the syndrome register, replacing $s(x)$ by $s(x) - s'(x)$. But $s'(x)$ can be nonzero in many places, and thus the subtraction affects many stages of the syndrome register and is a bother. To reduce this bother, change the definition of a syndrome to

$$s(x) = R_{g(x)}[x^{n-k}v(x)].$$

This is different from the original definition of a syndrome, but it is just as good, and we can do everything we did before with this modified definition. The advantage is that now

$$s'(x) = R_{g(x)}[x^{n-k}e_{n-1}x^{n-1}]$$
$$= R_{g(x)}[R_{x^n-1}[e_{n-1}x^{2n-k-1}]]$$
$$= R_{g(x)}[e_{n-1}x^{n-k-1}]$$
$$= e_{n-1}x^{n-k-1}$$

because $g(x)$ has degree $n - k$. But now $s'(x)$ is nonzero only in a single place, the high-order position of $s(x)$. When e_{n-1} is corrected, in order to replace $s(x)$ by $s(x) - s'(x)$ it suffices to subtract e_{n-1} from the high-order component of the syndrome. The syndrome then has the contribution from the corrected error symbol removed from it.

The premultiplication of $e(x)$ by x^{n-k} is accomplished by feeding $v(x)$ into a different place in the syndrome generator.

For the Hamming (15, 11) code already treated in Fig. 6.19, a modified Meggitt decoder is shown in Fig. 6.21. The received polynomial $v(x)$ is multiplied by x^4 and divided by $g(x)$, and thus the syndrome is

$$s(x) = R_{g(x)}[x^4 e(x)] = R_{g(x)}[R_{x^n-1}[x^4 e(x)]].$$

The advantage of this modification is that the syndrome corresponding to $e(x) = x^{14}$ is

$$s(x) = R_{x^4+x+1}[x^{18}]$$
$$= R_{x^4+x+1}[x^3] \quad ,$$
$$= x^3,$$

which can be corrected in the feedback signal.

The next example is a decoder for the BCH (15, 7) double-error-correcting code. This code will be defined in Chapter 7. For the present, we will only state without proof that it is the cyclic code defined by the generator polynomial $g(x) = x^8 + x^7 + x^6 + x^4 + 1$ and that it corrects two errors. There are

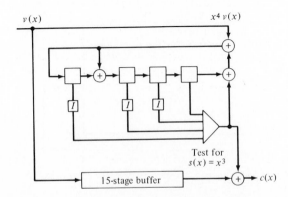

Figure 6.21   Another Meggitt decoder for a (15, 11) Hamming code.

15 correctable error patterns in which the high-order bit can be in error, 1 single-error pattern and 14 double-error patterns.

The received word is multiplied by x^8 and divided by $g(x)$. Hence, if $e(x) = x^{14}$, then

$$s(x) = R_{g(x)}[x^8 \cdot x^{14}] = x^7.$$

Similarly, if $e(x) = x^{14} + x^{13}$, then

$$s(x) = R_{g(x)}[x^8 \cdot (x^{14} + x^{13})] = x^7 + x^6.$$

Proceeding in this way, the 15 syndromes to be stored are computed. Hence the decoder must test for 15 syndromes corresponding to these error patterns. Figure 6.22 shows the Meggitt decoder. Notice that the content of the 8-bit syndrome register must be compared to each of 15 different 8-bit words to see if the higher-order bit is in error. This is repeated after each of 15 shifts so that each bit position in turn is examined for an error. A total of 30 shifts is required, 15 to compute the syndrome and 15 to locate the error.

It is possible to further simplify this circuit to obtain the circuit of Fig. 6.23. Notice that many of the 15 correctable error patterns appear twice as the received word is cyclically shifted. For example, (000000100000001) becomes (000000010000001) after 8 shifts (one bit is underlined just as a place marker). Each of these has a syndrome appearing in the table. If one of the two syndromes is deleted, the error pattern will still be caught eventually, after it is cyclically shifted. Hence, one needs only store the syndrome for one pattern of each such pair. There are eight syndromes that then need to be checked. These appear in the first column of the syndrome table in

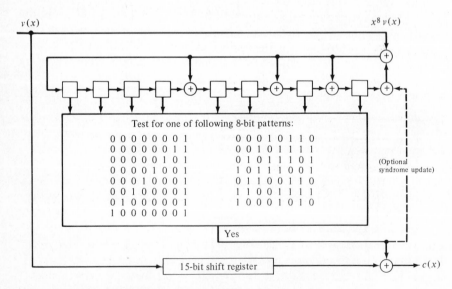

Figure 6.22 Meggitt decoder for BCH (15, 7) code.

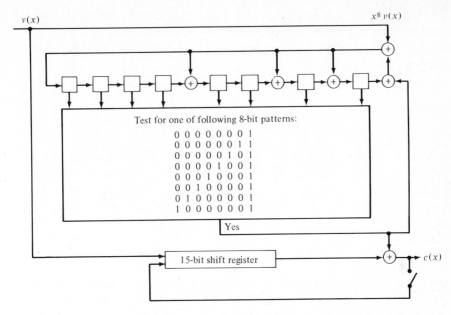

Figure 6.23   Another Meggitt Decoder for BCH (15, 7) code.

Fig. 6.22. Now, however, the first error reaching the end of the buffer might not be corrected at this time, but at least one error will be corrected during 15 shifts. It is necessary to execute two cycles of shifts to correct all errors. This results in a total of 45 shifts. The need for the syndrome update is now apparent, because otherwise, the second time an error reached the end of the buffer, the syndrome would again be unrecognized.

The decoder for the BCH (15, 7) code in Fig. 6.22 is nearly identical to the error-trapping decoder in the next section.

6.5 ERROR TRAPPING

The decoder variation described at the end of the previous section has a syndrome table that upon examination is seen to contain only words of weight 1 and weight 2. In fact, these syndromes look just like correctable error patterns but with the leftmost bits equal to zero and dropped. This decoder is known as an *error-trapping decoder*. An error-trapping decoder is a modification of a Meggitt decoder that can be used for certain cyclic codes.

Suppose that all errors in a received word occur close together. Then the syndrome, properly shifted, exhibits an exact copy of the error pattern. Let us define the length of an error pattern as the smallest number of sequential stages of a shift register that must be observed so that for some cyclic shift of the error pattern, all errors are within this segment of the shift register.

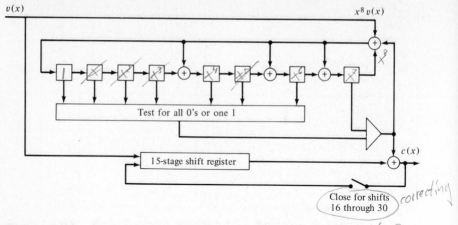

Figure 6.24 Error-trapping decoder for a BCH (15, 7) code. $t = 2$

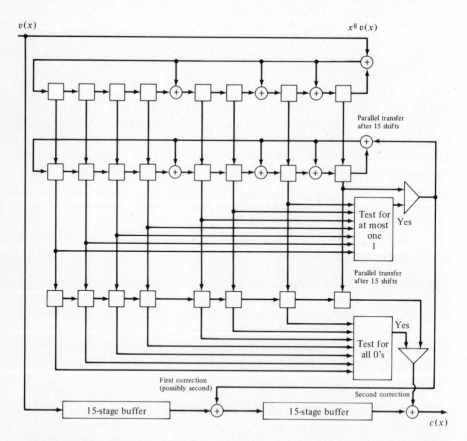

Figure 6.25 Pipelined version of the error-trapping decoder for a BCH (15, 7) code.

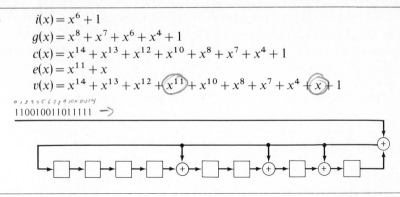

$$i(x) = x^6 + 1$$
$$g(x) = x^8 + x^7 + x^6 + x^4 + 1$$
$$c(x) = x^{14} + x^{13} + x^{12} + x^{10} + x^8 + x^7 + x^4 + 1$$
$$e(x) = x^{11} + x$$
$$v(x) = x^{14} + x^{13} + x^{12} + x^{11} + x^{10} + x^8 + x^7 + x^4 + x + 1$$

0 1 2 3 4 5 6 7 8 9 10 11 12 13 14
110010011011111 →

Shift No.	Syndrome Generator Register	Shift No.	Middle Register	Shift No.	Bottom Register
	LSB MSB				
0	0 0 0 0 0 0 0 0				
1	1 0 0 0 1 0 1 1	16	0 1 1 0 0 0 1 1	31	0 0 0 0 0 1 0 0
2	0 1 0 0 0 1 0 1	17	1 0 1 1 1 0 1 0	32	0 0 0 0 0 0 1 0
3	0 0 1 0 0 0 1 0	18	0 1 0 1 1 1 0 1	33	0 0 0 0 0 0 0 1
4	1 0 0 1 1 0 1 0	19	1 0 1 0 0 1 0 1	34	0 0 0 0 0 0 0 0
5	1 1 0 0 0 1 1 0	20	1 1 0 1 1 0 0 1	35	.
6	0 1 1 0 0 0 1 1	21	1 1 1 0 0 1 1 1	36	.
7	0 0 1 1 0 0 0 1	22	1 1 1 1 1 0 0 0	37	.
8	0 0 0 1 1 0 0 0	23	0 1 1 1 1 1 0 0	38	All zeros
9	0 0 0 0 1 1 0 0	24	0 0 1 1 1 1 1 0	39	.
10	0 0 0 0 0 1 1 0	25	0 0 0 1 1 1 1 1	40	.
11	1 0 0 0 1 0 0 0	26	1 0 0 0 0 1 0 0	41	.
12	0 1 0 0 0 1 0 0	27	0 1 0 0 0 0 1 0	42	.
13	0 0 1 0 0 0 1 0	28	0 0 1 0 0 0 0 1	43	.
14	1 0 0 1 1 0 1 0	29	0 0 0 1 0 0 0 0	44	.
15	1 1 0 0 0 1 1 0	30	0 0 0 0 1 0 0 0	45	.

Note: Errors trapped at shifts number 28 and 33.

Figure 6.26 Error-trapping example (15, 7) BCH code.

Suppose the longest-length error pattern that must be corrected is no longer than the syndrome. Then for some cyclic shift of the error pattern, the syndrome is equal to the error pattern. For such codes, the syndrome generator is shifted until a correctable pattern is observed. The content of the syndrome generator is subtracted from the cyclically shifted received polynomial and correction is complete.

Figure 6.24 shows an error-trapping decoder for a BCH (15, 7) code. A total of 45 shifts are required to correct the double error, 15 shifts to generate the syndrome, 15 shifts to correct the first error, and 15 shifts to correct the second error. Figure 6.25 shows a pipelined version of the decoder, in which three syndrome generators are employed. This allows decoding of continuously arriving 15-bit data blocks with the decoder shifting at line speed. Figure 6.26 works through the 45 cycles of the error-trapping decoder for a typical error pattern.

For a second example of error trapping, we will use the Reed-Solomon (7, 3) code. This is a code over $GF(8)$ with generator polynomial

$$g(x) = x^4 + (z+1)x^3 + x^2 + zx + (z+1),$$

where the field elements are expressed as polynomials in z. Alternatively,

$$g(x) = x^4 + \alpha^3 x^3 + x^2 + \alpha x + \alpha^3,$$

where the field elements are expressed in terms of the primitive element $\alpha = z$. In Chapter 7, we shall study Reed-Solomon codes and prove that this code is double-error-correcting. For the moment, we will accept this fact without proof.

The error pattern $e(x)$ has at most two nonzero terms and is a polynomial of degree 6 or less. It can always be cyclically shifted into a polynomial of

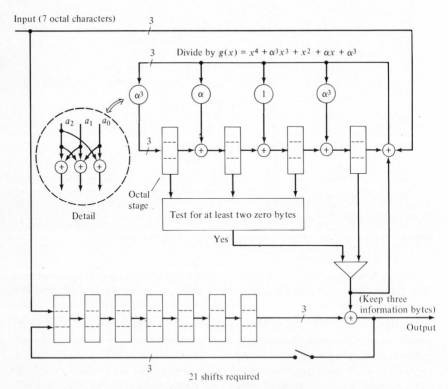

Figure 6.27   Error trapping for a (7, 3) Reed-Solomon code.

$$\alpha^0 = 1$$
$$\alpha^1 = z$$
$$\alpha^2 = z^2$$
$$\alpha^3 = z + 1$$
$$\alpha^4 = z^2 + z$$
$$\alpha^5 = z^2 + z + 1$$
$$\alpha^6 = z^2 + 1$$

$$g(x) = x^4 + \alpha^3 x^3 + x^2 + \alpha x + \alpha^3$$
$$c(x) = \alpha^4 x^6 + \alpha^4 x^4 + \alpha^3 x^3 + \alpha^6 x + \alpha^6$$
$$e(x) = \alpha^4 x^4 + \alpha^3$$
$$v(x) = \alpha^4 x^6 + \alpha^3 x^3 + \alpha^6 x + \alpha^4$$

Shift	Syndrome Register	Information Register
0	$0\ 0\ 0\ 0$	$0\ 0\ 0\ 0\ 0\ 0$
1	$1\ \alpha^5 \alpha^4 1$	$\alpha^4 0\ 0\ 0\ 0\ 0$
2	$\alpha^3 \alpha^3 \alpha^4 \alpha^6$	$0\ \alpha^4 0\ 0\ 0\ 0$
3	$\alpha^2 \alpha\ \alpha^4 \alpha$	$0\ 0\ \alpha^4 0\ 0\ 0$
4	$\alpha^3 \alpha^4 \alpha^3 \alpha^6$	$\alpha^3 0\ 0\ \alpha^4 0\ 0$
5	$\alpha^2 \alpha\ \alpha^3 \alpha^5$	$0\ \alpha^3 0\ 0\ \alpha^4 0$
6	$\alpha^4 0\ 0\ \alpha^6$	$\alpha^6 0\ \alpha^3 0\ 0\ \alpha^4$
7	$\alpha^6 0\ \alpha^3 \alpha^6$ Syndrome	$\alpha^4 \alpha^6 0\ \alpha^3 0\ 0\ \alpha^4$
8	$\alpha^2 \alpha^2 \alpha^6 \alpha^5$	$\alpha^4 \alpha^4 \alpha^6 0\ \alpha^3 0\ 0$
9	$\alpha\ 1\ \alpha^3 \alpha^5$	$0\ \alpha^4 \alpha^4 \alpha^6 0\ \alpha^3 0$
10	$\alpha\ \alpha^5 \alpha^4 1$	$0\ 0\ \alpha^4 \alpha^4 \alpha^6 0\ \alpha^3$
11	$\alpha^3 0\ \alpha^4 \alpha^6$	$\alpha^3 0\ 0\ \alpha^4 \alpha^4 \alpha^6 0$
12	$\alpha^2 \alpha\ \alpha^6 \alpha$	$0\ \alpha^3 0\ 0\ \alpha^4 \alpha^4 \alpha^6$
13	$\boxed{\alpha^4 0\ 0\ \alpha^3}$ ← Trapped error	$\alpha^6 0\ \alpha^3 0\ 0\ \alpha^4 \alpha^4$
14	$0\ \alpha^4 0\ 0$	$\alpha^6 \alpha^6 0\ \alpha^3 0\ 0\ \alpha^4$
15	$0\ 0\ \alpha^4 0$	$\alpha^6 \alpha^6 0\ \alpha^3 0\ 0\ \vert \alpha^4$
16	$\boxed{0\ 0\ 0\ \alpha^4}$ ← Trapped error	$\alpha^6 \alpha^6 0\ \alpha^3 0\ \vert 0\ \alpha^4$
17	$0\ 0\ 0\ 0$	$\alpha^6 \alpha^6 0\ \alpha^3 \vert \alpha^4 0\ \alpha^4$
18	$0\ 0\ 0\ 0$	$\alpha^6 \alpha^6 0\ \vert \alpha^3 \alpha^4 0$
19	$0\ 0\ 0\ 0$	$\alpha^6 \alpha^6 \vert 0\ \alpha^3 \alpha^4$
20	$0\ 0\ 0\ 0$	$\alpha^6 \vert \alpha^6 0\ \alpha^3$
21	$0\ 0\ 0\ 0$	$\vert \alpha^6 \alpha^6 0$

Figure 6.28 Error-trapping example.

degree 3 or less. Because the syndromes are of degree 3 or less, error trapping can be applied.

The error-trapping decoder is shown in Fig. 6.27. When implemented with binary circuits, the octal shift-register stages are three binary shift-register stages in parallel. All data paths are 3-bits wide. The multiply-by-$z+1$ (that is, by α^3) and -z (that is, by α) circuits in the feedback path are simple three-input three-output binary-logic circuits, which are easily determined. A total of 21 shifts are necessary for this decoder to correct all errors. The first set of 7 shifts computes the syndrome. The second set of 7 shifts corrects at least one error and sometimes both errors. The third set of 7 shifts corrects the second error if it is as yet uncorrected.

In Fig. 6.28, we trace through a sample decoding operation in detail. This is a valuable exercise because it illustrates error trapping and because it gives a concrete example of the relationship between the abstract concept of a Galois field and the logic design of a shift-register circuit.

For each shift, the content of both the syndrome register and the information buffer are listed in the table. After 7 shifts, the syndrome register contains the syndrome. Beginning with the eighth shift, the circuit will correct an error whenever it sees an error-trapped pattern. This is a pattern with at most two nonzero symbols and with one of the nonzero symbols in the rightmost place. Such a pattern must always occur at least once in the second 7 shifts if no more than two errors occur. In the example, it occurs at shift 13. Hence the error is trapped. Notice that the high-order syndrome symbols are normally to the right. When the error is trapped, we see a 4-symbol segment of the cyclically shifted error pattern (e_4, e_5, e_6, e_0). Because the error is trapped, e_0 is corrected in the information register and set equal to zero (or subtracted from itself) in the syndrome register. After 14 shifts, the syndrome register contains the syndrome of the remaining error pattern. The process repeats through a third set of 7 shifts, after which the error correction is complete.

If the syndrome is initially nonzero but no error is trapped during the second set of 7 shifts, then more than two errors occurred (but the converse is not true). Additional logic can easily be included to detect an uncorrectable error pattern.

For the final example of this section, we will describe an error-trapping decoder for a burst-error-correcting code. In contrast to the situation for random-error-correcting codes, every burst-error-correcting code can be decoded by an error-trapping decoder. We will give a decoder for a (14, 6) code that decodes all bursts of length 4. This code is obtained by interleaving two copies of the (7, 3) code from Table 5.1. The generator polynomial of the interleaved code is

$$g(x) = x^8 + x^6 + x^4 + 1.$$

To trap a burst error of length 4 or less, the proper procedure is to check that the four leftmost bits in the syndrome register are all zero. We can improve this a little, however. Notice that the even- and odd-numbered shift-register stages do not interact. The circuit can be thought of as performing two independent syndrome calculations, one for each of the two underlying codes, but with the syndrome bit positions interleaved. Hence, we can modify error-trapping to obtain the circuit shown in Fig. 6.29. This circuit will correct burst-error patterns of length 4 and also some other error patterns. Any pattern consisting of a burst of length 2 in the even-numbered components, and a burst-error of length 2 in the odd-numbered components, will be corrected.

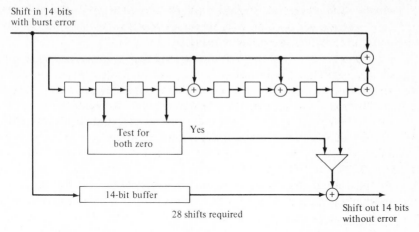

Figure 6.29 Error-trapping decoder for an interleaved burst-error-correcting code.

6.6 SHORTENED CYCLIC CODES

Any systematic cyclic code can be shortened, that is, changed from an (n, k) code to an $(n\text{-}b, k\text{-}b)$ code by dropping b information bits from each codeword. We will require that the b highest-order bits must be the ones dropped and that b must be less than k. Because the unused bits in a shortened code are always set to zero, they need not be transmitted, but the receiver can reinsert them and decode just as if the code were not shortened. If the original cyclic code has minimum distance d^*, then the shortened cyclic code has minimum distance d^* (or larger). Similarly, if the original code can correct burst errors of length t, then the shortened code can also correct burst errors of length t (or longer). Using the techniques of shortening and interleaving, the codes of Table 5.1 can be used to create a very large collection of good burst-error-correcting codes.

A shortened code is no longer cyclic because $R_{x^{n'}-1}[xc(x)]$ is not generally a codeword when $c(x)$ is a codeword. A shortened cyclic code, however, does have an algebraic structure as a subset of an appropriate ring. Whereas cyclic codes are ideals in the ring of polynomials modulo $x^n - 1$, shortened cyclic codes are ideals in the ring of polynomials modulo $f(x)$ for some polynomial $f(x)$ of degree $n' = n - b$. This is established by the following theorem.

☐ **Theorem 6.6.1** If $\mathscr{C}$ is a shortened cyclic code, then there exists a polynomial $f(x)$ such that whenever $c(x)$ is a codeword and $a(x)$ is any polynomial, then $R_{f(x)}[a(x)c(x)]$ is also a codeword.

Proof   Let $g(x)$ be the generator polynomial of the original cyclic code of blocklength n, and let n' be the blocklength of the shortened cyclic code. Then by the division algorithm we can write

$$x^{n'} = g(x)Q(x) + s(x).$$

Because $n' = n - b > n - k = \deg g(x)$, the remainder $s(x)$ has a degree smaller than n'. Let $f(x) = x^{n'} - s(x)$; then $f(x)$ has a degree of n', and $g(x)$ divides $f(x)$. Now if $c(x)$ is a multiple of $g(x)$ and $a(x)$ is any polynomial, then by the division algorithm we can write

$$a(x)c(x) = f(x)Q'(x) + r(x).$$

Because $g(x)$ divides both $c(x)$ and $f(x)$, $r(x)$ is clearly a multiple of $g(x)$; thus in the ring $GF(q)[x]/(f(x))$, $a(x)c(x) = r(x)$ is a multiple of $g(x)$, as was to be proved. □

A shortened cyclic code of blocklength $n' = n - b$ can be decoded by a Meggitt decoder designed for the original (n, k) code. The timing of this decoder is based on groups of n clock times, but the incoming codeword contains n' symbols. It may be that this mismatch in the timing can be easily accommodated somehow in the circuit design and thus is unimportant. In other applications, it may be worthwhile to balance the timing. We will discuss a way in which to modify the received word so that the timing of the Meggitt decoder can be based on groups of n' clock times instead. This speeds up the decoding of a shortened cyclic code.

We will redefine the syndrome so that those shift-register clock times corresponding to unused symbols can be bypassed. When b symbols are dropped, the syndrome is defined as

$$s(x) = R_{g(x)}[x^{n-k+b}v(x)]$$

instead of as the remainder of $x^{n-k}v(x)$. To see the reason for this choice, suppose that the high-order bit of the shortened code is in error. That is, let

$$e(x) = e_{n'-1}x^{(n-b)-1}.$$

Then

$$\begin{aligned}
s(x) &= R_{g(x)}[e_{n'-1}x^{2n-k-1}] \\
&= R_{g(x)}[R_{x^n-1}[e_{n'-1}x^{2n-k-1}]] \\
&= e_{n'-1}x^{n-k-1}.
\end{aligned}$$

Hence $s(x)$ is nonzero only in the high-order bit.
   Let

$$a(x) = R_{g(x)}[x^{n-k+b}].$$

Then by the rules of modulo computation, $s(x)$ can be written

$$s(x) = R_{g(x)}[a(x)v(x)].$$

All that need be done is to premultiply $v(x)$ by the fixed polynomial $a(x)$ prior to division by $g(x)$. This multiplication can be combined with the divide-by-$g(x)$ circuit by means of the way that $v(x)$ is fed into the circuit. The examples show how to do this.

We will give two examples of decoders for cyclic codes. The first example is a burst-correcting shortened cyclic code. Suppose the requirements of some application can be met by shortening the (511, 499) burst-correcting code of Table 5.1 to get a (272, 260) code. This code will correct all burst errors of length 4 or less. For this case, $g(x) = x^{12} + x^8 + x^5 + x^3 + 1$, $x^{n-k+b} = x^{251}$, and we need to compute

$$a(x) = R_{g(x)}[x^{251}].$$

One way to carry out this calculation is by writing

$$x^{251} = (x^{12})^{16}(x^{12})^4(x^{11})$$

and

$$x^{12} = x^8 + x^5 + x^3 + 1.$$

Repeated squaring of x^{12} reduced modulo $x^{12} + x^8 + x^5 + x^3 + 1$ gives $(x^{12})^4$ and $(x^{12})^{16}$, and from these x^{251} modulo $x^{12} + x^8 + x^5 + x^3 + 1$ can be quickly calculated. Then

$$a(x) = x^{11} + x^9 + x^7 + x^3 + x^2 + 1.$$

Finally,

$$s(x) = R_{x^{12} + x^8 + x^5 + x^3 + 1}[(x^{11} + x^9 + x^7 + x^3 + x^2 + 1)v(x)].$$

This can be implemented with a single divide-by-$g(x)$ circuit if at each iteration the incoming coefficient of $v(x)$ is added into the proper positions of the current remainder. A Meggitt decoder to decode the shortened code is shown in Fig. 6.30. This decoder is pipelined so that it will operate with a continuous stream of incoming bits.

We give as a second example a (64, 60) code over $GF(4)$, which is a shortened Hamming (85, 81) code. The Hamming (85, 81) code is a cyclic code, as was discussed in Section 5.5. The generator polynomial is $g(x) = x^4 + x^3 + 3x + 1$, and $x^{n-k+b} = x^{25}$. Then by carrying out the long division, we have

$$a(x) = R_{x^4 + x^3 + 3x + 1}[x^{25}] = x^3 + 3x^2 + 2.$$

The modified syndrome is then computed by

$$s(x) = R_{x^4 + x^3 + 3x + 1}[(x^3 + 3x^2 + 2)v(x)].$$

The circuit of Fig. 6.31 is a Meggitt decoder that will decode the shortened code in 128 clock times. It does this by multiplying the received polynomial by $x^3 + 3x^2 + 2$ and then dividing by $x^4 + x^3 + 3x + 1$ to produce the modified syndrome. Altogether, 64 clock times are used to compute the modified syndrome, and 64 clock times are used to correct the error pattern,

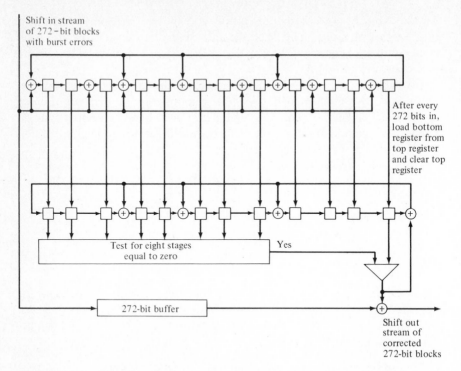

Shift in stream
of 272–bit blocks
with burst errors

After every
272 bits in,
load bottom
register from
top register
and clear top
register

Test for eight stages
equal to zero

Yes

272-bit buffer

Shift out
stream of
corrected
272-bit blocks

Figure 6.30   Error-trapping decoder for (272, 260) burst-error-correcting code.

for a total of 128 clock times. If desired, the decoder could be pipelined, or two decoders could be run in tandem, and then the decoder would run in step with the incoming data.

6.7 A MEGGITT DECODER FOR THE GOLAY CODE

Sometimes when error trapping cannot be used for a given code, it can be made to work by adding an extra circuit to remove a few troublesome error patterns. In general, this calls for a certain amount of ingenuity in order to obtain a satisfactory design. We shall illustrate such a decoder for the Golay (23, 12) code.

The error pattern is of length 23 and of weight 3 or less. The syndrome register has a length of 11. If an error pattern cannot be trapped, then it cannot be cyclically shifted so that all three errors appear in the 11 low-order places. In this case, one can convince oneself (perhaps with a few sketches) that one of the three error bits must have at least five zeros on one side of it and at least six zeros on the other side. Therefore, all error patterns can be cyclically shifted into one of the following three configurations (with bit positions numbered 0 through 22):

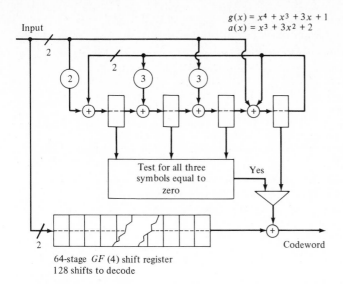

$g(x) = x^4 + x^3 + 3x + 1$
$a(x) = x^3 + 3x^2 + 2$

Test for all three symbols equal to zero

Yes

Codeword

64-stage $GF(4)$ shift register
128 shifts to decode

Figure 6.31 A Meggitt decoder for an (18, 15) shortened Hamming code over $GF(4)$.

1. All errors (three or less) are in the 11 high-order bits.
2. One error is in bit position 5 and the others are in the 11 high-order bits.
3. One error is in bit position 6 and the others are in the 11 high-order bits.

Therefore the decoder has the precomputed values $s_5(x) = R_{g(x)}[x^{n-k}x^5]$ and $s_6(x) = R_{g(x)}[x^{n-k}x^6]$. Then an error pattern is trapped if $s(x)$ has weight 3 or less, or if $s(x) - s_5(x)$ or $s(x) - s_6(x)$ has weight 2 or less. One can choose to correct all errors when this happens or to correct only the two errors in the 11 low-order bits and to wait for the third error to be shifted down.

Dividing x^{16} and x^{17} by the generator polynomial

$$g(x) = x^{11} + x^{10} + x^6 + x^5 + x^4 + x^2 + 1$$

gives

$$s_5(x) = x^9 + x^8 + x^6 + x^5 + x^3 + x^2 + x$$

$$s_6(x) = x^{10} + x^9 + x^7 + x^6 + x^4 + x^3 + x^2.$$

Therefore if an error occurs in bit position 5 or 6, the syndrome is (01110110110) or (11011011100), respectively. Two more errors occurring in the 11 high-order bit positions will cause two of these bits to be complemented at the appropriate locations.

The decoder looks for a syndrome pattern that differs from the all-zero syndrome in three or fewer places, or one that differs from either of the other two syndromes in two or fewer places.

PROBLEMS

6.1. **a.** Construct $GF(8)$ by means of the primitive irreducible polynomial $p(x) = x^3 + x + 1$. Let α be the primitive element $\alpha = x$.

    b. Design a simple logic circuit that evaluates $g(\alpha^3)$ given an arbitrary polynomial $g(x)$ over $GF(2)$.

    c. Design a circuit that multiplies two arbitrary field elements of $GF(8)$.

    d. Design a scaler that multiplies any element of $GF(8)$ by α^4.

    e. Identify those elements of $GF(8)$ that have square roots and tabulate them.

    f. Design a logic circuit that finds the square root of any field element in $GF(8)$ that has a square root.

6.2. Let $GF(16)$ be constructed with $x^4 + x + 1$. Two arbitrary elements of $GF(16)$ can be denoted as follows:

$$\beta = \beta_3 x^3 + \beta_2 x^2 + \beta_1 x + \beta_0,$$

$$\gamma = \gamma_3 x^3 + \gamma_2 x^2 + \gamma_1 x + \gamma_0,$$

where the coefficients are elements of $GF(2)$. Design a parallel logic circuit that will multiply two arbitrary elements of $GF(16)$.

6.3. Based on the relationships $\beta^{-1} = (\beta^{2^{m-1}-1})^2$ and $2^m - 1 = \sum_{k=0}^{m-1} 2^k$, design an iterative circuit that computes β^{-1} from β in m clocks using a squaring circuit and a multiplier.

6.4. A $(15, 9, 5)$ cyclic code over $GF(4)$ has a generator polynomial

$$g(x) = x^6 + 3x^5 + x^4 + x^3 + 2x^2 + 2x + 1.$$

    a. Design a shift-register encoder for this code.

    b. Design a Meggitt decoder for this code.

6.5. The cyclic binary code defined by the generator polynomial $g(x) = x^4 + x^3 + x^2 + 1$ corrects bursts of length 2.

    a. What are the blocklength and rate of this code?

    b. Find the minimum distance of the code.

    c. Design a systematic encoder for the code.

    d. Design an error-trapping decoder that will correct bursts of length 2.

6.6. The triple-error-correcting Golay $(23, 12)$ code is a cyclic code with a generator polynomial

$$g(x) = x^{11} + x^{10} + x^6 + x^5 + x^4 + x^2 + 1$$

or

$$g(x) = x^{11} + x^9 + x^7 + x^6 + x^5 + x + 1.$$

    a. Find the parity-check polynomial $h(x)$.

    b. Sketch a shift-register encoder.

    c. Can error trapping be used to correct triple errors? Why?

6.7. Design an encoder and decoder using 4-bit-wide shift registers for the Hamming (17, 15) hexadecimal code discussed in Section 3.4. Show all logic.

6.8. A 256-word by 8-bit computer memory is subject to occasional transients during the read/write cycle, and thus an occasional 8-bit word is incorrect. To remedy this problem, it is decided to use a shortened Hamming code over $GF(2^8)$ to correct a single-word error.

Describe the (256, 252) code, and design the encoder and an error-trapping decoder. (Notice that this scheme processes the content of the entire memory to find and correct one bad word.)

6.9. Design an encoder and an error-trapping decoder for the (19537, 19408) binary Fire code with the generator polynomial

$$g(x) = (x^{19} - 1)p(x),$$

where $p(x)$ is a primitive polynomial of degree 10.

6.10. The binary cyclic code of length 17 specified by the single zero at α^{15} in $GF(256)$ is a (17, 9, 5) code. It belongs to a class known as the quadratic residue codes. Find the generator polynomial and design a modified error-trapping decoder for correcting all double errors. Also, design a syndrome-table-lookup decoder. Make some comparisons concerning complexity and speed of the two decoders.

6.11. The (7, 5) Reed-Solomon code over $GF(8)$ has a generator polynomial $g(x) = x^2 + \alpha^4 x + \alpha^3$. Design a cyclic code for correcting bursts of length 2 over $GF(8)$ by the following steps.

a. Give the generator polynomial of a code that will correct octal bursts of length 2 by interleaving two copies of the Reed-Solomon code.

b. What are the blocklength and rate of this code?

c. Sketch a shift-register encoder for this code.

d. Design an error-trapping decoder to correct all bursts of length 2.

6.12. Construct a (1072, 1024) code for correcting burst errors of length 16 by shortening and interleaving a suitable code from Table 5.1. Construct a (1080, 1024) code for correcting bursts of length 20 by shortening and interleaving a Fire code.

6.13. A (31, 21) binary double-error-correcting code has the generator polynomial

$$g(x) = x^{10} + x^9 + x^8 + x^6 + x^5 + x^3 + 1.$$

a. Show that an error-trapping decoder cannot decode this code to the designed distance.

b. Show a simple modification of the error-trapping decoder that will decode to the designed distance.

c. Instead of a cyclic shift, use the permutation

$$v(x) \leftarrow v(x^2) \qquad (\bmod \ x^n - 1)$$

to design another variation of an error-trapping decoder that corrects all double errors.

NOTES

Many of the ideas of this chapter can now be clearly seen as a part of digital-filtering theory but with a Galois field in place of the real or complex field. This was vaguely realized at the outset and became more obvious as the subject developed. The basic shift-register circuits are immediately apparent to most designers and have entered the literature without any fanfare. Shift-register circuits for encoding and decoding can be found in the work of Peterson (1960) and Chien (1964). The ideas appear in textbook form in the book by Peterson (1961). Meggitt published the design for his decoder in 1960 and 1961. The origin of the idea of error-trapping is a little hazy, but credit is usually given to Prange.

Kasami (1964) studied ways to augment an error-trapping decoder to handle correctable but untrappable error patterns. The decoder for the Golay code in Section 6.7 uses the techniques of Kasami. The use of permutations other than cyclic shifts was studied by MacWilliams (1964). Other early work appears in the papers of Mitchell (1962) and Rudolph and Mitchell (1964).

CHAPTER 7

Bose-Chaudhuri-Hocquenghem Codes

The class of Bose-Chaudhuri-Hocquenghem (BCH) codes is a large class of multiple-error-correcting codes that occupies a prominent place in the theory and practice of error correction. This prominence is a result of at least four reasons: (1) Provided the blocklength is not excessive, there are good codes in this class (but often not the best known). (2) Relatively simple and instrumentable encoding and decoding techniques are known (although if simplicity is the only consideration, other codes are preferable). (3) The popular nonbinary subclass of Reed-Solomon codes has certain optimality properties and a well-understood distance structure. (4) A thorough understanding of BCH codes is probably the best single starting point for studying many other classes of codes.

In this chapter, we will develop the BCH codes directly in the time domain. This is the original historical approach to the subject. In Chapter 8, we shall develop many of the same ideas in terms of the Galois-field frequency domain.

We will first introduce BCH codes over $GF(q)$ by means of a procedure for constructing a generator polynomial $g(x)$ for a t-error-correcting code of blocklength $q^m - 1$. Codes with blocklength of this form are called *primitive BCH codes*. We will prove that these codes correct t errors by explicitly developing a decoding algorithm. We will later generalize our discussion to BCH codes whose blocklength is a divisor of $q^m - 1$.

7.1 DEFINITION OF THE CODES

The generator polynomial of a cyclic code can be expressed in the form

$$g(x) = \text{LCM}[f_1(x), f_2(x), \ldots, f_r(x)],$$

where $f_1(x), \ldots, f_r(x)$ are the minimal polynomials of the zeros of $g(x)$. We will develop this point of view and design codes by finding generator polynomials with desirable zeros.

Let $c(x)$ be a codeword polynomial and let $e(x)$ be an error polynomial. The received polynomial is

$$v(x) = c(x) + e(x),$$

where the polynomial coefficients are in $GF(q)$. We can evaluate this polynomial at elements of $GF(q^m)$, in particular at those elements that are zeros of $g(x)$, say at $\gamma_1, \ldots, \gamma_r$. Then, because $c(\gamma_j) = 0$ whenever γ_j is a zero of $g(x)$,

$$v(\gamma_j) = c(\gamma_j) + e(\gamma_j)$$

$$= e(\gamma_j).$$

Hence,

$$v(\gamma_j) = \sum_{i=0}^{n-1} e_i \gamma_j^i \qquad j = 1, \ldots, r$$

for all γ_j that are zeros of $g(x)$. This final set of r equations involves only the components of the error pattern, not those of the codeword. If this set of equations can be solved for e_i, then the error pattern can be determined. We will choose the γ_j so that this set of r equations can be solved for e_i whenever at most t components are nonzero.

For an arbitrary cyclic code whose generator polynomial $g(x)$ has zeros $\gamma_1, \ldots, \gamma_r$, define the syndromes

$$S_j = v(\gamma_j) \qquad j = 1, \ldots, r.$$

These field elements are different from the syndrome polynomial $s(x)$ but contain equivalent information. We wish to choose $\gamma_1, \ldots, \gamma_r$ such that t errors can be computed from $S_1, \ldots, S_r$. We will prove shortly that if α is primitive, then

$$\alpha, \alpha^2, \alpha^3, \ldots, \alpha^{2t}$$

is such a set. Accepting this fact for the moment, we choose $g(x)$ to have these as zeros. Given a primitive blocklength $n = q^m - 1$ for some m and t the number of errors to be corrected, proceed as follows:

1. Choose a prime polynomial of degree m and construct $GF(q^m)$.
2. Find $f_j(x)$, the minimal polynomial of α^j for $j = 1, \ldots, 2t$.
3. $g(x) = \text{LCM}[f_1(x), \ldots, f_{2t}(x)]$.

In the next section, by explicitly providing a decoding algorithm, we will prove that this cyclic code can correct t errors. Sometimes the BCH code designed in this way can correct more than t errors. For this reason,

$$d = 2t + 1$$

is called the *designed distance* of the code. The minimum distance d^* may be larger.

Table 7.1 gives $GF(16)$ as an extension field of $GF(2)$ constructed with the primitive polynomial $p(z) = z^4 + z + 1$. This table also gives the minimal polynomials over $GF(2)$ of all field elements in $GF(16)$ where $\alpha = z$ is primitive. Notice that the minimal polynomials of even powers of α always appear earlier in the list. This is a consequence of Theorem 5.3.4, which says that over $GF(2)$, and for any β, β and β^2 have the same minimal polynomial. This observation reduces slightly the work in finding $g(x)$.

Table 7.1 Representations of $GF(2^4)$.

Exponential Notation	Polynomial Notation	Binary Notation	Decimal Notation	Minimal Polynomial
0	0	0000	0	
α^0	1	0001	1	$x + 1$
α^1	z	0010	2	$x^4 + x + 1$
α^2	z^2	0100	4	$x^4 + x + 1$
α^3	z^3	1000	8	$x^4 + x^3 + x^2 + x + 1$
α^4	$z + 1$	0011	3	$x^4 + x + 1$
α^5	$z^2 + z$	0110	6	$x^2 + x + 1$
α^6	$z^3 + z^2$	1100	12	$x^4 + x^3 + x^2 + x + 1$
α^7	$z^3 + z + 1$	1011	11	$x^4 + x^3 + 1$
α^8	$z^2 + 1$	0101	5	$x^4 + x + 1$
α^9	$z^3 + z$	1010	10	$x^4 + x^3 + x^2 + x + 1$
α^{10}	$z^2 + z + 1$	0111	7	$x^2 + x + 1$
α^{11}	$z^3 + z^2 + z$	1110	14	$x^4 + x^3 + 1$
α^{12}	$z^3 + z^2 + z + 1$	1111	15	$x^4 + x^3 + x^2 + x + 1$
α^{13}	$z^3 + z^2 + 1$	1101	13	$x^4 + x^3 + 1$
α^{14}	$z^3 + 1$	1001	9	$x^4 + x^3 + 1$

The generator polynomial for the double-error-correcting BCH code of blocklength 15 is obtained as follows:

$$g(x) = \text{LCM}[f_1(x), f_2(x), f_3(x), f_4(x)]$$
$$= \text{LCM}[x^4 + x + 1, x^4 + x + 1, x^4 + x^3 + x^2 + x + 1, x^4 + x + 1]$$
$$= (x^4 + x + 1)(x^4 + x^3 + x^2 + x + 1)$$
$$= x^8 + x^7 + x^6 + x^4 + 1.$$

Because $g(x)$ has degree 8, $n - k = 8$. Therefore $k = 7$, and we have the generator polynomial for the BCH (15, 7) double-error-correcting code. Notice that BCH codes are designed from specification of n and t. The value of k is not known until after $g(x)$ is found.

Continuing in this way, we can construct generator polynomials for other primitive BCH codes of blocklength 15.

Let $t = 3$:

$$g(x) = \text{LCM}[f_1(x), f_2(x), f_3(x), f_4(x), f_5(x), f_6(x)]$$
$$= (x^4 + x + 1)(x^4 + x^3 + x^2 + x + 1)(x^2 + x + 1)$$
$$= x^{10} + x^8 + x^5 + x^4 + x^2 + x + 1.$$

This is the generator polynomial for a (15, 5) triple-error-correcting BCH code.

Let $t = 4$:

$$g(x) = \text{LCM}[f_1(x), f_2(x), f_3(x), f_4(x), f_5(x), f_6(x), f_7(x), f_8(x)]$$
$$= (x^4 + x + 1)(x^4 + x^3 + x^2 + x + 1)(x^2 + x + 1)(x^4 + x^3 + 1)$$
$$= x^{14} + x^{13} + x^{12} + x^{11} + x^{10} + x^9 + x^8 + x^7 + x^6 + x^5 + x^4$$
$$+ x^3 + x^2 + x + 1.$$

This is the generator polynomial for a (15, 1) BCH code. It is a simple repetition code and can correct seven errors.

Let $t = 5$, 6, and 7. Each of these cases results in the same generator polynomial as for $t = 4$. Beyond $t = 7$, the BCH code is undefined because the number of nonzero field elements is 15.

Table 7.2 gives $GF(16)$ as an extension field of $GF(4)$ constructed with the primitive polynomial $p(z) = z^2 + z + 2$. This table also gives the minimal polynomials over $GF(4)$ of all field elements in $GF(16)$ where $\alpha = z$ is primitive. The generator polynomial for the single-error-correcting BCH code over $GF(4)$ of blocklength 15 is obtained as follows:

$$g(x) = \text{LCM}[f_1(x), f_2(x)]$$
$$= (x^2 + x + 2)(x^2 + x + 3)$$
$$= x^4 + x + 1.$$

Table 7.2   Representations of $GF(4^2)$.

$$GF(4)$$

+	0 1 2 3		·	0 1 2 3
0	0 1 2 3		0	0 0 0 0
1	1 0 3 2		1	0 1 2 3
2	2 3 0 1		2	0 2 3 1
3	3 2 1 0		3	0 3 1 2

Exponential Notation	Polynomial Notation	Quaternary Notation	Decimal Notation	Minimal Polynomial
0	0	00	0	
α^0	1	01	1	$x+1$
α^1	z	10	4	x^2+x+2
α^2	$z+2$	12	6	x^2+x+3
α^3	$3z+2$	32	14	x^2+3x+1
α^4	$z+1$	11	5	x^2+x+2
α^5	2	02	2	$x+2$
α^6	$2z$	20	8	x^2+2x+1
α^7	$2z+3$	23	11	x^2+2x+2
α^8	$z+3$	13	7	x^2+x+3
α^9	$2z+2$	22	10	x^2+2x+1
α^{10}	3	03	3	$x+3$
α^{11}	$3z$	30	12	x^2+3x+3
α^{12}	$3z+1$	31	13	x^2+3x+1
α^{13}	$2z+1$	21	9	x^2+2x+2
α^{14}	$3z+3$	33	15	x^2+3x+3

This is the generator polynomial for a (15, 11) BCH single-error-correcting code over $GF(4)$. It encodes 11 quaternary symbols (equivalent to 22 bits) into 15 quaternary symbols. It is not a Hamming code.

Continuing, we can find the generator polynomials for other BCH codes over $GF(4)$ of blocklength 15.

Let $t = 2$:

$$g(x) = \text{LCM}[f_1(x),\ f_2(x),\ f_3(x),\ f_4(x)]$$
$$= (x^2+x+2)(x^2+x+3)(x^2+3x+1)$$
$$= x^6 + 3x^5 + x^4 + x^3 + 2x^2 + 2x + 1.$$

This is the generator polynomial for a (15, 9) double-error-correcting BCH code over $GF(4)$.

Let $t = 3$:

$$g(x) = x^9 + 3x^8 + 3x^7 + 2x^6 + x^5 + 2x^4 + x + 2.$$

This gives the (15, 6) triple-error-correcting BCH code over $GF(4)$.

Let $t = 4$:

$$g(x) = x^{11} + x^{10} + 2x^8 + 3x^7 + 3x^6 + x^5 + 3x^4 + x^3 + x + 3.$$

This gives the $(15, 4)$ four-error-correcting BCH code over $GF(4)$.

Let $t = 5$:

$$g(x) = x^{12} + 2x^{11} + 3x^{10} + 2x^9 + 2x^8 + x^7 + 3x^6 + 3x^4 + 3x^3 + x^2 + 2.$$

This gives the $(15, 3)$ five-error-correcting BCH code over $GF(4)$.

Let $t = 6$:

$$g(x) = x^{14} + x^{13} + x^{12} + x^{11} + x^{10} + x^9 + x^8 + x^7 + x^6 + x^5 + x^4$$
$$+ x^3 + x^2 + x + 1.$$

This gives the $(15, 1)$ six-error-correcting BCH code over $GF(4)$. It is a simple repetition code and can actually correct seven errors.

We will now formally define BCH codes. The definition is more general than that of the primitive BCH codes defined above, taking as the zeros of $g(x)$ $2t$ successive powers of any β, not necessarily a primitive element. The blocklength of the code is the order of β, that is, the smallest n for which $\beta^n = 1$.

□ **Definition 7.1.1**   Let q and m be given and let β be any element of $GF(q^m)$ of order n. Then for any positive integer t and any integer j_0, the corresponding BCH code is the cyclic code of blocklength n with the generator polynomial

$$g(x) = \text{LCM}[f_{j_0}(x), f_{j_0 + 1}(x), \ldots, f_{j_0 + 2t - 1}(x)],$$

where $f_j(x)$ is the minimal polynomial of β^j. □

Often one chooses $j_0 = 1$, which is usually—but not always—the choice that gives a $g(x)$ of smallest degree. Usually one desires a large blocklength, and thus β is chosen as an element with largest order, that is, as a primitive element.

7.2 THE PETERSON-GORENSTEIN-ZIERLER DECODER

BCH codes are cyclic codes and hence can be decoded by any technique for decoding cyclic codes. There are, however, much better algorithms that have been developed specifically for decoding BCH codes. The algorithm studied in this section was first developed by Peterson for binary codes. We will present the general case as developed by Gorenstein and Zierler. By proving that this algorithm can correct t errors, we prove that the construction of BCH codes of the previous section gives a t-error-correcting code. To simplify the equations we will take $j_0 = 1$, although arbitrary j_0 could be carried along with no change in the ideas.

Suppose that a BCH code is constructed based on the field element α, possibly nonprimitive. The error polynomial is

$$e(x) = e_{n-1}x^{n-1} + e_{n-2}x^{n-2} + \cdots + e_1 x + e_0,$$

where at most t coefficients are nonzero. Suppose that v errors actually occur, $0 \leqslant v \leqslant t$, and that they occur in unknown locations $i_1, i_2, \ldots, i_v$. The error polynomial can be written

$$e(x) = e_{i_1}x^{i_1} + e_{i_2}x^{i_2} + \cdots + e_{i_v}x^{i_v},$$

where e_{i_l} is the magnitude of the lth error ($e_{i_l} = 1$ for binary codes). We do not know $i_1, \ldots, i_v$, nor do we know $e_{i_1}, \ldots, e_{i_v}$. In fact, we do not even know the value of v. These must be computed to correct the errors. Evaluate the received polynomial at α to obtain the syndrome S_1:

$$S_1 = v(\alpha) = c(\alpha) + e(\alpha) = e(\alpha)$$

$$= e_{i_1}\alpha^{i_1} + e_{i_2}\alpha^{i_2} + \cdots + e_{i_v}\alpha^{i_v}.$$

This is a clumsy notation. To streamline it, we define the error magnitudes $Y_l = e_{i_l}$ for $l = 1, \ldots, v$, and the error-location numbers $X_l = \alpha^{i_l}$ for $l = 1, \ldots, v$, where i_l is the actual location of the lth error and X_l is the field element associated with this location. Notice that the error-location number of each component of the error pattern must be distinct because α is an element of order n.

With this notation, the syndrome is given by

$$S_1 = Y_1 X_1 + Y_2 X_2 + \cdots + Y_v X_v.$$

Similarly, we can evaluate the received polynomial at each of the powers of α used to define $g(x)$. Define the syndromes for $j = 1, \ldots, 2t$ by

$$S_j = v(\alpha^j) = c(\alpha^j) + e(\alpha^j) = e(\alpha^j).$$

Then we have the following set of $2t$ simultaneous equations in the v unknown error locations $X_1, \ldots, X_v$ and the v unknown error magnitudes $Y_1, \ldots, Y_v$:

$$S_1 = Y_1 X_1 + Y_2 X_2 + \cdots + Y_v X_v$$

$$S_2 = Y_1 X_1^2 + Y_2 X_2^2 + \cdots + Y_v X_v^2$$

$$S_3 = Y_1 X_1^3 + Y_2 X_2^3 + \cdots + Y_v X_v^3$$

$$\vdots \qquad\qquad \vdots$$

$$S_{2t} = Y_1 X_1^{2t} + Y_2 X_2^{2t} + \cdots + Y_v X_v^{2t}.$$

This set of equations must have at least one solution because of the way in which the syndromes are defined. We will see that the solution is unique.

Our task now is to find the unknowns given the syndromes. This is a problem in solving a system of nonlinear equations. The method of solution is valid for such a system of equations over any field.

The set of nonlinear equations is too difficult to solve directly. Instead, we judiciously define some intermediate variables that can be computed from the syndromes and from which the error locations can then be computed.

Consider the polynomial in x,

$$\Lambda(x) = \Lambda_v x^v + \Lambda_{v-1} x^{v-1} + \cdots + \Lambda_1 x + 1,$$

known as the error-locator polynomial and defined to be the polynomial with zeros at the inverse error locations X_l^{-1} for $l = 1, \ldots, v$. That is,

$$\Lambda(x) = (1 - xX_1)(1 - xX_2) \ldots (1 - xX_v).$$

If we knew the coefficients of $\Lambda(x)$, we could find the zeros of $\Lambda(x)$ to obtain the error locations. Therefore let us first try to compute $\Lambda_1, \ldots, \Lambda_v$ from the syndromes. If we can do this, the problem is nearly solved.

Multiply both sides of the above polynomial by $Y_l X_l^{j+v}$ and set $x = X_l^{-1}$. Then the left side is zero, and we have

$$0 = Y_l X_l^{j+v}(1 + \Lambda_1 X_l^{-1} + \Lambda_2 X_l^{-2} + \cdots + \Lambda_{v-1} X_l^{-(v-1)} + \Lambda_v X_l^{-v})$$

or

$$Y_l(X_l^{j+v} + \Lambda_1 X_l^{j+v-1} + \cdots + \Lambda_v X_l^j) = 0.$$

Such an equation holds for each l and each j. Sum up these equations from $l = 1$ to $l = v$. This gives, for each j,

$$\sum_{l=1}^{v} Y_l(X_l^{j+v} + \Lambda_1 X_l^{j+v-1} + \cdots + \Lambda_v X_l^j) = 0$$

or

$$\sum_{l=1}^{v} Y_l X_l^{j+v} + \Lambda_1 \sum_{l=1}^{v} Y_l X_l^{j+v-1} + \cdots + \Lambda_v \sum_{l=1}^{v} Y_l X_l^j = 0$$

The individual sums are recognized as syndromes, and thus the equation becomes

$$S_{j+v} + \Lambda_1 S_{j+v-1} + \Lambda_2 S_{j+v-2} + \cdots + \Lambda_v S_j = 0$$

Because $v \leq t$, the subscripts always specify known syndromes if j is in the interval $1 \leq j \leq v$. Hence, we have the set of equations

$$\Lambda_1 S_{j+v-1} + \Lambda_2 S_{j+v-2} + \cdots + \Lambda_v S_j = -S_{j+v} \qquad j = 1, \ldots, v.$$

This is the set of linear equations relating the syndromes to the coefficients of $\Lambda(x)$. We can write these equations in matrix form:

$$\begin{bmatrix} S_1 & S_2 & S_3 & \cdots & S_{v-1} & S_v \\ S_2 & S_3 & S_4 & \cdots & S_v & S_{v+1} \\ S_3 & S_4 & S_5 & \cdots & S_{v+1} & S_{v+2} \\ \vdots & & & & & \vdots \\ S_v & S_{v+1} & S_{v+2} & \cdots & S_{2v-2} & S_{2v-1} \end{bmatrix} \begin{bmatrix} \Lambda_v \\ \Lambda_{v-1} \\ \Lambda_{v-2} \\ \vdots \\ \Lambda_1 \end{bmatrix} = \begin{bmatrix} -S_{v+1} \\ -S_{v+2} \\ -S_{v+3} \\ \vdots \\ -S_{2v} \end{bmatrix}.$$

This equation can be solved by inverting the matrix if it is nonsingular. We will now prove that the matrix is nonsingular if there are v errors. The first step is to prove that the Vandermonde matrix is nonsingular.

□ **Theorem 7.2.1**   The *Vandermonde matrix*, defined as any matrix of the form

$$\mathbf{A} = \begin{bmatrix} 1 & 1 & \cdots & 1 \\ X_1 & X_2 & \cdots & X_\mu \\ X_1^2 & X_2^2 & \cdots & X_\mu^2 \\ \vdots & \vdots & & \vdots \\ X_1^{\mu-1} & X_2^{\mu-1} & \cdots & X_\mu^{\mu-1} \end{bmatrix},$$

has a nonzero determinant if and only if all of the X_i for $i = 1, \ldots, \mu$ are distinct.

Proof   The converse is obvious because if any two of the X_i are equal, then the matrix has two columns the same, and hence it has determinant zero.

To prove the direct part, use induction. The theorem is true if $\mu = 1$. We will show that if it is true for $\mu - 1$ by $\mu - 1$ Vandermonde matrices, then it is also true for μ by μ Vandermonde matrices. Replace X_1 by the indeterminate x. Then the determinant is a function of x given by

$$D(x) = \det \begin{bmatrix} 1 & x & x^2 & \cdots & x^{\mu-1} \\ 1 & X_2 & X_2^2 & \cdots & X_2^{\mu-1} \\ \vdots & & & & \vdots \\ 1 & X_\mu & X_\mu^2 & \cdots & X_\mu^{\mu-1} \end{bmatrix}.$$

The determinant can be expanded as elements of the first row times the cofactors of these elements of the first row. This will give a polynomial of degree $\mu - 1$ in x. This polynomial can be written

$$D(x) = d_{\mu-1} x^{\mu-1} + \cdots + d_1 x + d_0,$$

which has at most $\mu - 1$ zeros. The coefficient $d_{\mu-1}$ is itself the determinant of a Vandermonde matrix and by the induction hypothesis is nonzero. If for any i, $2 \leqslant i \leqslant \mu$, we set $x = X_i$, then two rows of the matrix are equal, and $D(X_i) = 0$. Thus each such X_i $(i \neq 1)$ is a zero of $D(x)$, and because they are all distinct and there are $\mu - 1$ of them, the polynomial can be easily factored:

$$D(x) = d_{\mu-1} \left[\prod_{i=2}^{\mu} (x - X_i) \right].$$

Therefore the determinant of the original Vandermonde matrix is

$$D(X_1) = d_{\mu-1} \left[\prod_{i=2}^{\mu} (X_1 - X_i) \right].$$

This is nonzero because $d_{\mu-1}$ is nonzero and X_1 is different from each of the remaining X_i. Hence, the determinant of the μ by μ Vandermonde matrix is nonzero, and by induction the theorem is true for all μ. $\square$

Now we are ready to prove the central theorem of the decoding algorithm. The theorem gives a condition that will determine v, the number of errors that actually occurred.

☐ **Theorem 7.2.2**   The matrix of syndromes

$$\mathbf{M} = \begin{bmatrix} S_1 & S_2 & \cdots & S_\mu \\ S_2 & S_3 & \cdots & S_{\mu+1} \\ \vdots & & & \vdots \\ S_\mu & S_{\mu+1} & \cdots & S_{2\mu-1} \end{bmatrix}$$

is nonsingular if μ is equal to v, the number of errors that actually occurred. The matrix is singular if μ is greater than v.

Proof   Let $X_\mu = 0$ for $\mu > v$. Let $\mathbf{A}$ be the Vandermonde matrix

$$\mathbf{A} = \begin{bmatrix} 1 & 1 & \cdots & 1 \\ X_1 & X_2 & \cdots & X_\mu \\ \vdots & \vdots & & \vdots \\ X_1^{\mu-1} & X_2^{\mu-1} & \cdots & X_\mu^{\mu-1} \end{bmatrix}$$

with elements $A_{ij} = X_j^{i-1}$, and let $\mathbf{B}$ be the diagonal matrix

$$\mathbf{B} = \begin{bmatrix} Y_1 X_1 & 0 & \cdots & 0 \\ 0 & Y_2 X_2 & \cdots & 0 \\ \vdots & & & \vdots \\ 0 & 0 & \cdots & Y_\mu X_\mu \end{bmatrix}$$

with elements $B_{ij} = Y_i X_i \delta_{ij}$, where $\delta_{ij} = 1$ if $i = j$ and is otherwise zero.

Then the matrix product $\mathbf{A}\mathbf{B}\mathbf{A}^T$ has elements

$$(\mathbf{A}\mathbf{B}\mathbf{A}^T)_{ij} = \sum_{l=1}^{\mu} X_l^{i-1} \sum_{k=1}^{\mu} Y_l X_l \delta_{lk} X_k^{j-1}$$

$$= \sum_{l=1}^{\mu} X_l^{i-1} Y_l X_l X_l^{j-1}$$

$$= \sum_{l=1}^{\mu} Y_l X_l^{i+j-1},$$

which is the ij element of the matrix $\mathbf{M}$. Therefore $\mathbf{M} = \mathbf{A}\mathbf{B}\mathbf{A}^T$. Hence the determinant of $\mathbf{M}$ satisfies

$$\det(\mathbf{M}) = \det(\mathbf{A}) \det(\mathbf{B}) \det(\mathbf{A}).$$

If μ is greater than v, then $\det(\mathbf{B}) = 0$. Hence, $\det(\mathbf{M}) = 0$, and $\mathbf{M}$ is singular. If μ is equal to v, then $\det(\mathbf{B}) \neq 0$. Further, the Vandermonde matrix $\mathbf{A}$ has a nonzero determinant if the columns are different and nonzero, which is true if μ is equal to v. Hence $\det(\mathbf{M}) \neq 0$. This completes the proof of the theorem. $\square$

The theorem provides the basis of the decoding algorithm. First find the correct value of v as follows. As a trial value, set $v = t$ and compute the determinant of $\mathbf{M}$. If it is nonzero, this is the correct value of v. Otherwise, if the determinant is zero, reduce the trial value of v by 1 and repeat. Continue in this way until a nonzero determinant is obtained. The actual number of errors that occurred is then known. Next, invert $\mathbf{M}$ and compute $\Lambda(x)$. Find the zeros of $\Lambda(x)$ to find the error locations. If the code is binary, the errors are known. Otherwise, return to the equations defining the syndromes.

$$S_1 = Y_1 X_1 + Y_2 X_2 + \cdots + Y_v X_v$$

$$S_2 = Y_1 X_1^2 + Y_2 X_2^2 + \cdots + Y_v X_v^2$$

$$\vdots \qquad\qquad\qquad \vdots$$

$$S_{2t} = Y_1 X_1^{2t} + Y_2 X_2^{2t} + \cdots + Y_v X_v^{2t}.$$

Because the error locations are now known, these are a set of $2t$ linear equations in the v unknown error magnitudes. The first v equations can be solved for the error magnitudes if the determinant of the matrix of coefficients is nonzero. But

$$\det \begin{bmatrix} X_1 & X_2 & \cdots & X_v \\ X_1^2 & X_2^2 & \cdots & X_v^2 \\ \vdots & \vdots & & \vdots \\ X_1^v & X_2^v & \cdots & X_v^v \end{bmatrix} = (X_1 X_2 \ldots X_v) \det \begin{bmatrix} 1 & 1 & \cdots & 1 \\ X_1 & X_2 & \cdots & X_v \\ \vdots & \vdots & & \vdots \\ X_1^{v-1} & X_2^{v-1} & \cdots & X_v^{v-1} \end{bmatrix}$$

By Theorem 7.2.1, the matrix does have a nonzero determinant if v errors occur because $X_1, X_2, \ldots, X_v$ are nonzero and distinct.

The decoding algorithm is summarized in Figure 7.1. Here we have made j_0 arbitrary, although the derivation has treated the special case $j_0 = 1$. The derivation for arbitrary j_0 is the same.

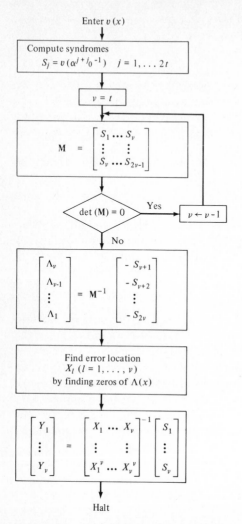

Figure 7.1 The Peterson-Gorenstein-Zierler decoder.

Usually, because there are only a finite number of field elements to check, the simplest way to find the zeros of $\Lambda(x)$ is by trial and error, a process known as a *Chien search*. One simply computes in turn $\Lambda(\alpha^j)$ for each j and checks for zero. A computationally simple way to evaluate the polynomial $\Lambda(x)$ at β is by Horner's rule:

$$\Lambda(\beta) = (\dots (((\Lambda_\nu \beta + \Lambda_{\nu-1})\beta + \Lambda_{\nu-2})\beta + \Lambda_{\nu-3})\beta + \dots + \Lambda_0).$$

Horner's rule needs only ν multiplications and ν additions to compute $\Lambda(\beta)$.

As an example of the decoding procedure, take the BCH (15, 5) triple-error-correcting code with the generator polynomial

$$g(x) = x^{10} + x^8 + x^5 + x^4 + x^2 + x + 1.$$

For the example, we will take the received polynomials to be $v(x) = x^7 + x^2$. Obviously, if three or fewer errors took place, the codeword must be the all-zero word, and $v(x) = e(x)$, but the decoder does not make this observation. We will proceed through the steps of the decoding algorithm. First compute the syndromes using the arithmetic of $GF(16)$:

$$S_1 = \alpha^7 + \alpha^2 = \alpha^{12}$$

$$S_2 = \alpha^{14} + \alpha^4 = \alpha^9$$

$$S_3 = \alpha^{21} + \alpha^6 = 0$$

$$S_4 = \alpha^{28} + \alpha^8 = \alpha^3$$

$$S_5 = \alpha^{35} + \alpha^{10} = \alpha^0$$

$$S_6 = \alpha^{42} + \alpha^{12} = 0.$$

Set $v = 3$. Then

$$\mathbf{M} = \begin{bmatrix} S_1 & S_2 & S_3 \\ S_2 & S_3 & S_4 \\ S_3 & S_4 & S_5 \end{bmatrix} = \begin{bmatrix} \alpha^{12} & \alpha^9 & 0 \\ \alpha^9 & 0 & \alpha^3 \\ 0 & \alpha^3 & 1 \end{bmatrix}.$$

The determinant of $\mathbf{M}$ is zero; hence set $v = 2$. Then

$$\mathbf{M} = \begin{bmatrix} S_1 & S_2 \\ S_2 & S_3 \end{bmatrix} = \begin{bmatrix} \alpha^{12} & \alpha^9 \\ \alpha^9 & 0 \end{bmatrix}.$$

The determinant is not zero; hence two errors occurred. Next,

$$\mathbf{M}^{-1} = \begin{bmatrix} 0 & \alpha^6 \\ \alpha^6 & \alpha^9 \end{bmatrix},$$

and

$$\begin{bmatrix} \Lambda_2 \\ \Lambda_1 \end{bmatrix} = \begin{bmatrix} 0 & \alpha^6 \\ \alpha^6 & \alpha^9 \end{bmatrix} \begin{bmatrix} 0 \\ \alpha^3 \end{bmatrix}$$

$$= \begin{bmatrix} \alpha^9 \\ \alpha^{12} \end{bmatrix}.$$

Hence

$$\Lambda(x) = \alpha^9 x^2 + \alpha^{12} x + 1.$$

By a Chien search, this factors as

$$\Lambda(x) = (\alpha^7 x + 1)(\alpha^2 x + 1) = \alpha^9(x - \alpha^8)(x - \alpha^{13}).$$

The error-locator polynomial $\Lambda(x)$ has zeros at α^8 and α^{13}, and the error locations are at the reciprocal of the zeros. Hence, errors occurred in the second and seventh components. Because the code is binary, the error magnitudes are 1, and $e(x) = x^7 + x^2$.

7.3 REED-SOLOMON CODES

An important and popular subset of the set of BCH codes is the class of Reed-Solomon codes. These are BCH codes in which the blocklength divides the multiplicative order of the symbol alphabet. That is, $m = 1$, and the symbol field $GF(q)$ and the error-locator field $GF(q^m)$ are the same. Usually, we take α as primitive. Then

$$n = q^m - 1 = q - 1.$$

The minimal polynomial over $GF(q)$ of an element β in the same $GF(q)$ is

$$f_\beta(x) = x - \beta.$$

Because the symbol field and the error-locator field are the same field, all minimal polynomials are linear. For a t-error-correcting Reed-Solomon code, $j_0 = 1$ is conventional, and the generator polynomial is

$$g(x) = (x - \alpha)(x - \alpha^2) \dots (x - \alpha^{2t}).$$

This always is a polynomial of degree of $2t$. Hence, a Reed-Solomon code satisfies

$$n - k = 2t.$$

One can just as well choose any j_0 for a Reed-Solomon code. Sometimes one can save circuit components by a clever choice. Then

$$g(x) = (x - \alpha^{j_0})(x - \alpha^{j_0 + 1}) \dots (x - \alpha^{j_0 + 2t - 1}).$$

As an example, we will find $g(x)$ for a $(15, 11)$ $t = 2$ Reed-Solomon code over $GF(16)$. Any j_0 will do. Choose $j_0 = 1$.

$$g(x) = (x - \alpha)(x - \alpha^2)(x - \alpha^3)(x - \alpha^4)$$
$$= x^4 + (z^3 + z^2 + 1)x^3 + (z^3 + z^2)x^2 + z^3 x + (z^2 + z + 1)$$
$$= x^4 + \alpha^{13}x^3 + \alpha^6 x^2 + \alpha^3 x + \alpha^{10},$$

where the field elements of $GF(16)$ are expressed as polynomials in z using Table 7.1. Because $g(x)$ has a degree of 4, $n - k = 4$, and $k = 11$. An information polynomial is a sequence of 11 16-ary (hexadecimal) symbols (equivalent to 44 bits).

As a second example, we will find $g(x)$ for a $(7, 3)$ $t = 2$ Reed-Solomon code over $GF(8)$. Any j_0 will do. Choose $j_0 = 4$.

$$g(x) = (x - \alpha^4)(x - \alpha^5)(x - \alpha^6)(x - \alpha^0)$$
$$= x^4 + (z^2 + 1)x^3 + (z^2 + 1)x^2 + (z + 1)x + z,$$

where the field elements of $GF(8)$ are expressed as polynomials in z. An information polynomial is a sequence of three 8-ary (octal) symbols (equivalent to nine bits). Suppose that

$$i(x) = (z^2 + z)x^2 + x + (z + 1).$$

The nonsystematic codeword is

$$c(x) = i(x)g(x)$$
$$= (\alpha^4 x^2 + x + \alpha^3)(x^4 + \alpha^6 x^3 + \alpha^6 x^2 + \alpha^3 x + \alpha)$$
$$= \alpha^4 x^6 + \alpha x^5 + \alpha^6 x^4 + 0x^3 + 0x^2 + \alpha^5 x + \alpha^4,$$

which is a sequence of seven octal symbols.

The Reed-Solomon codes are optimum in the sense of the Singleton bound.

☐ **Theorem 7.3.1**   A Reed-Solomon code is a maximum-distance code, and the minimum distance is $n - k + 1$.

Proof   Let $d = 2t + 1$ be the designed distance of the code. The minimum distance d^* satisfies

$$d^* \geqslant d = 2t + 1 = n - k + 1$$

because $2t = n - k$ for Reed-Solomon codes. But by the Singleton bound, for any linear code,

$$d^* \leqslant n - k + 1.$$

Hence $d^* = n - k + 1$, and $d^* = d$. ☐

This theorem tells us that for fixed (n, k), no code can have a larger minimum distance than a Reed-Solomon code. This is often a strong justification for using Reed-Solomon codes. It should not be read, however, as saying more than it does. Another code having parameters (n', k') for which no Reed-Solomon code exists is often preferred to any achievable (n, k) Reed-Solomon code. Reed-Solomon codes always have relatively short blocklength as compared to other cyclic codes over the same alphabet.

7.4 SYNTHESIS OF AUTOREGRESSIVE FILTERS

Most of the computations required to decode BCH codes using the algorithm of Section 7.2 centers on the solution of the matrix equation

$$
\begin{bmatrix}
S_1 & S_2 & S_3 & \cdots & S_v \\
S_2 & S_3 & S_4 & \cdots & S_{v+1} \\
S_3 & S_4 & S_5 & \cdots & S_{v+2} \\
\vdots & & & & \vdots \\
S_v & S_{v+1} & S_{v+2} & \cdots & S_{2v-1}
\end{bmatrix}
\begin{bmatrix}
\Lambda_v \\
\Lambda_{v-1} \\
\vdots \\
\Lambda_1
\end{bmatrix}
=
\begin{bmatrix}
-S_{v+1} \\
-S_{v+2} \\
\vdots \\
-S_{2v}
\end{bmatrix}.
$$

For moderate v, the obvious method of solution using matrix inversion is not unreasonable. The number of computations necessary to invert a v by v matrix is proportional to v^3. In many applications, however, one wants to use codes that correct large numbers of errors. In such cases, one wishes for a more efficient method of solution. Berlekamp found such a method. This method relies on the fact that the above matrix equation is not arbitrary in its form; rather, the matrix is highly structured. This structure is used to advantage to obtain the vector Λ by a method that is conceptually more intricate than direct matrix inversion, but computationally much simpler.

We will describe a variation of the algorithm by Massey, who recognized that the best way to derive the algorithm is as a problem in the design of linear-feedback shift registers. Suppose the vector Λ is known. Then the first row of the above matrix equation defines S_{v+1} in terms of $S_1, \ldots, S_v$. The second row defines S_{v+2} in terms of $S_2, \ldots, S_{v+1}$, and so forth. This sequential process is summarized by the equation

$$
S_j = - \sum_{i=1}^{v} \Lambda_i S_{j-i} \qquad j = v+1, \ldots, 2v.
$$

For fixed Λ, this is the equation of an autoregressive filter. It may be implemented as a linear-feedback shift register with taps given by Λ.

Seen in this way, the problem becomes one of designing the linear-feedback shift register shown in Fig. 7.2 that will generate the known sequence of syndromes. Many such shift registers exist, but we wish to find the smallest linear-feedback shift register with this property. This gives the least-weight error pattern that will explain the received data, that is, $\Lambda(x)$ of smallest degree. The polynomial of smallest degree will have degree v, and there is

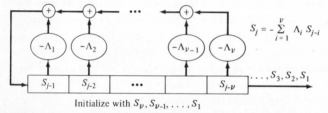

Initialize with $S_v, S_{v-1}, \ldots, S_1$

Figure 7.2 Error locator polynomial as a shift-register circuit.

only one of degree v because the v by v matrix of the original problem is invertible.

Any procedure for designing the autoregressive filter is also a method for solving the matrix equation for the Λ vector. We shall develop such a shift-register design procedure. The procedure applies in any field and does not assume any special properties for the sequence $S_1, S_2, \ldots, S_{2t}$. They need not be syndromes, but if they are the syndromes of a correctable error pattern, the procedure always designs a shift register with the rightmost tap nonzero. For an arbitrary linear-feedback shift register with feedback polynomial $\Lambda(x)$, the length of the shift register might be larger than the degree of $\Lambda(x)$, because some rightmost stages might not be tapped.

To design the required shift register, we must determine two quantities: the shift register length L, and the feedback-connection polynomial $\Lambda(x)$:

$$\Lambda(x) = \Lambda_v x^v + \Lambda_{v-1} x^{v-1} + \cdots + \Lambda_1 x + 1,$$

where $\deg \Lambda(x) \leqslant L$. We denote this pair by $(L, \Lambda(x))$. We must find a feedback shift register of shortest length that will produce the sequence $S_1, \ldots, S_{2t}$ when properly initialized.

The design procedure is inductive. For each r, starting with $r = 1$, we will design a shift register for generating the first r syndromes. Shift register $(L_r, \Lambda^{(r)}(x))$ is a minimum-length shift register for producing $S_1, \ldots, S_r$. This shift register need not be unique. Several choices may exist, but all will have the same length. At the start of iteration r, we will have constructed a list of shift registers

$$(L_1, \Lambda^{(1)}(x)),$$

$$(L_2, \Lambda^{(2)}(x)),$$

$$\vdots$$

$$(L_{r-1}, \Lambda^{(r-1)}(x)).$$

The main trick of the Berlekamp-Massey algorithm is to find a way to compute a new shortest-length shift-register design $(L_r, \Lambda^{(r)}(x))$ that will generate the sequence $S_1, \ldots, S_{r-1}, S_r$. This will be done by using the most recent shift register, and if necessary, modifying the length and the tap weights.

At iteration r, compute the next output of the $(r-1)$th shift register:

$$\hat{S}_r = -\sum_{j=1}^{n-1} \Lambda_j^{(r-1)} S_{r-j}.$$

Many terms in the sum are equal to zero because $n - 1$ is larger than the degree of $\Lambda^{(r-1)}$, and thus the sum could be written as a sum from 1 to deg $\Lambda^{(r-1)}(x)$. The notation is less cumbersome, however, if we write the sum extending to $n - 1$.

Subtract $\hat{S}_r$ from the desired output S_r to get a quantity Δ_r, known as the *rth discrepancy*:

$$\Delta_r = S_r - \hat{S}_r = S_r + \sum_{j=1}^{n-1} \Lambda_j^{(r-1)} S_{r-j}.$$

Equivalently,

$$\Delta_r = \sum_{j=0}^{n-1} \Lambda_j^{(r-1)} S_{r-j}.$$

If Δ_r is zero, then set $(L_r, \Lambda^{(r)}(x)) = (L_{r-1}, \Lambda^{(r-1)}(x))$, and the rth iteration is complete. Otherwise, the shift-register taps are modified as follows:

$$\Lambda^{(r)}(x) = \Lambda^{(r-1)}(x) + A x^l \Lambda^{(m-1)}(x),$$

where A is a field element, l is an integer, and $\Lambda^{(m-1)}(x)$ is one of the shift-register polynomials appearing earlier on the list. Now recompute the discrepancy (call it Δ_r') with this new polynomial:

$$\Delta_r' = \sum_{j=0}^{n-1} \Lambda_j^{(r)} S_{r-j}$$

$$= \sum_{j=0}^{n-1} \Lambda_j^{(r-1)} S_{r-j} + A \sum_{j=0}^{n-1} \Lambda_j^{(m-1)} S_{r-j-l}.$$

We are ready to specify m, l, and A. Choose an m smaller than r for which $\Delta_m \neq 0$, choose $l = r - m$, and choose $A = -\Delta_m^{-1}\Delta_r$. Then

$$\Delta_r' = \Delta_r - \frac{\Delta_r}{\Delta_m} \Delta_m = 0,$$

and thus the new shift register will generate the sequence $S_1, \ldots, S_{r-1}, S_r$. We do not want just any such shift register, however, we want one of smallest length. We still have not specified which m for which $\Delta_m \neq 0$ should be chosen. If we choose m as the most recent iteration at which $L_m > L_{m-1}$, we will get a shortest-length shift register at every iteration, but this last refinement will take some time to develop.

A physical interpretation of the development up to this point is shown in Fig. 7.3. The two shift registers at iteration m and at iteration r are shown in Fig. 7.3(a). Iteration m is chosen such that at iteration m, the shift register $(L_{m-1}, \Lambda^{(m-1)}(x))$ failed to produce syndrome S_m, and the shortest shift register that produced the required syndrome at iteration m was longer than L_{m-1}. We can also suppose that shift register $(L_{r-1}, \Lambda^{(r-1)}(x))$ failed to produce S_r because otherwise, we need not do anything to it.

In Fig. 7.3(b), we show the shift register $(L_{m-1}, \Lambda^{(m-1)}(x))$ made into an auxillary shift register by lengthening it, positioning it, and doctoring its output so that it can compensate for the failure of $(L_{r-1}, \Lambda^{(r-1)}(x))$ to produce S_r. Notice that the auxillary shift register has an extra tap with weight 1 coming from the term $\Lambda_0^{(m-1)}$. During the first $r-1$ iterations, the remaining taps are producing the negative of the term coming from the tap with weight 1, and thus a string of zeros comes from the auxillary register and does not affect the generated syndromes. At the rth iteration, the two terms do not cancel, and a nonzero comes from the auxillary shift register. The coefficient A is selected to adjust this nonzero value so that it can be added to the rth

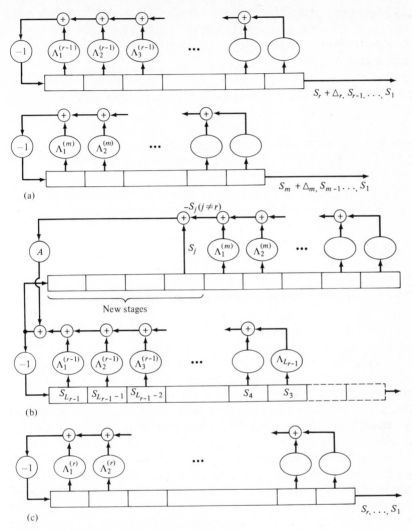

Figure 7.3 Berlekamp-Massey construction.

feedback of the main shift register, thereby producing the required syndrome S_r.

In Fig. 7.3(c), we show the two shift registers of part (b) physically merged into one shift register, which, because of superposition, does not change the behavior. This gives $(L_r, \Lambda^{(r)}(x))$. Sometimes $L_r = L_{r-1}$, sometimes $L_r > L_{r-1}$. When the latter happens, we replace m with r for use in future iterations.

A precise procedure for doing this is given by the following theorem, which asserts that it does produce a shortest shift register with the desired property. The proof is lengthy and occupies the remainder of the section.

☐ **Theorem 7.4.1 (The Berlekamp-Massey Algorithm)** In any field, let $S_1, \ldots, S_{2t}$ be given. Under the initial conditions $\Lambda^{(0)}(x) = 1$, $B^{(0)}(x) = 1$, and $L_0 = 0$, let the following set of recursive equations be used to compute $\Lambda^{(2t)}(x)$:

$$\Delta_r = \sum_{j=0}^{n-1} \Lambda_j^{(r-1)} S_{r-j}$$

$$L_r = \delta_r(r - L_{r-1}) + (1 - \delta_r) L_{r-1}$$

$$\begin{bmatrix} \Lambda^{(r)}(x) \\ B^{(r)}(x) \end{bmatrix} = \begin{bmatrix} 1 & -\Delta_r x \\ \Delta_r^{-1}\delta_r & (1 - \delta_r)x \end{bmatrix} \begin{bmatrix} \Lambda^{(r-1)}(x) \\ B^{(r-1)}(x) \end{bmatrix}$$

$r = 1, \ldots, 2t$ where $\delta_r = 1$ if both $\Delta_r \neq 0$ and $2L_{r-1} \leqslant r - 1$, and otherwise $\delta_r = 0$. Then $\Lambda^{(2t)}(x)$ is the smallest-degree polynomial with the properties that $\Lambda_0^{(2t)} = 1$, and

$$S_r + \sum_{j=1}^{n-1} \Lambda_j^{(2t)} S_{r-j} = 0 \qquad r = L_{2t} + 1, \ldots, 2t. \qquad \square$$

In the theorem, Δ_r may be zero, but only when δ_r is zero. The term $\Delta_r^{-1}\delta_r$ is then understood to be zero.

Notice that the matrix update requires at most $2t$ multiplications per iteration, and that the calculation of Δ_r requires no more than t multiplications per iteration. There are $2t$ iterations, and thus at most $6t^2$ multiplications. Thus using the algorithm will usually be much better than using a matrix inversion, which requires on the order of t^3 operations.

The proof of Theorem 7.4.1 is broken into two lemmas. First, in Lemma 7.4.2, we will find an inequality relationship between L_r and L_{r-1}. Then in Lemma 7.4.3, we will use the algorithm of Theorem 7.4.1 for the construction of a shift register that generates $S_1, \ldots, S_r$ from the shortest-length shift register that generates $S_1, \ldots, S_{r-1}$. We will conclude in Lemma 7.4.3 that the construction of Theorem 7.4.1 is the shortest such shift register because it satisfies the bound of Lemma 7.4.2.

☐ **Lemma 7.4.2** Suppose that $(L_{r-1}, \Lambda^{(r-1)}(x))$ is a linear-feedback shift register of shortest length that generates $S_1, \ldots, S_{r-1}$; $(L_r, \Lambda^{(r)}(x))$ is a linear-feedback shift register of shortest length that generates $S_1, \ldots, S_{r-1}, S_r$; and $\Lambda^{(r)}(x) \neq \Lambda^{(r-1)}(x)$. Then

$$L_r \geqslant \max[L_{r-1}, r - L_{r-1}].$$

Proof The inequality to be proved is a combination of two inequalities:

$$L_r \geqslant L_{r-1} \qquad \text{and} \qquad L_r \geqslant r - L_{r-1}.$$

The first inequality is obvious, because if a linear-feedback shift register generates a sequence, it must also generate any beginning portion of the sequence. The second inequality is obvious if $L_{r-1} \geq r$. Hence, assume $L_{r-1} < r$. Suppose the second inequality is not satisfied, and look for a contradiction. Then $L_r \leq r - 1 - L_{r-1}$. As a temporary shorthand, let $c(x) = \Lambda^{(r-1)}(x)$, let $b(x) = \Lambda^{(r)}(x)$, let $L = L_{r-1}$, and let $L' = L_r$. By assumption, we have: $r \geq L + L' + 1$, and $L' < r$. Next, by the assumptions of the lemma,

$$S_r \neq - \sum_{i=1}^{L} c_i S_{r-i},$$

$$S_j = - \sum_{i=1}^{L} c_i S_{j-i} \qquad j = L+1, \ldots, r-1,$$

and

$$S_j = - \sum_{k=1}^{L'} b_k S_{j-k} \qquad j = L'+1, \ldots, r.$$

Now establish the contradiction. First,

$$S_r = - \sum_{k=1}^{L'} b_k S_{r-k} = \sum_{k=1}^{L'} b_k \sum_{i=1}^{L} c_i S_{r-k-i},$$

where the expansion of S_{r-k} is valid because $r - k$ runs from $r - 1$ down to $r - L'$, which is in the range $L+1, \ldots, r-1$ because of the assumption $r \geq L + L' + 1$. Second,

$$S_r \neq - \sum_{i=1}^{L} c_i S_{r-i} = \sum_{i=1}^{L} c_i \sum_{k=1}^{L'} b_k S_{r-i-k},$$

where the expansion of S_{r-i} is valid because $r - i$ runs from $r - 1$ down to $r - L$, which is in the range $L'+1, \ldots, r-1$ again because of the assumption $r \geq L + L' + 1$. The summations on the right side can be interchanged to agree with the right side of the previous equation. Hence we get a contradiction: $S_r \neq S_r$, and the contradiction proves the lemma. $\square$

If we can find a shift-register design that satisfies the inequality of Lemma 7.4.2 with equality, then it must be of shortest length. The following lemma shows that Theorem 7.4.1 does this.

$\square$ **Lemma 7.4.3** Suppose that $(L_i, \Lambda^{(i)}(x))$ with $i = 1, \ldots, r$ is a sequence of minimum-length linear-feedback shift registers such that $\Lambda^{(i)}(x)$ generates $S_1, \ldots, S_i$. If $\Lambda^{(r)}(x) \neq \Lambda^{(r-1)}(x)$, then

$$L_r = \max [L_{r-1}, r - L_{r-1}],$$

and any shift register that generates $S_1, \ldots, S_r$ and has length equal to the right-hand side is a minimum-length shift register. Theorem 7.4.1 gives such a shift register.

Proof By Lemma 7.4.2, L_r cannot be smaller than the right-hand side. If we can construct any shift register that generates the required sequence and whose length equals the right-hand side, then this must be a minimum-length shift register. The proof is by induction. We give a construction for a shift register satisfying the theorem, assuming that we have iteratively constructed such shift registers for all $k \leqslant r - 1$. For each k, $k = 1, \ldots, r - 1$, let $(L_k, \Lambda^{(k)}(x))$ be the minimum-length shift register that generates $S_1, \ldots, S_k$. Assume for the induction argument that

$$L_k = \max[L_{k-1}, k - L_{k-1}] \qquad k = 1, \ldots, n - 1$$

whenever $\Lambda^{(k)}(x) \neq \Lambda^{(k-1)}(x)$. This is clearly true for $k = 0$ because $L_0 = 0$ and $L_1 = 1$. Let m denote the value k had at the most recent iteration step that required a length change. That is, at the end of iteration $r - 1$, m is that integer such that

$$L_{r-1} = L_m > L_{m-1}.$$

We now have

$$S_j + \sum_{i=1}^{L_{r-1}} \Lambda_i^{(r-1)} S_{j-i} = \sum_{i=0}^{L_{r-1}} \Lambda_i^{(r-1)} S_{j-i} = \begin{cases} 0 & j = L_{r-1}, \ldots, r-1 \\ \Delta_r & j = r. \end{cases}$$

If $\Delta_r = 0$, then the shift register $(L_{r-1}, \Lambda^{(r-1)}(x))$ also generates the first r digits, and thus

$$L_r = L_{r-1} \qquad \text{and} \qquad \Lambda^{(r)}(x) = \Lambda^{(r-1)}(x).$$

If $\Delta_r \neq 0$, then a new shift register must be designed. Recall that a change in shift-register length occurred at $k = m$. Hence

$$S_j + \sum_{i=1}^{L_{m-1}} \Lambda_i^{(m-1)} S_{j-i} = \begin{cases} 0 & j = L_{m-1}, \ldots, m-1 \\ \Delta_m \neq 0 & j = m, \end{cases}$$

and by the induction hypothesis,

$$L_{r-1} = L_m = \max[L_{m-1}, m - L_{m-1}]$$

$$= m - L_{m-1}$$

because $L_m > L_{m-1}$. Now choose the new polynomial

$$\Lambda^{(r)}(x) = \Lambda^{(r-1)}(x) - \Delta_r \Delta_m^{-1} x^{r-m} \Lambda^{(m-1)}(x),$$

and let $L_r = \deg \Lambda^{(r)}(x)$. Then, because $\deg \Lambda^{(r-1)}(x) \leqslant L_{r-1}$ and $\deg[x^{r-m} \Lambda^{(m-1)}(x)] \leqslant r - m + L_{m-1}$,

$$L_r \leqslant \max[L_{r-1}, r - m + L_{m-1}] \leqslant \max[L_{r-1}, r - L_{r-1}].$$

Hence recalling Lemma 7.4.2, if $\Lambda^{(r)}(x)$ generates $S_1, \ldots, S_r$, then $L_r = \max[L_{r-1}, r - L_{r-1}]$. It only remains to prove that the shift register $(L_r, \Lambda^{(r)}(x))$ generates the required sequence. This is done by direct computation of the difference between S_j and the shift-register feedback:

$$S_j - \left(-\sum_{i=1}^{L_r} \Lambda_i^{(r)} S_{j-i} \right) = S_j + \sum_{i=1}^{L_{r-1}} \Lambda_i^{(r-1)} S_{j-i}$$

$$- \Delta_r \Delta_m^{-1} \left[S_{j-r+m} + \sum_{i=1}^{L_{m-1}} \Lambda_i^{(m-1)} S_{j-r+m-i} \right]$$

$$= \begin{cases} 0 & j = L_r, L_r + 1, \ldots, r-1 \\ \Delta_r - \Delta_r \Delta_m^{-1} \Delta_m = 0 & j = r \end{cases}$$

Hence the shift register $(L_r, \Lambda^{(r)}(x)$ generates $S_1, \ldots, S_r$. In particular, $(L_{2t}, \Lambda^{(2t)}(x))$ generates $S_1, \ldots, S_{2t}$, and the lemma is proved. $\square$

7.5 FAST DECODING OF BCH CODES

Understanding the Peterson-Gorenstein-Zierler decoder is the best way to understand the decoding of BCH codes. But when building a decoder, one gives up the conceptually clear in favor of the computationally efficient. The Peterson-Gorenstein-Zierler decoder, as described in Section 7.2, requires that two t by t matrices be inverted. Although matrix inverses in a finite field do not suffer from problems of round-off error, the computational work may still be excessive, especially for large t. Both of these matrix inversions can be circumvented. The first matrix inversion is in the computation of the error-locator polynomial; it can be circumvented by using the Berlekamp-Massey algorithm. The second matrix inversion is in the computation of the error magnitudes; it can be circumvented by a procedure known as the Forney algorithm. We begin this section with a derivation of the Forney algorithm; then we return to the Berlekamp-Massey algorithm.

The Forney algorithm is derived starting with the error-locator polynomial

$$\Lambda(x) = \Lambda_v x^v + \Lambda_{v-1} x^{v-1} + \cdots + \Lambda_1 x + 1,$$

which was defined to have zeros at X_l^{-1} for $l = 1, \ldots, v$:

$$\Lambda(x) = \prod_{l=1}^{v} (1 - xX_l).$$

Define the syndrome polynomial

$$S(x) = \sum_{j=1}^{2t} S_j x^j = \sum_{j=1}^{2t} \sum_{i=1}^{v} Y_i X_i^j x^j,$$

and define the error-evaluator polynomial $\Omega(x)$ in terms of these known polynomials:

$$\Omega(x) = S(x)\Lambda(x) \qquad (\text{mod } x^{2t}).$$

The error-evaluator polynomial will play a minor role from time to time. It can be related to the error-locations and error magnitudes as follows.

☐ **Theorem 7.5.1**   The error-evaluator polynomial can be written

$$\Omega(x) = x \sum_{i=1}^{v} Y_i X_i \prod_{l \neq i} (1 - X_l x).$$

Proof   By the definition of the terms in $\Omega(x)$,

$$\Omega(x) = \left[\sum_{j=1}^{2t} \sum_{i=1}^{v} Y_i X_i^j x^j \right] \left[\prod_{l=1}^{v} (1 - X_l x) \right] \quad (\text{mod } x^{2t})$$

$$= \sum_{i=1}^{v} Y_i X_i x \left[(1 - X_i x) \sum_{j=1}^{2t} (X_i x)^{j-1} \right] \prod_{l \neq i} (1 - X_l x) \quad (\text{mod } x^{2t}).$$

The bracketted term is a factorization of $(1 - X_i^{2t} x^{2t})$. Therefore

$$\Omega(x) = \sum_{i=1}^{v} Y_i X_i x (1 - X_i^{2t} x^{2t}) \prod_{l \neq i} (1 - X_l x) \quad (\text{mod } x^{2t}).$$

Because this is modulo x^{2t}, it is the same as the expression to be proved. ☐

Now we are ready to give an expression for the error magnitudes that is much simpler than matrix inversion.

☐ **Theorem 7.5.2 (The Forney Algorithm)**   The error magnitudes are given by

$$Y_l = \frac{\Omega(X_l^{-1})}{\prod_{j \neq l} (1 - X_j X_l^{-1})} = - \frac{\Omega(X_l^{-1})}{X_l^{-1} \Lambda'(X_l^{-1})}.$$

Proof   Evaluate Theorem 7.5.1 at X_l^{-1} to get

$$\Omega(X_l^{-1}) = Y_l \prod_{j \neq l} (1 - X_j X_l^{-1})$$

which yields the first half of the theorem.
On the other hand, the derivative of $\Lambda(x)$ is

$$\Lambda'(x) = - \sum_{i=1}^{v} X_i \prod_{j \neq i} (1 - x X_j).$$

Hence

$$\Lambda'(X_l^{-1}) = - X_l \prod_{j \neq l} (1 - X_j X_l^{-1}),$$

from which the theorem follows. ☐

The Forney algorithm is a considerable improvement over matrix inversion but does require division. In Chapter 9, we will give alternative solutions that do not involve division.

Now we turn to the calculation of the error-locator polynomial using the Berlekamp-Massey algorithm of Theorem 7.4.1. Massey's view of the problem

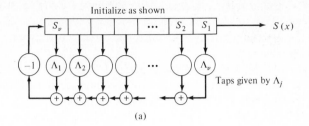

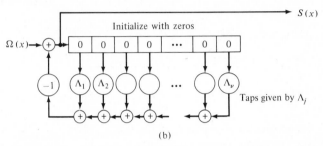

Figure 7.4 Generation of error spectrum. (a) Massey viewpoint. (b) Berlekamp viewpoint.

is shown in Fig. 7.4(a). Given S_j for $j = 1, \ldots, 2t$, find the smallest length vector Λ that satisfies the t equations

$$S_j + \sum_{k=1}^{t} S_{j-k}\Lambda_k = 0 \qquad j = t+1, \ldots, 2t.$$

That is, one is asked to solve a convolution given $2t$ components of **S**, and the a priori knowledge that $\Lambda_j = 0$ for j greater than t. The vector Λ that satisfies this equation gives the coefficients of the error-locator polynomial,

$$\Lambda(x) = \prod_{l=1}^{v} (1 - xX_l),$$

and X_l for $l = 1, \ldots, v$ are the error locations. The error-evaluator polynomial is not computed by the algorithm but can be computed later from $\Lambda(x)$ and $S(x)$ from the definition $\Omega(x) = S(x)\Lambda(x) \pmod{x^{2t}}$.

Berlekamp's formulation of the problem, shown in Fig. 7.4(b), portrays the error-evaluator polynomial in a more central role. This formulation asks for the vectors Λ and Ω, both zero for $t < k \leqslant n$, that satisfy the $2t$ equations

$$S_j + \sum_{k=1}^{t} S_{j-k}\Lambda_k = \Omega_j \qquad j = 1, \ldots, 2t,$$

where $S_j = 0$ for $j \leqslant 0$. Notice that j now runs over $2t$ values. The solution is described by two polynomials: the error-locator polynomial and the error-evaluator polynomial.

The two forms of the problem are equivalent. We have treated Massey's form of the problem. If desired, the Berlekamp-Massey algorithm can be modified to solve the Berlekamp form of the problem directly by introducing both $\Lambda^{(r)}(x)$ and $\Omega^{(r)}(x)$ as iterates.

Figure 7.5 gives the Berlekamp-Massey algorithm graphically in the form of a flowchart. As shown, the algorithm will compute the error-locator polynomial from the $2t$ syndromes $S_1, \ldots, S_{2t}$. If the code has some j_0 other than 1, simply define $S_j = V_{j+j_0-1}$ for $j = 1, \ldots, 2t$. These syndromes are

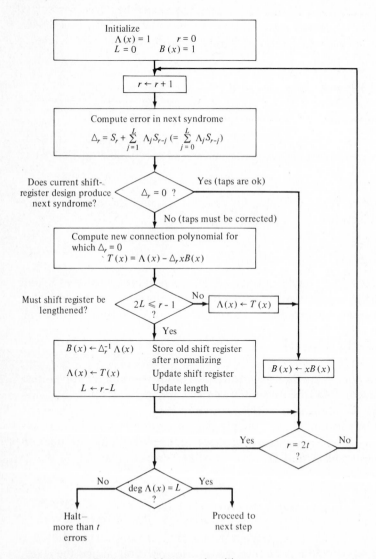

Figure 7.5 Berlekamp-Massey algorithm.

used just as before. There is no need to rederive the algorithm; this is merely a matter of properly labeling the internal variables of the algorithm.

The algorithm and its proof might be better understood by working through the details of Fig. 7.5 for specific examples. Table 7.3 gives the calculation for a (15, 9) Reed-Solomon triple-error-correcting code. These calculations should be checked by tracing through the six iterations in Fig. 7.5. Table 7.4 gives similar calculations for a (15, 5) BCH triple-error-correcting code.

The inner workings of the Berlekamp-Massey algorithm can appear somewhat mysterious. This difficulty might be softened by a few comments. At some iterations, say the rth, there may be more than one linear-feedback shift register of the minimum length that generate the required symbols.

Table 7.3   Sample Berlekamp-Massey computation

Reed-Solomon $(15, 9)$ $t = 3$ code:

$$g(x) = (x + \alpha)(x + \alpha^2)(x + \alpha^3)(x + \alpha^4)(x + \alpha^5)(x + \alpha^6)$$

$$= x^6 + \alpha^{10}x^5 + \alpha^{14}x^4 + \alpha^4 x^3 + \alpha^6 x^2 + \alpha^9 x + \alpha^6$$

$$i(x) = 0$$

$$v(x) = \alpha x^7 + \alpha^5 x^5 + \alpha^{11}x^2 = e(x)$$

$$S_1 = \alpha \alpha^7 \quad + \alpha^5 \alpha^5 \quad + \alpha^{11}\alpha^2 \quad = \alpha^{12}$$

$$S_2 = \alpha \alpha^{14} + \alpha^5 \alpha^{10} + \alpha^{11}\alpha^4 \quad = 1$$

$$S_3 = \alpha \alpha^{21} + \alpha^5 \alpha^{15} + \alpha^{11}\alpha^6 \quad = \alpha^{14}$$

$$S_4 = \alpha \alpha^{28} + \alpha^5 \alpha^{20} + \alpha^{11}\alpha^8 \quad = \alpha^{13}$$

$$S_5 = \alpha \alpha^{35} + \alpha^5 \alpha^{25} + \alpha^{11}\alpha^{10} = 1$$

$$S_6 = \alpha \alpha^{42} + \alpha^5 \alpha^{30} + \alpha^{11}\alpha^{12} = \alpha^{11}$$

r	Δ_r	$T(x)$	$B(x)$	$\Lambda(x)$	L
0			1	1	0
1	α^{12}	$1 + \alpha^{12}x$	α^3	$1 + \alpha^{12}x$	1
2	α^7	$1 + \alpha^3 x$	$\alpha^3 x$	$1 + \alpha^3 x$	1
3	1	$1 + \alpha^3 x + \alpha^3 x^2$	$1 + \alpha^3 x$	$1 + \alpha^3 x + \alpha^3 x^2$	2
4	1	$1 + \alpha^{14}x$	$x + \alpha^3 x^2$	$1 + \alpha^{14}x$	2
5	α^{11}	$1 + \alpha^{14}x + \alpha^{11}x^2 + \alpha^{14}x^3$	$\alpha^4 + \alpha^3 x$	$1 + \alpha^{14}x + \alpha^{11}x^2 + \alpha^{14}x^3$	3
6	0	$1 + \alpha^{14}x + \alpha^{11}x^2 + \alpha^{14}x^3$	$\alpha^4 x + \alpha^3 x^2$	$1 + \alpha^{14}x + \alpha^{11}x^2 + \alpha^{14}x^3$	3

$$\Lambda(x) = 1 + \alpha^{14}x + \alpha^{11}x^2 + \alpha^{14}x^3 = (1 + \alpha^7 x)(1 + \alpha^5 x)(1 + \alpha^2 x)$$

Table 7.4   Sample Berlekamp-Massey computation

BCH $(15, 5)$ $t = 3$ code:

$$g(x) = x^{10} + x^8 + x^5 + x^4 + x^2 + x + 1$$

$$i(x) = 0$$

$$v(x) = x^7 + x^5 + x^2 = e(x)$$

$$S_1 = \alpha^7 + \alpha^5 + \alpha^2 = \alpha^{14}$$

$$S_2 = \alpha^{14} + \alpha^{10} + \alpha^4 = \alpha^{13}$$

$$S_3 = \alpha^{21} + \alpha^{15} + \alpha^6 = 1$$

$$S_4 = \alpha^{28} + \alpha^{20} + \alpha^8 = \alpha^{11}$$

$$S_5 = \alpha^{35} + \alpha^{25} + \alpha^{10} = \alpha^5$$

$$S_6 = \alpha^{42} + \alpha^{30} + \alpha^{12} = 1$$

r	Δ_r	$T(x)$	$B(x)$	$\Lambda(x)$	L
0		1	1		0
1	α^{14}	$1 + \alpha^{14}x$	α	$1 + \alpha^{14}x$	1
2	0	$1 + \alpha^{14}x$	αx	$1 + \alpha^{14}x$	1
3	α^{11}	$1 + \alpha^{14}x + \alpha^{12}x^2$	$\alpha^4 + \alpha^3 x$	$1 + \alpha^{14}x + \alpha^{12}x^2$	2
4	0	$1 + \alpha^{14}x + \alpha^{12}x^2$	$\alpha^4 x + \alpha^3 x^2$	$1 + \alpha^{14}x + \alpha^{12}x^2$	2
5	α^{11}	$1 + \alpha^{14}x + \alpha^{11}x^2 + \alpha^{14}x^3$	$\alpha^4 + \alpha^3 x + \alpha x^2$	$1 + \alpha^{14}x + \alpha^{11}x^2 + \alpha^{14}x^3$	3
6	0	$1 + \alpha^{14}x + \alpha^{11}x^2 + \alpha^{14}x^3$	$\alpha^4 x + \alpha^3 x^2 + \alpha x^3$	$1 + \alpha^{14}x + \alpha^{11}x^2 + \alpha^{14}x^3$	3

$$\Lambda(x) = 1 + \alpha^{14}x + \alpha^{11}x^2 + \alpha^{14}x^3 = (1 + \alpha^7 x)(1 + \alpha^5 x)(1 + \alpha^2 x)$$

These all produce the same required sequence of r syndromes but differ in the future syndromes, which are not required of the rth iteration. During later iterations, whenever possible, another of the linear-feedback shift registers of this length is selected to produce the next required syndrome. If none such exists, then the shift register is lengthened. The test to see if lengthening is required, however, does not involve the next syndrome other than to determine that $\Delta_{r+1} \neq 0$. Hence, whenever one alternative shift register is available, then there are at least as many alternative shift registers as one less than the number of values that the $(r + 1)$th syndrome can assume.

The algorithm can be programmed on a general-purpose computer or on a special-purpose computer designed for Galois field computations. If very high decoding speeds are required, one can build special hardware circuits, possibly using shift registers, to implement the algorithm directly.

A shift-register implementation is outlined in Fig. 7.6. Registers are provided for the three polynomials $S(x)$, $\Lambda(x)$, and $B(x)$, and the length of each register is large enough to hold the largest degree of its polynomial, and possibly a little larger. Shorter polynomials are stored simply by filling out the register with zeros. The $S(x)$ and $B(x)$ registers are each one stage longer than needed to store the largest polynomial; notice the extra symbol in the syndrome register. This, and the number of clocks applied to each shift register during an iteration, are set up so that the polynomials will precess one position during each iteration. This supplies the multiplications of $B(x)$ by x and also offsets the index of S_j by r to provide S_{j-r}, which appears in the expression for Δ_r. To see this, refer to Fig. 7.6; the syndrome register is shown as it is initialized. During each iteration, it will be shifted to the right by one symbol so that it will be timed properly for multiplication with Λ. During one iteration, the Λ register is cycled twice, first to compute Δ, then to be updated.

In Fig. 7.7, we show all of the computations involved in a decoder that uses the Berlekamp-Massey algorithm and the Forney algorithm. This decoder will produce the correct error-locator polynomial as long as at most t errors occur. If more than t errors occur, the algorithm will fail, either by

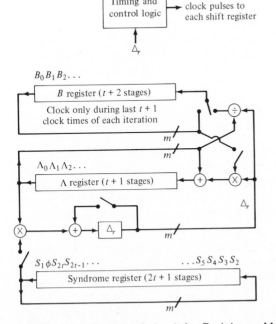

Figure 7.6 Outline of circuit for Berlekamp-Massey algorithm.
Notes: 2t iterations required. 2(t + 1) clocks per iterations. All data paths are *m* bits wide.

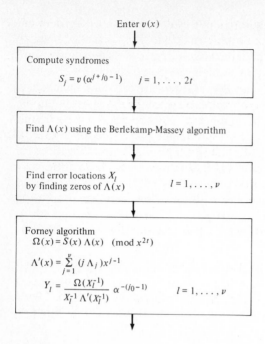

Figure 7.7 Fast decoding of BCH codes.

producing a polynomial that does not fit the requirements of an error-locator polynomial or by producing a legitimate, but incorrect, error-locator polynomial. We can recognize when the first case occurs, and thus the decoder can flag the message as uncorrectable. The tests that can be used to flag an uncorrectable error pattern are the following:

Number of distinct zeros of $\Lambda(x)$ in $GF(q^m)$ different from L.
Error symbols not in the symbol field.

The error-locator polynomial is tested first. If the error-locator polynomial is legitimate, the decoder proceeds to compute the error polynomial. If the symbol field is smaller than the error-locator field, it is possible that the decoder will find some error symbols outside of the symbol field. Such a symbol could not come through the channel, and hence this indicates a pattern of more than t errors has occurred.

In Section 9.6 we will discuss ways in which to decode BCH codes for some of the patterns of more than t errors. To end this section we will discuss the opposite situation—decoders that intentionally stop short of the designed distance. In practice, such decoders are used to greatly reduce the probability of decoding error, but the penalty is a greater probability of decoding failure.

To reduce the chance of a false decoding, a decoder may be designed to correct only up to t errors where $2t + 1$ is strictly smaller than d^* (this must always happen if d^* is even). The decoder will then be sure to detect an un-correctable error pattern if v, the number of errors that actually occur, satisfies

$$t + v < d^*,$$

because at least $d^* - t$ errors are needed to move any codeword into an incorrect decoding sphere.

The Berlekamp-Massey algorithm nicely fits into such a decoder. The procedure is to make $2t$ passes through the algorithm to generate $\Lambda(x)$. An additional $\tau - t$ iterations are then made to check if the discrepancy Δ_r is zero for each of these additional iterations where τ equals $d^* - 1 - t$. If Δ_n is nonzero for any of these iterations, the received word is flagged as having more than t errors.

The following theorem provides the justification for this procedure.

☐ **Theorem 7.5.3**   Given S_j for $j = 1, \ldots, t + \tau$, where $\tau > t$, and that at most τ errors occur, let $(L_{2t}, \Lambda^{(2t)}(x))$ describe a linear-feedback shift register that will produce S_j for $j = 1, \ldots, 2t$, and let

$$\Delta_r = \sum_{j=0}^{n-1} \Lambda_j^{(2t)} S_{r-j}.$$

Suppose that Δ_r equals zero for $r = 2t + 1, \ldots, \tau$ and $L_{2t} \leqslant t$. Then at most t errors have occurred, and $\Lambda^{(2t)}(x)$ is the correct error-locator polynomial.

Proof   We are given syndromes S_j for $j = 1, \ldots, t + \tau$. If we had $\tau - t$ more syndromes, S_j for $j = t + \tau + 1, \ldots, 2\tau$, then we could correct τ errors; that is, we could correct every error pattern assumed to occur. Suppose we are given these extra syndromes by a genie or an imaginary side channel. Then by the Berlekamp-Massey algorithm, we could compute an error-locator polynomial whose degree equals the number of errors. But at iteration $2t$, $L_{2t} \leqslant t$, and by assumption Δ_r equals zero for $r = 2t + 1, \ldots, t + \tau$, and thus L is not updated before iteration $t + \tau + 1$. Hence, by the rule for updating L,

$$L_{2\tau} \geqslant (t + \tau + 1) - L_{2t}$$
$$\geqslant (t + \tau + 1) - t = \tau + 1,$$

contrary to the assumption that there are at most τ errors. ☐

7.6 DECODING OF BINARY BCH CODES

The theory developed in this chapter holds for codes over any finite field. When the field is $GF(2)$, however, one can make some additional simplifica-tions. An obvious simplification is that it only is necessary to find the error location; the error magnitude is always one (but the decoder might compute the error magnitude as a check).

Further simplification is less obvious, but a clue suggesting a possibility occurs in the example of Table 7.4. Notice that Δ_r is always zero on even-numbered iterations. If this is always the case for binary codes, then even-numbered iterations can be skipped.

We shall prove in this section that this is so. The proof is based on the fact that over $GF(2)$ the even-numbered syndromes are easily determined from the odd-numbered syndromes by the formula

$$S_{2j} = \sum_{j=1}^{n} v(\alpha^{2j}) = \left[\sum_{j=1}^{n} v(\alpha^j) \right]^2 = S_j^2,$$

as follows from Theorem 5.3.3. Let us calculate algebraic expressions for the coefficients of $\Lambda^{(r)}(x)$ for the first several values of r. Tracing through the algorithm of Fig. 7.5 and using the fact that $S_4 = S_2^2 = S_1^4$ for all binary codes gives

$\Delta_1 = S_1$ $\qquad\qquad\qquad\qquad \Lambda^{(1)}(x) = S_1 x + 1$

$\Delta_2 = S_2 + S_1^2 = 0$ $\qquad\qquad\qquad \Lambda^{(2)}(x) = S_1 x + 1$

$\Delta_3 = S_3 + S_1 S_2$ $\qquad\qquad\qquad \Lambda^{(3)}(x) = (S_1^{-1} S_3 + S_2) x^2 + S_1 x + 1.$

$\Delta_4 = S_4 + S_1 S_3 + S_1^{-1} S_2 S_3 + S_2^2 = 0$

For any binary BCH code, this shows that Δ_2 and Δ_4 are always zero, but it is impractical to continue indefinitely in this explicit way to find other even-numbered syndromes. We will formulate instead a general argument to show that $\Delta_r = 0$ for all even r.

☐ **Theorem 7.6.1** In $GF(2)$, for any linear-feedback shift register $\Lambda(x)$ and any sequence $S_1, S_2, \ldots, S_{2v-1}$ satisfying $S_{2j} = S_j^2$ for $2j \leqslant 2v - 1$, suppose that

$$S_j = -\sum_{i=1}^{n-1} \Lambda_i S_{j-i} \qquad j = v, \ldots, 2v - 1.$$

If the next member of the sequence is given by

$$S_{2v} = -\sum_{i=1}^{n-1} \Lambda_i S_{2v-i},$$

then

$$S_{2v} = S_v^2.$$

Proof The proof consists of giving identical expressions for S_v^2 and S_{2v}. First, we have

$$S_v^2 = \left(\sum_{i=1}^{n-1} \Lambda_i S_{v-i} \right)^2 = \sum_{i=1}^{n-1} \Lambda_i^2 S_{v-1}^2 = \sum_{i=1}^{n-1} \Lambda_i^2 S_{2v-2i},$$

and also

$$S_{2v} = \sum_{k=1}^{n-1} \Lambda_k S_{2v-k} = \sum_{k=1}^{n-1} \sum_{i=1}^{n-1} \Lambda_k \Lambda_i S_{2v-k-i}.$$

By symmetry, every term in the double sum with $i \neq k$ appears twice, and in $GF(2)$ the two terms add to zero. Hence, only the diagonal terms with $i = k$ contribute:

$$S_{2v} = \sum_{i=1}^{n-1} \Lambda_i^2 S_{2v-2i},$$

which agrees with the expression for S_v^2 and thus proves the theorem. $\square$

Thus by induction, Δ_r is zero for even r, and we can analytically combine two iterations to give for odd r:

$$\Lambda^{(r)}(x) = \Lambda^{(r-2)}(x) - \Delta_r x^2 B^{(r-2)}(x),$$
$$B^{(r)}(x) = \delta_r \Delta_r^{-1} \Lambda^{(r-2)}(x) + (1 - \delta_r) x^2 B^{(r-2)}(x).$$

Using these formulas, iterations with r even can be skipped. This gives a faster decoder for binary codes. Notice that this improvement can be used even though the error pattern might contain more than t errors, because only the conjugacy relations of the syndromes were used in the proof of the theorem; nothing was assumed about the binary error pattern. Therefore subsequent tests for more than t errors are still valid.

7.7 DECODING WITH THE EUCLIDEAN ALGORITHM

The Euclidean algorithm can be used to develop alternative decoders to those we have discussed already. These decoders are a little easier to understand but have the reputation of being somewhat less efficient in practice. This latter observation, however, probably depends strongly on the application.

In Chapter 4 we gave the Euclidean algorithm as a recursive procedure for calculating the greatest common divisor of two polynomials. In a slightly expanded version the algorithm will also produce the polynomials $a(x)$ and $b(x)$ satisfying

$$GCD[s(x), t(x)] = a(x)s(x) + b(x)t(x).$$

For any polynomials $s(x)$ and $t(x)$, we repeat the algorithm in a convenient matrix form using the notation $s(x) = \left\lfloor \dfrac{s(x)}{t(x)} \right\rfloor t(x) + r(x)$ to represent the division algorithm.

□ **Theorem 7.7.1. (Euclidean Algorithm for Polynomials)** Given two polynomials $s(x)$ and $t(x)$ with $\deg s(x) \geq \deg t(x)$, let $s^{(0)}(x) = s(x)$ and $t^{(0)}(x) = t(x)$, and let $\mathbf{A}^{(0)}(x) = \begin{bmatrix} 1 & 0 \\ 0 & 1 \end{bmatrix}$. The following recursive equations,

$$Q^{(r)}(x) = \left\lfloor \frac{s^{(r)}(x)}{t^{(r)}(x)} \right\rfloor$$

$$\mathbf{A}^{(r+1)}(x) = \begin{bmatrix} 0 & 1 \\ 1 & -Q^{(r)}(x) \end{bmatrix} \mathbf{A}^{(r)}(x)$$

$$\begin{bmatrix} s^{(r+1)}(x) \\ t^{(r+1)}(x) \end{bmatrix} = \begin{bmatrix} 0 & 1 \\ 1 & -Q^{(r)}(x) \end{bmatrix} \begin{bmatrix} s^{(r)}(x) \\ t^{(r)}(x) \end{bmatrix} = \mathbf{A}^{(r+1)}(x) \begin{bmatrix} s(x) \\ t(x) \end{bmatrix},$$

satisfy

$$s^{(R)}(x) = \mathrm{GCD}[s(x), t(x)],$$

and for some scalar γ,

$$\gamma \mathrm{GCD}[s(x), t(x)] = A_{11}^{(R)}(x)s(x) + A_{12}^{(R)}(x)t(x)$$

where R is that r for which $t^{(R)}(x) = 0$.

Proof Because deg $t^{(r+1)}(x) <$ deg $t^{(r)}(x)$, eventually $t^{(R)}(x) = 0$ for some R, and thus the termination is well defined. Therefore,

$$\begin{bmatrix} s^{(R)}(x) \\ 0 \end{bmatrix} = \left\{ \prod_{r=R-1}^{0} \begin{bmatrix} 0 & 1 \\ 1 & -Q^{(r)}(x) \end{bmatrix} \right\} \begin{bmatrix} s(x) \\ t(x) \end{bmatrix},$$

and thus any divisor of both $s(x)$ and $t(x)$ divides $s^{(R)}(x)$.

The following matrix inverse is readily verified:

$$\begin{bmatrix} 0 & 1 \\ 1 & -Q^{(r)}(x) \end{bmatrix}^{-1} = \begin{bmatrix} Q^{(r)}(x) & 1 \\ 1 & 0 \end{bmatrix}.$$

Therefore

$$\begin{bmatrix} s(x) \\ t(x) \end{bmatrix} = \left\{ \prod_{r=0}^{R-1} \begin{bmatrix} Q^{(r)}(x) & 1 \\ 1 & 0 \end{bmatrix} \right\} \begin{bmatrix} s^{(R)}(x) \\ 0 \end{bmatrix},$$

and thus $s^{(R)}(x)$ must divide both $s(x)$ and $t(x)$ and hence divides $\mathrm{GCD}[s(x), t(x)]$. Hence, $\mathrm{GCD}[s(x), t(x)]$ divides $s^{(R)}(x)$ and is divisible by $s^{(R)}(x)$. Thus

$$s^{(R)}(x) = \gamma \mathrm{GCD}[s(x), t(x)].$$

Further,

$$\begin{bmatrix} s^{(R)}(x) \\ 0 \end{bmatrix} = \mathbf{A}^{(R)}(x) \begin{bmatrix} s(x) \\ t(x) \end{bmatrix},$$

and thus

$$s^{(R)}(x) = A_{11}^{(R)}(x)s(x) + A_{12}^{(R)}(x)t(x).$$

This proves the last part of the theorem. $\square$

In Theorem 7.7.1, we found a use for the matrix elements $A_{11}^{(R)}(x)$ and $A_{12}^{(R)}(x)$. The other two elements also have a direct interpretation. We will need the inverse of the matrix $\mathbf{A}^{(r)}(x)$. Recall that

$$\mathbf{A}^{(r)}(x) = \prod_{l=r-1}^{0} \begin{bmatrix} 0 & 1 \\ 1 & -Q^{(l)}(x) \end{bmatrix}.$$

From this it is clear that the determinant of $\mathbf{A}^{(r)}(x)$ is $(-1)^r$. The inverse is

$$\begin{bmatrix} A_{11}^{(r)}(x) & A_{12}^{(r)}(x) \\ A_{21}^{(r)}(x) & A_{22}^{(r)}(x) \end{bmatrix}^{-1} = (-1)^r \begin{bmatrix} A_{22}^{(r)}(x) & -A_{12}^{(r)}(x) \\ -A_{21}^{(r)}(x) & A_{11}^{(r)}(x) \end{bmatrix}.$$

☐ **Corollary 7.7.2**   The $A_{21}^{(R)}(x)$ and $A_{22}^{(R)}(x)$ produced by the Euclidean algorithm satisfy

$$s(x) = (-1)^R A_{22}^{(R)}(x)\gamma\mathrm{GCD}[s(x), t(x)],$$

$$t(x) = -(-1)^R A_{21}^{(R)}(x)\gamma\mathrm{GCD}[s(x), t(x)].$$

Proof   Using the above expression for the inverse gives

$$\begin{bmatrix} s(x) \\ t(x) \end{bmatrix} = (-1)^R \begin{bmatrix} A_{22}^{(R)}(x) & -A_{12}^{(R)}(x) \\ -A_{21}^{(R)}(x) & A_{11}^{(R)}(x) \end{bmatrix} \begin{bmatrix} s^{(R)}(x) \\ 0 \end{bmatrix},$$

from which the corollary follows. ☐

We will describe two methods of using the Euclidean algorithm for decoding that are quite different from each other, one method here and one in Section 9.1.

First recall that the syndrome polynomial, the error-locator polynomial, and the error-evaluator polynomial are related by the formula

$$\Omega(x) = S(x)\Lambda(x) \qquad (\mathrm{mod}\ x^{2t})$$

and the conditions that $\deg \Lambda(x) \leqslant t$ and $\deg \Omega(x) \leqslant t-1$. Let us look to the proof of the Euclidean algorithm to see how this equation can be solved for $\Lambda(x)$ and $\Omega(x)$. From this proof, it is easy to see that

$$\begin{bmatrix} s^{(r)}(x) \\ t^{(r)}(x) \end{bmatrix} = \begin{bmatrix} A_{11}^{(r)}(x) & A_{12}^{(r)}(x) \\ A_{21}^{(r)}(x) & A_{22}^{(r)}(x) \end{bmatrix} \begin{bmatrix} s(x) \\ t(x) \end{bmatrix},$$

and thus

$$t^{(r)}(x) = t(x)A_{22}^{(r)}(x) \qquad (\mathrm{mod}\ s(x)),$$

which is the form of the equation being solved if we take $t(x) = S(x)$ and $s(x) = x^{2t}$. Such an equation holds for each r. To solve the problem, we need to find an r for which $\deg A_{22}^{(r)}(x) \leqslant t$ and $\deg t^{(r)}(x) \leqslant t-1$, if such an r exists. We will satisfy the requirements by choosing r' as the value of r satisfying

$$\deg t^{(r-1)}(x) \geqslant t, \qquad \text{and} \qquad \deg t^{(r)}(x) \leqslant t-1.$$

This defines a unique value r' because $\deg t^{(0)}(x) = 2t$, and the degree of $t^{(r)}(x)$ is strictly decreasing as r is increasing.

Hence by the definition of r', we have that

$$\deg t^{(r')}(x) \leqslant t - 1.$$

As r is increasing, the degree of $A_{22}^{(r)}(x)$ is increasing. We only need to show that

$$\deg A_{22}^{(r')}(x) \leqslant t.$$

This we will prove by working with the inverse of the matrix $\mathbf{A}(x)$. First recall that

$$\mathbf{A}^{(r')}(x) = \prod_{r=1}^{r'} \begin{bmatrix} 0 & 1 \\ 1 & -Q^{(r)}(x) \end{bmatrix}.$$

From this equation it is clear that $\deg A_{22}^{(r)}(x) > \deg A_{12}^{(r)}(x)$. Also, recall that $\deg s^{(r)}(x) > \deg t^{(r)}(x)$. From these inequalities and the matrix equation

$$\begin{bmatrix} s(x) \\ t(x) \end{bmatrix} = (-1)^r \begin{bmatrix} A_{22}^{(r)}(x) & -A_{12}^{(r)}(x) \\ -A_{21}^{(r)}(x) & A_{11}^{(r)}(x) \end{bmatrix} \begin{bmatrix} s^{(r)}(x) \\ t^{(r)}(x) \end{bmatrix}$$

it is clear that $\deg s(x) = \deg A_{22}^{(r')}(x) + \deg s^{(r')}(x)$, and because $s^{(r')}(x) = t^{(r'-1)}(x)$, this becomes

$$\deg A_{22}^{(r')}(x) = \deg s(x) - \deg t^{(r'-1)}(x)$$

$$\leqslant 2t - t = t,$$

where the inequality follows from the definition of r'.

We now have most of the proof of the following theorem.

□ **Theorem 7.7.3**   Given $s^{(0)}(x) = x^{2t}$ and $t^{(0)}(x) = S(x)$, let $\mathbf{A}^{(0)}(x) = \begin{bmatrix} 1 & 0 \\ 0 & 1 \end{bmatrix}$, where $S(x)$ is the syndrome polynomial of a t-error-correcting BCH code. Solve the following recursive equations until $\deg t^{(r)}(x) \leqslant t - 1$:

$$Q^{(r)}(x) = \left\lfloor \frac{s^{(r)}(x)}{t^{(r)}(x)} \right\rfloor$$

$$\mathbf{A}^{(r+1)}(x) = \begin{bmatrix} 0 & 1 \\ 1 & -Q^{(r)}(x) \end{bmatrix} \mathbf{A}^{(r)}(x)$$

$$\begin{bmatrix} s^{(r+1)}(x) \\ t^{(r+1)}(x) \end{bmatrix} = \begin{bmatrix} 0 & 1 \\ 1 & -Q^{(r)}(x) \end{bmatrix} \begin{bmatrix} s^{(r)}(x) \\ t^{(r)}(x) \end{bmatrix},$$

and let

$$\Omega(x) = \Delta^{-1} t^{(r')}(x)$$

$$\Lambda(x) = \Delta^{-1} A_{22}^{(r')}(x),$$

where $\Delta = A_{22}^{(r)}(0)$. Then these are the unique solutions of

$$\Omega(x) = S(x)\Lambda(x) \qquad (\text{mod } x^{2t})$$

satisfying deg $\Lambda(x) \leqslant t$, and deg $\Omega(x) \leqslant t - 1$ and $\Lambda_0 = 1$.

Proof The division by Δ ensures that $\Lambda_0 = 1$. Otherwise, we have already seen that the final equation and conditions will be satisfied. Uniqueness holds because there is only one such solution for the syndrome of a t-error-correcting BCH code. $\square$

Once $\Lambda(x)$ and $\Omega(x)$ are known, the decoding can be completed in any of the ways derived for the Berlekamp-Massey algorithm. A flowchart of the resulting decoder is shown in Fig. 7.8. Here the decoder ends with the Forney algorithm, but there are other ways of ending it.

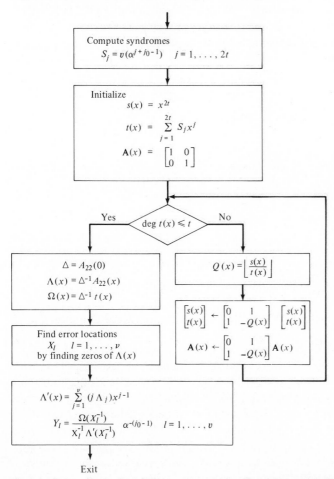

Exit

Figure 7.8 Decoding BCH codes by the Euclidean algorithm.

7.8 NESTED CODES

One way to achieve very long block codes is to nest codes.* This technique combines a code of small alphabet size and a code of larger alphabet size. Imagine a block of q-ary symbols of length kK. This block can be broken into K subblocks of k symbols, each subblock viewed as an element from a q^k-ary alphabet. A sequence of K such subblocks can be encoded with an (N, K) code over $GF(q^k)$. Later, each of the N q^k-ary symbols can be reinterpreted as k q-ary symbols and coded with an (n, k) q-ary code. In this way a nested code has two distinct levels of coding.

Let us recapitulate. Suppose one designs an (n, k) code for a q-ary channel. This code over $GF(q)$ has q^k codewords. The encoder input is a block of k input symbols, which can be viewed as a single element of $GF(q^k)$. This q^k-ary symbol enters the encoder and later leaves the decoder—possibly in error. Hence, the combination of the encoder, channel, and decoder can be thought of as a super-channel with the larger input/output alphabet $GF(q^k)$. We can construct super-codes for this super-channel. As shown in Fig. 7.9, we construct an (N, K) code over the q^k-ary alphabet.

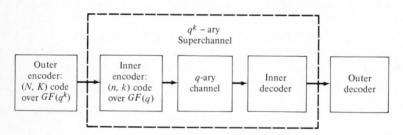

Figure 7.9 Nesting of codes.

EXAMPLE

Inner Code   The (7, 3) double-error-correcting Reed-Solomon code over $GF(8)$.

Outer Code   The (511, 505) triple-error-correcting Reed-Solomon code over $GF(8^3)$.

When these are nested, they form a (3577, 1515) code over $GF(8)$, which can correct any pattern of eleven errors and many, many error patterns with more errors. A way to visualize a codeword is shown in Fig. 7.10. Notice that the codeword is actually a vector of 3577 octal characters. It is shown as a two-dimensional array only to illustrate the method of construction. $\square$

---

*A nested code is also called a concatenated code because the encoders and the decoders are concatenated. We prefer to reserve this latter name for concatenated codewords—codewords that are strung together side by side.

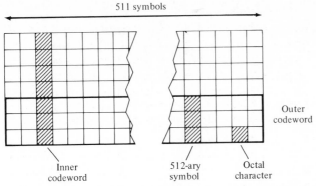

Figure 7.10 A nested (511, 505), (7, 3) Reed-Solomon code.

Another example of a codeword from a nested code is given in Fig. 7.11. This is a code for an octal channel obtained by nesting a (7, 4) Reed-Solomon code over $GF(8)$ with a (22, 18) shortened Reed-Solomon code over $GF(4096)$. The codeword, which contains 72 octal information characters, has a block-length of 154. Notice that the entire array produced by the inner encoder is a single codeword.

The received message shown in Fig. 7.11 has been corrupted by a channel that makes both errors and erasures. The receiver in such a channel declares a symbol to be erased if various internal validity checks fail. Symbols that are not erased may be correct or may be in error. In Fig. 7.11 the erasures are denoted by dashes, and the error symbols are underlined. Of course, the decoder knows the locations of the dashes but not of the underlines. Erasure decoding will be studied in Section 9.2.

This example dramatizes the strength of a nested code because of the highly broken message that is successfully decoded. Notice that the long string of erasures might correspond to a transient malfunction of the receiver or a transient interference if the symbols are transmitted row by row. Because the inner encoder generates one column at a time, however, this transmission scheme requires a so-called *corner-turning memory* between the inner encoder and the channel. Here the inner codewords are stored by columns until the entire nested codeword is assembled. It is then read into the channel by rows.

One can even mix block codes with convolutional codes using nesting. A simple convolutional code with a Viterbi decoder, as will be described in Chapter 12, will do quite well at correcting occasional errors in a long binary data stream, but too many errors occurring closely together will be decoded into an error burst by the Viterbi decoder. An outer Reed-Solomon code can be used to correct these bursts. This technique of nesting a Reed-Solomon code with a weak but simple convolutional code has proved to be a powerful technique for designing decoders for the gaussian-noise channel.

The original data—72 octal symbols

```
0 1 2 3 4 5 6 7 6 5 4 3 2 1 0 0 1 2
3 4 5 6 7 6 5 4 3 2 1 0 0 1 2 3 4 5
6 7 6 5 4 3 2 1 0 0 1 2 3 4 5 6 7 6
5 4 3 2 1 0 0 1 2 3 4 5 6 7 6 5 4 3
```

Outer codeword—(22, 18, 5) Reed-Solomon code over $GF(4096)$
(each column is one symbol, parity block in first four columns)

```
0 4 6 5 | 0 1 2 3 4 5 6 7 6 5 4 3 2 1 0 0 1 2
2 4 6 5 | 3 4 5 6 7 6 5 4 3 2 1 0 0 1 2 3 4 5
4 0 0 2 | 6 7 6 5 4 3 2 1 0 0 1 2 3 4 5 6 7 6
2 1 7 2 | 5 4 3 2 1 0 0 1 2 3 4 5 6 7 6 5 4 3
```

Inner codeword—22 copies of (7, 4, 4) Reed-Solomon code over $GF(8)$
(each column is one codeword, parity block in first three rows)

```
7 7 6 7   4 1 4 5 4 1 0 4 2 5 4 3 6 2 6 4 1 4
4 4 5 6   0 4 7 2 6 5 2 4 2 1 5 4 3 4 6 0 4 7
2 2 5 2   4 6 1 7 1 1 2 5 3 0 7 3 3 2 2 4 6 1
0 4 6 5 | 0 1 2 3 4 5 6 7 6 5 4 3 2 1 0 0 1 2
2 4 6 5 | 3 4 5 6 7 6 5 4 3 2 1 0 0 1 2 3 4 5
4 0 0 2 | 6 7 6 5 4 3 2 1 0 0 1 2 3 4 5 6 7 6
2 1 7 2 | 5 4 3 2 1 0 0 1 2 3 4 5 6 7 6 5 4 3
```

The received message with errors and erasures

```
4 7 – 7 4 – 4 5 4 1 – 4 2 1 4 – 6 2 6 4 – 4
4 3 – – 0 2 7 2 – – 2 4 2 4 5 4 3 4 5 0 4 7
2 2 – 2 4 4 1 7 1 1 2 5 3 5 7 3 3 – 2 4 6 1
0 4 – – 1 6 0 – – – – – – – – – – – – – – –
– – – – – – – – – – – – – 1 0 0 1 2 2 4 5
4 0 – 2 6 1 6 5 4 3 2 – – – 4 – 0 – 5 6 – 6
2 1 5 2 5 2 3 – 1 0 0 1 2 6 4 5 6 7 6 5 4 1
```

The message after the inner decoder

```
0 4 – 5 0 – 2 3 4 5 6 7 6 7 4 3 2 1 0 0 1 2
2 4 – 5 3 – 5 6 7 6 5 4 3 3 1 0 0 1 2 3 4 5
4 0 – 2 6 – 6 5 4 3 2 1 0 0 1 2 3 4 5 6 7 6
2 1 – 2 5 – 3 2 1 0 0 1 2 6 4 5 6 7 6 5 4 3
```

The message after the outer decoder

```
0 1 2 3 4 5 6 7 6 5 4 3 2 1 0 0 1 2
3 4 5 6 7 6 5 4 3 2 1 0 0 1 2 3 4 5
6 7 6 5 4 3 2 1 0 0 1 2 3 4 5 6 7 6
5 4 3 2 1 0 0 1 2 3 4 5 6 7 6 5 4 3
```

Figure 7.11   An octal nested code.

7.9 JUSTESEN CODES

Any code over $GF(q^m)$ can be converted into a code over $GF(q)$ simply by "tilting" each q^m-ary symbol into a sequence of m q-ary symbols. This changes an (N, K) linear code over $GF(q^m)$ into an (mN, mK) linear code over $GF(q)$. The d^* nonzero symbols of a minimum-weight codeword will tilt into md^* symbols, but only a fraction of these will be nonzero. The rate of the new code is the same as that of the original code, but the minimum distance is a much smaller fraction of blocklength.

The principal use of this tilting construction is to create a simple form of a multiple burst-error-correcting code. If the original code has a minimum distance of 5, then any single burst of $m + 1$ q-ary symbols can be corrected, as well as many patterns consisting of two shorter bursts. For example, an (n, k) Reed-Solomon code over $GF(2^m)$ can be tilted into an (mn, mk) binary code for multiple burst-error correction. Such a code, however, is usually not attractive as a code for correcting random errors.

Justesen realized that he could get good codes by cleverly adding an extra twist to the construction. This gives the class of Justesen codes—a class that, as we will show, contains some very good codes. Unfortunately, the Justesen codes are good codes only for long blocklengths, and there has been little interest in using these codes in practice. The codes are used as an example to show that good codes of long blocklength can be constructed. The Justesen codes do not have a well-developed collection of decoding algorithms.

A codeword in a $(2mN, mK)$ Justesen code is a $2m$ by $q^m - 1$ array of elements from $GF(q)$. The codewords are constructed starting with all the codewords of a single fixed (N, K) Reed-Solomon code that has the same number of codewords as the desired Justesen code. Starting with codeword $\mathbf{c} = (c_0, c_1, \ldots, c_{N-1})$ from the Reed-Solomon code, first form the 2 by N array of $GF(q^m)$-ary symbols:

$$\begin{bmatrix} c_0 & c_1 & c_2 & \cdots & c_{N-1} \\ \alpha^0 c_0 & \alpha^1 c_1 & \alpha^2 c_2 & \cdots & \alpha^{N-1} c_{N-1} \end{bmatrix}.$$

Each element of the array is an element of the field $GF(q^m)$. Now replace each element by a column vector of m $GF(q)$-ary symbols. The resulting $2m$ by N array of $GF(q)$-ary symbols gives one codeword of the Justesen code. The array can be mapped into a vector in any convenient way. Repeating this construction for each codeword of the Reed-Solomon code gives the Justesen code.

Notice first of all that the construction gives a linear code. This is important because in order to find the minimum distance of the code, it suffices to find the minimum weight. But now we can see the twist that makes the codes good. There are at least $N - K + 1$ nonzero columns in any codeword array, because every Reed-Solomon codeword has at least this weight. Further, if two columns are the same in the top m elements, then they must be different in the bottom m elements. Hence, no two nonzero columns can be the same.

To bound the minimum weight, we assume that the $N - K + 1$ nonzero columns have smallest possible weight under the constraint that they are all different. That is, we sum up the weights of the $N - K + 1$ smallest-weight vectors of length $2m$.

◻ **Theorem 7.9.1** The minimum distance of the $(2mN, \; mK)$ Justesen code constructed from an (N, K) Reed-Solomon code is bounded by

$$d^* \geq \sum_{i=1}^{I} i(q - 1)^i \binom{2m}{i}$$

for any I satisfying

$$\sum_{i=1}^{I} (q - 1)^i \binom{2m}{i} \leq N - K + 1.$$

Proof The minimum weight codeword has $N - K + 1$ distinct nonzero columns. The weight is at least as great as a word constructed by filling in $N - K + 1$ columns with the $N - K + 1$ distinct $2m$-tuples of smallest weight. In an m-tuple, there are $\binom{2m}{i}$ ways of picking i nonzero places and $(q - 1)$ different nonzero values. Hence, there is a column of weight I for every I that satisfies

$$\sum_{i=1}^{I} (q - 1)^i \binom{2m}{i} \leq N - K + 1,$$

The minimum distance is at least as large as the sum of the weights of these columns. That is

$$d^* \geq \sum_{i=1}^{I} i(q - 1)^i \binom{2m}{i}.$$

This completes the proof. ◻

Making the best use of the bound of Theorem 7.9.1 requires a computer. But even with the aid of a computer, for large N the binomial coefficients can be impractical to evaluate. Therefore we will develop an alternative description to investigate the behavior for large blocklength. The following discussion is necessary only to describe the asymptotic behavior in blocklength of the bound; no new coding theory is developed.

◻ **Lemma 7.9.2** For p such that $0 < p < \frac{1}{2}$ and np is an integer,

$$\sum_{k=0}^{pn} \binom{n}{k} \leq 2^{nH(p)},$$

where $H(p) = -p \log_2 p - (1 - p) \log_2 (1 - p)$.

Proof   Let λ be any positive number. We have the following string of inequalities:

$$2^{\lambda(1-p)n} \sum_{k=0}^{pn} \binom{n}{k} = 2^{\lambda(1-p)n} \sum_{k=(1-p)n}^{n} \binom{n}{k} \leqslant \sum_{k=(1-p)n}^{n} 2^{\lambda k} \binom{n}{k}$$

$$\leqslant \sum_{k=0}^{n} 2^{\lambda k} \binom{n}{k} = (1+2^{\lambda})^n.$$

Thus

$$\sum_{k=0}^{pn} \binom{n}{k} \leqslant (2^{-\lambda(1-p)} + 2^{\lambda p})^n.$$

Now choose $\lambda = \log_2[(1-p)/p]$. Then

$$\sum_{k=0}^{pn} \binom{n}{k} \leqslant [2^{-(1-p)\log_2[(1-p)/p]} + 2^{p\log_2[(1-p)/p]}]^n$$

$$= [2^{-(1-p)\log_2(1-p)-p\log_2 p}(2^{\log_2 p} + 2^{\log_2(1-p)})]^n$$

$$= 2^{nH(p)}(p+1-p)^n,$$

which proves the lemma. $\square$

$\square$ **Lemma 7.9.3**   In any set of M distinct nonzero binary words of length $2m$, the sum of the weights W satisfies

$$W \geqslant 2m\lambda(M - 2^{2mH(\lambda)}).$$

For any λ between 0 and $\frac{1}{2}$.

Proof   By Lemma 7.9.2, for any $0 < \lambda < \frac{1}{2}$, the number of $2m$-tuples in the set having weight at most $2m\lambda$ satisfies

$$\sum_{i=1}^{2m\lambda} \binom{2m}{i} < 2^{2mH(\lambda)}.$$

Therefore for each λ, there are at least $M - 2^{2mH(\lambda)}$ words of weight greater than $2m\lambda$. Hence, the sum of the weights of the M words in the set satisfies

$$W \geqslant 2m\lambda(M - 2^{2mH(\lambda)}).$$

This completes the proof of the lemma. $\square$

$\square$ **Theorem 7.9.4**   For fixed R $(0 < R < \frac{1}{2})$ and for each integer m, let $K = \lceil 2NR \rceil$. Then the (n, k) Justesen code where $n = 2mN$ and $k = mK$ has a rate at least as large as R and a minimum distance satisfying

$$\frac{d^*}{n} \geqslant (1 - 2R)(H^{-1}(\tfrac{1}{2}) - o(1)),$$

where $o(1)$ is a function of n that goes to zero as n goes to infinity.

Proof Because $K = \lceil 2NR \rceil$, $K > 2NR$, and the code rate $K/2N$ is greater than R. Now the codeword $\mathbf{c}$ has at least $N - K + 1$ distinct nonzero columns; it contains at least $N - K + 1$ distinct nonzero binary $2m$-tuples. Further,

$$N - K + 1 \geqslant N(1 - 2R).$$

Next, choose $N(1 - 2R)$ of these $2m$-tuples. This fits the requirements of Lemma 7.9.3. Therefore by Lemma 7.9.3,

$$d^* \geqslant W \geqslant 2m\lambda [N(1 - 2R) - 2^{2mH(\lambda)}]$$

Therefore,

$$\frac{d^*}{n} \geqslant \lambda(1 - 2R)\left[1 - \frac{2^{mH(\lambda)}}{1 - 2R}\right]$$

Set

$$\lambda = H^{-1}\left(\frac{1}{2} - \frac{1}{\log_2 2m}\right)$$

to complete the proof of the theorem. $\square$

The significance of Justesen codes is a result of Theorem 7.9.4. This theorem says that, asymptotically for large n,

$$\frac{d^*}{n} \geqslant 0.11(1 - 2R).$$

For fixed R less than $1/2$, the ratio d^*/n is bounded away from zero as n does to infinity. The Justesen codes are the only known class of codes having an explicitly defined construction for which this property is known to be true.

The Justesen codes have rate smaller than one-half. It is possible to get codes of higher rate by puncturing the code. These codes, again, are only of academic interest as an example of codes whose performance is good at very large blocklengths.

PROBLEMS

7.1. Find $g(x)$ for a binary double-error-correcting code of blocklength $n = 31$. Use a primitive α and the primitive polynomial $p(x) = x^5 + x^2 + 1$.

7.2. Find the codeword that corresponds to the information polynomial $\alpha^5 x + \alpha^3$ corresponding to the single-error-correcting Reed-Solomon code of blocklength 15 based on the primitive element α of $GF(2^4)$.

7.3. **a.** Find $g(x)$ for the double-error-correcting Reed-Solomon code based on the primitive element $\alpha \in GF(2^4)$ and $j_0 = 1$.

b. If $S_1 = \alpha^4$, $S_2 = 0$, $S_3 = \alpha^8$, and $S_4 = \alpha^2$, find the error-locator polynomial, the error locations, and the error values by using the Peterson-Gorenstein-Zierler decoder.

c. Repeat part (b) using the Berlekamp-Massey algorithm.

7.4. Section 7.1 gives a generator polynomial for a $(15, 6, 7)$ BCH code over $GF(4)$. Find the generator polynomial for a $(15, 7, 7)$ BCH code over $GF(4)$.

7.5. The double-error-correcting BCH (15, 7) code has the generator polynomial $g(x) = x^8 + x^7 + x^6 + x^4 + 1$. Combine the ideas of a Meggitt decoder and those of the PGZ algorithm to obtain a decoder with the spirit of the Meggitt decoder, but using the extension field syndromes S_1, S_2, S_3, S_4 rather than the syndrome polynomial $s(x)$.

7.6. Find the generator polynomial for a (63, 55, 5) code over $GF(8)$.

7.7. Suppose that a Reed-Solomon code has minimum distance of $2t + 1$ and that v is an integer smaller than t. We wish to correct the message if at most v errors occur and to detect a bad message if more than v and at most $2t - v$ errors occur. Describe how to do this using the Berlekamp-Massey algorithm. Repeat for a BCH code.

7.8. Show that every BCH code is a subfield-subcode of a Reed-Solomon code of the same designed distance. Under what conditions is the rate of the subfield-subcode the same as the rate of the Reed-Solomon code? For a nonsystematically encoded (7, 5) Reed-Solomon code, describe the 16 information sequences that will produce codewords in the Hamming (7, 4) code.

7.9. Find the generator polynomial for a (23, 12) double-error-correcting BCH code over $GF(2)$. Notice that the resulting code is the Golay code. This gives an example of a BCH code whose minimum distance is larger than the designed distance.

7.10. A ternary channel transmits one of three symbols at each symbol time: a sinusoidal pulse at $0°$ phase angle, a sinusoidal pulse at $120°$ phase angle, or a sinusoidal pulse at $240°$ phase angle. Errors are made randomly and with equal probability. Represent the channel symbols with the set $\{0, 1, 2\}$.

Design a triple-error-correcting code of blocklength 80 for this channel. A primitive polynomial of degree of 4 over $GF(3)$ is

$$p(x) = x^4 + x + 2.$$

What is the rate of the code? How might this code be used to transmit blocks of binary data?

7.11. A tape memory stores 8-bit bytes as a single 256-ary character. Design a (15, 13) single-error-correcting code for this alphabet. Design a decoder circuit.

7.12. The polynomial $y^{20} + y^3 + 1$ is a primitive polynomial over $GF(2)$. The primitive element $\alpha = y$ with minimal polynomial $y^{20} + y^3 + 1$ is used to construct a double-error-correcting BCH code of blocklength $2^{20} = 1,048,576$.

a. A received message has syndromes

$$S_1 = y^4 \qquad S_3 = y^{12} + y^9 + y^6.$$

Find the remaining syndromes.

b. Find the error-locator polynomial.

c. Find the location of the error or errors.

7.13. a. Find $g(x)$ for a binary BCH code of blocklength $n = 15$ with $d = 7$. Use a primitive α, $j_0 = 1$, and the irreducible polynomial $x^4 + x + 1$.

b. In the code of part (a), suppose a sequence v is received such that

$$S_1 = v(\alpha) = \alpha + \alpha^2, \qquad S_3 = v(\alpha^3) = \alpha^2, \qquad \text{and} \qquad S_5 = v(\alpha^5) = 1.$$

(i) Find S_2, S_4, and S_6.
(ii) Assuming that $v \leqslant 3$ errors took place, find v.
(iii) Find the error-locator polynomial.
(iv) Find the error.

NOTES

The BCH codes were discovered independently by Hocquenghem (1959) and by Bose and Ray-Chaudhuri (1960). It was noticed quickly by Gorenstein and Zierler (1961) that the codes discovered earlier by Reed and Solomon (1960) are a special case of nonbinary BCH codes.

The behavior of the minimum distance and rate of BCH codes of large blocklength has been determined only slowly and by many authors. The BCH codes with blocklength $q^m - 1$ become unsatisfactory as the blocklength becomes very large in comparison to q. For moderate blocklength, this is because for the binary case, it takes something on the order of m parity bits for each error to be corrected; and for other q it takes on the order of $2m$ parity symbols per error to be corrected. The asymptotic behavior is better, but still not satisfactory. This vague description requires considerable work to make it precise.

Kasami and Tokura (1969) found an infinite subfamily of primitive BCH codes for which the BCH bound is strictly smaller than the true minimum distance; the first example is the (127, 43) BCH code with $d = 29$ and $d^* = 31$. Chen (1970) found examples of cyclic codes that are better than BCH codes; an example is a (63, 28, 15) cyclic code.

The first error-correction procedure for BCH codes was found by Peterson (1960) for the binary codes and by Gorenstein and Zierler (1961) for the nonbinary codes. Simplifications were found by Chien (1964) and Forney (1965). The iterative algorithm for finding the error-locator polynomial was discovered by Berlekamp (1968), and Massey (1969) rederived the algorithm as a procedure for designing autoregressive filters. Burton (1971) showed how to implement the Berlekamp-Massey algorithm without division, but divisions are still needed to compute the error magnitudes.

The use of the Euclidean algorithm for decoding was first discovered by Sugiyama, Kasahara, Hirasawa, and Namekawa (1975). Welch and Scholtz (1979) derived a decoder using continued fractions that is quite similar to the use of the Euclidean algorithm. A second way of using the Euclidean algorithm of Mandelbaum (1977) is discussed in Section 9.1.

CHAPTER 8

Codes Based on Spectral Techniques

T he subject of digital signal processing is permeated with applications of the Fourier transform. When the time variable is continuous, the study of real-valued or complex-valued signals relies heavily on the Fourier transform. When the time variable is discrete, the discrete Fourier transform plays a parallel role. Fourier transforms also exist on the vector space of n-tuples over the Galois field $GF(q)$ for many values of n. Fourier transforms in a Galois field can play an important role in the study and processing of $GF(q)$-valued signals; that is, of codewords. By using Fourier transforms, the ideas of coding theory can be described in a setting that is much different from that seen thus far. Cyclic codes can be defined as codes whose codewords have certain specified spectral components equal to zero. Also, the decoding of BCH codes and Reed-Solomon codes can be described spectrally.

In this chapter and the next, we study codes and algorithms from a frequency-domain point of view. By revisiting many topics by way of the frequency domain, we can deepen our understanding and also find alternative encoding and decoding techniques. We also will use the frequency-domain setting to introduce some additional classes of codes.

8.1 FOURIER TRANSFORMS IN A GALOIS FIELD

In the complex field, the definition of the discrete Fourier transform of $\mathbf{p} = \{p_i \quad i = 0, \ldots, N-1\}$, a vector of complex numbers, is a vector $\mathbf{P} = \{P_k \quad k = 0, \ldots, N-1\}$ given by

$$P_k = \sum_{i=0}^{N-1} e^{-j2\pi N^{-1}ik} p_i \qquad k = 0, \ldots, N-1,$$

where $j = \sqrt{-1}$. The Fourier kernel $\exp(-j2\pi N^{-1})$ is an Nth root of unity in the field of complex numbers. In the finite field $GF(q^m)$, an element α of order n is an nth root of unity. Drawing on the analogy between $\exp(-j2\pi N^{-1})$ and α, we have the following definition.

☐ **Definition 8.1.1** Let $\mathbf{v} = \{v_i \quad i = 0, \ldots, n-1\}$ be a vector over $GF(q)$, where n divides $q^m - 1$ for some m, and let α be an element of $GF(q^m)$ of order n. The Galois-field Fourier transform of the vector $\mathbf{v}$ is the vector $\mathbf{V} = \{V_j \quad j = 0, \ldots, n-1\}$ given by

$$V_j = \sum_{i=0}^{n-1} \alpha^{ij} v_i \qquad j = 0, \ldots, n-1.$$

☐

It is natural to call the discrete index i *time* and to call $\mathbf{v}$ the *time-domain function* or the *signal*. Also, we might call the discrete index j *frequency* and $\mathbf{V}$ the *frequency-domain function* or the *spectrum*.

Any factor of $q^m - 1$ can be used as the blocklength of a Fourier transform, but the most important values for n are the primitive blocklengths, $n = q^m - 1$. Then α is a primitive element of $GF(q^m)$. In contrast to the situation for the complex field, Fourier transforms of every blocklength do not exist in a Galois field because elements of every order do not exist. There are enough, however, for most purposes. If m is the smallest integer such that n divides $q^m - 1$, then there is a Galois-field Fourier transform over $GF(q)$ of blocklength n, and the components of the Fourier transform are in $GF(q^m)$. Unfortunately, for some values of n, although the transform exists, it will be in a very large extension field and may not be practical for a given application.

In the case of the discrete Fourier transform, even though the time-domain function $\mathbf{p}$ is real, the transform $\mathbf{P}$ is complex. Similarly, in the Galois-field Fourier transform, even though the time-domain function $\mathbf{v}$ is over the field $GF(q)$, the spectrum $\mathbf{V}$ is over the extension field $GF(q^m)$. In error-control applications, all the decoding action really takes place in the big field $GF(q^m)$;

it is just that we happen to start with a vector consistent with the channel input; that is, in the small field $GF(q)$.

☐ **Theorem 8.1.2** Over $GF(q)$, a field of characteristic p, a vector and its spectrum are related by

$$V_j = \sum_{i=0}^{n-1} \alpha^{ij} v_i$$

$$v_i = \frac{1}{n} \sum_{j=0}^{n-1} \alpha^{-ij} V_j,$$

where n is interpreted as an integer of the field; that is, modulo p.

Proof In any field,

$$x^n - 1 = (x - 1)(x^{n-1} + x^{n-2} + \cdots + x + 1).$$

By the definition of α, α^r is a zero of the left side for all r. Hence for all $r \neq 0$ modulo n, α^r is a zero of the last term. But this is equivalent to

$$\sum_{j=0}^{n-1} \alpha^{rj} = 0 \qquad r \neq 0 \ (\text{mod } n)$$

whereas if $r = 0$ modulo n,

$$\sum_{j=0}^{n-1} \alpha^{rj} = n \qquad (\text{mod } p),$$

which is not zero if n is not a multiple of the field characteristic p. Combining these facts, we have

$$\sum_{j=0}^{n-1} \alpha^{-ij} \sum_{k=0}^{n-1} \alpha^{kj} v_k = \sum_{k=0}^{n-1} v_k \sum_{j=0}^{n-1} \alpha^{(k-i)j} = (n \bmod p) v_i.$$

Finally, $q^m - 1 = p^M - 1$ is a multiple of n, and consequently n is not a multiple of p. Hence $n \neq 0 \ (\text{mod } p)$. This proves the theorem. ☐

The Fourier transform has many strong properties that carry over to the finite field case. An example is the convolution property of the next theorem. A dual theorem can be proved with the time domain and the frequency domain interchanged.

☐ **Theorem 8.1.3 (Convolution Theorem)** Suppose that

$$e_i = f_i g_i \qquad i = 0, \ldots, n-1.$$

Then

$$E_j = \frac{1}{n} \sum_{k=0}^{n-1} F_{((j-k))} G_k \qquad j = 0, \ldots, n-1,$$

where the double parentheses denote modulo-n arithmetic on the indices.

Proof Take the Fourier transform of $e_i = f_i g_i$

$$E_j = \sum_{i=0}^{n-1} \alpha^{ij} f_i \left(\frac{1}{n} \sum_{k=0}^{n-1} \alpha^{-ik} G_k \right) = \frac{1}{n} \sum_{k=0}^{n-1} G_k \left(\sum_{i=0}^{n-1} \alpha^{i(j-k)} f_i \right) = \frac{1}{n} \sum_{k=0}^{n-1} G_k F_{((j-k))}.$$

$\square$

Note also that setting $j = 0$ in the convolution formula,

$$E_j = \sum_{i=0}^{n-1} \alpha^{ij} f_i g_i = \frac{1}{n} \sum_{k=0}^{n-1} F_{((j-k))} G_k,$$

yields the Parseval-type formula

$$\sum_{i=0}^{n-1} f_i g_i = \frac{1}{n} \sum_{k=0}^{n-1} F_{((n-k))} G_k.$$

$\square$ **Theorem 8.1.4 (Translation Property)**   If $\{v_i\} \leftrightarrow \{V_j\}$ is a Fourier transform pair, then the following are Fourier transform pairs:

$$\{\alpha^i v_i\} \leftrightarrow \{V_{((j+1))}\}$$
$$\{v_{((i-1))}\} \leftrightarrow \{\alpha^j V_j\}.$$

Proof Immediate substitutions prove the theorem. $\square$

Sometimes we represent a vector **v** by a polynomial $v(x)$. The polynomial

$$v(x) = v_{n-1} x^{n-1} + \cdots + v_1 x + v_0$$

can be transformed into a polynomial

$$V(x) = V_{n-1} x^{n-1} + \cdots + V_1 x + V_0$$

by means of the Galois-field Fourier transform. The latter polynomial is called the *spectrum polynomial* or the *associated polynomial* of $v(x)$. Properties of the spectrum are closely related to the zeros of polynomials, as stated in the following theorem.

$\square$ **Theorem 8.1.5**

   (i) The polynomial $v(x)$ has a zero at α^j if and only if the jth frequency component V_j equals zero.
   (ii) The polynomial $V(x)$ has a zero at α^{-i} if and only if the ith time component v_i equals zero.

Proof The proof of part (i) is immediate because

$$v(\alpha^j) = \sum_{i=0}^{n-1} v_i \alpha^{ij} = V_j.$$

The proof of part (ii) follows in the same way. $\square$

Thus in finite fields, when one speaks of zeros of polynomials or of spectral components equal to zero, one really speaks of the same thing, but the terminology and the insights are different. In the first formulation, one draws on insight into the factoring of polynomials; in the second, one draws on understanding of the Fourier transform.

8.2 CONJUGACY CONSTRAINTS AND IDEMPOTENTS

The Fourier transform over $GF(q)$ of blocklength n takes values in an extension field $GF(q^m)$. If we start with an arbitrary n-vector over $GF(q^m)$ and take the inverse Fourier transform, we generally do not get a time-domain vector over $GF(q)$; there may be components in the larger field. We must find constraints on the spectrum that will ensure a time-domain vector over $GF(q)$.

Constraints of this sort are familiar in the field of complex numbers. Recall that over the complex field, a spectrum $P(f)$ has a real-valued inverse Fourier transform if and only if $P^*(-f) = P(f)$. The next theorem gives a set of constraints, known as *conjugacy constraints*, that provide an analogous condition for a finite field.

☐ **Theorem 8.2.1** Let **V** be a vector of length n of elements of $GF(q^m)$ where n is a divisor of $q^m - 1$. Then the inverse Fourier transform **v** is a vector of elements of $GF(q)$ if and only if the following equations are satisfied:

$$V_j^q = V_{((qj))} \qquad j = 0, \ldots, n-1.$$

Proof By definition,

$$V_j = \sum_{i=0}^{n-1} \alpha^{ij} v_i \qquad j = 0, \ldots, n-1.$$

For a field of characteristic p, $(a+b)^{p^r} = a^{p^r} + b^{p^r}$ for any integer r. Further, if v_i is an element of $GF(q)$ for all i, then $v_i^q = v_i$. Consequently, combining these gives

$$V_j^q = \left(\sum_{i=0}^{n-1} \alpha^{ij} v_i \right)^q = \sum_{i=0}^{n-1} \alpha^{qij} v_i^q = \sum_{i=0}^{n-1} \alpha^{qij} v_i = V_{((qj))}.$$

Conversely, suppose that for all j, $V_j^q = V_{((qj))}$. Then

$$\sum_{i=0}^{n-1} \alpha^{iqj} v_i^q = \sum_{i=0}^{n-1} \alpha^{iqj} v_i \qquad j = 0, \ldots, n-1.$$

Let $k = qj$. Because q is relatively prime to $n = q^m - 1$, as j ranges over all values between 0 and $n-1$, k also takes on all values between 0 and $n-1$. Hence

$$\sum_{i=0}^{n-1} \alpha^{ik} v_i^q = \sum_{i=0}^{n-1} \alpha^{ik} v_i \qquad k = 0, \ldots, n-1,$$

and by uniqueness of the Fourier transform, $v_i^q = v_i$ for all i. Thus v_i is a zero of $x^q - x$ for all i, and such zeros are all elements of $GF(q)$. $\square$

To apply the theorem, the integers modulo n are divided into a collection of sets, known as *conjugacy classes*, as follows:

$$A_j = \{j, jq, jq^2, \ldots, jq^{m_j - 1}\},$$

where m_j is the smallest positive integer satisfying $jq^{m_j} = j$ modulo n. Because the field is finite, there must be such an m_j. For example, when $q = 2$ and $n = 7$, the conjugacy classes are

$$A_0 = \{0\}$$
$$A_1 = \{1, 2, 4\}$$
$$A_3 = \{3, 6, 5\}.$$

The conjugacy class A_j specifies a set of frequencies in the spectrum. We call this set of frequencies a *chord*. Theorem 8.2.1 asserts that if the time-domain signal is in $GF(q)$, then the value of the spectrum at any frequency in the chord specifies the value of the spectrum at all other frequencies in the chord. In the next section we will develop this line of thought to give a spectral description of codes.

Figure 8.1 tabulates the conjugacy classes for some small fields using a slightly different notation. We have written the conjugacy classes using negative integers because this emphasizes the symmetries that arise. The negative integers in Fig. 8.1 may be replaced by positive integers if desired by replacing j by $n + j$ whenever j is negative. We have also included the conjugacy classes of the integers modulo 21 as a reminder that any integer might be used as the modulus. Notice that the members of the conjugacy classes modulo 21 can be multiplied by 3, and the classes then become some of the conjugacy classes modulo 63.

$\square$**Definition 8.2.2** The *q-ary trace* of an element β of $GF(q^m)$ is the sum

$$\mathrm{trace}(\beta) = \sum_{i=0}^{m-1} \beta^{q^i}. \qquad \square$$

Clearly, by Theorem 4.6.10, the q-th power of the q-ary trace of β is equal to the q-ary trace of β, and thus the q-ary trace is an element of $GF(q)$. If β has m elements in its conjugacy class, then trace (β) is the sum of all the elements in the conjugacy class. Otherwise, the number of elements in the conjugacy class divides m, and the number of times each element is added into the trace is given by this ratio.

It follows from the definition of the trace and Theorem 4.6.10 that

$$\mathrm{trace}(\beta + \gamma) = \mathrm{trace}(\beta) + \mathrm{trace}(\gamma)$$

and that all conjugates have the same trace.

Modulo 7	Modulo 63
{-1, -2, 3}	{-11, -22, 19, -25, 13, 26}
{ 0}	{ -9, -18, 27}
{ 1, 2, -3}	{ -5, -10, -20, 23, -17, 29}
	{ -3, -6, -12, -24, 15, 30}
	{ -1, -2, -4, -8, -16, 31}
	{ 0}
Modulo 15	{ 1, 2, 4, 8, 16, -31}
	{ 3, 6, 12, 24, -15, -30}
{-1, -2, -4, 7}	{ 5, 10, 20, -23, 17, -29}
{ 0}	{ 7, 14, 28, -7, -14, -28}
{ 1, 2, 4, -7}	{ 9, 18, -27}
{ 3, 6, -3, -6}	{ 11, 22, -19, 25, -13, -26}
{ 5, -5}	{ 21, -21}

Modulo 31	Modulo 127
{-5, -10, 11, -9, 13}	{-21, -42, 43, -41, 45, -37, 53}
{-3, -6, -12, 7, 14}	{-19, -38, 51, -25, -50, 27, 54}
{-1, -2, -4, -8, 15}	{-13, -26, -52, 23, 46, -35, 57}
{ 0}	{-11, -22, -44, 39, -49, 29, 58}
{ 1, 2, 4, 8, -15}	{ -9, -18, -36, 55, -17, -34, 59}
{ 3, 6, 12, -7, -14}	{ -7, -14, -28, -56, 15, 30, 60}
{ 5, 10, -11, 9, -13}	{ -5, -10, -20, -40, 47, -33, 61}
	{ -3, -6, -12, -24, -48, 31, 62}
	{ -1, -2, -4, -8, -16, -32, 63}
	{ 0}
	{ 1, 2, 4, 8, 16, 32, -63}
	{ 3, 6, 12, 24, 48, -31, -62}
Modulo 21	{ 5, 10, 20, 40, -47, 33, -61}
	{ 7, 14, 28, 56, -15, -30, -60}
{-3, -6, 9}	{ 9, 18, 36, -55, 17, 34, -59}
{-1, -2, -4, -8, 5, 10}	{ 11, 22, 44, -39, 49, -29, -58}
{ 0}	{ 13, 26, 52, -23, -46, 35, -57}
{ 1, 2, 4, 8, -5, -10}	{ 19, 38, -51, 25, 50, -27, -54}
{ 3, 6, -9}	{ 21, 42, -43, 41, -45, 37, -53}
{ 7, -7}	

Figure 8.1   Conjugacy classes.

☐ **Theorem 8.2.3**   Over $GF(q^m)$, the q-ary trace takes on each value of $GF(q)$ equally often; that is, q^{m-1} times.

Proof Let γ be an element of $GF(q)$. Suppose β is an element of $GF(q^m)$ whose q-ary trace is γ. Then β is a zero of the polynomial

$$x^{q^{m-1}} + x^{q^{m-2}} + \cdots + x^q + x - \gamma.$$

This polynomial has a degree of q^{m-1}, and thus it has at most q^{m-1} zeros. But there are only q such polynomials, and every element of $GF(q^m)$ is a zero of one of them. The theorem follows. $\square$

One useful property of the trace is as follows.

$\square$ **Theorem 8.2.4** The quadratic equation

$$x^2 + x + a = 0,$$

where a is an element of $GF(2^m)$, has a root in $GF(2^m)$ if and only if the binary trace of a equals zero.

Proof Let β be a root of the quadratic equation. Then the binary trace of the quadratic equation evaluated at β gives

$$\text{trace}(\beta^2 + \beta + a) = \text{trace}(0) = 0.$$

The trace distributes across addition, and the traces of β and β^2 are the same elements of $GF(2)$. Hence

$$\text{trace}(a) = 0.$$

Conversely, every β is a zero of $x^2 + x + a$ for some a, namely, a equal to $-(\beta + \beta^2)$. There are 2^{m-1} such a with zero trace, and this is just enough to form 2^{m-1} equations, each with two roots. The proof is complete. $\square$

Suppose now that we choose a chord A_k and define the spectrum:

$$W_j = \begin{cases} 0 & j \in A_k \\ 1 & j \notin A_k \end{cases}$$

By Theorem 8.2.1 the inverse Fourier transform of this spectrum is a vector over $GF(q)$, which can be represented by the polynomial $w(x)$. It has the special property that

$$w(x)^2 = w(x) \qquad (\text{mod } x^n - 1),$$

because the convolution $w(x)^2$ transforms into the product W_j^2 in the frequency domain, and clearly $W_j^2 = W_j$. Any polynomial $w(x)$ satisfying $w(x)^2 = w(x)$ (mod $x^n - 1$) is called an *idempotent*.

Every idempotent can be obtained in the following way. Choose several chords; set $W_j = 0$ if j is in one of the chosen chords, and otherwise set $W_j = 1$. The inverse Fourier transform gives a polynomial in the time domain that is an idempotent, and every idempotent can be obtained in this way.

We close this section with an application to cyclic codes.

☐ **Theorem 8.2.5** Every cyclic code has a unique codeword polynomial $w(x)$ with the property that $c(x)$ is a codeword polynomial if and only if

$$c(x)w(x) = c(x) \qquad (\bmod\ x^n - 1).$$

The polynomial $w(x)$ is an idempotent.

Proof Let $g(x)$ be the generator polynomial, and let

$$W_j = \begin{cases} 0 & \text{if } g(\alpha^j) = 0 \\ 1 & \text{if } g(\alpha^j) \neq 0. \end{cases}$$

Then $w(x)$ is an idempotent. It has the same zeros as $g(x)$ and thus is a codeword. In addition, $W_j G_j = G_j$ for all j, and therefore $w(x)g(x) = g(x)$. Next, $c(x)$ is a codeword if and only if for some $a(x)$, $c(x) = a(x)g(x)$, and thus

$$c(x)w(x) = a(x)w(x)g(x) = a(x)g(x) = c(x) \qquad (\bmod\ x^n - 1),$$

which proves the theorem. ☐

8.3 SPECTRAL DESCRIPTION OF CYCLIC CODES

In a cyclic code every codeword $c(x)$ is represented by a polynomial of degree $n - 1$. A nonsystematic form can be written as $c(x) = g(x)d(x)$, where $d(x)$ is a data polynomial of degree of $k - 1$. This is a (cyclic) convolution in the time domain:

$$c_i = \sum_{k=0}^{n-1} g_{((i-k))} d_k.$$

Therefore in the frequency domain, the encoding operation can be written as a product

$$C_j = G_j D_j.$$

Any spectrum that satisfies this expression is a frequency-domain codeword, provided that all components in the time domain are $GF(q)$-valued. Because the data spectrum is arbitrary, the only significant role of G_j is to specify frequencies where the codeword spectrum C_j is zero. Thus we can define a cyclic code alternatively as follows. Given a set of spectral components $j_1, \ldots, j_{n-k}$ called *parity frequencies*, the cyclic code $\mathscr{C}$ is the set of words over $GF(q)$ whose spectrum is zero in components $j_1, \ldots, j_{n-k}$.

Although each codeword in a cyclic code is a vector over $GF(q)$, the codeword spectrum is a vector over $GF(q^m)$. Hence a cyclic code can be described as the set of inverse Fourier transforms of the set of all spectral vectors that are constrained to zero in several prescribed components, provided that these inverse Fourier transforms are $GF(q)$-valued. It is not possible to choose any spectrum that is zero in the prescribed components; some of these may have inverse transforms with components that are not in $GF(q)$. To get codewords in $GF(q)$, we must choose only spectra that satisfy the conjugacy constraints of Theorem 8.2.1.

The BCH codes are the cyclic codes that one obtains if the parity frequencies are chosen consecutively. A t-error-correcting BCH code of blocklength $n = q^m - 1$ is the set of all words over $GF(q)$ whose spectrum is zero in a specified block of $2t$ consecutive components.

The BCH bound is proved simply and intuitively in the frequency domain. It is worth the trouble to present this second proof in order to develop different insights and familiarity.

☐ **Theorem 8.3.1 (BCH Bound)**   Let n be a factor of $q^m - 1$ for some m. The only vector in $GF(q)^n$ of weight $d - 1$ or less that has $d - 1$ sequential values of its spectrum equal to zero is the all-zero vector.

Proof   Let $i_1, \ldots, i_v$ denote the indices of the v nonzero components of the vector $\mathbf{c}$, $v \leqslant d - 1$. Define a frequency-domain vector whose inverse Fourier transform is zero whenever $c_i \neq 0$. There are many such frequency-domain vectors that could be used. One choice is based on the locator polynomial $\Lambda(x)$:

$$\Lambda(x) = \prod_{k=1}^{v} (1 - x\alpha^{-i_k}) = \Lambda_v x^v + \Lambda_{v-1} x^{v-1} + \cdots + \Lambda_1 x + \Lambda_0.$$

As a vector, $\mathbf{\Lambda}$ is a frequency spectrum that has been judiciously defined so that its inverse transform $\lambda = \{\lambda_i\}$ equals zero at every time i at which $c_i \neq 0$. The product in the time domain is zero ($\lambda_i c_i = 0$ for $i = 0, \ldots, n - 1$); therefore, the cyclic convolution in the frequency domain is zero:

$$\mathbf{\Lambda} * \mathbf{C} = \mathbf{0}.$$

Because $\Lambda_0 = 1$ and $\Lambda_k = 0$ if $k > d - 1$, this convolution can be written

$$C_j = -\sum_{k=1}^{d-1} \Lambda_k C_{((j-k))}$$

But $\mathbf{C}$ is zero in a block of length $d - 1$. Consequently, the recursion implies that $\mathbf{C}$ is everywhere zero and that $\mathbf{c}$ must be the all-zero vector. ☐

When $n = q - 1$ (or a factor of $q - 1$), the BCH code is a Reed-Solomon code; the codeword and the spectrum are in the same field. One can encode directly in the frequency domain by using the information symbols to specify spectral components. Every spectrum consistent with the parity constraints yields a codeword. Encoding is as follows. Some set of $2t$ consecutive frequencies (e.g., the first $2t$) are chosen as the symbols constrained to zero. The $n - 2t$ unconstrained components of the spectrum are filled with information symbols from $GF(q)$. The inverse Fourier transform then produces a (nonsystematic) codeword, as shown in Fig. 8.2. Because there are $n - 2t$ frequency

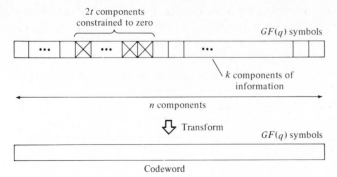

Figure 8.2   Encoding a Reed-Solomon code via the transform.

components that can take on information values, we obtain a codeword of an $(n, n - 2t)$ Reed-Solomon code.

For the more general BCH codes, the encoding is more complex. Now there are two fields: the symbol field $GF(q)$ and the locator field $GF(q^m)$ used for the spectrum. Again, $2t$ consecutive components of the spectrum are chosen to be zero. The remaining symbols must be chosen from $GF(q^m)$ to represent the k information symbols only in those q^k possible ways that have inverse Fourier transforms that are q-ary valued. This is illustrated in Fig. 8.3, which deals with a binary code of blocklength 63. Here, each component of the spectrum vector is a 6-bit binary number, and the spectrum vector is depicted as a list of 63 6-bit binary numbers. The codeword is also depicted as a list of 63 6-bit binary numbers, but with the constraint that only the low-order bit in each 6-bit number can be nonzero. That is, the codeword is actually a 63-bit binary word. We want to specify the spectrum vector in such a way that the signal vector is such a binary codeword. Theorem 8.2.1 gives the constraints needed to construct a suitable spectrum vector.

We will construct some codes of blocklength 63 in a moment, but first we will work through an even simpler example. Using Theorem 8.2.1, we can easily construct the Hamming (7, 4) code in the frequency domain. This is shown in Fig. 8.4. Components C_1 and C_2 are chosen as parity frequencies so that a single error can be corrected. The information is contained at frequency components C_0 and C_3. The remaining frequencies are constrained by the theorem, because $C_1^4 = C_2^2 = C_4 = 0$ and $C_3^4 = C_6^2 = C_5$. Theorem 8.2.1 also requires that $C_0^2 = C_0$, and thus C_0 can only have the value of zero or one. The equivalent "bit content" of C_0 is one bit. The equivalent bit content of C_3 is three bits. Thus the four information bits of the Hamming code can be used to uniquely specify the spectrum. The information bits are inserted into the frequency domain rather than the time domain.

In the general case, the integers modulo n are divided into conjugacy classes:

$$A_j = \{j, jq, jq^2, \ldots, jq^{m_j - 1}\}.$$

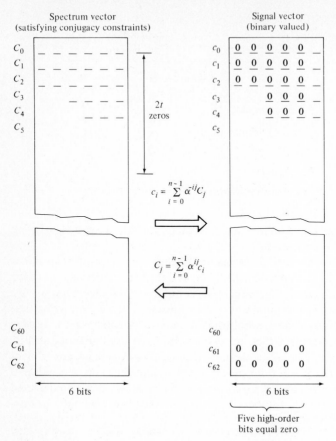

Figure 8.3 Encoding a BCH code via the transform.

If the spectral component C_j is specified, then every other spectral component whose index is in the conjugacy class of j must be a power of C_j and hence cannot be separately specified. Further, if the conjugacy class has r members, then we must have

$$C_j^{q^r} = C_j$$

and

$$C_j^{q^r - 1} = 1$$

Consequently, we are not free to choose any element of $GF(q^m)$ for C_j, but only those of order dividing $q^r - 1$ or the zero element. Every element of $GF(q^m)$ has order dividing $q^m - 1$; hence $q^r - 1$ divides $q^m - 1$, and it is clear that the size of every conjugacy class divides m.

To specify an encoder, we break the first $q^m - 1$ integers into conjugacy classes, and select one integer to represent each class. These representatives

Frequency-Domain Codewords							Time-Domain Codewords						
C_0	C_1	C_2	C_3	C_4	C_5	C_6	c_0	c_1	c_2	c_3	c_4	c_5	c_6
0	0	0	0	0	0	0	0	0	0	0	0	0	0
0	0	0	α^0	0	α^0	α^0	1	1	1	0	1	0	0
0	0	0	α^1	0	α^4	α^2	0	0	1	1	1	0	1
0	0	0	α^2	0	α^1	α^4	0	1	0	0	1	1	1
0	0	0	α^3	0	α^5	α^6	1	1	0	1	0	0	1
0	0	0	α^4	0	α^2	α^1	0	1	1	1	0	1	0
0	0	0	α^5	0	α^6	α^3	1	0	0	1	1	1	0
0	0	0	α^6	0	α^3	α^5	1	0	1	0	0	1	1
1	0	0	0	0	0	0	1	1	1	1	1	1	1
1	0	0	α^0	0	α^0	α^0	0	0	0	1	0	1	1
1	0	0	α^1	0	α^4	α^2	1	1	0	0	0	1	0
1	0	0	α^2	0	α^1	α^4	1	0	1	1	0	0	0
1	0	0	α^3	0	α^5	α^6	0	0	1	0	1	1	0
1	0	0	α^4	0	α^2	α^1	1	0	0	0	1	0	1
1	0	0	α^5	0	α^6	α^3	0	1	1	0	0	0	1
1	0	0	α^6	0	α^3	α^5	0	1	0	1	1	0	0

Figure 8.4   Hamming (7, 4) code.

specify the uniquely assignable symbols. To form a BCH code, a block of $2t$ spectral components are chosen as parity frequencies and set to zero. The remaining assignable symbols are information symbols, arbitrary except for occasional constraints on the order. All other symbols indexed from the same conjugacy class are not free; they are obligatory frequencies.

Figure 8.5 shows the situation for $GF(64)$. We choose the first column to be free symbols. If we take C_1, C_2, C_3, C_4, C_5, and C_6 to be parity frequencies, then we have a triple-error-correcting BCH code. Then C_0, C_7, C_9, C_{11}, C_{13}, C_{15}, C_{21}, C_{23}, C_{27}, and C_{31} are the information symbols. C_9 and C_{27} must be zero or symbols of order 7 (because $C_9^8 = C_9$ and $C_{27}^8 = C_{27}$). These are the elements of the subfield $GF(8)$. C_{21} must be zero or an element of order 3, (because $C_{21}^4 = C_{21}$). These are the elements of the subfield $GF(4)$. C_0 must be zero or an element of order 1. These are the elements of the subfield $GF(2)$. All other symbols are arbitrary elements of $GF(64)$. It requires a total of 45 information bits to specify these symbols. Hence, we have the (63, 45) triple-error-correcting BCH code.

After loading these free symbols, the obligatory symbols are padded with appropriate powers. The completed spectrum is then transformed into the codeword. The set of 2^{45} codewords that one obtains by encoding in this way is the same as the set of 2^{45} codewords that one obtains by encoding in

Free Frequencies	Obligatory Frequencies	Bit Content
$\{C_0\}$		1
$\{C_1$	$C_2 \; C_4 \; C_8 \; C_{16} \, C_{32}\}$	6
$\{C_3$	$C_6 \; C_{12} \, C_{24} \, C_{48} \, C_{33}\}$	6
$\{C_5$	$C_{10} \, C_{20} \, C_{40} \, C_{17} \, C_{34}\}$	6
$\{C_7$	$C_{14} \, C_{28} \, C_{56} \, C_{49} \, C_{35}\}$	6
$\{C_9$	$C_{18} \, C_{36}\}$	3
$\{C_{11}$	$C_{22} \, C_{44} \, C_{25} \, C_{50} \, C_{37}\}$	6
$\{C_{13}$	$C_{26} \, C_{52} \, C_{41} \, C_{19} \, C_{38}\}$	6
$\{C_{15}$	$C_{30} \, C_{60} \, C_{57} \, C_{51} \, C_{39}\}$	6
$\{C_{21}$	$C_{42}\}$	2
$\{C_{23}$	$C_{46} \, C_{29} \, C_{58} \, C_{53} \, C_{43}\}$	6
$\{C_{27}$	$C_{54} \, C_{45}\}$	3
$\{C_{31}$	$C_{62} \, C_{61} \, C_{59} \, C_{55} \, C_{47}\}$	6

Figure 8.5   Structure of the spectrum over $GF(64)$.

the time domain. Up until the point at which the information is recovered, the decoder need not care how the information was encoded. At the last step, however, when the information is extracted from the corrected codeword, the decoder must know how the information is stored in the codeword. If the information bits were encoded in the frequency domain, then they must be read out of the frequency domain.

8.4 EXTENDED REED-SOLOMON CODES

It is possible, in general, to add two extra components onto a Reed-Solomon code; we will always place one new symbol at the beginning and one at the end of the codeword. Codes obtained by adding one or both of the extra components are called *extended Reed-Solomon codes*. Each of these extra components can be used either as information or as parity, that is, either to expand the code by increasing the rate or to lengthen the code by increasing the minimum distance. We use the less-specific term, extended Reed-Solomon code, because the codes can be considered as codes constructed either by expanding Reed-Solomon codes of minimum distance d^* or by lengthening Reed-Solomon codes of minimum distance $d^* - 2$. The same extended Reed-Solomon code is obtained in either case.

The two new locations must be identified, and several notations are in use. If the original components are labeled by field elements, then the zero field element can be used to identify one new component, and an additional symbol is needed to identify the other. Usually, ∞ is used.* If the original components are labeled by exponents on a primitive element, then zero is not available to identify a new symbol, and two new symbols are needed. We will use $-$ and $+$ for these. Thus an augmented codeword is

$$(c_-, c_0, c_1, c_2, \ldots, c_{q^m-3}, c_{q^m-2}, c_+),$$

and $n = q^m + 1$. The vector obtained by excluding c_- and c_+ will be called the *interior*. We shall study extended codes by means of Fourier transform properties of the interior, together with additional properties of the extended vector space. When we speak of the spectrum of the codeword, we mean the spectrum of the interior.

First we will give a definition of an extended cyclic code, then that of the special case of an extended Reed-Solomon code.

□ **Definition 8.4.1** An extended (n, k) cyclic code over $GF(q)$ is a linear code of blocklength $n = q^m + 1$ consisting of the set of words with the properties that each codeword $(c_-, c_0, c_1, \ldots, c_{n-3}, c_+)$ has a spectrum $(C_0, C_1, \ldots, C_{n-3})$ that is equal to zero in a specified set of $n - k - 2$ components with indices $j_1, \ldots, j_{n-k-2}$, and that two other spectral components satisfy $C_{j_0} = c_-$, $C_{j_{n-k-1}} = c_+$. □

An extended cyclic code is generally not cyclic.

□ **Definition 8.4.2** Let j_0 and t be arbitrary integers. An extended Reed-Solomon code is a linear code over $GF(q)$ of blocklength $n = q + 1$ whose codewords $(c_-, c_0, c_1, \ldots, c_{q-2}, c_+)$ have spectra satisfying:

(1) $C_j = 0 \qquad j = j_0 + 1, \ldots, j_0 + 2t - 2$
(2) $C_{j_0} = c_-$
(3) $C_{j_0 + 2t - 1} = c_+$. □

The integer $2t + 1$ is the designed distance of the extended Reed-Solomon code. The definition constrains $2t - 2$ successive spectral components to be equal to zero, and the spectral components on either side of these $2t - 2$ components are equal to c_- and c_+, respectively. The two special frequencies are called the *edge frequencies*.

Compared to the Reed-Solomon code obtained by deleting c_- and c_+ and setting $C_{j_0} = C_{j_0 + 2t - 1} = 0$, the extended Reed-Solomon code always gives two extra information components without changing the minimum

---

*It is a common and convenient practice to extend the field of real numbers by adding the extra symbols $+\infty$ and $-\infty$ and to define arithmetic operations for these. The extended reals do not form a field. One can do the same with a Galois field, adding the symbol ∞ and the operations $a + \infty = \infty, a \cdot \infty = \infty$. The set is no longer a field.

distance. Later, we will examine this statement in the frequency domain, but first we will give a proof using properties of the Vandermonde matrix.

☐ **Theorem 8.4.3** An extended Reed-Solomon code over $GF(q)$ is a $(q+1, k)$ code with minimum distance $2t + 1 = n - k + 1 = q - k + 2$.

Proof First, suppose for simplicity that $j_0 = 0$. The parity-check matrix is

$$\mathbf{H} = \begin{bmatrix} -1 & 1 & 1 & \cdots & 1 & 1 & 0 \\ 0 & \alpha & \alpha^2 & \cdots & \alpha^{q-2} & \alpha^{q-1} & 0 \\ 0 & \alpha^2 & \alpha^4 & \cdots & \alpha^{2(q-2)} & \alpha^{2(q-1)} & 0 \\ \vdots & & & & & & \vdots \\ 0 & \alpha^{q-k-1} & \alpha^{(q-k-1)2} & \cdots & \alpha^{(q-k-1)(q-2)} & \alpha^{(q-k-1)(q-1)} & 0 \\ 0 & \alpha^{q-k} & \alpha^{(q-k)2} & \cdots & \alpha^{(q-k)(q-2)} & \alpha^{(q-k)(q-1)} & -1 \end{bmatrix}.$$

The code has minimum distance of at least d if the vectors in every set of $d - 1$ columns of the parity-check matrix are linearly independent. If the first and last columns are excluded, then any set of $q - k + 1$ columns is a Vandermonde matrix and thus is nonsingular, and hence all the interior columns are linearly independent in sets of $d - 1$. But if we choose a set of $q - k + 1$ columns including the first column and the last column, then the determinant can be computed by expanding in turn about the one in the first column, then the one in the last column. This chops off the first row and the last row leaving a Vandermonde matrix that again has a nonzero determinant. Hence, any $q - k + 1$ columns are linearly independent, and thus the minimum distance is at least $q - k + 2$.

Next, if $j_0 \neq 0$, the parity-check matrix only changes in that every element, except those in the first and last columns, is multiplied by α^{j_0}. This, however, has no effect on subsequent arguments. ☐

Figure 8.6 shows a frequency-domain encoder for an extended Reed-Solomon code. We can best understand these codes by thinking of the encoder as a modification of a frequency-domain encoder for a conventional Reed-Solomon code of minimum distance d^*. The latter encoder constrains to zero a block of $d^* - 1$ contiguous frequencies of the spectrum. The remaining components of the spectrum contain arbitrary information symbols from $GF(q)$. To extend this code in information, the two values of the spectrum on the edges of the block of parity frequencies are used to represent two arbitrary information symbols, and these two information symbols are also appended to the codeword in the time domain. This gives an extended Reed-Solomon code, still with minimum distance d^*, but with two more information symbols. If instead we wish to extend the original code in minimum distance, the two information components adjacent to the original block of parity frequencies are declared to be new parity frequencies. The values of these frequency components are not changed, but rather the two components are appended to the codeword in the time domain. This gives a code of minimum distance $d^* + 2$, and the same number of information symbols as the original codeword. Of course, the same extended code is obtained if we start instead with a Reed-Solomon code of minimum distance $d^* + 2$ and extend it in information.

A time-domain encoder for an (n, k) extended Reed-Solomon code is shown in Fig. 8.7. For this encoder, we view the purpose of the extended symbols as a way to lengthen an $(n - 2, k)$ Reed-Solomon code of minimum

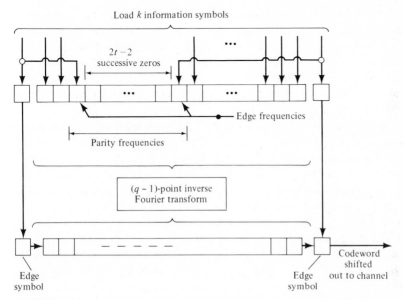

Figure 8.6 Encoding an extended Reed-Solomon code in the frequency domain.

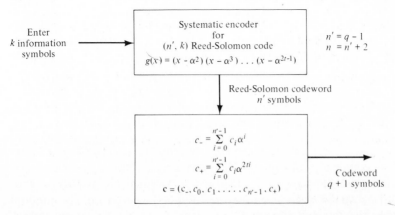

Figure 8.7 Systematic encoder for an extended Reed-Solomon code.

distance $d* - 2$ to get a code of distance $d*$. Take the generator polynomial with zeros $\alpha^2, \ldots, \alpha^{2t-1}$ to encode k information symbols into the interior of the codeword. Then the edge symbols are defined by

$$c_- = \sum_{i=0}^{n'-1} c_i \alpha^i \quad \text{and} \quad c_+ = \sum_{i=0}^{n'-1} c_i \alpha^{2ti},$$

and these are attached to the interior to produce the codeword.

8.5 EXTENDED BCH CODES

Now consider codes for the channel alphabet $GF(q)$ constructed using the locator field $GF(q^m)$. An extended Reed-Solomon code over $GF(q^m)$ can be used to create a code over $GF(q)$ by taking the subfield-subcode of the extended Reed-Solomon code in the smaller field $GF(q)$. Sometimes, because of constraints over the subfield $GF(q)$, the extended components might not be useable as information places. That is, they might contain the same symbol in every codeword and may just as well be dropped.

In this section, we shall take a somewhat different approach to constructing a code over $GF(q)$ from an extended code over $GF(q^m)$. The approach is to take from the extended Reed-Solomon code those words that have components only in $GF(q)$ in the $q^m - 1$ interior symbols. The two extended symbols are allowed to be arbitrary in $GF(q^m)$ but are represented in the codeword by leading and trailing "tails," each consisting of m q-ary symbols.

As we shall see, it takes a little effort to make this work, but the resulting codes are transform decodable, and many good codes can be obtained in this way. We call these codes *extended BCH codes*. One can find the original BCH code in the extended BCH code by picking all codewords whose tails are equal to zero.

A vector $\mathbf{C}$ over $GF(q^m)$ of length $q^m - 1$ is a valid spectrum for the interior of a $GF(q)$-ary codeword if the conjugacy constraints

$$C_j^{\,q} = C_{((qj))}$$

are satisfied. To get an extended BCH code of designed distance d, we proceed as for the extended Reed-Solomon codes. Choose $d - 1$ contiguous frequencies starting at j_0 as parity frequencies, and set

$$C_{j_0} = c_-$$
$$C_j = 0 \qquad\qquad j = j_0 + 1, \ldots, j_0 + d - 3$$
$$C_{j_0 + d - 2} = c_+$$

where c_- and c_+ are arbitrary elements of $GF(q^m)$, provided they do not violate the conjugacy constraints. The remaining spectral components are chosen in any of the ways that satisfy the constraints. The interior of the codeword is then the inverse Fourier transform of this spectrum. The interior is preceded by a tail consisting of at most m $GF(q)$-ary symbols representing

c_- and is followed by a similar tail representing c_+. It may be that constraints on C_{j_0} or C_{j_0+d-2} force c_- or c_+ to have an order smaller than $q^m - 1$, in which case c_- or c_+ represents less than m q-ary information symbols. In such a case, the tail length is a divisor of m.

When we studied BCH codes, we usually chose $j_0 = 1$, which usually gave the best codes. In this section we will find good extended BCH codes, usually by choosing $j_0 = 0$ or -1, but sometimes other values for j_0 will prove worthwhile.

First, take $j_0 = 0$ and d odd $(d = 2t + 1)$. All of the extended codes obtained from primitive BCH codes of blocklength $n = 255$ are shown in Fig. 8.8. The BCH codes that are extended have parity frequencies $C_0, \ldots, C_{2t-1}$, but for comparison purposes, we give the parameters of the primitive BCH code with parity frequencies $C_1, \ldots, C_{2t}$. As an example of the construction, we will construct some codes with $n' = 63$ by using the conjugacy classes shown in Fig. 8.1. Because $C_0^2 = C_0$, it must be either zero or one, and c_- is a single binary symbol. C_{2t-1} (and hence c_+) is an arbitrary element of $GF(64)$ unless $2t - 1 = 9$, 18, 36, 27, 54, or 45, in which case c_+ contains three bits, or if $2t - 1 = 21$ or 42, in which case c_+ contains two bits. Further, $2t - 1$ must be the smallest integer in its conjugacy class, because if there is another integer in its conjugacy class, that component of the spectrum is constrained to zero, and thus C_{2t-1} must also be zero.

Let $t = 4$. Then $2t - 1 = 7$, and $C_0, C_1, \ldots, C_7$ are parity frequencies, with $C_0 = c_-$ any element of $GF(2)$ and $C_7 = c_+$ any element of $GF(64)$. Further, C_0 corresponds to one parity bit, and C_1, C_3, C_5, and C_7 each correspond to six parity bits. Hence $n = 63 + 1 + 6$, and we have a $(70, 45)$ code whose minimum distance is at least 9.

Let $t = 8$. Then $2t - 1 = 15$ and $C_0, C_1, \ldots, C_{15}$ are parity frequencies, with $C_0 = c_-$ any element of $GF(2)$ and $C_{15} = c_+$ any element of $GF(64)$. Further, C_0 corresponds to one parity bit, C_1, C_3, C_5, C_7, C_{11}, C_{13}, and C_{15} each correspond to six parity bits, and C_9 corresponds to three parity bits. Hence, we have a $(70, 24)$ code whose minimum distance is at least 17.

This second example illustrates a case where the extended BCH code has a designed distance d that is smaller than the minimum distance of the original BCH code. This occurs several times in Fig. 8.8, whenever the BCH code of designed distance d is the same as the BCH code of designed distance $d + 2$.

Next, take $j_0 = -1$. With this choice of j_0, and if c_+ is nonzero, the minimum distance of the code is even, because the upper parity frequency must have odd index. To make the minimum distance odd, we add one extra bit as a parity check on the bits of one of the tails. The extra parity bit allows the decoder to detect a single error in this tail. This is enough to increase the minimum distance of the code by one. We will not prove this fact immediately; rather, we will prove it in Section 9.3, where we will give a decoding procedure to correct $d/2$ errors. The existence of this decoder proves that the minimum distance is increased by one.

d_{BCH}	Primitive BCH Code	Extended BCH Code	$n-k$	Primitive BCH Code	Extended BCH Code	$n-k$	Primitive BCH Code	Extended BCH Code	$n-k$
3	(15, 11)	(20, 15)	5	(31, 26)	(37, 31)	6	(63, 57)	(70, 63)	7
5	(15, 7)	(20, 11)	9	(31, 21)	(37, 26)	11	(63, 51)	(70, 57)	13
7	(15, 5)	(18, 7)	11	(31, 16)	(37, 21)	16	(63, 45)	(70, 51)	19
9							(63, 39)	(70, 45)	25
11				(31, 11)	(37, 16)	21	(63, 36)	(67, 39)	28
13							(63, 30)	(70, 36)	34
15				(31, 6)	(37, 11)	26	(63, 24)	(70, 30)	40
17								(70, 24)	46
19									
21							(63, 18)	(66, 18)	48
23							(63, 16)	(70, 16)	54
25									
27							(63, 10)		
29									

d_{BCH}	Primitive BCH Code	Extended BCH Code	$n-k$	Primitive BCH Code	Extended BCH Code	$n-k$
3	(127, 120)	(135, 127)	8	(255, 247)	(264, 255)	9
5	(127, 113)	(135, 120)	15	(255, 239)	(264, 247)	17
7	(127, 106)	(135, 113)	22	(255, 231)	(264, 239)	25
9	(127, 99)	(135, 106)	29	(255, 223)	(264, 231)	33
11	(127, 92)	(135, 99)	36	(255, 215)	(264, 223)	41
13	(127, 85)	(135, 92)	43	(255, 207)	(264, 215)	49
15	(127, 78)	(135, 85)	50	(255, 199)	(264, 207)	57
17		(135, 78)	57	(255, 191)	(264, 199)	65
19	(127, 71)	(135, 71)	64	(255, 187)	(260, 191)	69
21	(127, 64)	(135, 64)	71	(255, 179)	(264, 187)	77
23	(127, 57)	(135, 57)	78	(255, 171)	(264, 179)	85
25				(255, 163)	(264, 171)	93
27	(127, 50)	(135, 50)	85	(255, 155)	(264, 163)	101
29	(127, 43)			(255, 147)	(264, 155)	109

Figure 8.8 Table of extended BCH codes, $i_0 = 0$

d_{BCH}	Primitive BCH Code	Extended BCH Code	$n-k$	Primitive BCH Code	Extended BCH Code	$n-k$	Primitive BCH Code	Extended BCH Code	$n-k$
3	(15, 11)			(31, 26)	(42, 30)	12	(63, 57)	(76, 62)	14
5	(15, 7)	(24, 14)	10	(31, 21)	(42, 25)	17	(63, 51)	(76, 56)	20
7	(15, 5)	(24, 10)	14	(31, 16)	(42, 20)	22	(63, 45)	(76, 50)	26
9							(63, 39)	(76, 44)	32
11				(31, 11)	(42, 15)	27	(63, 36)	(73, 38)	35
13							(63, 30)	(76, 35)	41
15				(31, 6)	(42, 10)	32	(63, 24)	(76, 29)	47
17								(76, 23)	53
19									
21							(63, 18)		
23							(63, 16)		
25								(72, 17)	55
27							(63, 10)	(76, 15)	61
29									

d_{BCH}	Primitive BCH Code	Extended BCH Code	$n-k$	Primitive BCH Code	Extended BCH Code	$n-k$
3	(127, 120)	(142, 126)	16	(255, 247)	(272, 254)	18
5	(127, 113)	(142, 119)	23	(255, 239)	(272, 246)	26
7	(127, 106)	(142, 112)	30	(255, 231)	(272, 238)	34
9	(127, 99)	(142, 105)	37	(255, 223)	(272, 230)	42
11	(127, 92)	(142, 98)	44	(255, 215)	(272, 222)	50
13	(127, 85)	(142, 91)	51	(255, 207)	(272, 214)	58
15	(127, 78)	(142, 84)	58	(255, 199)	(272, 206)	66
17				(255, 191)	(272, 198)	74
19	(127, 71)	(142, 77)	65	(255, 187)	(268, 190)	78
21	(127, 64)	(142, 70)	72	(255, 179)	(272, 186)	86
23	(127, 57)	(142, 63)	79	(255, 171)	(272, 178)	94
25				(255, 163)	(272, 170)	102
27	(127, 50)	(142, 56)	86	(255, 155)	(272, 162)	110
29	(127, 43)	(142, 49)	93	(255, 147)		

Figure 8.9 Table of extended BCH codes, $j_0 = -1$.

All of the extended codes obtained from primitive BCH codes of block-length $n \leqslant 255$ and $j_0 = -1$ are shown in Fig. 8.9. We can also take other values for j_0, but we will find no new codes of interest in the range $n \leqslant 500$, $d \leqslant 29$. The only exception is in $GF(64)$. With $j_0 = -9$ one can obtain a $(70, 20, 21)$ code as an extended BCH code, which is better than any other known code of this n and k.

An encoder for an (n, k, d) extended BCH code is shown in Fig. 8.10. The encoder uses the generator polynomial of an $(n', k, d - 2)$ BCH code with zeros at $\alpha^{j_0+1}, \ldots, \alpha^{j_0+d-3}$. The values of the spectrum at the two edge frequencies are then appended to the codeword as tails. One of the tails may have its own parity bit attached to it if necessary.

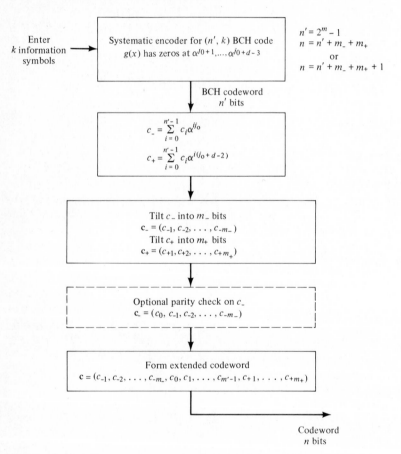

Figure 8.10 Systematic encoder for an extended BCH code.

8.6 ALTERNANT CODES

A BCH code over $GF(q)$ of blocklength $n = q^m - 1$ is a subfield-subcode of a Reed-Solomon code over $GF(q^m)$. That is, the BCH code consists of all those

Reed-Solomon codewords that are $GF(q)$-valued. As such, the BCH code has at least as large a minimum distance as the Reed-Solomon code. Unfortunately, BCH codes of large blocklength and large minimum distance do not contain enough codewords to satisfy us. Stated more precisely, in any sequence of BCH codes of increasing blocklength and bounded rate (for some fixed R', all codes in the sequence satisfy $k/n \geqslant R'$) the normalized minimum distance d^*/n approaches zero with increasing n. The original Reed-Solomon code has a great many codewords, but the subfield-subcode uses very few of them or else has poor distance structure. In this section, we will study ways to increase the minimum distance by reducing the Reed-Solomon code to a subfield code in another way.

Alternant codes are a class of linear codes that are a variation of BCH codes defined such that at fixed rate, large minimum distance can be obtained (at least in principle). Let $n = q^m - 1$. Choose **h**, a fixed n-vector of nonzero components over $GF(q^m)$, which will be called the (time-domain) *template*; and choose a Reed-Solomon code over $GF(q^m)$ with designed distance $2t + 1$. The alternant code consists of all $GF(q)$-valued vectors **c** such that $c_i' = h_i c_i$ for $i = 0, \ldots, n-1$ is a codeword in the Reed-Solomon code.

To put the same thing another way, suppose h_i is always nonzero and let $g_i = h_i^{-1}$. Then for each codeword **c**′ in the Reed-Solomon code, form the vector $c_i = g_i c_i'$ for $i = 0, \ldots, n-1$. If the vector **c** is $GF(q)$-valued, it is in the alternant code. The alternant code is the set of all $GF(q)$-valued codewords that can be obtained in this way.

Normally one would select a template **h** with all components nonzero, but if a template with some zero components is chosen, the codeword must be zero in those components. The zero components contain no information and are simply not transmitted. The decoder can reinsert them if necessary to fit the needs of a decoding algorithm.

Alternant codes have true minimum distances that are very large if the templates are selected properly; for large blocklength they are essentially as good as any known codes. Unfortunately, a practical rule for choosing the template at large n is not known, even though good templates are plentiful, as we shall prove in the next section.

The definition of the alternant codes is easily translated into the frequency domain. Suppose **h** is everywhere nonzero. Let **H** be the transform of **h**, which will be called the *frequency-domain template*. Because $h_i c_i$ for $i = 0, \ldots, n-1$ gives a Reed-Solomon codeword, the cyclic convolution **H** ∗ **C** gives a Reed-Solomon codeword spectrum. That is,

$$\sum_{k=0}^{n-1} H_{((j-k))} C_k = 0 \qquad j = j_0, \ldots, j_0 + 2t - 1.$$

Because **h** is everywhere nonzero, **H** is invertible; that is, there is a **G** (the transform of the vector $g_i = h_i^{-1}$ for $i = 0, \ldots, n-1$) such that **H** ∗ **G** is a delta function. (If $j = 0$, $(\mathbf{H} * \mathbf{G})_j = 1$; otherwise $(\mathbf{H} * \mathbf{G})_j = 0$.)

In the language of polynomials, this convolution becomes

$$H(x)G(x) = 1 \qquad (\text{mod } x^n - 1).$$

If $H(x)$ is a polynomial over the small field $GF(q)$, then so is $G(x)$. The argument is as follows for primitive n. $H(x)$ has no zeros in $GF(q^m)$ because $H(\alpha^{-i}) = nh_i \neq 0$. Hence $H(x)$ is relatively prime to $x^n - 1 = x^{q^m - 1} - 1$, and by the Euclidean algorithm there exist $G(x)$ and $F(x)$ over $GF(q)$ such that

$$H(x)G(x) + (x^n - 1)F(x) = 1.$$

That is,

$$H(x)G(x) = 1 \pmod{x^n - 1}.$$

The alternant codes can be defined in the frequency domain as follows'

☐ **Definition 8.6.1.** Let **H** be a fixed n-vector in the frequency domain and let j_0 and t be fixed integers. The alternant code $\mathscr{C}$ (in the frequench domain) is the set containing every vector whose transform **C** satisfies two conditions:

$$(1) \sum_{k=0}^{n-1} H_{((j-k))} C_k = 0 \qquad j = j_0, \ldots, j_0 + 2t - 1,$$

and

$$(2) \ C_k^q = C_{((qk))}. \qquad\qquad\qquad ☐$$

The first of these conditions is a convolution corresponding to the time-domain product of the more usual definition; the second condition ensures that the time-domain codewords are $GF(q)$-valued. The vector

$$T_j = \sum_{k=0}^{n-1} H_{((j-k))} C_k \qquad j = 0, \ldots, n-1$$

will be called the *filtered spectrum* of the codeword.

Because the alternant codes are so closely related to the Reed-Solomon codes, it is apparant that the minimum distance is at least as large as the designed distance $2t + 1$. The following theorem says that the dimension also satisfies $k \geqslant n - 2tm$.

☐ **Theorem 8.6.2** Let $\mathscr{C}$ be an (n, K, D) linear code over $GF(q^m)$ and let $\mathscr{C}'$ be an (n, k, d) subfield-subcode of $\mathscr{C}$ over $GF(q)$. Then

$$D \leqslant d \leqslant n \qquad \text{and} \qquad (n - K) \leqslant (n - k) \leqslant m(n - K).$$

Proof The only nontrivial inequality is the last one. Each parity-check equation for the code over $GF(q^m)$ yields at most m linearly independent parity-check equations over $GF(q)$. The last inequality follows from this. ☐

☐ **Corollary 8.6.3** An alternant code of designed distance $2t + 1$ has dimension k satisfying

$k \geqslant n - 2tm$.

Proof Use Theorem 8.6.2 and $n - K = 2t$. ☐

We will see in the next section that some alternant codes have a minimum distance much larger than the designed distance, but the proof is nonconstructive.

We can extend the BCH bound to an instructive frequency-domain derivation of the distance structure inherited by alternant codes from Reed-Solomon codes.

☐ **Theorem 8.6.4** If a vector **c** has less than d nonzero components, and if the filtered spectrum is zero on any $d - 1$ successive components $(T_k = 0, k = k_0, \ldots, k_0 + d - 2)$, then $c_i = 0$ for all i, where $\mathbf{T} = \mathbf{H} * \mathbf{C}$ and **H** is an invertible filter.

Proof The locator polynomial $\Lambda(x)$ is defined in such a way that its transform λ_i is zero whenever $c_i \neq 0$. Then $\lambda_i c_i = 0$, which implies that $\Lambda * \mathbf{C} = \mathbf{0}$. Hence, $\Lambda * (\mathbf{H} * \mathbf{C}) = \mathbf{H} * (\Lambda * (\Lambda * \mathbf{C})) = \mathbf{0}$. But Λ is nonzero only in a block of at most d, and $\mathbf{H} * \mathbf{C}$ is zero in a block of length $d - 1$. Consequently, $\mathbf{H} * \mathbf{C} = \mathbf{0}$, and in turn $\mathbf{C} = \mathbf{0}$. Hence **c** is the all-zero vector. ☐

8.7 PERFORMANCE OF ALTERNANT CODES

Alternant codes are attractive because in this class there are codes of long blocklength that are good. By this we mean that there are sequences of increasingly long codes with rate k/n and relative minimum distance d^*/n that remain bounded away from zero as n goes to infinity. This we will now show. The technique used is to show that there are not too many low-weight words over $GF(q)$ and that each cannot appear in too many alternant codes. Because there are many alternant codes by comparison, some alternant code has no low-weight word. Hence, this code has large minimum distance.

In the proof of the theorem, we will not find k and d^* for any code; instead we will find only lower bounds on them. For purposes of this theorem, by an (n, k, d) code, we mean a code of blocklength n whose dimension is *at least* k and whose minimum distance is *at least* d.

☐ **Theorem 8.7.1** For any $GF(q)$ and m, let $n = q^m - 1$, and let d and r be any integers. Then there exists an $(n, n - mr, d)$ alternant code, provided d and r satisfy

$$\sum_{j=1}^{d-1} \binom{n}{j} (q - 1)^j < (q^m - 1)^r.$$

Proof The idea of the proof given below is to count the number of alternant codes of a certain type and then count the number of such codes to which belongs a given vector $\mathbf{v}$ of weight $j < d$. There are not enough such $\mathbf{v}$ to account for all of the codes, and thus some codes have no $\mathbf{v}$ of weight $j < d$.

(i) Let $\mathscr{C}$ be a Reed-Solomon code over $GF(q^m)$ of designed distance $r + 1$ and rate $K = n - r$. Let $\mathscr{C}(\mathbf{h})$ be the alternant code over $GF(q)$ generated from $\mathscr{C}$ by template $\mathbf{h}$, where $\mathbf{h}$ is a vector over $GF(q^m)$ with all components nonzero. Then

$$\mathscr{C}(\mathbf{h}) = \{c \in GF(q)^n : \mathbf{hc} \in \mathscr{C}\},$$

and $\mathbf{hc}$ denotes the vector $\{h_i c_i \ i = 0, \ldots, n - 1\}$. Because $h_i \neq 0$ for all i, there are $(q^m - 1)^n$ such codes. Each such code is a sub-field-subcode of the linear code $\{\mathbf{c} \in GF(q^m)^n : \mathbf{hc} \in \mathscr{C}\}$ and hence, by Theorem 8.6.2, for each such code,

$$k \geq n - mr.$$

(ii) Choose a vector $\mathbf{v}$ over $GF(q)$ of weight $j < d$. There are $\binom{n}{j}(q - 1)^j$ vectors of weight j, and

$$\sum_{j=1}^{d-1} \binom{n}{j}(q - 1)^j$$

vectors of weight less than d.

(iii) A vector $\mathbf{v}$ of weight j appears in at most $(q^m - 1)^{n-r}$ of the alternant codes defined in (i). This is because any $n - r$ places in a Reed-Solomon codeword specify the codeword. If we fix $\mathbf{v}$, then there are only $n - r$ places in $\mathbf{h}$ that can be independently specified such that $\mathbf{hv}$ is in $\mathscr{C}$.

(iv) Now combine (i), (ii), and (iii). From (i), the number of alternant codes is $(q^m - 1)^n$. The maximum number that can have a vector of weight less than d is $(q^m - 1)^{n-r} \sum_{j=1}^{d-1} \binom{n}{j}(q - 1)^j$. Suppose

$$(q^m - 1)^n > (q^m - 1)^{n-r} \sum_{j=1}^{d-1} \binom{n}{j}(q - 1)^j.$$

(iii) Then some code of rate $n - mr$ has minimum distance at least as large as d. This is equivalent to the statement of the theorem. $\square$

Notice from the proof that the class of alternant codes is a very large class. For any k and primitive blocklength, the number of alternant (n, k) codes over $GF(q)$ is $(q^m - 1)^n = n^n$. The theorem only tells us that some of these are good codes but it does not say how to find them.

Let q equal 2. Theorem 8.7.1 asserts that binary alternant codes exist that satisfy

$$\sum_{j=1}^{d-1} \binom{n}{j} < 2^{n-k}.$$

The left-hand side was bounded in Lemma 7.9.2, but in the wrong direction. Later, in Chapter 14, we will study how to estimate $\binom{n}{d}$ using Stirling's approximation. Theorem 14.4.1 then implies that

$$\sum_{k=0}^{pn} \binom{n}{k} > \binom{n}{pn} \geq 2^{n[H(p) - o(1)]}$$

where $o(1)$ is a term that goes to zero as n goes to infinity. If we ignore this term, the theorem asserts that for large-enough n, binary codes of rate R and relative minimum distance d/n exist provided

$$-\frac{d}{n} \log \frac{d}{n} - \left(1 - \frac{d}{n}\right) \log \left(1 - \frac{d}{n}\right) < 1 - R.$$

The important thing here is that there are nonzero solutions to this inequality and that the inequality involves only R and d/n. Hence, it is a strong statement about the existence of asymptotically good binary alternant codes.

This form of the bound is equivalent to a bound known as the *Gilbert bound*, which preceded the introduction of alternant codes by many years. The Gilbert bound asserted that codes this good exist, and thus alternant codes are one class of codes that fulfill the promise of the Gilbert bound. In fact, at the present time, there is no definite evidence that a class of binary codes asymptotically better than the Gilbert bound exists. Hence, asymptotically optimum codes may very well be contained in the class of alternant codes. The alternant codes are a very large class, however, and without some constructive methods for isolating the good codes, the bound of Theorem 8.7.1 is another unfulfilled promise. Although the bound of Theorem 8.7.1 implies that good alternant codes are better than the Justesen codes studied in Section 7.9, the Justesen codes nevertheless are defined by an explicit construction, whereas we do not yet know how to explicitly find the good alternant codes of long blocklength.

8.8 GOPPA CODES

The Goppa codes constitute a special class of alternant codes that were discovered earlier than the general class and remain worthy of individual attention.

☐ **Definition 8.8.1** A *Goppa code* of designed distance d is an alternant code of designed distance d, with the additional property that the inverse frequency template **G** has width d. That is, the inverse frequency template can be described as a polynomial $G(x)$ of degree $d - 1$, called the *Goppa polynomial*. A *narrow-sense Goppa code* is a Goppa code with the $2t$ parity frequencies at locations $\alpha^{n - 2t + 1}, \alpha^{n - 2t + 2}, \ldots, \alpha^0$. ☐

☐ **Theorem 8.8.2** In a Goppa code with Goppa polynomial $G(x)$, **c** is a codeword if and only if

$$\sum_{i=0}^{n-1} c_i \frac{\alpha^{ij}}{G(\alpha^{-i})} = 0 \qquad j = 0, \ldots, 2t - 1.$$

Proof The proof follows directly from the convolution theorem. ☐

☐ **Theorem 8.8.3** A Goppa code with Goppa polynomial of degree $2t$ has minimum distance d^* and dimension k satisfying

$$d^* \geqslant 2t + 1,$$

$$k \geqslant n - 2tm.$$

Proof The proof follows immediately from Corollary 8.6.3. ☐

As stated, Definition 8.8.1 allows Goppa codes to have only blocklengths that divide $q^m - 1$. Shortened codes or extended codes obtained from Goppa codes, however, are also called Goppa codes. The techniques of Section 8.4 can be used to get extended Goppa codes of blocklength q^m or $q^m + 1$ by extending the code by a single q-ary symbol on each end. In principle, even longer extended Goppa codes can be obtained by tilting q^m-ary extension symbols, as was done for BCH codes in Section 8.5.

As a subclass of the class of alternant codes, the class of Goppa codes retains the property that it includes many codes whose minimum distance is much larger than d. Just as for the general case of an alternant code, however, not much is known about finding the good Goppa codes. Similarly, there are not yet good encoding algorithms for general Goppa codes, nor are there algorithms for decoding to the minimum distance. The known Goppa codes are interesting primarily because they give a way to extend a narrow-sense BCH code ($j_0 = 1$) by an extra information symbol and to extend other codes by even more extension symbols. Consequently, the good Goppa codes that are known are good not because they are the good codes in the sense promised by Theorem 8.7.1, but for another reason.

We can describe the Goppa codes in the frequency domain using the shift-register circuit of Fig. 8.11. Instead of inserting the information into the time-domain codeword, it is inserted in the frequency domain, either into the spectrum or into the filtered spectrum, as shown in Fig. 8.11, and in either case it is done in such a way that all constraints are satisfied. There is no general yet practical procedure known for doing this, but in codes of modest size, it is possible to set up and solve algebraic equations that describe the constraints. We will give an example of this later. Once the filtered spectrum is loaded with the information, it is filtered by a finite-impulse-response filter whose tap weights are given by the Goppa polynomial. The filter operation is cyclic. That is, the input is treated as periodic. Finally, the inverse Fourier transform of the spectrum is taken to produce a codeword.

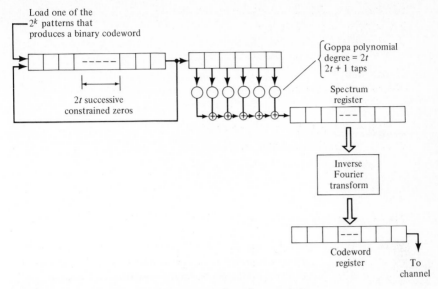

Figure 8.11   Goppa-code frequency-domain templating.

An alternative description of the Goppa codes is contained in the following theorem.

☐ **Theorem 8.8.4**   The narrow-sense Goppa code over $GF(q)$ with blocklength $n = q^m - 1$ and with Goppa polynomial $G(x)$ is given by the set of all vectors $\mathbf{c} = (c_0, \dots, c_{n-1})$ over $GF(q)$ satisfying

$$\sum_{i=0}^{n-1} c_i \prod_{i' \neq i} (x - \alpha^{-i'}) = 0 \qquad (\text{mod } G(x))$$

Proof   The condition of the theorem is

$$\sum_{i=0}^{n-1} c_i \prod_{i' \neq i} (x - \alpha^{-i'}) = A(x)G(x).$$

Because $G(x)$ is a polynomial of degree $2t$ and the left-hand side is a polynomial of degree at most $n - 1$, the degree of $A(x)$ is at most $n - 2t - 1$. That is, $A_j = 0$ for $j = n - 2t, \dots, n - 1$. Evaluate the above expression at $x = \alpha^{-i}$:

$$c_i \prod_{i' \neq i} (\alpha^{-i} - \alpha^{-i'}) = A(\alpha^{-i})G(\alpha^{-i})$$

or

$$c_i \left[(\alpha^{-i})^{n-1} \prod_{i' \neq i} (1 - \alpha^{-(i' - i)}) \right] = A(\alpha^{-i})G(\alpha^{-i})$$

or

$$c_i \alpha^i \prod_{k \neq 0} (1 - \alpha^k) = A(\alpha^{-i}) G(\alpha^{-i}).$$

Hence, define

$$T(x) = \prod_{k \neq 0} (1 - \alpha^k)^{-1} x A(x) \qquad (\text{mod } x^n - 1)$$

so that

$$T(\alpha^{-1}) = \prod_{k \neq 0} (1 - \alpha^k)^{-1} [\alpha^{-i} A(\alpha^{-1})]$$

and

$$c_i = T(\alpha^{-1}) G(\alpha^{-1}).$$

Finally, notice that because $A_j = 0$ for $j = n - 2t, \ldots, n - 1$, $T_j = 0$ for $j = n - 2t + 1, \ldots, n$ (mod n), and thus the condition of the theorem is equivalent to the condition defining the narrow-sense Goppa code:

$$C(x) = T(x) G(x) \qquad (\text{mod } x^n - 1),$$

which completes the proof of the theorem. $\square$

The form in Theorem 8.8.4 makes it easy to extend the Goppa code by one symbol to get a code with blocklength q^m. Simply add the field element zero as another location number. We then have an alternative definition.

□ **Definition 8.8.5** The Goppa code over $GF(q)$ with blocklength $n = q^m$ and with Goppa polynomial $G(x)$ is given by the set of all vectors $\mathbf{c} = (c_0, \ldots, c_{n-1})$ over $GF(q)$ satisfying

$$\sum_{i=0}^{n-1} c_i \prod_{i' \neq i} (x - \beta_{i'}) = 0 \qquad (\text{mod } G(x)),$$

where β_i now ranges over all elements of $GF(q^m)$. $\square$

We now turn to the special case of binary Goppa codes, restricting attention to those codes whose Goppa polynomial has no repeated zeros in any extension field. Such a code is called a *separable* Goppa code. For separable and binary Goppa codes, we will see that the minimum distance is at least $2r + 1$, where r is the degree of $G(x)$. This is more striking than the general bound for any Goppa code, $d^* \geq r + 1$. The key to the proof of this fact can be summarized by the following theorem, which gives a condition on the reciprocal form of the locator polynomial. The reciprocal form of the locator polynomial is given by

$$\tilde{\Lambda}_c(x) = \prod_{i=1}^{v} (x - \beta_i),$$

where β_i is the location of the ith one of codeword $\mathbf{c}$ and v is the number of ones in the codeword.

☐ **Theorem 8.8.6**   Suppose that $G(x)$, a polynomial with no zeros in $GF(2^m)$, is a Goppa polynomial of a narrow-sense binary Goppa code. Then $\mathbf{c}$ is a codeword if and only if its reciprocal locator polynomial $\tilde{\Lambda}_c(x)$ has formal derivative $\tilde{\Lambda}'_c(x)$ divisible by $G(x)$.

Proof   The formal derivative is

$$\tilde{\Lambda}'_c(x) = \sum_{i=1}^{v} \prod_{i' \neq i} (x - \beta_{i'}).$$

Now in a binary code, c_i is either zero or one, and thus the formula of Theorem 8.8.4 reduces to the expression for $\tilde{\Lambda}'_c(x)$. ☐

Notice that the formal derivative of any polynomial over an extension field of $GF(2)$ is a perfect square, because the coefficients of odd powers of x vanish. Suppose that we have a separable Goppa code with polynomial $G(x)$. Then not only does $G(x)$ divide $\tilde{\Lambda}'_c(x)$, but because $\tilde{\Lambda}'_c(x)$ is a perfect square, $G(x)^2$ must also divide $\tilde{\Lambda}'_c(x)$. In fact for such a $G(x)$, we will get the same code if we use $\bar{G}(x) = G(x)^2$ instead as the Goppa polynomial. This has a degree of $2r$, and thus $d^* \geq 2r + 1$.

Although a separable Goppa code has a minimum distance of at least $2r + 1$, Definition 8.8.1 produces only t syndromes rather than $2t$, and the usual decoding techniques do not apply directly. We could describe a special variation of decoding algorithm for this case that uses only t syndromes. Instead, we will modify the description of the code so that the decoders of Chapter 7 and Chapter 9 can be used directly. We can do this with no change in the code, only a change in its description. We use $G(x)^2$ as the Goppa polynomial instead of $G(x)$. This gives the same code, but the performance bounds become

$$d^* \geq \bar{r} + 1 = 2r + 1$$

and

$$k \geq n - \tfrac{1}{2}m\bar{r} = n - mr,$$

where $\bar{r}$ is the degree of $G(x)^2$. This is the same code and the same performance as in the previous case, but now there are $2t$ parity frequencies, and all the familiar decoding techniques apply directly.

The smallest example of a Goppa code is an $(8, 2, 5)$ binary Goppa code. Take $G(x) = x^2 + x + 1$. The zeros of this polynomial are distinct and are in $GF(4)$ or in any extension of $GF(4)$, and thus none are in $GF(8)$. Hence $G(x)$ can be used to obtain a Goppa code with blocklength 8, minimum distance of at least 5, and at least two information symbols. We will see below that there are exactly two information symbols. We will first describe this code using Definition 8.8.1. Then we will describe the code in the time-domain using Theorem 8.8.2.

We have

$$G(x) = x^2 + x + 1 \qquad \text{and} \qquad H(x) = x^6 + x^5 + x^3 + x^2 + 1$$

because

$$H(x)G(x) + x(x^7 - 1) = 1.$$

Further,

$$\bar{G}(x) = x^4 + x^2 + 1 \qquad \text{and} \qquad \bar{H}(x) = x^6 + x^5 + x^4 + x^3 + 1.$$

The polynomials $H(x)$ and $\bar{H}(x)$ can be calculated from $G(x)$ and $\bar{G}(x)$ using the Euclidean algorithm.

The parity frequencies are at $\alpha^{-3}, \alpha^{-2}, \alpha^{-1}$, and α^0, and $T_0 = c_+$, $T_{-1} = 0$, $T_{-2} = 0$, and $T_{-3} = 0$. From these and the defining equation

$$T_k = \sum_{j=0}^{n-1} \bar{H}_{k-j} C_j$$

we get the equations

$$c_+ = C_0 + C_1 + C_2 + C_3 + C_4$$
$$0 = C_6 + C_0 + C_1 + C_2 + C_3$$
$$0 = C_5 + C_6 + C_0 + C_1 + C_2$$
$$0 = C_4 + C_5 + C_6 + C_0 + C_1.$$

We also have the constraints

$$C_j^2 = C_{((2j))},$$

Any spectrum that satisfies the parity equations and the constraints is an information spectrum. Using the constraints to eliminate C_2, C_4, C_5, and C_6 gives

$$c_+ = C_0 + (C_1 + C_1^2 + C_1^4) + C_3$$
$$0 = C_0 + (C_1 + C_1^2) + (C_3 + C_3^2)$$
$$0 = C_0 + (C_1 + C_1^2) + (C_3^2 + C_3^4)$$
$$0 = C_0 + (C_1 + C_1^4) + (C_3^2 + C_3^4).$$

If we take $C_0 = 0$, C_1 and C_3 each as an arbitrary element of $GF(2)$, and the extension symbol c_+ equal to C_1 plus C_3, all of the equations are satisfied. Thus we have two binary information symbols. An encoder for this code in the frequency domain is shown in Fig. 8.12.

We can get the same code by encoding in the time domain according to Theorem 8.8.2. The parity-check matrix $\mathbf{H}$ has elements given by $\alpha^{ij}/G(\alpha^{-i})$. That is,

$$\mathbf{H} = \begin{bmatrix} 1 & 1 & \alpha^2 & \alpha^4 & \alpha^2 & \alpha & \alpha & \alpha^4 \\ 0 & 1 & \alpha^3 & \alpha^6 & \alpha^5 & \alpha^5 & \alpha^6 & \alpha^3 \end{bmatrix},$$

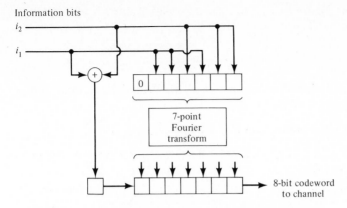

Figure 8.12 An encoder for an (8, 2, 5) Goppa code.

where the first column is appended to give the (8, 2) extended code. Replacing each field element by its 3-bit representation gives

$$\mathbf{H} = \begin{bmatrix} 1 & 1 & 0 & 0 & 0 & 0 & 0 & 0 \\ 0 & 0 & 0 & 1 & 0 & 1 & 1 & 1 \\ 0 & 0 & 1 & 1 & 1 & 0 & 0 & 1 \\ 0 & 1 & 1 & 1 & 1 & 1 & 1 & 1 \\ 0 & 0 & 1 & 0 & 1 & 1 & 0 & 1 \\ 0 & 0 & 0 & 1 & 1 & 1 & 1 & 0 \end{bmatrix}.$$

The rows are linearly independent, and hence this specifies an (8, 2) code.

For a more difficult example of a binary Goppa code, we will choose the Goppa polynomial

$$G(x) = x^3 + x + 1,$$

which has three distinct zeros in $GF(8)$ or in any extension of $GF(8)$ and hence has no zeros in $GF(32)$. Then by Theorem 8.8.2, either $G(x)$ or $G(x)^2$ can be used as the Goppa polynomial for a (31, 16, 7) Goppa code or a (32, 17, 7) extended Goppa code. The (31, 16, 7) Goppa code is not better than a (31, 16, 7) BCH code except that it can be extended to a (32, 17, 7) code, whereas the BCH code cannot be so extended.

The square of $G(x)$ is

$$\bar{G}(x) = x^6 + x^2 + 1,$$

and the inverse Goppa polynomials are

$$H(x) = x^{30} + x^{27} + x^{25} + x^{24} + x^{23} + x^{20} + x^{18} + x^{17} + x^{16} + x^{13}$$
$$+ x^{11} + x^{10} + x^9 + x^6 + x^4 + x^3 + x^2$$

and

$$\bar{H}(x) = x^{29} + x^{26} + x^{23} + x^{22} + x^{20} + x^{19} + x^{18} + x^{17} + x^{15} + x^{12}$$
$$+ x^9 + x^8 + x^6 + x^5 + x^4 + x^3 + x.$$

For the example, we choose to insert the information directly into the spectrum. Then the filtered spectrum is given by

$$T_k = \sum_{j=0}^{n-1} \bar{H}_{((k-j))} C_j \qquad k = 0, \ldots, n-1,$$

and the parity frequencies are $k = -5, -4, \ldots, 0$, Writing these out, with edge syndromes c_+ and c_-, we have

$$c_+ = C_2 + C_5 + C_8 + C_9 + C_{11} + C_{12} + C_{13} + C_{14} + C_{16} + C_{19}$$
$$+ C_{22} + C_{23} + C_{25} + C_{26} + C_{27} + C_{28} + C_{30}$$

$$0 = C_1 + C_4 + C_7 + C_8 + C_{10} + C_{11} + C_{12} + C_{13} + C_{15} + C_{18}$$
$$+ C_{21} + C_{22} + C_{24} + C_{25} + C_{26} + C_{27} + C_{29}$$

$$0 = C_0 + C_3 + C_6 + C_7 + C_9 + C_{10} + C_{11} + C_{12} + C_{14} + C_{17}$$
$$+ C_{20} + C_{21} + C_{23} + C_{24} + C_{25} + C_{26} + C_{28}$$

$$0 = C_{30} + C_2 + C_5 + C_6 + C_8 + C_9 + C_{10} + C_{11} + C_{13} + C_{16}$$
$$+ C_{19} + C_{20} + C_{22} + C_{23} + C_{24} + C_{25} + C_{27}$$

$$0 = C_{29} + C_1 + C_4 + C_5 + C_7 + C_8 + C_9 + C_{10} + C_{12} + C_{15}$$
$$+ C_{18} + C_{19} + C_{21} + C_{22} + C_{23} + C_{24} + C_{26}$$

$$c_- = C_{28} + C_0 + C_3 + C_4 + C_6 + C_7 + C_8 + C_9 + C_{11} + C_{14} + C_{17}$$
$$+ C_{18} + C_{20} + C_{21} + C_{22} + C_{23} + C_{25}.$$

Any c_+, c_-, and C_j for $j = 0, \ldots, 30$ over $GF(32)$ satisfying these equations defines a codeword provided the conjugacy constraints

$$C_j^2 = C_{((2j))} \qquad j = 0, \ldots, n-1$$

are satisfied. Using the constraint equations, the parity-check equations become

$$c_+ = (C_1^2 + C_1^8 + C_1^{16}) + C_3^4 + (C_5 + C_5^8) + (C_7^2 + C_7^4 + C_7^8 + C_7^{16})$$
$$+ (C_{11} + C_{11}^2 + C_{11}^4 + C_{11}^8) + (C_{15}^2 + C_{15}^8 + C_{15}^{16})$$

$$0 = (C_1 + C_1^4 + C_1^8) + (C_3^4 + C_3^8) + (C_5^2 + C_5^{16}) + (C_7 + C_7^8)$$
$$+ (C_{11} + C_{11}^2 + C_{11}^4 + C_{11}^8 + C_{11}^{16}) + (C_{15} + C_{15}^4 + C_{15}^8)$$

$$0 = C_0 + (C_3 + C_3^2 + C_3^4 + C_3^8 + C_3^{16}) + (C_5^2 + C_5^4 + C_5^8)$$
$$+ (C_7 + C_7^2 + C_7^4 + C_7^8) + (C_{11} + C_{11}^8 + C_{11}^{16}) + C_{15}^{16}$$

$$0 = (C_1^2 + C_1^8 + C_1^{16}) + (C_3^2 + C_3^8) + (C_5 + C_5^2 + C_5^4 + C_5^8)$$
$$+ (C_7^8 + C_7^{16}) + (C_{11} + C_{11}^2 + C_{11}^4) + (C_{15}^2 + C_{15}^8 + C_{15}^{16})$$

$$0 = (C_1 + C_1^4 + C_1^8) + (C_3^4 + C_3^8) + (C_5 + C_5^2 + C_5^8 + C_5^{16})$$
$$+ (C_7 + C_7^{16}) + (C_{11}^2 + C_{11}^8 + C_{11}^{16}) + (C_{15} + C_{15}^4 + C_{15}^{16})$$

$$c_- = C_0 + (C_1^4 + C_1^8) + (C_3 + C_3^2 + C_3^{16}) + (C_5^4 + C_5^8 + C_5^{16})$$
$$+ (C_7 + C_7^2 + C_7^4 + C_7^8) + (C_{11} + C_{11}^2 + C_{11}^{16}) + C_{15}^{16}$$

We will work through the solution of these equations in detail. First, square the third equation and solve for C_{15}:

$$C_{15} = C_0 + (C_3 + C_3^2 + C_3^4 + C_3^8 + C_3^{16}) + (C_5^4 + C_5^8 + C_5^{16})$$
$$+ (C_7^2 + C_7^4 + C_7^8 + C_7^{16}) + (C_{11} + C_{11}^2 + C_{11}^{16}).$$

Use this equation to eliminate C_{15}. This yields five equations:

$$c_+ = C_0 + (C_1^2 + C_1^8 + C_1^{16}) + (C_3 + C_3^2 + C_3^8 + C_3^{16}) + (C_5 + C_5^8 + C_5^{16})$$
$$+ (C_7 + C_7^2 + C_7^8 + C_7^{16}) + (C_{11} + C_{11}^2 + C_{11}^8)$$

$$0 = C_0 + (C_1 + C_1^4 + C_1^8) + (C_3 + C_3^2 + C_3^{16}) + (C_5^2 + C_5^8 + C_5^{16})$$
$$+ (C_7 + C_7^2 + C_7^8 + C_7^{16}) + (C_{11}^2 + C_{11}^4 + C_{11}^8 + C_{11}^{16})$$

$$0 = C_0 + (C_1^2 + C_1^8 + C_1^{16}) + (C_3 + C_3^4 + C_3^{16})$$
$$+ (C_5 + C_5^2 + C_5^4 + C_5^8 + C_5^{16}) + (C_7 + C_7^4 + C_7^8 + C_7^{16})$$
$$+ (C_{11} + C_{11}^4)$$

$$0 = C_0 + (C_1 + C_1^4 + C_1^8) + (C_3 + C_3^2 + C_3^{16}) + (C_5^2 + C_5^8 + C_5^{16})$$
$$+ (C_7 + C_7^2 + C_7^8 + C_7^{16}) + (C_{11}^2 + C_{11}^4 + C_{11}^8 + C_{11}^{16})$$

$$c_- = (C_1^4 + C_1^8) + (C_3^4 + C_3^8) + (C_5^2 + C_5^{16}) + (C_{11}^2 + C_{11}^8).$$

The fourth equation is the same as the second and can be discarded. Add the second equation, the third equation, and the square of the third equation. This gives

$$C_1 = C_0 + (C_3 + C_3^2 + C_3^8) + (C_5^2 + C_5^8 + C_5^{16}) + (C_7 + C_7^8) + (C_{11}^2 + C_{11}^{16}).$$

Substituting this for C_1, we now have four equations:

$$c_+ = C_3^2 + (C_5 + C_5^2 + C_5^4 + C_5^{16}) + (C_7 + C_7^2 + C_7^4 + C_7^{16})$$
$$+ (C_{11} + C_{11}^4 + C_{11}^{16})$$

$$0 = (C_3^4 + C_3^8) + (C_5 + C_5^{16}) + (C_7 + C_7^{16}) + (C_{11} + C_{11}^4 + C_{11}^8 + C_{11}^{16})$$

$$0 = (C_3 + C_3^2 + C_3^4 + C_3^8) + (C_5 + C_5^4 + C_5^8 + C_5^{16}) + (C_7 + C_7^{16})$$
$$+ (C_{11} + C_{11}^4 + C_{11}^8 + C_{11}^{16})$$

$$c_- = (C_3 + C_3^2 + C_3^8 + C_3^{16}) + (C_5 + C_5^2 + C_5^4 + C_5^8)$$
$$+ (C_7 + C_7^2 + C_7^4 + C_7^8) + (C_{11}^4 + C_{11}^{16})'$$

Take the fourth power of the last equation and compare it to the second equation. This shows that $c_- = 0$, and the fourth equation can be dropped. Add the eighth power of the third equation to the third equation. This gives the second equation, and thus the second equation can be dropped. Two equations remain:

$$c_+ = C_3^2 + (C_5 + C_5^2 + C_5^4 + C_5^{16}) + (C_7 + C_7^2 + C_7^4 + C_7^{16})$$
$$+ (C_{11} + C_{11}^4 + C_{11}^{16})'$$

$$0 = (C_3^4 + C_3^8) + (C_5 + C_5^{16}) + (C_7 + C_7^{16}) + (C_{11} + C_{11}^4 + C_{11}^8 + C_{11}^{16}).$$

Form the sixteenth power of the first equation:

$$C_3 = c_+^{16} + (C_5 + C_5^2 + C_5^8 + C_5^{16}) + (C_7 + C_7^2 + C_7^8 + C_7^{16})$$
$$+ (C_{11}^2 + C_{11}^8 + C_{11}^{16}).$$

Substituting this into the last equation gives

$$0 = c_+^2 + c_+^4.$$

Taking the sixteenth power gives

$$0 = c_+(1 + c_+),$$

which requires c_+ to equal zero or one.

We now have derived the following rule: C_0 and c_+ are arbitrary elements of $GF(2)$; C_5, C_7, and C_{11} are arbitrary elements of $GF(32)$; and C_1, C_3, and C_{15} are specified by the equations

$$C_1 = c_+ + C_0 + C_5^8 + (C_7 + C_7^2 + C_7^8 + C_7^{16}) + (C_{11} + C_{11}^2 + C_{11}^8)$$
$$C_3 = c_+ + (C_5 + C_5^2 + C_5^8 + C_5^{16}) + (C_7 + C_7^2 + C_7^8 + C_7^{16})$$
$$+ (C_{11}^2 + C_{11}^8 + C_{11}^{16})$$
$$C_{15} = c_+ + C_0 + (C_5^4 + C_5^8 + C_5^{16}) + (C_7^2 + C_7^4 + C_7^8 + C_7^{16})$$
$$+ (C_{11}^4 + C_{11}^8).$$

All other C_j are specified by the conjugacy constraints. An inverse Fourier transform gives 31 components of the time-domain codeword. To these, c_+ is appended as a tail. The code is a (32, 17, 7) extended Goppa code. Because the constraint equations force c_- to equal zero, it is not possible to add a second tail to the codeword.

8.9 PREPARATA CODES

A few good classes of nonlinear codes are known, and among them is the class of Preparata codes. We will study these codes by constructing one example, the Preparata (15, 8) code, by working in the frequency domain.

Before we study the Preparata codes, let us return to the procedure for decoding double-error-correcting binary BCH codes described in Section 5.6, where the reciprocal error-locator polynomial was written down explicitly. It is

$$\tilde{\Lambda}(x) = x^2 + S_1 x + S_1^{-1}(S_1^3 + S_3) = 0$$

unless $S_1 = 0$. This special case arises only when there are no errors and is easily checked. If we define $0/0 = 0$, then the error-locator polynomial even includes the case of no errors. In this case, the equation degenerates to

$$x^2 = 0,$$

with roots at $X_1 = 0$ and $X_2 = 0$. If there is one error, it degenerates to

$$x^2 + S_1 x = 0,$$

with roots at $X_1 = 0$ and $X_2 = S_1$.

We make the change in variable $x = S_1 z$. Then we have the new polynomial, also called $\tilde{\Lambda}$, given by

$$\tilde{\Lambda}(z) = z^2 + z + (1 + S_1^{-3} S_3).$$

Over $GF(2^m)$, this polynomial has two zeros if and only if $\text{trace}(1 + S_1^{-3} S_3) = 0$. Over extensions of $GF(4)$, $\text{trace}(1) = 0$, and the condition becomes

$$\text{trace}(S_1^{-3} S_3) = 0.$$

Now in any field of characteristic 2, by Theorem 8.2.3, exactly half the elements have trace equal to zero. For each value of S_1, S_3 can take on only one of 2^{m-1} values, and in fact these form a vector space in $GF(2^m)$ of dimension $m - 1$. One bit of S_3 is "not used." It seems superficially that it may be possible to put one extra bit of information into frequency C_3 of the codeword. This is not possible because the unused bit of S_3 depends on S_1, but the Preparata codes do manage something as good. If the spectrum is in an extension of $GF(4)$, one extra bit can be slipped into the spectrum by rearranging the way the other information bits are specified.

For each even m greater than 2, there is a $(2^m - 1, 2^m - 2m, 5)$ Preparata code over $GF(2)$. The Preparata code always contains one more information bit than the corresponding double-error-correcting BCH code. We will develop only the (15, 8, 5) Preparata code.

☐ **Definition 8.9.1** The Preparata (15, 8) binary code† is the set of binary words of blocklength 15 whose spectrum satisfies the constraints $C_1 = 0$, $C_3 = A$, and $C_5 = B$, where either

(1) $A \in \{1, \alpha^3, \alpha^6, \alpha^9, \alpha^{12}\}$ and $B = 0$,

or

(2) $B \in \{1, \alpha^5, \alpha^{10}\}$ and $A = 0$,

and all other spectral components are arbitrary insofar as conjugacy constraints allow. ☐

Notice that the conjugacy constraints require that $C_5^4 = C_5$, and thus C_5 can only be an element of $GF(4)$. Because C_0 is an arbitrary element of $GF(2)$ and C_7 is an arbitrary element of $GF(16)$, C_0 and C_7 together contain five bits. An additional three bits describe the eight choices for A and B. Hence, the code is a (15, 8) code.

† With this definition, the all-zero word is not a codeword. Other definitions in use translate the code to place one codeword on the all-zero word.

We will show how to correct double errors and thus show that the minimum distance is at least 5. Let V_j for $j = 0, \ldots, n-1$ be the spectral components of the received word. Define the syndromes:

$$S_1 = E_1 = \quad V_1$$
$$S_2 = E_2 = \quad V_2$$
$$S_3 = E_3 + A = V_3$$
$$S_4 = E_4 = \quad V_4$$
$$S_5 = E_5 + B = V_5.$$

The terms A and B are unknown to the receiver but constrained by the choices allowed by Definition 8.9.1. Then

$$S_1 = X_1 + X_2$$
$$S_3 = X_1^3 + X_2^3 + A$$
$$S_5 = X_1^5 + X_2^5 + B.$$

We will first solve these for A and B; A can then be subtracted from S_3, reducing the problem to the decoding of a double-error-correcting BCH code. A simple calculation gives

$$S_1^3 + (S_3 + A) \qquad = X_1 X_2 S_1$$
$$(S_3 + A)^2 + S_1(S_5 + B) = X_1 X_2 S_1^4.$$

Eliminate $X_1 X_2$ to obtain the quadratic equation

$$A^2 + S_1^3 A + (S_1^3 S_3 + S_3^2 + S_1^6 + S_1 S_5 + S_1 B) = 0.$$

We can solve for A and B as follows. First, set $B = 0$ and solve the quadratic equation for A. Then set $A = 0$ and solve the linear equation for B. In this way, up to three solutions are found for the pair (A, B). In the proof of the following theorem, we will show that only one such solution can agree with the constraints of Definition 8.9.1.

☐ **Theorem 8.9.2** The minimum distance of the Preparata $(15, 8)$ code is 5.

Proof We will prove only that the minimum distance is at least 5 by giving a decoding procedure to correct double errors. It suffices to give a procedure to find (A, B) from the received word, because when A and B are known, the problem reduces to the decoding of a double-error-correcting BCH code.

Suppose there are at most two errors. If S_1 equals zero, there are no errors. We will assume that S_1 has been tested and found to be nonzero.

First, set $B = 0$ and find the roots of the quadratic equation in A:

$$A^2 + S_1^3 A + (S_1^3 S_3 + S_3^2 + S_1^6 + S_1 S_5) = 0.$$

The only solutions for A that satisfy the constraints are nonzero cubes. Next, set A equal to zero and find the solution of the linear equation in B:

$$(S_1^3 S_3 + S_3^2 + S_1^6 + S_1 S_5) + S_1 B = 0.$$

Step 1. We first show that the quadratic equation cannot have two solutions that are both nonzero cubes. If A_1 and A_2 are roots of the quadratic equation, then $A_1 + A_2 = S_1^3$. The sum of the roots is a nonzero cube. We only need to show that in $GF(16)$ the sum of two nonzero cubes can never be a nonzero cube. Let the set of nonzero cubes be given by

$$U_3 = \{1, \alpha^3, \alpha^6, \alpha^9, \alpha^{12}\}.$$

Then by direct computation of all possible sums,

$$U_3 + U_3 = \{0, \alpha, \alpha^2, \alpha^4, \alpha^5, \alpha^7, \alpha^8, \alpha^{10}, \alpha^{11}, \alpha^{13}, \alpha^{14}\},$$

which contains no nonzero cubes. The sum of two nonzero cubes in $GF(16)$ is never a nonzero cube, and thus A_1 and A_2 do not both satisfy the constraints.

Step 2. Now suppose that $(A, 0)$ and $(0, B)$ are two solutions. We will show that they cannot both satisfy the constraints. Subtract the two equations to get

$$A^2 + S_1^3 A + S_1 B = 0.$$

Let $A = S_1^3 A'$. Then

$$(A')^2 + A' + S_1^{-5} B = 0.$$

But both S_1^5 and B are nonzero elements of $GF(4)$. Hence A' must satisfy one of the following:

$$(A')^2 + A' + 1 \quad = 0$$
$$(A')^2 + A' + \alpha^5 \quad = 0$$
$$(A')^2 + A' + \alpha^{10} = 0.$$

Hence, collecting the roots of these three equations gives

$$A' \in \{\alpha^5, \alpha^{10}, \alpha, \alpha^2, \alpha^4, \alpha^8\}.$$

There is no cube in this set. But A' must be a cube because it is equal to $S_1^{-3} A$ and A is a cube. Thus $(A, 0)$ and $(0, B)$ cannot both satisfy the constraints. This completes proof of the theorem. $\square$

PROBLEMS

8.1. Prove the following standard properties of the discrete Fourier transform, starting with the Fourier transform pair $\{c_i\} \leftrightarrow \{C_j\}$:

    a. Linearity:

$$\{ac_i + bc'_i\} \leftrightarrow \{aC_j + bC'_j\}.$$

    b. Cyclic shift:

$$\{c_{((i-1))}\} \leftrightarrow \{\alpha^j C_j\}.$$

    c. Modulation:

$$\{\alpha^i c_i\} \leftrightarrow \{C_{((j+1))}\}.$$

8.2. Show that the Fourier transform of the signal vector $c_i = \alpha^{ri}$ has a single nonzero spectral component. Which is it if $r = 0$? Show that a vector that is nonzero in only a single component has a nonzero spectrum everywhere.

8.3. Prove that $E_j = F_j G_j$ if and only if

$$e_i = \frac{1}{n} \sum_{k=0}^{n-1} f_{((i-k))} g_k,$$

8.4. How many idempotents are there in the ring of polynomials modulo $x^{15} - 1$? List them.

8.5. The fundamental theorem of algebra says that a polynomial of degree of d can have at most d zeros. Given a Reed-Solomon code with a codeword spectrum C_j that is zero for $j > n - k$, use the fundamental theorem of algebra to prove the BCH bound.

8.6. **a.** Find the generator polynomial for the binary (42, 25, 7) extended BCH code. Sketch an encoder.

    b. Find the generator polynomial for a (17, 9, 7) extended BCH code over $GF(4)$. Sketch an encoder.

8.7. Let $G(x) = x^2 + x + 1$ be the Goppa polynomial for a (32, 22, 5) Goppa code. Derive an encoding rule, and give a decoding procedure.

8.8. Let $G(x) = x^2 + x + \alpha^3$ be the Goppa polynomial for a (16, 8, 5) Goppa code where α is a primitive element in $GF(16)$. Find a parity-check matrix for this code.

8.9. Design an encoder for the Preparata (15, 8) code by modifying a nonsystematic encoder for a BCH (15, 5) code.

8.10. A Preparata code can be decoded by using the Berlekamp-Massey algorithm for binary codes for three iterations ($r = 1, 3$, and 5) and choosing A and B so that $\Delta_5 = 0$. By working through the iterations of this algorithm, set up an equation that A and B must solve.

8.11. The Preparata (63, 52) binary code can be defined in terms of its spectrum as follows: $C_1 = 0$, $C_3 = A$, and $C_9 = B$, where either

    (1) $A \in \{1, \alpha^7, \alpha^{14}, \alpha^{21}, \alpha^{28}, \alpha^{35}, \alpha^{42}, \alpha^{49}, \alpha^{56}\}$ and $B = 0$,

    or

    (2) $B \in \{1, \alpha^9, \alpha^{18}, \alpha^{27}, \alpha^{36}, \alpha^{45}, \alpha^{54}\}$ and $A = 0$,

and all other spectral components are arbitrary insofar as the conjugacy constraints allow.

    a. Prove that the code encodes 52 information bits.

b. By deriving the equation

$$A^4 + S_1^6 A^2 + S_1^9 A + [S_1^3 S_9 + S_3^4 + S_1^6 S_3^2 + S_1^9 S_3] + S_1^3 B = 0$$

and studying its solutions, prove that the code has a minimum distance of at least 5.

NOTES

Although the relationship to the Fourier transform was not then explicitly recognized, what we would now call spectral descriptions of error-control codes can be found in early papers. The original paper of Reed and Solomon (1960) introduced a spectral decoder for use in the proof of their codes' minimum distance, but as that decoder was not practical, spectral decoding techniques were not studied further for many years. Mattson and Solomon (1961) described the spectral polynomial, which played a useful role in theoretical developments, but again the essence of the spectral polynomial as a Fourier transform was not widely recognized, and the close relationship with the subject of signal processing was hidden. Mandelbaum (1979) developed similar ideas, but using the language of interpolation.

Fourier transforms over a finite field were discussed by Pollard (1971), and their use in error-control codes was introduced by Gore (1973) and discussed further by Chien and Choy (1975) and Lempel and Winograd (1977). The proof of the BCH bound given in this chapter is based in part on a proof of Chien (1972), but transferred into the frequency domain.

The idea of an extended code is widespread. Extended Reed-Solomon codes were discussed by Wolf (1969). Constructions for extending BCH codes were discussed by Andryanov and Saskovets (1966); by Sloane, Reddy, and Chen (1972); and by Kashara, Sugiyama, Hirasawa, and Namekawa (1975). The construction in the transform domain was discussed by Blahut (1980).

Alternant codes were introduced by Helgert (1974), who named them as such because the parity-check matrix can be put in a form known to mathematics as an alternant matrix. The alternant codes subsumed the earlier Goppa codes (1970). Delsarte (1975) discussed the alternant codes as subfield-subcodes of modified Reed-Solomon codes, a description much different from the original.

The Preparata codes have an interesting history. Preparata (1968) discovered the class based on studying the properties of the smallest code in the class, the (15, 8, 5) code, which was already known under the name of the Nordstrom-Robinson code (1967). Using a computer, these two men had constructed the (15, 8, 5) nonlinear code as an extension of the still earlier Nadler (12, 5, 5) nonlinear code (1962) and Green (13, 6, 5) nonlinear code (1966). In turn, the Preparata codes have recently stimulated the discovery of even more difficult nonlinear codes, the Kerdock low-rate codes (1972) and the Goethals triple-error-correcting codes (1976).

CHAPTER 9

Algorithms Based on Spectral Techniques

An error-control code must be judged not only by its rate and minimum distance, but also by whether a decoder can be built economically for it. Usually there are many ways to decode a given code. A designer can choose between several different decoding algorithms or algorithmic variations and must be familiar with all of them so that the best one for a particular application can be chosen. The choice will depend not only on the code parameters, such as blocklength and minimum distance, but also on how the implementation is divided between hardware and software, on the required decoding speed, and even on the economics of available circuit components.

In this chapter we will broaden our collection of decoding techniques by working in the frequency domain. Included here are techniques for decoding erasures and errors and for decoding beyond the designed distance of a code.

9.1 SPECTRAL TECHNIQUES FOR DECODING

We begin this chapter by returning to the problem of decoding BCH codes. Some of the ideas already studied will be reinterpreted from the point of view of the frequency domain. We shall develop alternative decoding procedures using the terminology of the Fourier transform.

A received word $\mathbf{v}$ with components $v_i = c_i + e_i$ for $i = 0, \ldots, n-1$ is the sum of a codeword $\mathbf{c}$ and an error word $\mathbf{e}$. The decoder must process the received word so as to remove the error word $\mathbf{e}$; the information is then recovered from $\mathbf{c}$. The syndromes of this noisy BCH codeword $\mathbf{v}$ are given by the following set of equations:

$$S_j = \sum_{i=0}^{n-1} \alpha^{i(j+j_0-1)} v_i = v(\alpha^{j+j_0-1}) \qquad j = 1, \ldots, 2t.$$

Obviously, the syndromes are computed as $2t$ components of a Fourier transform. The received noisy codeword $\mathbf{v} = \mathbf{c} + \mathbf{e}$ has Fourier transform with components $V_j = C_j + E_j$ for $j = 0, \ldots, n-1$, and the syndromes are the $2t$ components of this spectrum from j_0 to $j_0 + 2t - 1$. But by construction of the BCH code, the parity frequencies (for $j = j_0, \ldots, j_0 + 2t - 1$) have spectral components equal to zero:

$$C_j = 0 \qquad j = j_0, \ldots, j_0 + 2t - 1.$$

Hence

$$S_j = V_{j+j_0-1} = E_{j+j_0-1} \qquad j = 1, \ldots, 2t.$$

The block of syndromes gives us a window through which we can look at $2t$ of the n components of the spectrum of the error pattern. But we know from the BCH bound that if the error pattern has weight of at most t, then these $2t$ syndromes are enough to uniquely determine the error pattern.

Suppose there are $v < t$ errors at locations α^{i_k} for $k = 1, \ldots, v$. The error-locator polynomial is

$$\Lambda(x) = \prod_{k=1}^{v} (1 - x\alpha^{i_k}).$$

The inverse Fourier transform of the vector $\mathbf{\Lambda}$ is the same as $\Lambda(\alpha^{-i})$, which is $\Lambda(x)$ evaluated at α^{-i}. Clearly, $\Lambda(\alpha^{-i})$ equals zero if and only if i is an error location. Thus $\Lambda(x)$ has been defined so that in the time domain, $\lambda_i = 0$ whenever $e_i \neq 0$. Therefore $\lambda_i e_i = 0$ for all i, and thus, by the convolution theorem, the convolution in the frequency domain is zero:

$$\sum_{j=0}^{n-1} \Lambda_j E_{k-j} = 0 \qquad k = 0, \ldots, n-1.$$

Because $\Lambda(x)$ is a polynomial of degree of at most t, $\Lambda_j = 0$ for $j > t$. Then

$$\sum_{j=0}^{t} \Lambda_j E_{k-j} = 0 \qquad k = 0, \ldots, n-1.$$

Because Λ_0 equals one, this can be written in the form

$$E_k = -\sum_{j=1}^{t} \Lambda_j E_{k-j} \qquad k = 0, \ldots, n-1.$$

This is a set of n equations in $n-t$ unknowns—t coefficients of $\Lambda(x)$ and $n - 2t$ components of $\mathbf{E}$—and in $2t$ known values of $\mathbf{E}$ given by the syndromes. Of the n equations, there are t equations that involve only components of Λ and the known components of $\mathbf{E}$ given by the syndromes. That is, the t equations

$$S_k = -\sum_{j=1}^{t} \Lambda_j S_{k-j} \qquad k = t+1, \ldots, 2t$$

involve only the known syndromes and the t unknown components of Λ. These are always solvable for Λ, as we saw in Chapter 7, using for example the Berlekamp-Massey algorithm.

The remaining components of $\mathbf{S}$ can then be obtained by recursive extension; that is, using the above convolution equation to find S_{2t+1} from the known components of $\mathbf{S}$ and Λ, then to find S_{2t+2}, and so on. This computation can be described as the operation of a linear-feedback shift register with tap weights given by the coefficients Λ and initialized with $S_1, \ldots, S_t$. In this way S_j is computed for all j, E_j equals S_{j-j_0+1}, and

$$C_j = V_j - E_j.$$

An inverse Fourier transform completes the decoding.

Figure 9.1 shows a flow to implement the above procedure (except for the Fourier transforms). The decoder can be used with an encoder that is either in the time domain or the frequency domain. If the encoder is a time-domain encoder, then the inverse Fourier transform of the corrected spectrum must be taken to obtain the time-domain codeword, from which the information is recovered. If the encoder uses the information symbols in the frequency domain to specify the values of the spectrum, then the corrected spectrum gives the information symbols directly. The decoder does not have an inverse transform.

The computations can be arranged in a number of ways. Figure 9.2 shows four different schemes. The first scheme is as developed in Chapter 7. In the second scheme, the information is encoded in the frequency domain so that once the spectrum is corrected, the decoding is complete. The third and fourth circuit illustrate that although the error pattern is computed by recursive extension in the frequency domain, the final correction may be done either in the time domain or in the frequency domain.

The fourth scheme resembles the first scheme, although the development is much different. The syndrome generator is the same as the direct Fourier transform. The Chien search is similar to an inverse Fourier transform. It is an n-point transform with v nonzero input components and a $GF(q^m)$-valued output vector, as compared to an n-point transform with n nonzero

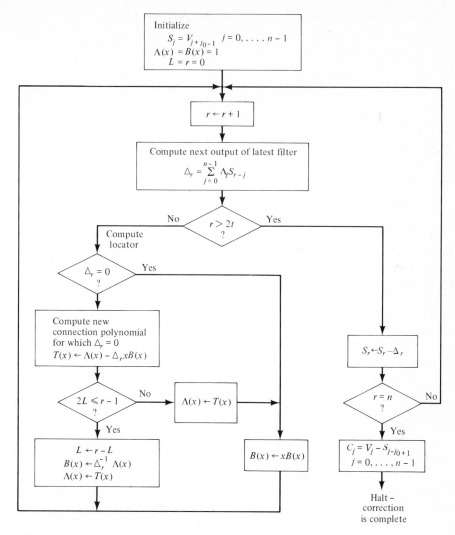

Figure 9.1 A frequency-domain decoder.

input components and a $GF(q)$-valued output. The Forney algorithm is replaced by the recursive extension. The fourth scheme has an advantage of a simpler appearance than the first, which can be reflected in the construction of the decoder circuitry.

A choice from among these options by the designer will depend in part on available techniques for computing the Fourier transform, and thus we shall study a number of different computational algorithms for the Fourier transform in a later section. When choosing from these Fourier-transform algorithms and decoder options, the designer may also wish to arrange things so that only a portion of the spectral components need to be computed. For example, the fourth circuit of Fig. 9.2 requires that only $2t$ components of the spectrum be computed. A further simplification is as follows. Let the received polynomial be written

$$v(x) = Q(x)g(x) + s(x),$$

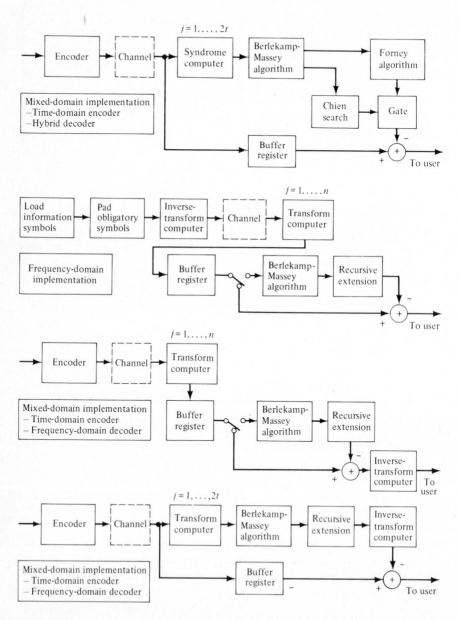

Figure 9.2 Some encoder/decoder schemes for BCH codes.

where $g(x)$ is the generator polynomial of the BCH code and $s(x)$ is the syndrome polynomial. The syndrome polynomial can be computed by a divide-by-$g(x)$ circuit. Then

$$S_j = v(\alpha^j) = Q(\alpha^j)g(\alpha^j) + s(\alpha^j)$$

$$= s(\alpha^j) \qquad\qquad j = j_0 + 1, \ldots, j_0 + 2t$$

because for these j, $g(\alpha^j) = 0$. Now the syndromes are obtained as the Fourier transform of $s(x)$, which has only $n - k$ nonzero components rather than n. This technique is useful only if it is easier to divide by $g(x)$ than to compute a Fourier transform of n input points. This is sometimes the case for small n.

There is another decoding method that uses the Euclidean algorithm but is quite different from that of Section 7.7. This method has a frequency-domain orientation, and we will discuss it in this section.

In $GF(q^m)$ we have the factorization

$$x^n - 1 = \prod_{i=0}^{n-1} (x - \alpha^i)$$

Define the truth-locator polynomial $\Lambda^0(x) = (x^n - 1)/\Lambda(x)$. This is a polynomial because $\Lambda(x)$ only has distinct linear factors dividing $x^n - 1$. By the location of its zeros, the polynomial $\Lambda^0(x)$ locates the correct components of the received word.

□ **Theorem 9.1.1** The error polynomial $E(x)$ and the locator polynomials satisfy

$$\mathrm{GCD}[x^n - 1, E(x)] = \frac{x^n - 1}{\Lambda(x)} = \Lambda^0(x).$$

Proof The polynomials $E(x)$ and $\Lambda(x)$ have no common zeros because by definition $\Lambda(\alpha^j) = 0$ if and only if $E(\alpha^j) \neq 0$. Every α^i must be a zero of either $E(x)$ or $\Lambda(x)$. Therefore

$$\Lambda(x)E(x) = P(x)(x^n - 1)$$

for some polynomial $P(x)$ relatively prime to $\Lambda(x)$. Then

$$\mathrm{GCD}[x^n - 1, E(x)] = \frac{x^n - 1}{\Lambda(x)} = \Lambda^0(x),$$

as was to be proved. □

Apply the Euclidean algorithm as given in Theorem 7.7.1 with $s(x) = x^n - 1$ and $t(x) = E(x)$, and ignore for the moment the fact that in general, only the $2t$ high-order coefficients of $E(x)$ are known. Since

$$\Lambda(x)\mathrm{GCD}[x^n - 1, E(x)] = x^n - 1,$$

Corollary 7.7.2 says that

$$\Lambda(x) = (-1)^R A_{22}^{(R)}(x),$$

which polynomial is computed by the Euclidean algorithm.

If we knew $E(x)$, then this gives a way of computing $\Lambda(x)$ using the Euclidean algorithm. But we only know those coefficients of $E(x)$ where the like coefficients of $C(x)$ are zero, and thus it superficially appears that this formula for $\Lambda(x)$ is useless. Actually, we can use the formula knowing only $2t$ values of $E(x)$, as long as they are the right ones.

Consider a BCH code whose generator polynomial has zeros at α^{n-2t}, $\ldots, \alpha^{n-1}$. (These are the usual zeros from 1 to $2t$ but using α^{-1} as the primitive element). We will derive a decoding algorithm for a BCH code with these zeros. We must show that if at most t errors occur, then the iterations of the Euclidean algorithm depend on $E(x)$ only in the high-order $2t$ coefficients. The other unknown coefficients may be filled arbitrarily.

☐ **Theorem 9.1.2** Let E_j be given for $j = n - 2t, \ldots, n-1$. There is at most one way to fill in E_j for $j = 0, \ldots, n - 2t - 1$ such that

$$\Lambda(x)\text{GCD}[x^n - 1, E(x)] = x^n - 1$$

is solved by a $\Lambda(x)$ of degree t or less.

Proof The theorem is proved by showing it to be a variation of the BCH bound. Suppose $\Lambda(x)$ has degree t or less and satisfies the condition of the theorem. Write the result of the Euclidean algorithm in the form of Corollary 7.7.2:

$$\begin{bmatrix} x^n - 1 \\ E(x) \end{bmatrix} = (-1)^R \begin{bmatrix} A_{22}^{(R)}(x) & -A_{12}^{(R)}(x) \\ -A_{21}^{(R)}(x) & -A_{11}^{(R)}(x) \end{bmatrix} \begin{bmatrix} \text{GCD}[x^n - 1, E(x)] \\ 0 \end{bmatrix}.$$

This shows that $(-1)^R A_{22}^{(R)}(x) = \Lambda(x)$, whereas the direct form

$$\begin{bmatrix} \text{GCD}[x^n - 1, E(x)] \\ 0 \end{bmatrix} = \begin{bmatrix} A_{11}^{(R)}(x) & A_{12}^{(R)}(x) \\ A_{21}^{(R)}(x) & A_{22}^{(R)}(x) \end{bmatrix} \begin{bmatrix} x^n - 1 \\ E(x) \end{bmatrix}$$

requires that

$$0 = (-1)^R A_{21}^{(R)}(x)(x^n - 1) + \Lambda(x)E(x),$$

and thus $\Lambda(x)E(x)$ is a multiple of $(x^n - 1)$. Hence $E(x)$ has zeros in $GF(q^m)$ everywhere that $\Lambda(x)$ does not. Because $\Lambda(x)$ has a degree of at most t, it has at most t zeros. Then the inverse Fourier transform e_i is zero in at least $n - t$ places. By the BCH bound, there can be at most one such e_i whose Fourier transform agrees with the known $2t$ coefficients of $E(x)$ in the places $j = n - 2t, \ldots, n-1$. This completes the proof of the theorem.
☐

One naive way to apply the theorem is to try every possible way to fill in the unknown components of $E(x)$, and then to use the Euclidean algorithm to find $\Lambda(x)$. Only one $\Lambda(x)$ will have a degree of t or less. This is the correct error-locator polynomial, and the corresponding $E(x)$ is the correct error spectrum. Because $\Lambda(x)$ is uniquely determined by the known components of $E(x)$, however, it seems reasonable to suppose that we can arrange the computations to avoid using the missing components of $E(x)$. This is shown in Figure 9.3.

Consider the division algorithm

$$s(x) = Q(x)t(x) + r(x)$$

where deg $t(x) = a$ and deg $s(x) = b$. Then the quotient polynomial $Q(x)$ has degree $b - a$ and depends on $t(x)$ only through the coefficients $t_a, t_{a-1}, \ldots,$

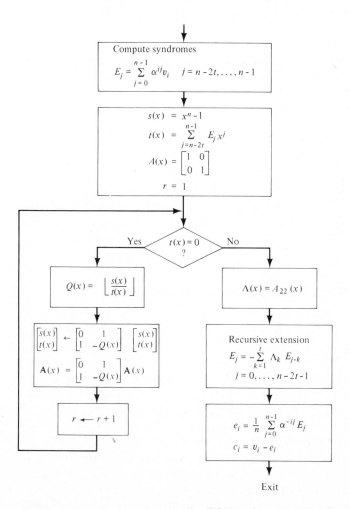

Figure 9.3 Another decoder for BCH codes using the Euclidean algorithm.

t_{b-a}. To compute $Q(x)$, use the following iterative procedure for $r = 0, \ldots,$ $b - a$.

$$Q_{b-a-r} = \frac{s_{b-r} - \sum_{l=0}^{r-1} Q_{b-a-l}t_{a+l-r}}{t_a}.$$

This is a slight variation of conventional long division of polynomials.

We use this procedure to compute the quotient at each step of the Euclidean algorithm. At iteration r of Theorem 7.7.1, only compute the coefficients $s_j^{(r+1)}$ and $t_j^{(r+1)}$ for j running from $n - 2t + \sum_{l=1}^{r} \deg Q^{(l)}(x)$ to $n - 1$. These high-order fragments of $s^{(r+1)}(x)$ and $t^{(r+1)}(x)$ are all that is needed to continue the iterations of the Euclidean algorithm insofar as obtaining the series of quotient polynomials is concerned. Since

$$\begin{bmatrix} \text{GCD}[x^n - 1, E(x)] \\ 0 \end{bmatrix} = \left\{ \prod_{l=R-1}^{0} \begin{bmatrix} 0 & 1 \\ 1 & -Q^{(l)}(x) \end{bmatrix} \right\} \begin{bmatrix} x^n - 1 \\ E(x) \end{bmatrix}$$

$$= \left\{ \prod_{l=R-1}^{r+1} \begin{bmatrix} 0 & 1 \\ 1 & -Q^{(l)}(x) \end{bmatrix} \right\} \begin{bmatrix} s^{(r+1)}(x) \\ t^{(r+1)}(x) \end{bmatrix},$$

we can write

$$\left\{ \prod_{l=R-1}^{r+1} \begin{bmatrix} Q^{(l)}(x) & 1 \\ 1 & 0 \end{bmatrix} \right\} \begin{bmatrix} \text{GCD}[x^n - 1, E(x)] \\ 0 \end{bmatrix} = \left\{ \prod_{l=r}^{0} \begin{bmatrix} 0 & 1 \\ 1 & -Q^{(l)}(x) \end{bmatrix} \right\} \begin{bmatrix} x^n - 1 \\ E(x) \end{bmatrix}$$

$$= \begin{bmatrix} s^{(r+1)}(x) \\ t^{(r+1)}(x) \end{bmatrix}.$$

Because $\text{GCD}[x^n - 1, E(x)]$ has a degree of at least $n - t$, this says that $t^{(r+1)}(x)$ has degree at least $n - t + \sum_{l=r+1}^{R-1} Q^{(l)}(x)$. That is, $t_j^{(r+1)}$ is known for $j = n - 2t + \sum_{l=1}^{r} Q^{(l)}(x)$ to $n - t + \sum_{l=r+1}^{R} Q^{(l)}(x)$ and nonzero at the upper index. This range is sufficient to determine $Q^{(l+1)}(x)$, and the iteration can continue.

9.2 CORRECTION OF ERASURES AND ERRORS

An error-control code can be used on a channel that makes both errors and erasures. A received word on such a channel consists of channel input symbols (of which some may be in error) and blanks (or an equivalent symbol) denoting erasures. The decoder must correct the errors and fill the erasures. Given a code with minimum distance d^*, any pattern of v errors and ρ erasures can be decoded provided that

$$d^* \geqslant 2v + 1 + \rho.$$

The largest v that satisfies this inequality is denoted by t_ρ.

To decode a received word with ρ erasures, it is necessary to find a codeword that differs from the unerased portion of the received word in at most t_ρ places. Any such word will do because by the definition of t_ρ, such a word is unique. We need only seek some solution, because we are confident that only one exists.

One way to decode is to guess the erased symbols and then apply any error-correction procedure. If the procedure finds that less than t_ρ of the unerased symbols are in error (and possibly some of the guesses for the erased symbols), then these errors can be corrected, and the codeword is restored. If too many errors are found, then a new guess is made for the erased symbols. In this way any error-correction procedure suitable for a given code can be adapted to a procedure for decoding both errors and erasures. It is practical if the number of combinations that must be tried for the erasures is small. Otherwise, such a trial-and-error procedure becomes impractical. In the latter case, it is necessary to incorporate erasure filling into the decoding algorithm in a more central way.

As we have seen, the special class of BCH codes is supported by a variety of strong decoding algorithms. These can be extended to algorithms for decoding both errors and erasures. For simplicity, we treat $j_0 = 1$.

Let v_i for $i = 0, \ldots, n-1$ be the vector of received symbols. Suppose that erasures are made in locations $i_1, i_2, \ldots, i_\rho$. At these known locations, the received word has blanks, which we will initially fill with zeros. Define the erasure vector as that n-vector having component f_{i_l} for $l = 1, \ldots, \rho$ equal to the erased symbol, and in other components f_i equals zero. Then

$$v_i = c_i + e_i + f_i \qquad i = 0, \ldots, n-1.$$

Let ψ be any vector that is zero at every erased location and otherwise nonzero. Then

$$\psi_i v_i = \psi_i(c_i + e_i + f_i) = \psi_i c_i + \psi_i e_i.$$

Define the modified received word $v_i' = \psi_i v_i$, the modified error vector $e_i' = \psi_i e_i$, and the modified codeword $c_i' = \psi_i c_i$. The modified error vector has errors in the same locations as **e**. The last equation becomes

$$v_i' = c_i' + e_i'.$$

The problem now is to decode **v**′ to find **e**′, which we know how to do if there are enough syndromes.

The next step in the development is to choose ψ by working in the frequency domain. Let $U_l = \alpha^{i_l}$ for $l = 1, \ldots, \rho$ denote the erasure locations. Define the erasure-locator polynomial:

$$\Psi(x) = \sum_{k=0}^{n-1} \Psi_k x^k = \prod_{l=1}^{\rho} (1 - xU_l).$$

This is defined so that the inverse transform of the vector Ψ has components ψ_i equal to zero whenever $f_i \neq 0$. Therefore, $\psi_i f_i = 0$. In the frequency domain,

$$\mathbf{V}' = (\mathbf{\Psi} * \mathbf{C}) + \mathbf{E}'.$$

But Ψ is nonzero only in a block of length $\rho + 1$, and by the construction of a

BCH code, $\mathbf{C}$ is zero in a block of length $2t$. Consequently, the convolution $\mathbf{\Psi} * \mathbf{C}$ is zero in a block of length $2t - \rho$. In this block, define the modified syndrome S'_j by $S'_j = V'_j$. Then

$$S'_j = (\mathbf{\Psi} * \mathbf{V})_j = E'_j,$$

which has enough syndrome components to describe the correctable patterns of modified errors.

Hence just as in the errors-only case, from these $2t - \rho$ known values of $\mathbf{E}'$ we can find the error-locator polynomial $\Lambda(x)$, provided the number of errors v is not more than $(2t - \rho)/2$. Once the error-locator polynomial is known, we can combine it with the erasure-locator polynomial and proceed as in the errors-only case. To do this, first define the error-and-erasure locator polynomial

$$\bar{\Lambda}(x) = \mathbf{\Psi}(x)\Lambda(x).$$

The inverse Fourier transform of $\bar{\Lambda}$ is zero at every erasure or error. That is, $\bar{\lambda}_i = 0$ if $e_i \neq 0$ or $f_i \neq 0$. Therefore $\bar{\lambda}_i(e_i + f_i) = 0$,

$$\bar{\Lambda} * (\mathbf{E} + \mathbf{F}) = \mathbf{0},$$

and $\bar{\Lambda}$ is nonzero in a block of length of at most $v + \rho + 1$. Hence, the $2t$ known values of $\mathbf{E} + \mathbf{F}$ can be recursively extended to n values by using this convolution equation and the known value of $\bar{\Lambda}$. Then

$$C_i = V_i - (E_i + F_i).$$

An inverse Fourier transform completes the decoding.

The step of computing the error-locator polynomial from the modified syndromes can use the Berlekamp-Massey algorithm. It is possible to do much better, however, by combining several steps. The idea of the Berlekamp-Massey algorithm is to compute $\Lambda(x)$ by a recursive procedure, starting with the initial estimates of $\Lambda^{(0)}(x) = 1$ and $B^{(0)}(x) = 1$, and proceeding through $2t$ iterations.

In the case of erasures, the syndrome is replaced with the modified syndromes in the equation for Δ_r:

$$\Delta_r = \sum_{j=0}^{n-1} \Lambda_j^{(r-1)} S'_{r-j}.$$

After n iterations starting with the initial values $\Lambda^{(0)}(x) = B^{(0)}(x) = 1$, the error-locator polynomial $\Lambda(x)$ is obtained.

But what happens if we start instead with the values $\Lambda^{(0)}(x) = B^{(0)}(x) = \mathbf{\Psi}(x)$? Then notice that

$$\Lambda^{(r)}(x)\mathbf{\Psi}(x) = \Lambda^{(r-1)}(x)\mathbf{\Psi}(x) - \Delta_r x B^{(r-1)}(x)\mathbf{\Psi}(x)$$

$$B^{(r)}(x)\mathbf{\Psi}(x) = (1 - \delta_r)x B^{(r-1)}(x)\mathbf{\Psi}(x) + \delta_r \Delta_r^{-1} \Lambda^{(r-1)}(x)\mathbf{\Psi}(x).$$

If we temporarily define $\bar{\Lambda}^{(r)}(x) = \Lambda^{(r)}(x)\Psi(x)$ and compute Δ_r by

$$\Delta_r = \sum_{j=0}^{n-1} \bar{\Lambda}_j^{(r-1)} S_{r-j} = \sum_{j=0}^{n-1} \bar{\Lambda}_{r-j}^{(r-1)} S_j,$$

then

$$\Delta_r = \sum_{j=0}^{n-1} \left(\sum_{k=0}^{n-1} \Lambda_k^{(r-1)} \Psi_{r-j-k} \right) S_j = \sum_{k=0}^{n-1} \Lambda_k^{(r-1)} S_{r-k}'.$$

Therefore if we initialize the Berlekamp-Massey algorithm with $\Psi(x)$ instead of with 1, the modified syndromes are computed implicitly and need not explicitly appear. We will now drop the notation $\bar{\Lambda}(x)$, replacing it with $\Lambda(x)$, which will now be called the *error-and-erasure-locator polynomial*. The Berlekamp-Massey algorithm initialized with $\Psi(x)$ generates recursively the error-and-erasure-locator polynomial according to the equations:

$$\Lambda^{(r)}(x) = \Lambda^{(r-1)}(x) - \Delta_r x B^{(r-1)}(x)$$

$$B^{(r)}(x) = (1 - \delta_r) x B^{(r-1)}(x) + \delta_r \Delta_r^{-1} \Lambda^{(r-1)}(x)$$

$$\Delta_r = \sum_{j=0}^{n-1} \Lambda_j^{(r-1)} S_{r-j}$$

The Berlekamp-Massey algorithm, revised to also handle erasures, is shown in Fig. 9.4. This should be compared to Fig. 9.1. The only change from the decoder for errors only is the computation of the erasure-locator polynomial, which is trivial compared to other decoding computations. This is provided by a special loop for the first ρ iterations, as shown in Fig. 9.4. The index r is used to count out the·first ρ iterations while the erasure polynomial is being computed and then continues to count out the iterations of the Berlekamp-Massey algorithm, stopping when r exceeds $2t$. The shift-register length L is increased once for each erasure, and thereafter the length changes according to the procedure of the Berlekamp-Massey algorithm. Because this algorithm was developed in the absence of erasures, however, and erasure correction was added later, the length test must be modified by replacing r and L by $r - \rho$ and $L - \rho$, respectively.

Before ending this section, we mention that instead of using a blank to denote an erased symbol, we can leave a best guess of a symbol in this component and denote that it is erased by attaching a flag bit to this component. This is called a *readable erasure*. It does not matter to the decoding algorithm because in effect this position is multiplied by zero. Sometimes, outside of the main decoder, one may devise various schemes for making use of the weak information that is contained in a readable erasure. For example, one may refuse to accept a decoder output if too many of the readable erasures disagree with the decoder output word.

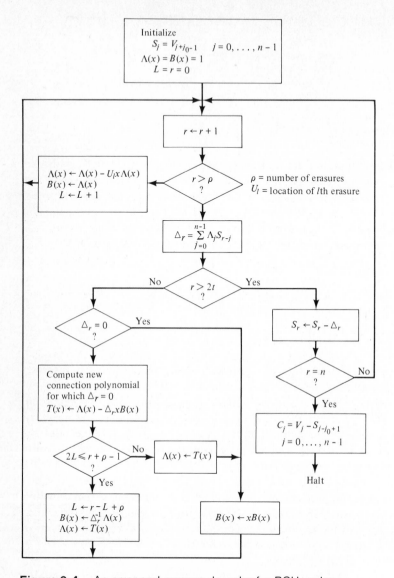

Figure 9.4 An error-and-erasure decoder for BCH codes.

9.3 DECODING OF EXTENDED REED-SOLOMON CODES

Any decoder for a Reed-Solomon code can be slightly modified to obtain a decoder for an extended Reed-Solomon code. One way is to simply guess in turn each of the q^2 possible error patterns in the two extended symbols, and then decode based on the guess. Every trial guess that results in a codeword with t or less corrected symbols must result in the same codeword, because only one codeword lies within a distance of t of the received word.

A better procedure is to divide the possible error patterns into two cases: either at least one error has occurred in an extended symbol; or no errors have occurred in an extended symbol. The message can be decoded twice, once for each of these hypotheses. Let* $S_j = V_{j+j_0}$ for $j = 1, \ldots, 2t-2$; and whenever v_- or v_+ is correct, let $S_0 = V_{j_0} - v_-$ and $S_{2t-1} = V_{j_0+2t-1} - v_+$. For the first hypothesis, the $2t-2$ interior syndromes $S_1, \ldots, S_{2t-2}$ are sufficient to find the entire spectrum of the error pattern in the interior, because at most $t-1$ errors have occurred in the interior. These $2t-2$ syndromes can be recursively extended to give the $n-2$ components of the error spectrum, because $S_j = E_{j+j_0}$. For the second hypothesis, the $2t$ syndromes $S_0, \ldots, S_{2t-1}$ are sufficient to find the entire spectrum of the error pattern, because it is certain that all errors are in the $n-2$ interior symbols. Although two trial decodings are made, in general one of these will not be successful, because we know the code has a minimum distance of $2t+1$, and only one pattern of t or less errors can be found.

Instead of doubling the decoding complexity by using two decoders, we will now describe how to share the computations so the complexity increases only a little. In this section, we will modify the Berlekamp-Massey algorithm to decode extended Reed-Solomon codes, and in the next section we will do the same to decode extended BCH codes. Because we already know how to do the other steps, we will develop a decoder only as far as computing the error-locator polynomial.

The most important extended Reed-Solomon codes are those extended by a single symbol, because among these are the codes whose blocklength is 2^m. A power of 2 is often a convenient blocklength in applications. We will begin with the singly extended case because it is important in practice, because the decoder is simple, and because it is easily explained.

The code has spectral components $C_{j_0}, \ldots, C_{j_0+2t-2}$ equal to zero, and the single extended parity symbol $c_+ = C_{j_0+2t-1}$. The $2t-1$ components equal to zero ensure that the code has distance $2t$ so that it can correct $t-1$ errors and detect t errors. The block of $2t$ syndromes begins with S_1 equal to V_{j_0} and ends with S_{2t} equal to $V_{j_0+2t-1} - v_+$. Suppose that at most t errors have occurred; start the Berlekamp-Massey algorithm at syndrome S_1 and iterate out to syndrome S_{2t-1}. If $L_{2t-2} \leqslant t-1$, and the discrepancy Δ_{2t-1} is zero, then by Theorem 7.5.3 at most $t-1$ errors have occurred in the interior, and the error-locator polynomial is correct. Otherwise, t errors have occurred in the interior, and thus v_+ is correct. The extra syndrome S_{2t} allows the Berlekamp-Massey algorithm to be continued through one more iteration for a total of $2t$ iterations, and hence a t-error-correcting

---

*It is convenient here to modify our usual practice and label the syndromes from S_0 to S_{2t-1} for a doubly extended code.

error-locator polynomial is found. In Fig. 9.5 a decoder for a singly extended Reed-Solomon code is shown.

A decoder for a doubly extended Reed-Solomon code is more intricate and difficult to describe. Suppose that at most t errors have occurred. There are $2t - 2$ interior syndromes available, starting with S_1 equal to $V_{j_0 + 1}$. Use these to correct up to $t - 2$ errors in the interior and to detect up to t errors as in Theorem 7.5.3. That is, starting with S_1, perform $2t - 4$ iterations of the Berlekamp-Massey algorithm to find an error-locator polynomial.

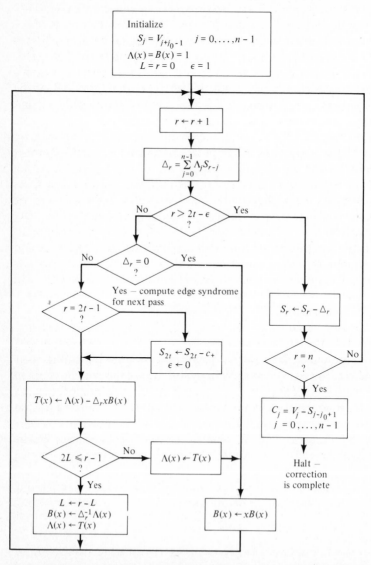

Figure 9.5   A decoder for a singly extended Reed-Solomon code.

If $L_{2t-4} \leqslant t-2$, proceed through two more iterations, stopping if either discrepancy Δ_{2t-3} or Δ_{2t-2} is nonzero. If both are zero, then at most $2t-2$ errors have occurred in the interior. The error-locator polynomial is correct and can be used to correct the interior. Because all information can be recovered from the interior, the error correction is complete. Otherwise, the interior has either $t-1$ or t errors and, consequently, at most a single error in an edge symbol. Therefore at least one of the two edge syndromes S_0 or S_{2t-1} is correct, and both are correct if all errors are in the interior. Attaching first one then the other of these edge syndromes gives two blocks, each of $2t-1$ syndromes, and at least one of these two blocks is a correct set of $2t-1$ syndromes.

Now apply the Berlekamp-Massey algorithm twice, first with one of these blocks of $2t-1$ syndromes (S_0 through S_{2t-2}), then with the other (S_1 through S_{2t-1}). Each time correct $t-1$ errors and detect t errors. If t errors are in the interior, then both trials will detect t errors in the interior and hence no errors are in the extended symbols. If one or both of these trials fails to detect t errors, then there are only $t-1$ errors in the interior; thus the error-locator polynomial is correct and can be used to correct the interior. Because all information can be recovered from the interior, the error correction is complete.

Finally, if t errors are detected in the interior, there are no errors in the edge symbols. Hence, both edge syndromes are correct, and thus there are $2t$ syndromes available to correct the t errors in the interior.

The above procedure still uses two applications of the Berlekamp-Massey algorithm. It has been stretched out above for the purpose of explanation; it can be collapsed into a more concise procedure.

9.4 DECODING OF EXTENDED BCH CODES

Now we are ready to decode the doubly extended BCH codes of Section 8.5. If the designed distance d of the code is odd, then the code with its tails represented in the extension field is just a subcode of a Reed-Solomon code, and the decoder for the doubly extended Reed-Solomon code already described can be used. If the designed distance of the code is even, then an extra parity bit is attached to one of the tails. We have claimed, but not yet proved, that this forces the minimum distance to be at least $d+1$. We now give this proof in the form of the decoding algorithm. The decoder is similar to the decoder for the doubly extended Reed-Solomon code.

☐ **Theorem 9.4.1** The doubly extended binary BCH code with designed distance d an even integer and an extra parity check on one tail has a minimum distance of at least $d+1$.

Proof Let $t = d/2$. We give a decoder that corrects t errors. There are $2t-3$ interior syndromes and two edge syndromes, $S_0 = V_{j_0} - v_-$ and

$S_{2t-2} = V_{j_0+2t-2} - v_+$, which are correct syndromes if v_- and v_+ contain no errors. The conjugacy constraints require j_0 and $j_0 + 2t - 2$ to be chosen as odd integers, and by assumption the designed distance $d = 2t$ is even. This can only occur when $j_0 < 0$ and $j_0 + 2t - 2 > 0$. Therefore the conjugacy constraints also ensure that $C_{j_0-1} = 0$ and $C_{j_0+2t-1} = 0$ because $(j_0 - 1)/2$ and $(j_0 + 2t - 1)/2$ are both parity frequencies. Hence, we have two more valid syndromes: $S_{-1} = V_{j_0-1}$ and $S_{2t-1} = V_{j_0+2t-1}$.

Because v_+ has a simple parity check, we can determine whether v_+ has an even number or an odd number of errors. Suppose the parity check on v_+ detects an error. Then there are at most $t - 1$ errors in the interior. There are $2t - 3$ interior syndromes. These allow $t - 2$ errors in the interior to be corrected and $t - 1$ errors in the interior to be detected. If $t - 1$ errors are detected in the interior, then v_- has no error, and S_0 is a correct syndrome and can be used for one more iteration to find the error-locator polynomial for $t - 1$ errors. The correction is complete for the case where the parity check on v_+ detects an error.

Otherwise, the parity check on v_+ detects no error, and thus v_+ has an even number of errors. Then use the Berlekamp-Massey algorithm starting at S_1 for $2t - 6$ iterations to correct $t - 3$ errors in the interior, followed by three more iterations (using $2t - 3$ interior syndromes) to detect t or less errors in the interior. If $t - 3$ errors are not corrected, then there are either $t - 2$, $t - 1$, or t errors in the interior and thus at most two in the edge symbols. Therefore, either v_+ is correct or v_+ contains two errors and v_- is correct.

At least one of the edge syndromes is correct. Attach either S_{-1} and S_0 to one end of the block of syndromes, or attach S_{2t-1}, and S_{2t} to the other end. This gives two blocks of $2t - 1$ syndromes, and at least one of the two blocks is correct. Use the Berlekamp-Massey algorithm twice, once for each block to correct $t - 1$ errors and to detect t errors in the interior. If t errors have occurred in the interior, then no errors are in the edge syndromes, and both blocks will detect t errors. If one or both of the trials fail to detect t errors, then there are at most $t - 1$ errors in the interior, the error-locator polynomial is correct, and the error correction is complete.

Finally, if t errors are detected in the interior, there are no errors in the edge symbols. Hence, there are $2t + 1$ syndromes available to correct t errors. $\square$

9.5 DECODING IN THE TIME DOMAIN

We saw in Section 9.1 that the decoding procedures for BCH codes can be developed in terms of a problem in spectral estimation. The decoder consists of a Fourier transform (syndrome computer) followed by an autoregressive spectral analysis (the Berlekamp-Massey algorithm) followed by an inverse

Fourier transform. Such a decoder is best derived and studied using these blocks, but the actual implementation can be quite different.

In this section, we will show how to transform the computational algorithm rather than the data. This will eliminate both Fourier transforms from the decoder. The idea is to note that the Berlekamp-Massey recursion is linear in the two updated polynomials (although nonlinear in the discrepancy). The recursive equations have a counterpart in the time domain, which can be found by analytically taking the Fourier transform. This gives a set of decoding equations that operate directly on the raw data, and the error correction is completed without transforms.

To eliminate the Fourier transform from the computations, take the Fourier transform of all variables in Theorem 7.4.1. The transform of $\mathbf{\Lambda}$ is $\lambda = \{\lambda_i | i = 0, \ldots, n-1\}$, which is the time-domain error locator. The transform of $\mathbf{B}$ is the vector $\mathbf{b} = \{b_i | i = 0, \ldots, n-1\}$. The Berlekamp-Massey algorithm then transforms into a recursive process in the time domain, as described in the following theorem.

☐ **Theorem 9.5.1** Let $\mathbf{v}$ be the received noisy BCH codeword. Let the following set of recursive equations be used to compute $\lambda_i^{(2t)}$ for $i = 0, \ldots, n-1$:

$$\Delta_r = \sum_{i=0}^{n-1} \alpha^{ir} (\lambda_i^{(r-1)} v_i)$$

$$L_r = \delta_r(r - L_{r-1}) + \bar{\delta}_r L_{r-1}$$

$$\begin{bmatrix} \lambda_i^{(r)} \\ b_i^{(r)} \end{bmatrix} = \begin{bmatrix} 1 & -\Delta_r \alpha^i \\ \Delta_r^{-1} \delta_r & \bar{\delta}_r \alpha^i \end{bmatrix} \begin{bmatrix} \lambda_i^{(r-1)} \\ b_i^{(r-1)} \end{bmatrix},$$

$r = 1, \ldots, 2t$; the initial conditions are $\lambda_i^{(0)} = 1$, $b_i^{(0)} = 1$ for all i, and $\delta_r = (1 - \bar{\delta}_r) = 1$ if both $\Delta_r \neq 0$ and $2L_{r-1} \leqslant r-1$, and otherwise $\delta_r = 0$. Then $\lambda_i^{(2t)} = 0$ if and only if $e_i \neq 0$.

Proof Take the Fourier transform of all vector quantities. Then the recursive equations of Theorem 7.4.1 are obtained, except for the equation

$$\Delta_r = \sum_{j=0}^{n-1} \Lambda_j^{(r-1)} V_{r-j},$$

which has $\mathbf{V}$ in place of $\mathbf{S}$. But $\Lambda_j^{(r-1)} = 0$ for $j > 2t$, and $V_j = S_j$ for $j = 1, \ldots, 2t$. Therefore

$$\Delta_r = \sum_{j=0}^{n-1} \Lambda_j^{(r-1)} S_{r-j},$$

and the time-domain algorithm reduces exactly to the form of Theorem 7.4.1. ☐

For binary codes, once the vector λ is known correction is nearly complete, because the received word is in error in component i if and only if $\lambda_i = 0$. In Fig. 9.6 a time-domain decoder for a binary code is shown.

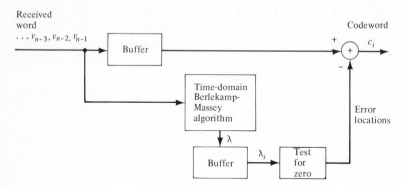

Figure 9.6 A time-domain decoder for a binary BCH code.

For nonbinary codes, it does no good to compute only the error locations in the time domain; we must also compute the error magnitudes. In the frequency domain, the error magnitudes can be computed by the following recursion:

$$E_k = - \sum_{j=1}^{t} \Lambda_j E_{k-j} \qquad k = 2t + 1, \ldots, n-1.$$

Once the error-locator polynomial is known, this recursion can be used to extend the $2t$ known components of $\mathbf{E}$ to all components of $\mathbf{E}$, by iterating $n - 2t$ times.

We will give the corresponding process in the time domain in the next theorem. It is not possible to just write the Fourier transform of this equation; some restructuring is necessary.

$\square$ **Theorem 9.5.2** Let $\mathbf{v} = \mathbf{c} + \mathbf{e}$ be a received noisy BCH codeword. Given the time-domain error locator λ, the following set of recursive equations

$$\Delta_r = \sum_{i=0}^{n-1} \alpha^{ir} v_i^{(r-1)} \lambda_i$$

$$v_i^{(r)} = v_i^{(r-1)} - \Delta_r \alpha^{-ri}$$

results in

$$v_i^{(n)} = e_i \qquad i = 0, \ldots, n-1.$$

Proof The equation of the recursion in the frequency domain is rewritten by breaking it into two steps, starting with the received spectrum **V** and changing it to **E** one component at a time:

$$\Delta_r = V_r - \left(-\sum_{j=1}^{n-1} \Lambda_j V_{r-j} \right) = \sum_{j=0}^{n-1} \Lambda_j V_{r-j}$$

$$V_j^{(r)} = \begin{cases} V_j^{(r-1)} & j \neq r \\ V_j^{(r-1)} - \Delta_r & j = r \end{cases}$$

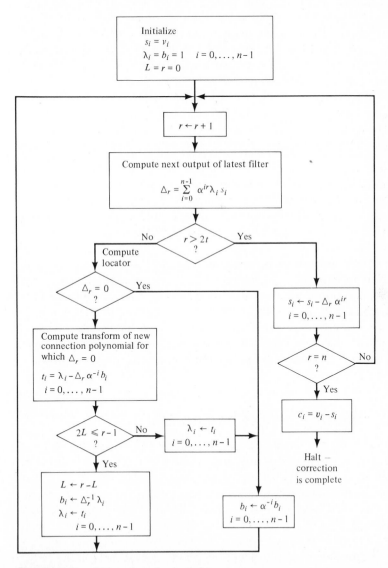

Figure 9.7 A time-domain decoder.

Because $V_j^{(2t)} = E_j$ for $j = 1, \ldots, 2t$ and $\Lambda_j = 0$ for $j > t$, the above equations are equivalent to

$$E_r = -\sum_{j=1}^{n-1} \Lambda_j E_{r-j}.$$

This equivalence proves the theorem. $\square$

A time-domain decoder is shown in Fig. 9.7 for fields of characteristic 2. The left side of the diagram is based on Theorem 9.5.1, and the right side is based on Theorem 9.5.2. During the iterations on the left side, the Fourier transform of the error-locator polynomial is being formed. During each pass on the right side, the received word is modified in such a way that one component of the spectrum of the received word is changed into one component of the spectrum of the error word. Hence, after the last iteration, the received word has been changed into the error word.

The time-domain decoder can be attractive for two reasons:

1. There is only one major step in the computation. That is, there is no syndrome computer or Chien search. This leads to an economy of design, especially if the decoder circuits are built into hardware.
2. The computational work can be much less than that of a decoder that performs the Fourier transforms directly and uses a conventional Berlekamp-Massey algorithm. This is usually the case for moderate n.

The number of major clocks required is n, which is independent of the number of errors corrected. During each clock, vectors of length n are processed, and thus the complexity of the decoder is $O(n^2)$. For large n, decoders with fewer computations can be found. The time-domain decoder is simple in structure and attractive for small n, however, including the range of practical values of n. In the era of large-scale integrated circuits, structural simplicity is at least as important as the number of arithmetic operations.

9.6 DECODING BEYOND THE BCH BOUND

Error patterns slightly outside the packing radius of a code often will not fall into any decoding sphere. These error patterns between the spheres are loosely called *uncorrectable error patterns*. They are detected but are not usually corrected. Sometimes one may choose to enlarge the set of correctable error patterns and correct some of these as well. We will give some decoding techniques to do this.

An uncorrectable error pattern in a BCH codeword can be recognized if the error-locator polynomial does not have a number of zeros in the error-locator field equal to its degree, or if the error pattern has components outside of the symbol field $GF(q)$. It is possible to catch these cues without completing all of the decoding calculations. They can be recognized by properties of the recursively computed error spectrum:

$$E_j = - \sum_{k=1}^{t} \Lambda_k E_{j-k}$$

According to Theorem 8.2.1, the requirement that the error pattern be in $GF(q)$ can be recognized in the error spectrum by the condition

$$E_j^q = E_{((jq))}$$

for all j. If this equation is tested as each E_j is computed, then an uncorrectable error pattern may be detected and the computation can be halted. The requirement that deg $\Lambda(x)$ should equal the number of zeros of $\Lambda(x)$ in $GF(q^m)$ can be tested by the condition that E_j is periodic. That is,

$$E_{((n+j))} = E_j$$

for all j. This condition gives another test that can be used to detect an uncorrectable error pattern and halt the decoding. It is established by the following theorem.

☐ **Theorem 9.6.1** Suppose $\Lambda(x)$ is a nonzero polynomial of smallest degree satisfying

$$E_j = - \sum_{k=1}^{\deg \Lambda(x)} \Lambda_k E_{j-k}$$

for $j = 2t + 1, \ldots, n + 2t$. The number of distinct zeros of $\Lambda(x)$ in $GF(q^m)$ is equal to deg $\Lambda(x)$ if and only if

$$E_{((n+j))} = E_j$$

for $j = 1, \ldots, 2t$, where $n = q^m - 1$.

Proof Suppose the number of distinct zeros of $\Lambda(x)$ in $GF(q^m)$ equals deg $\Lambda(x)$. Then $\Lambda(x)$ divides $x^n - 1$, and there is a polynomial $\Lambda^0(x)$ with $\Lambda^0(x)\Lambda(x) = x^n - 1$. Hence, because

$$\sum_{k=0}^{t} \Lambda_k E_{j-k} = 0,$$

we have $\Lambda(x)E(x) = 0$, and thus $\Lambda^0(x)\Lambda(x)E(x) = (x^n - 1)E(x) = 0$. This implies that $E_j = E_{n+j}$ for all j.

Conversely, suppose that $E_j = E_{n+j}$ for all j. Then $(x^n - 1)E(x) = 0$. But we are given that $\Lambda(x)$ is the smallest-degree nonzero polynomial with the property that $\Lambda(x)E(x) = 0 \pmod{x^n - 1}$. By the division algorithm, write

$$(x^n - 1) = \Lambda(x)Q(x) + r(x)$$

so that

$$(x^n - 1)E(x) = \Lambda(x)E(x)Q(x) + r(x)E(x).$$

Therefore

$$r(x)E(x) = 0 \qquad (\text{mod } x^n - 1).$$

But $r(x)$ has a degree smaller than the degree of $\Lambda(x)$, and thus $r(x)$ must equal zero. Then $\Lambda(x)$ divides $x^n - 1$, and thus all of its zeros are also zeros of $x^n - 1$. $\square$

If either of the two conditions fails, that is, if

$$E_j^q \neq E_{((qj))} \qquad \text{for some } j$$

or

$$E_{((n+j))} \neq E_j \qquad \text{for some } j,$$

then a pattern with more than t errors has been detected.

Sometimes one may wish to push the decoding beyond the designed distance. Techniques that decode a small distance beyond the designed distance can be obtained by forcing the Berlekamp-Massey algorithm to continue past $2t$ iterations. The basic idea is to introduce as unknowns extra syndromes (or extra discrepancies). The decoder analytically continues its decoding algorithm, leaving the extra syndromes as unknowns, and the error polynomial is computed as a function of these unknowns. The unknowns are then selected by trial and error to obtain a smallest-weight error pattern in the symbol field of the code. Unfortunately, the complexity of these techniques increases very quickly as one passes beyond the designed distance, and thus only a limited penetration is possible.

There are many situations in which the techniques can be applied. Some of these are illustrated by the following examples:

1. A binary BCH code with all of the parity frequencies in a block of length $2t$ but with the actual minimum distance larger than $2t + 1$. (The Golay code is one example of such a code. Another is the $(127, 43, 31)$ BCH code, which has a designed distance of only 29.)
2. A cyclic code with parity frequencies that are not contiguous.
3. A decoder for some of the $(t + 1)$-error patterns in a t-error-correcting Reed-Solomon code or BCH code.
4. A decoder for an alternant code.

One may proceed either in the time domain, in the frequency domain, or in some hybrid fashion. One must develop both the error-locator polynomial $\Lambda(x)$ (or $\lambda(x)$) and the error polynomial $e(x)$. The complexity of the processing depends on the approach. If the code is in a subfield of the error-locator field, then schemes that first find the error-locator polynomial can generate many ambiguities, and these must be resolved by computing each error polynomial in turn and rejecting those not in the code symbol field. In this case, it is wise to build additional tests into the computations so that false ambiguities in the solution for $\Lambda(x)$ can be rejected immediately.

We will start the discussion with a Reed-Solomon code in $GF(q)$ of designed distance $2t + 1$. Any polynomial $\Lambda(x)$ of degree $t + v$ with $t + v$ distinct zeros in $GF(q)$ is a legitimate error-locator polynomial if

$$\sum_{j=0}^{n-1} \Lambda_j S_{r-j} = 0 \qquad r = 1 + t + v, \ldots, 2t.$$

The smallest-degree such polynomial with $\Lambda_0 = 1$, if it is unique, corresponds to the codeword at minimum distance. If it is of degree of at most t, this polynomial is produced by the Berlekamp-Massey algorithm. Even when there are more than t errors, the smallest-degree polynomial with these properties may be unique, and the received word can be uniquely decoded whenever that polynomial can be found. There is no need to check the error magnitude in a Reed-Solomon code because the errors are always in $GF(q)$. If the smallest-degree polynomial is not unique, then there are several possible error patterns, all of the same weight, that agree with the received word.

Suppose there are $t + 1$ errors; then the two unknown syndromes S_{2t+1} and S_{2t+2}, if they were known, would be enough to find $\Lambda(x)$. Equivalently, the discrepancies Δ_{2t+1} and Δ_{2t+2}, if they were known, would be enough to find $\Lambda(x)$. Hence, analytically continue the Berlekamp-Massey algorithm through two more iterations with these the discrepancies as unknowns. Then we have

$$\begin{bmatrix} \Lambda^{(2t+2)}(x) \\ B^{(2t+2)}(x) \end{bmatrix} = \begin{bmatrix} 1 & -\Delta_{2t+2}x \\ \Delta_{2t+2}^{-1}\delta_{2t+2} & \bar{\delta}_{2t+2}x \end{bmatrix} \begin{bmatrix} 1 & -\Delta_{2t+1}x \\ \Delta_{2t+1}^{-1}\delta_{2t+1} & \bar{\delta}_{2t+1}x \end{bmatrix} \begin{bmatrix} \Lambda^{(2t)}(x) \\ B^{(2t)}(x) \end{bmatrix},$$

where the unknowns satisfy $\Delta_{2t+1}, \Delta_{2t+2} \in GF(q)$; $\delta_{2t+1}, \delta_{2t+2} \in \{0, 1\}$. Everything else on the right is known from the $2t$ syndromes. Transform the frequency-domain expression into the time domain:

$$\begin{bmatrix} \lambda_i^{(2t+2)} \\ b_i^{(2t+2)} \end{bmatrix} = \begin{bmatrix} 1 & -\Delta_{2t+2}\alpha^{-i} \\ \Delta_{2t+2}^{-1}\delta_{2t+2} & \bar{\delta}_{2t+2}\alpha^{-i} \end{bmatrix} \begin{bmatrix} 1 & -\Delta_{2t+1}\alpha^{-i} \\ \Delta_{2t+1}^{-1}\delta_{2t+1} & \bar{\delta}_{2t+1}\alpha^{-i} \end{bmatrix} \begin{bmatrix} \lambda_i^{(2t)} \\ b_i^{(2t)} \end{bmatrix},$$

where we have used the general fact that if $E_j' = E_{j-1}$, then the inverse transform satisfies $e_i' = \alpha^{-i}e_i$. We must now choose the unknowns, if possible, so that the error pattern contains at most $t + 1$ nonzero components.

Rewrite this as the two cases:

(1) $\lambda_i^{(2t+2)} = \lambda_i^{(2t)} - A_1\alpha^{-i}b_i^{(2t)} - A_2\alpha^{-2i}b_i^{(2t)}$

(2) $\lambda_i^{(2t+2)} = \lambda_i^{(2t)} - A_1\alpha^{-i}b_i^{(2t)} - A_2\alpha^{-2i}\lambda_i^{(2t)}$

where A_1 and A_2 are constants not both zero, and A_1 is nonzero in the second equation. Each of these cases is to be searched over A_1 and A_2 for a solution with $\lambda_i^{(2t+2)} = 0$ for exactly $t + 1$ values of i. This locates $t + 1$ errors and the decoding can continue as for erasure decoding.

Searching through these cases appears tedious, but it is quite orderly and simple in structure, and shift-register circuits can be easily designed to search for a solution. One can organize the search in a variety of ways. One possibility is a histogram approach. For case (2), for each value of A_1 prepare a histogram of $(\lambda_i^{(2t)} - A_1\alpha^{-i}b_i^{(2t)})^{-1}(\alpha^{-2i}\lambda_i^{(2t)})$. Any component of the histogram that takes the value $t + 1$ corresponds to a possible $t + 1$ error pattern.

The decoder can be further extended to decode $t + v$ errors. Although the equations become lengthy, it seems that such an approach may be practical out to $t + 3$ or $t + 4$, depending on the blocklength of the code.

Now consider binary codes. These differ from Reed-Solomon codes in that the decoder can be simplified by using Theorem 7.6.1 but is also complicated by the fact that many of the $t + v$ error patterns found may correspond to nonbinary error patterns and thus must be discarded.

Suppose that we have a binary BCH code of designed distance $2t + 1$, and we wish to correct all uniquely decodable patterns of at most $t + 1$ errors. The only measurement data available to the decoder are the $2t$ syndromes $S_1, S_2, \ldots, S_{2t}$. All other frequencies either can take on arbitrary values or are completely determined by the constraints. The binary algorithm can be iterated again to give

$$\Lambda^{(2t+2)}(x) = \Lambda^{(2t)}(x) - \Delta_{2t+1}xB^{(2t)}(x).$$

In the time domain this is

$$\lambda_i^{(2t+2)} = \lambda_i^{(2t)} - \Delta_{2t+1}\alpha^{-i}b_i^{(2t)},$$

and suppose a pattern of t or less errors was not found.

Prepare a histogram of $\alpha^i\lambda_i^{(2t)}/b_i^{(2t)}$ over the nonzero components of $GF(q)$. Each component of the histogram that equals $t + 1$ corresponds to a candidate error pattern. Once the error locations are known, the error pattern can be computed. If it is unique and binary-valued, the decoding is successful.

Next consider a binary code for which the parity frequencies are not contiguous. The (63, 28, 15) binary cyclic code has parity frequencies $C_1, C_3, C_5, C_7, C_9, C_{11}$, and C_{21}. The minimum distance is 15, as may be verified by a computer search. This code should be preferred to the (63, 24, 15) BCH code because of a superior rate, but the BCH code might be chosen because of its well-known decoding algorithms. With a little extra complexity, however, we can modify a frequency-domain BCH decoder to handle the (63, 28, 15) code. Using the procedure discussed previously, all patterns of seven or less errors that agree with the 12 contiguous parity frequencies are found. Then S_{21} is computed for each of these candidates. Only one will agree with the measured value of S_{21}.

9.7 DECODING OF ALTERNANT CODES

An alternant code is a subfield-subcode of a simple modification of a Reed-Solomon code. The minimum distance d^* of the alternant code is at least as large as d, the designed distance of the Reed-Solomon code. Any procedure for decoding the Reed-Solomon code can be used to decode the alternant code. All that needs to be added is a step to modify the syndromes by the inverse of the template, either by multiplying in the time domain or by convolving in the frequency domain. No other change is necessary. Hence, any frequency-domain or time-domain BCH decoder can decode alternant codes out to the designed distance. The appeal of alternant codes, however, is that their minimum distance is much larger than their designed distance. An alternant code used with a BCH decoder has little advantage over a BCH code used with a BCH decoder. Of course, although it can only correct to the designed distance, the BCH decoder can detect error patterns up to the minimum distance, and this can be a reason to use an alternant code. In Section 9.6 we discussed techniques to decode slightly beyond the designed distance, but these techniques are of limited usefulness. The full potential of alternant codes will not be realized until a constructive procedure is found for finding templates that give good codes, and a decoding algorithm is found for decoding out to the minimum distance.

The filtered spectrum of the received word is given by

$$T_j = \sum_{k=0}^{n-1} H_{((j-k))} V_k,$$

and the spectrum itself can be recovered from **T** by

$$V_j = \sum_{k=0}^{n-1} G_{((j-k))} T_k = \sum_{k=0}^{2t} G_k T_{((j-k))},$$

for a Goppa code, where the Goppa polynomial $G(x)$ has degree $2t$, and

$$G(x)H(x) = 1 \qquad (\mod x^n - 1)$$

Since

$$\sum_{k=0}^{n-1} H_{((j-k))} C_k = 0 \qquad j = n - 2t + 1, \ldots, n,$$

the syndromes are defined by

$$S_{j-(n-2t)} = \sum_{k=0}^{n-1} H_{((j-k))} V_k \qquad j = n - 2t + 1, \ldots, n$$

or

$$S_j = \sum_{k=0}^{n-1} H_{((j+n-2t-k))} V_k \qquad j = 1, \ldots 2t.$$

From these syndromes, compute an error-locator polynomial, and then recursively extend to obtain S_j for $j = 1, \ldots, n$. The error spectrum can be obtained from

$$E_j = \sum_{k=0}^{n-1} G_k S_{((j-k-n+2t))} \qquad j = 0, \ldots, n-1.$$

Figure 9.8 shows a frequency-domain decoder for an alternant code. The syndromes are modified in the frequency domain by a convolution. Fewer multiplications are required in principle if this function is performed by a componentwise multiplication in the time domain before the Fourier transform. The received word, however, will consist of symbols from a small alphabet, say $GF(2)$. It may be preferable to do the Fourier transform on the small field and modify the syndromes by a convolution in the frequency domain.

Except for the step of removing the template, the decoding of an alternant code proceeds just as does the decoding of a Reed-Solomon code. Alternant

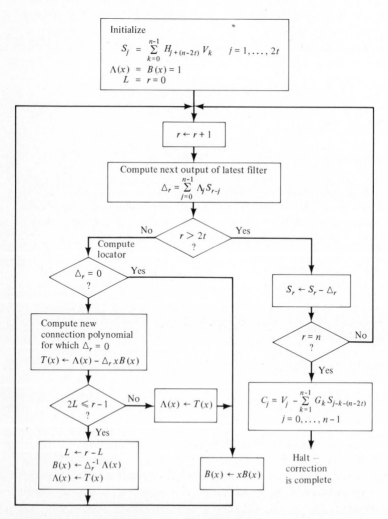

Figure 9.8   A decoder for an alternant code.

codes can be decoded beyond the designed distance just as Reed-Solomon codes. Only a single codeword can be within the minimum distance of the code. Other words may be found by the Reed-Solomon decoder, but these will have some components not in the symbol field of the code and these words can be rejected.

When decoding a narrow-sense Goppa code, one can avoid these false words by only appending syndromes that do not violate the constraint that $E_{2j} = E_j^2$. The two additional syndromes S_{2t+1} and S_{2t+2}, needed to correct $t + 1$ errors, are unknown. But

$$E_j = \sum_{k=0}^{2t} G_k S_{((j-k-n+2t))}.$$

Therefore

$$E_1 = G_0 S_{2t+1} + \sum_{k=1}^{2t} G_k S_{((2t+1-k))},$$

$$E_2 = G_0 S_{2t+2} + \sum_{k=1}^{2t} G_k S_{((2t+2-k))},$$

and because $E_2 = E_1^2$,

$$S_{2t+2} = G_0^{-1}\left[\sum_{k=1}^{2t} G_k S_{2t+2-k} + G_0^2 S_{2t+1}^2 + \sum_{k=1}^{2t} G_k^2 S_{2t+1-k}^2\right].$$

Only S_{2t+1} has to be introduced as an unknown. In a more general case, odd-numbered syndromes appear as unknowns, while even-numbered syndromes are computed. Only half as many new syndromes are needed, and the error pattern is always binary. If the resulting error-locator polynomial is legitimate, the decoding is complete. Unfortunately, to correct s errors beyond the designed distance, one still has to search through q^s possibilities for the unknown syndromes.

9.8 COMPUTATION OF THE FINITE FIELD TRANSFORMS

Consider the Fourier transform

$$V_j = \sum_{i=0}^{n-1} \alpha^{ij} v_i,$$

where α is an element of order n in $GF(q^m)$. For a small blocklength, it is practical to compute this just as it is written, but the computation involves n^2 multiplications and therefore becomes impractical for a large blocklength. We need efficient methods for computing the Fourier transform, and several techniques are available. The most powerful techniques, useful for some blocklengths, are techniques that turn a one-dimensional Fourier transform into a multidimensional Fourier transform. These techniques are known collectively as the *fast Fourier transform*. We shall postpone the study of them until Chapter 11. In this section we will study other ways to compute the Fourier transform. The methods we will study here are the Bluestein chirp algorithm, the Rader prime algorithm, and the Goertzel algorithm.

The Bluestein chirp algorithm and the Rader prime algorithm shown in Figure 9.9 are two different ways of turning a Fourier transform into a convolution; the first turns an n-point Fourier transform into an n-point convolution, and the second turns an n-point Fourier transform into an $(n-1)$-point convolution whenever n is a prime.

The Bluestein chirp algorithm can be used whenever the element α has a square root. Theorem 4.6.15 shows that every element of a Galois field has a square root. For finite fields of characteristic 2, $\sqrt{\alpha} = \alpha^{(n+1)/2}$ because

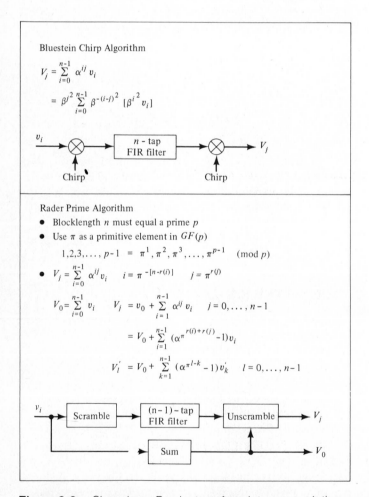

Figure 9.9 Changing a Fourier transform into a convolution.

$n+1$ is always even. For finite fields of characteristic other than 2, α has a square root either in $GF(q^m)$ or in $GF(q^{2m})$.

The Bluestein chirp algorithm is given by the expression

$$V_j = \beta^{j^2} \sum_{i=0}^{n-1} \beta^{-(j-i)^2} (\beta^{i^2} v_i),$$

where β is a square root of α. This variation of the Fourier transform is based on the calculation

$$\beta^{j^2} \sum_{i=0}^{n-1} \beta^{-(j-i)^2} (\beta^{i^2} v_i) = \sum_{i=0}^{n-1} \beta^{2ij} v_i = \sum_{i=0}^{n-1} \alpha^{ij} v_i = V_j.$$

Notice that the chirp transform consists of a pointwise product of v_i by β^{i^2} (n multiplications) followed by a cyclic convolution with β^{-i^2} (an n-tap FIR filter) followed by a pointwise product with β^{j^2} (n multiplications). The number of operations is still on the order of n^2, and thus the chirp algorithm is not asymptotically more efficient than the direct Fourier transform. It can be easier to implement in hardware in some applications, however. It is also possible to replace the direct convolution by a fast convolution algorithm of Section 11.1.

The Rader prime algorithm can be used to compute the Fourier transform in any field $GF(q)$ whenever the blocklength n is a prime. Because n is a prime, we can make use of the structure of $GF(n)$. This prime field is not to be confused with $GF(q)$ or with any subfield or extension of $GF(q)$.

Choose a primitive element π in the prime field $GF(n)$. Then each integer less than n can be expressed as a power of π. The Fourier transform in $GF(q)$ can be rewritten as follows, with the zero-frequency component and the zero-time component treated specially:

$$V_0 = \sum_{i=0}^{n-1} v_i$$

$$V_j = v_0 + \sum_{i=1}^{n-1} \alpha^{ij} v_i$$

$$= V_0 + \sum_{i=1}^{n-1} (\alpha^{ij} - 1) v_i \qquad j = 1, \ldots, n-1$$

For each i from 1 to $n-1$, let $r(i)$ be the unique integer from 1 to $n-1$ such that in $GF(p)$, $\pi^{r(i)} = i$. The function $r(i)$ is a permutation on $\{1, 2, \ldots, n-1\}$. Then V_j can be written

$$V_{\pi^{r(j)}} = V_0 + \sum_{i=1}^{n-1} (\alpha^{\pi^{r(i)+r(j)}} - 1) v_{\pi^{r(i)}}$$

Because $r(i)$ is a permutation, we can set $l = r(j)$, set $k = n - r(i)$, and use k as the index of summation, to get

$$V_{\pi^l} = V_0 + \sum_{k=1}^{n-1} (\alpha^{\pi^{l-k}} - 1) v_{\pi^{n-1-k}}$$

or

$$V_l' - V_0 = \sum_{k=1}^{n-1} (\alpha^{\pi^{l-k}} - 1)v_k',$$

where $V_l' = V_{\pi l}$ and $v_k' = v_{\pi^{n-k}}$ are scrambled input and output data sequences. This is now the equation of a cyclic convolution between $\{v_k'\}$ and $\{\alpha^{\pi^k} - 1\}$. By scrambling the input and output indices, we have turned the Fourier transform into a convolution. As it is written, the number of operations needed to implement the convolution is still on the order of n^2. As for the Bluestein chirp algorithm, however, the convolution may be computed by a fast convolution algorithm of Section 11.1.

Using the Rader prime algorithm, let us construct a binary five-point Fourier transform that will compute

$$V_j = \sum_{i=0}^{4} \alpha^{ij} v_i \qquad j = 0, \dots, 4.$$

This transform is in $GF(16)$ because the smallest m for which 5 divides $2^m - 1$ is 4. In $GF(5)$, the element 2 is primitive, and thus in $GF(5)$ we have:

$$2^0 = 1 \qquad 2^0 = 1$$
$$2^1 = 2 \qquad 2^{-1} = 3$$
$$2^2 = 4 \qquad 2^{-2} = 4$$
$$2^3 = 3 \qquad 2^{-3} = 2.$$

from which we obtain the scrambled indices. Then,

$$V_l' - V_0 = \sum_{k=0}^{3} (\alpha^{2^{l-k}} - 1)v_k'.$$

The summation is recognized as a four-point cyclic convolution. By identifying terms, we can write the Rader filter as a polynomial $g(x)$ over $GF(16)$ where coefficient g_k equals $\alpha^{2^{-k}} - 1$. Then

$$g(x) = (\alpha^3 - 1)x^3 + (\alpha^4 - 1)x^2 + (\alpha^2 - 1)x + (\alpha - 1)$$
$$= \alpha^{14}x^3 + \alpha x^2 + \alpha^8 x + \alpha^4.$$

The input to the filter and the output from the filter can also be expressed as polynomials whose coefficients are scrambled coefficients of v and V:

$$a(x) = v_3 x^3 + v_4 x^2 + v_2 x + v_1$$

and

$$b(x) = (V_2 - V_0)x^3 + (V_4 - V_0)x^2 + (V_3 - V_0)x + (V_1 - V_0)$$

and

$$b(x) = g(x)a(x) \qquad (\mod x^4 - 1).$$

The polynomial $g(x)$ is fixed. The polynomial $a(x)$ is formed by scrambling the coefficients of $v(x)$. The polynomial $V(x)$ is obtained by unscrambling the coefficients of the polynomial $b(x)$. The algorithm is summarized in Fig. 9.10. Any convenient method may be chosen to do the cyclic convolution.

To end this section, we give an algorithm for computing a Fourier transform on a Galois field that relies on the fact that an element of a finite field has a rich set of conjugates. The algorithm involves about $n \log n$ multiplications in $GF(q^m)$ but also requires about n^2 additions; hence it is called a *semifast algorithm*. It is an analog in the finite field of an algorithm for computing the Fourier transform in the complex field that is known to the subject of digital signal processing as the *Goertzel algorithm*. The algorithm involves at most $\log n$ multiplications and $n \log n$ additions in the symbol field per spectral component computed. When all spectral components are computed, it involves at most $n \log n$ multiplications and n^2 additions in the symbol field.

The jth Fourier component $V_j = \sum_i \alpha^{ij} v_i$ is the polynomial $v(x)$ evaluated at α^j. Let $f_j(x)$ be the minimal polynomial of α^j. It has a degree m_j that is less than or equal to m. We can write

$$v(x) = f_j(x)Q(x) + r(x)$$

and

$$v(\alpha^j) = f_j(\alpha^j)Q(\alpha^j) + r(\alpha^j) = r(\alpha^j).$$

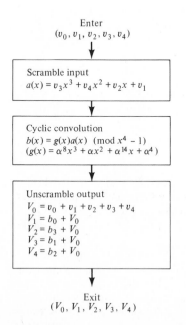

Figure 9.10   A five-point Fourier transform using the Rader algorithm.

Hence to compute V_j, we divide $v(x)$ to obtain the remainder $r(x)$ and then evaluate $r(\alpha^j)$. Because $f_j(x)$ is a polynomial over $GF(q)$ with degree m_j, the division by $f_j(x)$ involves $(n - m_j)m_j$ multiplications of elements of $GF(q^m)$ by elements of $GF(q)$, and $(n - m_j)m_j$ additions in $GF(q^m)$. The remainder polynomial $r(x)$ has a degree equal to $m_j - 1$. Then, computation of $r(\alpha^j)$ involves $m_j - 1$ multiplications in $GF(q^m)$ and the same number of additions in $GF(q^m)$. Therefore the single component V_j can be computed from $v(x)$ with $m_j - 1$ multiplications in $GF(q^m)$, $(n - m_j)m_j$ multiplications of elements in $GF(q^m)$ by elements of $GF(q)$, and $(n - m_j + 1)m_j - 1$ additions in $GF(q^m)$.

Because there are a total of n components in the transform, this process must be repeated $n = q^m - 1$ times, for a total of at most $m(q^m - 1)$ multiplications in $GF(q^m)$. If two elements are conjugates, then they have the same minimal polynomial, and therefore $r(x)$ is the same for each of these. Consequently, the intermediate polynomial $r(x)$ need not be computed separately for every component but must be computed only once for each conjugacy class. The number of additions is at most $(n - 1)n + n(m - 1) = n^2 + nm - 2m$. In particular, if $q = 2$, there are at most $n \log_2 (n + 1)$ multiplications in $GF(2^m)$. This holds even though $2^m - 1$ may be prime, in contrast to the fast-Fourier-transform algorithm. On the other hand, the number of additions required is still $O(n^2)$.

If the input vector is over the small field $GF(q)$, then even though the transform gives a vector over $GF(q^m)$, it requires no multiplications in $GF(q^m)$. This is because in this case, $v(x)$ is a polynomial over $GF(q)$, and the computation of V_j uses only multiplications of elements from $GF(q)$ by elements from $GF(q^m)$. If $q = 2$, this becomes an addition of elements of $GF(q^m)$ as selected by the nonzero coefficients of $r(x)$. Thus a syndrome of a binary code can be computed with no multiplications in $GF(2^m)$ at all and with at most $n \log n$ additions in $GF(2)$ and at most $\log n$ additions in $GF(2^m)$.

PROBLEMS

9.1. a. Devise a decoder for a Preparata (15, 8) code by augmenting the binary form of the Berlekamp-Massey algorithm with one extra iteration.

   b. Using part (a), derive a time-domain decoder for a Preparata code.

9.2. Describe how an errors-only decoder for a binary code can be used twice to decode a received word with $2t$ erasures. How can it be used to correct both errors and erasures?

9.3. Refer to Problem 7.3 (Chapter 7). Repeat part (b) using the Euclidean algorithm as discussed in Section 9.1.

9.4. Draw a flow for an errors-and-erasures decoder that works in the time domain.

9.5. Draw a flow for decoding a singly extended Reed-Solomon code in the time domain.

9.6. A time-domain decoder with $2t$ clocks that uses Forney's algorithm can be developed if the inverse Fourier transforms of $\Omega(x)$ and $\Lambda'(x)$ are available. Develop iterative equations similar to those of the Berlekamp-Massey algorithm for iteratively computing $\Omega(x)$ and $\Lambda'(x)$. Use the inverse Fourier transforms of these equations to describe a time-domain decoder with $2t$ clocks.

9.7. Combine the results of Problem 8.1 with Theorem 7.5.2 to derive Forney's algorithm for arbitrary j_0.

9.8. Write down explicitly the equations of a five-point Fourier transform over $GF(16)$ computed by the Rader prime algorithm. Sketch a circuit diagram showing the scrambling and unscrambling rules, and an FIR filter with the proper tap weights.

9.9. Use the Goertzel algorithm to compute the Fourier transform in $GF(8)$ of the vector represented by the polynomial

$$v(x) = \alpha^3 x^6 + \alpha^5 x^5 + x^4 + \alpha x^3 + \alpha^3 x^2 + x + 1.$$

NOTES

The decoding technique described by Reed and Solomon (1960) is somewhat similar to the frequency-domain techniques developed in this chapter, but thereafter techniques evolved primarily in the time domain. What amounts to a frequency-domain decoder was first proposed by Mandelbaum (1971), although in the terminology of the Chinese remainder theorem. Such a decoder was implemented in a computer program by Paschburg (1974).

The first discussion of decoding from the spectral point of view can be found in Gore (1973). He pointed out that the information can be encoded into the frequency domain and also that the error spectrum can be obtained by recursive extension. Implementation of transform domain decoders was also discussed by Michelson (1976). General discussion of spectral decoding techniques can be found in Blahut (1979). The reflection of these decoders back into the time domain is from Blahut (1980, 1981). The method of using the Euclidean algorithm for decoding is from Mandelbaum (1977).

The notion of an erasure channel is from Elias (1954). Early work on extending decoding algorithms for BCH codes to erasures as well as errors was done by Blum and Weiss (1960) and by Forney (1965). The approach described in this chapter is from Blahut (1979).

The decoding of extended codes appeared in Wolf (1969) and in Kasahara et al. (1975). The version of these techniques that appears in this chapter is from Blahut (1981). The decoding of alternant codes and Goppa codes has been treated by Patterson (1975) and by Helgert (1977). Delsarte (1975) pointed out that these codes can be decoded by any decoder of Reed-Solomon codes.

Decoding beyond the BCH bound can be found in Berlekamp (1968), Hartmann (1972), and Blahut (1979). A complete algebraic decoding algorithm for double-error-correcting BCH codes was given by Berlekamp (1968), and a complete algebraic decoding algorithm for some triple-error-correcting BCH codes was given by Vanderhorst and Berger (1976).

The Bluestein algorithm, (1970), the Rader algorithm (1968), and the Goertzel algorithm (1958) were described by these men in conjunction with signal-processing problems in the complex field. Additional discussion can be found in such textbooks as Oppenheim and Schafer (1975) or Rabiner and Gold (1975). Sarwate (1978) has proposed another variation of a semifast algorithm.

CHAPTER 10

Multi-dimensional Spectral Techniques

Just as one can define a Fourier transform in a finite field, so can one define a multidimensional Fourier transform in a finite field. These are transforms defined on multidimensional arrays of data, and they are useful in many ways. One can define new codes based on multidimensional transforms that are more efficiently decodable or so as to obtain new properties. Multidimensional transforms also are useful as tools for analyzing the structure of cyclic codes, such as BCH codes. The multidimensional codes are closely related to modern topics in digital signal processing that exploit the Chinese remainder theorems. The best-known multidimensional codes are the product codes, and we will begin with a study of these.

The codes obtained using multidimensional techniques have random-error-correcting ability that is generally inferior to that of codes already studied. They are studied for the sharpened insights they give; because it is sometimes convenient to process codewords as multidimensional arrays; and because one can obtain good codes that combine random- and burst-error correction.

10.1 PRODUCT CODES

The components of a codeword of a linear code of blocklength n can be arranged in an n_1 by n_2 array if $n = n_1 n_2$. This array, with elements denoted by $c_{ii'}$ or c_{ij} as is convenient, is a more natural array for defining and processing certain kinds of codes because the rows and columns may be treated individually. In such a case, the code is referred to as a *multidimensional code*. Of course as a vector space, the dimension of the code is still k—the number of information symbols. It is the array of indices that is referred to as multidimensional. Although all of the ideas also apply for more than two dimensions, we shall state them only for two dimensions.

We will begin the study with product codes, the simplest kind of multidimensional code.

□ **Definition 10.1.1** The *product code* $\mathscr{C} = \mathscr{C}_1 \otimes \mathscr{C}_2$ of two codes $\mathscr{C}_1$ and $\mathscr{C}_2$ is the code whose codewords are all the two-dimensional arrays for which columns are codewords in $\mathscr{C}_1$ and rows are codewords in $\mathscr{C}_2$. □

We can obtain a systematic representation of $\mathscr{C}$ by using systematic representations for $\mathscr{C}_1$ and $\mathscr{C}_2$ with the first k_1 and k_2 symbols, respectively, as information symbols. A codeword for $\mathscr{C}$ then appears as in Fig. 10.1. From this figure it is clear how to encode: first, encode each of the first k_1 rows with an encoder for $\mathscr{C}_1$, then encode all columns with an encoder for $\mathscr{C}_2$. It is simple to verify that one obtains the same codeword if the first k_2 columns are first encoded, then all the rows. The codeword is then serialized for passage through the channel, for example, by reading it out by rows or by columns.

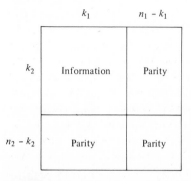

Figure 10.1 Structure of a systematic ($n_1 n_2$, $k_1 k_2$) codeword.

Codewords in a product code can be represented by polynomials in two variables. That is, if $c_{ii'}$ for $i = 0, \ldots, n_1 - 1$ and $i' = 0, \ldots, n_2 - 1$ is a codeword, then one has the polynomial representation

$$c(x, y) = \sum_{i=0}^{n_1 - 1} \sum_{i'=0}^{n_2 - 1} c_{ii'} x^i y^{i'}.$$

This can be parenthesized in either of two ways:

$$c(x, y) = \sum_{i=0}^{n_1 - 1} \left(\sum_{i'=0}^{n_2 - 1} c_{ii'} y^{i'} \right) x^i$$

or

$$c(x, y) = \sum_{i'=0}^{n_2 - 1} \left(\sum_{i=0}^{n_1 - 1} c_{ii'} x^i \right) y^{i'}.$$

By the definition of a product code, each of the parenthesized terms (one for each i) in the first expression is a codeword in $\mathscr{C}_2$, and each of the parenthesized terms (one for each i') in the second expression is a codeword in $\mathscr{C}_1$.

The component codes $\mathscr{C}_1$ and $\mathscr{C}_2$ may be cyclic, but this does not necessarily mean that $\mathscr{C}$ is cyclic. In Section 10.2 we will give a condition for which $\mathscr{C}$ is cyclic.

□ **Theorem 10.1.2**   If the minimum distances of $\mathscr{C}_1$ and $\mathscr{C}_2$ are d_1^* and d_2^*, respectively, then the minimum distance of $\mathscr{C}$ is $d_1^* d_2^*$.

Proof   The code is linear, a codeword of minimum weight has at least d_1^* nonzero entries in every nonzero column, and each row with such an entry has at least d_2^* nonzero entries; thus the minimum weight is at least $d_1^* d_2^*$. Further, at least one such codeword exists. □

The theorem implies that if the two codes can correct t_1 and t_2 errors, respectively, then the product code can correct $2t_1 t_2 + t_1 + t_2$ errors.

If in the array of Fig. 10.1 we set $n_2 - k_2$ equal to zero and read the codeword out to the channel by columns, then all we have done is interleave the n_2 codewords of the (n_1, k_1) code that appear as rows. Thus a product code is a generalization of an interleaved code. It is like an interleaved code, but some of the rows contain only parity. Hence it is clear that the product code can be used as a burst-error-correcting code. It corrects bursts of length $n_2 b_1$ if the row code corrects bursts of length b_1. If the same product codeword is read out to the channel by rows, then it corrects bursts of length $n_1 b_2$ if the column code corrects bursts of length b_2. By choosing the appropriate way in which to serialize the codeword, it can be used to correct bursts of length $\max(n_2 b_1, n_1 b_2)$. We have seen that it can be used to correct $(d_1^* d_2^* - 1)/2$ random errors. The following theorem says that it can be used in both of these ways at the same time.

□ **Theorem 10.1.3** The code formed as the product of a linear (n_1, k_1, d_1^*) code and a linear (n_2, k_2, d_2^*) code does not have any coset containing both a word of weight t or less, where $t = (d_1^* d_2^* - 1)/2$, and another word that is a burst of length $\max(n_2 t_1, n_1 t_2)$ or less, where $t_1 \leqslant (d_1^* - 1)/2$ and $t_2 \leqslant (d_2^* - 1)2$.

Proof To be specific, assume that $n_2 t_1 \geqslant n_1 t_2$, and thus the code is to be serialized by columns. If a burst error of length $n_2 t_1$ or less and a different random-error pattern of weight t or less are in the same coset, then their difference is a codeword. Each row of such a codeword has either a weight of zero or a weight of at least d_1^*. Because the burst has a length of at most $n_2 t_1$, each nonzero row can contain at most t_1 errors from the burst and thus must contain at least $d_1^* - t_1$ of the random errors. Thus the t random errors occur in at most $\lfloor t/(d_1^* - t_1) \rfloor$ rows. Hence the codeword contains at most this many nonzero rows, each with at most t_1 errors from the burst. The total number of errors is at most $\lfloor t/(d_1^* - t_1) \rfloor t_1 + t$. But this is less than $2t$ because $d_1^* - t_1$ is greater than t_1. Because the code has minimum weight of at least $2t + 1$, this is a contradiction. Such a codeword cannot exist, and thus the burst error and the random error cannot be in the same coset. □

Any product code can be used in the manner allowed by this theorem. One way to build the decoder is to combine a burst-error-correcting decoder and a random-error-correcting decoder side-by-side in a composite decoder, where each decoder corrects only up to the required number of errors and otherwise detects an uncorrectable error pattern. Either both decoders will yield the same error pattern or only one of the two decoders will successfully decode; the other will detect a pattern that it finds uncorrectable. Sometimes the random-error-correcting decoder will also catch all of the burst errors. In Section 10.3 we will describe a random-error-correcting decoder that decodes to the designed distance of the product of two BCH codes.

10.2 THE CHINESE REMAINDER THEOREMS

When is it possible to uniquely determine an integer given only its moduli with respect to each of several integers? An answer to this question was known to ancient China. We shall study this theorem next, as well as a more modern analogue dealing with the uniqueness of a set of polynomial moduli. The Chinese remainder theorem for integers will be proved in two parts. First we will prove the uniqueness of a solution, and then we will prove the existence of a solution.

□ **Theorem 10.2.1** Given a set of positive integers $m_1, m_2, \ldots, m_k$ that are pairwise relatively prime, and a set of nonnegative integers

$c_1, c_2, \ldots, c_k$ with $c_i < m_i$, the system of equations

$$c_i = c \pmod{m_i} \qquad i = 1, \ldots, k$$

has at most one solution for c in the interval $0 \leqslant c < \prod_{i=1}^{k} m_i$.

Proof Suppose that c and c' are solutions in this interval. Then

$$c = Q_i m_i + c_i$$

and

$$c' = Q_i' m_i + c_i,$$

and thus $c - c'$ is a multiple of m_i for each i. Then $c - c'$ is a multiple of $\prod_{i=1}^{k} m_i$ because the m_i are relatively prime. But $c - c'$ lies between $-(\prod_{i=1}^{k} m_i - 1)$ and $\prod_{i=1}^{k} m_i - 1$. The only possibility is $c - c' = 0$. Hence $c = c'$. $\square$

To actually find the solution to the system of congruences of Theorem 10.2.1, we make use of the corollary to the Euclidean algorithm (Corollary 4.1.4), which says that in the ring of integers,

$$GCD(r, s) = ar + bs$$

for some integers a and b.

Given the set of pairwise relatively prime positive integers $m_1, m_2, \ldots, m_k$, let $M = \prod_{i=1}^{k} m_i$, and let $M_i = M/m_i$. Then $GCD(M_i, m_i) = 1$, and thus there exist integers N_i and n_i with

$$N_i M_i + n_i m_i = 1.$$

We are now ready to prove the following theorem.

□ **Theorem 10.2.2** Let $M = \prod_{i=1}^{k} m_i$ be a product of pairwise-relatively prime positive integers, let $M_i = M/m_i$, and let N_i satisfy $N_i M_i + n_i m_i = 1$. Then the system of congruences

$$c_i = c \pmod{m_i} \qquad i = 1, \ldots, k$$

is uniquely solved by

$$c = \sum_{i=1}^{k} c_i N_i M_i \qquad \pmod{M}.$$

Proof We need only show that this c solves the specified system of congruences because we already know the solution is unique. But for this c,

$$c = \sum_{r=1}^{k} c_r N_r M_r \qquad \pmod{m_i}$$

$$= c_i N_i M_i \qquad \pmod{m_i}$$

because m_i divides M_r if $r \neq i$. Finally, because

$$N_i M_i + n_i m_i = 1,$$

we have $N_i M_i = 1$ (mod m_i), and $c = c_i$ (mod m_i), which completes the proof. $\square$

Now we turn to a ring of polynomials over any field. For any such ring we have the Chinese remainder theorem for polynomials, which is developed just as for the case of integers.

$\square$ **Theorem 10.2.3** Given a set of polynomials $m_1(x)$, $m_2(x), \ldots$, $m_k(x)$ that are pairwise relatively prime, and a set of polynomials $c_1(x)$, $c_2(x), \ldots, c_k(x)$ with deg $c_i(x) <$ deg $m_i(x)$, then the system of equations

$$c_i(x) = c(x) \qquad (\text{mod } m_i(x)) \qquad i = 1, \ldots, k$$

has at most one solution for $c(x)$ satisfying

$$\deg c(x) < \sum_{i=1}^{k} \deg m_i(x).$$

Proof The proof is essentially the same as the proof of Theorem 10.2.1. Suppose that $c(x)$ and $c'(x)$ are solutions:

$$c(x) = Q_i(x)m_i(x) + c_i(x)$$

and

$$c'(x) = Q'_i(x)m_i(x) + c_i(x),$$

and thus $c(x) - c'(x)$ is a multiple of $m_i(x)$ for each i. That is, $c(x) - c'(x)$ is a multiple of $\prod_{i=1}^{k} m_i(x)$ with $\deg[c(x) - c'(x)] < \deg[\prod_{i=1}^{k} m_i(x)]$. That is, $c(x) - c'(x) = 0$, and the proof is complete. $\square$

As in the case of the integer ring, in a ring of polynomials over a field, for some $a(x)$ and $b(x)$,

$$\text{GCD}[r(x), s(x)] = a(x)r(x) + b(x)s(x)$$

Hence given $m_i(x)$, let $M(x) = \prod_{r=1}^{k} m_r(x)$ and $M_i(x) = M(x)/m_i(x)$, and let $N_i(x)$ and $n_i(x)$ satisfy $N_i(x)M_i(x) + n_i(x)m_i(x) = 1$. They do exist, by Corollary 4.3.7.

$\square$ **Theorem 10.2.4** Let $M(x) = \prod_{r=1}^{k} m_r(x)$ be a product of pairwise relatively prime polynomials; let $M_i(x) = M(x)/m_i(x)$ and $N_i(x)$ satisfy $N_i(x)M_i(x) + n_i(x)m_i(x) = 1$. Then the system of congruences

$$c_i(x) = c(x) \qquad (\text{mod } m_i(x)) \qquad i = 1, \ldots, k$$

is uniquely solved by

$$c(x) = \sum_{i=1}^{k} c_i(x) N_i(x) M_i(x) \qquad (\bmod\ M(x)).$$

Proof We need only show that this $c(x)$ satisfies every congruence in the system of congruences, because we know there is only one solution. But

$$c(x) = c_i(x) N_i(x) M_i(x) \qquad (\bmod\ m_i(x)),$$

because $M_r(x)$ has $m_i(x)$ as a factor if $r \neq i$. Finally, because

$$N_i(x) M_i(x) + n_i(x) m_i(x) = 1,$$

we have $N_i(x) M_i(x) = 1$ (mod $m_i(x)$) and $c(x) = c_i(x)$ (mod $m_i(x)$), which completes the proof. $\square$

The Chinese remainder theorem can be used to see if the product of cyclic codes is itself cyclic.

$\square$ **Theorem 10.2.5** If $\mathscr{C}_1$ and $\mathscr{C}_2$ are cyclic codes whose blocklengths n_1 and n_2 are relatively prime, then $\mathscr{C}$ is a cyclic code when appropriately serialized.

Proof By the Chinese remainder theorem, if $0 \leqslant i \leqslant n_1 - 1$ and $0 \leqslant i' \leqslant n_2 - 1$, then there is a unique integer $I(i, i')$ with $0 \leqslant I(i, i') \leqslant n_1 n_2 - 1$ satisfying

$$I(i, i') = i \qquad (\bmod\ n_1)$$

$$I(i, i') = i' \qquad (\bmod\ n_2).$$

We can replace the codeword $c(x, y)$ by the serialization

$$c(z) = \sum_{I=0}^{n_1 n_2 - 1} c_{(I \bmod n_1)(I \bmod n_2)} z^I.$$

To see that the set of such $c(z)$ forms a cyclic code, notice that $zc(z)$ (mod $z^{n_1 n_2} - 1$) corresponds to $xyc(x, y)$ (mod $x^{n_1} - 1$) (mod $y^{n_2} - 1$). Because this is a codeword, $zc(z)$ (mod $z^{n_1 n_2} - 1$) is a codeword. $\square$

The relationship between $c(z)$ and $c(x, y)$ can be better understood in terms of the following two-dimensional array:

$$c_{ii'} = \begin{bmatrix} c_{00} & c_{01} & c_{02} & \cdots & c_{0(n_1-1)} \\ c_{10} & c_{11} & c_{12} & \cdots & c_{1(n_1-1)} \\ \vdots & \vdots & \vdots & & \vdots \\ c_{(n_2-1)0} & c_{(n_2-1)1} & c_{(n_2-1)2} & \cdots & c_{(n_2-1)(n_1-1)} \end{bmatrix}$$

The coefficients of $c(z)$ are obtained by reading down the diagonal starting with c_{00} and folding back at the edges as if the matrix were periodically repeated in both directions. Because n_1 and n_2 are relatively prime, the extended diagonal does not repass through any element until all $n_1 n_2$ elements have been used.

10.3 DECODING OF PRODUCT CODES

A product code can correct v errors when $v \leqslant (d_1^* d_2^* - 1)/2$. This theoretical capability of the code is worthless, however, without a practical decoding algorithm. In this section, we will give such an algorithm, which uses as subalgorithms an errors-only decoder for one of the component codes and an errors-and-erasures decoder for the other. We have described such decoders for BCH codes, so we shall speak only of decoding products of BCH codes.

We will discuss the case where $d_1^* d_2^*$ is odd. Without loss of generality, we will assume that $d_2^* \geqslant d_1^*$. A decoder for correcting the random errors in a product of two BCH codewords only needs to find any codeword within the packing radius $t = (d_1^* d_2^* - 1)/2$ of the received word, because there is only one such codeword. The decoder consists of an inner BCH decoder and an outer processing loop built around any available errors-and-erasures decoder for a BCH code. First, we will describe a simplified decoder; later we will improve it and then prove that it works.

The decoder will first "correct" each column. It does not matter to the decoding algorithm whether the codeword is actually transmitted by rows or by columns, but it will help the discussion if we think of the codeword as transmitted by columns; each column can be thought of as a subblock which will be decoded separately. Later, when decoding rows, the miscorrected subblocks will be caught and repaired.

Let v_j be the number of errors in the jth column of the received data. Then

$$v = \sum_{j=0}^{n_1 - 1} v_j.$$

The first step is to use the BCH decoder to correct each column. To the corrected jth column is appended the integer ω_j, the number of errors corrected. This is the weight of the estimated column error pattern $\hat{e}_i(j)$ and equals v_j if the decoding is correct. If an uncorrectable error pattern is detected, then the jth column is erased. Unerased columns with the largest value of ω_j will be considered the least reliable by the row decoder.

Next, the BCH errors-and-erasures decoder is used to correct each row. Now, however, side information is available, which will be used to judiciously erase additional columns. Start with the first row, ignoring side information, and decode each row, if possible. The row decoder may fail to decode or may put out a nonzero error pattern. Either case implies that some of the column decodings were incorrect. We need a test to decide whether to accept the row decoding or whether to erase a least reliable column and try again.

We will derive the basic theorem under the condition that no columns have been erased by the column decoder. Later we will use this theorem in the presence of erasures simply by reducing d_1^* by the number of erased columns. The methods of proof will appear again later, in Chapter 15, where we will study soft-decision decoding.

Given that the product code can correct $t = (d_1^* d_2^* - 1)/2$ errors and that the column decoder has already corrected ω_j errors in the jth column, what can be said about the row decoder? Suppose that the ith row is decoded and a row error pattern $\hat{e}_j(i)$ is found in the ith row. Let U_i be the set of j for which $\hat{e}_j(i)$ is nonzero. If j is in U_i, then the jth column decoding was incorrect; there are now at least d_2^* errors in the jth column, of which ω_j errors may have been introduced by the column decoder, and ω_j is less than d_2^*. Consequently, if the row decoder found a correct error pattern, there were at least $d_2^* - \omega_j$ errors in the jth column of the original received word for each j in U_i, and as far as we yet know, there were ω_j errors in the jth column of the original received word for each j not in U_i. Thus a reasonable condition for the acceptance of the decoded ith row is the following:

$$\sum_{j \in U_i} (d_2^* - \omega_j) + \sum_{j \notin U_i} \omega_j \leq t.$$

The next theorem says that this inequality is both necessary and sufficient for the ith row decoder to be correct. First we put the inequality in the form of an inner product, which will be useful in proving the theorem. Rewrite it as

$$2 \sum_{j \in U_i} \left(1 - \frac{\omega_j}{d_2^*}\right) + 2 \sum_{j \notin U_i} \frac{\omega_j}{d_2^*} < d_1^*$$

Then

$$\sum_{j \in U_i} 1 + \sum_{j \notin U_i} 1 - 2 \sum_{j \in U_i} \left(1 - \frac{\omega_j}{d_2^*}\right) - 2 \sum_{j \notin U_i} \frac{\omega_j}{d_2^*} > n_1 - d_1^*.$$

Let ξ_j equal -1 if j is an element of U_i and otherwise equal 1. Then

$$\sum_{j=0}^{n_1 - 1} \xi_j \left(1 - \frac{2\omega_j}{d_2^*}\right) > n_1 - d_1^*.$$

Finally, let $a_j = [1 - (2\omega_j/d_2^*)]$. The inequality becomes

$$\sum_{j=0}^{n_1 - 1} \xi_j a_j > n_1 - d_1^*.$$

Now we are ready for the theorem.

☐ **Theorem 10.3.1** Let ω_j be the number of places in which the jth column of the column-corrected array differs from the received word. For each i, there is exactly one row codeword satisfying

$$\sum_{j \in U_i} (d_2^* - \omega_j) + \sum_{j \notin U_i} \omega_j \leq t,$$

where U_i is the set of j in which the row codeword differs from the jth component of the column-corrected array.

Proof   In the first step, we will prove that a correct row codeword in the ith row satisfies the inequality. In the second step, we will prove there is no other.

Step 1   Let ϕ denote the number of columns decoded incorrectly, and let U_ϕ be their index set. Then, $n_1 - \phi$ are decoded correctly. But

$$\sum_{j \in U_\phi} v_j + \sum_{j \notin U_\phi} v_j \leq t,$$

and the number of errors v_j actually occurring in the jth column of the received word satisfies

$$v_j = \omega_j$$

if the jth column is correctly decoded and satisfies

$$v_j \geq d_2^* - \omega_j > \omega_j$$

if the jth column is incorrectly decoded. The set U_i of decoded columns in which errors occur in the ith row satisfies $U_i \subset U_\phi$. Hence,

$$\sum_{j \in U_i} (d_2^* - \omega_j) + \sum_{j \notin U_i} \omega_j \leq t,$$

thereby proving that for every row, the correct row codeword satisfies the given inequality.

Step 2   Consider the ith row. Suppose that $\mathbf{c}_r$ and $\mathbf{c}_{r'}$ are row codewords, and let $\boldsymbol{\mu}$ denote the ith row after all columns have been "corrected." Let ξ_j equal 1 if $\mathbf{c}_r$ agrees with $\boldsymbol{\mu}$ in component j, and otherwise $\xi_j = -1$. Let ξ_j' be defined similarly from codeword $\mathbf{c}_{r'}$. Define the sets

$$T = \{j | c_{rj} = c_{r'j}\}$$
$$V = \{j | c_{rj} \neq c_{r'j} \quad \text{and} \quad c_{rj} = \mu_j\}$$
$$W = \{j | c_{rj} \neq c_{r'j} \quad \text{and} \quad c_{rj} \neq \mu_j\}.$$

Every value of j is in one of the three sets. Then

$$\sum_{j=0}^{n_1-1} \xi_j a_j = \sum_{j \in T} \xi_j a_j + \sum_{j \in V} a_j - \sum_{j \in W} a_j = A_T + A_V - A_W,$$

with the obvious definition of A_T, A_V, and A_W. The number of elements in T is no more than $n_1 - d_1^*$. If $\mathbf{c}_r$ satisfies the condition of the theorem

$$\sum_{j=0}^{n_1-1} \xi_j a_j = A_T + A_V - A_W > n_1 - d_1^*.$$

Therefore $A_V - A_W > 0$. Now we are ready for $\mathbf{c}_{r'}$.

$$\sum_{j=0}^{n_1-1} \xi'_j a_j = \sum_{j \in T} \xi'_j a_j + \sum_{j \in V} \xi'_j a_j + \sum_{j \in W} \xi'_j a_j,$$

$$= A_T - A_V + B_W$$

with the obvious definition of B_W and noting that $\mathbf{c}_{r'j} \neq \mu_j$ in set V. But $B_W \leqslant A_W$ and we have seen that $A_W - A_V < 0$. Hence

$$\sum_{j=0}^{n_1-1} \xi'_j a_j \leqslant A_T - A_V + A_W < A_T \leqslant n_1 - d_1^*,$$

which proves that $\mathbf{c}_{r'}$ does not satisfy the inequality. $\square$

We will now describe a practical way to find this codeword. We already know how to build decoders to correct errors and erasures based on hard decisions. We will build an outer processing loop around any available errors-and-erasures decoder. Based on the ith column-corrected row, we form a series of trial hard-decision-with-erasure vectors. The indices are ordered such that $\omega_{j_1} \geqslant \omega_{j_2} \geqslant \cdots \geqslant \omega_{j_{n_1}}$ or $a_{j_1} \leqslant a_{j_2} \leqslant \cdots \leqslant a_{j_{n_1}}$. For each l from 0 to $d_1^* - 1$, we will erase the l components for which ω_j is the largest (breaking ties arbitrarily). In this way, a vector $\mu^{(l)}$ with erasures is formed. Decode $\mu^{(l)}$ using an errors-and-erasures decoder. If it decodes into $\mathbf{c}_r$, test it using Theorem 10.3.1. If it passes, then $\mathbf{c}_r$ is the decoded codeword for that row. Otherwise, increase l and repeat. The next theorem proves that this process reaches the correct codeword.

$\square$ **Theorem 10.3.2** If for codeword $\mathbf{c}_r$,

$$\sum_{j=0}^{n_1-1} \xi_j a_j > n_1 - d_1^*,$$

then for at least one l

$$\sum_{j=0}^{n_1-1} \xi_j b_j^{(l)} > n_1 - d_1^*,$$

where

$$b_{j_1}^{(l)} = b_{j_2}^{(l)} = \cdots = b_{j_l}^{(l)} = 0$$

$$b_{j_{l+1}}^{(l)} = b_{j_{l+2}}^{(l)} = \cdots = b_{j_{n_1}}^{(l)} = 1$$

and consequently $\mathbf{c}_r$ is the unique codeword found by an errors-and-erasures decoder.

Proof It is sufficient to prove the theorem for l running from 0 to n_1, because the conclusion is clearly not possible for $l \geqslant d_1^*$.

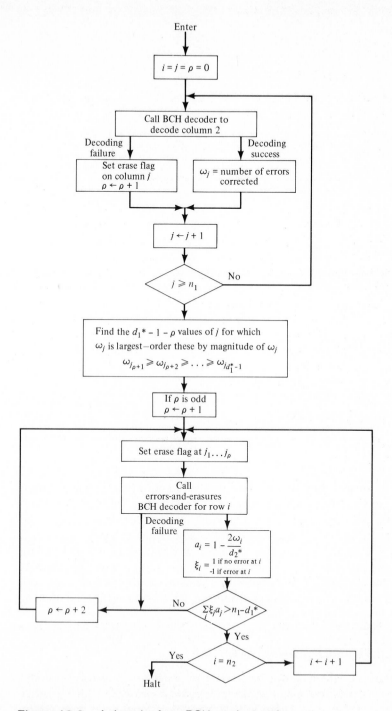

Figure 10.2   A decoder for a BCH product code.

The idea of the proof is that μ lies in the convex hull of the set $\{\mu^{(l)}\}$. Let

$$\lambda_0 = a_{j_1}$$

$$\lambda_l = a_{j_{l+1}} - a_{j_l} \qquad 1 \leqslant l \leqslant n_1 - 1$$

$$\lambda_{n_1} = 1 - a_{j_{n_1}}.$$

Then $0 \leqslant \lambda_l \leqslant 1$, and $\sum_{l=0}^{n_1} \lambda_l = 1$. Furthermore,

$$\sum_{l=0}^{l'-1} \lambda_l = a_{j_{l'}}$$

and

$$a_j = \sum_{l=0}^{n_1} \lambda_l b_j^{(l)}.$$

Now suppose that

$$\sum_{j=0}^{n_1-1} \xi_j b_j^{(l)} \leqslant n_1 - d_1^*$$

for all l. Then

$$\sum_{j=0}^{n_1-1} \xi_j a_j = \sum_{l=0}^{n_1} \lambda_l \sum_{j=0}^{n_1-1} \xi_j b_j^{(l)}$$

$$\leqslant \sum_{l=0}^{n_1} \lambda_l (n_1 - d_1^*)$$

$$\leqslant n_1 - d_1^*,$$

in contradiction to the assumption of the theorem. Hence, the theorem is proved. $\square$

The decoder of Fig. 10.2 is based on the previous two theorems. When decoding row i, if some columns have been erased, then the same procedure is used, but only treating the unerased columns and with d_2^* reduced by the number of erasures. Further, if while decoding row i any columns are erased or found to contain an error, then these columns stay erased while decoding all subsequent rows. The decoder always erases two columns whenever it needs to erase one, and thus the number of erasures is always even. This does not reduce the error-correcting performance, but it reduces the total number of iterations to at most $n_2 + (d_1^* - 1)/2$.

10.4 MULTIDIMENSIONAL SPECTRA

A two-dimensional array can be studied by means of a two-dimensional Fourier transform, provided the dimensions are compatible with a Fourier transform size. Let $\{v_{ii'}\}$ be an n by n two-dimensional array over $GF(q)$, which will be called a *two-dimensional signal*, and suppose n divides $q^m - 1$ for some m. Let α be an element of $GF(q^m)$ of order n. The array with elements

$$V_{jj'} = \sum_{i=0}^{n-1} \sum_{i'=0}^{n-1} \alpha^{ij}\alpha^{i'j'} v_{ii'}$$

will be called the *two-dimensional spectrum*, and the indices j and j' are the frequency variables. It is obvious that

$$v_{ii'} = \frac{1}{n}\frac{1}{n} \sum_{j=0}^{n-1} \sum_{j'=0}^{n-1} \alpha^{-ij}\alpha^{-i'j'} V_{jj'}$$

by inspection of the one-dimensional inverse transform. Figure 10.3 shows a two-dimensional spectrum over $GF(8)$. Each square in the grid contains an octal symbol.

To define an error-control code, select a set of $N - K$ of these components to be (two-dimensional) parity frequencies and constrain these to be zero, as in Fig. 10.3. The remaining set of K components is filled with K information symbols over $GF(q^m)$, and the inverse two-dimensional Fourier transform is taken to produce the codeword corresponding to the given information symbols. Clearly, this is a linear code, but in general it is not cyclic.

If the desired code is in a subfield of $GF(q^m)$ [in the example, $GF(2)$ is the only subfield of $GF(8)$], then one must restrict the set of codewords to those that only have components in the subfield, and thus one obtains a two-dimensional subfield-subcode. One could also obtain a two-dimensional alternant code by multiplying by a two-dimensional template before extracting the subfield-subcode.

The two-dimensional spectrum need not be square, but if it is, and $n + 1 = q^m$, then the largest field in the discussion is $GF(n + 1)$. If the spectrum is an n_1 by n_2 array ($n_1 \neq n_2$), one must deal with the smallest field $GF(q^m)$ for some m such that both n_1 and n_2 divide $q^m - 1$. Let $\{v_{ii'}\}$ be an n_1 by n_2 two-dimensional signal. Let β and γ be elements of $GF(q^m)$ of order n_1 and n_2, respectively. Then

$$V_{jj'} = \sum_{i=0}^{n_1-1} \sum_{i'=0}^{n_2-1} \beta^{ij}\gamma^{i'j'} v_{ii'}.$$

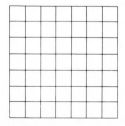

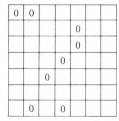

(a) Unconstrained spectrum   (b) Constrained spectrum

Figure 10.3   Two-dimensional spectrum over $GF(8)$.

Again, it is obvious that

$$v_{ii'} = \frac{1}{n_1} \frac{1}{n_2} \sum_{j=0}^{n_1-1} \sum_{j'=0}^{n_2-1} \beta^{-ij} \gamma^{-i'j'} V_{jj'}$$

by inspection of the one-dimensional inverse transform.

For an example, choose all of the elements in a set of vertical stripes and a set of horizontal stripes to be parity frequencies of a two-dimensional code, as shown in Fig. 10.4. All the two-dimensional time-domain functions with these frequencies equal to zero are the codewords. That is,

$$\sum_{i=0}^{n_1-1} \sum_{i'=0}^{n_2-1} \beta^{ij} \gamma^{i'j'} c_{ii'} = 0$$

for each parity frequency (j, j'). This can be interpreted in another way by defining the two-dimensional polynomial

$$c(x, y) = \sum_{i=0}^{n_1-1} \sum_{i'=0}^{n_2-1} c_{ii'} x^i y^{i'}$$

so that the code satisfies

$$c(\beta^j, \gamma^{j'}) = 0$$

for every j and every j' that are parity frequencies. Because the parity frequencies are defined on vertical and horizontal stripes, we have

$$c(\beta^j, y) = 0 \qquad \text{and} \qquad c(x, \gamma^{j'}) = 0$$

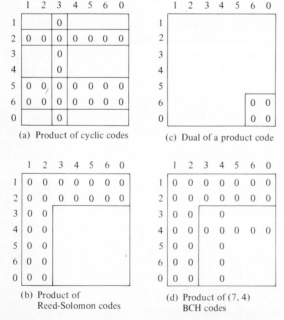

(a) Product of cyclic codes

(b) Product of Reed-Solomon codes

(c) Dual of a product code

(d) Product of (7, 4) BCH codes

Figure 10.4　Spectra of some codes over $GF(8)$.

for every j and every j' that are parity frequencies. This says that $c_{ii'}$ is a product code.

If we take the stripes of parity frequencies to be contiguous, we have a code that is the product of two Reed-Solomon codes. Figure 10.4(b) illustrates a (49, 25, 9) code over $GF(8)$ defined spectrally. Each of the 25 information symbols can be loaded with an octal information character. The result is transformed to the time domain in order to obtain the codeword.

The same structure can be used to obtain a code over $GF(2)$ by selecting only binary codewords. In the frequency domain, only a spectrum that yields a binary codeword may be specified. The two-dimensional conjugacy constraints are

$$C_{jj'}^2 = C_{(2j \bmod n)(2j' \bmod n)}$$

We can construct the table shown in Fig. 10.5 with this property. Each set in the table shows a constrained set of frequencies. Any member of a conjugacy set can be specified. The remaining symbols in a set are not arbitrary. The frequency C_{00} can be only 0 or 1 because it is its own square. The remaining information symbols are octal. Altogether 49 bits specify the spectrum, but of course some of these are parity and contain no information. Using this table, the code of Fig. 10.4(b) when restricted to the binary subfield-subcode has spectrum as shown in Fig. 10.4(b). There are only 16 open frequencies which, because of the constraints, can encode 16 bits. This is a consequence of the fact that row 1 and column 1 have their parity symbols scattered among different conjugacy sets. The code is an unimpressive (49, 16, 9) code. By following the details of the construction, we can see that because of conjugacy constraints, product codes often will have poor performance. To get good product codes one must generally make the dimensions relatively prime. Hence the underlying field becomes large, and one usually winds up with cyclic codes with zeros in this larger field.

	Bit Content		Bit Content
$\{C_{11}\ C_{22}\ C_{44}\}$	3	$\{C_{33}\ C_{66}\ C_{55}\}$	3
$\{C_{12}\ C_{24}\ C_{41}\}$	3	$\{C_{35}\ C_{63}\ C_{56}\}$	3
$\{C_{21}\ C_{42}\ C_{14}\}$	3	$\{C_{53}\ C_{36}\ C_{65}\}$	3
$\{C_{13}\ C_{26}\ C_{45}\}$	3	$\{C_{01}\ C_{02}\ C_{04}\}$	3
$\{C_{31}\ C_{62}\ C_{54}\}$	3	$\{C_{10}\ C_{20}\ C_{40}\}$	3
$\{C_{15}\ C_{23}\ C_{46}\}$	3	$\{C_{03}\ C_{06}\ C_{05}\}$	3
$\{C_{51}\ C_{32}\ C_{64}\}$	3	$\{C_{30}\ C_{60}\ C_{50}\}$	3
$\{C_{16}\ C_{25}\ C_{43}\}$	3	$\{C_{00}\}$	1
$\{C_{61}\ C_{52}\ C_{34}\}$	3		

Figure 10.5 Two-dimensional conjugacy sets.

The second case, called a *dual product code*, is illustrated in Fig. 10.4(c). It is a dual to a product code. A dual product code does not have a large minimum distance and so it is not very good for correcting random errors. It is good for correcting multiple low-density burst errors as is discussed in Section 10.7. For the parity frequencies, choose a rectangle, b frequencies wide and a frequencies high. It is easily seen that the minimum distance satisfies

$$d \geqslant 1 + \min(a, b).$$

Hence, the example gives a (49, 45, 3) code over $GF(8)$. The binary subfield-subcode is a (49, 39) $d \geqslant 3$ code.

10.5 FAST BCH CODES

We saw in Chapter 9 that the encoder/decoder for a BCH code usually involves two Fourier transforms. If n is composite, then one of the fast-Fourier-transform (FFT) algorithms that will be studied in the next chapter can be used to compute the Fourier transforms in order to reduce considerably the computational load. The Cooley-Tukey FFT requires some adjustment terms, however, and the Good-Thomas FFT requires address shuffling. We can make these vanish by a slight redefinition of the BCH code to get an equivalent code, which we give in this section. We call this version of the BCH code a *fast BCH code* because it is set up to reduce the work of the decoder. It amounts to a form of the Good-Thomas algorithm (to be derived in Section 11.2) but with the time-domain symbols left in a shuffled order.

Let $n = n_1 n_2 = q^m - 1$, where n_1 and n_2 are relatively prime. Let the code consist of all two-dimensional $GF(q)$-valued time functions $c_{ii'}$ for $i = 0, \ldots, n_1 - 1$, and for $i' = 0, \ldots, n_2 - 1$ such that the two-dimensional transforms $C_{jj'}$ satisfy the following parity relationships:

$$C_{11} = C_{22} = C_{33} = \cdots = C_{2t, 2t} = 0,$$

where the subscripts are modulo n_1 and modulo n_2, respectively. This is a linear t-error-correcting code, which is different from a BCH code in only a trivial way. The rate and minimum distance are unchanged. The rate is the same because of the following theorem.

□ **Theorem 10.5.1** The two-dimensional conjugacy class of j (mod n_1) and j (mod n_2) has the same number of elements as the conjugacy class of j (mod $n_1 n_2$).

Proof Let r be the smallest positive integer such that $q^r j = j$ (mod n_1) and $q^r j = j$ (mod n_2). Let s be the smallest positive integer such that $q^s j = j$ (mod $n_1 n_2$). Then

$$q^r j = a n_1 n_2 + j$$

$$q^s j = b n_1 n_2 + j$$

for some a and for some b. Obviously, the smallest such r and the smallest such s are identical. $\square$

The distance of the code is at least $2t + 1$, as is proved by the following decoding procedure for t errors. Given a received word with two-dimensional transform $V_{jj'}$, define the syndromes

$$S_j = V_{(j \bmod n_1, \, j \bmod n_2)} \qquad j = 1, \ldots, 2t.$$

If a single error of value $e_{i_1 i_1'}$ takes place in row i_1 and in column i_1', then

$$S_j = e_{i_1 i_1'}(\beta^{i_1}\gamma^{i_1'})^j = Y_1 X_1^j,$$

where X_1 is a power of α. This power of the primitive element is unique for each row and column. Thus for v errors, the syndromes are of the form

$$S_j = \sum_{k=1}^{v} Y_k X_k^j.$$

This has a unique solution if t or less errors have occurred. Use the Berlekamp-Massey algorithm and a recursive extension to obtain S_j for $j = 1, \ldots, n$; and set

$$E_{(j \bmod n_1, \, j \bmod n_2)} = S_j \qquad j = 1, \ldots, n.$$

Because n_1 and n_2 are relatively prime, every syndrome S_j for $j = 1, \ldots, n$ has a unique place in the two-dimensional array. Finally,

$$C_{jj'} = V_{jj'} - E_{jj'},$$

and a two-dimensional inverse transform completes the decoding.

All that this procedure amounts to graphically is working down the extended diagonal of the n_1 by n_2 array shown in Fig. 10.6. The $2t$ parity frequencies are defined down the extended diagonal. The Berlekamp-Massey algorithm works down the extended diagonal, and because n_1 and n_2 are relatively prime, the recursive extension fills in the entire array to give the two-dimensional Fourier transform of the error pattern.

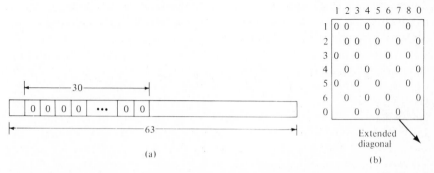

Figure 10.6 Spectrum of a fast BCH code. (a) Spectrum of a $(63, 33, 31)$ Reed-Solomon code. (b) Two-dimensional spectrum of a $(63, 33, 31)$ fast Reed-Solomon code.

10.6 DECODING OF MULTIDIMENSIONAL CODES

A multidimensional codeword defined by a two-dimensional spectrum has certain two-dimensional spectral components equal to zero. We saw one example in the previous section. Suppose the code is defined so that for certain pairs of indices, (j_k, j'_k) indexed by k, we have

$$\sum_{i=0}^{n_1-1} \sum_{i'=0}^{n_2-1} c_{ii'} \beta^{ij_k} \gamma^{i'j'_k} = 0.$$

Then the two-dimensional syndrome $S_{j_k j'_k}$ of the t-error pattern $e_{ii'}$ is defined as

$$S_{j_k j'_k} = \sum_{i=0}^{n_1-1} \sum_{i'=0}^{n_2-1} e_{ii'} \beta^{ij_k} \gamma^{i'j'_k},$$

which can be evaluated from the received word $v_{ii'}$.

The error patterns will be described now in terms of row locators, column locators, and error magnitudes. For an error in row i_l and column i'_l, the locators are defined as $X_l = \beta^{i_l}$ and $Y_l = \gamma^{i'_l}$. The lth error magnitude is denoted by Z_l. Then the syndrome becomes

$$S_{j_k j'_k} = \sum_{l=1}^{t} Z_l X_l^{j_k} Y_l^{j'_k}.$$

Two-dimensional codes can be defined so that the above set of equations can be solved for X_l, Y_l, and Z_l, for $l = 1, \ldots, t$. For example, we can choose the parity frequencies to get the set of equations

$$S_{11} = Z_1 X_1 Y_1 + Z_2 X_2 Y_2 + \cdots + Z_v X_v Y_v = E_{11}$$

$$S_{12} = Z_1 X_1 Y_1^2 + Z_2 X_2 Y_2^2 + \cdots + Z_v X_v Y_v^2 = E_{12}$$

$$\vdots$$

$$S_{1,2t} = Z_1 X_1 Y_1^{2t} + Z_2 X_2 Y_2^{2t} + \cdots + Z_v X_v Y_v^{2t} = E_{1,2t},$$

which is familiar from the decoding of a Reed-Solomon code. There is one difference; here, the Y_l need not be distinct because several errors might occur in the same column. It is, however, a simple matter to combine the terms with the same Y_l to obtain a similar set of equations with smaller v, and this smaller set also satisfies $v \leqslant t$. Then the Berlekamp-Massey algorithm, followed by recursive extension, will yield $E_{11}, E_{12}, \ldots, E_{1n}$, although because errors can occur in the same column, the procedure cannot be used to uniquely give (X_l, Y_l) for $l = 1, \ldots, v$. In general, we have the following theorem for the case where $n_1 = n_2 = n$. It can be proved more generally by replacing n by LCM (n_1, n_2).

□ **Theorem 10.6.1** Suppose that $v \leqslant t$ errors occur, and for any integers j_0, j'_0 and a, a' the syndromes $S_{j_0+ak, j'_0+a'k}$ for $k = 1, \ldots, 2t$ are known. Then these uniquely define the syndromes $S_{j_0 + ak,\, j'_0 + a'k}$ for $k = 1, \ldots, n$.

Proof Given the $2t$ equations for $k = 1, \ldots, 2t$,

$$S_{j_0 + ak,\, j'_0 + a'k} = \sum_{l=1}^{v} Z_l X_l^{j_0 + ak} Y_l^{j'_0 + a'k}$$

$$= \sum_{l=1}^{v} Z_l (X_l^{j_0} Y_l^{j'_0})(X_l^{a} Y_l^{a'})^k.$$

Let v' be the number of distinct $X_l^a Y_l^{a'}$ over l, and let $\bar{Y}_{l'}$ for $l' = 1, \ldots, v'$ denote these. Let $\bar{X}_{l'}$ denote the sum of the factors multiplying $\bar{Y}_{l'}$ in each equation. It is the same for each k. Then

$$S_{j_0 + ak,\, j'_0 + a'k} = \sum_{l'=1}^{v} \bar{X}_{l'} \bar{Y}_{l'}^{k} \qquad k = 1, \ldots, 2t,$$

where the $\bar{Y}_{l'}$ are now distinct and $v \leqslant t$. The Berlekamp-Massey algorithm followed by recursive extension will produce the remaining syndromes:

$$S_{j_0 + ak,\, j'_0 + a'k} = \sum_{l'=1}^{v} \bar{X}_{l'} \bar{Y}_{l'}^{k} \qquad k = 1, \ldots, n. \qquad \square$$

Hence by this theorem, any $2t$ syndromes in a straight line (horizontal, vertical, or at any angle) can be extended to all syndromes in that line. Further, because of conjugacy constraints, each of these new syndromes also determines all syndromes in its conjugacy class. It need not be the case, however, that the set of syndromes computed is equal to the set of all possible syndromes. The array need not have relatively prime dimensions, and thus the extended straight line does not necessarily include all components.

Now let us see how the BCH bound generalizes to two (or more) dimensions. Suppose that we have $2t$ contiguous syndromes anywhere in the first row. These can be extended to give all syndromes in the first row. Similarly, $2t$ contiguous syndromes anywhere in the second row can be extended to give all syndromes in the second row. Further, $2t$ contiguous syndromes anywhere in each of the first $2t$ rows can be extended to give all syndromes in each of the first $2t$ rows and hence $2t$ contiguous syndromes in every column. These can be extended to give all syndromes in every column and hence suffice to give the error pattern. The simplest example has a square array of $2t$ by $2t$ known syndromes. The general situation is as follows.

☐ **Theorem 10.6.2 (Two-Dimensional BCH Bound)** Given any a, a', and m_k for $k = 1, \ldots, 2t$, the set of syndromes

$$S_{a(m_k + k'),\, a'(m_k + k') + k} \qquad k' = 1, \ldots, 2t;\; k = 1, \ldots, 2t$$

uniquely determines the error pattern, provided $v \leqslant t$ errors took place and a is relatively prime to n.

Proof Apply the previous theorem for each k to determine the syndromes

$$S_{a(m_k+k'),\, a'(m_k+k')+k} \qquad k' = 1, \ldots, n;\, k = 1, \ldots, 2t.$$

We can now redefine the index k' to absorb m_k so that the known syndromes are

$$S_{ak',\, a'k'+k} \qquad k' = 1, \ldots, n;\, k = 1, \ldots, 2t.$$

Apply the previous theorem again for each k' to determine the syndromes

$$S_{ak',\, a'k'+k} \qquad k' = 1, \ldots, n;\, k = 1, \ldots, n.$$

Now, because k ranges over all n values, we can redefine the index k to absorb $a'k'$, so that we know

$$S_{ak',\, k} \qquad k' = 1, \ldots, n;\, k = 1, \ldots, n.$$

Because a is relatively prime to n, the index ak' ranges over all n values. Hence all syndromes are determined, and so is the error pattern. □

10.7 LARGE CODES IN SMALL FIELDS

For codes of very large blocklength and high rate, the complexity of the decoder can be of far more concern than the rate of the code. The difference between a rate of 0.98 and a rate of 0.99 may be of minor practical importance if the decoders for the two codes are very different in cost. In this section, we will study codes of very large size whose decoders are of limited complexity. The codes we will study are multidimensional codes whose performance is generally superior to that of product codes, and these codes can be decoded with computations in a Galois field much smaller than the blocklength. Such codes may be contrasted with BCH codes.

For a BCH code of blocklength $n = q^m - 1$, a practical decoder requires computations in $GF(q^m)$. If n is large this is a large Galois field. The codes we will describe can be decoded with computations in a small Galois field. One example we will give is a binary code defined as a square two-dimensional code with $n = 2^m - 1$ rows and the same number of columns. Hence, the blocklength of the code is n^2, but we can hope to do all of the decoding with computations in the field $GF(2^m)$. Although the rate of these codes is inferior to that of BCH codes of the same n and d, one may prefer them in some applications because of the smaller wordlength in the decoder.

The first example we will consider is the product of two BCH codes—an (n_1, k_1, d_1) code and an (n_2, k_2, d_2) code to yield an $(n_1 n_2, k_1 k_2, d_1 d_2)$ code. For example, the product of a (256, 232, 25) extended Reed-Solomon code with itself yields a (65,536, 53,824, 625) code over $GF(256)$, which can correct 312 8-bit bytes and also bursts of length 3072 8-bit bytes, as well as many patterns with more than 312 error bytes. One could use instead a (65,536, 64,289, 625) BCH code, which has a much higher rate, to correct the 312 random byte errors, but its decoder requires the 16-bit wide arithmetic of $GF(2^{16})$. The product code has another compensating advantage in that it corrects many patterns with more than 312 errors, whereas the BCH code does not. The product code can be decoded by the decoder given in Section 10.3.

The second example is the dual of the product of two Reed-Solomon codes or its subfield-subcode. A dual product code corrects random errors and also patterns of multiple low-density burst errors, defined as codeword segments where the number of errors is greater than is typical. Codes that correct multiple low-density bursts are useful on channels whose probability of error intermittently degrades, such as a fading channel. For example, the dual product code of a (255, 239, 17) Reed-Solomon code with itself is a (65,025, 64,769, 17) code over $GF(256)$, which can correct all random patterns of eight 8-bit bytes and all patterns of 64 8-bit bytes arranged as low-density bursts in the form of eight bad columns, each with eight bad bytes.

This code has two-dimensional parity frequencies (j, j') for $j = 1, \ldots, 16$ and $j' = 1, \ldots, 16$. A decoding procedure, based on Theorem 10.6.1, is as follows. Given the received word $v_{ii'}$, compute the syndromes $S_{jj'}$ by $S_{jj'} = \sum_{i=0}^{255} \sum_{i'=0}^{255} \alpha^{ij} \alpha^{i'j'} v_{ii'}$ for $j = 1, \ldots, 16$ and $j' = 1, \ldots, 16$. Use the Berlekamp-Massey algorithm followed by recursive extension on the jth row to extend the syndromes to that entire row. After 16 rows are passed through the decoder, $S_{jj'}$ for $j = 1, \ldots, 255$ and $j' = 1, \ldots, 16$ are known. The inverse Fourier transform of each of the 16 rows has nonzero values only in the eight (or fewer) columns containing errors. Identify these eight columns. In each column, the transforms in the 16 rows provide 16 field elements, $T_{j'}^{(i)}$ for $i = 1, \ldots, 255$ and $j' = 1, \ldots, 16$. The set of magnitudes for column i can be written in terms of the error magnitudes and row locators for that column:

$$T_1^{(i)} = Z_1^{(i)}(X_1^{(i)})^1 + Z_2^{(i)}(X_2^{(i)})^1 + \cdots + Z_{v(i)}^{(i)}(X_{v(i)}^{(i)})^1$$

$$T_2^{(i)} = Z_1^{(i)}(X_1^{(i)})^2 + Z_2^{(i)}(X_2^{(i)})^2 + \cdots + Z_{v(i)}^{(i)}(X_{v(i)}^{(i)})^2$$

$$\vdots$$

$$T_{16}^{(i)} = Z_1^{(i)}(X_1^{(i)})^{16} + Z_2^{(i)}(X_2^{(i)})^{16} + \cdots + Z_{v(i)}^{(i)}(X_{v(i)}^{(i)})^{16},$$

where $v(i)$ is the number of errors in the ith column. If $v(i) \leqslant 8$ for each i, this

	1	2	3	4	5	6	7	8	9	10	11	12	13	14	15	16	17	18	19	20	21 ....
1	0	0	0	0	0	0	0	0	0	0	0	0	0	0	0	0					
2																					
3	0	0	0	0	0	0	0	0	0	0	0	0	0	0	0	0					
4																					
5	0	0	0	0	0	0	0	0	0	0	0	0	0	0	0	0					
6																					
7	0	0	0	0	0	0	0	0	0	0	0	0	0	0	0	0					
7																					
9	0	0	0	0	0	0	0	0	0	0	0	0	0	0	0	0					
10																					
11	0	0	0	0	0	0	0	0	0	0	0	0	0	0	0	0					
12																					
13	0	0	0	0	0	0	0	0	0	0	0	0	0	0	0	0					
14																					
15	0	0	0	0	0	0	0	0	0	0	0	0	0	0	0	0					
16																					
17																					
18																					
19																					

(a) Row-organized parity symbols

	1	2	3	4	5	6	7	8	9	10	11	12	13	14	15	16	17	18	19	20	21 ...
1	0	0	0	0	0	0	0	0	0	0	0	0	0	0	0	0					
2																					
3	0		0		0	0	0			0	0	0	0	0	0	0					
4																					
5	0		0		0			0	0	0			0	0	0						
6	0																				
7	0		0		0		0		0			0	0	0							
8																					
9	0		0		0		0		0		0			0							
10	0		0																		
11	0		0		0		0		0		0			0							
12	0																				
13	0		0		0		0		0		0			0							
14	0		0	0																	
15	0		0		0		0		0		0			0							
16																					
17																					
18																					
19																					

(b) Alternative parity symbols

Figure 10.7 Two-dimensional parity frequencies.

set of equations can also be solved with the Berlekamp-Massey algorithm to complete the decoding.

We can also form dual product codes from BCH codes. These codes, however, are contained in much larger codes, described next, that have the same minimum distance and low-density burst-error correction capability. Generally, the larger codes would be preferred.

We will use the specific case of a binary code with $t = 8$, $n = 255$, and blocklength $n^2 = 65,025$ to illustrate the ideas. We will work through the selection of parity frequencies shown in Fig. 10.7 so that all of the syndromes in the block $j = 1, \ldots, 2t$, $j' = 1, \ldots, 2t$ can be computed. Theorem 10.4.2 then guarantees that the remaining syndromes can be computed.

We will need to choose 128 parity frequencies to get an eight-error-correcting code. First choose $(1, 1), (1, 2), \ldots, (1, 2t)$ as parity frequencies so that $C_{11} = C_{12} = \cdots = C_{1, 2t} = 0$. Each of the parity frequencies is in a different conjugacy class, and each class has eight elements; thus each of these parity frequencies is equivalent to eight parity bits. The syndromes at these frequencies can be extended to $S_{1j'}$ for $j' = 1, \ldots, n$ if less than t errors have occurred. Then, by the conjugacy constraints on this top row, rows 2, 4, 8, and 16 are also known. Next, choose $(3, 1), (3, 2), \ldots, (3, 2t)$ as parity frequencies. This adds 16×8 more parity bits. From the syndromes at these frequencies, the third row can be computed, and thus also rows 6 and 12. Continue in this way to choose all the parity frequencies shown in Fig. 10.7. These determine the remaining frequencies in the $2t$ by $2t$ corner and hence all of the frequencies, as long as less than t errors have occurred. Each parity symbol is equivalent to eight parity bits, and thus there are a total of 1024 parity bits. The code is a $(65,025, 64,001, 17)$ code. It has a larger overhead than the $(65,535, 65,407, 17)$ BCH code. Its virtue is that it is relatively easily decoded despite its large blocklength and, with the decoder we will describe, the code will correct many burst-error patterns.

The decoder is similar to the decoder described previously. Given a two-dimensional received word, compute only those components of its two-dimensional Fourier transform at the 128 parity frequencies. The values of the error spectrum $E_{jj'}$ are then known at the parity frequencies. We will show how to compute all other components of the error spectrum from these known components. Perform a Berlekamp-Massey algorithm along the first row, recursively extend to all 255 components, and use conjugacy constraints to fill in rows 2, 4, 8, and 16. Do the same along the third row, then fill in rows 3, 6, and 12. Repeat for the fifth row, and so on. Continue until $2t$ rows are complete.

After $2t$ rows of $E_{jj'}$ are known, the columns are decoded. One method is to use the Berlekamp-Massey algorithm down each column to obtain the entire $E_{jj'}$ array. An inverse two-dimensional Fourier transform completes the decoding. A simpler procedure is as follows. Take the inverse one-dimensional Fourier transform of the $2t$ known rows of $E_{jj'}$. This gives a set of $2t$ syndromes for each column; at most $2t$ columns can have nonzero syndromes, and only these $2t$ columns need be processed by the Berlekamp-Massey algorithm.

Figure 10.7 also shows an alternative definition of the two-dimensional parity frequencies that gives a higher code rate but a more complicated decoder. In this case, the Berlekamp-Massey algorithm must alternate between decoding rows and decoding columns. The conjugacy constraints will then provide new components of $E_{jj'}$ as they are needed.

PROBLEMS

10.1. The set of all 7-by-7 matrices over $GF(2)$ is a vector space. Give a basis for this space. How many vectors are in the space? Is the set of all such matrices with zeros on the diagonal a subspace? If so, how many vectors are in it?

10.2. Over $GF(2)$ let $p(x) = x^2 + x + 1$, and let $q(x) = x^4 + x + 1$. Find the "Chinese polynomials" $a(x)$ and $b(x)$ satisfying $a(x)p(x) + b(x)q(x) = 1$.

10.3. Let $\mathscr{C}$ be an $(n, n-1)$ simple parity-check code, and let $\mathscr{C}^3$ be the $(n^3, (n-1)^3)$ code obtained as the three-dimensional product code with $\mathscr{C}$ as each component code.

    a. How many errors can $\mathscr{C}^3$ correct?

    b. Give two error patterns of the same weight that are detectable but that have the same syndrome and thus cannot be corrected.

10.4. **a.** Design a (3840, 3360) interleaved extended Reed-Solomon code over $GF(64)$ to correct bursts of length 240 6-bit bytes. What is the minimum distance of the interleaved code?

    b. Upgrade the code to a (4096, 3360) product code that also corrects bursts of length 240 bytes and, in addition, all random patterns of 22 bytes.

    c. Discuss the decoders for the codes in parts (a) and (b).

10.5. How many errors can be corrected by the product of a (7, 4) Hamming code with itself? Using a Hamming (7, 4) decoder as an "off-the-shelf" building block, design a simple decoder that corrects to the packing radius of the product code.

10.6. Let a and b satisfy

$$an_1 + bn_2 = 1,$$

where n_1 and n_2 are relatively prime. Given an (n_1, k_1) cyclic code with generator polynomial $g_1(x)$ and an (n_2, k_2) cyclic code with generator polynomial $g_2(x)$, prove that the cyclic product code with blocklength $n = n_1 n_2$ has generator polynomial

$$g(x) = \text{GCD}[g_1(x^{bn_2}), g_1(x^{an_1}), x^n - 1].$$

NOTES

Product codes were introduced by Elias (1954), who showed that the minimum distance is the product of the minimum distances of the two codes. It was proved by Burton and

Weldon (1965) that the product of two cyclic codes is a cyclic code if the dimensions of the two cyclic codes are relatively prime. The same paper also studied the correction of burst and random errors by product codes. The technique for decoding product codes was given by Reddy and Robinson (1972) and by Weldon (1971). The discussions in Sections 10.4 through 10.6 are based on ideas found in Blahut (1979). The use of dual product codes for the correction of multiple low-density bursts was discussed by Chien and Ng (1973).

CHAPTER 11
Fast Algorithms

G ood codes of large blocklength and large alphabet size, such as Reed-Solomon codes, are coming into widespread use. Future requirements will be for ever-larger error-control codes, and thus it becomes important to reduce the complexity of the decoding algorithms. We have already studied a number of efficient decoding algorithms for Reed-Solomon codes and related codes, and we have seen how to build decoders that require on the order of n^2 computational steps. In this chapter we will sharpen the attack on the complexity of the decoders. We will start with the decoders already studied and find ways to do the computations even more efficiently. The measure of computational complexity we will use is the number of multiplications (and, sometimes, the number of additions) in the computation. In this sense, we will find techniques to reduce the computational complexity. The price one pays for the improvement is a more intricate structure. To reduce the number of multiplications and additions, one increases the organizational complexity, using algorithms that contain more complicated indexing and branching. Of course in many applications, the regularity of an algorithm is more important than the number of multiplications and additions. This aspect of complexity is difficult to quantify and is not treated.

11.1 LINEAR CONVOLUTION AND CYCLIC CONVOLUTION

The linear convolution

$$c_i = \sum_{k=0}^{n-1} g_{i-k}d_k$$

can also be written as the polynomial product

$$c(x) = g(x)d(x).$$

The obvious way to compute this polynomial product requires approximately $(\deg d(x) \times \deg g(x))$ multiplications and additions, but there may be other ways to compute it that involve fewer computations. Because convolution is such a common computation, it is worthwhile to find efficient ways to compute it. Moreover, the cyclic convolution

$$c(x) = g(x)d(x) \qquad (\bmod\ x^n - 1)$$

can be computed by first finding the linear convolution, and then reducing it modulo $x^n - 1$. Hence, efficient ways of computing linear convolutions also lead to efficient ways of computing cyclic convolutions. Conversely, efficient algorithms for cyclic convolutions can be easily turned into efficient algorithms for linear convolutions.

The cyclic convolution can be written

$$c_i = \sum_{k=0}^{n-1} g_{((i-k))}d_k \qquad i = 0, \ldots, n-1$$

where the double parentheses denote that the indices are modulo n. The convolution theorem says that in the frequency domain,

$$C_j = G_j D_j,$$

and thus we can compute the convolution with a Fourier transform, a point-by-point product, and an inverse Fourier transform. If n is highly composite, a fast Fourier transform (described in later sections) may be used to reduce the number of computations. The Fourier transform only exists for an n that is a divisor of $q^m - 1$, and some such n are not convenient for FFT algorithms. The well-known techniques of digital signal processing, however, can be used to lengthen the vectors $\mathbf{d}$, $\mathbf{g}$, and $\mathbf{c}$ to length n' in such a way that components $i = 0, \ldots, n-1$ agree with the designated values, and $\mathbf{c}$ is still related to **d** and **g** by a cyclic convolution—now, however, with a length n' that is a convenient Fourier transform size.

For example, take a convenient n' satisfying $n' \geqslant 2n$ for which the Fourier transform is easy to compute, and let

$$a_i' = \begin{cases} a_i & i = 0, \ldots, n-1 \\ 0 & i = n, \ldots, n'-1 \end{cases}$$

$$b_i' = \begin{cases} b_i & i = 0, \ldots, n-1 \\ 0 & i = n, \ldots, n'-n-1 \\ b_{i+n-n'} & i = n'-n, \ldots, n'-1 \end{cases}$$

and

$$c_i' = \sum_{k=0}^{n'-1} a_k' b_{((i-k))}',$$

where now the double parentheses denotes modulo n'. Then $c_i' = c_i$ for i in the range $i = 0, \ldots, n-1$. The other values of c_i' are of no interest and can be discarded.

Techniques also are available for reducing a long linear convolution to a set of short cyclic convolutions. We will describe a technique known as the *overlap-save method* which has proved quite useful in digital signal processing. It also applies to long convolutions in a Galois field.

Suppose we have a device for doing cyclic convolutions of length n, and we wish to multiply $a(x)$, a polynomial whose degree A is smaller than n, and $b(x)$, a polynomial whose degree B is larger than n, to obtain $c(x) = a(x)b(x)$. From $b(x)$, form a set of polynomials $\{b^{(1)}(x), b^{(2)}(x), \ldots, b^{(s)}(x)\}$, each polynomial of degree of $n-1$ or less. The definition is as follows:

$$b_i^{(1)} = \begin{cases} b_i & i = 0, \ldots, n-1 \\ 0 & \text{otherwise} \end{cases}$$

$$b_i^{(2)} = \begin{cases} b_{i+(n-A)} & i = 0, \ldots, n-1 \\ 0 & \text{otherwise} \end{cases}$$

$$b_i^{(3)} = \begin{cases} b_{i+2(n-A)} & i = 0, \ldots, n-1 \\ 0 & \text{otherwise} \end{cases}$$

$$\vdots$$

$$b_i^{(s)} = \begin{cases} b_{i+(s-1)(n-A)} & i = 0, \ldots, n-1 \\ 0 & \text{otherwise} \end{cases}$$

where s is chosen large enough so that all coefficients of $b(x)$ are assigned. Notice that the coefficients of the new polynomials are overlapped. Let

$$c^{(l)}(x) = a(x)b^{(l)}(x) \qquad (\text{mod } x^n - 1) \qquad l = 1, \ldots, s.$$

The coefficients of $c(x)$, except for the first A coefficients, can be found among the coefficients of the $c^{(l)}(x)$. Thus

$$
\begin{aligned}
c_i &= c_i^{(1)} & i &= A, \ldots, n-1 \\
c_{i+(n-A)} &= c_i^{(2)} & i &= A, \ldots, n-1 \\
c_{i+2(n-A)} &= c_i^{(3)} & i &= A, \ldots, n-1,
\end{aligned}
$$

and so on. The A low-order coefficients of $c(x)$ are lost. In many applications of linear convolution, not all of the output coefficients are needed, and this illustrates such an application. If all output coefficients are needed, simply replace $b(x)$ with the polynomial $x^A b(x)$ in the foregoing discussion. All output coefficients will then be obtained, but with the index offset by A.

Each cyclic convolution except the last produces $n - A$ coefficients of the linear convolution and A useless coefficients, which are discarded. Because $b^{(s)}(x)$ can have a degree smaller than $n - 1$, the last convolution may produce more than $n - A$ meaningful coefficients.

11.2 FAST CONVOLUTION ALGORITHMS

Many algorithms for cyclic convolution are known, and often these are more efficient than using a fast Fourier transform and the convolution theorem. We will develop the Winograd algorithm for fast convolution in this section. The technique can be used in any field, but we are interested only in a finite field $GF(q)$. The technique breaks a convolution into a number of short convolutions that are easy to compute. The short convolutions are recombined using the Chinese remainder theorem for polynomials.

The Winograd algorithm computes the remainder

$$
c(x) = g(x)d(x) \qquad (\text{mod } b(x)),
$$

where $b(x)$ is any fixed polynomial. To obtain an algorithm for the linear convolution

$$
c(x) = g(x)d(x),
$$

choose any integer N larger than deg $c(x)$, and any polynomial $b(x)$ of degree N. We then have a trivial statement:

$$
c(x) = c(x) \qquad (\text{mod } b(x)),
$$

and thus the theory applies to computing linear convolutions.

To break a convolution modulo $b(x)$ into pieces, factor $b(x)$ into relatively prime polynomials over some subfield of $GF(q)$:

$$
b(x) = b_1(x)b_2(x) \ldots b_s(x).
$$

Usually one would choose the prime subfield $GF(p)$ for the factorization, and we refer to this case; but the theory can admit other subfields as well. The procedure minimizes the number of multiplications in $GF(q)$ but does not attempt to minimize the number of multiplications in $GF(p)$. In most practical cases, the prime field is $GF(2)$, and the multiplications are trivial.

The Winograd convolution algorithm makes use of the residues

$$c_k(x) = R_{b_k(x)}[c(x)] \qquad k = 1, \ldots, s.$$

We will divide the cyclic convolution into two steps. First, compute the residues

$$c_k(x) = g(x)d(x) \qquad (\text{mod } b_k(x))$$

$$= g_k(x)d_k(x) \qquad (\text{mod } b_k(x))$$

for $k = 1, \ldots, s$. Computation of the residues $g_k(x)$ and $d_k(x)$ requires no multiplications.

By the Chinese remainder theorem for polynomials, $c(x)$ can be computed from this set of residues by

$$c(x) = a_1(x)c_1(x) + \cdots + a_s(x)c_s(x) \qquad (\text{mod } b(x))$$

for appropriate polynomials $a_1(x), \ldots, a_s(x)$, all with coefficients in $GF(p)$. Because $a_k(x)$ only has coefficients in the prime field, this last step involves no multiplications. Only the short convolutions represented by the polynomial products $g_k(x)d_k(x)$ require multiplications in $GF(q)$; a total of

$$\sum_{k=1}^{s} [\deg b_k(x)]^2$$

multiplications are required for the obvious implementation of the polynomial products, because $g_k(x)$ and $d_k(x)$ each have $\deg b_k(x)$ coefficients. This can be a considerable savings in multiplications. Even further savings can be obtained in general by breaking one or more of the short convolutions down into even smaller pieces by repeating the same procedure.

A variation of the procedure is to choose a $b(x)$ with a somewhat smaller degree. This will produce an incorrect convolution, but a few extra computations can make it right. This is done as follows. By the division algorithm, we can write

$$c(x) = Q(x)b(x) + R_{b(x)}[c(x)].$$

If $\deg b(x) > \deg c(x)$, the quotient polynomial $Q(x)$ is identically zero, and we have the situation discussed earlier. If $\deg b(x) \leqslant \deg c(x)$, the Winograd algorithm will produce only the remainder $R_{b(x)}[c(x)]$. The term $Q(x)b(x)$ can be determined by a side computation and added in. The simplest case is the case where $\deg b(x) = \deg c(x)$. Then $Q(x)$ must have a degree of zero. If $b(x)$ is a monic polynomial of degree N, then clearly $Q(x) = c_N$, the coefficient of x^N in the polynomial $c(x)$. Consequently

$$c(x) = c_N b(x) + R_{b(x)}[c(x)],$$

and c_N can be easily computed as the product of the leading coefficients of $d(x)$ and $g(x)$.

For a cyclic convolution modulo $x^n - 1$, one can first compute the linear convolution and then reduce it modulo $x^n - 1$. It is usually better, however, to choose $x^n - 1$ for $b(x)$ and to allow the reduction modulo $x^n - 1$ to occur when the Chinese remainder theorem is applied. In the linear convolution, the degree of $b(x)$ must be greater than the sum of the degrees of $g(x)$ and $d(x)$, whereas the degree of $x^n - 1$ may be much smaller. The modulus polynomials will then be smaller in degree or fewer in number. However, the prime factors of $x^n - 1$ are what they are, whereas a general $b(x)$, although of larger degree, can be chosen to have convenient factors; the relatively prime factors of $b(x)$ need not even be prime.

A set of general cyclic-convolution algorithms for fields of characteristic 2 developed using the techniques discussed previously is given in Fig. 11.1. The algorithms are expressed compactly in matrix form as

$$c = B[(Cg) \cdot (Ad)],$$

where Cg and Ad are vectors of equal length and the (componentwise) product of Cg and Ad is the vector denoted by $[(Cg) \cdot (Ad)]$. The matrix representation of these algorithms is concise but leaves the order of doing the additions unspecified. By cleverly ordering the additions and reusing partial sums, one can also minimize the number of additions. When the polynomial $g(x)$ is fixed, the product Cg can be precomputed. The convolution algorithm then can be written in matrix form as $c = BGAd$, where G is a diagonal matrix whose elements are the components of Cg. As an example, the four-point cyclic-convolution algorithm is shown in Fig. 11.2.

We will conclude this section with a simple example, an encoder for the (7, 3) Reed-Solomon code. This is only a small problem, and thus the power of the techniques will not be illustrated properly; but the development of the algorithm will be easy to follow. Further, we will not attempt to find the most efficient algorithm. Rather, we will develop the algorithm in a way that illustrates many of the ideas.

A (7, 3) Reed-Solomon code with generator polynomial $g(x) = x^4 + \alpha^3 x^3 + x^2 + \alpha x + \alpha^3$ has deg $d(x) \leqslant 2$. Direct computation of $g(x)d(x)$ requires 15 multiplications. Because this particular $g(x)$ has only two distinct nonunity coefficients, however, it is a trivial task to arrange the computations so that only 6 multiplications are needed. The fast algorithm that we will derive should be judged in comparison both to 15 and to 6 multiplications. Also, notice that the seven-point cyclic-convolution algorithm of Fig. 11.1 could be used, but it has 13 multiplications.

We can choose any $b(x)$ of degree not less than 7. We will choose $b(x) = x^7 + 1$. Then

$$x^7 + 1 = (x + 1)(x^3 + x + 1)(x^3 + x^2 + 1)$$

$$= b_1(x)b_2(x)b_3(x).$$

We could also choose such a polynomial as

$$b(x) = x^2(x + 1)^2(x^3 + x + 1)$$

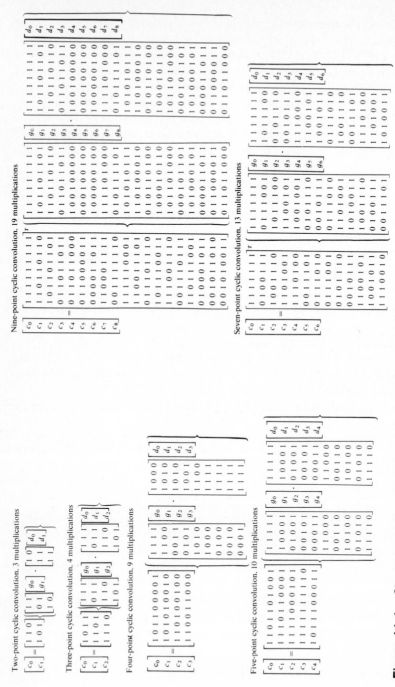

Figure 11.1 Short convolution algorithms for fields of characteristic 2.

$$
\begin{bmatrix} c_0 \\ c_1 \\ c_2 \\ c_3 \end{bmatrix} =
\begin{bmatrix}
1 & 0 & 1 & 1 & 0 & 0 & 0 & 0 & 1 \\
1 & 0 & 1 & 0 & 1 & 0 & 0 & 1 & 0 \\
1 & 1 & 0 & 1 & 0 & 0 & 1 & 0 & 0 \\
1 & 1 & 0 & 0 & 1 & 1 & 0 & 0 & 0
\end{bmatrix}
\begin{bmatrix}
G_0 & & & & & & & & 0 \\
& G_1 & & & & & & & \\
& & G_2 & & & & & & \\
& & & G_3 & & & & & \\
& & & & G_4 & & & & \\
& & & & & G_5 & & & \\
& & & & & & G_6 & & \\
& & & & & & & G_7 & \\
0 & & & & & & & & G_8
\end{bmatrix}
\begin{bmatrix}
1 & 0 & 0 & 0 \\
1 & 0 & 1 & 0 \\
1 & 0 & 1 & 0 \\
1 & 0 & 0 & 1 \\
1 & 1 & 0 & 0 \\
1 & 1 & 1 & 1 \\
1 & 1 & 1 & 1 \\
1 & 1 & 1 & 1 \\
1 & 1 & 1 & 1
\end{bmatrix}
\begin{bmatrix} d_0 \\ d_1 \\ d_2 \\ d_3 \end{bmatrix}
$$

where

$$
\begin{bmatrix} G_0 \\ G_1 \\ G_2 \\ G_3 \\ G_4 \\ G_5 \\ G_6 \\ G_7 \\ G_8 \end{bmatrix} =
\begin{bmatrix}
1 & 1 & 1 & 1 \\
1 & 1 & 0 & 0 \\
0 & 0 & 1 & 1 \\
0 & 1 & 0 & 1 \\
1 & 0 & 1 & 0 \\
1 & 0 & 0 & 0 \\
0 & 1 & 0 & 0 \\
0 & 0 & 1 & 0 \\
0 & 0 & 0 & 1
\end{bmatrix}
\begin{bmatrix} g_0 \\ g_1 \\ g_2 \\ g_3 \end{bmatrix}
$$

Figure 11.2 A four-point Winograd convolution.

so that the degrees of some of the relatively prime factors are a little smaller, but our choice works out nicely.

First we will find all of the fixed polynomials needed in the algorithm:

$$g^{(1)}(x) = R_{b_1(x)}[g(x)] = \alpha$$

$$g^{(2)}(x) = R_{b_2(x)}[g(x)] = 1$$

$$g^{(3)}(x) = R_{b_3(x)}[g(x)] = \alpha^3 x^2 + \alpha^3 x + 1.$$

By the Chinese remainder theorem for polynomials,

$$a^{(1)}(x) = x^6 + x^5 + x^4 + x^3 + x^2 + x + 1$$

$$a^{(2)}(x) = x^4 + x^2 + x + 1$$

$$a^{(3)}(x) = x^6 + x^5 + x^3 + 1.$$

We now have three short convolutions to compute:

$$c^{(1)}(x) = g^{(1)}(x)d^{(1)}(x) = \alpha d^{(1)}(x)$$

$$c^{(2)}(x) = g^{(2)}(x)d^{(2)}(x) = d^{(2)}(x)$$

$$c^{(3)}(x) = g^{(3)}(x)d^{(3)}(x) = (\alpha^3 x^2 + \alpha^3 x + 1)d^{(3)}(x).$$

From the data polynomial $d(x)$, we compute the residues:

$$d^{(1)}(x) = d_2 + d_1 + d_0$$
$$d^{(2)}(x) = d_2 x^2 + d_1 x + d_0$$
$$d^{(3)}(x) = d_2 x^2 + d_1 x + d_0.$$

Computing $c^{(1)}(x)$ requires one multiplication, computing $c^{(2)}(x)$ requires none, and computing $c^{(3)}(x)$ requires three multiplications. By combining all of these pieces, the convolution can be written

$$c(x) = (A_1 + A_2 + A_4 + A_6 + A_8)x^6 + (A_1 + A_3 + A_4 + A_7)x^5$$
$$+ (A_1 + A_2 + A_4 + A_5 + A_8)x^4 + (A_1 + A_2 + A_3 + A_4 + A_5 + A_6)x^3$$
$$+ (A_1 + A_2 + A_3 + A_4 + A_5 + A_6 + A_7)x^2$$
$$+ (A_1 + A_3 + A_4 + A_6 + A_7 + A_8)x + (A_1 + A_5 + A_7 + A_8),$$

where

$$A_1 = \alpha(d_2 + d_1 + d_0)$$
$$A_2 = d_2$$
$$A_3 = d_1$$
$$A_4 = d_0$$
$$A_5 = \alpha^3 d_2$$
$$A_6 = \alpha^3 d_2 + \alpha^3 d_1$$
$$A_7 = \alpha^3 d_1 + \alpha^3 d_0$$
$$A_8 = \alpha^3 d_0 + d_1.$$

In this form, a total of 4 multiplications and 35 additions in $GF(8)$ are necessary to compute $c(x)$ as written. It is apparent, however, that intermediate partial sums can be saved and reused to reduce the number of additions.

If we wish to go further, we may try to reduce the number of multiplications in computing $c^{(3)}(x)$:

$$c^{(3)}(x) = g^{(3)}(x)d^{(3)}(x)$$
$$= (\alpha^3 x^2 + \alpha^3 x + 1)(d_2 x^2 + d_1 x + d_0).$$

Choose

$$b'(x) = x(x + 1)(x^2 + x + 1).$$

Then

$$c^{(3)}(x) = (\alpha^3 d_2)b(x) + R_{b(x)}[c^{(3)}(x)].$$

One multiplication is needed to compute $\alpha^3 d_2$. The residues are

$$g^{(3)(1)}(x) = 1$$
$$g^{(3)(2)}(x) = 1$$
$$g^{(3)(3)}(x) = \alpha$$

and

$$d^{(3)(1)}(x) = d_0$$
$$d^{(3)(2)}(x) = d_0 + d_1 + d_2$$
$$d^{(3)(3)}(x) = (d_1 + d_2)x + (d_0 + d_2).$$

Then

$$c^{(3)(1)}(x) = d^{(3)(1)}(x)$$
$$c^{(3)(2)}(x) = d^{(3)(2)}(x)$$
$$c^{(3)(3)}(x) = \alpha d^{(3)(3)}(x).$$

Computing $c^{(3)(3)}(x)$ requires two multiplications. We already used one multiplication to compute $\alpha^3 d_2$, and thus a total of three multiplications are needed to compute $c^{(3)}(x)$ by this procedure. Because a direct computation of $c^{(3)}(x)$ also uses three multiplications, the direct computation should be preferred.

11.3 FAST FOURIER TRANSFORMS

The Fourier transform

$$V_j = \sum_{i=0}^{n-1} \alpha^{ij} v_i,$$

as it is written, requires on the order of n^2 multiplications and n^2 additions. If n is composite, there are several ways to change this Fourier transform into a two-dimensional Fourier transform, or something similar to it. This changes the computation to a form that is much more efficient, but the price is an increased difficulty of understanding. Algorithms of this type are known collectively as the *fast Fourier transform (FFT)*. Figure 11.3 summarizes the structures of the Cooley-Tukey FFT algorithm and the Good-Thomas FFT algorithm, the algorithms that will be studied in this section.

We will start with the Cooley-Tukey FFT algorithm. Suppose that $n = n'n''$. Replace each of the indices in the expression for the Fourier transform by a coarse index and a vernier index as follows:

$$i = i' + n'i'' \qquad i' = 0, \ldots, n' - 1$$
$$i'' = 0, \ldots, n'' - 1$$

DFT

$$V_j = \sum_{i=0}^{n-1} \alpha^{ij} v_i$$

Number of multiplications $\approx n^2$

Cooley-Tukey FFT (1965)

$$n = n'n''$$

$$i = i' + n'i'' \qquad i' = 0, \ldots, n'-1; \; i'' = 0, \ldots, n''-1$$

$$j = n''j' + j'' \qquad j' = 0, \ldots, n'-1; \; j'' = 0, \ldots, n''-1$$

$$V_{j',j''} = \sum_{i'=0}^{n'-1} \beta^{i'j'} \left[\alpha^{i'j''} \sum_{i''=0}^{n''-1} \gamma^{i''j''} v_{i',i''} \right]$$

Number of multiplications $\approx n(n' + n'') + n$

Good-Thomas FFT (1960–63)

$$n = n'n'' \text{ relatively prime}$$

Scramble input indices

$$\left. \begin{array}{l} i' = i \quad (\mathrm{mod}\ n') \\ i'' = i \quad (\mathrm{mod}\ n'') \end{array} \right\} \;\leftrightarrow\; \left\{ \begin{array}{l} i = i'N''n'' + i''N'n' \quad (\mathrm{mod}\ n) \\ \text{where} \\ 1 = N'n' + N''n'' \end{array} \right.$$

Scramble output indices

$$\left. \begin{array}{l} j' = N''j \quad (\mathrm{mod}\ n') \\ j'' = N'j \quad (\mathrm{mod}\ n'') \end{array} \right\} \;\leftrightarrow\; j = n''j' + n'j'' \quad (\mathrm{mod}\ n)$$

$$V_{j',j''} = \sum_{i'=0}^{n'-1} \beta^{i'j'} \left[\sum_{i''=0}^{n''-1} \gamma^{i''j''} v_{i',i''} \right]$$

Number of multiplications $\approx n(n' + n'')$

Figure 11.3 Summary of FFT algorithms.

$$j = n''j' + j'' \qquad \begin{array}{l} j' = 0, \ldots, n'-1 \\ j'' = 0, \ldots, n''-1 \end{array}.$$

Then

$$V_{n''j'+j''} = \sum_{i''=0}^{n''-1} \sum_{i'=0}^{n'-1} \alpha^{(i'+n'i'')(n''j'+j'')} v_{i'+n'i''}.$$

Expand the product in the exponent and let $\alpha^{n'} = \gamma$ and $\alpha^{n''} = \beta$. Because α has order $n'n''$, the term $\alpha^{n'n''i''j'} = 1$ and can be dropped. Now define the two-dimensional variables, also called v and V, given by

$$v_{i', i''} = v_{i' + n'i''} \qquad \begin{array}{l} i' = 0, \ldots, n' - 1 \\ i'' = 0, \ldots, n'' - 1 \end{array}$$

$$V_{j', j''} = V_{n''j' + j''} \qquad \begin{array}{l} j' = 0, \ldots, n' - 1 \\ j'' = 0, \ldots, n'' - 1 . \end{array}$$

In this way, the input and output data vectors are mapped into two-dimensional arrays. Then

$$V_{j', j''} = \sum_{i' = 0}^{n' - 1} \beta^{i'j'} \left[\alpha^{i'j''} \sum_{i'' = 0}^{n'' - 1} \gamma^{i''j''} v_{i', i''} \right].$$

Although this form is more difficult to understand than the original, the number of additions and multiplications is much smaller. In fact, at most $n(n' + n'' + 1)$ multiplications are required, as compared to about n^2 previously required. Notice that the inner sum is an n''-point Fourier transform for each value of i' and that the outer sum is an n'-point Fourier transform for each value of i''. Each of these, if composite, can in turn be simplified by another application of the fast Fourier transform. In this way, a transform whose size n has factors n_i can be broken down into a form requiring about $n \sum_i n_i$ multiplications.

The Cooley-Tukey FFT can be visualized as the mapping of a two-dimensional array into a two-dimensional array, as shown in Fig. 11.4 for $n = 15$ and for $n = 21$. The computation consists first of a Fourier transform on each row and concludes with a Fourier transform on each column. Before the Fourier transforms on columns, there is an element-by-element multiplication. Observe that the components of the spectrum are arranged differently in the array than are the components of the signal. This is known as address shuffling.

The Galois fields in which the computation of a Fourier transform is simplest are those of the form $GF(2^m + 1)$, which is a field whenever $2^m + 1$ is a prime. It is known that $2^m + 1$ is not a prime if m is not a binary power. The converse is not true, however, because $2^{32} + 1$ is known to be composite. But primes are found for $m = 2, 4, 8$, or 16, and thus $2^m + 1 = 5, 17, 257$, or 65,537—a set of integers known as *Fermat primes*. In a Galois field $GF(q)$ when q is a Fermat prime, $q - 1$ or any factor of $q - 1$ is a power of 2. The Fourier transform

$$V_j = \sum_{i = 0}^{n - 1} \alpha^{ij} v_i$$

exists whenever n is a divisor of 2^m and α is an element of order n. Thus the field $GF(2^{16} + 1)$ has Fourier transforms of sizes $2^{16}, 2^{15}, 2^{14}, \ldots, 2^2, 2$. A systematic Reed-Solomon code based on such a field can be tilted into a binary burst-error-correcting code. The code can be used to systematically encode r-bit bytes; the single value 2^r will never occur as an information symbol. The parity symbols can take on $2^r + 1$ values, and thus their binary representation requires $r + 1$ bits.

The Fourier transforms over $GF(2^{16} + 1)$ with blocklength 32 or less are quite simple because the element 2 has order 32. To see this, notice that $2^{16} + 1 = 0$ in $GF(2^{16} + 1)$. Hence $2^{16} = -1$ and $2^{32} = 1$. The Fourier transform is

$$V_j = \sum_{i=0}^{31} 2^{ij} v_i$$

and the multiply operation is actually a shift in a binary arithmetic system because it is a multiplication by a power of 2. This Fourier transform is very easy to compute using a radix-2 Cooley-Tukey FFT, but a blocklength of 32 is too short for many applications. Longer Fourier transforms must have some nontrivial multiplications. However one can reduce these in number by using a radix-32 Cooley-Tukey FFT. For example, consider a 1024-point transform in $GF(2^{16} + 1)$:

$$V_j = \sum_{i=0}^{1023} \alpha^{ij} v_i,$$

where now α is an element of order 1024. The Cooley-Tukey FFT puts this in the form

$$V_{n''j' + j''} = \sum_{i'=0}^{31} 2^{i'j'} \left[\alpha^{i'j''} \sum_{i''=0}^{31} 2^{i''j''} v_{i' + n'i''} \right].$$

The inner sum is a Fourier transform for each value of i', and the outer sum is a 32-point Fourier transform for each value of i''. The term in α is a nontrivial multiplication, but there are only 1024 such multiplications. In general, a Fourier transform in $GF(2^{16} + 1)$ can be computed in about $n(\lceil \log_{32} n \rceil - 1)$ multiplications in $GF(2^{16} + 1)$, with $\frac{1}{2} n \log_2 n$ additions and $\frac{1}{2} n \log_2 n$ shifts.

The second type of FFT algorithm is the Good-Thomas prime-factor algorithm. This is a little more complicated conceptually than the Cooley-Tukey algorithm, but it is a little simpler computationally. The Good-Thomas algorithm is another way of organizing a linear array of $n = n'n''$ numbers into a n' by n'' array, but in such a way that a one-dimensional Fourier transform can be done by a true two-dimensional Fourier transform. The idea is much different than the idea of the Cooley-Tukey algorithm. Now n' and n'' must be relatively prime, and the mapping is based on the Chinese remainder theorem. Refer to Fig. 11.4 to see how the input data is arranged. It is stored in the two-dimensional array by starting in the upper left-hand corner and listing the components down the extended diagonal. Because the number of rows and the number of columns are relatively prime, the extended diagonal passes through every element of the array. After a true two-dimensional Fourier transform, the spectrum appears in another

Actual input file

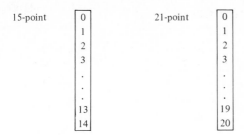

Cooley-Tukey Shuffling

15-point input

0	1	2	3	4
5	6	7	8	9
10	11	12	13	14

21-point input

0	1	2	3	4	5	6
7	8	9	10	11	12	13
14	15	16	17	18	19	20

15-point output

0	3	6	9	12
1	4	7	10	13
2	5	8	11	14

21-point output

0	3	6	9	12	15	18
1	4	7	10	13	16	19
2	5	8	11	14	17	20

Good-Thomas Shuffling

15-point input

0	6	12	3	9
10	1	7	13	4
5	11	2	8	14

21-point input

0	15	9	3	18	12	6
7	1	16	10	4	19	13
14	8	2	17	11	5	20

15-point output

0	3	6	9	12
5	8	11	14	2
10	13	1	4	7

21-point output

0	3	6	9	12	15	18
7	10	13	16	19	1	4
14	17	20	2	5	8	11

Figure 11.4 Shuffling examples.

two-dimensional array. The output components, however, appear in a different order in the output array.

The derivation of the Good-Thomas FFT algorithm is based on the Chinese remainder theorem for integers. The input index is described by its residues as follows:

$$i' = i \quad (\mathrm{mod}\ n')$$

$$i'' = i \quad (\mathrm{mod}\ n'').$$

This is the map of the input index i down the extended diagonal of a two-dimensional array indexed by (i', i''). By the Chinese remainder theorem, there exist integers N' and N'' such that

$$N'n' + N''n'' = 1.$$

Then the input index can be recovered as follows:

$$i = i'N''n'' + i''N'n' \pmod{n}.$$

The output index is described somewhat differently. Define

$$j' = N''j \pmod{n'}$$
$$j'' = N'j \pmod{n''}.$$

These can be written in the equivalent form $j'' = ((N' \bmod n'')j \bmod n'')$ and $j' = ((N'' \bmod n')j \bmod n')$. The output index j can be recovered as follows:

$$j = n''j' + n'j'' \pmod{n}.$$

To verify this, write it out:

$$j = n''(N''j + Q_1 n') + n'(N'j + Q_2 n'') \pmod{n'n''}$$
$$= j(n''N'' + n'N') \pmod{n}$$
$$= j.$$

Now with these new indices, we convert the formula

$$V_j = \sum_{i=0}^{n-1} \alpha^{ij} v_i$$

into

$$V_{n''j' + n'j''} = \sum_{i''=0}^{n''-1} \sum_{i'=0}^{n'-1} \alpha^{(i'N''n'' + i''N'n')(n''j' + n'j'')} v_{i'N''n'' + i''N'n'}.$$

Multiply out the exponent. Because α has order $n'n''$, terms in the exponent involving $n'n''$ can be dropped. Treat the input and output vectors as two-dimensional arrays using the index transformations given above. Then

$$V_{j',j''} = \sum_{i'=0}^{n'-1} \sum_{i''=0}^{n''-1} \alpha^{N''(n'')^2 i'j'} \alpha^{N'(n')^2 i''j''} v_{i',i''}$$
$$= \sum_{i'=0}^{n'-1} \sum_{i''=0}^{n''-1} \beta^{i'j'} \gamma^{i''j''} v_{i',i''},$$

where $\beta = \alpha^{N''(n'')^2}$ is an element of order n' and $\gamma = \alpha^{N'(n')^2}$ is an element of order n''. This is now in the form of a two-dimensional n'-by-n'' point Fourier transform. The number of multiplications is about $n(n' + n'')$, and the number of additions is about the same. The Fourier transform on the rows or on the columns, if the size is composite, can in turn be simplified by another application of the fast Fourier transform. In this way, a transform whose size n has relatively prime factors n_i can be broken down into a form requiring about $n \sum_i n_i$ multiplications and additions.

One can choose either the Cooley-Tukey algorithm or the Good-Thomas algorithm to do the Fourier transforms. It is even possible to build a Fourier transform algorithm using both the Cooley-Tukey FFT and the Good-Thomas FFT. For example, a 63-point transform can be broken into a 7-point transform and a 9-point transform using the Good-Thomas FFT; the 9-point transform can then be broken into two 3-point transforms using the Cooley-Tukey FFT. One then has a computation in a form similar to a 3-by-3-by-7-point three-dimensional Fourier transform.

11.4 AGARWAL-COOLEY CONVOLUTIONS

The same indexing scheme used by the Good-Thomas algorithm to turn a one-dimensional Fourier transform into a multidimensional Fourier transform can be used to turn a one-dimensional cyclic convolution into a multidimensional cyclic convolution. This method of breaking down a convolution is known as the Agarwal-Cooley convolution algorithm. It does not reduce the number of multiplications to as low a level as the Winograd convolution algorithm. In compensation, it does not have any tendency for the number of additions to get out of hand for large n as does the Winograd algorithm. Further, it is better structured, and thus when n is large, this method is more manageable because it can be broken into subroutines. Good convolution algorithms will use the Agarwal-Cooley convolution algorithm to break a long convolution into short convolutions and use the Winograd convolution algorithm to do the short convolutions efficiently.

In contrast to the Winograd convolution algorithm, which uses the polynomial version of the Chinese remainder theorem, the Agarwal-Cooley convolution uses the integer version of the Chinese remainder theorem and can only be used when the blocklength n has relatively prime factors. Given the vectors g_i and d_i for $i = 0, \ldots, n-1$, we wish to compute the cyclic convolution

$$c_i = \sum_{k=0}^{n-1} g_{((i-k))} d_k \qquad i = 0, \ldots, n-1,$$

where the double parentheses on the indices designate modulo n.

We will turn this one-dimensional convolution into a two-dimensional convolution. In the last section, by using the Chinese remainder theorem, we saw how to map the one-dimensional input data into a two-dimensional array and how to map the two-dimensional output array back into a one-dimensional vector. Replace the indices i and k by double indices (i', i'') and (k', k'') such that

$$i = n''i' + n'i'' \qquad \begin{aligned} i' &= 0, \ldots, n'-1 \\ i'' &= 0, \ldots, n''-1 \end{aligned}$$

$$k = n''k' + n'k'' \qquad k' = 0, \ldots, n' - 1$$
$$k'' = 0, \ldots, n'' - 1$$

We have already seen in the discussion of the Good-Thomas algorithm how the new indices should be defined to make this work. They are:

$$i' = N''i \quad (\text{mod } n') \qquad k' = N''k \quad (\text{mod } n')$$
$$i'' = N'i \quad (\text{mod } n'') \qquad k'' = N'k \quad (\text{mod } n''),$$

where N' and N'' are those integers that satisfy

$$N'n' + N''n'' = 1.$$

The convolution can be written

$$c_{n''i' + n'i''} = \sum_{k'=0}^{n'-1} \sum_{k''=0}^{n''-1} d_{n''k' + n'k''} g_{n''(i'-k') + n'(i''-k'')}$$

The double summation on (k', k'') is equivalent to the single summation on k because it picks up the same terms. Now define the two-dimensional variables, also called g, d, and c, given by

$$g_{k', k''} = g_{n''k' + n'k''} \qquad k' = 0, \ldots, n' - 1$$
$$k'' = 0, \ldots, n'' - 1$$

$$d_{k', k''} = d_{n''k' + n'k''} \qquad k' = 0, \ldots, n' - 1$$
$$k'' = 0, \ldots, n'' - 1$$

$$c_{k', k''} = c_{n''k' + n'k''} \qquad k' = 0, \ldots, n' - 1$$
$$k'' = 0, \ldots, n'' - 1$$

so that the convolution now becomes

$$c_{i', i''} = \sum_{k'=0}^{n'-1} \sum_{k''=0}^{n''-1} d_{k', k''} g_{i'-k', i''-k''},$$

where the first and second indices are interpreted modulo n' and modulo n'', respectively. This is now a true two-dimensional cyclic convolution.

For the algorithm to be useful, we must give an efficient way of doing the two-dimensional cyclic convolutions. The Winograd convolution algorithm will be used along each of the two dimensions. This may be easier to see if the two-dimensional arrays are thought of as one-dimensional arrays of polynomials. Define the set of n'' polynomials

$$d_{k''}(x) = \sum_{k'=0}^{n'-1} d_{k', k''} x^{k'} \qquad k'' = 0, \ldots, n'' - 1.$$

Similarly, define

$$g_{k''}(x) = \sum_{k'=0}^{n'-1} g_{k', k''} x^{k'} \qquad k'' = 0, \ldots, n'' - 1$$

and

$$c_{k''}(x) = \sum_{k'=0}^{n'-1} c_{k',k''}x^{k'} \qquad k'' = 0, \ldots, n'' - 1.$$

The two-dimensional convolution now becomes a one-dimensional convolution of polynomials:

$$c_{i''}(x) = \sum_{k''=0}^{n''-1} g_{((i''-k''))}(x)d_{k''}(x) \qquad (\text{mod } x^{n'} - 1)$$

for $i'' = 0, \ldots, n'' - 1$. For each i'', the sum is a summation of n'' polynomial products. There are $(n'')^2$ polynomial products. Each polynomial product is a convolution and can be computed by any convenient algorithm for computing convolutions. The Winograd convolution algorithm is one such algorithm.

In order to finish developing the Agarwal-Cooley convolution, we also need to use the Winograd convolution algorithm on the other dimension. First we will pause and compute the complexity of this intermediate form. Let $M(l)$ and $A(l)$ denote the number of multiplications and additions, respectively, needed by some available library of cyclic convolution algorithms to perform a convolution of length l. Then the two-dimensional convolution requires $(n'')^2 M(n')$ multiplications and $(n'')^2 A(n') + (n'' - 1)n''n'$ additions. We can do even better, however, by also using the Winograd convolution algorithm on the other axis.

Because the Winograd convolution algorithm is an identity involving additions and multiplications, it still holds when the arithmetic elements are replaced by polynomials. Therefore $c_{i''}(x)$ can be computed with $M(n'')$ multiplications of polynomials and $A(n'')$ additions of polynomials, and each multiplication of polynomials takes $M(n')$ arithmetic multiplications and $A(n')$ arithmetic additions. The total computational work is $M(n'')M(n')$ arithmetic multiplications and $M(n'')A(n') + A(n'')n'$ arithmetic additions. The number of additions is not symmetric in n' and n'', and thus one should assign the labels n' and n'' with care in order to minimize the number of additions.

Similarly if the blocklength n of the cyclic convolution has three or more relatively prime factors, then the Agarwal-Cooley algorithm can be used to break the convolution into a multidimensional cyclic convolution; each dimension is computed by a Winograd convolution algorithm. The structure of the multidimensional cyclic convolution can also be described in terms of the one-dimensional cyclic convolutions as a Kronecker product. The Kronecker product is described in Section 11.5. Figure 11.5 tabulates the multiplicative complexity of some Agarwal-Cooley convolutions over fields of characteristic 2.

Blocklength	Multiplications*
2	3
3	4
4	9
5	10
6	12
7	13
9	19
10	30
14	39
15	40
21	76
35	130
45	190
63	247
105	520
315	2,470
630	7,410
1,260	22,230

*Using the short convolutions of Fig. 11.1.

Figure 11.5   Performance of some Agarwal-Cooley cyclic convolutions.

11.5 THE WINOGRAD FAST FOURIER TRANSFORM

The Winograd fast Fourier transform is another method of efficiently computing the discrete Fourier transform. It is built from four separate ideas: the Rader prime algorithm; the small Winograd convolution algorithm of Section 11.2; the Good-Thomas prime-factor indexing scheme; and Winograd's nesting algorithm. The Winograd FFT is better than the Cooley-Tukey FFT and the Good-Thomas FFT as measured by the number of multiplications, but it is more intricate. The price paid for having fewer multiplications is more extensive indexing and shuffling operations.

The Winograd FFT algorithm will be subdivided into the small Winograd FFT and the large Winograd FFT. The first gives an FFT whose blocklength is a small prime or a small prime power. The large Winograd FFT binds together small Winograd FFTs to get one with large blocklength.

The first step is to construct the small Winograd FFT algorithm. If n is a small prime, use the Rader prime algorithm to express the transform as a convolution, which is computed using a small Winograd convolution algorithm. Generally, one writes out the equations in longhand, and thus it is not practical to take n too large. The Rader prime algorithm changes the discrete Fourier transform into a convolution using only scrambling of the indices; no additions or multiplications are needed in that step. The convolution algorithm itself has the structure of a set of additions followed by a set of multiplications followed by another set of additions. If n is a small prime power, then the same procedure can be followed, provided the Rader algorithm is replaced by a more general form which we will not discuss.

Let us construct a binary five-point Winograd FFT that will compute

$$V_j = \sum_{i=0}^{4} \alpha^{ij} v_i \qquad j = 0, \ldots, 4.$$

in the field $GF(16)$. The five-point Winograd FFT uses the equations of the Rader prime algorithm which were developed in Section 9.8 for this same example. There the Fourier transform was changed into the convolution

$$b(x) = g(x)a(x) \qquad (\text{mod } x^4 - 1),$$

where

$$g(x) = \alpha^{14} x^3 + \alpha x^2 + \alpha^8 x + \alpha^4$$

$$a(x) = v_3 x^3 + v_4 x^2 + v_2 x + v_1$$

$$b(x) = (V_2 - V_0) x^3 + (V_4 - V_0) x^2 + (V_3 - V_0) x + (V_1 - V_0).$$

The polynomial $g(x)$ is fixed. The polynomial $a(x)$ is formed by scrambling the coefficients of $v(x)$. The polynomial $V(x)$ is obtained by unscrambling the coefficients of the polynomial $b(x)$.

The five-point small Winograd FFT is obtained if the product $g(x)a(x)$ is computed by a small convolution algorithm. Refer to Fig. 11.2, which shows a four-point cyclic convolution algorithm with nine multiplications. We can rewrite this to do the Fourier transform. Incorporate the scrambling and unscrambling operations into the matrices of the convolution by scrambling the appropriate rows and columns. Also the coefficients of $g(x)$ are fixed constants in $GF(16)$, and thus the product of **g** and its matrix is precomputed. When these changes are made to the four-point convolution algorithm, and the terms V_0 and v_0 are included, it becomes the five-point small Winograd FFT. Figure 11.6 shows the five-point transform in the matrix form

V = BDAv.

Notice that the matrix of preadditions **A** and the matrix of postadditions **B** are not square. The five-point input vector is expanded to a ten-point vector, and this is where the multiplications occur, as represented by the diagonal matrix **D**. The top row has to do with V_0 and has no multiplications. The other nine rows come from the four-point cyclic convolution algorithms. One of the multiplying constants turns out to be a one, and thus there are really only eight multiplications in the algorithm.

$$
\begin{bmatrix} V_0 \\ V_1 \\ V_2 \\ V_3 \\ V_4 \end{bmatrix} = \begin{bmatrix} 1 & 0 & 0 & 0 & 0 & 0 & 0 & 0 & 0 & 0 \\ 0 & 1 & 0 & 1 & 1 & 0 & 0 & 0 & 0 & 1 \\ 0 & 1 & 1 & 0 & 0 & 1 & 1 & 0 & 0 & 0 \\ 0 & 1 & 0 & 1 & 0 & 1 & 0 & 0 & 1 & 0 \\ 0 & 1 & 1 & 0 & 1 & 0 & 0 & 1 & 0 & 0 \end{bmatrix} \begin{bmatrix} 1 & & & & & & & & & 0 \\ & \alpha^{13} & & & & & & & & \\ & & \alpha^{9} & & & & & & & \\ & & & \alpha^{10} & & & & & & \\ & & & & \alpha^{6} & & & & & \\ & & & & & 1 & & & & \\ & & & & & & \alpha^{4} & & & \\ & & & & & & & \alpha^{14} & & \\ & & & & & & & & \alpha & \\ 0 & & & & & & & & & \alpha^{8} \end{bmatrix} \begin{bmatrix} 1 & 1 & 1 & 1 & 1 \\ 0 & 1 & 0 & 0 & 0 \\ 0 & 1 & 0 & 0 & 1 \\ 0 & 1 & 0 & 0 & 1 \\ 0 & 1 & 0 & 1 & 0 \\ 0 & 1 & 1 & 0 & 0 \\ 0 & 1 & 1 & 1 & 1 \\ 0 & 1 & 1 & 1 & 1 \\ 0 & 1 & 1 & 1 & 1 \\ 0 & 1 & 1 & 1 & 1 \end{bmatrix} \begin{bmatrix} v_0 \\ v_1 \\ v_2 \\ v_3 \\ v_4 \end{bmatrix}
$$

Figure 11.6   A five-point small Winograd FFT.

The small Winograd FFT of length n can be derived in this way whenever n is a prime. A small Winograd FFT also can be derived whenever n is a prime power. Generally, one constructs the small Winograd FFT only for fairly small blocklengths. For large blocklengths, one prefers to use something with a little more structure, even if there is a slight penalty in the number of multiplications. The large Winograd FFT satisfies this need.

The general case of the Winograd FFT has a blocklength n that is a product of small primes or small prime powers. We will discuss the case with two factors. Then $n = n'n''$. The prime-factor Good-Thomas algorithm decomposes an n-point Fourier transform into a two-dimensional n'-by-n''-point Fourier transform. The individual components of this two-dimensional Fourier transform can be computed by an n'-point Winograd transform and an n''-point Winograd transform, respectively. This consists of taking an n'-point Fourier transform of each row followed by an n''-point Fourier transform of each column.

There is yet one more step before we have the Winograd FFT. Because it does not matter whether the rows or the columns of the two-dimensional Fourier transform are transformed first, it would seem possible somehow to do them together. This is what the Winograd FFT does. It binds together the row computations and the column computations in a way that reduces the total number of multiplications. The technique uses the notion of a Kronecker product of matrices. We will pause to define the Kronecker product and to prove one important theorem. Then we will complete the development of the Winograd FFT.

$\square$ **Definition 11.5.1**   Let $\mathbf{A} = (a_{ik})$ be an I by K matrix, and let $\mathbf{B} = (b_{jl})$ be a J by L matrix. Then the *Kronecker product* of $\mathbf{A}$ and $\mathbf{B}$, denoted $\mathbf{A} \times \mathbf{B}$, is a matrix with IJ rows and KL columns whose entry in row $(i-1)J + j$ and column $(k-1)L + l$ is given by

$$c_{ij,kl} = a_{ik}b_{jl}. \qquad \square$$

The easiest way to comprehend the structure of the Kronecker product is to envision $\mathbf{A} \times \mathbf{B}$ as an I by K array of J by L blocks, with the (i, k)th such block being $a_{ik}\mathbf{B}$. It is immediately apparent from the definition that the Kronecker product is not commutative but is associative:

$$\mathbf{A} \times \mathbf{B} \neq \mathbf{B} \times \mathbf{A}$$

$$(\mathbf{A} \times \mathbf{B}) \times \mathbf{C} = \mathbf{A} \times (\mathbf{B} \times \mathbf{C}).$$

The elements of $\mathbf{B} \times \mathbf{A}$ are the same as those of $\mathbf{A} \times \mathbf{B}$, but they are arranged differently. It is also clear that the Kronecker product distributes over ordinary matrix addition.

The following theorem says that the Kronecker product of the matrix product of two matrices is the matrix product of the Kronecker products.

☐ **Theorem 11.5.2** The Kronecker product satisfies $(\mathbf{A} \times \mathbf{B})(\mathbf{C} \times \mathbf{D})$ $= (\mathbf{AC}) \times (\mathbf{BD})$, provided the matrix products all exist.

Proof Let the matrices $\mathbf{A}$, $\mathbf{B}$, $\mathbf{C}$, and $\mathbf{D}$ have respective dimensions I by K, J by L, K by M and L by N. Because $\mathbf{A} \times \mathbf{B}$ has KL columns and $\mathbf{C} \times \mathbf{D}$ has KL rows, the matrix product $(\mathbf{A} \times \mathbf{B})(\mathbf{C} \times \mathbf{D})$ is defined. It has IJ rows, which we doubly index by (i, j), and MN columns, which we doubly index by (m, n). The entry in row (i, j) and column (m, n) is $\sum_{kl} a_{ik}b_{jl}c_{km}d_{ln}$. Because $\mathbf{AC}$ has I rows and M columns, and $\mathbf{BD}$ has J rows and L columns, $(\mathbf{AC}) \times (\mathbf{BD})$ is also an IJ by MN matrix. Its entry in row (i, j) and column (m, n) is

$$\sum_k a_{ik}c_{km} \sum_l b_{jl}d_{ln} = \sum_{kl} a_{ik}b_{jl}c_{km}d_{ln},$$

which completes the proof. ☐

The Kronecker product has application to the Fourier transform. Let $\mathbf{W}'$ and $\mathbf{W}''$ be the matrix representations of Fourier transforms of size n' and n'', respectively. That is,

$$\mathbf{V}' = \mathbf{W}'\mathbf{v}'$$

and

$$\mathbf{V}'' = \mathbf{W}''\mathbf{v}''$$

are matrix representations of the Fourier transforms

$$V'_j = \sum_{i=0}^{n'-1} \beta^{ij}v'_i$$

and

$$V''_j = \sum_{i=0}^{n''-1} \gamma^{ij}v''_i.$$

An n' by n'' two-dimensional Fourier transform of the two-dimensional signal $v_{i'i''}$ is obtained by applying $\mathbf{W}'$ to each row and then applying $\mathbf{W}''$ to each column. An n' by n'' two-dimensional signal $v_{i'i''}$ can be turned into a one-dimensional signal by reading it by rows. (Possibly, the two-dimensional signal was previously formed from a one-dimensional signal by the Chinese remainder theorem. Reading it by rows results in a new one-dimensional signal whose components are a permutation of the components of the original one-dimensional signal.)

If we think of $v_{i'i''}$ and $V_{j'j''}$ arranged as one-dimensional $n'n''$-point vectors in this way, then the two-dimensional transform can be written using a Kronecker product as

$$\mathbf{V} = (\mathbf{W}' \times \mathbf{W}'')\mathbf{v}.$$

Whenever we have Winograd transforms of length n' and n'', then we have the matrix factorizations

$$\mathbf{W}' = \mathbf{B}'\mathbf{D}'\mathbf{A}'$$

$$\mathbf{W}'' = \mathbf{B}''\mathbf{D}''\mathbf{A}'',$$

where $\mathbf{A}'$, $\mathbf{A}''$, $\mathbf{B}'$, and $\mathbf{B}''$ are matrices of integers of the field, and $\mathbf{D}'$ and $\mathbf{D}''$ are diagonal matrices with elements from $GF(q)$. The multiplication by matrix $\mathbf{D}'$ or $\mathbf{D}''$ is where the Winograd algorithm collects all of its multiplications. Let $\mathbf{W} = \mathbf{W}' \times \mathbf{W}''$, and apply Theorem 11.7.2 twice to get

$$\mathbf{W} = (\mathbf{B}'\mathbf{D}'\mathbf{A}') \times (\mathbf{B}''\mathbf{D}''\mathbf{A}'')$$

$$= (\mathbf{B}' \times \mathbf{B}'')(\mathbf{D}' \times \mathbf{D}'')(\mathbf{A}' \times \mathbf{A}'')$$

$$= \mathbf{BDA},$$

where the Kronecker products $\mathbf{B} = \mathbf{B}' \times \mathbf{B}''$ and $\mathbf{A} = \mathbf{A}' \times \mathbf{A}''$ have only elements from $GF(p)$, and the Kronecker product $\mathbf{D} = \mathbf{D}' \times \mathbf{D}''$ is again a diagonal matrix with elements from $GF(q)$. Hence, we have an $n'n''$-point Fourier transform algorithm, again in the form of the Winograd FFT. In this way large Winograd FFT algorithms can be built up from small ones.

The derivation of $\mathbf{W}$ requires that the $n'n''$-point vector be written as a two-dimensional Fourier transform using the Good-Thomas prime-factor algorithm, and then, the two-dimensional vector $\mathbf{v}$ be turned back into a one-dimensional vector by reading it by rows. Hence, the $n'n''$-point transform

$$\mathbf{V} = (\mathbf{BDA})\mathbf{v}$$

that we have derived presumes that $\mathbf{v}$ is in a scrambled order and computes $\mathbf{V}$ in a scrambled order. Once $\mathbf{A}$ and $\mathbf{B}$ are derived, however, it is trivial to rearrange the columns of $\mathbf{A}$ and the rows of $\mathbf{B}$ so that $\mathbf{v}$ and $\mathbf{V}$ are in their natural order.

Let $M(n')$ and $M(n'')$ be the number of multiplications required of the n'- and n''-point Winograd FFT, respectively. Then $M(n)$, the number of multiplications needed by the $n'n''$-point Winograd FFT, is about $M(n')M(n'')$. More precisely,

$$\dim \mathbf{D} = (\dim \mathbf{D}')(\dim \mathbf{D}''),$$

and $M(n')$, $M(n'')$, and $M(n)$ are less than the dimensions of $\mathbf{D}'$, $\mathbf{D}''$, and $\mathbf{D}$, respectively, because the diagonal matrices have one or more multiplications by one. If we count all multiplications by elements of the diagonal matrix, even those by one, then we have the simple formula

$$M(n) = M(n')M(n'').$$

11.6 AN ACCELERATED BERLEKAMP-MASSEY ALGORITHM

The Berlekamp-Massey algorithm, described in Section 7.4, requires a number of multiplications in the rth iteration that is approximately equal to twice the degree of $\Lambda^{(r)}(x)$. Because deg $\Lambda^{(r)}(x)$ is on the order of r, typically $r/2$, and there are $2t$ iterations, about $2t^2$ multiplications are required, and about the same number of additions. This is quadratic in t. In brief, we say there are on the order of t^2 multiplications, or formally $O(t^2)$ multiplications, in the Berlekamp-Massey algorithm. For very large codes and large t, the number of multiplications can be a burden. In this section, we will show a way to reduce the computational complexity for long codes.

The accelerated algorithm can be motivated as follows. The frequency domain Berlekamp-Massey algorithm has few multiplications in the initial iterations—on the order of the degree of $\Lambda(x)$. But the degree of $\Lambda(x)$ approaches a significant fraction of n, and thus the average number of multiplications per iteration is on the order of n. The accelerated algorithm will take advantage of the simplicity of the early iterations in the frequency domain by doing a few iterations at a time. After each such batch of iterations, the partial result is used to modify the syndromes in order to absorb the $\Lambda(x)$ and $B(x)$ computed in that batch into the modified syndromes. The next batch of iterations starts the Berlekamp-Massey algorithm anew using these modified syndromes and $\Lambda(x)$ reinitialized to one. The accelerated decoder is efficient for some large, but still practical codes. Other decoders that are even more efficient will be studied in the next section.

The development will begin with a more compact organization of the Berlekamp-Massey algorithm. We replace the polynomials $\Lambda^{(r)}(x)$ and $B^{(r)}(x)$ by a 2 by 2 matrix of polynomials:

$$\Lambda^{(r)}(x) = \begin{bmatrix} \Lambda^{(r)}_{11}(x) & \Lambda^{(r)}_{12}(x) \\ \Lambda^{(r)}_{21}(x) & \Lambda^{(r)}_{22}(x) \end{bmatrix}.$$

We will need several indices on the elements of $\Lambda^{(r)}(x)$. The symbol $\Lambda^{(r)}_{ab,j}$ denotes the jth coefficient of the polynomial element at row a, column b of the matrix at the rth iteration.

Recall that the computations of the Berlekamp-Massey algorithm reside primarily in the two equations

$$\Delta_r = \sum_{j=0}^{n-1} \Lambda_j^{(r-1)} S_{r-j}$$

and

$$\begin{bmatrix} \Lambda^{(r)}(x) \\ B^{(r)}(x) \end{bmatrix} = \begin{bmatrix} 1 & -\Delta_r x \\ \Delta_r^{-1}\delta_r & (1-\delta_r)x \end{bmatrix} \begin{bmatrix} \Lambda^{(r-1)}(x) \\ B^{(r-1)}(x) \end{bmatrix}.$$

The second equation can be expanded:

$$\begin{bmatrix} \Lambda^{(r)}(x) \\ B^{(r)}(x) \end{bmatrix} = \left\{ \prod_{l=1}^{r} \begin{bmatrix} 1 & -\Delta_l x \\ \Delta_l^{-1}\delta_l & (1-\delta_l)x \end{bmatrix} \right\} \begin{bmatrix} 1 \\ 1 \end{bmatrix}.$$

Define the matrix $\boldsymbol{\Lambda}^{(r)}(x)$ by

$$\boldsymbol{\Lambda}^{(r)}(x) = \prod_{l=1}^{r} \begin{bmatrix} 1 & -\Delta_l x \\ \Delta_l^{-1}\delta_l & (1-\delta_l)x \end{bmatrix}.$$

From this matrix, $\Lambda^{(r)}(x)$ and $B^{(r)}(x)$ can be obtained by the expression

$$\begin{bmatrix} \Lambda^{(r)}(x) \\ B^{(r)}(x) \end{bmatrix} = \boldsymbol{\Lambda}^{(r)}(x)\begin{bmatrix} 1 \\ 1 \end{bmatrix} = \begin{bmatrix} \Lambda_{11}^{(r)}(x) + \Lambda_{12}^{(r)}(x) \\ \Lambda_{21}^{(r)}(x) + \Lambda_{22}^{(r)}(x) \end{bmatrix}.$$

It serves just as well to update $\boldsymbol{\Lambda}^{(r)}(x)$ as to update $\Lambda^{(r)}(x)$ and $B^{(r)}(x)$, although updating $\boldsymbol{\Lambda}^{(r)}(x)$ directly can involve about twice as many multiplications because it has four elements rather than two. We will replace the iterates $\Lambda^{(r)}(x)$ and $B^{(r)}(x)$ with the iterate $\boldsymbol{\Lambda}^{(r)}(x)$ and accept the doubling of the number of multiplications. This penalty will be overcome later by reorganizing the computations.

The revised form of the Berlekamp-Massey algorithm is built around the two equations

$$\Delta_r = \sum_{j=0}^{n-1} \Lambda_{11,j}^{(r-1)} S_{r-j} + \sum_{j=0}^{n-1} \Lambda_{12,j}^{(r-1)} S_{r-j}$$

and

$$\boldsymbol{\Lambda}^{(r)}(x) = \begin{bmatrix} 1 & -\Delta_r x \\ \Delta_r^{-1}\delta_r & (1-\delta_r)x \end{bmatrix} \boldsymbol{\Lambda}^{(r-1)}(x).$$

Next we will reduce the number of computations by grouping the iterations into batches. Define the matrix

$$\mathbf{M}^{(r)}(x) = \begin{bmatrix} 1 & -\Delta_r x \\ \Delta_r^{-1}\delta_r & (1-\delta_r)x \end{bmatrix}$$

so that

$$\boldsymbol{\Lambda}^{(r)}(x) = \mathbf{M}^{(r)}(x)\mathbf{M}^{(r-1)}(x) \ldots \mathbf{M}^{(1)}(x).$$

This product must be multiplied out one term at a time from the right, because $\mathbf{M}^{(r)}(x)$ is not computed until after $\Lambda^{(r-1)}(x)$ is computed.

Define the following partial product of such matrices:

$$\Lambda^{(r,r')}(x) = \mathbf{M}^{(r)}(x)\mathbf{M}^{(r-1)}(x) \ldots \mathbf{M}^{(r'+1)}(x).$$

Then

$$\Lambda^{(r)}(x) = \Lambda^{(r,0)}(x)$$

and

$$\Lambda^{(r)}(x) = \Lambda^{(r,r')}(x)\Lambda^{(r')}(x).$$

Also define the vector of modified syndrome polynomials $\mathbf{S}^{(r)}(x)$ by

$$\mathbf{S}^{(r)}(x) = \Lambda^{(r)}(x)\begin{bmatrix} S(x) \\ S(x) \end{bmatrix}$$

$$= \Lambda^{(r,r')}(x)\mathbf{S}^{(r')}(x).$$

The discrepancy

$$\Delta_r = \sum_{j=0}^{n-1} \Lambda_{11,j}^{(r-1)}S_{r-j} + \sum_{j=0}^{n-1} \Lambda_{12,j}^{(r-1)}S_{r-j}$$

is the rth term of a convolution equation that can be expressed as a polynomial equation:

$$\Delta(x) = \Lambda_{11}^{(r-1)}(x)S(x) + \Lambda_{12}^{(r-1)}(x)S(x)$$

$$= [\Lambda_{11}^{(r-1,r')}(x)\Lambda_{11}^{(r')}(x) + \Lambda_{12}^{(r-1,r')}(x)\Lambda_{21}^{(r')}(x)]S(x)$$

$$+ [\Lambda_{11}^{(r-1,r')}(x)\Lambda_{12}^{(r')}(x) + \Lambda_{12}^{(r-1,r')}(x)\Lambda_{22}^{(r')}(x)]S(x).$$

Rearrange terms to obtain

$$\Delta(x) = \Lambda_{11}^{(r-1,r')}(x)[\Lambda_{11}^{(r')}(x)S(x) + \Lambda_{12}^{(r')}(x)S(x)]$$

$$+ \Lambda_{12}^{(r-1,r')}(x)[\Lambda_{21}^{(r')}(x)S(x) + \Lambda_{22}^{(r')}(x)S(x)].$$

The terms in brackets are recognized as components of $\mathbf{S}^{(r')}(x)$, the vector of modified syndrome polynomials. Consequently, we can replace the equation for Δ_r by

$$\Delta_r = \sum_{j=0}^{r-r'} \Lambda_{11,j}^{(r-1,r')}S_{1,r-j}^{(r')} + \sum_{j=0}^{r-r'} \Lambda_{12,j}^{(r-1,r')}S_{2,r-j}^{(r')},$$

where $S_{1,j}^{(r)}$ and $S_{2,j}^{(r)}$ denote the jth coefficient of the polynomials in the first or second component of $\mathbf{S}^{(r)}(x)$, respectively.

To accelerate the Berlekamp-Massey algorithm, take batches of τ iterations. If τ divides $2t$, then each of $2t/\tau$ batches is treated the same. Otherwise, the last batch will have less than τ iterations but will otherwise be the same. The index r now looks like

$$r = 1, 2, \ldots, \tau, \tau + 1, \ldots, 2\tau, 2\tau + 1, \ldots, 3\tau, 3\tau + 1, \ldots$$

In the rth iteration of the kth batch, the Berlekamp-Massey algorithm in modified form is used to update $\Lambda^{(r,r')}(x)$ according to the equation

$$\Lambda^{(r,r')}(x) = \begin{bmatrix} 1 & -\Delta_r x \\ \Delta_r^{-1}\delta_r & (1-\delta_r)x \end{bmatrix} \Lambda^{(r-1,r')}(x),$$

where $r' = k\tau$ and where Δ_r is computed by

$$\Delta_r = \sum_{j=0}^{r-r'} \Lambda_{11,j}^{(r-1,r')}S_{1,r-j}^{(r')} + \sum_{j=0}^{r-r'} \Lambda_{12,j}^{(r-1,r')}S_{2,r-j}^{(r')}.$$

At the end of the kth batch, when r equals $(k+1)\tau$, the error-locator matrix and the vector of modified syndrome polynomials are updated by the equations

$$\Lambda^{(r)}(x) = \Lambda^{(r,r')}(x)\Lambda^{(r')}(x)$$

and

$$S^{(r)}(x) = \Lambda^{(r,r')}(x)S^{(r')}(x),$$

where $r' = k\tau$ and $r = (k+1)\tau$. The accelerated algorithm is now ready to begin the $(k+1)$th batch.

A flowchart of an accelerated algorithm is shown in Fig. 11.7, but with some obvious abbreviated notation. The left-hand side is our standard form of the Berlekamp-Massey algorithm, which is exercised for only τ iterations. The right-hand side is a bridge to link together these batches of τ iterations. If the right-hand side is executed just as it is written, there will be no net savings. The polynomial multiplications in the major block of the right-hand side, however, are equivalent to convolutions. Convolutions can be done efficiently as described in Sections 11.1 and 11.3, or by the use of fast Fourier transforms and the convolution theorem. An example will illustrate some of the possibilities.

The (4096, 2048) extended Reed-Solomon code is a code of rate $\frac{1}{2}$ over $GF(2^{12})$ that will correct error patterns with 1024 12-bit bytes in error. The Berlekamp-Massey algorithm typically requires $2t^2$ (or 2,097,152) multiplications of the 12-bit numbers of $GF(2^{12})$ and a worst-case error pattern might contain about 1.5 times this many multiplications. The accelerated Berlekamp-Massey algorithm will do better.

We will count multiplications for a slight variation of the accelerated Berlekamp-Massey algorithm. Rather than make the batches the same size, branching out every τ iterations, we will branch when the degree of $\Lambda(x)$ reaches a limit. We will branch out when the degree of any polynomial element of $\Lambda(x)$ equals 128, with a terminating branch after 2048 iterations. Whenever there are exactly 1024 errors, there will be eight batches, each of about 128 iterations. This is the case we will analyze.

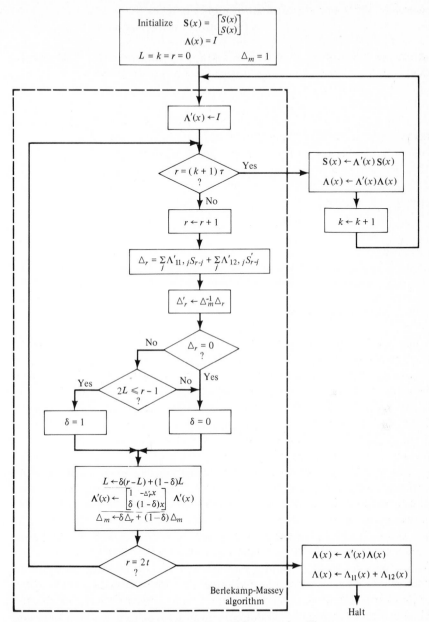

Figure 11.7   An accelerated Berlekamp-Massey algorithm.

During each iteration, the left side of Fig. 11.7 requires a number of multiplications equal to about four times the degree $\Lambda'(x)$ has during that iteration. This is twice as many multiplications as in the original form of the Berlekamp-Massey algorithm. Hence, there are about τ^2 iterations per batch on the left side of Fig. 11.7. There are eight batches, and τ equals 128; thus there are 524,288 multiplications within the batches. To this must be added the number of multiplications in the convolutions on the right side, which are used to link the batches together. We choose to do these linear convolutions using a 315-point cyclic convolution algorithm requiring 2470 multiplications. This is an Agarwal-Cooley convolution built from three short convolutions, with a five-point, a seven-point, and a nine-point convolution as the subroutines.

After each batch, we need to compute terms of the form $\Lambda(x)S(x)$, where $S(x)$ has degree $2048-k\tau$ and $\Lambda(x)$ has degree 128. We will use the overlap-save method with the 315-point convolution algorithm. This will produce $315 - \deg \Lambda(x)$ or 188 correct output points of the linear convolution $\Lambda(x)S(x)$. Producing $2048 - 256$ points requires 10 applications of the cyclic convolution algorithm. Because $\Lambda'(x)S(x)$ has four linear convolutions, a total of 40 applications of the cyclic convolution algorithms are needed.

Continuing in this way, we can count a total of 168 applications of the cyclic convolution algorithm—a total of 480,480 multiplications.

After each batch, we also need to compute the matrix products of $\Lambda'(x)\Lambda(x)$. Breaking up the convolutions in the matrix product $\Lambda'(x)\Lambda(x)$ and counting as indicated, we can find that 216 applications of the 315-point cyclic convolution algorithm are required.

The total number of multiplications needed to decode the (4096, 2048) Reed-Solomon code is obtained by adding the three counts. This gives a multiplication load of 1,462,768 as compared to 2,097,152 for the direct implementation.

11.7 A RECURSIVE BERLEKAMP-MASSEY ALGORITHM

We can construct a decoder that is even more efficient than the decoder of the previous section. The improved decoder is not only of practical interest but also of theoretical interest. With it we can show that the asymptotic complexity of decoding Reed-Solomon codes is at most $O(n \log^2 n)$ (and very nearly $O(n \log n)$). Besides the good asymptotic behavior, the same algorithm is also practical for moderate blocklengths.

For simplicity of exposition, we will treat mainly the case where $2t$ is a power of 2. Let $2t = 2^p$. The recursive algorithm works by splitting a problem of length 2^p into two problems, each of length 2^{p-1}, which are linked together using a 2^{p-1}-point convolution algorithm. Each of the two half-problems is, in turn, split into two problems. This continues until problems of only one iteration are reached. If the half-problems can be made to look the same as the original problem, then a recursive implementation can be realized.

There are several ways to modify the procedure to handle cases where $2t$ is not a power of 2. One way is to write $2t$ as a product of primes. If p_l

is the lth factor, then at the lth level the problem is divided into p_l subproblems instead of two. Otherwise, the algorithm works just as before.

A second method is to replace the number of iterations by the smallest power of 2 greater than $2t$ and again break this problem into halves at each level. Each time the procedure is called, it looks at the global value of the iteration counter r to see if r exceeds $2t$. If it does, it returns immediately without performing any iterations. Otherwise, the algorithm works just as before.

The way to formulate the recursive step becomes obvious if we only note that the computations described in the last section for computing Δ_r and $\Lambda^{(r,k\tau)}(x)$ from $S^{(k\tau)}(x)$ are of exactly the same form described by Theorem 7.4.1, except $2t$ is replaced by τ, $\Lambda^{(r)}(x)$ is replaced by $\Lambda^{(r,k\tau)}(x)$, and the vector of syndrome polynomials $S(x)$ is replaced by $S^{(k\tau)}(x)$. Therefore the same algorithm can be used to compute $\Lambda^{(r,k\tau)}(x)$ as is used to compute $\Lambda^{(2t)}(x)$.

The recursive algorithm, which we call *procedure BerMas*, is shown in Fig. 11.8. Procedure BerMas uses itself. It has a push-down stack, where it can temporarily store a copy of data at one level of the recursion when it proceeds to the next level. The next level behaves the same way, pushing down yet another set of data. Eventually, the problem segment has only one iteration and cannot be divided in half. When it is called to do one iteration, procedure BerMas simply executes the single iteration and returns.

Each time procedure BerMas calls itself, it must store its local variables in a push-down stack. If the problem requires 2^ρ iterations at the start, then the recursion will go ρ levels deep. The push-down stack must be large enough to hold this many sets of temporary variables.

The lth level will be visited 2^l times—the zero level once, the first level twice, and so on, with the final level visited 2^ρ times. At the lth level, the computation $S(x) \leftarrow \Lambda(x)S(x)$ involves four polynomial products. The polynomials of $\Lambda'(x)$ have degree approximately equal to $2^{\rho-l-1}-1$, and they multiply polynomials of degree of $2^{\rho-l+1}-1$. Only $2^{\rho-1}$ coefficients of the product polynomial need be computed correctly, namely, the coefficients of $x^{2^{\rho-1}}$ up to $x^{2^{\rho-l+1}}-1$, because these are the only coefficients of the updated vector $S(x)$ that will be used in the second call of procedure BerMas. Also at the lth level is the matrix product $\Lambda'(x)\Lambda(x)$, which involves the product of polynomials of degree $2^{\rho-l-1}$ each.

The multiplication load of procedure BerMas is almost entirely in the convolutions. This is because when an iteration of the Berlekamp-Massey algorithm is finally executed, it occurs as a single iteration and has just one multiplication (by Δ_m^{-1}), which can be neglected when counting multiplications. The computational complexity of procedure BerMas depends directly on the computational complexity of the convolution algorithms. Its successful use presumes the availability of a good set of convolution algorithms.

Figure 11.9 gives an accounting of the number of multiplications used by a recursive implementation applied to the same (4096, 2048) Reed-Solomon code used as an example in the previous section. Convolutions are done by

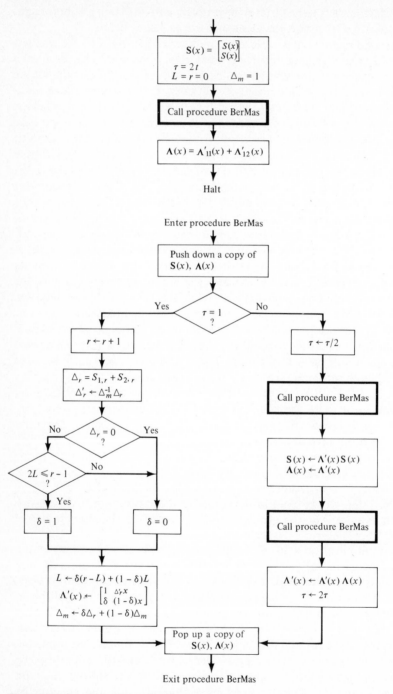

Figure 11.8   Procedure BerMas.

Level	Number of Visits	deg Λ(x)	deg S(x) In	Convolution Size Used	Number of Convolutions Λ'(x)**S**(x) Computation	Number of Convolutions Λ'(x)**Λ**(x) Computation	Number of Multiplications
1	1	511	2041	1260	8	8	355,680
2	2	255	1023	630	2×8	2×8	237,120
3	4	127	511	315	4×8	4×8	158,080
4	8	63	255	140	8×8	8×8	149,760
5	16	31	127	70	16×8	16×8	99,840
6	32	15	63	35	32×8	32×8	66,560
7	64	7	31	21	64×8	64×8	77,824
8	128	3	15	9	128×8	128×8	38,912
9	256	1	7	4	256×8	256×8	36,864
10	512	0	3	2	–	512×8	12,288
11	1024	0	1	1	–	–	–
							1,232,928

Figure 11.9   Multiplication count for procedure BerMas.

the overlap-save method in two sections using the convolutions listed in Fig. 11.5. The detail of the table is convincing evidence that the algorithm has an intricate structure. This structure, however, resides in an executive section of software or hardware, which schedules the computational resources. It calls the convolution algorithms from a library of them as they are needed.

In the general case of $2t$ iterations the Berlekamp-Massey algorithm has a computational complexity, as measured by the number of multiplications, that is on the order of $(\log_2 2t)C(t)$, where $C(t)$ is the number of multiplications required to convolve polynomials of degree of t. This is because there are 2^l visits to level l, and level l requires convolutions of length $2^{-l}t$. The computational complexity of 2^l convolutions, each of length $2^{-l}t$, is greatest when l equals zero, and l takes on $\log_2 2t$ values.

A bound on the asymptotic computational complexity depends on a bound on the asymptotic complexity of convolution in a Galois field. Recall that the Winograd convolutions require a set of relatively prime factors over $GF(p)$. In order to minimize the number of multiplications, these should be chosen to have small degree. If n is large, however, there will not be enough polynomials of small degree. Some polynomials whose degree is on the order of $\log n$ will be needed. The convolution of size n will be replaced by a number of convolutions, the largest of which has a size on the order of $\log n$. The same process can be used in turn to replace a convolution of size $\log n$ by a number of smaller convolutions, the largest of which has a size of about $\log (2 \log n)$. By formalizing this argument, one can say that the asymptotic complexity of convolution in a Galois field is $O(n2^{\log^* n})$, where $\log^* n$ is the number of times that a base 2 logarithm must be iterated starting with argument n to get a number less than or equal to one. That is,

$$\log_2(\log_2(\ldots (\log_2 n))) \leqslant 1,$$

and $\log^* n$ is the number of iterations. The term $2^{\log^* n}$ goes to infinity more slowly than any finite number of iterated logarithms.

The best bound on $C(n)$ known says that $C(n)$ is $O(n2^{\log^* n})$, and thus the recursive Berlekamp-Massey algorithm has complexity $O(n2^{\log^* n} \log n)$. Hence, the recursive Berlekamp-Massey algorithm has complexity greater than $O(n \log n)$ by the thinnest of margins.

11.8 ACCELERATED DECODING OF BCH CODES

The techniques of the previous sections will now be applied to obtain an accelerated decoder. It suffices to discuss only primitive Reed-Solomon codes. BCH codes and nonprimitive Reed-Solomon codes are decoded in the same way. A primitive t-error-correcting Reed-Solomon code of block-length $n = q - 1$ is the set of all words of length n over $GF(q)$ whose spectrum is zero in a specified block of $2t$ consecutive components.

The decoder works with the Fourier transform of $\mathbf{v}$, the received word. The complexity of the Fourier transform is typically of the order of $n \log_2 n$.

The codeword spectrum $\mathbf{C}$ is zero on a block of $2t$ components, and thus we have the $2t$ syndromes:

$$S_j = E_j = V_j \qquad j = 1, \ldots, 2t.$$

The error-locator polynomial

$$\Lambda(x) = \prod_{k=1}^{v} (1 - x\alpha^{i_k}),$$

where $v \leqslant t$ is the number of errors, satisfies

$$\sum_{j=0}^{t} \Lambda_j E_{k-j} = 0.$$

The convolution is a set of n equations in $n - t$ unknowns—t coefficients of $\Lambda(x)$ and $n - 2t$ components of $\mathbf{E}$. Of the n equations, there are t equations that involve only components of Λ and known components of $\mathbf{E}$. Using convolution algorithms of complexity $n \log_2 n$, the recursive Berlekamp-Massey algorithm of the previous section will solve these equations for the unknown components of Λ with complexity of at most $O(n \log_2^2 n)$. The remaining components of $\mathbf{E}$ can be recursively computed from Λ and the known components of $\mathbf{E}$ by

$$E_j = -\sum_{k=1}^{t} \Lambda_k E_{j-k}.$$

In this way E_j is computed for all j, and C_j equals $V_j - E_j$. An inverse Fourier transform completes the decoding.

The computation of E_j for $j = 2t + 1, \ldots, n$ requires $t(n - 2t)$ multiplications and therefore has complexity of order n^2. In the remainder of this section, we will show how to reduce the computational complexity of this step to a complexity of at most $O(n \log_2 n)$.

The form of the Berlekamp-Massey algorithm given by Massey treats the spectrum $\mathbf{E}$ on an interval of length n and as periodically continued outside of this interval. The relationship between $E(x)$ and $\Lambda(x)$ can be written

$$E(x)\Lambda(x) = 0 \qquad (\mathrm{mod}\ x^n - 1).$$

The Fourier transform of the cyclic convolution gives

$$e_i \lambda_i = 0 \qquad i = 0, \ldots, n-1.$$

These time-domain equations are indeterminate because the solution is $e_i = 0/\lambda_i$, and $\lambda_i = 0$ whenever $e_i \neq 0$. They cannot be solved in this form.

Berlekamp takes a slightly different approach to the algorithm. With the Berlekamp point of view, the shift-register output is no longer periodic, but periodic only after a start-up transient. The shift register is initially empty, and the known polynomial Ω is shifted in. The equation becomes

$$E_j = -\sum_{k=1}^{t} \Lambda_k E_{j-k} + \Omega_j.$$

and the excitation Ω_j, which is zero for $j > t$, brings the shift register from the initially quiescent state into the periodic state described previously.

The error-spectrum polynomial $E(x)$ satisfies the linear convolution

$$E(x)\Lambda(x) = \Omega(x).$$

The polynomial $\Omega(x)$ can be calculated by the recursive algorithm with no asymptotic increase in complexity, and $E(x)$ can be computed by polynomial division. But this last step also has complexity that grows as n^2. Because the expression is neither periodic nor of finite duration, transform techniques are not immediately applicable. In solving this equation, however, the Forney algorithm is an indirect method that does the job. From $\Lambda(x)$ compute $\Omega(x)$ by

$$\Omega(x) = E(x)\Lambda(x) \qquad (\mathrm{mod}\ x^{2t}),$$

and compute $\Lambda'(x)$ as the formal derivative of $\Lambda(x)$. Then take inverse Fourier transforms of Λ, Ω, and Λ' to get vectors λ_i, ω_i, and λ_i'. The error value is given by (see Problem 11.5)

$$e_i = -\frac{\omega_i}{\alpha^{-i}\lambda_i'}$$

whenever λ_i is equal to zero. Because the Forney algorithm can be done with three Fourier transforms and a convolution, it has complexity $O(n \log_2 n)$.

11.9 CONVOLUTION IN SURROGATE FIELDS

Computations in one field can be executed in a different field. Perhaps to meet the needs of a large diversity of signal processing tasks with a few standard computational modules, one may wish to fit one kind of computational task into a different kind of structure. For example, one may wish to do Galois field computations using the complex field as a surrogate field.

The cyclic convolution in the prime field $GF(p)$

$$c_i = \sum_{k=0}^{n-1} a_k b_{((i-k))} \qquad i = 0, \ldots, n-1$$

can be replaced by a convolution in the integer ring. One only needs to suspend the modulo p aspect of computation. The convolution equation then has the same appearance, but the arithmetic operations are interpreted as ordinary integer arithmetic. Later, c_i in the $GF(p)$ convolution can be obtained from c_i in the integer convolution by computing its residue modulo p; hence, we only need to convolve integer sequences. The integer ring then can be embedded in a suitable field, such as the complex field. The integer convolution in the complex field can be computed using any convolution algorithm in the complex field, such as the discrete Fourier transform and the convolution theorem. In practice, the Fourier transform in the complex field is computed with finite wordlength, and thus roundoff error will enter the computations. It is a simple matter, however, to select the wordlength such that roundoff error in c_i is always less than 0.5. Therefore rounding each component of the answer to the nearest integer must give the correct integer convolution. The residue of each integer modulo p then gives the convolution in $GF(p)$.

It may be impossible to justify the use of the complex field as a surrogate field by simply counting multiplications. Devices that do convolutions in a complex field are widely available, however, and the use of a surrogate field also may be justified if it fits the computational problem into an available device.

Next suppose that the signals to be convolved are over $GF(q)$, where q is no longer a prime. We can think of each individual product of field elements as a convolution of polynomials modulo an irreducible polynomial. The computation of the residue modulo the irreducible polynomial $p(x)$ will be held pending until after all convolutions are complete. The original convolution then becomes a two-dimensional convolution.

Let **a** and **b** be vectors over $GF(q)$. The vector components are polynomials over the prime field $GF(p)$:

$$a_i = \sum_{l=0}^{m-1} a_{il} z^l$$

and

$$b_i = \sum_{l=0}^{m-1} b_{il} z^l,$$

where $q = p^m$ and a_{il} and b_{il} are nonnegative integers less than p. The linear convolution of a and b is

$$c_i = \sum_{k=0}^{n-1} a_k b_{i-k}$$

$$= \sum_{k=0}^{n-1} \sum_{l=0}^{m-1} \sum_{l'=0}^{m-1} a_{kl} b_{(i-k)l'} z^{l+l'} \qquad (\text{mod } p)(\text{mod } p(x)),$$

where p is the characteristic of the field and $p(x)$ is a prime polynomial of degree of m. Define

$$c_{ii'} = \sum_{k=0}^{n-1} \sum_{k'=0}^{m-1} a_{kk'} b_{(i-k)(i'-k')} \qquad \begin{array}{l} i = 0, \ldots, n-1 \\ i' = 0, \ldots, 2m-1, \end{array}$$

interpreted as a two-dimensional convolution of integers; each integer in the two-dimensional array is between zero and $p-1$. This convolution can be computed in any convenient surrogate field, such as the real field or the complex field. Then

$$c_i(z) = \sum_{i'=0}^{2m-1} c_{ii'} z^{i'} \qquad (\text{mod } p)(\text{mod } p(x)).$$

The residue computations are done last; first the residue of each integer modulo p is found, and then the residue of the polynomial $c_i(z)$ is found modulo $p(x)$. The complexity of the residue computations can be neglected as compared to the complexity of the two-dimensional convolution.

Instead of the complex field, one may also use as the surrogate field any convenient finite field, even one whose characteristic is different from that of the original field. To convolve sequences in $GF(2)$ whose blocklength n is smaller than one-half of a Fermat prime $2^m + 1$ for $m = 2, 4, 8,$ or 16, one can use $GF(2^m + 1)$. The sequences in $GF(2)$ can be regarded as sequences of integers that only take the values zero or one. The linear convolution of the integer sequences has length smaller than $2^m + 1$ and is nowhere larger than n. Hence the linear convolution in $GF(2)$ can be done as a cyclic convolution in $GF(2^m + 1)$ followed by a modulo 2 computation. The cyclic convolution in $GF(2^m + 1)$ may be done by any fast convolution algorithm; one method is to use a fast Fourier transform with the convolution theorem.

For example, two sequences of length 2^{15} in $GF(2)$ can be convolved directly, with about 2^{31} bit operations. Instead, one can use the convolution theorem with the field $GF(2^{16} + 1)$. A Fourier transform requires about 2^{18} multiplications and 2^{20} additions in this field; each multiplication requires about $(17)^2$ bit operations, and each addition requires about 17 bit operations. Therefore the convolution can be computed with about $3 \times (17^2 \times 2^{18}) \approx 3 \times 2^{26}$ bit operations.

Now suppose we wish to convolve two sequences in $GF(2^m)$. As before, we can represent the field elements by polynomials over $GF(2)$. If we leave pending the operation of finding the residue modulo $p(x)$ until all other computations are finished, then the original convolution becomes a two-dimensional convolution. The problem can be imbedded in a surrogate field $GF(2^{m'} + 1)$ as long as the convolution of integers will not exceed $2^{m'} + 1$, that is, as long as

$$m \cdot n < 2^{m'} + 1.$$

For example, we will linearly convolve two sequences of length 8192 over $GF(2^8)$. Because 8(8192) is smaller than $2^{16} + 1$, we can use $GF(2^{16} + 1)$ as the surrogate field. A two-dimensional 16-by-16,384-point cyclic convolution will accommodate the two-dimensional 8-by-8192-point linear convolution with no terms spoiled. The 16-by-16,384-point cyclic convolution can be done by Fourier transform techniques. The 16-point transform has no multiplications—only shifts. The 16,384-point transform can be broken down using the Cooley-Tukey FFT, as was discussed earlier. Three transforms are needed to employ the convolution theorem, and each requires 2048 multiplications. Also, $16 \times 16,384$ multiplications are needed in the transform domain. Thus 268,288 multiplications in $GF(2^{16} + 1)$ are needed to compute the 8192-point convolution over $GF(2^8)$.

PROBLEMS

11.1. Construct a fast convolution algorithm for encoding the (7, 3) Reed-Solomon code whose generator polynomial has zeros at α^0, α^1, α^2, and α^3.

11.2. Construct a fast convolution algorithm for encoding the (15, 11) Reed-Solomon code having the generator polynomial $g(x) = x^4 + \alpha^{13}x^3 + \alpha^6 x^2 + \alpha^3 x + \alpha^{10}$.

11.3. a. Construct a three-point Winograd FFT in $GF(16)$.

    b. Using the Winograd nesting technique, combine a 3-point Winograd FFT and a 5-point Winograd FFT to get a 15-point Winograd FFT over $GF(16)$.

11.4. Set up the indexing equations for a 35-point Cooley-Tukey FFT.

11.5. The Forney algorithm $e_i = -\omega_i/(\alpha^{-i}\lambda_i')$ is similar to the expression $E(x)\Lambda(x) = \Omega(x)$. The second expression is not periodic, however, and thus Fourier transform techniques cannot be used to derive the Forney algorithm directly. Develop the following line of reasoning in order to derive the Forney algorithm using the Fourier transform. Choose n' so that an element of order $n'n$ exists in some extension field. Show that $E(x)\Lambda(x) = -(x^n - 1)\Omega(x)$ can be interpreted as a periodic expression with period $n'n$. Use a Fourier transform of blocklength $n'n$ to complete the proof.

11.6. Give an outline of a procedure for constructing an 8-point cyclic convolution algorithm for fields of characteristic 2 that uses 28 or fewer multiplications. The description should be complete except for straightforward calculations.

11.7. Suppose it is necessary to write a program that computes a 31-point cyclic convolution in $GF(32)$ or an extension of $GF(32)$.

    a. Estimate the complexity of a program that uses a 31-point DFT and the convolution theorem.

    b. Construct a program that uses a 75-point fast Fourier transform in $GF(2^{20})$. Build the FFT out of three-point and five-point Winograd Fast Fourier Transforms. Estimate the complexity of the convolution program.

11.8. A $(256, 256 - 2t)$ Reed-Solomon code over $GF(2^8 + 1)$ is used to systematically encode 8-bit bytes into codewords of 8-bit bytes. Whenever a parity symbol takes on the value 2^8 it cannot be represented with 8 bits. It is replaced by zero, and the codeword contains an error at the time of encoding which can be corrected by the code. What is the rate of the binary code? Discuss the degradation in performance due to assigning only 8 bits to the parity symbols.

NOTES

The material in this chapter is based on techniques that have been developed within the literature of digital signal processing and the design of efficient computer algorithms. For the most part, these techniques were formulated without noticing that they could be applied to the subject of error-control codes. The original papers only use computations in the real or complex field, but it is a trivial matter to apply the same ideas in a Galois field, and this we have done here.

Fast-Fourier-transform algorithms came into widespread use in digital signal processing as a result of the well-known paper of Cooley and Tukey (1965). A different FFT, however, appeared earlier in the papers of Good (1960) and Thomas (1963). The relationship between the FFT and the complexity of decoding was discussed by Justesen (1976) and by Sarwate (1977).

Fast convolution algorithms were first constructed by Agarwal and Cooley (1977) using brute-force techniques. Winograd (1978) gave the general method of construction that we have described and also proved important theorems concerning the nonexistence of better convolution algorithms in the real or complex field. The Winograd theorems have less punch in a Galois field because multiplications there can be easily disguised as additions. The use of the Chinese remainder theorem for integers to break long convolutions into short convolutions was discussed by Agarwal and Cooley (1977). The Winograd FFT was published by him in 1978. Our description breaks it apart and relates it to other signal-processing techniques. The Winograd FFT and other efficient algorithms were discussed by Nussbaumer (1981).

The application of the Winograd FFT to the decoding of Reed-Solomon codes was discussed by Miller, Truong, and Reed (1980).

The accelerated and recursive Berlekamp-Massey algorithms, previously unpublished, are from Blahut (1981). The use of surrogate fields for convolution was treated by Preparata and Sarwate (1977).

CHAPTER 12
Convolutional Codes

Modern communication systems often must be designed to transmit at very high data rates—sometimes many millions of bits per second. To protect such systems from error, block codes are often used. The data stream is segmented into blocks of k information symbols, and each block is encoded into n codeword symbols. The codewords for successive k-symbol blocks are not coupled in any way by the encoder.

An alternative scheme divides the data stream into much smaller blocks of length k_0, which we will call information frames. These information frames typically contain no more than a few symbols. The information frames are encoded into codeword frames of length n_0. Rather than coding a single information frame into a single codeword frame, however, an information frame together with the previous m information frames are encoded into a single codeword frame. Hence successive codeword frames are coupled together by the encoding procedure.

The codes that one obtains in this way are called *tree codes*. The most important tree codes are those known as *convolutional codes*. Convolutional codes are tree codes that satisfy certain additional linearity and time-invariance properties. We shall first study the general notion of a tree code, but primarily we will be concerned with convolutional codes as a special case of tree codes.

12.1 TREE CODES AND TRELLIS CODES

We will begin the discussion of tree codes with the shift-register encoder of Fig. 12.1. Many of the basic definitions can be introduced using this circuit. An information sequence is shifted in, beginning at time zero, and continuing indefinitely. The stream of incoming information symbols is broken into segments, each of k_0 symbols, called *information frames*. An information frame may be as short as one symbol, and in practice it often is this short. The encoder can store m frames. During each frame time, a new information frame is shifted into the shift register, and the oldest information frame is shifted out and discarded. At the end of any frame time the encoder has stored the most recent m frames (a total of mk_0 information symbols). At the beginning of a frame, from the incoming information frame and the m stored frames, the encoder computes a single codeword frame of length n_0 symbols. This codeword frame is shifted out of the encoder as the next information frame is shifted in. Hence the channel must transmit n_0 codeword symbols for each k_0 information symbols.

The infinite set of all infinitely long codewords that one obtains by exciting this encoder with every possible input sequence is called an (n_0, k_0) *tree code*. The rate R of the tree code is defined as

$$R = \frac{k_0}{n_0}.$$

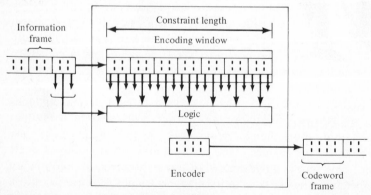

Figure 12.1 A shift-register encoder.

Let $v = mk_0$. This v is an important descriptor of a convolutional code. It is called the *constraint length*. This loose definition of constraint length is enough for most purposes (although a sharper definition is necessary in some cases). The formal definition will be given in the next section. The encoder of Fig. 12.1 has $k_0 = 3$, $n_0 = 5$, and $v = 21$.

There are several other length measures for a tree code. Let $k = (m + 1)k_0$. This k is closely related to the constraint length. We call it the *wordlength* of the convolutional code. The corresponding measure after encoding is called the *blocklength n*. It is given by

$$n = (m + 1)n_0 = k \frac{n_0}{k_0}.$$

The encoder of Fig. 12.1 has a blocklength of 40. The blocklength is the length of codeword that can be influenced by a single information frame. Because of implementation considerations, practical tree codes use very small integers for k_0 and n_0; typically k_0 is one. This means that the choice for the code's rate is limited. One cannot design a practical tree code with a rate very close to one, as can be conveniently done with a block code (such as a Reed-Solomon code).

A formal definition of a tree code follows.

□ **Definition 12.1.1** An (n_0, k_0) *tree code* is a mapping from the set of semi-infinite sequences of elements of $GF(q)$ into itself such that if for any M, two semi-infinite sequences agree in the first Mk_0 components, then their images agree in the first Mn_0 components. □

We can visualize a tree code mechanistically in terms of the encoder of Fig. 12.1. A tree code has associated with it a constraint length, possibly infinite, and a rate.

Four properties are imposed in various combinations to obtain special cases of tree codes. These properties should be examined in the context of Fig. 12.1.

Finite Constraint Length   The constraint length may be finite or may be infinite. Practical tree codes always have finite constraint length. Infinite-constraint-length codes are sometimes useful in theoretical studies, however. An (n_0, k_0) tree code with finite constraint length v, wordlength $k = v + k_0$, and blocklength n is also called an (n, k) *trellis code*.

Time Invariance   If two different input sequences agree except for a time shift by an integer number of frames, then the codeword sequences agree except for a time shift by the same integer number of frames.

Linearity   Any linear combination of two information sequences has a codeword that is the same linear combination of the codewords of the two information sequences. That is, if d_1 and d_2 are two information sequences with codewords $G(d_1)$ and $G(d_2)$, then $ad_1 + bd_2$ has codeword

$$G(ad_1 + bd_2) = aG(d_1) + bG(d_2).$$

Systematic A systematic tree code is one in which each information frame appears unaltered within the first k_0 symbols of the first codeword frame that it affects.

□ **Definition 12.1.2** An (n_0, k_0) tree code that is linear, time invariant, and has finite wordlength $k = (m + 1)k_0$ is called an (n, k) *convolutional code*. An (n, k) convolutional code that is systematic is called an (n, k) *systematic convolutional code.* □

Notice that we can refer to the same code as an (n_0, k_0) tree code or as an (n, k) convolutional code. In practical examples k is significantly larger than k_0, and there is no confusion.

□ **Definition 12.1.3** An (n_0, k_0) tree code that is time invariant and has finite wordlength k is called an (n, k) *sliding block code*. Hence a linear sliding block code is a convolutional code. □

A graphical illustration of the relationship between various classes of tree codes is shown in Fig. 12.2. Other possibilities exist, but these are the cases of major interest. Examples of encoders for two different convolutional codes are shown in Fig. 12.3, both with $n_0 = 2$, $k_0 = 1$. The first example is an encoder for a systematic (12, 6) binary convolutional code of constraint length 5. It has all of the special properties described previously. The second example is an encoder for a nonsystematic (6, 3) binary convolutional code of constraint length 2. In each case the input data is filtered twice, by the upper and lower taps coming off of the shift register. The two filter outputs are interleaved in time by inserting the filter outputs at each clock time into a buffer that is clocked out twice as fast as the incoming information.

Convolutional codes, and other trellis codes, can be described usefully in terms of a type of graph called a *trellis*; hence the name trellis code. A trellis is a graph whose nodes are in a rectangular grid, semi-infinite to the right; the number of nodes in each column is finite. The configuration of the branches connecting each column of nodes to the column of nodes on the right is the same for each column of nodes. Usually, nodes that cannot be reached by starting at the top left node and moving only to the right are not shown.

A typical trellis for a binary code alphabet is shown in the diagram of Fig. 12.4. This trellis is the right one for describing the second encoder of Fig. 12.3. In Fig. 12.5, it is shown labeled for use with that encoder. The nodes in each column of a trellis represent the q^v states that can be assumed by the

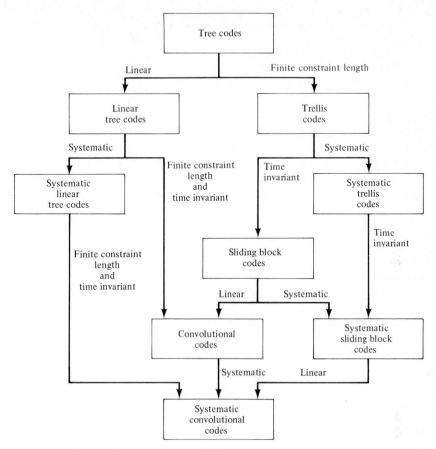

Figure 12.2 A hierarchy of tree codes.

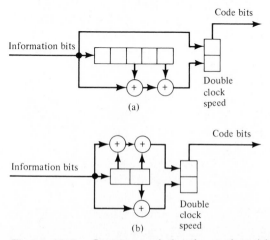

Figure 12.3 Some convolutional encoders. (a) An encoder for a binary (12, 6) convolutional code. (b) An encoder for a binary (6, 3) convolutional code.

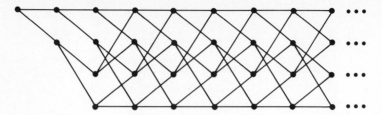

Figure 12.4 Trellis for a convolutional code.

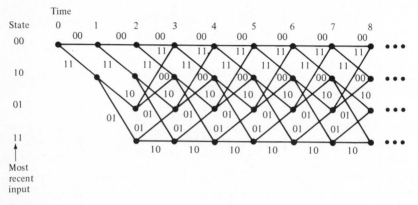

Figure 12.5 Trellis diagram for a (6, 3) convolutional code.

shift register. Each subsequent column represents the set of states at a subsequent bit time.

Each input frame causes the shift register to change state. This is represented by a branch to the next node. In the example, each branch is labeled with the two bits transmitted to the channel as the shift register enters the next state. In this simple example, the higher line leaving a node represents a zero input bit, and the lower line leaving a node represents a one input bit. In general, one would also label each branch with the k_0 input symbols to which it corresponds.

The labeled trellis represents the convolutional code in the sense that every path from left to right through the trellis specifies a codeword. The labels on the branches are identical for each segment and are linear in the sense that the linear combination of labels on any set of branches is a label on some branch.

The trellis diagram can be labeled under weaker constraints. If the labels are not linear, then as we have seen, the code is called a sliding block code. If the labels do not stay the same from frame to frame, the code is known by the general name of trellis code. Finally, if the number of states in successive frame times continues to increase without limit, the code is a general tree code.

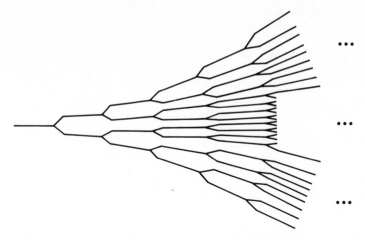

Figure 12.6   A tree for a binary tree code of rate ½.

A trellis code can also be represented as a kind of a graph known as a *tree*, shown in Fig. 12.6, in which the number of nodes and branches increases without limit as the tree grows to the right. Hence the name tree code. We then regard each node as a state corresponding to the total number of patterns of information symbols since time zero. For codes with an infinite constraint length, or even a moderately large constraint length, a tree is the right kind of graph to visualize. The codewords correspond to paths through the tree. For codes with a small constraint length, however, it is more convenient to use a trellis. As we have seen, everything about the code is described in terms of the most recent v symbols, and these suffice to define a state.

12.2 POLYNOMIAL DESCRIPTION OF CONVOLUTIONAL CODES

An $((m+1)n_0, (m+1)k_0)$ convolutional code over $GF(q)$ with constraint length $v = mk_0$ can be encoded by n_0 sets of finite-impulse-response (FIR) filters, each set consisting of k_0 FIR filters in $GF(q)$. The input to the encoder is a stream of symbols with a rate of k_0 symbols per unit time, and the output to the channel is a stream of n_0 symbols per unit time. Figure 12.7 shows an encoder for a binary convolutional code with $n_0 = 5$, $k_0 = 1$. Such an encoder consists of a bank of filters as well as an output timing buffer, which is needed to match the output rate to the filter rate. Figure 12.8 shows a similar encoder for a binary convolutional code with $n_0 = 5$, $k_0 = 3$. An input buffer is added to match the input rate to the filter rate.

Each FIR filter can be represented by a polynomial of degree of at most m. If the input stream is written as a polynomial—possibly of infinite length— the operation of the filter can be written as polynomial multiplication. In this way, the encoder for the convolutional code can be represented by a set

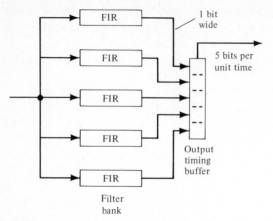

Figure 12.7 A convolutional encoder.

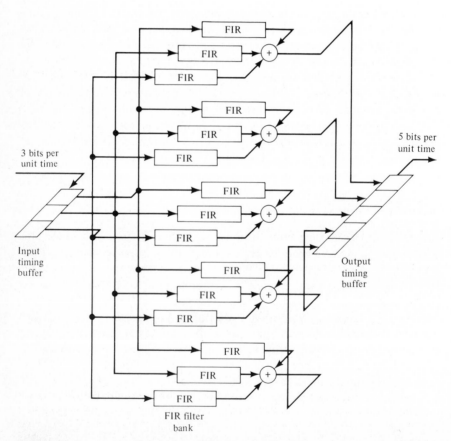

Figure 12.8 A convolutional encoder ($n_0 = 5$, $k_0 = 3$).

of polynomials, and thus the code itself can also be represented by this same set of polynomials. That is, the code is the set of codewords that this set of polynomials will produce. These polynomials are called the *generator polynomials* of the code. A generator polynomial of largest degree has degree equal to m.

In contrast to block codes, which are described by a single generator polynomial, a convolutional code requires multiple generator polynomials to describe it—a total of $k_0 n_0$ polynomials. Let $g_{ij}(x)$ for $i = 1, \ldots k_0$ and $j = 1, \ldots, n_0$ be the set of generator polynomials. These can be put together in a *generator-polynomial matrix*, a k_0 by n_0 matrix of polynomials given by

$$\mathbf{G}(x) = [g_{ij}(x)].$$

When k_0 is greater than one, it is not unusual for some of the generator polynomials to be the zero polynomial.

For example, the matrices of generator polynomials for the encoders shown in Figure 12.3 are

$$\mathbf{G}(x) = [1 \quad x^5 + x^3 + 1]$$

and

$$\mathbf{G}(x) = [x^2 + x + 1 \quad x^2 + 1].$$

Starting with the matrix of generator polynomials $\mathbf{G}(x)$, we give the formal definition of constraint length.

□ **Definition 12.2.1** Given the matrix of generator polynomials $[g_{ij}(x)]$, the *constraint length* of the convolutional code is*

$$v = \sum_{i=1}^{k_0} \max_j [\deg g_{ij}(x)].$$

The *wordlength* of the code is

$$k = k_0 \max_{i,j} [\deg g_{ij}(x) + 1],$$

and the *blocklength* of the code is

$$n = n_0 \max_{i,j} [\deg g_{ij}(x) + 1]. \qquad \square$$

For example, the convolutional codes whose encoders are shown in Fig. 12.9 have $v = 3$, $k = 6$, $n = 9$; and $v = 4$, $k = 6$, $n = 9$, respectively.

---

*Several different definitions of the term *constraint length* are in use. We find as compelling reasons for our choice its properties that a code with a smaller trellis has a smaller constraint length; the trellis always has q^v nodes; and any minimal encoder—either feedback or feedforward—always has v storage elements. Hence, v measures the complexity of the convolutional code. Our definitions of k and n also are useful at times and are also called "the constraint length" in the literature.

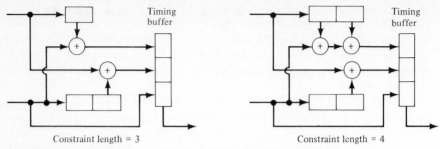

Constraint length = 3   Constraint length = 4

Figure 12.9   Encoders for two convolutional codes of rate ⅔.

Consider the input frame as k_0 symbols in parallel, and consider the sequence of input frames as k_0 sequences of symbols in parallel. These may be represented by k_0 information polynomials $d_i(x)$ for $i = 1, \ldots, k_0$, or as a row vector of such polynomials:

$$\mathbf{d}(x) = [d_1(x), d_2(x), \ldots, d_{k_0}(x)].$$

Similarly, the output codeword can be represented by n_0 codeword polynomials $c_j(x)$ for $j = 1, \ldots, n_0$, or as a vector of such polynomials

$$\mathbf{c}(x) = [c_j(x)] = [c_1(x), c_2(x), \ldots, c_{n_0}(x)].$$

The coefficients of the codeword polynomials are interleaved in order to pass them through the channel.

The encoding operation can now be described compactly as a vector-matrix product,

$$\mathbf{c}(x) = \mathbf{d}(x)\mathbf{G}(x),$$

or equivalently,

$$c_j(x) = \sum_{i=1}^{k_0} d_i(x)g_{ij}(x).$$

A *parity-check-polynomial matrix* $\mathbf{H}(x)$ is an $(n_0 - k_0)$ by n_0 matrix of polynomials that satisfies

$$\mathbf{G}(x)\mathbf{H}(x)^T = \mathbf{0}.$$

The *syndrome-polynomial vector* is given by

$$\mathbf{s}(x) = \mathbf{v}(x)\mathbf{H}(x)^T.$$

It is an $(n_0 - k_0)$-component row-vector of polynomials.

A systematic encoder for a convolutional code has a generator-polynomial matrix of the form

$$\mathbf{G}(x) = [\mathbf{I} \vdots \mathbf{P}(x)],$$

where $\mathbf{I}$ is a k_0 by k_0 identity matrix, and $\mathbf{P}(x)$ is a k_0 by $(n_0 - k_0)$ matrix of polynomials. For a systematic convolutional code, a parity-check-polynomial matrix can be written down immediately as

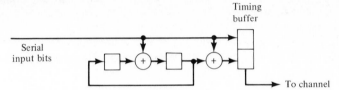

Figure 12.10   A systematic feedback encoder for a (6, 3) convolutional code.

$$H(x) = [-P(x)^T \mid I],$$

where I is an $(n_0 - k_0)$ by $(n_0 - k_0)$ identity matrix. It is straightforward to verify that

$$G(x)H(x)^T = 0.$$

Just as for block codes, it is more precise to speak of systematic encoders for convolutional codes rather than to speak of systematic convolutional codes. Systematic encoders for convolutional codes seem more satisfying because the information is visible and can be read directly if no errors are made. Contrary to the case for block codes, however (but in a restricted sense), not every convolutional code is equivalent to a systematic convolutional code, and some nonsystematic convolutional codes have superior distance structure. Because codewords that have not been encoded systematically do not display the information directly, they must be designed so that the information can be recovered in the absence of errors. The restricted notion of equivalence that is implicit here presumes that all encoders are feedforward devices made out of FIR filters. By using the feedback of polynomial division circuits, one can build a systematic encoder for any convolutional code. Figure 12.10 gives a systematic feedback encoder for the code corresponding to the trellis in Fig. 12.5.

We will first discuss the important special case where $k_0 = 1$. We simplify the notation when $k_0 = 1$ and write

$$G(x) = [g_1(x) \ g_2(x) \ \ldots \ g_{n_0}(x)]$$

and

$$c_j(x) = d(x)g_j(x) \qquad j = 1, \ldots, n_0.$$

For a systematic code $g_1(x) = 1$.

☐ **Definition 12.2.2**   A convolutional code whose generator polynomials $g_1(x), \ldots, g_{n_0}(x)$ satisfy

$$GCD[g_1(x), \ldots, g_{n_0}(x)] = x^a$$

for some a is called a *noncatastrophic convolutional code*. Otherwise, it is called a *catastrophic convolutional code*. ☐

Without loss of meaningful generality we can take $x^a = 1$, because otherwise it corresponds to a simple (and pointless) delay in each filter.

A noncatastrophic convolutional code can be decoded in the absence of errors by using the Euclidean algorithm for polynomials. This states that there exist polynomials $a_1(x), \ldots, a_{n_0}(x)$ with

$$a_1(x)g_1(x) + \cdots + a_{n_0}(x)g_{n_0}(x) = 1.$$

Therefore if the data polynomial $d(x)$ is encoded by

$$c_j(x) = d(x)g_j(x) \qquad j = 1, \ldots, n_0,$$

we can recover $d(x)$ by

$$d(x) = a_1(x)c_1(x) + \cdots + a_{n_0}(x)c_{n_0}(x),$$

as is readily checked by simple substitution.

An example is shown in Fig. 12.11. The data polynomial enters the circuit from the left, and the same data polynomial leaves from the right. The combined bit rate at points a and b is twice the input rate, however, and these points can be combined to form the channel codeword for a rate $\frac{1}{2}$ convolutional code. The redundancy at this point is used to find and correct errors; the more errors that can be corrected, the better the code.

The task of finding a good convolutional code is the task of finding a good set of relatively prime generator polynomials. It is not hard finding arbitrary sets of relatively prime polynomials. What is hard is finding sets that have good error-correcting ability.

In the general case, k_0 is greater than one. A noncatastrophic code is defined in terms of the $\binom{n_0}{k_0}$ different k_0 by k_0 submatrices of $\mathbf{G}(x)$. Let the set of these submatrices be indexed by l, and let $\Delta_l(x)$ be the determinant of the lth k_0 by k_0 submatrix.

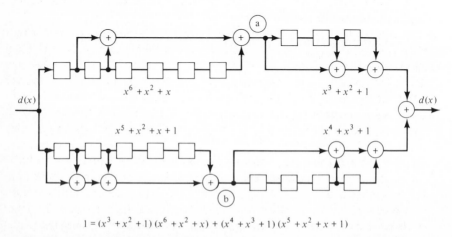

$$1 = (x^3 + x^2 + 1)(x^6 + x^2 + x) + (x^4 + x^3 + 1)(x^5 + x^2 + x + 1)$$

Figure 12.11 A transparent shift-register circuit.

☐ **Definition 12.2.3** A convolutional code whose generator-polynomial matrix $\mathbf{G}(x)$ has determinants $\Delta_l(x)$ for $l = 1, \ldots, \binom{n_0}{k_0}$ that satisfy

$$\mathrm{GCD}\left[\Delta_l(x) \quad l = 1, \ldots, \binom{n_0}{k_0}\right] = x^a$$

for some a is called a *noncatastrophic convolutional code*. Otherwise, it is called a *catastrophic convolutional code*. ☐

Just as in the previous case, a noncatastrophic code can be inverted. That is, there exists an n_0 by k_0 matrix of polynomials $\mathbf{G}^*(x)$ such that

$$\mathbf{G}^*(x)\mathbf{G}(x) = x^a\mathbf{I},$$

where $\mathbf{I}$ is the k_0 by k_0 identity matrix and x^a represents some fixed delay. It is generally difficult to find $\mathbf{G}^*(x)$, and we shall not deal with it further in the abstract case. If we deal only with systematic codes, then the condition of Definition 12.2.3 is always satisfied. Systematic codes are always noncatastrophic.

12.3 ERROR CORRECTION AND DISTANCE NOTIONS

When a convolutional codeword is passed through a channel, errors are made from time to time in the codeword symbols. The decoder must correct these errors by processing the codeword. The convolutional codeword, however, is so long that the decoder can only remember a part of it at a time. Although the codeword is infinite in length, all decoding decisions are made on codeword segments of finite length. But because of the structure of the code, no matter how one chops out a part of the received word for the decoder to work with, there is some interaction with other parts of the received word that the decoder does not see. Thus there may be useful information available that the decoder does not use.

Most of the study of decoding procedures for convolutional codes has been devoted to the task of correcting errors in the first frame. If this frame can be corrected and decoded, then the first frame of information is known. The effect of these information symbols on subsequent codeword frames can be computed and subtracted from subsequent codeword frames. Hence, the problem of decoding the second codeword frame is then the same as the problem of decoding the first codeword frame. Continuing in this way, if the first j frames can be successfully corrected, then the problem of decoding the $(j + 1)$th frame is the same as the problem of decoding the first frame. Many such decoding procedures are known. A procedure that uses the information symbols in a corrected frame explicitly to subtract the effect of these symbols in subsequent frames is called a *feedback procedure*. In other decoders, the computations are arranged so that the effect of earlier frames, properly decoded, on the current frame is zero.

In any decoder, occasionally the first frame of the codeword will not be corrected properly because too many errors have occurred. In some decoders, this can introduce decoding errors into subsequent frames, causing them to be decoded incorrectly. If it is possible for a single decoding-error event to induce an infinite number of additional errors in the codeword, then the decoder is said to be subject to *error propagation*. The existence of error propagation may be inherent in the choice of decoding algorithm, in which case it is called *ordinary error propagation*. It also may be endemic in the choice of a catastrophic generator polynomial for the convolutional code, in which case it is called *catastrophic error propagation*. A properly designed system can avoid both of these possibilities.

The number of symbols that the decoder can store is called the *decoding-window width*. In general, if one tries to detect as many error patterns as possible, then one can always get better performance by increasing the decoding-window width, but one eventually reaches a point of diminishing return. The decoding-window width must be at least as large as the block-length *n*, and often it is several times larger.

A convolutional code has many minimum distances, determined by the length of the initial codeword segment over which the minimum distance is measured. The distance measure is defined such that if two codewords both decode into the same first information frame, then they can be considered equivalent.

□ **Definition 12.3.1** The *lth minimum distance* d_l^* of a convolutional code is equal to the smallest Hamming distance between any two initial codeword segments *l* frames long that disagree in the initial frame. If *l* equals $m + 1$, then this is called simply the *minimum distance* and is denoted d^*. The sequence $d_1^*, d_2^*, d_3^*, \ldots$ is called the *distance profile* of the convolutional code. □

Because a convolutional code is linear, one of the two codewords might just as well be the all-zero word. The *l*th minimum distance is then equal to the weight of the smallest-weight codeword segment *l* frames long that is nonzero in the first frame. This can be read off a labeled trellis. From Fig. 12.5 we can see that that convolutional code has $d_1^* = 2$, $d_2^* = 3$, $d_3^* = 5$, and $d_i^* = 5$ for all *i* greater than 3.

Suppose that a convolutional code has *l*th minimum distance d_l^*. If at most *t* errors satisfying

$$2t + 1 \leqslant d_l^*$$

occur in the first *l* frames, then those that occur in the first codeword frame can be corrected. In particular, take $l = m + 1$; the minimum distance d^* of the code is equal to d_{m+1}^*. Then if t satisfies

$$2t + 1 \leqslant d^*,$$

the code can correct the first codeword frame if at most t errors have occurred in the first blocklength. Such a code is called a *t-error-correcting convolutional code*. A more appropriate name, although too cumbersome to actually use, is a *t-error-per-blocklength-correcting convolutional code*.

□ **Definition 12.3.2** The *free distance* of a convolutional code $\mathscr{C}$ is given by

$$d_\infty = \max_l d_l. \qquad \qquad \square$$

It is apparent that

$$d_{m+1} \leqslant d_{m+2} \leqslant \cdots \leqslant d_\infty.$$

□ **Definition 12.3.3** The *free length* n_∞ of a convolutional code is the length of the nonzero segment of a smallest-weight convolutional codeword of nonzero weight. Thus $d_l = d_\infty$ if $l = n_\infty$, and $d_l < d_\infty$ if $l < n_\infty$. □

In the example of Fig. 12.5, the free distance equals 5, and the free length equals 6. In this example the free length is equal to the blocklength of the convolutional code. In general it will be longer than the blocklength.

12.4 MATRIX DESCRIPTION OF CONVOLUTIONAL CODES

A convolutional code consists of an infinite number of infinitely long codewords. It is linear and can be described by an infinite generator matrix. A great many generator matrices can be used to describe each code, but only a few of them are convenient to deal with. Even in the best case, a generator matrix for a convolutional code is more cumbersome than a generator matrix for a block code.

The generator polynomials, indexed by i and j, can be written

$$g_{ij}(x) = \sum_l g_{ijl} x^l.$$

To get a generator matrix, the coefficients g_{ijl} are arranged into matrix form. For each l, let $\mathbf{G}_l$ be the k_0 by n_0 matrix

$$\mathbf{G}_l = [g_{ijl}].$$

Then the generator matrix for the convolutional code truncated to a block code of blocklength n is

$$
\mathbf{G}^{(n)} = \begin{bmatrix}
\mathbf{G}_0 & \mathbf{G}_1 & \mathbf{G}_2 & \cdots & \mathbf{G}_m \\
\mathbf{0} & \mathbf{G}_0 & \mathbf{G}_1 & \cdots & \mathbf{G}_{m-1} \\
\mathbf{0} & \mathbf{0} & \mathbf{G}_0 & \cdots & \mathbf{G}_{m-2} \\
\vdots & & & & \vdots \\
\mathbf{0} & \mathbf{0} & \mathbf{0} & & \mathbf{G}_0
\end{bmatrix},
$$

where each $\mathbf{0}$ is a k_0 by n_0 matrix of zeros. The generator matrix for the convolutional code is

$$
\mathbf{G} = \begin{bmatrix}
\mathbf{G}_0 & \mathbf{G}_1 & \mathbf{G}_2 & \cdots & \mathbf{G}_m & \mathbf{0} & & \mathbf{0} & \mathbf{0} & \mathbf{0} & \cdots \\
\mathbf{0} & \mathbf{G}_0 & \mathbf{G}_1 & \cdots & \mathbf{G}_{m-1} & \mathbf{G}_m & & \mathbf{0} & \mathbf{0} & \mathbf{0} & \cdots \\
\mathbf{0} & \mathbf{0} & \mathbf{G}_0 & \cdots & \mathbf{G}_{m-2} & \mathbf{G}_{m-1} & & \mathbf{G}_m & \mathbf{0} & \mathbf{0} & \cdots \\
& \vdots
\end{bmatrix},
$$

where the matrix continues indefinitely down and to the right. Except for the diagonal band of m nonzero submatrices, all other entries are equal to zero.

For a systematic convolutional code, these two matrices can also be written

$$
\mathbf{G}^{(n)} = \begin{bmatrix}
\mathbf{I} & \mathbf{P}_0 & \mathbf{0} & \mathbf{P}_1 & \mathbf{0} & \mathbf{P}_2 & \cdots & \mathbf{0} & \mathbf{P}_m \\
\mathbf{0} & \mathbf{0} & \mathbf{I} & \mathbf{P}_0 & \mathbf{0} & \mathbf{P}_1 & \cdots & \mathbf{0} & \mathbf{P}_{m-1} \\
\mathbf{0} & \mathbf{0} & \mathbf{0} & \mathbf{0} & \mathbf{I} & \mathbf{P}_0 & \cdots & \mathbf{0} & \mathbf{P}_{m-2} \\
\vdots & & & & & & & \vdots \\
\mathbf{0} & \mathbf{0} & \mathbf{0} & \mathbf{0} & \mathbf{0} & \mathbf{0} & \cdots & \mathbf{I} & \mathbf{P}_0
\end{bmatrix}
$$

and

$$
\mathbf{G} = \begin{bmatrix}
\mathbf{I} & \mathbf{P}_0 & \mathbf{0} & \mathbf{P}_1 & \mathbf{0} & \mathbf{P}_2 & \cdots & \mathbf{0} & \mathbf{P}_m & \mathbf{0} & \mathbf{0} & \mathbf{0} & \mathbf{0} & \cdots \\
\mathbf{0} & \mathbf{0} & \mathbf{I} & \mathbf{P}_0 & \mathbf{0} & \mathbf{P}_1 & \cdots & \mathbf{0} & \mathbf{P}_{m-1} & \mathbf{0} & \mathbf{P}_m & \mathbf{0} & \mathbf{0} & \cdots \\
\mathbf{0} & \mathbf{0} & \mathbf{0} & \mathbf{0} & \mathbf{I} & \mathbf{P}_0 & \cdots & \mathbf{0} & \mathbf{P}_{m-2} & \mathbf{0} & \mathbf{P}_{m-1} & \mathbf{0} & \mathbf{P}_m & \cdots \\
\vdots & & & & & & & & \vdots & \mathbf{0} & \mathbf{P}_{m-2} & \mathbf{0} & \mathbf{P}_{m-1} & \cdots \\
& & & & & & & & & & \vdots & \mathbf{0} & \mathbf{P}_{m-2} & \cdots \\
& & & & & & & & & & & & \vdots
\end{bmatrix}
$$

where the pattern repeats right-shifted in every row, and unspecified matrix entries to the left and right are filled with zeros. Here $\mathbf{I}$ is a k_0 by k_0 identity matrix, $\mathbf{0}$ is a k_0 by k_0 matrix of zeros, and $\mathbf{P}_0, \ldots, \mathbf{P}_m$ are k_0 by $(n_0 - k_0)$ matrices. The first row describes the encoding of the first information frame into the first m codeword frames. One should interpret this matrix expression in terms of the shift-register description of the encoder.

The first information frame is encoded into the first codeword frame by the upper left-hand block of $\mathbf{G}$:

$$
\mathbf{G}^{(n_0)} = \begin{bmatrix} \mathbf{I} & \mathbf{P}_0 \end{bmatrix}.
$$

Similarly, the first two information frames are encoded into the first two codeword frames by

$$G^{(2n_0)} = \begin{bmatrix} I & P_0 & 0 & P_1 \\ 0 & 0 & I & P_0 \end{bmatrix}.$$

A parity-check matrix is any matrix **H** that satisfies

$$G^{(ln_0)}H^{(ln_0)T} = 0 \qquad l = 0, 1, 2, \ldots,$$

where $G^{(ln_0)}$ and $H^{(ln_0)}$ are the upper left-hand submatrices of **G** and **H** corresponding to l frames. A parity-check matrix **H**, which is an infinite-dimensional matrix, can be constructed from inspection of **G**. Choose the matrix

$$H = \begin{bmatrix} P_0^T & -I & & & & & & & & \cdots \\ P_1^T & 0 & P_0^T & -I & & & & & \\ P_2^T & 0 & P_1^T & 0 & P_0^T & -I & & & \\ \vdots & & & & & & & & \\ P_m^T & 0 & P_{m-1}^T & 0 & P_{m-2}^T & 0 & \cdots & P_0^T & -I & \cdots \\ & & P_m^T & 0 & P_{m-1}^T & 0 & \cdots & & \\ & & & & P_m^T & 0 & \cdots & & \end{bmatrix},$$

where, again, unspecified entries are all zeros.

☐ **Example** A systematic (4, 2) binary convolutional code with $k_0 = 1$ and $m = 1$ is described by the 1 by 1 matrices $P_0 = 1$ and $P_1 = 1$. Hence

$$G = \begin{bmatrix} 1 & 1 & 0 & 1 & & & \\ & & 1 & 1 & 0 & 1 & \\ & & & & 1 & 1 & 0 & 1 \\ & & & & & \cdots & \\ & & & & & & \cdots \end{bmatrix}$$

and

$$H = \begin{bmatrix} 1 & 1 & & & \\ 1 & 0 & 1 & 1 & \\ & & 1 & 0 & 1 & 1 \\ & & & \cdots & \\ & & & & \cdots \end{bmatrix}.$$

☐

☐ **Example** A systematic (12, 4) binary convolutional code with $k_0 = 1$ and $m = 3$ is given by $P_0 = [11]$, $P_1 = [01]$, $P_2 = [10]$, and $P_3 = [11]$. Hence

$$G = \begin{bmatrix} 1 & 1 & 1 & 0 & 0 & 1 & 0 & 1 & 0 & 0 & 1 & 1 & & & & \\ & & & 1 & 1 & 1 & 0 & 0 & 1 & 0 & 1 & 0 & 0 & 1 & 1 & \\ & & & & & & 1 & 1 & 1 & 0 & 0 & 1 & 0 & 1 & 0 & 0 & 1 & 1 \\ & & & & & & & & & 1 & 1 & 1 & 0 & 0 & 1 & 0 & 1 & 0 & 0 & 1 & 1 \\ & & & & & & & & & & & \vdots \end{bmatrix}$$

and

$$
\mathbf{H} = \begin{bmatrix}
1\ 1\ 0 \\
1\ 0\ 1 \\
0\ 0\ 0\ 1\ 1\ 0 \\
1\ 0\ 0\ 1\ 0\ 1 \\
1\ 0\ 0\ 0\ 0\ 0\ 1\ 1\ 0 \\
0\ 0\ 0\ 1\ 0\ 0\ 1\ 0\ 1 \\
1\ 0\ 0\ 1\ 0\ 0\ 0\ 0\ 0\ 1\ 1\ 0 \\
1\ 0\ 0\ 0\ 0\ 0\ 1\ 0\ 0\ 1\ 0\ 1 \\
\quad\ 1\ 0\ 0\ 1\ 0\ 0\ 0\ 0\ 0\ 1\ 1\ 0 \\
\quad\ 1\ 0\ 0\ 0\ 0\ 0\ 1\ 0\ 0\ 1\ 0\ 1 \\
\quad\ \vdots
\end{bmatrix}.
$$

12.5 SOME SIMPLE CONVOLUTIONAL CODES

Only a few constructive classes of convolutional codes are known. No classes with an algebraic structure comparable to that of the t-error-correcting BCH codes are known, and thus no constructive method exists for finding convolutional codes of long constraint length. Most of the best convolutional codes known and in use today have been discovered by computer search.

This section will first describe a general class of single-error-correcting convolutional codes. The section will then close with lists of some of the best convolutional codes known to the current literature.

A class of single-error-correcting binary convolutional codes, called *Wyner-Ash codes*, is analogous to the class of Hamming codes. For each positive integer m, there is an $((m+1)2^m, (m+1)(2^m-1))$ Wyner-Ash code. The code is defined in terms of the parity-check matrix $\mathbf{H}'$ of the Hamming $(2^m-1, 2^m-1-m)$ code. This is an m by (2^m-1) parity-check matrix in which all 2^m-1 columns are distinct and nonzero. Choose such a matrix; use the rows to define a set of 1 by (2^m-1) matrices $\mathbf{P}_1^T,\ldots,\mathbf{P}_m^T$; and let $\mathbf{P}_0^T$ be the row vector whose 2^m-1 elements are all ones. Then the parity-check matrix for the Wyner-Ash code is

$$
\mathbf{H} = \begin{bmatrix}
\mathbf{P}_0^T & 1 & 0 & 0 & 0 & 0 & 0 & \cdots \\
\mathbf{P}_1^T & 0 & \mathbf{P}_0^T & 1 & 0 & 0 & 0 & 0 \\
\mathbf{P}_2^T & 0 & \mathbf{P}_1^T & 0 & \mathbf{P}_0^T & 1 & 0 & 0 \\
\vdots & & \vdots & & \mathbf{P}_1^T & & & \\
\mathbf{P}_m^T & 0 & & & & & & \\
0 & 0 & \mathbf{P}_m^T & 0 & & & & \\
\vdots & \vdots & & & & & &
\end{bmatrix}
$$

and

$$\mathbf{H}^{((m+1)2m)} = \begin{bmatrix} \mathbf{P}_0^T & 1 & 0 & & 0 & 0 & & 0 \\ \mathbf{P}_1^T & 0 & \mathbf{P}_0^T & & 1 & 0 & & 0 \\ \mathbf{P}_2^T & 0 & \mathbf{P}_1^T & & 0 & \mathbf{P}_0^T & & 1 \\ \vdots & & & & & & & \\ \mathbf{P}_m^T & 0 & \mathbf{P}_{m-1}^T & 0 & \mathbf{P}_{m-2}^T & 0 & \cdots & \mathbf{P}_0^T & 1 \end{bmatrix}$$

where **1** is a 1 by 1 matrix containing a single one, and **0** is a 1 by 1 matrix containing a single zero.

□ **Theorem 12.5.1** The Wyner-Ash code has minimum distance d^* equal to 3 and thus is a single-error-correcting convolutional code.

Proof The definition of minimum distance requires that the two codewords differ in the first frame. The code is linear, and thus we can take one codeword to be the all-zero codeword and the second to have a one in the first frame. Because $\mathbf{c}\mathbf{H}^T = 0$ for codewords, the sum of those columns of **H** where **c** is nonzero equals zero. The top row of **H** is nonzero only in the first frame, and thus there must be at least two ones in the first frame. Finally, because any two columns of **H** in the first frame are linearly independent, there must be another one somewhere in the codeword, and the minimum distance is at least 3.

To show that it is exactly 3, it suffices to show that there are three columns adding to zero. Take the column where $\mathbf{P}_0^T, \ldots, \mathbf{P}_m^T$ are all equal to one. The sum of this column in the first frame with the same column in the second frame equals $(1, 0, 0, \ldots, 0)^T$, and this column appears in the first frame. Hence, there are three columns adding to zero. □

For example, the Wyner-Ash (12, 9) code is constructed with $m = 2$. The parity-check matrix is

$$\mathbf{H} = \begin{bmatrix} 1 & 1 & 1 & 1 & & & & & & & & \\ 1 & 1 & 0 & 0 & 1 & 1 & 1 & 1 & & & & \\ 1 & 0 & 1 & 0 & 1 & 1 & 0 & 0 & 1 & 1 & 1 & 1 \\ 0 & 0 & 0 & 0 & 1 & 0 & 1 & 0 & 1 & 1 & 0 & 0 & 1 & 1 & 1 & 1 \\ 0 & 0 & 0 & 0 & 0 & 0 & 0 & 0 & 1 & 0 & 1 & 0 & 1 & 1 & 0 & 0 \\ \vdots & & & & \vdots & & & & \vdots & & & & \vdots \end{bmatrix} \cdots$$

When the code is truncated to a parity-check matrix of blocklength 12, the parity-check matrix is

$$\mathbf{H}^{(12)} = \begin{bmatrix} 1 & 1 & 1 & 1 & 0 & 0 & 0 & 0 & 0 & 0 & 0 & 0 \\ 1 & 1 & 0 & 0 & 1 & 1 & 1 & 1 & 0 & 0 & 0 & 0 \\ 1 & 0 & 1 & 0 & 1 & 1 & 0 & 0 & 1 & 1 & 1 & 1 \end{bmatrix}.$$

The generator matrix is

$$G = \begin{bmatrix} 1\ 0\ 0 & 1 & 0\ 0\ 0 & 1 & 0\ 0\ 0 & 1 \\ 0\ 1\ 0 & 1 & 0\ 0\ 0 & 1 & 0\ 0\ 0 & 0 \\ 0\ 0\ 1 & 1 & 0\ 0\ 0 & 0 & 0\ 0\ 0 & 1 \\ & 1\ 0\ 0 & 1 & 0\ 0\ 0 & 1 & 0\ 0\ 0 & 1 \\ & 0\ 1\ 0 & 1 & 0\ 0\ 0 & 1 & 0\ 0\ 0 & 0 \\ & 0\ 0\ 1 & 1 & 0\ 0\ 0 & 0 & 0\ 0\ 0 & 1 \\ & & 1\ 0\ 0 & 1 & 0\ 0\ 0 & 1 & 0\ 0\ 0 & 1 \\ & & 0\ 1\ 0 & 1 & 0\ 0\ 0 & 1 & 0\ 0\ 0 & 0 \cdots \\ & & 0\ 0\ 1 & 1 & 0\ 0\ 0 & 0 & 0\ 0\ 0 & 1 \\ \vdots & & \vdots & & & \end{bmatrix},$$

and the generator matrix for a code truncated to a blocklength of 12 is

$$G^{(12)} = \begin{bmatrix} 1\ 0\ 0 & 1 & 0\ 0\ 0 & 1 & 0\ 0\ 0 & 1 \\ 0\ 1\ 0 & 1 & 0\ 0\ 0 & 1 & 0\ 0\ 0 & 0 \\ 0\ 0\ 1 & 1 & 0\ 0\ 0 & 0 & 0\ 0\ 0 & 1 \end{bmatrix}.$$

It is clear by inspection of $G^{(12)}$ that within the block of length 12, every non-zero codeword has a weight of 3 or greater. Consequently, the code can correct one error in a block of length 12.

An encoder for the (12, 9) Wyner-Ash code is shown in Fig. 12.12. The circuit shows a separate FIR filter for each generator polynomial.

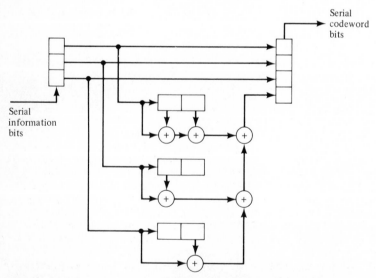

Figure 12.12   An encoder for the (12, 9) Wyner-Ash code.

Most of the best-regarded convolutional codes known have been obtained by computer search. Figure 12.13 tabulates many such codes.

(n, k, d_∞)	Matrix of Generator Polynomials (in Terms of Polynomial Coefficients)		
$(6, 3, 5)$	$(x^2 + 1)$ 101	$(x^2 + x + 1)$ 111	
$(8, 4, 6)$	$(x^3 + x + 1)$ 1011	$(x^3 + x^2 + x + 1)$ 1111	
$(10, 5, 7)$	11001	10111	
$(12, 6, 8)$	110101	101111	
$(14, 7, 10)$	1101101	1001111	
$(16, 8, 10)$	11100101	10011111	
$(18, 9, 12)$	100011101	110101111	
$(20, 10, 12)$	1110111001	1010011011	
$(22, 11, 14)$	10111011001	10001101111	
$(24, 12, 15)$	101110110001	110010111101	
$(26, 13, 16)$	1101101010001	1000110111111	
$(28, 14, 16)$	10111101110001	1100101001101	

(n, k, d_∞)			
$(9, 3, 8)$	101	111	111
$(12, 4, 10)$	1101	1011	1111
$(15, 5, 12)$	10101	11011	11111
$(18, 6, 13)$	111001	110101	101111
$(21, 7, 15)$	1101101	1010011	1011111
$(24, 8, 16)$	10101001	10011011	11101111
$(27, 9, 18)$	111101101	110011011	100100111
$(30, 10, 20)$	111001001	1010111101	1101100111
$(33, 11, 22)$	11010111001	10011101101	10111110011
$(36, 12, 24)$	11101111001	110010111101	10101010011
$(39, 13, 24)$	1101101010001	1011110110001	1000110111111
$(42, 14, 26)$	10100101110001	10001101110111	1011101001111

(n, k, d_∞)				
$(12, 3, 10)$	101	111	111	111
$(16, 4, 13)$	1101	1011	1011	1111
$(20, 5, 16)$	10101	11011	10111	11111
$(24, 6, 18)$	110101	111011	100111	101111
$(28, 7, 20)$	1011101	1011101	1110011	1100111
$(32, 8, 22)$	10111001	10111101	11010011	11110111
$(36, 9, 24)$	110011001	101110101	110110111	101001111
$(40, 10, 27)$	1111001001	1010111101	1101100111	1101010111
$(44, 11, 29)$	11101011001	11010111001	10011101101	10111110011
$(48, 12, 32)$	111011111001	110010111101	101011010011	101101001111
$(52, 13, 33)$	1010011001001	1111110010101	1101111011011	1110101110111
$(56, 14, 36)$	11010010010001	1011110011001	11101010110111	11111010110111

Figure 12.13   Noncatastrophic binary convolutional codes with maximum free distance.

12.6 SYNDROME DECODING ALGORITHMS

Suppose that we receive an infinite-length sequence $\mathbf{v}$ that consists of a convolutional codeword and an error pattern:

$$\mathbf{v} = \mathbf{c} + \mathbf{e}.$$

Just as for block codes, we can compute the syndrome:

$$\mathbf{s} = \mathbf{v}\mathbf{H}^T = \mathbf{e}\mathbf{H}^T.$$

Now, however, the syndrome has infinite length. The decoder does not look at the entire syndrome at once. It works from the end, computing components of $\mathbf{s}$ as it goes, correcting errors, and discarding components of $\mathbf{s}$ when they are too old. The decoder contains a table of syndrome segments and the error-pattern segment that causes each syndrome segment. When the decoder sees a syndrome segment that is in the table, it can correct the initial segment of the codeword.

We will develop the various forms of syndrome decoders by way of examples. First, we will give a decoder for the (12, 9) Wyner-Ash code. This is shown in Fig. 12.14. The incoming serial bit stream is converted to n_0

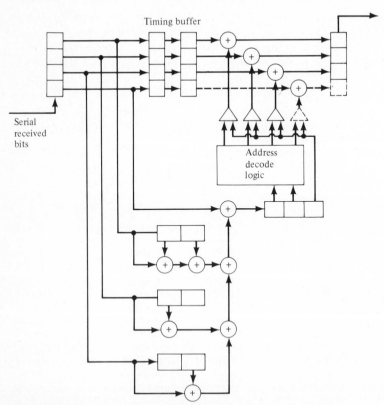

Figure 12.14 Decoding table for the (12, 9) Wyner-Ash code.

parallel lines, and the syndrome is computed by recomputing the parity bit from the received information bits and comparing it with the received parity bit. We need to compute only enough syndrome bits so that a single error in the first frame can be corrected. The possible patterns of a single error in the first three frames and the first three syndrome bits are tabulated in Fig. 12.15. Notice that the rightmost bit is a one if and only if an error has occurred in the first frame. The other two syndrome bits then specify the location of the error in the first frame.

The elements shown with dotted lines in Figure 12.14 can be included if it is desired to reconstruct the codeword including the parity bits. Otherwise, these elements can be eliminated.

One more problem must be dealt with. After the first frame is corrected, the syndrome must be modified so that it does not cause a false correction in the next frame. Several techniques are available for handling this, and although they are all satisfactory for this code, they can be quite different in a more powerful code. Two options are:

1. Set the syndrome register to zero each time an error is corrected.
2. Subtract the syndrome of the correction from the syndrome register.

The first option is peculiar to single-error-correcting codes. We will explore the second option with the aid of a somewhat more difficult example.

The (6, 3) double-error-correcting code is given by the encoder of Fig. 12.3. A decoder is shown in Fig. 12.16. The decoder is based on the syndromes tabulated in Fig. 12.17. This circuit will correct two errors within the first

Error Pattern				Syndrome
Fourth Frame	Third Frame	Second Frame	First Frame	
· · · · · · ·	0 0 0 0	0 0 0 0	0 0 0 1	1 1 1
	0 0 0 0	0 0 0 0	0 0 1 0	0 1 1
	0 0 0 0	0 0 0 0	0 1 0 0	1 0 1
	0 0 0 0	0 0 0 0	1 0 0 0	0 0 1
	0 0 0 0	0 0 0 1	0 0 0 0	1 1 0
	0 0 0 0	0 0 1 0	0 0 0 0	1 1 0
	0 0 0 0	0 1 0 0	0 0 0 0	0 1 0
	0 0 0 0	1 0 0 0	0 0 0 0	0 1 0
	0 0 0 1	0 0 0 0	0 0 0 0	1 0 0
	0 0 1 0	0 0 0 0	0 0 0 0	1 0 0
	0 1 0 0	0 0 0 0	0 0 0 0	1 0 0
	1 0 0 0	0 0 0 0	0 0 0 0	1 0 0

Figure 12.15 Decoding table for (12.9) Wyner-Ash code.

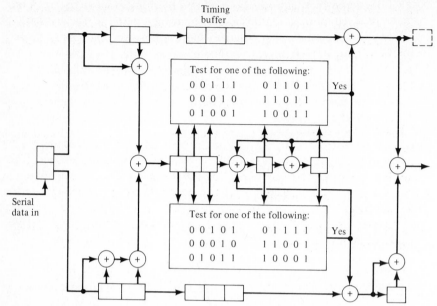

Figure 12.16   Decoding table for a (6, 3) convolutional code.

	Error Pattern			Syndrome
Fourth Frame	Third Frame	Second Frame	First Frame	
. . . .	0 0	0 0	0 1	· · · 0 0 1 1 1
	0 0	0 0	1 0	0 0 1 0 1
	0 0	0 0	1 1	0 0 0 1 0
	0 0	0 1	0 1	0 1 0 0 1
	0 0	1 0	0 1	0 1 1 0 1
	0 1	0 0	0 1	1 1 0 1 1
	1 0	0 0	0 1	1 0 0 1 1
	0 0	0 1	1 0	0 1 0 1 1
	0 0	1 0	1 0	0 1 1 1 1
	0 1	0 0	1 0	1 1 0 0 1
	1 0	0 0	1 0	1 0 0 0 1

Figure 12.17   Decoding table for a (6, 3) convolutional code.

six bits. The feedback will remove from the syndrome register the contribution of each error that is corrected. Because the code is not a systematic code, the information bit must be recovered from the corrected codeword. The circuit uses the relationship

$$1 = GCD[x^2 + x + 1, x^2 + 1]$$
$$= x(x^2 + x + 1) + (x + 1)(x^2 + 1)$$

to recover the information.

The decoder of Fig. 12.16 is not a complete decoder because many syndromes exist that are not used. In principle one could decode some additional error patterns by tabulating other syndromes and expanding the length of the syndrome memory. In practice, however, selecting another code of longer blocklength is probably a better way to improve performance. Further, before trying to extend a syndrome decoder to a complete decoder, one should consider the Viterbi decoder described in Section 12.8.

Error Pattern	Syndrome
$\cdots$ 0 0 0 0 0 0 0 0 0 0 0 1	$\cdots$ 1 1 1 0 0 1
0 0 0 0 0 0 0 0 0 0 1 1	1 1 1 0 0 0
0 0 0 0 0 0 0 0 0 1 0 1	0 0 1 0 1 1
0 0 0 0 0 0 0 0 1 0 0 1	1 1 1 0 1 1
0 0 0 0 0 0 0 1 0 0 0 1	0 1 1 1 0 1
0 0 0 0 0 0 1 0 0 0 0 1	1 1 1 1 0 1
0 0 0 0 0 1 0 0 0 0 0 1	1 1 0 0 0 1
0 0 0 0 1 0 0 0 0 0 0 1	1 1 0 0 0 1
0 0 0 1 0 0 0 0 0 0 0 1	1 0 1 0 0 1
0 0 1 0 0 0 0 0 0 0 0 1	1 1 0 0 0 1
0 1 0 0 0 0 0 0 0 0 0 1	0 1 1 0 0 1
1 0 0 0 0 0 0 0 0 0 0 1	0 1 1 0 0 1
0 0 0 0 0 0 0 0 0 0 1 0	0 0 0 0 0 1
0 0 0 0 0 0 0 0 0 1 1 0	1 1 0 0 1 1
0 0 0 0 0 0 0 0 1 0 1 0	0 0 0 0 1 1
0 0 0 0 0 0 0 1 0 0 1 0	1 0 0 1 0 1
0 0 0 0 0 0 1 0 0 0 1 0	0 0 0 1 0 1
0 0 0 0 0 1 0 0 0 0 1 0	0 0 1 0 0 1
0 0 0 0 1 0 0 0 0 0 1 0	0 0 1 0 0 1
0 0 0 1 0 0 0 0 0 0 1 0	0 1 0 0 0 1
0 0 1 0 0 0 0 0 0 0 1 0	0 1 0 0 0 1
0 1 0 0 0 0 0 0 0 0 1 0	1 0 0 0 0 1
1 0 0 0 0 0 0 0 0 0 1 0	1 0 0 0 0 1

Figure 12.18 Decoding table for a (12, 6) convolutional code.

The final example of this section is a systematic (12, 6) convolutional code. This code can correct two errors in a block of length 12. We will study this code again later, in Section 13.4, as a majority-decodable code. In this section, however, we use syndrome decoding. A decoding table is shown in

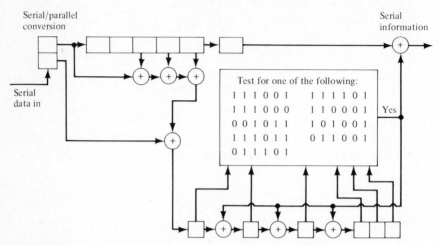

Figure 12.19 A decoder for a (12, 6) convolutional code.

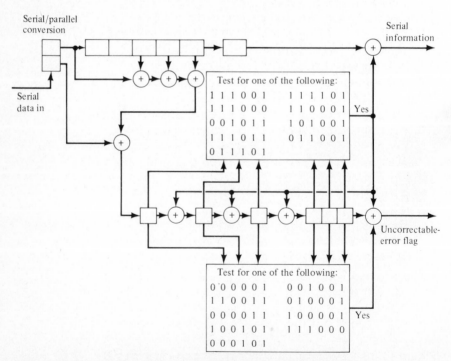

Figure 12.20 Another decoder for a (12, 6) convolutional code.

Fig. 12.18. The syndromes above the horizontal line are for error patterns with an error in the rightmost information bit, and those below the line are for error patterns with an error in the rightmost parity bit but no error in the rightmost information bit. The decoder of Fig. 12.19 only tests for syndromes above the horizontal line and thus provides correct information bits whenever the error pattern is within the design limits of the code. The decoder will not detect uncorrectable, but detectable, error patterns, however. This requires that syndromes below the line also be tested. Such a decoder, with provision for error detection, is shown in Fig. 12.20.

12.7 CONVOLUTIONAL CODES FOR CORRECTING BURST ERRORS

A burst error of length t is any sequence of t symbols, the first and last of which are nonzero. In an infinitely long word received by a decoder for a convolutional code, many errors may occur, and we may think of these errors as grouped into a number of bursts of various lengths. If the individual bursts come infrequently, then the decoder must only contend with one burst error at a time. A convolutional code for which a decoder can correct any single burst error of length t provided that other burst errors are far enough away is called a convolutional code with burst-correcting ability t.

Any t-error-correcting (n, k) convolutional code will of course correct any burst of length t. Convolutional codes for correcting longer bursts can be obtained by interleaving. To get a (jn, jk) convolutional code from an (n, k) code, take j copies of the encoder and merge the codewords by alternating the symbols. If the original code can correct any burst error of length t, it is apparent that the interleaved code can correct any burst error of length jt. For example, the (14, 7) systematic convolutional code of constraint length 6 with generator polynomials

$$g_1(x) = 1 \qquad g_2(x) = x^6 + x^5 + x^2 + 1$$

can correct any two bit errors in any interval of length 14. By taking four copies of the (14, 7) code and interleaving the bits, one obtains a (56, 28) code that will correct any burst of length 8.

The technique of interleaving creates a convolutional code from a convolutional code. If $g(x)$ is a generator polynomial of the original code, then $g(x^j)$ is the generator polynomial of the interleaved code. The generator polynomials of the above example become stretched into the new polynomials

$$g_1(x) = 1 \qquad g_2(x) = x^{24} + x^{20} + x^8 + 1.$$

This is the same behavior as was seen for interleaving cyclic block codes.

One can construct many burst-error-correcting convolutional codes by interleaving the short random-error-correcting convolutional codes tabulated in Section 12.5. The interleaved codes will correct not only burst errors but also many patterns of random errors. If only burst errors are to be corrected, however, one can get better performance by using a code developed specifically for correcting burst errors. The Iwadare codes are such a class of codes, capable of correcting any burst of length λn_0 or less, where λ is a design parameter.

□ **Definition 12.7.1** Let λ and n_0 be any positive integers. An *Iwadare code* is a systematic binary burst-error-correcting convolutional code with an $(n_0 - 1)$ by n_0 matrix of generator polynomials given by

$$\mathbf{G}(x) = \begin{bmatrix} 1 & & & g_1(x) \\ & 1 & & g_2(x) \\ & & \ddots & \vdots \\ & & & 1 & g_{(n_0-1)}(x) \end{bmatrix},$$

where matrix element $g_{in_0}(x)$ has been abbreviated to $g_i(x)$ and is given by

$$g_i(x) = x^{(\lambda+1)(2n_0-i)+i-3} + x^{(\lambda+1)(n_0-i)-1} \qquad \text{for } i = 1, \ldots, n_0 - 1. \quad □$$

The largest-degree generator polynomial is $g_1(x)$, which has a degree of $(\lambda+1)(2n_0-1)-2$. Therefore an Iwadare code is an $((m+1)n_0, (m+1)(n_0-1))$ convolutional code where m, the number of frames, is

$$m = (\lambda+1)(2n_0-1)-2.$$

As we shall see, this code corrects any burst error of length λn_0 or less.

The parity-check-polynomial matrix is

$$\mathbf{H}(x) = [g_1(x) \; g_2(x) \; \cdots \; g_{(n_0-1)}(x) \; 1].$$

Because $n_0 - k_0 = 1$, there is only a single syndrome polynomial:

$$s(x) = \sum_{i=1}^{n_0-1} g_i(x)e_i(x) + e_{n_0}(x)$$

$$= e_{n_0}(x) + \sum_{i=0}^{n_0-1} [x^{(\lambda+1)(n_0-i)-1} + x^{(\lambda+1)(2n_0-i)+i-3}]e_i(x).$$

The decoder uses this polynomial to find the bursts. Suppose a burst begins in the first frame and lasts for λn_0 bits. If it does not begin in the first bit of frame one, then it may extend into frame $\lambda+1$. In order to show that the code can correct this burst error, we must show that the decoder can recover the burst error from the syndrome, and also that the decoder will not be fooled by a burst error beginning in a later frame.

The best way to understand the decoding of Iwadare codes is in terms of a single example, because the structure of all of the codes is the same. We will use as an example the (72, 48) Iwadare code with $n_0 = 3$, $\lambda = 4$, and thus $m = 24$. An encoder is shown in Fig. 12.21.

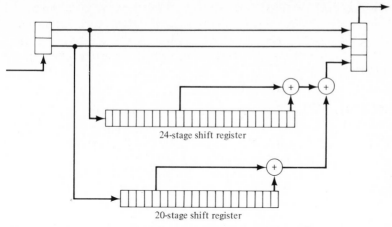

Figure 12.21 An encoder for the (72, 48) Iwadare code.

The polynomial $c_3(x)$ is the polynomial of parity symbols, and $c_1(x)$ and $c_2(x)$ are the polynomials of information symbols. The corresponding error polynomials are $e_1(x)$, $e_2(x)$, and $e_3(x)$. The syndrome polynomial is

$$s(x) = e_3(x) + (x^4 + x^{19})e_2(x) + (x^9 + x^{23})e_1(x),$$

where for a burst error beginning in the first frame,

$$e_3(x) = e_{30} + e_{31}x + e_{32}x^2 + e_{33}x^3$$
$$e_2(x) = e_{20} + e_{21}x + e_{22}x^2 + e_{23}x^3 + e_{24}x^4$$
$$e_1(x) = e_{10} + e_{11}x + e_{12}x^2 + e_{13}x^3 + e_{14}x^4.$$

Notice that e_{34} must be zero if the burst begins in the first frame. Further, if e_{24} is not zero, then e_{20} and e_{10} are zero; and if e_{14} is not zero, then e_{10} is zero. This is because the burst has a length of at most 12. Figure 12.22 shows the coefficients of $s(x)$ for the three cases, in which the burst error begins at e_{10}, e_{20}, or e_{30}. The generator polynomials have been chosen so that every syndrome bit is affected by only a single error bit. Also, notice that although the error polynomials start out interleaved and in the order $e_1(x)$, $e_2(x)$, $e_3(x)$, when they reach the syndrome, images of them appear deinterleaved and in the reverse order $e_3(x)$, $e_2(x)$, $e_1(x)$.

Each bit of $e_2(x)$ produces a doublet in the syndrome; the first occurrence is followed by an echo after a delay of 15 bits. Similarly, each bit of $e_1(x)$ produces a doublet in the syndrome; the first occurrence is followed by an echo after a delay of 14 bits. Because e_{24} and e_{10} cannot both be nonzero, the doublets never overlap. Each bit of $e_3(x)$ produces a singlet in the syndrome; the only occurrence of each bit is followed by a zero after a delay of 14 bits and by another zero after a delay of 15 bits. These zeros characterize $e_3(x)$.

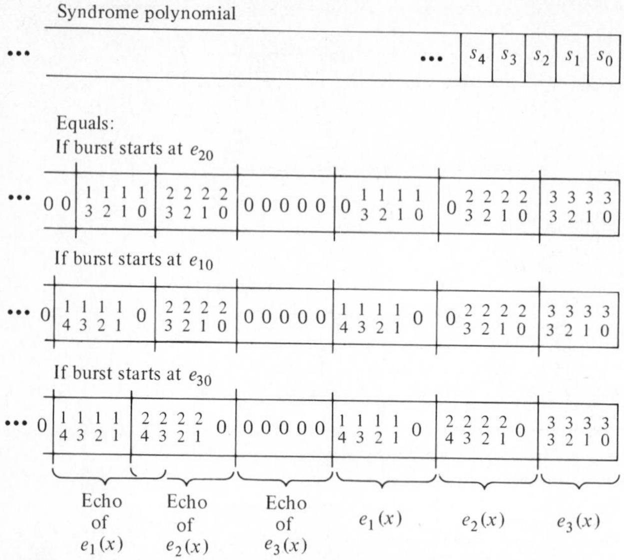

Syndrome polynomial

Figure 12.22 Syndrome structure for the (72, 48) Iwadare code.

If the burst error actually begins in the *l*th frame, then the syndrome is shifted to the right by *l* bits and is prefixed by *l* zeros. The decoding procedure is designed so that it will not inadvertently interpret such a pattern as a burst error beginning in the first frame.

We are now ready to describe the decoder shown in Fig. 12.23. After the first 20 frames have been shifted in, the syndrome register has the first 20 syndrome bits stored in it, with s_0 at the right. Similarly, the first received bit of $v_2(x)$ is in the rightmost stage of the $v_2(x)$ register. The first received bit of $v_1(x)$ will not reach the rightmost stage of the $v_1(x)$ register for four more clocks. We begin the description at this time. The first four syndrome bits depend only on errors in the received parity bits and are not of interest. Hence, the portion of Fig. 12.23 shown in dotted lines could be dropped. The crosshatched shift-register stages can be removed by taking s_{19} directly from the preceding modulo-2 adder.

The decoder first corrects the second bit in each frame of the burst error and then returns to the beginning of the burst and corrects the first bit in each frame. This is why the decoder has four shift-register stages for $c_2(x)$ after the correction is complete. The third bit of each frame is a parity bit; it is not corrected.

To correct an error in $v_2(x)$, the decoder tests syndrome positions s_4 and s_{19}. If both are equal to one, the rightmost bit in the $v_2(x)$ register is in error. An appropriate correction is made to the data stream and to the syndrome register. This test cannot be fooled by an $e_3(x)$ starting in a later frame because the echo of $e_3(x)$ is zero. Simultaneously, to find an error in $v_1(x)$ four frames

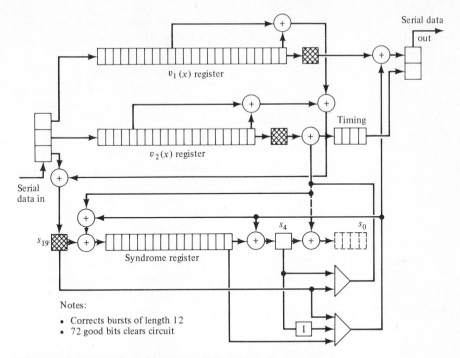

Figure 12.23 A decoder for the (72, 48) Iwadare code.

later, the decoder tests syndrome positions s_5 and s_{19}. If both are equal to one and s_4 is equal to zero, the rightmost bit in the $v_1(x)$ register is in error. This test on $v_1(x)$ must fail to find an error during the first four clock times, but thereafter it will begin to correct errors in $v_1(x)$. The test cannot be fooled by an $e_3(x)$ starting in a later frame because the echo of $e_3(x)$ is zero. The test cannot be fooled by an as yet uncorrected bit of $e_2(x)$ because of the qualifying test; s_4 is equal to zero.

After a burst error of length 12 occurs, there must be no more errors so that the syndrome will not be disturbed while the burst error is being corrected. This will be the case if no more errors occur until the twenty-ninth frame. Hence, at least 24 error-free frames (72 good bits) must occur between burst errors. As long as this is true, the decoder will successfully correct many successive burst-error patterns, each of length 12 or less.

12.8 THE VITERBI DECODING ALGORITHM

The Viterbi decoding algorithm is a complete decoding algorithm for convolutional codes. Because it is complete, the probability of decoding failure is zero; but for a given code, the probability of decoding error will be larger than with an incomplete decoder. The algorithm is practical for binary codes of small constraint length—today's limit is a constraint length of perhaps from 7 to 10. Nonbinary codes can be decoded by the Viterbi decoder only with difficulty and only for very small constraint length.

The following procedure—known as the *minimum-distance decoder*—gives in principle a good decoder for a convolutional code. It is a maximum-likelihood decoder for memoryless binary noise. Choose a decoding-window width b in excess of the blocklength n. Compute all codewords of length b, and compare the received word to each of them. Select that codeword closest to the received word. The first information frame of the estimated codeword is taken as the first information frame that produced the selected codeword. The decoded first information frame is then reencoded and subtracted from the received word. Then n_0 new symbols are shifted into the decoder, the first n_0 symbols are discarded, and the process is repeated to find the next information frame.

Of course, for a convolutional code of even quite modest complexity, this procedure is hopelessly impractical, but it is worthwhile to have the minimum-distance decoding procedure in mind as a point of reference. Further, for small convolutional codes, we will see how the minimum distance decoder can be implemented practically.

The direct implementation of the minimum-distance decoder is complex. Just as one can evaluate a discrete Fourier transform with a Cooley-Tukey FFT algorithm and an autoregressive filter synthesis problem with a Berlekamp-Massey algorithm, however, so too is there an efficient method of implementing the minimum-distance decoder. This is known as the Viterbi algorithm, and it is based on techniques drawn from the subject of dynamic programming. As with other efficient algorithms, one accepts a conceptually intricate algorithm because it is computationally efficient. Therefore in theoretical studies it is usually best to think of the minimum-distance decoder, but it is best to use the Viterbi algorithm in the actual decoder if possible.

The Viterbi decoder operates iteratively frame by frame, tracing through a trellis identical to that used by the encoder in an attempt to emulate the encoder's behavior. At any frame time the decoder does not know which node the encoder reached and thus does not try to decode this node yet. Instead, given the received sequence, the decoder determines the most likely path to every node, and it also determines the distance between each such path and the received sequence. This distance is called the *discrepancy* of the path. If all paths in the set of most likely paths begin in the same way, the decoder knows how the encoder began.

Then in the next frame, the decoder determines the most likely path to each of the new nodes of that frame. But to get to any one of the new nodes the path must pass through one of the old nodes. One can get the candidate paths to a new node by extending to this new node each of the old paths that can be thus extended. The most likely path is found by adding the incremental discrepancy of each path extension to the discrepancy of the path to the old node. There are q^ν such paths to each new node, and the path with the smallest discrepancy is the most likely path to the new node. This process is repeated for each of the new nodes. At the end of the iteration, the decoder knows the most likely path to each of the nodes in the new frame.

Consider the set of surviving paths to the set of nodes at the rth frame time. One or more of the nodes at the first frame time will be crossed by these paths. If all of the paths cross through the same node at the first frame time, then regardless of which node the encoder visits at the rth frame time, we know the most likely node it visited at the first frame time. That is, we know the first information frame even though we have not yet made a decision for the rth frame.

To build a Viterbi decoder, one must choose a decoding-window width b, usually several times as big as the blocklength and validated by computer simulation of the decoder. At frame time n, the decoder examines all surviving paths to see that they agree in the first branch. This branch defines a decoded information frame, which is passed out of the decoder.

Next, the decoder drops the first branch and takes in a new frame of the received word for the next iteration. If again all surviving paths pass through the same node of the oldest surviving frame, then this information frame is decoded. The process continues in this way, decoding frames indefinitely.

If b is chosen long enough, then a well-defined decision will almost always be made at a frame time. If the code is properly designed for the channel, this decision will be the correct one with high probability. Several things can go wrong, however. The surviving paths might not all go through a common node. This is a decoding failure. The decoder can break the tie using any arbitrary rule. Alternatively, the decoder can retain a record of the tie, using it later to flag an uncorrectable codeword segment. To this limited extent, the decoder then becomes an incomplete decoder. This point will be best understood from the example given shortly.

Sometimes, the decoder will reach a well-defined decision, but a wrong one. When this happens, the decoder will necessarily follow this with additional wrong decisions, but it will soon recover if the code is a noncatastrophic code.

It may be helpful to think of the Viterbi decoder as a window through which a portion of the trellis may be viewed. This is shown in Fig. 12.24. One can only see a finite-length section of the trellis, and on this is marked the surviving paths, each labeled with a discrepancy. As time goes by, the trellis slides to the left—quite rapidly in practical applications. As new nodes appear on the right, some paths are extended to them, other paths disappear, and an old column of nodes on the left is shifted out of sight. By the time a column of nodes is lost on the left side, only one of its nodes (in normal operation) has a path through it.

An example is shown in Fig. 12.25 based on the (6, 3) convolutional code

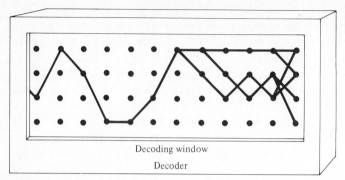

Figure 12.24 Conceptualizing the Viterbi decoder.

with generator polynomials $g_1(x) = x^2 + x + 1$ and $g_2(x) = x^2 + 1$. An encoder for this code is shown in Fig. 12.3. For simplicity of explanation, we will take the information sequence to be all zeros. Also, to keep the example simple, we will choose a decoder with a decoding-window width b equal to 15. Suppose that

$$\mathbf{v} = 1010000010000000000000000000 \dots,$$

which is actually the all-zero codeword with three errors.

The sequence of states of the decoder is shown in Fig. 12.25. At the third iteration, the decoder has already identified the shortest path to each node of the third frame. Then, at iteration r, the decoder finds the shortest path to each node of the rth frame by extending the paths to each node of the $(r-1)$th frame and keeping the shortest path to each node. Sometimes a tie may result. In the example, two ties are present at iteration five. The decoder may either break a tie by guessing or keep both paths in the tie. In the example, ties are retained either until they are replaced by a more likely path, or until they disappear out the end of the decoder. As the decoder penetrates into deeper frames, the earlier frames reach the end of the decoder memory. If a path exists to only one node of the oldest frame, the decoding is complete. If several paths exist, then an uncorrectable error pattern has been detected. It can either be flagged as such, or a guess can be made.

In the example, the information sequence has been decoded as either

$$\mathbf{i} = 0\ 0\ 0\ 0\ 0\ 0 \dots$$

or

$$\mathbf{i} = 1\ 0\ 1\ 0\ 0\ 0\ 0 \dots.$$

Increasing the decoding-window width above 15 would not make the error correctable. A code with a larger free distance is necessary if this error pattern must be corrected.

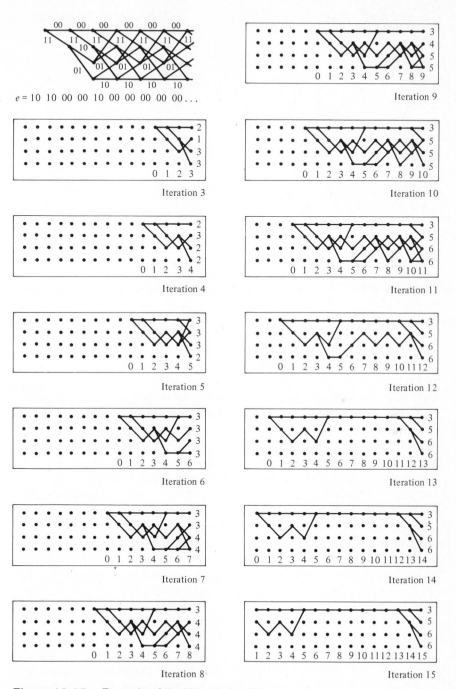

Figure 12.25   Example of the Viterbi algorithm.

The decoder shown symbolically in Fig. 12.25 might look much different in its actual implementation. For example, the active paths through the trellis could be represented by a table of 15-bit numbers. At each iteration some of the 15-bit numbers are shifted left, dropping the leftmost bit and adding a bit at the right. Other 15-bit numbers are not extended and are dropped from the table.

As the decoder progresses through many frames, the accumulating discrepancies continue to increase. To avoid overflow problems, they must be reduced occasionally. A simple procedure is periodically subtracting the smallest discrepancy from all of them. This does not affect the choice of the maximum discrepancy.

Viterbi decoders can be very fast as long as the code constraint length is small. For example, it is quite practical to build such a decoder with 128 nodes at each level that will iterate 10 million times per second.

12.9 TRELLIS SEARCHING ALGORITHMS

The performance of a convolutional code can be improved by increasing the constraint length. The Viterbi decoder, however, quickly becomes impractical; at a constraint length of 10, the decoder of a binary code already must store 1024 surviving paths. For moderate to long constraint lengths, one devises strategies that ignore the improbable paths through the trellis, at least for as long as they appear to be improbable. Such strategies usually leave pending most decisions to drop paths permanently. Occasionally, the decoder will decide to back up and extend a path previously ignored.

All such strategies for searching only the high-probability paths through a trellis are known collectively as *sequential decoding*. Sequential decoding is quite general and can be used with channels that make hard decisions, which we will treat in this section, or with channels that can make erasures or even softer decisions, which we will treat in Chapter 15.

Imagine the trellis for a convolutional code with a large constraint length, say a constraint length of 40. This trellis must be searched over several hundred levels in order to make a decision. Even more overwhelming is the number of nodes at each level. There are 2^{40} such nodes, or approximately 1000 billion. The decoder must find the path through this trellis that most closely matches the received word in Hamming distance—at least it should do this with very high probability, although we will allow it to fail occasionally. This failure is an additional error mode not found in a Viterbi decoder; the decoder may be wrong even though the minimum-distance decision would be correct.

Rather than follow the optimum procedure of the Viterbi algorithm, the decoder we will begin with looks at only the first frame, makes a decision, and proceeds to a trellis node at the first level. It then repeats this procedure. At each level it is at a single node; it looks at the next frame, choosing the branch closest to the received frame, and proceeds to a single node at the next level. If there are no errors, this procedure works fine. If there are errors, however, the decoder will occasionally choose the wrong branch. As the decoder proceeds past a wrong choice, the decoder will suddenly perceive that it is finding many errors. But this is the fault of the decoder, not the channel. A sequential decoder will back up through the last few frames and explore alternative paths until it finds a likely path, and then it will proceed along this alternative path. The rules controlling this search will be developed shortly. The performance of the decoder depends on b, the decoding-window width in codeword frames. When the decoder has found a path that penetrates b frames into the trellis, it makes an irrevocable decision on the oldest frame, outputs these bits, and shifts a new frame into its window.

We can think of a sequential decoder working its way along a convolutional codeword at an erratic pace. Usually it moves along smoothly, producing corrected output bits. Occasionally it has a little trouble and slows down to get past this troublesome spot. Even more rarely, it has considerable trouble and pauses while it works itself past this difficult spot. Detailed algorithms for doing this have been developed. The most popular is the Fano algorithm, which we will now describe.

This algorithm requires that we know p, the probability of bit error through the channel, or at least an upper bound on p. As long as the decoder is following the right path, we expect to see about $p n_0 l$ errors through the first l frames. The decoder will tolerate an error rate a little higher than this, but if it is too much higher, the decoder concludes that it is on the wrong path. Choose a parameter p' (perhaps by simulation), larger than p but smaller than one-half, and define the tilted distance as†

$$t(l) = p' n_0 l - d(l),$$

where $d(l)$ is the measured Hamming distance between the received word and the current path through the trellis. For the correct path, $d(l)$ is approximately $p n_0 l$, and $t(l)$ is positive and increasing. As long as $t(l)$ is increasing, the decoder continues threading its way through the trellis. If $t(l)$ ever starts to decrease, the decoder concludes that at some node it might have chosen the wrong branch. It then begins to back up through the trellis, testing other paths. It may find a better path and follow it, or it may return to the same node, but now with more confidence, and continue past it. To decide when $t(l)$ is beginning to decrease, the decoder uses a running threshold T, which is always a multiple of a threshold increment Δ. As long as the decoder is moving forward, it keeps the threshold as large as possible with the constraints that it is not larger than $t(l)$ and that it is a multiple of Δ. The quantization of T allows $t(l)$ to decrease a little without falling through the threshold.

The Fano algorithm requires that at each node, the q^{k_0} branches leaving that node must be numbered according to some ordering rule. The ordering

---

†We have chosen the sign convention so that a positive sign occurs when the decoder is performing properly.

rule assigns an index j for $j = 0, \ldots, q^{k_0} - 1$ to each branch. This index need not be stored for each branch. It only is necessary that the rule be known so that when the decoder backs up to a node along the branch with known index j, it can reorder the branches by the rule, find branch j, and thence find branch $j + 1$. The most common rule is the minimum-distance rule. The branches are ordered according to their Hamming distance from the corresponding frame of the received word, and ties are broken by any convenient subrule. The algorithm will work if the branches are preassigned any fixed order, however, such as one where the branches are ordered lexicographically according to their information symbols. This latter ordering rule will result in more back-and-forth searching but eliminates the need to compute or recompute an order when reaching each node. Which ordering rule results in a simpler implementation depends on the details of the design. For ease of under-standing the structure of the algorithm, it is best to leave the ordering rule a little vague; we only suppose that at each node the branch closest in Hamming distance to the received branch is ordered first. The decoder will search the branches out of each node according to this arbitrary order.

A shift-register implementation of a decoder based on the Fano algo-rithm is outlined in Fig. 12.26. The heart of the decoder is a replica of the

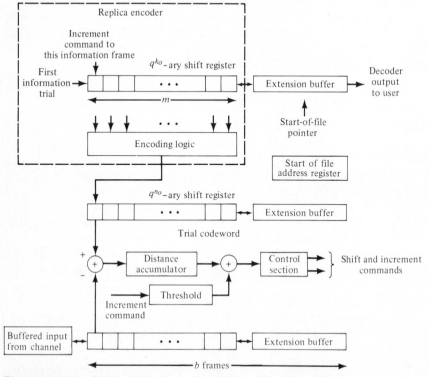

Figure 12.26   Shift-register implementation of the Fano algorithm.

encoder together with some auxillary storage registers. The decoder attempts to insert symbols into the replica encoder in such a way as to generate a codeword that is sufficiently close to the received word. At each iteration, it has immediate access to the content of the latest frame entered into the replica encoder. It can change the information in this frame, or it can back up to an earlier frame, or it can shift in a new frame. It decides what to do based on the value of the tilted distance $t(l)$ as compared to the running threshold T.

The Fano algorithm, which controls the decoder, is shown in simplified form in Fig. 12.27. Practical details, concerned with the finite buffer size, are ignored for the moment.

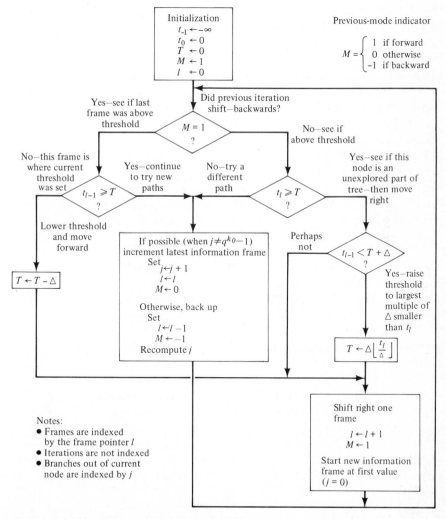

Figure 12.27 An annotated Fano algorithm.

When the channel is quiet and errors are rare, the decoder will circle around the rightmost loop of Fig. 12.27, each time, shifting all the registers of Fig. 12.26 one frame to the right. As long as $t(l)$ remains above the threshold, the decoder continues to shift right and continues to raise the threshold to keep it tight. If $t(l)$ drops below the threshold, the decoder will test alternative branches in that frame, trying to find one above the threshold. If it cannot, it backs up. As we shall see later, once it begins to back up, the logic will force it to continue to back up until it finds an alternative path that stays above the current threshold or until it finds the node at which the current threshold was set. Then the decoder moves forward again with a lowered threshold; but now, as we shall also see, the threshold is not raised again until the decoder reaches new nodes that were previously unexplored. Each time it visits the same node while moving forward, it has a smaller threshold. The decoder will never advance to the same node twice with the same threshold. Consequently, it can only visit any node a finite number of times. This behavior assures us that the decoder cannot be trapped in a loop. It must continue to work through the data with or without correct decoding.

Now we must prove two earlier assertions: that if it cannot find an alternative path, the decoder will move back to the node where the current threshold was set and lower it; and that the decoder will not raise the threshold again until it reaches a previously unexplored node. In the first assertion, it is obvious that if the decoder cannot find a new branch on which to move forward, it must eventually back up to the specified node. But, if at any node the tilted distance $t(l-1)$ at the previous frame is smaller than the current threshold T, then the threshold must have been increased at the lth frame. This is just the test contained in Fig. 12.27 to find the node at which the current threshold was set, and at this node the threshold is now reduced.

To prove the second assertion, notice that after the threshold is lowered by Δ, the decoder will search the subsequent branches in exactly the same sequence as before until it finds a place at which the threshold test is now passed where previously it failed. Until this point the logic will not allow the threshold T to be changed. This is because once the threshold is lowered by Δ, the tilted distance will never be smaller than $T + \Delta$ at any node where it previously exceeded the original threshold. When it penetrates into a new part of the tree, it will eventually reach the condition that $t(l-1) < T + \Delta$ while $t(l) \geqslant T$. This is the point at which the threshold is raised. This then is the test to determine if a new node is being visited. There is no need to keep an explicit record of the nodes previously visited. This test appears in Fig. 12.27.

The Fano algorithm depends on the two parameters p' and Δ, which can be chosen by means of computer simulation. In practice it will also be necessary to reduce $t(l)$ and T occasionally so that the numbers do not get too large. Subtraction of any multiple of Δ from both will not affect subsequent computations.

In practical implementations one must also choose the decoding-window width b, usually at least several times the blocklength. Figure 12.28

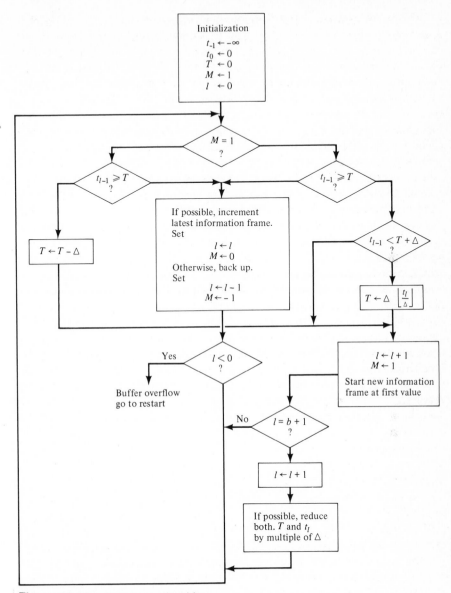

Figure 12.28   The Fano algorithm.

gives a more complete flowchart for the Fano algorithm, showing the important role of b. Whenever the oldest information frame reaches the end of the buffer, as indicated by the frame pointer, it is passed out of the decoder, and the frame pointer is decremented so that it is always a reference to the oldest available frame. The algorithm may otherwise occasionally try to back up far enough to look at a frame that has been passed out of the decoder.

Sometimes the sequential decoder makes so many computations that the input buffer is not big enough. This is called *buffer overflow* and is the major limitation on the performance of the Fano algorithm. The probability of buffer overflow decreases very slowly with buffer size, and thus no matter how large one makes the buffer the problem does not completely go away.

Two ways to handle buffer overflows are available. The most certain is to periodically insert into the encoder a known sequence of information symbols—typically a sequence of zeros—of length equal to the constraint length of the convolutional code. Upon buffer overflow, the decoder declares a decoding failure and waits for the start of the next known sequence, where it starts decoding again. All of the intervening data between buffer overflow and the next start-up is lost. This approach reduces slightly the rate of the code and also introduces a time-synchronization problem into the decoder design. Alternatively, if the constraint length is not too large, one can just force the pointer forward. The decoder can recover if it can find a correct node. If the probability that no error has occurred over a blocklength is not too small, the decoder assumes that no error has occurred and inverts the codeword to obtain the information word. This is immediate if the code is systematic and otherwise involves a simple application of the Chinese remainder theorem for polynomials. If it obtains an error-free received-word segment whose length is one constraint length, the decoder has found the correct node and can continue to decode. If, contrary to the assumption, an error did occur, then the node is wrong, and the buffer will quickly overflow again. This process of forcing the decoder forward is repeated until correct decoding resumes.

PROBLEMS

12.1. a. Design an encoder for a systematic, noncatastrophic, binary (16, 4) convolutional code with minimum distance $d^* = 9$ and constraint length $v = 3$.
   b. What is the free distance of this code?

12.2. Every Hamming code over $GF(q)$ can be used to build a single-error-correcting convolutional code over $GF(q)$.
   a. Give a parity-check matrix for a systematic (9, 7) octal Hamming code.
   b. Based on this Hamming code, find the parity-check matrix for a (30, 27) Wyner-Ash code over $GF(8)$.
   c. Design an encoder and a syndrome decoder.
   d. What is the rate of this code? What is the rate of a Wyner-Ash hexadecimal code based on the (17, 15) Hamming code over $GF(16)$?

12.3. Design an encoder for the (12, 9) Wyner-Ash code that uses a single binary shift register of length 3.

12.4. Design an encoder and a syndrome decoder for the (32, 28) Wyner-Ash code.

12.5. Reconstruct the example of Fig. 12.25 using instead the received word

$$\mathbf{v} = 1\ 0\ 0\ 0\ 1\ 0\ 0\ 0\ 0\ 0\ 1\ 0\ 0\ 0\ 0\ 0\ 0\ 0\ 0\ \ldots .$$

12.6. Determine which of the following rate $\frac{1}{2}$ convolutional codes are catastrophic:

   a. $g_1(x) = x^2$, $g_2(x) = x^3 + x + 1$.

   b. $g_1(x) = x^4 + x^2 + 1$, $g_2(x) = x^4 + x^3 + x + 1$.

   c. $g_1(x) = x^4 + x^2 + x + 1$, $g_2(x) = x^4 + x^3 + 1$.

   d. $g_1(x) = x^6 + x^5 + x^4 + 1$, $g_2(x) = x^5 + x^3 + x + 1$.

12.7. A rate $\frac{1}{3}$, constraint length 2 convolutional code has generator polynomials $g_1(x) = x^2 + x + 1$, $g_2(x) = x^2 + x + 1$, and $g_3(x) = x^2 + 1$; and d_∞ equals 8.

   a. What is the minimum distance of the code?

   b. What decoding-window width should be used if all triple errors are to be corrected?

   c. Design a decoder for this code with a decoding-window width equal to 9 that will correct all double errors.

12.8. A rate $\frac{1}{2}$ convolutional code over $GF(4)$ has generator polynomials $g_1(x) = 2x^3 + 2x^2 + 1$ and $g_2(x) = x^3 + x + 1$.

   a. Show that this code is noncatastrophic.

   b. Show that the minimum distance is 5.

   c. How many double-error patterns are within the decoding constraint length of 8?

   d. Design a syndrome decoder for correcting all double errors.

12.9. Find a systematic feedback shift-register encoder for the binary convolutional code with generator matrix of polynomials

$$\mathbf{G}(x) = \begin{bmatrix} x & x^2 & 1 \\ 0 & 1 & x \end{bmatrix}.$$

NOTES

The notion of a convolutional code originated with Elias (1954) and was developed by Wozencraft (1957). Wyner and Ash (1963) gave a general construction, akin to that of the Hamming codes, for a family of single-error-correcting convolutional codes. A class of multiple-error-correcting convolutional codes was found by Massey (1963). Massey's codes were easy to decode, but not otherwise notable in performance. No general method is known for constructing a family of high-performance multiple-error-correcting codes. Costello (1969) has described some ways of finding good convolutional codes of moderate blocklength. The codes now in common use have been found by computer search, principally by Bussgang (1965), Oldenwalder (1970), Bahl and Jelinek (1971), Larsen (1973), Paaske (1974), and Johannesson (1975). We have summarized this work in Fig. 12.13.

A general study of the algebraic structure of convolutional codes was carried out by Massey and Sain (1968) and by Forney (1970), who introduced the use of a trellis. Our polynomial treatment is based on these papers. Costello (1969) showed that every convolutional code can be encoded systematically if feedback is allowed in the encoder. Additional treatment of the abstract structure can be found in Lindner and Staiger (1977).

The design of decoders for convolutional codes began with complex decoders of high performance and slowly evolved toward the simple decoders of lower performance that are so popular today. The trellis-searching algorithm we have described originated with Fano (1963). Our formulation relies heavily on a version of the Fano algorithm given by Gallager (1968). Viterbi (1967) published his algorithm more as a pedagogical device than as a serious algorithm. Shortly thereafter Heller (1968) pointed out that the Viterbi algorithm is quite practical if the constraint length is not too large.

General discussions of convolutional codes can be found in the book by Viterbi and Omura (1970) and the tutorial articles by Forney (1974) and Massey (1975).

CHAPTER 13

Codes and Algorithms for Decoding with Majority Logic

Majority decoding is a method of decoding that is relatively simple to implement. Hence if one wishes for extremely fast decoders, one should turn to a majority decoder. Unfortunately, only a small class of codes can be decoded in this way, and these codes are usually not as strong as other codes. Hence majority decoding is of only minor importance in practice. Nevertheless, it is the only way to satisfy some requirements. In addition, these codes are of theoretical interest and provide another well-developed view of the subject of error-control codes.

Most known codes that can be decoded with majority logic are cyclic codes or extended cyclic codes. For these codes, the majority decoders can always be implemented as Meggitt decoders and characterized by an especially simple logic tree for examining the syndrome. Thus one can take the pragmatic view and define majority-decodable codes as those cyclic codes for which the Meggitt decoder can be put in a standard simple form. But in order to find these codes, we must travel a winding road.

13.1 DECODING WITH MAJORITY LOGIC

The Reed-Muller codes, studied in Section 3.6, were decoded by taking for each information symbol a majority vote of a set of the parity-check equations. Other codes that can be majority decoded exist. The history of such codes can usually be traced back to the Reed-Muller codes.

Recall that any linear (n, k) code over $GF(q)$ has a parity-check matrix $\mathbf{H}$, and codewords satisfy $\mathbf{cH}^T = \mathbf{0}$. If we restrict attention to the jth row of $\mathbf{H}$ we have the parity-check equation

$$\sum_{i=0}^{n-1} H_{ij}c_i = 0.$$

We can also take any linear combination of rows of $\mathbf{H}$ to form another parity-check equation. A total of q^{n-k} parity-check equations can be formed in this way. The art of majority decoding lies in choosing a good subset of these parity checks, provided a good subset does exist.

In this and the next section, we will construct majority decoders. In later sections, we will study the construction of codes that allow majority decoding.

□ **Definition 13.1.1** A set of parity-check equations is *concurring** on coordinate k if c_k appears in every parity-check equation of the set, and every c_j $(j \neq k)$ appears in at most one parity-check equation of the set. □

As shown in the following theorem, the majority decoder estimates e_k by a majority vote of the parity-check equations. It is not known a priori whether or not there is an error in the kth received bit, and an error value of zero is one of the candidates in the vote. If J, the number of parity-check equations, is even, then ties are broken in the direction of no error. If J is even, a true majority will always occur if the number of errors is less than $(J-1)/2$.

□ **Theorem 13.1.2** If a set of J parity-check equations is concurring on coordinate k, then c_k can be correctly estimated provided that no more than $J/2$ errors occurred in the received word.

Proof The proof is given by exhibiting the correction procedure. Because c_k appears in every parity-check equation in this set, H_{kj} is not

---

*The term *orthogonal* is often used here. We avoid this term because it directly conflicts with usage of the same term in the study of vector spaces.

zero. Set

$$s_j = H_{kj}^{-1} \sum_{i=0}^{n-1} H_{ij} v_i = H_{kj}^{-1} \sum_{i=0}^{n-1} H_{ij} e_i.$$

The division by H_{kj} ensures that the coefficient of e_k equals one. But now $s_j = e_k$ for at least half of the values of j because there are J equations; at most $J/2$ of the other e_i are nonzero, and each of the other e_i appears at most once in the set of parity-check equations. Hence, at least $J/2$ of the s_j are equal to e_k if e_k equals zero, and more than $J/2$ of the s_j are equal to e_k if e_k is not equal to zero. We can find e_k by a majority decision over the s_j. $\square$

☐ **Corollary 13.1.3** If each coordinate has a set of J parity-check equations concurring on it, the code can correct $\lfloor J/2 \rfloor$ errors.

Proof The proof is immediate. $\square$

If J is even, $J/2$ is an integer, and the code can correct $J/2$ errors. This implies that the code has a minimum distance of at least $J + 1$. The next theorem gives a direct proof of this and includes the case where J is odd. Hence, $J + 1$ is called the *majority-decodable distance*, sometimes denoted d_{MD}. The true minimum distance may be larger.

☐ **Theorem 13.1.4** If each coordinate of a linear code has a set of J parity-check equations concurring on it, the code has a minimum distance of at least $J + 1$.

Proof Choose any nonzero codeword, and pick any place k where it is nonzero. There are J parity-check equations concurring on k. Each equation involves a nonzero component c_k, and thus it must involve at least one other nonzero component because the parity-check equation is equal to zero. Hence, there are at least J other nonzero components, and the theorem is proved. $\square$

☐ **Corollary 13.1.5** If any coordinate of a cyclic code has a set of J parity-check equations concurring on it, the code has a minimum distance of at least $J + 1$.

Proof Every cyclic shift of a codeword in a cyclic code is another codeword in the same code; therefore a set of J parity-check equations on one coordinate can be readily used to write down a set of J parity-check equations on any other coordinate. $\square$

☐ **Theorem 13.1.6** Let $\bar{d}$ be the minimum distance of the dual code of $\mathscr{C}$, a code over $GF(q)$. Not more than $\frac{1}{2}(n-1)(\bar{d}-1)^{-1}$ errors can be corrected by a majority decoder for $\mathscr{C}$.

Proof Linear combinations of rows of **H** are codewords in the dual code $\mathscr{C}^{\perp}$. Consider a set of J parity-check equations concurring on the first coordinate. Each equation has at least $\bar{d}-1$ nonzero components in the remaining $n-1$ coordinates, and each of the remaining $n-1$ coordinates is nonzero at most once in the J equations. Hence

$$J(\bar{d}-1) \leqslant n-1,$$

and $J/2$ errors can be corrected by a majority decoder. $\square$

Hence, majority decoding cannot decode to the packing radius of a code unless

$$d^* \leqslant \frac{n-1}{\bar{d}-1} + 1.$$

This is a necessary, but not sufficient, condition. Most interesting codes fail to meet this condition.

The majority decoder is quite simple, but it generally can be used only for codes of low performance. Therefore we introduce something a little more complex—an L-step majority decoder.

A 2-step majority decoder uses a majority decision to localize an error to a set of components rather than to a specific component. Then a majority decision is made within this set to find the error. An L-step majority decoder uses L levels of majority logic. At each level, the logic begins with an error already localized to a set of components and by a majority decision localizes the error to a subset of these components.

$\square$ **Definition 13.1.7** A set of parity-check equations is concurring on the set of components $i_1, i_2, \ldots, i_r$ if for some coefficients $A_1, A_2, \ldots, A_r$, the sum $A_1 c_{i_1} + A_2 c_{i_2} + \cdots + A_r c_{i_r}$ appears in every parity-check equation of the set and every c_i for $i \neq i_1, i_2, \ldots, i_r$ appears in at most one parity-check equation of the set. $\square$

An L-step majority decoder may correct more errors than a single-step majority decoder, but it still will not generally reach the packing radius of the code, as shown by the following theorem.

$\square$ **Theorem 13.1.8** Let $\bar{d}$ be the minimum distance of the dual code of $\mathscr{C}$, a code over $GF(q)$. Not more than $(n/\bar{d}) - \frac{1}{2}$ errors can be corrected by an L-step majority-logic decoder for $\mathscr{C}$.

Proof In order to correct t errors, it is first necessary to construct J parity-check equations concurring on some set B that contains b components, with $J = 2t$. Each such equation corresponds to a linear combination of rows of **H**, and these linear combinations are codewords in the dual code $\mathscr{C}^{\perp}$. Excluding components in the set B, let the number of nonzero components in the lth parity-check equation be denoted by a_l for $l = 1, \ldots, J$. These equations correspond to codewords in the dual code, and thus

$$b + a_l \geqslant \bar{d}.$$

Summing these J equations gives

$$Jb + \sum_{l=1}^{J} a_l \geqslant J\bar{d}.$$

Because each component other than those in set B can be nonzero in at most one of the parity-check equations,

$$\sum_{l=1}^{J} a_l \leqslant n - b.$$

Eliminating b gives

$$Jn + \sum_{l=1}^{J} a_l \geqslant J\left(\bar{d} + \sum_{l=1}^{J} a_l\right).$$

Now we need to derive a second condition. Subtracting two codewords in the dual code produces another codeword in which the b places have zeros. That is,

$$a_l + a_{l'} \geqslant \bar{d} \qquad \text{for } l \neq l'.$$

There are $J(J-1)$ such equations, and each a_l appears in $2(J-1)$ of them. Adding all such equations together gives

$$2(J-1)\sum_{l=1}^{J} a_l \geqslant J(J-1)\bar{d}.$$

Finally, eliminate $\sum_{l=1}^{J} a_l$ using this equation and the earlier equation. This gives

$$2J(n - \bar{d}) \geqslant J(J-1)\bar{d}.$$

Because a majority decoder can correct $J/2$ errors, the theorem follows. $\qquad\square$

An an application of this theorem, we observe that the Golay (23, 12) code cannot be decoded by majority logic.

13.2 CIRCUITS FOR MAJORITY DECODING

Majority-decodable codes are studied because the decoders are simple and fast. Thus an important part of their story is a description of the decoders. We shall study the decoders by way of examples.

As a first example, we take the (7, 3) code dual to the Hamming (7, 4) code. This code, known as a *simplex code*, has minimum distance 4 and can correct one error. Because $1 \leqslant \frac{1}{2}(7-1)(3-1) = 3/2$, Theorem 13.1.6 does not preclude majority decoding. One way to get a parity-check matrix for this code is to note that the cyclic code has α^0 and α^3 as zeros in $GF(8)$. Hence

$$\mathbf{H} = \begin{bmatrix} \alpha^0 & \alpha^0 & \alpha^0 & \alpha^0 & \alpha^0 & \alpha^0 & \alpha^0 \\ \alpha^4 & \alpha & \alpha^5 & \alpha^2 & \alpha^6 & \alpha^3 & \alpha^0 \end{bmatrix}.$$

Over $GF(2)$ this becomes

$$\mathbf{H} = \begin{bmatrix} 1 & 1 & 1 & 1 & 1 & 1 & 1 \\ 1 & 0 & 1 & 1 & 1 & 0 & 0 \\ 1 & 1 & 1 & 0 & 0 & 1 & 0 \\ 0 & 0 & 1 & 0 & 1 & 1 & 1 \end{bmatrix}.$$

The parity-check equations that involve c_0 have a one in the rightmost component. There are eight of these equations that can be formed with coefficients given by

$$
\begin{array}{ccccccc}
1 & 1 & 1 & 1 & 1 & 1 & 1 \\
0 & 0 & 1 & 0 & 1 & 1 & 1 \\
0 & 1 & 0 & 0 & 0 & 1 & 1 \\
0 & 0 & 0 & 1 & 1 & 0 & 1 \\
1 & 0 & 0 & 1 & 0 & 1 & 1 \\
1 & 1 & 0 & 0 & 1 & 0 & 1 \\
1 & 0 & 1 & 0 & 0 & 0 & 1 \\
0 & 1 & 1 & 1 & 0 & 0 & 1 \, .
\end{array}
$$

We choose from these the third, fourth, and seventh, which give the parity-check equations

$$c_0 + c_1 + c_5 = 0$$

$$c_0 + c_2 + c_3 = 0$$

$$c_0 + c_4 + c_6 = 0$$

as the desired set of three equations concurring on c_0. Based on these, we have the decoder of Fig. 13.1. If the shift register initially contains the received vector, after seven shifts it will contain the corrected codeword provided a single error took place.

Of course to correct one error, we only need use any two of the above parity-check equations. Adding the third equation gives a decoder based on a two-out-of-three decision rather than a two-out-of-two decision. As long as only one error occurs, the two decoders behave in the same way. But if two errors occur, the decoders behave differently. The two-out-of-three decoder will correct a slightly larger fraction of the double-error patterns, although both decoders will fail to correct or miscorrect most double-error patterns.

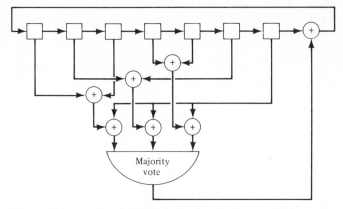

Figure 13.1   A majority decoder for the (7, 3) simplex code.

If desired, the decoder could require all three parity-checks to be satisfied. Then the decoder would correct all single-error patterns and detect all double-error patterns.

It is possible to turn the structure of a majority decoder into that of a Meggitt decoder. Recall that the syndrome polynomial is defined either as

$$s(x) = R_{g(x)}[v(x)]$$

or as

$$s(x) = R_{g(x)}[x^{n-k}v(x)]$$

The syndrome polynomial is related linearly to the received polynomial $v(x)$ by the parity-check matrix. We can write each coefficient as

$$s_j = \sum_{i=0}^{n-1} H_{ij}v_i \qquad j = 0, \ldots, k-1.$$

Any other parity-check relationship is defined by some linear combination of the rows of $\mathbf{H}$; that is, as a linear combination of syndromes. Therefore, all of the parity checks used by a majority decoder can be obtained as a linear combination of the syndrome coefficients of a Meggitt decoder. In this way, any majority decoder for a cyclic code can be implemented as a Meggitt decoder.

The simplex (7, 3) code is a cyclic code and has generator polynomial $g(x) = x^4 + x^2 + x + 1$. Let

$$s(x) = R_{g(x)}[x^4 v(x)]$$
$$= v_6 x^3 + v_5 x^2 + v_4 x + v_3 + v_2(x^3 + x + 1) + v_1(x^3 + x^2 + x)$$
$$+ v_0(x^2 + x + 1).$$

We can write this in the form

$$[s_0 \ s_1 \ s_2 \ s_3] = [v_0 \ v_1 \ v_2 \ v_3 \ v_4 \ v_5 \ v_6] \begin{bmatrix} 1 & 1 & 1 & 0 \\ 0 & 1 & 1 & 1 \\ 1 & 1 & 0 & 1 \\ 1 & 0 & 0 & 0 \\ 0 & 1 & 0 & 0 \\ 0 & 0 & 1 & 0 \\ 0 & 0 & 0 & 1 \end{bmatrix}.$$

For majority decoding, we used the parity-check equations

$$c_0 + c_1 + c_5 = 0$$

$$c_0 + c_2 + c_3 = 0$$

$$c_0 + c_4 + c_6 = 0.$$

The first of these is the same as s_2, the second is the same as s_0, and the third is the same as $s_1 + s_3$. Figure 13.2 shows the majority decoder implemented as a Meggitt decoder.

Majority decoders, without any additional circuitry, will decode many error patterns beyond the packing radius of the code. This might seem like an attractive advantage for majority decoders. In order to employ majority decoding, however, one usually must use a code whose packing radius is small as compared to other codes of comparable rate and blocklength. The ability of the decoder to decode beyond the packing radius can only be viewed as a partial compensation for using an inferior code.

When using a majority decoder implemented as a Meggitt decoder, it is necessary to add feedback if the decoder is to correct many patterns beyond

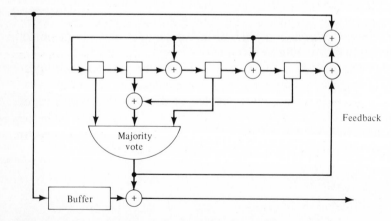

Figure 13.2 A Meggitt decoder for the (7, 3) simplex code.

the packing radius. This is the function of the feedback path in Fig. 13.2. If decoding beyond the packing radius is unimportant, the feedback path can be deleted.

13.3 AFFINE PERMUTATIONS FOR CYCLIC CODES

A cyclic shift of any codeword in a cyclic code gives another codeword. Hence, the entire code is invariant under a cyclic shift. A cyclic shift is a simple example of a permutation. A cyclic code may also be invariant under other permutations. In this section, we will show that many cyclic codes, when extended, are invariant under a large group of permutations called affine permutations. The affine permutations can be used to design codes, to analyze codes, or to design decoders—particularly majority decoders.

Let $\mathscr{C}$ be a cyclic code of blocklength $n = q^m - 1$ generated by the polynomial $g(x)$. Let $\overline{\mathscr{C}}$ be the code of blocklength q^m obtained from $\mathscr{C}$ by appending an overall parity-check symbol to every codeword in $\mathscr{C}$. That is, if $(c_{n-1}, \ldots, c_1, c_0)$ is a codeword in $\mathscr{C}$, then $(c_{n-1}, \ldots, c_1, c_0, c_\infty)$ is a codeword in $\overline{\mathscr{C}}$, where c_∞ is the overall parity-check symbol given by $c_\infty = -(c_{n-1} + \cdots + c_1 + c_0)$.

To index the components of a codeword, we will use $GF(q^m)$ as a set of location numbers. The nonzero elements in $GF(q^m)$ are given by α^i, where α is primitive. The zero element 0 in $GF(q^m)$ will be represented by α^∞. We number the components of a vector $(c_{n-1}, \ldots, c_1, c_0, c_\infty)$ in $\overline{\mathscr{C}}$ by the elements of $GF(q^m)$ as follows: component c_∞ is numbered α^∞, and, for $0 \leqslant i < q^m - 1$, component c_i is numbered α^i.

A group of permutations is called *transitive* if for every pair of locations (X, Y) in a codeword, there is a permutation in the group that interchanges them, possibly rearranging other locations as well. A group of permutations is called *doubly transitive* if for every two pairs of locations $((X_1, Y_1), (X_2, Y_2))$ with $X_1 \neq X_2$ and $Y_1 \neq Y_2$, there is a permutation in the group that interchanges the locations in the first pair and also interchanges the locations in the second pair, possibly rearranging other locations as well.

An *affine permutation* is a permutation that carries the component with location number X to the component with location number $aX + b$, where a and b are any fixed elements in $GF(q^m)$ and $a \neq 0$. The set of all affine permutations is a group under composition, because (1) if location X goes to location $Y = aX + b$ and location Y goes to location $Z = a'Y + b'$, then X goes to $Z = a'aX + a'b + b'$; and (2) the permutation $a^{-1}X - a^{-1}b$ is the inverse permutation to $aX + b$. The group of affine permutations is doubly transitive because given the pairs (X_1, Y_1) and (X_2, Y_2), the pair of equations

$$Y_1 = aX_1 + b$$

$$Y_2 = aX_2 + b$$

has a unique solution for a and b.

□ **Theorem 13.3.1** Any code of blocklength $n = q^m$ that is invariant under the group of affine permutations can be made into a cyclic code by dropping the location with location number α^∞.

Proof Let α be the primitive element used to define the location numbers. The permutation $Y = \alpha X$ is an affine permutation. But this permutation is a cyclic shift of all locations but α^∞. Hence, the code is cyclic. □

It is more difficult to give a condition that works in the other direction, that is, stating when a cyclic code can be extended to get a code that is invariant under the group of affine permutations. Such cyclic codes, identified in Theorem 13.3.4, are called cyclic codes with the doubly-transitive-invariant property. Before we can study this theorem we need a little background.

□ **Definition 13.3.2** Let j be an integer with radix-q representation

$$j = j_0 + j_1 q + j_2 q^2 + \cdots + j_{m-1} q^{m-1} \qquad 0 \leqslant j_i < q.$$

Another integer k with radix-q representation

$$k = k_0 + k_1 q + k_2 q^2 + \cdots + k_{m-1} q^{m-1} \qquad 0 \leqslant k_i < q$$

is called a *radix-q descendent of j* if

$$k_l \leqslant j_l \quad l = 0, \ldots, m-1. \qquad \qquad \square$$

It can be awkward to determine whether a given integer k is a radix-q descendent of an integer j. For the case where q is a prime p, the next theorem will be used to give a simple yet equivalent condition in terms of $\binom{j}{k}$. In reading this theorem recall the convention that if $m > n$, $\binom{n}{m} = 0$.

□ **Theorem 13.3.3 (Lucas's Theorem)** Let p be a prime and let

$$j = j_0 + j_1 p + \cdots + j_{m-1} p^{m-1}$$

and

$$k = k_0 + k_1 p + \cdots + k_{m-1} p^{m-1}$$

be any two integers expressed in their radix-p representations. Then the following congruence holds:

$$\binom{j}{k} = \prod_{i=0}^{m-1} \binom{j_i}{k_i} \pmod{p}.$$

Further, $\binom{j}{k}$ equals zero modulo p if and only if k is not a radix-p descendent of j.

Proof The last statement follows from the first because $\binom{j_i}{k_i}$ is not equal to zero modulo p for all i if and only if k is a radix-p descendent of j. We only need to prove the first phrase of the theorem.

The proof will consist of expanding the polynomial $(1+x)^j$ in two different ways and then equating coefficients of like powers of x. Using Theorem 4.6.10, we can write the polynomial identity over $GF(p)$:

$$(1+x)^{p^i} = 1 + x^{p^i}.$$

We then have for arbitrary j:

$$(1+x)^j = (1+x)^{j_0 + j_1 p + j_2 p^2 + \cdots + j_{m-1} p^{m-1}}$$
$$= (1+x)^{j_0}(1+x^p)^{j_1}(1+x^{p^2})^{j_2} \cdots (1+x^{p^{m-1}})^{j_{m-1}}.$$

Next use the binomial expansion on both sides of the above equation to write it in the following form:

$$\sum_{k=0}^{j} \binom{j}{k} x^k =$$

$$\left[\sum_{k_0=0}^{j_0} \binom{j_0}{k_0} x^{k_0}\right]\left[\sum_{k_1=0}^{j_1} \binom{j_1}{k_1} x^{k_1 p}\right] \cdots \left[\sum_{k_{m-1}=0}^{j_{m-1}} \binom{j_{m-1}}{k_{m-1}} x^{k_{m-1} p^{m-1}}\right],$$

where each k_i is less than or equal to j_i and thus is less than p. Now equate coefficients of x^k. This gives

$$\binom{j}{k} = \sum \binom{j_0}{k_0}\binom{j_1}{k_1} \cdots \binom{j_{m-1}}{k_{m-1}} \quad (\bmod\ p),$$

where the sum is over all m-tuples $(k_0, k_1, \ldots, k_{m-1})$ having each component less than p and

$$k = k_0 + k_1 p + k_2 p^2 + \cdots + k_{m-1} p^{m-1}.$$

But this is the radix-p expansion of k, which is unique. Thus there is only one term in the sum, and the sum collapses to

$$\binom{j}{k} = \binom{j_0}{k_0}\binom{j_1}{k_1} \cdots \binom{j_{m-1}}{k_{m-1}} \quad (\bmod\ p).$$

This completes the proof of the theorem. □

We are now ready to characterize those cyclic codes whose extensions are invariant under the group of affine permutations. The characterization is in terms of the zeros of the generator polynomial. We exclude from consideration generator polynomials $g(x)$ with a zero at α^0 because otherwise, indeterminate expressions would occur.

□ **Theorem 13.3.4** Let α be a primitive element of $GF(q^m)$, a field of characteristic p. Let $\mathscr{C}$ be a cyclic code of blocklength $q^m - 1$ generated by $g(x)$, a polynomial for which α^0 is not a zero, and let $\overline{\mathscr{C}}$ be the extended code obtained by appending an overall parity-check symbol. The extended code $\overline{\mathscr{C}}$ is invariant under the group of affine permutations if and only if whenever α^k is a zero of $g(x)$ and k' is a nonzero radix-p descendent of k, then $\alpha^{k'}$ is also a zero of $g(x)$.

Proof Let $X' = aX + b$ denote an affine permutation. Let $X_1, X_2, \ldots,$ X_v be the location numbers of the nonzero components of a codeword **c**, and let $Y_1, Y_2, \ldots, Y_v$ denote the values of these components. Further, let $X'_1, X'_2, \ldots, X'_v$ denote the location numbers of the nonzero components of the codeword under the affine permutation. That is, $X'_i = aX_i + b$.

First, suppose that whenever α^k is a zero of $g(x)$ then so is $\alpha^{k'}$ for every k' that is a nonzero radix-p descendent of k. We must show the permutation of a codeword produces another codeword.

The codeword polynomial satisfies $c(x) = g(x)d(x)$, and the extension symbol is $c_\infty = -(c_{n-1} + \cdots + c_0)$. Let $C_j = c(\alpha^j) = \sum_{i=0}^{n-1} \alpha^{ij}c_i$. Then

$$C_j = \sum_{i=0}^{n-1} c_i\alpha^{ij} = \sum_{l=1}^{v} Y_l X_l^j = 0$$

for every j for which α^j is a zero of $g(x)$. Notice that there may be a nonzero symbol at location number α^∞. But α^∞ is a representation for the zero element, and thus this X_l is zero. Even though the term $Y_l X_l^j$ when X_l is zero was not included in the definition of C_j, we may consider it to be included on the right because it is zero anyway.

The permuted word **c**′ is a codeword if $c'_\infty + c'_{n-1} + \cdots + c'_0 = 0$, which clearly is still true after the permutation, and if

$$C'_j = \sum_{l=1}^{v} Y_l X_l'^j = 0$$

for every j for which α^j is a zero of $g(x)$. Consider such j:

$$
\begin{aligned}
C'_j &= \sum_{l=1}^{v} Y_l(aX_l + b)^j \\
&= \sum_{l=1}^{v} Y_l \sum_{k=0}^{j} \binom{j}{k} a^k X_l^k b^{j-k} \\
&= \sum_{k=0}^{j} \binom{j}{k} b^{j-k} a^k C_k
\end{aligned}
$$

By Theorem 5.9.3, $\binom{j}{k}$ is equal to zero unless k is a radix-p descendent of j, and by assumption C_k is zero for such k. Hence in every term of the sum, either $\binom{j}{k}$ equals zero or C_k equals zero. Thus C'_j equals zero, and the permuted codeword is again a codeword.

Now prove the converse. Assume that the extended code is invariant under the affine group of permutations. Then every codeword satisfies

$$C'_j = \sum_{l=1}^{v} Y_l(aX_l + b)^j = 0$$

for every a and b, and every j for which α^j is a zero of $g(x)$. As before, this becomes

$$C'_j = \sum_{k=0}^{j} \binom{j}{k} b^{j-k} a^k C_k = 0.$$

Let K be the number of radix-p descendents of j, and let k_l for $l = 1, \ldots, K$ index them. The sum can be written as

$$C'_j = \sum_{l=0}^{K} \binom{j}{k_l} b^{j-k_l} a^{k_l} C_{k_l} = 0.$$

Now a and b are arbitrary. We choose in turn b equal to 1 and a equal to the first K successive powers of α to get

$$\begin{bmatrix} (\alpha^{k_1})^0 & (\alpha^{k_2})^0 & \cdots & (\alpha^{k_K})^0 \\ (\alpha^{k_1})^1 & (\alpha^{k_2})^1 & \cdots & (\alpha^{k_K})^1 \\ \vdots & & & \vdots \\ (\alpha^{k_1})^{K-1} & (\alpha^{k_2})^{K-1} & \cdots & (\alpha^{k_K})^{K-1} \end{bmatrix} \begin{bmatrix} \binom{j}{k_1} C_{k_1} \\ \binom{j}{k_2} C_{k_2} \\ \vdots \\ \binom{j}{k_K} C_{k_K} \end{bmatrix} = \begin{bmatrix} 0 \\ 0 \\ \vdots \\ 0 \end{bmatrix}.$$

This matrix is a Vandermonde matrix. It is invertible because all columns are distinct. Therefore $C_{k_l} = 0$ for $l = 1, \ldots, K$. Hence, α^{k_l} is a zero of $g(x)$ whenever k_l is a radix-p descendent of j. This completes the proof of the theorem. $\square$

13.4 CYCLIC CODES BASED ON PERMUTATIONS

We will now describe a method for constructing some one-step majority-decodable codes. The technique makes use of the affine permutations described in Section 13.3. This technique can be used to obtain cyclic codes over $GF(q)$ of blocklength n, provided that n is composite; that is, $n = L \cdot J$. In addition, we must have $L \neq 0$ modulo p, where p is the characteristic of $GF(q)$. This condition is always satisfied for n that is a primitive blocklength or a divisor thereof.

Choose a primitive and composite blocklength n equal to $q^m - 1$, and let $n = L \cdot J$. Then

$$x^n - 1 = (x^J)^L - 1$$
$$= (x^J - 1)(x^{J(L-1)} + x^{J(L-2)} + \cdots + x^J + 1).$$

Denote the second term in this factorization by $a(x)$ so that

$$x^n - 1 = (x^J - 1)a(x).$$

The nonzero elements of $GF(q^m)$ are zeros of either $x^J - 1$ or $a(x)$. If α is primitive in $GF(q^m)$, then $\alpha^{LJ} = 1$ and $\alpha^{L(J-1)}, \alpha^{L(J-2)}, \ldots, \alpha^L, 1$ are the J zeros of $x^J - 1$. Therefore, for each j, α^j is a zero of $a(x)$ unless j is a multiple of L.

Define as follows a polynomial $\tilde{h}(x)$ whose reciprocal will be the parity-check polynomial for the desired code. For each j, α^j is a zero of $\tilde{h}(x)$ unless

j or a radix-q descendent of j is a multiple of L. Because every zero of $\tilde{h}(x)$ is then a zero of $a(x)$, we see that $a(x)$ is a multiple of $\tilde{h}(x)$.

Let $h(x)$ be the reciprocal polynomial of $\tilde{h}(x)$, and let $g(x)$ be defined by

$$g(x)h(x) = x^n - 1.$$

We now have two cyclic codes that are duals. Let $\mathscr{C}$ be the cyclic code with generator polynomial $g(x)$, and let $\mathscr{C}^\perp$ be the cyclic code with generator polynomial $\tilde{h}(x)$. By the definition of $\tilde{h}(x)$ and Theorem 13.3.4, the code $\mathscr{C}^\perp$ is a cyclic code with the doubly-transitive-invariant property. That is, we can extend $\mathscr{C}^\perp$ to a code $\overline{\mathscr{C}^\perp}$ that is invariant under the group of affine permutations.

We will form J parity-check equations for the cyclic code $\mathscr{C}$ that are concurring on a single component. Because the code is cyclic, it is therefore majority decodable, and the minimum distance is at least $J + 1$. We will find these parity-check equations for the code $\mathscr{C}$ by working with the dual code $\mathscr{C}^\perp$.

As we have seen previously, the polynomial

$$a(x) = x^{J(L-1)} + x^{J(L-2)} + \cdots + x^J + 1$$

has α^j as a zero if and only if j is not a multiple of L. Hence, $a(x)$ is a multiple of $\tilde{h}(x)$ and is a codeword in the dual code. Therefore, the elements of the set

$$\{a(x), xa(x), x^2 a(x), \ldots, x^{J-1} a(x)\}$$

of polynomials are all codewords in $\mathscr{C}^\perp$. Each of these designated codewords has Hamming weight L, and by inspection of $a(x)$ it is clear that no two of them have a common nonzero component.

Now we will find another set of codewords in $\mathscr{C}^\perp$ that can be used to define parity checks for $\mathscr{C}$. We will do this by temporarily adding an extended symbol to $\mathscr{C}^\perp$. This symbol will later serve as a kind of pivot point on which to develop the J concurring parity-check equations. In order to move the extended symbol into the interior of the cyclic code, it will be permuted to another component, and then the new extended symbol will be dropped.

Thus, append an overall parity-check symbol to each of the designated codewords. This gives J codewords in the extended code $\overline{\mathscr{C}^\perp}$ of blocklength $\bar{n} = n + 1$. If $L \neq 0$ (modulo p), the extended symbol is nonzero and is the same for every one of the J codewords constructed. Divide the codewords by this extended symbol to get a new set of codewords. We now have established the existence of a set of J codewords in $\overline{\mathscr{C}^\perp}$ with the following properties:

1. Each codeword in the set of J codewords has a one in location α^∞.
2. One and only one codeword in the set of J codewords has a nonzero component at location α^j for $j = 0, 1, \ldots, n - 1$.

We are now ready to make use of Theorem 13.3.4. In fact, the preceding definitions were designed so that the theorem applies. Because the code $\mathscr{C}^\perp$

has the doubly-transitive-invariant property, it is invariant under any affine permutation. In particular, choose

$$Y = \alpha X + \alpha^{n-1}.$$

This permutation carries the set of codewords in $\overline{\mathscr{C}^{\perp}}$ into another set of codewords in $\overline{\mathscr{C}^{\perp}}$ with the properties that:

1. Each codeword in the new designated set of J codewords has a one in location α^{n-1}.
2. One and only one codeword in the new set of J codewords has a nonzero component at location α^j for $j = \infty, 0, 1, \ldots, n-2$.

We can now drop location α^{∞} to get a set of codewords in $\mathscr{C}^{\perp}$ that are concurring on location $n-1$. In fact, these J codewords are orthogonal to the codewords of the code $\mathscr{C}$ and thus form parity-check equations. These are J parity-check equations concurring on location $n-1$, and the code is a cyclic code. We are now ready for the following theorem.

☐ **Theorem 13.4.1** Let $n = q^m - 1$ be factorable as $n = J \cdot L$. Suppose that a cyclic code $\mathscr{C}$ over $GF(q)$ has a generator polynomial constructed by the following rule. For each j, if j is a multiple of L or any radix-q descendent of j is a multiple of L, then α^{-j} is a zero of $g(x)$, and otherwise α^{-j} is not such a zero. Then $\mathscr{C}$ is a majority-decodable code over $GF(q)$ with a minimum distance of at least J.

Proof By definition of $\tilde{h}(x)$, α^{-j} is not a zero of $g(x)$ if and only if α^j is a zero of $\tilde{h}(x)$. Then $\tilde{h}(x)$ has α^j as a zero if and only if j is not a nonzero multiple of L and every nonzero radix-q descendent of j is not a multiple of L. Hence as we have seen, by reference to the dual code, there are J concurring parity-check equations on each component.

The code is over $GF(q)$ if each conjugate of a zero of $g(x)$ is also a zero. If α^{-j} is a zero because j is a multiple of L, then qj is a multiple of qL (mod LJ), and thus α^{-jq} is a zero, also. Otherwise, if α^{-j} is a zero because j', a radix-q descendent of j, is a multiple of L, then qj' (mod LJ), a radix-q descendent of qj (mod LJ), is a multiple of qL (mod LJ). ☐

We will illustrate the theorem with a simple example over $GF(2)$. Because

$$x^{15} - 1 = (x^3 - 1)(x^{12} + x^9 + x^6 + x^3 + 1)$$

$$= (x^5 - 1)(x^{10} + x^5 + 1),$$

we can take $J = 3$ and $L = 5$ or $J = 5$ and $L = 3$ to get either a single-error-correcting code or a double-error-correcting code. We will construct the single-error-correcting code.

The nonzero multiples of 5 are 5 and 10; 7 and 13 have 5 as a binary descendent; and 11 and 14 have 10 as a binary descendent. Hence, the zeros of $\tilde{h}(x)$ are α, α^2, α^3, α^4, α^6, α^8, α^9, and α^{12}, where α is a primitive element in $GF(16)$, and the zeros of $g(x)$ are α, α^2, α^4, α^5, α^8, α^{10}, and α^0. Hence

$$g(x) = (x-1)(x-\alpha)(x-\alpha^2)(x-\alpha^4)(x-\alpha^5)(x-\alpha^8)(x-\alpha^{10})$$
$$= x^7 + x^3 + x + 1,$$

and the code has eight information bits.

Table 13.1 tabulates some of these codes and also gives the parameters of some corresponding BCH codes. In each case, the minimum distance listed is that promised by the respective bounds. The actual minimum distance may be larger.

Notice from the table that a few cases occur where the choice of a majority-decodable code does not involve a serious penalty in k, although in most cases the penalty is substantial. It is important to realize, however, that the majority decoder is quick and simple and usually will readily correct many patterns with more than J errors. Simulations are worthwhile before a final judgement is made for a given application.

Table 13.1. Some binary one step-decodable codes compared to BCH codes

	Majority-Decodable		BCH	
n	k	d_{MD}	k	d_{BCH}
15	8	3	11	3
	6	5	7	5
63	48	3	57	3
	36	9	39	9
	12	21	18	21
255	224	3	247	3
	206	5	239	5
	174	17	191	17
	36	51	91	51
	20	85	47	85
511	342	7	484	7
	138	73	241	73
1023	960	3	1013	3
	832	11	973	11
	780	33	863	33
	150	93	598	93
	30	341	123	341

13.5 CONVOLUTIONAL CODES FOR MAJORITY DECODING

Some convolutional codes can be decoded by a majority decoder. Just as for block codes, these decoders are simple and extremely fast, but the codes are not as strong as other codes. One usually prefers a code with a higher rate.

The majority-decodable codes are decoded by taking a majority vote of certain of the syndromes, or a majority vote of certain linear combinations of the syndromes. A number of majority-decodable convolutional codes have been found by computer search. We shall tabulate some of these below.

The (12, 6) convolutional code produced by the encoder of Fig. 12.3 and decoded by the decoder of Fig. 12.20 can be decoded by majority logic. We will give two different majority decoders for this code to illustrate the nature of such decoders. In Fig. 13.3 we give the syndromes of all single-error patterns. The table contains modified syndromes computed according to two different rules. Notice that for either rule, the modified syndromes are concurring on the first bit position. In either case, because there are four modified syndromes, an error in the first bit position can be corrected, even in the presence of a second error. Figure 13.4 shows a majority decoder based on the first set of modified syndromes. This decoder will correct any double-error

Single Error Patterns	Syndromes $s_5\ s_4\ s_3\ s_2\ s_1\ s_0$	Modified Syndromes Rule 1 $s_3'\ s_2'\ s_1'\ s_0'$	Modified Syndromes Rule 2 $s_3''\ s_2''\ s_1''\ s_0''$
0 0 0 0 0 0 0 0 0 0 0 1	1 1 1 0 0 1	1 1 1 1	1 1 1 1
0 0 0 0 0 0 0 0 0 0 1 0	0 0 0 0 0 1	0 0 0 1	0 0 0 1
0 0 0 0 0 0 0 0 0 1 0 0	1 1 0 0 1 0	0 1 0 0	1 0 0 0
0 0 0 0 0 0 0 0 1 0 0 0	0 0 0 0 1 0	0 0 1 0	0 1 0 0
0 0 0 0 0 0 0 1 0 0 0 0	1 0 0 1 0 0	0 0 0 0	1 0 0 0
0 0 0 0 0 0 1 0 0 0 0 0	0 0 0 1 0 0	0 1 0 0	0 0 0 0
0 0 0 0 0 1 0 0 0 0 0 0	0 0 1 0 0 0	1 0 0 0	0 0 1 0
0 0 0 0 1 0 0 0 0 0 0 0	0 0 1 0 0 0	1 0 0 0	0 0 1 0
0 0 0 1 0 0 0 0 0 0 0 0	0 1 0 0 0 0	0 0 1 0	0 1 0 0
0 0 1 0 0 0 0 0 0 0 0 0	0 1 0 0 0 0	0 0 1 0	0 1 0 0
0 1 0 0 0 0 0 0 0 0 0 0	1 0 0 0 0 0	0 1 0 0	1 0 0 0
1 0 0 0 0 0 0 0 0 0 0 0	1 0 0 0 0 0	0 1 0 0	1 0 0 0

Rule 1	Rule 2
$s_0' = s_0$	$s_0'' = s_0$
$s_1' = s_1 + s_4$	$s_1'' = s_3$
$s_2' = s_2 + s_5$	$s_2'' = s_1 + s_4$
$s_3' = s_3$	$s_3'' = s_5$

Figure 13.3 Modified syndromes for a (12,6) convolutional code.

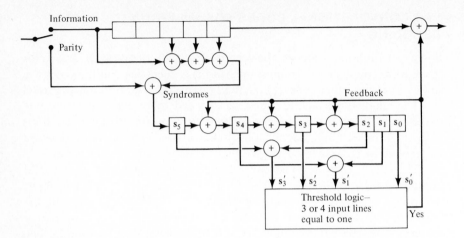

Figure 13.4   A majority decoder for a (12, 6) convolutional code.

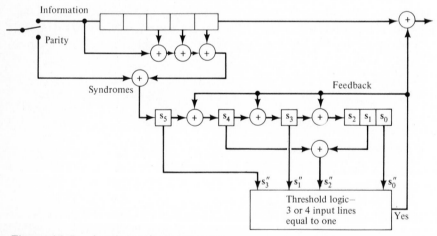

Figure 13.5   Another majority decoder.

pattern and is simpler than the decoder of Fig. 12.20. It has a fatal flaw, however, to which many majority decoders for convolutional codes are subject. Some patterns of more than two errors will pass the majority test and cause a false correction. For some of these, the feedback signal will modify the syndrome in such a way as to reproduce the same syndrome, even in the absence of further errors. For example, in the absence of further errors, the syndrome pattern 011010 leads to no error corrected, followed by the syndrome 001101 with one error corrected, followed by the syndrome 011010, which renews the cycle. This kind of an error is called an *ordinary error propagation*. It is a property of a majority decoder, and it can occur even with a noncatastrophic code. Ordinary error propagation cannot occur in a normal syndrome decoder.

(n_0, k_0)	(n, k)	t_{MD}	$G(x)$
(2, 1)	(6, 3)	1	$[x+1]^T$
(2, 1)	(14, 7)	2	$[x^6 + x^5 + x^2 + 1]^T$
(2, 1)	(36, 18)	3	$[x^{17} + x^{16} + x^{13} + x^7 + x^2 + 1]^T$
(2, 1)	(72, 36)	4	$[x^{35} + x^{31} + x^{30} + x^{18} + x^{16} + x^{10} + x^7 + 1]^T$
(2, 1)	(112, 56)	5	$[x^{55} + x^{54} + x^{49} + x^{45} + x^{32} + x^{29} + x^{21} + x^{14} + x^2 + 1]^T$
(3, 2)	(9, 6)	1	$[x+1]^T$
(3, 2)	(42, 28)	2	$[x^{12} + x^9 + x^8 + 1 \quad x^{13} + x^{11} + x^6 + 1]^T$
(3, 2)	(123, 82)	3	$[x^{30} + x^{29} + x^{24} + x^6 + x^2 + 1 \quad x^{36} + x^{35} + x^{28} + x^{15} + x^3 + 1]^T$
(4, 3)	(16, 12)	1	$[x+1 \quad x^2+1 \quad x^3+1]^T$
(4, 3)	(80, 60)	2	$[x^{19} + x^{15} + x^3 + 1 \quad x^{18} + x^{17} + x^8 + 1 \quad x^{13} + x^{11} + x^6 + 1]^T$

Figure 13.6 A short list of majority decodable convolutional codes.

In Fig. 13.5, we give another majority decoder for the same code but now based on the second set of modified syndromes from Fig. 13.3. This decoder is not subject to ordinary error propagation. From this example, we see that some majority decoders for convolutional codes are subject to ordinary error propagation, but that it may be possible to eliminate the error propagation by careful selection of the modified syndromes. If this is not possible for the desired code, then a normal syndrome decoder should be used.

A short list of convolutional codes that can be corrected by majority-logic is given in Fig. 13.5. These codes have been obtained by computer search.

13.6 GENERALIZED REED-MULLER CODES

The original Reed-Muller codes were introduced as binary codes. We will now study the Reed-Muller codes over a general Galois field $GF(q)$. The class of generalized Reed-Muller (GRM) codes contains subclasses that are majority decodable, but it also contains many codes that are of no practical interest. All of these are carried along in the same general theory.

The GRM codes, including the binary codes, will be defined by extending a cyclic code called a cyclic GRM code. We will limit the discussion in this section to cyclic GRM codes of primitive blocklength $q^m - 1$ and to GRM codes obtained from these by appending an overall parity-check symbol.

The zeros of the codewords are specified in a seemingly roundabout and mysterious way. We must define the radix-q weight of an integer.

☐ **Definition 13.6.1** Let j be an integer with radix-q representation

$$j = j_0 + j_1 q + j_2 q^2 + \cdots + j_{m-1} q^{m-1}.$$

The *radix-q weight* of j is

$$w_q(j) = j_0 + j_1 + j_2 + \cdots + j_{m-1},$$

with addition as integers. ☐

☐ **Definition 13.6.2** The *cyclic GRM code*† of order r and blocklength $n = q^m - 1$ over the field $GF(q)$ is the cyclic code whose generator polynomial $g(x)$ has zeros at all α^j for $j = 1, \ldots, q^m - 1$ such that

$$0 < w_q(j) \leqslant (q-1)m - r - 1.$$

The expansion of this cyclic code to a code of blocklength $n = q^m$ by a simple parity check is called a *GRM code* of order r. ☐

---

†An alternative definition is to choose $g(x)$ with zeros for all j satisfying $0 \leqslant w_q(j) \leqslant (q-1)m - r - 1$, where the first inequality now includes equality. The GRM code will then be obtained by lengthening the cyclic GRM code, adding the all-one vector to **G** rather than to **H**. With our definition, the Hamming codes are cyclic GRM codes.

Notice in Definition 13.6.1 that j and jq (mod $q^m - 1$) have the same radix-q weight. Therefore if β is a zero of $g(x)$, then so are all conjugates of β, and Definition 13.6.2 does indeed define a code over $GF(q)$.

When $q = 2$, the GRM code reduces to a code equivalent to the Reed-Muller code; it is the same but for a permutation of the components—hence the name generalized Reed-Muller code. This code can correct $2^{m-r-1} - 1$ errors by majority logic. The cyclic Reed-Muller codes of order $m - 2$ are Hamming codes, because then j is a zero of $g(x)$ whenever $w_2(j) = 1$; that is, when j equals 1 or a conjugate of 1. The Hamming codes are the simplest examples of GRM codes.

It is instructive to construct some of the binary GRM codes. Take $m = 5$ and $r = 2$. This code has blocklength 31 and can correct three errors by majority decoding. The code has parity frequencies indexed by all nonzero j for which

$$w_2(j) \leq 3.$$

that is, for which the binary representation of j has at most two ones. These are the binary numbers

$$0\ 0\ 0\ 0\ 1$$
$$0\ 0\ 0\ 1\ 1$$
$$0\ 0\ 1\ 0\ 1$$

and all cyclic shifts of these binary numbers. Thus parity frequencies occur at $j = 1$, 3, and 5 and all members of their conjugacy classes. This second-order cyclic GRM code is identical to the (31, 16, 7) BCH code over $GF(2)$. The expansion of the cyclic code is a (32, 16, 8) GRM code.

Next take $m = 5$ and $r = 1$. This code can correct seven errors by majority decoding. The indices of the parity frequencies now satisfy

$$w_2(j) \leq 3.$$

These indices have binary representations

$$0\ 0\ 0\ 0\ 1$$
$$0\ 0\ 0\ 1\ 1$$
$$0\ 0\ 1\ 0\ 1$$
$$0\ 0\ 1\ 1\ 1$$
$$0\ 1\ 0\ 1\ 1$$

and all cyclic shifts of these binary numbers. Thus parity frequencies occur at $j = 1$, 3, 5, 7, and 11 and at all members of their conjugacy classes. This first-order cyclic GRM code is a (31, 6, 15) code. The expansion is a (32, 6, 16) GRM code. Because 9 is in the conjugacy class of 5, and 13 is in the conjugacy of 11, the cyclic code is identical to the (31, 6, 15) BCH code.

Thus we see that both the BCH (31, 16) code and the BCH (31, 6) code can be corrected by majority decoding. To see a different situation, take $m = 6$ and $r = 2$. This Reed-Muller code can correct seven errors by majority decoding. The indices of the parity frequencies satisfy

$$w_2(j) \leqslant 3.$$

These indices have binary representations

$$
\begin{array}{cccccc}
0 & 0 & 0 & 0 & 0 & 1 \\
0 & 0 & 0 & 0 & 1 & 1 \\
0 & 0 & 0 & 1 & 0 & 1 \\
0 & 0 & 0 & 1 & 1 & 1 \\
0 & 0 & 1 & 0 & 0 & 1 \\
0 & 0 & 1 & 0 & 1 & 1 \\
0 & 0 & 1 & 1 & 0 & 1 \\
0 & 1 & 0 & 1 & 0 & 1 \\
\end{array}
$$

and all cyclic shifts of these binary numbers. Thus parity frequencies occur at $j = 1, 3, 5, 7, 9, 11, 13,$ and 21 and at all members of their conjugacy classes. This second-order cyclic GRM code is a (63, 22, 15) code. There is also a (63, 24) seven-error-correcting BCH code. The binary GRM code has inferior rate but can be decoded by majority logic. The expansion of the cyclic GRM code is a (64, 22, 16) GRM code.

We can restate the definition of the cyclic GRM code in terms of the spectrum of the codewords. The cyclic GRM code of order r and blocklength $n = q^m - 1$ over the field $GF(q)$ is the set of words whose spectral component C_j equals zero for all j satisfying

$$0 < w_q(j) \leqslant (q-1)m - r - 1.$$

We can encode such a code in the frequency domain by setting the spectrum at all these frequencies equal to zero, filling the remaining frequencies with information insofar as the conjugacy constraints allow, and taking the inverse Fourier transform. A time-domain encoder will usually be simpler, however.

The minimum distance of cyclic GRM codes must satisfy the BCH bound. The following theorem evaluates this bound.

□ **Theorem 13.6.3** The cyclic GRM code over $GF(2)$ of order r and blocklength $n = 2^m - 1$ is a subcode of the BCH code of designed distance $d = 2^{m-r} - 1$ and thus has a minimum distance at least this large.

Proof In radix 2, $2^{m-r} - 1$ is represented by an $(m-r)$-bit binary number consisting of all ones. Numbers smaller than $2^{m-r} - 1$ have less than $m - r$ ones. Therefore $w_2(j) \leqslant m - r - 1$ for $j = 1, 2, \ldots, 2^{m-r} - 2$, and $g(x)$ has α^j as a zero for $j = 1, 2, \ldots, 2^{m-r} - 2$. Consequently, the code is a subcode of the BCH code of designed distance $d = 2^{m-r} - 1$. $\square$

For nonbinary codes, the cyclic GRM code of order r is again a subcode of the BCH code of designed distance $q^{m-r} - 1$, provided that r is less than $q - 1$. Otherwise, the condition is a little more complicated, as given by the following theorem.

□ **Theorem 13.6.4** Let $r = (q-1)Q + R$, with $0 \leqslant R < q - 1$. The cyclic GRM code over $GF(q)$ of order r and blocklength $n = q^m - 1$ is a subcode of the BCH code over $GF(q)$ of designed distance

$$d = (q - R)q^{(m-Q-1)} - 1$$

and thus has a minimum distance at least this large.

Proof   Consider the q-ary representation of $(q - R)q^{(m-Q-1)} - 1$. It is equal to $q - R - 1$ in the most significant digit and is equal to $q - 1$ in each of the $m - Q - 1$ other digits. Hence

$$w_q((q - R)q^{(m-Q-1)} - 1) = (q - 1)(m - Q - 1) + q - R - 1$$

$$= (q - 1)m - r.$$

But then for all j less than $(q - R)q^{(m-Q-1)} - 1$, the q-ary weight is smaller than $(q - 1)m - r$. Hence for all j satisfying $0 < j \leqslant (q - R)q^{(m-Q-1)} - 2$, α^j is a zero of the generator polynomial, and the cyclic GRM code is a subcode of the BCH code with these zeros. This completes the proof. $\square$

The performance of some generalized Reed-Muller codes is shown in Fig. 13.7. When q equals 2, the codes are equivalent to Reed-Muller codes. The minimum distance listed is actually the lower bound on minimum distance given by Theorem 13.6.4. The number of information symbols is obtained by counting. Because the definition of the code specifies all zeros of $g(x)$, one can easily find the number of parity symbols by counting the positive integers less than n for which $w_q(j) \leqslant (q - 1)m - r - 1$.

□ **Theorem 13.6.5**   The dual of a GRM code over $GF(q)$ of order r and blocklength $n = q^m$ is equivalent to a GRM code of order $(q - 1)m - r - 1$ and blocklength $n = q^m$.

Proof   Let $\overline{\mathscr{C}}$ be the GRM code, and let $\mathscr{C}$ be the cyclic GRM code obtained by shortening $\overline{\mathscr{C}}$. The proof will be in three steps. In step 1, a generator polynomial $h(x)$ for the dual $\mathscr{C}^{\perp}$ of the cyclic GRM code $\mathscr{C}$ is found. In step 2, the parity-check polynomials of both $\mathscr{C}$ and $\mathscr{C}^{\perp}$ are observed to have $(x - 1)$ as a factor. In step 3, $\mathscr{C}$ and $\mathscr{C}^{\perp}$ are extended to GRM codes $\overline{\mathscr{C}}$ and $\overline{\mathscr{C}^{\perp}}$, which are shown to be duals.

$q=2$				$q=4$				$q=8$			
m	r	(n,k)	d_{BCH}	m	r	(n,k)	d_{BCH}	m	r	(n,k)	d_{BCH}
4	1	(15, 5)	7	2	1	(15, 3)	11	2	1	(63, 3)	55
4	2	(15, 11)	3	2	2	(15, 6)	7	2	2	(63, 6)	47
5	1	(31, 6)	15	2	3	(15, 10)	3	2	3	(63, 10)	39
5	2	(31, 16)	7	2	4	(15, 13)	2	2	4	(63, 15)	31
5	3	(31, 26)	3	3	1	(63, 4)	47	2	5	(63, 21)	23
6	1	(63, 7)	31	3	2	(63, 10)	31	2	6	(63, 28)	15
6	2	(63, 22)	15	3	3	(63, 20)	15	2	7	(63, 36)	7
6	3	(63, 42)	7	3	4	(63, 32)	11	2	8	(63, 43)	6
6	4	(63, 57)	3	3	5	(63, 44)	7	2	9	(63, 49)	5
7	1	(127, 8)	63	3	6	(63, 54)	3	2	10	(63, 54)	4
7	2	(127, 29)	31	3	7	(63, 60)	2	2	11	(63, 58)	3
7	3	(127, 64)	15	4	1	(255, 5)	191	2	12	(63, 61)	2
7	4	(127, 99)	7	4	2	(255, 15)	127	3	1	(511, 4)	447
7	5	(127, 120)	3	4	3	(255, 35)	63	3	2	(511, 10)	383
8	1	(255, 9)	127	4	4	(255, 66)	47	3	3	(511, 20)	319
8	2	(255, 37)	63	4	5	(255, 106)	31	3	4	(511, 35)	255
8	3	(255, 93)	31	4	6	(255, 150)	15	3	5	(511, 56)	191
8	4	(255, 163)	15	4	7	(255, 190)	11	3	6	(511, 84)	127
8	5	(255, 219)	7	4	8	(255, 221)	7	3	7	(511, 120)	63
8	6	(255, 247)	3	4	9	(255, 241)	3	3	8	(511, 162)	55
9	1	(511, 10)	255	4	10	(255, 251)	2	3	9	(511, 208)	47
9	2	(511, 46)	127					3	10	(511, 256)	39
9	3	(511, 130)	63					3	11	(511, 304)	31
9	4	(511, 256)	31					3	12	(511, 350)	23
9	5	(511, 382)	15					3	13	(511, 392)	15
9	6	(511, 466)	7					3	14	(511, 428)	7
9	7	(511, 502)	3					3	15	(511, 456)	6
								3	16	(511, 477)	5
								3	17	(511, 492)	4
								3	18	(511, 502)	3
								3	19	(511, 508)	2

Figure 13.7   Parameter of some generalized Reed-Muller codes.

Step 1 $\mathscr{C}$ is the set of words with parity frequencies at all j satisfying

$$0 < j \leqslant q^m - 1$$

and

$$w_q(j) \leqslant (q-1)m - r - 1.$$

The generator polynomial $g(x)$ has as zeros all α^j for such j. For convenience, we have replaced 0 with $q^m - 1$ in the range of j so that $w_q(j) > 0$ for all j. By the theory of cyclic codes, the parity frequencies of the dual code are described if j is replaced by $q^m - 1 - j$ and the inequality is reversed. That is, the parity frequencies are indexed by those j for which

$$w_q(q^m - 1 - j) > (q-1)m - r - 1.$$

But if

$$j = j_0 + j_1 q + j_2 q^2 + \cdots + j_{m-1} q^{m-1},$$

then

$$q^m - 1 - j = (q - 1 - j_0) + (q - 1 - j_1)q + \cdots + (q - 1 - j_{m-1})q^{m-1},$$

which can be verified by adding both sides of the equations. Hence $w_q(q^m - 1 - j) = (q - 1)m - w_q(j)$. Thus the dual code has parity frequencies at j satisfying $0 < j \leqslant q^{m-1}$ and

$$w_q(j) = (q - 1)m - w_q(q^m - 1 - j)$$

$$< r + 1.$$

The generator polynomial $\tilde{h}(x)$ for the dual code $\mathscr{C}^\perp$ has such α^j as zeros.
Step 2 α^0 is not a zero of either $g(x)$ or of $\tilde{h}(x)$. Hence the parity-check polynomials of both $\mathscr{C}$ and $\mathscr{C}^\perp$ have $x - 1$ as a factor.

Step 3 Now extend $\mathscr{C}$ and $\mathscr{C}^\perp$ to obtain two GRM codes. The parity-check matrices for the extended codes are

$$\begin{bmatrix} 1\ 1\ \cdots\ 1 \\ 0 \\ \vdots\quad \mathbf{H} \\ 0 \end{bmatrix} \quad \text{and} \quad \begin{bmatrix} 1\ 1\ \cdots\ 1 \\ 0 \\ \vdots\quad \mathbf{H'} \\ 0 \end{bmatrix}$$

where $\mathbf{H}$ and $\mathbf{H'}$ are parity-check matrices for $\mathscr{C}$ and $\mathscr{C}^\perp$. Excluding the first row of each matrix for the moment, all rows of the left matrix are orthogonal to all rows of the right matrix, because this is true of $\mathbf{H}$ and $\mathbf{H'}$. Next, the all-one row is orthogonal to itself because the blocklength is a multiple of q. Finally, the all-one row is orthogonal to every other row of both matrices because $x - 1$ is a factor of both parity-check polynomials. Therefore the left and right matrices are orthogonal, and the dimensions of the lengthened cyclic codes have sum q^m. The proof is complete. □

One can also define nonprimitive GRM codes in an obvious way. This definition will end the section.

□ **Definition 13.6.6** Let b divide $q^m - 1$. The cyclic nonprimitive GRM code of order r and blocklength $n = (q^m - 1)/b$ over the field $GF(q)$ is the cyclic code whose generator polynomial $g(x)$ has zeros at all α^{bj} for $j = 1, \ldots, (q^m - 1)/b$ such that $0 < w_q(bj) \leqslant (q - 1)m - r - 1$. □

13.7 EUCLIDEAN GEOMETRY CODES

A finite geometry is a finite set within which one specifies certain subsets called lines, planes, or flats that satisfy a collection of axioms. A finite geometry takes its terminology from conventional elementary geometry. This latter case consists of a set containing an infinite number of points together with subsets known as lines and planes. Each finite geometry is defined by its own set of axioms, and within each, one can develop a list of theorems. The most meaningful finite geometries are the Euclidean geometries and the projective geometries. These finite geometries can be used to invent codes.

Several classes of codes that are defined in terms of finite geometries are majority decodable—the Euclidean-geometry codes and the projective-geometry codes. We will introduce these classes of codes in terms of the generalized Reed-Muller codes. Both of these classes were originally introduced in a different way, using the theory of finite geometries, and this is how they get their names. This section will treat Euclidean-geometry codes, and the next will treat projective-geometry codes. We will study only codes over the prime-symbol field $GF(p)$. Three Galois fields play a role: $GF(p)$, the symbol field of the Euclidean-geometry code; $GF(q)$, the symbol field of the GRM code, which is an extension of $GF(p)$ with $q = p^s$; and the locator field $GF(q^m)$.

□ **Definition 13.7.1** Let r, s, and m be any positive integers, and let $q = p^s$, with p as a prime. The *Euclidean-geometry code* over $GF(p)$ of blocklength $n = q^m$ and order r is the dual of the subfield subcode of the GRM code over $GF(q)$ of blocklength q^m and of order $(q-1)(m-r-1)$.

□

Equivalently, a Euclidean-geometry code is the extended form of a cyclic code over $GF(p)$, also called a Euclidean-geometry code, with blocklength $q^m - 1$, given by the following theorem.

□ **Theorem 13.7.2** Let α be a primitive element of $GF(p^{sm})$. A Euclidean-geometry code over $GF(p)$ with parameters r and s and blocklength q^m is an extended cyclic code generated by the polynomial having zeros at α^j for $0 < j \leqslant q^m - 1$ if j satisfies

$$0 < \max_{0 \leqslant i < s} w_q(jp^i) \leqslant (q-1)(m-r-1).$$

Proof The $GF(p)$ subfield-subcode of the cyclic GRM code of order $(q-1)(m-r-1)$ has a generator polynomial with zero at α^j for $0 < j \leqslant q^m - 1$ if j satisfies

$$w_q(j) \leqslant (q-1)m - [(q-1)(m-r-1)] - 1 = (q-1)(r+1) - 1,$$

or if any p-ary conjugate of j satisfies this inequality. Conversely, α^j is a zero of the parity-check polynomial $h(x)$ if

$$w_q(j') > (q-1)(r+1) - 1$$

for every j' that is a p-ary conjugate of j. But now by the theory of cyclic codes, the generator polynomial of the dual code is the reciprocal polynomial of $h(x)$. Then j' is a zero of this reciprocal polynomial if $n - j'$ is a zero of $h(x)$, that is, if

$$w_q(n - j') > (q - 1)(r + 1) - 1$$

for every j' that is a p-ary conjugate of j. But as shown in the proof of Theorem 13.6.5, $w_q(n - j') = (q - 1)m - w_q(j')$. Hence

$$w_q(j') \leqslant (q - 1)(m - r - 1)$$

for every j' that is a p-ary conjugate of j. The theorem follows. $\square$

The simplest example of a Euclidean-geometry code is when $s = 1$ and $p = 2$. Then

$$w_2(j) \leqslant m - r - 1$$

if α^j is a zero of $g(x)$. This is just a Reed-Muller code of order r. The Euclidean-geometry codes are a generalization of the Reed-Muller codes. The parameters of the other Euclidean-geometry codes are given in Fig. 13.8.

Our goal is to show that the Euclidean-geometry codes can be majority decoded in $r + 1$ steps, and that $d_{\text{MD}} = (q^{m-r} - 1)/(q - 1)$. We will develop the decoder in terms of a suggestive geometric language, the language of a Euclidean geometry, which we will now introduce.

A Euclidean geometry, denoted by $EG(m, q)$, of dimension m over the field $GF(q)$ consists of q^m points (the vector space $GF(q)^m$) together with certain subsets called *flats* (or *affine subspaces*†), which are defined recursively as follows. The 0-flats (zero-dimensional affine subspaces) are the points of EG(m, q). They are the q^m m-tuples of the vector space. The $(t + 1)$-flats are obtained from the t-flats; each translation of the smallest vector sub-

t	Euclidean-Geometry Code (n, k)	BCH Code (n, k)
4	(63, 37)	(63, 39)
10	(63, 13)	(63, 18)
2	(255, 231)	(255, 239)
8	(255, 175)	(255, 191)
10	(255, 127)	(255, 179)
42	(255, 19)	(255, 47)

Figure 13.8 Parameters of some Euclidean-geometry codes and some BCH codes.

---

†A vector subspace must contain the origin of the vector space. An affine subspace is a translation of a vector subspace (i.e., a coset).

space containing a t-flat is a $(t + 1)$-flat. That is, if E_t is a t-flat, then the set $\{\gamma_t \mathbf{u} | \gamma_t \in GF(q), \mathbf{u} \in E_t\}$ is the smallest vector subspace containing E_t. If $\mathbf{v}_{t+1}$ is any specified point in $GF(q)^m$ not belonging to E_t, then a $(t + 1)$-flat E_{t+1} is obtained as the set

$$E_{t+1} = \{\mathbf{v}_{t+1} + \gamma_t \mathbf{u} | \gamma_t \in GF(q), \mathbf{u} \in E_t\}.$$

A more formal definition is as follows.

☐ **Definition 13.7.3** The Euclidean geometry EG(m, q) is the vector space $GF(q)^m$ together with all subspaces and translations of subspaces of $GF(q)^m$. ☐

The next theorem follows immediately from this definition.

☐ **Theorem 13.7.4** A t-flat contains exactly q^t points and itself has the structure of a Euclidean geometry EG(t, q). A t-flat can be expressed as the set of q^t points

$$\mathbf{v}_t + \gamma_{i_{t-1}} \mathbf{v}_{t-1} + \gamma_{i_{t-2}} \mathbf{v}_{t-2} + \cdots + \gamma_{i_0} \mathbf{v}_0,$$

where γ_i ranges over all elements of $GF(q)$, including the zero element, and the $GF(q)^m$-vectors $\mathbf{v}_0, \mathbf{v}_1, \ldots, \mathbf{v}_t$ are a fixed set of linearly independent elements of the t-flat. ☐

One might also call 1-flats and 2-flats *lines* and *planes*. This is because the definition of Euclidean geometry corresponds to the idea of conventional Euclidean space, only it is built on a finite field instead of on the real field. We might as well think of EG(m, q), $GF(q^m)$, and $GF(q)^m$ as containing the same elements. When we call it $GF(q^m)$, however, we are thinking of its algebraic structure, rules of multiplication, and so forth. When we call it EG(m, q), we are interested in the geometric structure created by Definition 13.7.3. When we call it $GF(q)^m$, we are interested in its vector-space structure.

The Euclidean geometry EG$(3, 2)$ is given in Fig. 13.9. This example suggests that the number of t-flats in a Euclidean geometry can be quite large. We will count the number of t-flats in EG(m, q). This will make use of the quantities known as q-ary gaussian coefficients, defined by

$$\begin{bmatrix} m \\ i \end{bmatrix} = \prod_{j=0}^{i-1} \frac{q^m - q^j}{q^i - q^j}$$

for $i = 1, 2, \ldots, m$, and $\begin{bmatrix} m \\ 0 \end{bmatrix} = 1$.

☐ **Theorem 13.7.5**
    (i) EG(m, q) contains $q^{m-t} \begin{bmatrix} m \\ t \end{bmatrix}$ distinct t-flats, for $t = 0, 1, \ldots m$.
    (ii) For any s and t, with $0 \leqslant s \leqslant t \leqslant m$, each s-flat is contained properly in exactly $\begin{bmatrix} m-s \\ t-s \end{bmatrix}$ distinct t-flats in EG(m, q).

0-Flats	1-Flats	2-Flats
000	000,001	000,001,010,011
001	000,010	000,001,100,101
010	000,011	000,001,110,111
011	000,100	000,010,100,110
100	000,101	000,010,101,111
101	000,110	000,011,100,111
110	000,111	000,011,101,110
111	001,010	001,011,101,111
	001,011	001,011,100,110
	001,100	001,010,101,110
	001,101	001,010,100,111
	001,110	010,011,110,111
	001,111	010,011,100,101
	010,011	100,101,110,111
	010,100	
	010,101	
	010,110	
	010,111	
	011,100	
	011,101	
	011,110	
	011,111	
	100,101	
	100,110	
	100,111	
	101,110	
	101,111	
	110,111	

Figure 13.9   The Euclidean geometry EG(3,2).

Proof   (i) We can construct a t-dimensional subspace by choosing an ordered set of t linearly independent points in EG(m, q). This can be done in

$$(q^m - 1)(q^m - q) \ldots (q^m - q^{t-1})$$

different ways: Many of these sets of independent points, however, will lead to the same t-dimensional subspace; in fact

$$(q^t - 1)(q^t - q) \ldots (q^t - q^{t-1})$$

sets will lead to the same t-dimensional subspace, because this is the number of ways of picking an ordered sequence of independent points from the t-dimensional subspace. Hence there are

$$\frac{(q^m - 1)(q^m - q) \cdots (q^m - q^{t-1})}{(q^t - 1)(q^t - q) \cdots (q^t - q^{t-1})} = \begin{bmatrix} m \\ t \end{bmatrix}$$

distinct t-dimensional subspaces. Each subspace has q^{m-t} cosets, and thus there are $q^{m-t} \begin{bmatrix} m \\ t \end{bmatrix}$ t-flats.

(ii) Given an s-flat, it can be extended to a t-flat by choosing a sequence of $t - s$ independent points not yet included in the s-flat. This can be done in

$$(q^m - q^s)(q^m - q^{s+1}) \cdots (q^m - q^{t-1})$$

ways. Many of these sequences of independent points, however, will extend the s-flat to the same t-flat; in fact

$$(q^t - q^s)(q^t - q^{s+1}) \cdots (q^t - q^{t-1})$$

sequences will lead to the same t-flat, because this is the number of ways of picking an ordered sequence of independent points from the t-flat without using points from the s-flat. The ratio of these two products is the number of distinct t-flats in which the s-flat is contained. This is equivalent to the statement to be proved. $\square$

☐ **Definition 13.7.6** The *incidence vector* of a subset of a set of q^m elements indexed by i is a vector of length q^m that has a one at component i if the element indexed by i is in the subset and otherwise has a zero at component i. $\square$

In our description of a GRM code, the elements of $GF(q^m)$ are used to number the components of the vector space of dimension $n = q^m$ (which itself contains q^{q^m} vectors). In other words, the elements of the vector space $GF(q)^m$ are being used to index the n components of the vector space $GF(q)^{q^m}$. The incidence vector of a subset of $GF(q)^m$ is a vector in $GF(q)^{q^m}$. When $GF(q)^m$ is given the structure of a Euclidean geometry $EG(m, q)$, then the incidence vector of a flat in $EG(m, q)$ is a vector in $GF(q)^{q^m}$. As we will see, the incidence vector of a flat in $EG(m, q)$ is a codeword in a GRM code contained in $GF(q)^{q^m}$.

We are now ready to find an alternative way in which to define the Euclidean-geometry codes.

☐ **Theorem 13.7.7** An rth order Euclidean-geometry code of blocklength $n = q^m$ over $GF(p)$ is the largest linear code over $GF(p)$ having in its null space the incidence vectors of all of the $(r + 1)$-flats in $EG(m, q)$.

Proof It suffices to prove that the GRM code that contains the dual of the Euclidean-geometry code is the smallest linear code over $GF(q)$

that contains all of the incidence vectors. This is because the components of an incidence vector can only be zero or one, and thus it always has all components in the subfield $GF(p)$. Hence an incidence vector is in the dual of the Euclidean-geometry code if it is in the GRM code that contains the dual.

The incidence vector is in the GRM code if it is in the cyclic GRM code and also has the correct extension symbol. But the incidence vector of an $(r + 1)$-flat has q^{r+1} nonzero components that add to zero modulo p, and thus the extension symbol is always correct. It is only necessary to show that the incidence vector with the last component deleted is in the cyclic GRM code. That is, we must show that the Fourier transform of each incidence vector $\mathbf{f}$ has component F_j equal to zero if

$$w_q(j) \leqslant (q-1)m - [(q-1)(m-r-1)] - 1,$$

which reduces to

$$w_q(j) < (q-1)(r+1).$$

The proof consists of evaluating F_j and showing that it is zero for all such j but may be nonzero for other j.

Step 1   Use the representation of Theorem 13.7.4 to express the $(r+1)$-flat as the set $\{\mathbf{v}_{r+1} + \gamma_{i_r}\mathbf{v}_r + \gamma_{i_{r-1}}\mathbf{v}_{r-1} + \cdots + \gamma_{i_0}\mathbf{v}_0\}$ where

$$i_0 = 0, 1, \ldots, q-1$$
$$i_1 = 0, 1, \ldots, q-1$$
$$\vdots$$
$$i_r = 0, 1, \ldots, q-1$$

index the q elements of $GF(q)$, and $\mathbf{v}_0, \ldots, \mathbf{v}_{r+1}$ are a fixed set of independent points in the $(r+1)$-flat. The incidence vector $\mathbf{f}$ has a one in component i when the field element α^i is in the preceding set and otherwise has a zero. The spectral component

$$F_j = \sum_{i=0}^{n-1} \alpha^{ij} f_i$$

now can be written as a sum of those terms where f_i equals one, dropping the terms where f_i equals zero:

$$F_j = \sum_{i_0=0}^{q-1} \sum_{i_1=0}^{q-1} \cdots \sum_{i_r=0}^{q-1} (v_{r+1} + \gamma_{i_r}v_r + \gamma_{i_{r-1}}v_{r-1} + \cdots + \gamma_{i_0}v_0)^j.$$

where now $v_0, \ldots, v_{r+1}$ are thought of as elements of $GF(q^{r+1})$. We need to determine those values of j for which F_j equals zero. A multinomial expansion gives

$$F_j = \sum_{i_0=0}^{q-1} \cdots \sum_{i_r=0}^{q-1} \sum_{\mathbf{h}} \frac{j!}{h_0! h_1! \ldots h_{r+1}!} v_{r+1}^{h_{r+1}} (\gamma_{i_r}v_r)^{h_r} \cdots (\gamma_{i_0}v_0)^{h_0},$$

where the sum on $\mathbf{h}$ is over all $(r+1)$-tuples $(h_0, h_1, \ldots, h_{r+1})$ such that

$h_0 + h_1 + \cdots + h_{r+1} = j$. Now interchange the summations and work with the terms of the form $\sum_{i=0}^{q-1} (\gamma_i v)^h$ with h fixed.

Step 2   The sum $\sum_{i=0}^{q-1} \gamma_i^h$ is over all field elements of $GF(q)$ and thus can be rewritten in terms of the primitive element α. For h not equal to zero,

$$\sum_{i=0}^{q-1} \gamma_i^h = 0 + \sum_{k=0}^{q-2} \alpha^{kh}.$$

This is the hth component of the Fourier transform of the all-one vector. It is zero except when h is a multiple of $q-1$. Then it is equal to $q-1$ mod p, which is equal to -1. For h equal to zero,

$$\sum_{i=0}^{q-1} \gamma_i^0 = \sum_{i=0}^{q-1} 1 = 0 \qquad (\text{mod } p),$$

using the convention $\gamma^0 = 1$ for all γ in $GF(q)$.

Every term in the sum for F_j is zero and can be dropped except when h_l is a nonzero multiple of $(q-1)$ for $l = 0, \ldots, r$. The sum becomes

$$F_j = (-1)^r \sum_{h_0} \sum_{h_1} \cdots \sum_{h_{r+1}} \frac{j!}{h_0! h_1! \cdots h_{r+1}!} v_0^{h_0} v_1^{h_1} \cdots v_{r+1}^{h_{r+1}},$$

where the sum is over $(h_0, \ldots, h_{r+1})$ such that

$$\sum_{l=0}^{r+1} h_l = j,$$

h_l is a nonzero multiple of $q-1$ for $l = 0, \ldots, r$, and $h_{r+1} \geqslant 0$.

Step 3   By Lucas's theorem (Theorem 13.3.3), in the equation for F_j the multinomial coefficient is zero in every term for which h_l is not a radix-p descendent of j for $l = 0, \ldots, r+1$. Therefore if h_l contributes to the sum, h_l is a radix-p descendent of j for $l = 0, \ldots, r+1$; hence h_l is a radix-q descendent of j for $l = 0, \ldots, r+1$. This follows from Lucas's theorem by writing

$$\frac{j!}{h_0! h_1! \ldots h_{r+1}!} = \frac{j!}{h_0! (j-h_0)!} \frac{(j-h_0)!}{h_1! \ldots h_{r+1}!}$$

$$= \frac{j!}{h_0! (j-h_0)!} \frac{(j-h_0)!}{h_1! \ldots h_{r+1}!} \frac{(j-h_0-h_1)!}{h_2! \ldots h_{r+1}!} = \cdots.$$

Further, any sum of the h_l contributing to the sum is a radix-p descendent of j and therefore is a radix-q descendent of j.

We can now summarize the conditions on the terms that contribute to F_j as follows:

(i) $\sum_{l=0}^{r+1} h_l = j$.

(ii) h_l is a nonzero multiple of $q-1$ for $l = 0, \ldots, r$, and $h_{r+1} \geqslant 0$.

(iii) Each place in the radix-q representation of j is the sum of the corresponding places of the radix-q representations of the h_l.

In order to complete the proof, we must show that there are no such terms if j satisfies

$$w_q(j) < (q-1)(r+1).$$

Step 4 Consider a radix-q representation of some integer k:

$$k = k_0 + k_1 q + k_2 q^2 + \cdots k_{m-1} q^{m-1}.$$

Then $k \pmod{q-1}$ can be evaluated as follows:

$$k = k_0 + k_1 q + \cdots + k_{m-1} q^{m-1}$$
$$k = k_0 + k_1 + \cdots + k_{m-1} \quad \pmod{q-1}$$
$$= w_q(k),$$

because q can be replaced by 1 without changing values modulo $q-1$. Hence

$$k = w_q(k) \quad \pmod{q-1}.$$

If k is a nonzero multiple of $q-1$, then $w_q(k)$ is a nonzero multiple of $q-1$.

Now consider a radix-q representation of j and h_l. Each place in the radix-q representation of j is the sum of the corresponding places of the radix-q representations of the h_l. Hence

$$w_q(j) = \sum_{l=0}^{r+1} w_q(h_l),$$

and for $l = 0, \ldots, r$, $w_q(h_l)$ is a nonzero multiple of $q-1$. Hence

$$w_q(j) \geq (q-1)(r+1)$$

if F_j can be nonzero. The theorem is proved. $\square$

The proof of the next theorem contains the majority-decoding algorithm.

$\square$ **Theorem 13.7.8** Let $q = p^s$. An rth order Euclidean-geometry code of blocklength $n = q^m$ over $GF(p)$ can be majority-decoded in $r+1$ steps in the presence of up to $\frac{1}{2}(q^{m-r} - 1)/(q-1)$ errors.

Proof The proof uses a recursive argument, showing that from a set of parity-check equations based on the incidence vectors of t-flats, one can get parity-check equations based on the incidence vectors of the $(t-1)$-flats. This shows that the parity-check equations based on the incidence vectors of the $(r+1)$-flats, as established by Theorem 13.7.7, can be pushed down in $r+1$ steps to parity checks on the individual symbols. The argument is as follows.

It follows from the definition of a t-flat in a finite geometry that the incidence vectors of all t-flats that contain a given $(t-1)$-flat define a set of $r = \begin{bmatrix} m-(t-1) \\ t-(t-1) \end{bmatrix}$ parity checks that are concurring on the sum of the error symbols associated with the points of that $(t-1)$-flat. For, given a $(t-1)$-flat E, any point not belonging to E is contained in precisely one t-flat that contains E. Hence, by a majority decision, a new parity check that corresponds to the incidence vector of the $(t-1)$-flat E can be obtained. This can be done for all of the $(t-1)$-flats that contain a given $(t-2)$-flat, which in turn define a set of parity checks concurring on that $(t-2)$-flat. Hence, by induction, we obtain after t steps a set of parity checks concurring on a 0-flat, that is, on a single error symbol. At the ith step, the number of concurring parity checks that can be used is $\begin{bmatrix} m-t+i \\ 1 \end{bmatrix}$. Hence, there are at least $\begin{bmatrix} m-t+1 \\ 1 \end{bmatrix}$ parity checks at each step, and the error-correction capability of the algorithm is given by

$$\frac{1}{2}\begin{bmatrix} m-t+1 \\ 1 \end{bmatrix} = \frac{\frac{1}{2}(q^{m-t+1}-1)}{(q-1)}.$$

This completes the proof of the theorem. $\square$

13.8 PROJECTIVE GEOMETRY CODES

The projective-geometry codes constitute a class of codes that is similar to the class of Euclidean-geometry codes. The codes differ in that they are constructed from nonprimitive cyclic GRM codes with blocklength $(q^m - 1)/(q-1)$, rather than from GRM codes with blocklength q^m. The development will proceed as before. Three fields play a role: $GF(p)$, the symbol field of the code, with p as a prime; $GF(q)$, the symbol field of a nonprimitive GRM code, where $q = p^s$; and $GF(q^m)$, the locator field.

$\square$ **Definition 13.8.1** Let r, s, and m be any positive integers, and let $q = p^s$, with p as a prime. The *projective-geometry code* over $GF(p)$ of blocklength $n = (q^m - 1)/(q-1)$ and order r is the dual of the subfield-subcode of the nonprimitive cyclic GRM code over $GF(q)$ of the same blocklength and of order $(q-1)(m-r-1)$. $\square$

Equivalently, a projective-geometry code is a nonprimitive cyclic code with a generator polynomial given by the following theorem.

$\square$ **Theorem 13.8.2** A projective-geometry code over $GF(p)$ with parameters r and s and blocklength $(q^m - 1)/(q-1)$ is a cyclic code generated by the polynomial having zeros at β^j for $0 < j \leqslant (q^m - 1)/(q-1)$ if j satisfies

$$0 < \max_{0 \leqslant i < s} \; w_q(j(q-1)p^i) \leqslant (q-1)(m-r-1),$$

where $q = p^s$, $\beta = \alpha^{q-1}$, and α is primitive in $GF(q)$.

Proof   The proof is the same as that of Theorem 13.7.2. $\square$

The parameters of some projective-geometry codes are given in Fig. 13.10. A projective-geometry code is r-step majority decodable. Our remaining tasks are to develop the majority decoder and to show that $d_{MD} = 1 + (q^{m-r+1} - 1)/(q-1)$.

The decoding procedure can be developed with the geometric language of a projective geometry. A projective geometry is closely related to a Euclidean geometry. In fact, for a quick description one may say that a projective-geometry is a Euclidean geometry augmented by some extra points, which may be called points at infinity, and with some new flats defined that involve these extra points. A formal definition is quite technical.

The projective geometry PG(m, q) has $(q^{m+1} - 1)/(q-1)$ points and is defined by working with the nonzero points of $GF(q)^{m+1}$. There are $q^{m+1} - 1$ such nonzero points, and they are divided into $(q^{m+1} - 1)/(q-1)$ sets, each set constituting one point of PG(m, q). Each point of PG(m, q) has $q - 1$ points of $GF(q)^{m+1}$ mapped onto it, and this projection suggests the name projective geometry.

The rule for forming these sets is that whenever $\mathbf{v}$ is a nonzero vector in $GF(q)^{m+1}$ and λ is a nonzero field element from $GF(q)$, $\mathbf{v}$ and $\lambda\mathbf{v}$ are in the same set V; that is, they are mapped onto the same point of PG(m, q). There are $q - 1$ such nonzero λ and so $q - 1$ vectors in the set. Hence, the points of

t	Projective Geometry Code (n, k)	Shortened Primitive BCH Code (n, k)
2	(21, 11)	(21, 11)
4	(73, 45)	(73, 45)
2	(85, 68)	(85, 71)
10	(85, 24)	(85, 22)
8	(273, 191)	(273, 201)
2	(341, 315)	(341, 323)
10	(341, 195)	(341, 251)
42	(341, 45)	(341, 32)
4	(585, 520)	(585, 545)
36	(585, 184)	(585, 250)
16	(1057, 813)	
2	(1365, 1328)	
10	(1365, 1063)	
42	(1365, 483)	
170	(1365, 78)	

Figure 13.10   Parameters of some projective geometry codes and some BCH codes.

the projective geometry can be identified with the $(q^{m+1} - 1)/(q - 1)$ distinct one-dimensional subspaces of $GF(q)^{m+1}$.

The projective geometry $PG(m, q)$ of dimension m over the field $GF(q)$ is the set of these $(q^{m+1} - 1)/(q - 1)$ points together with collections of subsets called t-flats for $t = 0, 1, \ldots, m$.

The 1-flat containing V_0 and V_1 is defined as follows. Let $\mathbf{v}_0 \in V_0$ and $\mathbf{v}_1 \in V_1$; it does not matter which elements are chosen (see Problem 13.9). Then the 1-flat (or line) containing V_0 and V_1 is the set of points in $PG(m, q)$ that are the images of the points $\beta_0 \mathbf{v}_0 + \beta_1 \mathbf{v}_1$ in $GF(q)^{m+1}$, where β_0 and β_1 are arbitrary field elements not both zero. There are $q^2 - 1$ choices for β_0 and β_1, and these map into $(q^2 - 1)/(q - 1)$ points in $PG(m, q)$. Thus a 1-flat in $PG(m, q)$ has $q + 1$ points.

Similarly, the t-flat containing V_i for $i = 0, \ldots, t$ is defined as follows. Let $\mathbf{v}_i \in V_i$ for $i = 0, \ldots, t$. The set of points $\mathbf{v}_i$ must be linearly independent in $GF(q)^{m+1}$, because the set of V_i are distinct points in $PG(m, q)$. Then the t-flat containing $V_0, \ldots, V_t$ is the set of points in $PG(m, q)$ that are the images of the points

$$\beta_0 \mathbf{v}_0 + \beta_1 \mathbf{v}_1 + \cdots + \beta_t \mathbf{v}_t$$

in $GF(q)^{m+1}$, where $\beta_0, \ldots, \beta_t$ are arbitrary field elements not all zero. There are $q^{t+1} - 1$ choices for $\beta_0, \ldots, \beta_t$, and these map into $(q^{t+1} - 1)/(q - 1)$ points in $PG(m, q)$. Thus a $(t + 1)$-flat has $q^t + q^{t-1} + \cdots + q + 1$ points.

☐ **Theorem 13.8.3** A t-flat in $PG(m, q)$ contains $\begin{bmatrix} t-1 \\ 1 \end{bmatrix}$ points and itself has the structure of a projective geometry $PG(t, q)$.

Proof The number of points is immediate because $\begin{bmatrix} t-1 \\ 1 \end{bmatrix} = (q^{t+1} - 1)/(q - 1)$. The structure of the t-flat is inherited from the structure of $PG(t, q)$. ☐

☐ **Theorem 13.8.4**
   (i) $PG(m, q)$ contains $\begin{bmatrix} m+1 \\ t+1 \end{bmatrix}$ distinct t-flats for $t = 0, 1, \ldots, m$.
   (ii) For any s and t, with $0 \leqslant s \leqslant t \leqslant m$, each s-flat is properly contained in exactly $\begin{bmatrix} m-s \\ t-s \end{bmatrix}$ distinct t-flats in $PG(m, q)$.

Proof The proof is essentially the same as that of Theorem 13.7.5. ☐

An alternative way in which to define the projective-geometry codes is given by the following theorem. This theorem parallels Theorem 13.7.6, and the proof is the same. It will be used to show that projective-geometry codes are majority decodable, just as Theorem 13.7.7 was used to show the Euclidean-geometry codes are majority decodable.

☐ **Theorem 13.8.5** An rth order projective-geometry code of block-length $n = (q^m - 1)/(q - 1)$ over $GF(p)$ is the largest linear code over $GF(p)$

having in its null space the incidence vectors of all of the r-flats in $PG(m, q)$.

Proof   It suffices to prove that the nonprimitive cyclic GRM code that contains the dual of the projective-geometry code is the smallest linear code over $GF(q)$ that contains all of the incidence vectors of the r-flats. This is because the components of an incidence vector can only be zero or one, and thus it always has all components in the subfield $GF(p)$. Hence an incidence vector is in the dual of the projective-geometry code if it is in the GRM code that contains the dual.

The incidence vector $\mathbf{f}$ is the nonprimitive cyclic GRM code if the Fourier transform has component F_j equal to zero for

$$w_q((q-1)j) \leqslant (q-1)m - [(q-1)(m-r-1)] - 1$$

or

$$w_q((q-1)j) < (q-1)(r+1).$$

The proof consists of evaluating F_j and showing that it is zero for such j.

Step 1   Express the r-flat as the image of the set

$$\{\gamma_{i_r}\mathbf{v}_r + \gamma_{i_{r-1}}\mathbf{v}_{r-1} + \cdots + \gamma_{i_0}\mathbf{v}_0\},$$

where $i_0, i_1, \ldots, i_r$ each index the q elements of $GF(q)$, and $\mathbf{v}_0, \ldots, \mathbf{v}_r$ represent a fixed set of independent points in the r-flat. It is not necessary here to exclude the case where all the γ coefficients are zero. This point will not contribute to F_j. The incidence vector $\mathbf{f}$ has a one in component i when the field element α^i is in this set and otherwise has a zero. Let $j' = (q-1)j$ for $j = 0, \ldots, (q^m - 1)/(q-1) - 1$, and compute the spectral component $F_{j'}$ by

$$F_{j'} = \sum_{i=0}^{n-1} \alpha^{ij'} f_i$$

$$= \sum_{i_0=0}^{q-1} \sum_{i_1=0}^{q-1} \cdots \sum_{i_r=0}^{q-1} (\gamma_{i_r}v_r + \gamma_{i_{r-1}}v_{r-1} + \cdots + \gamma_{i_0}v_0)^{j'}.$$

where now $v_0, \ldots, v_{r-1}$ are thought of as elements of $GF(q^r)$. We need to determine those values of j' for which this equals zero. A multinomial expansion gives

$$F_{j'} = \sum_{i_0=0}^{q-1} \cdots \sum_{i_r=0}^{q-1} \sum_{\mathbf{h}} \frac{j'!}{h_0! h_1! \ldots h_r!} (\gamma_{i_r}v_r)^{h_r} \cdots (\gamma_{i_0}v_0)^{h_0},$$

where the sum on $\mathbf{h}$ is over all solutions of $h_0 + h_1 + \cdots + h_r = j'$. Now interchange the summations and work with the terms $\sum_{i=0}^{q-1} (\gamma_i v)^h$.

Step 2   The sum $\sum_{i=0}^{q-1} \gamma_i^h$ is over all field elements and thus can be rewritten in terms of the primitive element α. As in the proof of Theorem

13.7.7, this will imply that only terms with h_l as a nonzero multiple of $q - 1$ contribute to $F_{j'}$. Then

$$F_{j'} = (-1)^r \sum_{h_0} \sum_{h_1} \cdots \sum_{h_{r+1}} \frac{j'!}{h_0! h_1! \ldots h_r!} v_0^{h_0} v_1^{h_1} \cdots v_r^{h_r},$$

where the sum is over $(h_0, \ldots, h_r)$ such that

$$\sum_{l=0}^{r+1} h_l = j'$$

and h_l is a nonzero multiple of $q - 1$ for $l = 0, \ldots, r$.

Steps 3 and 4 As in the proof of Theorem 13.7.7, Lucas's theorem implies that for each l, h_l is a radix-q descendent of j'. Hence

$$w_q(j') = \sum_{l=0}^{r} w_q(h_l).$$

But, as shown in the proof of Theorem 13.7.7, $w_q(h_l)$ is a nonzero multiple of $q - 1$ whenever h_l is. Hence

$$w_q(j') \geq (q - 1)(r + 1)$$

if $F_{j'}$ can be nonzero. The theorem is proved. $\square$

The proof of the following theorem contains the majority-decoding algorithm.

$\square$ **Theorem 13.8.6** Let $q = p^s$. An rth order projective-geometry code of blocklength $n = (q^m - 1)/(q - 1)$ over $GF(p)$ can be majority-decoded in r steps in the presence of up to $\frac{1}{2}(q^{m-r+1} - 1)/(q - 1)$ errors.

Proof The proof uses a recursive argument showing that from a set of parity-check equations based on the incidence vectors of t-flats, one can get parity-check equations based on the incidence vectors of the $(t - 1)$-flats. This shows that the parity-check equations based on the incidence vectors of the r-flats can be pushed down in r steps to parity checks on the individual symbols. The argument is the same as that given in the proof of Theorem 13.7.8. $\square$

PROBLEMS

13.1. Show that the binary (15, 7) double-error-correcting BCH code is majority decodable by implementing the Meggitt decoder as a majority decoder.

13.2. Design a two-step majority decoder for the (7, 4) binary Hamming code.

13.3. Construct a majority decoder for the binary (21, 12) double-error-correcting projective-geometry code.

13.4. Find the generator polynomial for a (15, 6) triple-error-correcting code over $GF(4)$ that is majority decodable. Design the decoder. Find the generator polynomial for a triple-error-correcting BCH code over $GF(4)$.

13.5. If $GF(q)$ is a field of characteristic 2, some majority-decodable codes over $GF(q)$ of modest performance can be obtained by taking $J = (q^m - 1)/q - 1$ and using a permutation technique. Verify the existence of the following codes:

$(255, 156)$, $t = 8$, over $GF(16)$.
$(4095, 2800)$, $t = 32$, over $GF(64)$.
$(65,535, 47,040)$, $t = 128$, over $GF(256)$.

If this is done by hand, some kind of four-dimensional array describing the radix-q representation of the exponents should be used to reduce the work.

13.6. Prove that no Reed-Solomon code can be decoded to its packing radius by a majority decoder.

13.7. Give a majority decoder for the $(42, 28)$ convolutional code given in Fig. 13.6.

13.8. Show that if an r-flat of EG(m, q) contains the origin, then it is a linear subspace of EG(m, q) regarded as a vector space. Given an r-flat in EG(m, q), how many other r-flats are disjoint from it?

13.9. In the definition of a 1-flat in a projective geometry, show that it does not matter which points representing V_0 and V_1 in $GF(q)^m$ are chosen.

13.10. Prove that no two lines are parallel in a projective geometry. That is, prove that every pair of 1-flats have nonzero intersection.

13.11. Construct a high-speed decoder for the $(63, 24, 15)$ binary BCH code by using in parallel four majority-logic decoders designed for the $(63, 22, 15)$ GRM code.

NOTES

The notion of the class of majority-decodable codes as constituting a special subclass of error-control codes was crystallized by Massey (1963). He established the general framework for treating such codes. Earlier, majority decoding had been used for some special cases. The first use was by Reed (1954), who used it to decode the Reed-Muller codes. Massey, in his work, was especially interested in convolutional codes, and he defined a class of majority-decodable convolutional codes. These convolutional codes were developed further by Robinson and Bernstein (1967) and by Wu (1976).

Finding constructive classes of majority-decodable block codes has proved to be a difficult task, and the work accumulates slowly. The key contributions were the application of finite geometries to code construction, first introduced by Rudolph (1964, 1967), and the realization by Kasami, Lin, and Peterson (1968) and by Kolesnik and Mironchikov (1968) that Reed-Muller codes are cyclic (but for an overall parity bit) and can be generalized to an arbitrary alphabet. The generalized Reed-Muller codes are from Kasami, Lin, and Peterson (1968). These leads were quickly developed by Weldon (1967, 1968); by Kasami, Lin, and Peterson (1968) in a second paper; by Goethals and Delsarte (1968); and by Delsarte, Goethals, and MacWilliams (1970). The simple method of construction of Section 13.4 is taken from Lin and Markowsky (1980). Finite-geometry codes were discussed in detail in a tutorial by Goethals (1975).

CHAPTER 14

Composition and Performance of Error-Control Codes

*I*n any engineering discipline, one first looks for methods of solving a given class of problems. Later, after these methods are in hand, one turns to questions of optimality. Are these methods the best methods, and if not, in what way and by how much are they inferior?

In order to answer such questions, one needs to know how good known codes are, and how good the best possible codes are. Generally, we cannot answer either of these questions satisfactorily. Although the best possible error-control code of a certain rate and blocklength is not known, a number of bounds are known—bounds beyond which no codes can exist, and bounds within which codes are sure to exist. A knowledge of these bounds deepens one's understanding of the subject.

In this chapter, we will study the composition structure of block codes and the probabilities of decoding error and of decoding failure. We will then give bounds on the best possible codes.

14.1 WEIGHT DISTRIBUTIONS

If a linear block code has a minimum distance d^*, then we know at least one codeword of weight d^* exists. Sometimes we are not content with this single piece of information; we wish to know how many codewords have weight d^*, and what are the weights of the other codewords. For example, in Table 5.3, we gave a list of code weights for the Golay (23, 12) binary code. For any small code, we can find such a table of all the weights by an exhaustive search. For a large code, this is not possible. Instead, one must employ analytical techniques if such techniques can be found. It is clear that such techniques will be difficult to find in general, because even the minimum distance is unknown for many codes.

Let A_l denote the number of codewords of weight l in an (n, k) linear code. The $(n + 1)$-dimensional vector with components A_l for $l = 0, \ldots, n$ is called the *weight distribution* of the code. Obviously, if the minimum distance is d^*, then $A_0 = 1, A_1, \ldots, A_{d^*-1}$ are all zero, and A_{d^*} is not zero. To say more than this requires some work.

Analytically describing the weight distribution of a code is a difficult problem and is unsolved for most codes, but for the important case of the Reed-Solomon codes (or any maximum-distance code), an analytical solution is known. This section will provide an introduction to the problem, giving a formula for the number of codewords of each weight in a maximum-distance code. For an arbitrary linear code, we will not be able to give such a formula, but we will give a little information. The MacWilliams identities will be derived; these relate the weight distribution of a code to the weight distribution of its dual code. The MacWilliams identities are useful if the dual code is small enough for its weight distribution to be found by computer search.

First we will give the exact solution for maximum-distance codes.

□ **Theorem 14.1.1**   In a maximum-distance code, any set of k places may be chosen as information places, taking on arbitrary values in $GF(q)$. The values in the remaining $n - k$ places are then forced by the code.

Proof   A code of minimum distance d^* can correct any $d^* - 1$ erasures. Because $d^* = n - k + 1$ for maximum-distance codes, the theorem is proved. □

It is clear from the proof of the theorem that if the code is not a maximum-distance code, then it is not true that any set of k places may be used as information places. This converse applies to all binary codes because no binary code is a maximum-distance code.

For maximum-distance codes, we can easily compute the number of codewords of weight d^*. Partition the set of integers from 0 to $n - 1$ into two sets, T_{d*} and T_{d*}^c, with T_{d*} having $d*$ integers. There are $\binom{n}{d*}$ ways of forming this partition. Consider all the codewords that are zero in those places indexed by the integers in T_{d*}^c. Any set of $k = n - d* + 1$ places in a maximum-distance codeword uniquely determines that codeword. Pick $n - d* + 1$ information places as the $n - d*$ places indexed by the integers in T_{d*}^c plus one additional place. This additional place can take on any of q values, and the remaining $d* - 1$ places are then determined. Hence, there are exactly q codewords for which a given set of $n - d*$ places is zero. One of these is the all-zero codeword, and $q - 1$ are of weight $d*$. Because the $n - d*$ zero locations as indexed by elements of T_{d*}^c can be chosen in $\binom{n}{d*}$ ways, we have

$$A_{d*} = \binom{n}{d*}(q - 1).$$

To find A_l for $l > d*$, we use a similar but considerably more difficult argument. This is done in proving the following theorem.

□ **Theorem 14.1.2** The weight distribution of a maximum-distance (n, k) code over $GF(q)$ is given by $A_0 = 1$; $A_l = 0$ for $l = 1, \ldots, d* - 1$; and, for $l \geq d*$,

$$A_l = \binom{n}{l}(q - 1) \sum_{j=0}^{l-d*} (-1)^j \binom{l-1}{j} q^{l-d*-j}.$$

Proof The theorem is obvious for $l < d*$. The proof of the remainder is divided into three steps.

Step 1 Partition the set of integers from 0 to $n - 1$ into two sets, T_l and T_l^c, with T_l having l integers, and consider only codewords that are equal to zero in those places indexed by the integers in T_l^c and are equal to zero nowhere else. Let M_l be the number of such codewords of weight l. For the total code,

$$A_l = \binom{n}{l} M_l,$$

and thus we only need to prove that

$$M_l = (q - 1) \sum_{j=0}^{l-d*} (-1)^j \binom{l-1}{j} q^{l-d*-j}.$$

This will be proved by developing an implicit relationship between M_l and $M_{l'}$ for l' less than l and l greater than $d*$.

Choose a set of $n - d* + 1$ information components as follows. All of the $n - l$ components indexed by the integers in T_l^c are information components, and any $l - d* + 1$ of the components indexed by the integers in T_l are also information components. Recall that the components indexed by T_l^c have been set to zero. By arbitrarily specifying the latter $l - d* + 1$ components, we get $q^{l-d*+1} - 1$ nonzero codewords, all of weight of at most l.

From the set of l places indexed by T_l, we can choose any subset of

l' places. There will be $M_{l'}$ codewords of weight l' with nonzero components confined to these l' places. Hence

$$\sum_{l'=d*}^{l} \binom{l}{l'} M_{l'} = q^{l-d*+1} - 1.$$

This recursion implicitly gives M_{d*+1} in terms of M_{d*}; M_{d*+2} in terms of M_{d*} and M_{d*+1}, and so forth. We will next solve the recursion to give an explicit formula for M_l.

Step 2 In this step we will rearrange the equation stated in the theorem into a form that will be more convenient to prove. Treat q as an indeterminate for the purpose of manipulating the equations as if they were polynomials. Define the notation

$$\left[\sum_{n=-N_1}^{N_2} a_n q^n \right] = \sum_{n=0}^{N_2} a_n q^n$$

as an operator keeping only coefficients of nonnegative powers of q. Notice that this is a linear operation. With this convention, the expression to be proved can be written

$$M_l = (q-1) \left[q^{-(d*-1)} \sum_{j=0}^{l-1} (-1)^j \binom{l-1}{j} q^{l-1-j} \right].$$

The extra terms included in the sum correspond to negative powers of q and do not contribute to M_l. Now we can collapse this using the binomial theorem:

$$M_l = (q-1) [q^{-(d*-1)}(q-1)^{l-1}].$$

Step 3 Finally, we will show that the expression for M_l derived in step 2 solves the recursion derived in step 1:

$$\sum_{l'=d*}^{l} \binom{l}{l'} M_{l'} = \sum_{l'=0}^{l} \binom{l}{l'} M_{l'}$$

$$= (q-1) \sum_{l'=0}^{l} \binom{l}{l'} [q^{-(d*-1)}(q-1)^{l'-1}]$$

$$= (q-1) \left[q^{-(d*-1)}(q-1)^{-1} \sum_{l'=0}^{l} \binom{l}{l'} (q-1)^{l'} \right]$$

$$= (q-1) \left[q^{-d*} \left(1 - \frac{1}{q} \right)^{-1} q^l \right]$$

$$= (q-1) \left[\sum_{i=0}^{\infty} q^{l-d*-i} \right]$$

$$= (q-1) \sum_{i=0}^{l-d*} q^{l-d*-i}$$

$$= q^{l-d*+1} - 1,$$

as was to be proved. □

☐ **Corollary 14.1.3** The weight distribution of a maximum-distance (n, k) code over $GF(q)$ is given by $A_0 = 1$; $A_l = 0$ for $l = 1, \ldots, d^* - 1$; and, for $l \geq d^*$,

$$A_l = \binom{n}{l} \sum_{j=0}^{l-d^*} (-1)^j \binom{l}{j} (q^{l-d^*+1-j} - 1)$$

Proof Use the identity

$$\binom{l}{j} = \binom{l-1}{j} + \binom{l-1}{j-1}$$

to rewrite the equation to be proved as

$$A_l = \binom{n}{l} \sum_{j=0}^{l-d^*} (-1)^j \left[\binom{l-1}{j} + \binom{l-1}{j-1} \right] (q^{l-d^*+1-j} - 1)$$

$$= \binom{n}{l} \left[\sum_{j=0}^{l-d^*} (-1)^j \binom{l-1}{j} (q q^{l-d^*-j} - 1) \right.$$

$$\left. - \sum_{j=1}^{l-d^*+1} (-1)^{j-1} \binom{l-1}{j-1} (q^{l-d^*+1-j} - 1) \right]$$

$$= \binom{n}{l} \sum_{i=0}^{l-d^*} (-1)^i \binom{l-1}{i} (q-1) q^{l-d^*-i},$$

which is known to be true from Theorem 14.1.2. ☐

Corollary 14.1.3 is useful for calculating the weight distribution of a Reed-Solomon code. An example, the weight distribution of the (31, 15) Reed-Solomon code, is shown in Fig. 14.1. Even for small Reed-Solomon codes, such as this one, the number of codewords of weight l can be very large. This is why it is generally not practical to find the weight distribution of a code by simple enumeration of the codewords.

We do not have anything like Theorem 14.1.2 for the case of codes that are not maximum-distance codes. For small n, the weight distribution can be found by a computer search, but for large n this quickly becomes impractical.

The strongest tool we have is an expression of the relationship between the weight distributuon of a linear code and the weight distribution of its dual code—the so-called *Mac Williams identities*. The MacWilliams identities hold for any linear code and are based on the vector-space structure of linear codes and on the fact that the dual code of a code $\mathscr{C}$ is the orthogonal complement of $\mathscr{C}$. Before we can derive the MacWilliams identities, we must return to the study of abstract finite-dimensional vector spaces, which was started in Section 2.6. We need to introduce the ideas of the intersection and direct sum of two subspaces and prove some properties.

Let U and V be subspaces of F^n. Then $U \cap V$, called the *intersection* of U and V, denotes the set of vectors that are in both U and V; and $U \oplus V$, called the *direct sum* of U and V, denotes the set of all linear combinations $a\mathbf{u} + b\mathbf{v}$,

l	A_l
0	1
1	0
2	0
3	0
4	0
5	0
6	0
7	0
8	0
9	0
10	0
11	0
12	0
13	0
14	0
15	0
16	0
17	8.22×10^9
18	9.59×10^{10}
19	2.62×10^{12}
20	4.67×10^{13}
21	7.64×10^{14}
22	1.07×10^{16}
23	1.30×10^{17}
24	1.34×10^{18}
25	1.17×10^{19}
26	8.37×10^{19}
27	4.81×10^{20}
28	2.13×10^{21}
29	6.83×10^{21}
30	1.41×10^{22}
31	1.41×10^{22}

Figure 14.1   Weight distribution
for the (31,15) Reed-Solomon code.

where **u** and **v** are in U and V, respectively, and a and b are scalars. Both $U \cap V$ and $U \oplus V$ are subspaces of F^n.

□ Theorem 14.1.4

$$\dim [U \cap V] + \dim [U \oplus V] = \dim [U] + \dim [V].$$

Proof A basis for $U \cap V$ has dim $[U \cap V]$ vectors. This basis can be extended to a basis for U by adding dim $[U] -$ dim $[U \cap V]$ more basis vectors and can be extended to a basis for V by adding dim $[V] -$ dim $[U \cap V]$ more basis vectors. All of these basis vectors taken together form a basis for $U \oplus V$. That is,

$$\dim[U \oplus V] = \dim[U \cap V]$$
$$+ (\dim[U] - \dim[U \cap V]) + \dim[V] - \dim[U \cap V],$$

from which the theorem follows. $\square$

$\square$ Theorem 14.1.5

$$U^{\perp} \cap V^{\perp} = (U \oplus V)^{\perp}$$

Proof U is contained in $U \oplus V$, and thus $(U \oplus V)^{\perp}$ is contained in $U^{\perp}$. Similarly, $(U \oplus V)^{\perp}$ is contained in $V^{\perp}$. Therefore $(U \oplus V)^{\perp}$ is contained in $U^{\perp} \cap V^{\perp}$. On the other hand, write an element of $U \oplus V$ as $a\mathbf{u} + b\mathbf{v}$, and let $\mathbf{w}$ be any element of $U^{\perp} \cap V^{\perp}$. Then $\mathbf{w} \cdot (a\mathbf{u} + b\mathbf{v}) = \mathbf{0}$, and thus $U^{\perp} \cap V^{\perp}$ is contained in $(U \oplus V)^{\perp}$. Hence the two are equal. $\square$

Let A_l for $l = 0, \ldots, n$ and B_l for $l = 0, \ldots, n$ be the weight distributions of a linear code and its dual code, respectively. Define the weight polynomials

$$A(x) = \sum_{l=0}^{n} A_l x^l \qquad \text{and} \qquad B(x) = \sum_{l=0}^{n} B_l x^l.$$

The following theorem relates these two polynomials and allows one to be computed from the other.

$\square$ Theorem 14.1.6 The weight polynomial $A(x)$ of an (n, k) linear code over $GF(q)$ and the weight polynomial of its dual code are related by

$$q^k B(x) = [1 + (q-1)x]^n A\left(\frac{1-x}{1+(q-1)x}\right).$$

Proof Let $\mathscr{C}$ be the code, and let $\mathscr{C}^{\perp}$ be the dual code. The proof will be in two parts. In part 1 we will prove that

$$\sum_{i=0}^{n} B_i \binom{n-i}{m} = q^{n-k-m} \sum_{j=0}^{n} A_j \binom{n-j}{n-m}$$

for $m = 0, \ldots, n$. In part 2 we will prove that this is equivalent to the condition of the theorem.

Part 1 For a given m, partition the integers from 0 to $n-1$ into two subsets, T_m and T_m^c, with set T_m having m elements. In the vector space $GF(q)^n$, let V be the m-dimensional subspace consisting of all vectors that have zeros in components indexed by the elements of T_m. Then

$V^\perp$ is the $(n-m)$-dimensional subspace consisting of all vectors that have zeros in components indexed by the elements of T_m.

By Theorem 14.1.5,

$$(\mathscr{C} \cap V)^\perp = \mathscr{C}^\perp \oplus V^\perp.$$

Therefore

$$\dim[\mathscr{C}^\perp \oplus V^\perp] = n - \dim[\mathscr{C} \cap V].$$

On the other hand, by Theorem 14.1.4,

$$\dim[\mathscr{C}^\perp \oplus V^\perp] = (n-k) + (n-m) - \dim[\mathscr{C}^\perp \cap V^\perp].$$

Equating these gives

$$\dim[\mathscr{C}^\perp \cap V^\perp] = \dim[\mathscr{C} \cap V] + n - k - m.$$

Now for each choice of T_m, there are $q^{\dim[\mathscr{C} \cap V]}$ vectors in $\mathscr{C} \cap V$ and $q^{\dim[\mathscr{C}^\perp \cap V^\perp]}$ vectors in $\mathscr{C}^\perp \cap V^\perp$. Consider $\{T_m\}$, the collection of all such T_m. Enumerate the vectors in each of the $\mathscr{C} \cap V$ that can be produced from some subset T_m in the collection $\{T_m\}$. There will be $\sum_{\{T_m\}} q^{\dim[\mathscr{C} \cap V]}$ vectors in the enumeration, many of them repeated appearances. Similarly, an enumeration of all vectors in each $\mathscr{C}^\perp \cap V^\perp$ produced from T_m in $\{T_m\}$ is given by

$$\sum_{\{T_m\}} q^{\dim[\mathscr{C}^\perp \cap V^\perp]} = q^{n-k-m} \sum_{\{T_m\}} q^{\dim[\mathscr{C} \cap V]}.$$

To complete part 1 of the proof, we must evaluate the two sums in the equation. This we do by counting how many times a vector of weight j in $\mathscr{C}$ shows up in a set $\mathscr{C} \cap V$. It is in $\mathscr{C} \cap V$ whenever the j positions fall in the m positions in which vectors in V are allowed to be nonzero, or equivalently, whenever the $n-m$ positions where vectors in V must be zero fall in the $n-j$ zero positions of the codeword. There are $\binom{n-j}{n-m}$ choices for the $n-m$ zero components, and thus the given codeword of weight j shows up in $\binom{n-j}{n-m}$ sets. There are A_j codewords of weight j. Therefore

$$\sum_{\{T_m\}} q^{\dim[\mathscr{C} \cap V]} = \sum_{j=0}^{n} A_j \binom{n-j}{n-m}.$$

We can similarly count the vectors in $\mathscr{C}^\perp \cap V^\perp$. The earlier equation then becomes

$$\sum_{j=0}^{n} B_i \binom{n-i}{m} = q^{n-k-m} \sum_{j=0}^{n} A_j \binom{n-j}{n-m}.$$

Because m is arbitrary, the first part of the proof is complete.

Part 2 Starting with the conclusion of part 1, write the polynomial identity

$$\sum_{m=0}^{n} y^m \sum_{i=0}^{n} B_i \binom{n-i}{m} = \sum_{m=0}^{n} y^m q^{n-k-m} \sum_{j=0}^{n} A_j \binom{n-j}{n-m}.$$

Interchange the order of the summations

$$\sum_{i=0}^{n} B_i \sum_{m=0}^{n-i} \binom{n-i}{m} y^m = q^{n-k} \sum_{j=0}^{n} A_j \sum_{m=0}^{n} \binom{n-j}{n-m} \left(\frac{y}{q}\right)^n \left(\frac{q}{y}\right)^{n-m},$$

recalling that $\binom{n-i}{m} = 0$ if $m > n - i$. Using the binomial theorem, this becomes

$$\sum_{i=0}^{n} B_i (1+y)^{n-i} = q^{n-k} \sum_{j=0}^{n} A_j \left(\frac{y}{q}\right)^n \left(1 + \frac{q}{y}\right)^{n-j}.$$

Finally, make the substitution $y = (1/x) - 1$, to get

$$q^k x^{-n} \sum_{i=0}^{n} B_i x^i = q^n \sum_{j=0}^{n} A_j \left(\frac{1-x}{xq}\right)^n \left(\frac{1+(q-1)x}{1-x}\right)^{n-j}$$

or

$$q^k \sum_{i=0}^{n} B_i x^i = (1+(q-1)x)^n \sum_{j=0}^{n} A_j \left(\frac{1-x}{1+(q-1)x}\right)^j,$$

which completes the proof of the theorem. $\square$

We close this section with a simple application of this theorem. From Table 1.1, we see that the weight enumerator of the Hamming (7, 4) code is given by

$$(A_0, A_1, \ldots, A_7) = (1, 0, 0, 7, 7, 0, 0, 1),$$

and thus

$$A(x) = x^7 + 7x^4 + 7x^3 + 1.$$

The dual code is the binary cyclic code known as the simplex code. Its generator polynomial

$$g(x) = x^4 + x^3 + x^2 + 1$$

has zeros at α^0 and α^1. By Theorem 14.1.6, the weight polynomial $B(x)$ of the simplex code is given by

$$2^4 B(x) = (1+x)^7 A\left(\frac{1-x}{1+x}\right)$$

$$= (1-x)^7 + 7(1+x)^3(1-x)^4 + 7(1+x)^4(1-x)^3 + (1+x)^7.$$

This reduces to

$$B(x) = 7x^4 + 1.$$

The (7, 3) simplex code has one codeword of weight 0 and seven codewords of weight 4.

14.2 PROBABILITIES OF DECODING ERROR AND DECODING FAILURE

An incomplete decoder for a t-error-correcting code that corrects to the packing radius corrects all error patterns of weight t or less and corrects no patterns of weight larger than t. When more than t errors occur, the decoder sometimes declares that it has an uncorrectable message and sometimes makes a decoding error. Hence, the decoder output can be the correct message, an incorrect message, or a decoding failure (an erased message). In general, how to compute the probabilities of these events is not known, but for some special cases of practical interest, satisfactory formulas are known. We will study the case of linear codes used on channels that make symbol errors independently and symmetrically. The probability expressions are in terms of the weight distribution $\{A_l\}$ of the code and thus are only useful when the weight distribution is known. We saw in the previous section that the weight distribution is known for all Reed-Solomon codes; thus for these codes, we can compute the probabilities of decoding error and decoding failure.

The channels we will consider are q-ary channels that make independent errors with probability P in each component and transmit correctly with probability $1 - P$. Each of the $q - 1$ wrong symbols occurs with probability $P/(q - 1)$. Each pattern of k errors has a probability of

$$p(k) = \left(\frac{P}{q-1}\right)^k (1 - P)^{n-k}$$

of occurring. We consider only incomplete decoders that do not decode beyond the packing radius of the code. The decoder will decode every received word to the closest codeword provided that it is within distance t of the codeword, where t is a fixed number that satisfies

$$2t + 1 \leq d^*.$$

For a linear code, we can analyze the case conditioned on the all-zero word being transmitted. Every other codeword will have the same conditional probabilities, and thus the results are also the unconditional probabilities. Figure 14.2 illustrates the three regions into which the received word can fall. The probability of correct decoding is the probability that the received word is in the crosshatched region. The probability of incorrect decoding is the probability that the received word is in the shaded region. The probability of decoding failure is the probability that the received word lies in the white region. The sum of these three probabilities equals 1, and thus only formulas for two of them are needed.

We will first dispense with the easy part of the work.

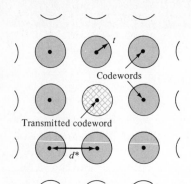

Figure 14.2   Decoding regions.

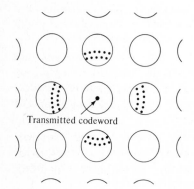

Figure 14.3   Some words that will cause a decoding error.

□ **Theorem 14.2.1**   A decoder that corrects to the packing radius of a code has a probability of correct decoding given by

$$p_c = \sum_{v=0}^{t} \binom{n}{v} P^v (1 - P)^{n - v}$$

Proof   There are $\binom{n}{v}$ ways that the v places with errors can be selected; each occurs with probability $P^v (1 - P)^{n - v}$. The theorem follows. □

Although the theorem holds for any channel-alphabet size, only the probability of making an error enters the formula. It does not matter how this probability of symbol error is broken down into the individual symbols. In the next theorem, dealing with decoding failure, it is necessary to count the ways in which errors can be made. Figure 14.3 illustrates some of the error patterns whose probabilities must be summed.

Let $N(l, h; s)$ be the number of error patterns of weight h that are at distance s from a codeword of weight l. Clearly, $N(l, h; s)$ is the same for every codeword of weight l. Notice that if $N(l, h; s) \neq 0$, then $l - s \leqslant h \leqslant l + s$. In the following theorem, this is taken care of automatically by using the convention $\binom{n}{m} = 0$ if m is negative or larger than n.

☐ **Theorem 14.2.2** The number of error patterns of weight h that are at distance s from a particular codeword of weight l is

$$N(l, h; s) = \sum_{\substack{0 \leqslant i \leqslant n \\ 0 \leqslant j \leqslant n \\ i + 2j + h = s + l}} \binom{n-l}{j+h-l}\binom{l}{i}\binom{l-i}{j}(q-1)^{j+h-l}(q-2)^i.$$

Proof An equivalent expression is

$$N(l, h; s) = \sum_{\substack{i,j,k \\ i+j+k=s \\ l+k-j=h}} \left[\binom{n-l}{k}(q-1)^k\right]\left[\binom{l}{i}(q-2)^i\right]\left[\binom{l-i}{j}\right],$$

which can be verified with the substitution $k = j + h - l$. This form has three summation indices and two constraints. The summand is the number of words that can be obtained by changing any k of the $n - l$ zero components of the codeword to any of the $(q - 1)$ nonzero elements, any i of the l nonzero elements to any of the other $(q - 2)$ nonzero elements, and any j of the remaining nonzero elements to zeros. The constraint $i + j + k = s$ ensures that the resulting word is at distance s from the codeword. The constraint $l + k - j = h$ ensures that the resulting word has a weight of h. ☐

☐ **Theorem 14.2.3** If $2t + 1 \leqslant d^*$, and the decoding is limited to t apparent errors, the probability of decoding error is

$$p_e = \sum_{h=0}^{n} \left(\frac{P}{q-1}\right)^h (1 - P)^{n-h} \sum_{s=0}^{t} \sum_{l=1}^{n} A_l N(l, h; s).$$

Proof The number of error words of weight h that will be decoded is $\sum_{s=0}^{t} \sum_{l=1}^{n} A_l N(l, h; s)$, where no point has been counted twice because $2t + 1 \leqslant d^*$. Each such word occurs with probability $[P/(q-1)]^h(1-P)^{n-h}$, and the theorem follows. ☐

Theorems 14.2.2, 14.2.3, and 14.1.3 contain all of the equations necessary in order to compute the error probability for a Reed-Solomon code. Evaluating them by using a computer program is straightforward. These equations are easily modified for an errors-and-erasures decoder. For ρ erasures, simply replace n with $n - \rho$ and replace p_e with the conditional error probability $p_{e|\rho}$. Then if $Q(\rho)$, the probability distribution on ρ, is known, p_e can be obtained as $p_e = \sum_{\rho} p_{e|\rho} Q(\rho)$.

14.3 WEIGHT DISTRIBUTIONS FOR CONVOLUTIONAL CODES

The weight of a convolutional codeword, infinitely long, is the number of nonzero components it has. The free distance is the weight of the codeword of smallest weight. The free length is the length of the codeword segment up to the last nonzero frame of the minimum-weight codeword. If the code is simple enough for the trellis to be drawn, all of these parameters can be read from the trellis. For example, in Fig. 14.4 the trellis of the (6, 3) convolutional code studied in Chapter 12 is redrawn. There is one path of weight 5, and this is the minimum distance of the code. This path occupies three frames, and the free length of the code is 6. The path that determines the free distance is excited by a single one in the information sequence. Looking further, we see two paths of weight 6, one of length 8 and one of length 10. In the same way we can enumerate the number of paths of each weight, but this quickly becomes tedious. In this section, we will present a more powerful procedure.

Figure 14.5(a) collapses the trellis into a state diagram by removing the time axis. For convenience, the state diagram is redrawn in Fig. 14.5(b) with

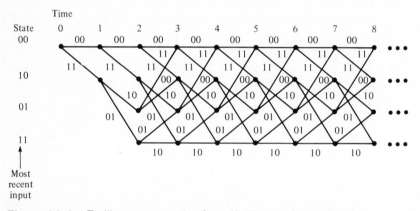

Figure 14.4 Trellis representation for a (6, 3) convolutional code.

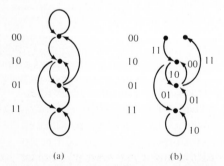

Figure 14.5 State diagram for a (6, 3) convolutional code.

the paths labeled. The node labeled 00 is shown twice, once as input and once as output, because we are only interested in paths starting at 00 and ending at 00. In the state diagram, it is easy to recognize the path of weight 5.

Measuring the weight of a path can be simplified by attaching a gain to each path as a power of a dummy variable D and using the techniques developed for the analysis of signal flow diagrams. The modified state diagram is shown in Fig. 14.6. The weight of a branch now appears as the power of D. The weight of a path is obtained by multiplying all the gains along the path.

Now compute the gain $T(D)$ of the whole network between input and output by simultaneous solution of the following equations obtained from Fig. 14.6:

$$b = Dc + Dd$$

$$c = D^2a + b$$

$$d = Dc + Dd$$

$$e = D^2b.$$

Solution of these equations gives

$$e = \frac{D^5}{1 - 2D}\, a,$$

and thus the transfer function is

$$T(D) = \frac{D^5}{1 - 2D}$$

$$= D^5 + 2D^6 + 4D^7 + \cdots + 2^kD^{k+5} + \cdots.$$

Hence, there are 2^k paths of weight $k + 5$.

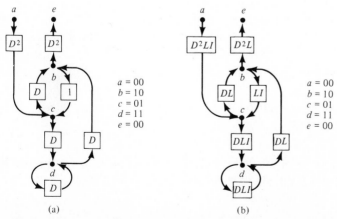

Figure 14.6 Signal flow diagrams for a (6, 3) convolutional code. (a) With delay-counting variables. (b) With delay-, length-, and input-counting variables.

The same technique can be used to count other properties of the code. We will introduce two new dummy variables, L to count frames, and I to count input ones. Each branch gain has a single L in it; each branch entered because of an input bit equal to one has a single I, and other branches have no I. Then as before,

$$
\begin{aligned}
T(D, L, I) &= \frac{D^5 L^3 I}{1 - DL(1 + L)I} \\
&= D^5 L^3 I + D^6 L^4 (1 + L) I^2 + D^7 L^5 (1 + L)^2 I^3 \\
&\quad + \cdots + D^{5+k} L^{3+k} (1 + L)^k I^{1+k} + \cdots .
\end{aligned}
$$

We see that the path of weight 5 has a length of 3 and is caused by a single input bit equal to one. There are two paths of weight 6, each caused by two input ones; one path has a length of 5, and one has a length of 6.

Thus we have fully determined the properties of the convolutional code. These properties are useful for comparing the structures of two convolutional codes. The distance structure also is needed for bounding the probability of error when the code is used on a specified channel.

14.4 BOUNDS ON MINIMUM DISTANCE FOR BLOCK CODES

An error-control code of blocklength n and rate R is judged by its minimum distance d^*. If we have two codes of the same n and R, we generally prefer the code with the larger d^*. If we have a code $\mathscr{C}$, we would like to know if d^* is as large as it can be for any code of this n and R. Generally, unless n is quite small, we do not know how to answer this question. We can usually give only some coarse bounds. We have already encountered the Singleton bound, which is a very coarse bound when n is much greater than q.

We will only give an asymptotic analysis. For a fixed alphabet size q, define

$$
\bar{d}(n, R) = \max_{\mathscr{C}} d^*(\mathscr{C}),
$$

where the maximum is over all codes of blocklength n and rate R, and

$$
d^*(\mathscr{C}) = \min_{\substack{x, y \in \mathscr{C} \\ x \neq y}} d(x, y)
$$

is the minimum distance of the code $\mathscr{C}$. The function $\bar{d}(n, R)$ is the largest minimum distance of any code over $GF(q)$ of rate R and blocklength n. Except for small n, we do not know $\bar{d}(n, R)$. Next, define

$$
\bar{d}(R) = \lim_{n \to \infty} \frac{1}{n} \bar{d}(n, R),
$$

provided the limit exists. Given the function $\bar{d}(R)$, we can say that for large enough n, the best block code of rate R has a minimum distance d^* approximately equal to $n\bar{d}(R)$. Thus if known, the function $\bar{d}(R)$ would give us a way in which to judge existing classes of error-control codes. Also, the derivation of $\bar{d}(R)$ might give some clues about the structure of good codes and how to find them.

Although we would like to know the functions $\bar{d}(n, R)$ and $\bar{d}(R)$, we do not know them. All that we know are lower bounds and upper bounds, some of which will be derived in this section. We will only study those bounds that can be derived with moderate effort; in particular, we will derive bounds known as the *Gilbert lower bound* and the *Elias upper bound*.

In order to obtain these bounds, we will employ counting arguments and estimate the composition of typical codewords. The composition of a q-ary codeword is a q-vector $(n_0, \ldots, n_{q-1})$, where $\sum_l n_l = n$, whose lth component specifies the number of times that letter l appears in the codeword. The relative frequency of a q-ary codeword is the q-vector $(p_0, \ldots, p_{q-1})$, where $p_l = n_l/n$. We will find bounds on the minimum distance in terms of the multinomial coefficients $n!/\Pi_l n_l!$, where $\Pi_l n_l!$ denotes the product $\prod_{l=0}^{q-1} (n_l!)$. The entropy function $H(p)$ is defined by

$$H(p) = -\sum_l p_l \log p_l.$$

We wish to prove the asymptotic equality for large n

$$\frac{n!}{\Pi_l(n_l!)} \approx e^{nH(p)},$$

which will be made precise shortly. This treatment will make use of Stirling's approximation:

$$\sqrt{2n\pi} \left(\frac{n}{e}\right)^n < n! < \sqrt{2n\pi} \left(\frac{n}{e}\right)^n \left(1 + \frac{1}{12n-1}\right).$$

□ **Theorem 14.4.1**

$$e^{n[H(p) - o_2(1)]} < \frac{n!}{\Pi_l(n_l!)} < e^{n[H(p) - o_1(1)]},$$

where

$$o_1(1) = \frac{1}{2n}(q-1)\log(2n\pi) + \frac{1}{2n}\sum_l \log p_l - \frac{1}{n}\log\left(1 + \frac{1}{12n-1}\right)$$

$$o_2(1) = \frac{1}{2n}(q-1)\log(2n\pi) + \frac{1}{2n}\sum_l \log p_l + \frac{1}{n}\sum_l \log\left(1 + \frac{1}{12np_l-1}\right).$$

Proof

$$\log \frac{n!}{\Pi_l(n_l!)} < \log \frac{\sqrt{2n\pi}\left(\frac{n}{e}\right)^n\left(1 + \frac{1}{12n-1}\right)}{\Pi_l\left[\sqrt{2n_l\pi}\left(\frac{n_l}{e}\right)^{n_l}\right]}$$

$$= \log \frac{\Pi_l n^{n_l}}{\Pi_l n_l^{n_l}} + \log \frac{\sqrt{2n\pi}\left(1 + \frac{1}{12n-1}\right)}{\Pi_l\sqrt{2n_l\pi}}$$

Letting $n_l = np_l$ proves the right-hand inequality. The left-hand inequality is proved in the same way. $\square$

We are now ready to develop the Gilbert bound. We do this by counting the number of codewords within a sphere surrounding each point in the space—not necessarily a codeword—and then averaging. The number of points in a sphere of radius d is called the *volume* of the sphere. It is

$$V = \binom{n}{0} + (q-1)\binom{n}{1} + \cdots + (q-1)^d\binom{n}{d}.$$

$\square$ **Theorem 14.4.2** In the vector space $GF(q)^n$, let V be the number of points in a sphere of radius d around any point. Given a code $\mathscr{C}$ with q^k codewords, the average number of codewords in a sphere of radius d around an arbitrary point in the space is

$$\bar{T} = q^k \frac{V}{q^n}.$$

Proof The argument proceeds by considering a sphere of radius d around each point in the space. Count the number of codewords in each sphere, and then sum over all spheres. Because a codeword has V points within distance d, it lies in V such spheres. Therefore the sum over all spheres of the number of codewords in each sphere must equal $q^k V$, and thus the average number of codewords per sphere is $(q^k V)/q^n$. $\square$

$\square$ **Theorem 14.4.3** There exist codes of rate R and minimum distance d over $GF(q)$ that satisfy

$$R \geq 1 - \frac{1}{n}\log_q V$$

where V is the volume of a sphere of radius d.

Proof Use Theorem 14.4.2 and assume that $\bar{T} \geq 1$. Otherwise, we could choose any point that has no codeword within distance d and declare it to be a codeword, thereby enlarging the code. Hence

$$q^{k-n}V \geqslant 1,$$

or

$$n - k \leqslant \log_q V,$$

from which the theorem follows. $\square$

□ **Theorem 14.4.4 (Gilbert Bound)** $\bar{d}(R) \geqslant \delta$ for all δ that satisfy

$$R \geqslant 1 - \delta \log_q (q-1) + \delta \log_q \delta + (1-\delta)\log_q(1-\delta).$$

Proof V consists of the sum of d terms, of which the last is the largest. Therefore

$$V < d(q-1)^d \binom{n}{d}.$$

Using Theorem 14.4.1, with $\delta = d/n$,

$$V < d(q-1)^{n\delta} q^{n[-\delta \log_q \delta + (1-\delta)\log_q (1-\delta) - o(1)]},$$

where $o(1)$ is a term that goes to zero as n goes to infinity. Then

$$\frac{1}{n} \log_q V < \delta \log_q (q-1) - \delta \log_q \delta - (1-\delta) \log_q (1-\delta) - o'(1).$$

Substitute this into Theorem 14.4.3 and asymptotically drop the term $o'(1)$ to complete the proof. $\square$

For a binary code, the Gilbert bound is

$$R \geqslant 1 - H_b(\bar{d}),$$

where

$$H_b(\bar{d}) = -\bar{d} \log_2 \bar{d} - (1-\bar{d}) \log_2 (1-\bar{d}).$$

This is shown graphically in Fig. 14.7.

An upper bound on $\bar{d}(R)$, called the Elias bound is derived next. Suppose that a code has $M = e^{nR}$ codewords of blocklength n. The *joint composition* of codeword $\mathbf{c}$ and codeword $\mathbf{c}'$ is the q by q array $\{n_{ll'}^{cc'}\}$, wherein the element $n_{ll'}^{cc'}$ gives the number of components in which codeword $\mathbf{c}$ contains an l and codeword $\mathbf{c}'$ contains an l'. Hence

$$d(\mathbf{c}, \mathbf{c}') = \sum_{\substack{l, l \\ l \neq l'}} n_{ll'}^{cc'}.$$

Each word has a total of

$$A_t = (q-1)^t \binom{n}{t}$$

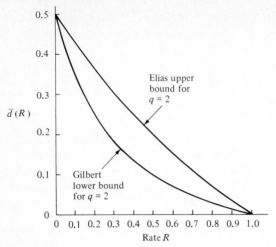

Figure 14.7 Some known bounds on the function $\bar{d}(R)$.

words at a distance t from it, so there are this many words on the surface of a sphere of radius t.

☐ **Theorem 14.4.5** In the vector space $GF(q)^n$, let A_t be the number of vectors on the surface of a sphere of radius t around any point. Given a code $\mathscr{C}$ with q^k codewords, the average number of codewords on the surface of a sphere around an arbitrary point in the space is

$$\bar{T}_s = q^k \frac{A_t}{q^n}.$$

Proof Because a codeword has A_t points at distance t, it lies on the surface of A_t such spheres. Therefore the sum of the number of codewords on each sphere is $q^k A_t$, and the average number of codewords per sphere surface is $(q^k A_t)/q^n$. ☐

We will choose such a sphere with at least an average number of codewords on its surface. It is convenient to visualize the all-zero vector as the center of this sphere, and thus we will translate the entire space, including the codewords, to place the center of the chosen sphere at the all-zero vector. This has no effect on the minimum distance of the code.

We now have a sphere of radius t centered at the origin with T codewords on its surface, where T is at least as large as $q^{k-n}A_t$. We can later choose t so that T is large enough for our needs. The next step is to bound the distance between two of these codewords on the sphere's surface. We do this by bounding the average distance between such codewords

$$d_{av} = \frac{1}{T(T-1)} d_{tot},$$

where d_{tot} is the total distance obtained as the sum of the distances between all unordered pairs of codewords on the surface, not necessarily distinct:

$$d_{tot} = \sum_{c, c'} d(\mathbf{c}, \mathbf{c}')$$

$$= \sum_{c, c'} \sum_{\substack{l, l' \\ l \neq l'}} n_{ll'}^{cc'}.$$

Recall that $\{n_{ll'}^{cc'}\}$ is the joint composition of codewords $\mathbf{c}$ and $\mathbf{c}'$. We now can simplify the sum on $\mathbf{c}$ and $\mathbf{c}'$. Let $n_{ll'|i}^{cc'}$ equal one if $\mathbf{c}$ has an l in the ith place and $\mathbf{c}'$ has an l' in the ith place, and otherwise equal zero. Let $T_{l|i}$ be the number of codewords on the sphere's surface having an l in the ith place. Then

$$n_{ll'}^{cc'} = \sum_{i=0}^{n-1} n_{ll'|i}^{cc'}$$

and

$$d_{tot} = \sum_{c, c'} \sum_{\substack{l, l' \\ l \neq l'}} \sum_{i} n_{ll'|i}^{cc'}$$

$$= \sum_{i} \sum_{\substack{l, l' \\ l \neq l'}} \sum_{c, c'} n_{ll'|i}^{cc'}$$

$$= \sum_{i} \sum_{\substack{l, l' \\ l \neq l'}} T_{l|i} T_{l'|i}.$$

Next, define

$$\lambda_{l|i} = \frac{T_{l|i}}{T}.$$

This is the fraction of codewords on the sphere's surface with an l in the ith place. The total distance between these codewords is

$$d_{tot} = T^2 \sum_{i} \sum_{l, l'} \lambda_{l|i} \lambda_{l'|i} D_{ll'},$$

where $D_{ll'}$ equals one if $l \neq l'$ and otherwise equals zero. We do not know $\lambda_{l|i}$, but we do know it satisfies the following two constraints:

$$\sum_{l=0}^{q-1} \lambda_{l|i} = 1 \quad \text{and} \quad \sum_{l=1}^{q-1} \sum_{i=0}^{n-1} \lambda_{l|i} = t.$$

Because we do not know $\lambda_{l|i}$, we will take the worst case by choosing it so as to make the right side as large as possible consistent with the known constraints. One way to solve this maximization problem is by using Lagrange multipliers for the constraints, provided the argument is first proved to be a concave function of the probability vector λ. We will instead use an elementary proof that avoids most of the work. We will postulate a maximizing value for $\lambda_{l|i}$, and then prove that it does indeed give a maximum.

□**Lemma 14.4.6** Let $F(\lambda) = \sum_i \sum_{l,l'} \lambda_{l|i} \lambda_{l'|i} D_{ll'}$, where $D_{ll'}$ equals one if $l \neq l'$ and otherwise equals zero. If λ satisfies the constraints

$$\sum_{l=0}^{q-1} \lambda_{l|i} = 1 \quad \text{and} \quad \sum_{l=1}^{q-1} \sum_{i=0}^{n-1} \lambda_{l|i} = t,$$

then

$$F(\lambda) \leq t \left[\frac{q}{q-1} - \frac{1 + (q-1)^2}{(q-1)^2} \frac{t}{n} \right].$$

Proof First notice that the constraints imply that

$$\sum_{i=0}^{n-1} \lambda_{0|i} = n - t.$$

Let

$$\lambda_{l|i}^* = \begin{cases} 1 - (t/n) & l = 0 \\ (t/n)/(q-1) & l = 1, \ldots, q-1 \end{cases}$$

for all i. We will see that this maximizes $F(\lambda)$. Notice that

$$\sum_{l=0}^{q-1} \lambda_{l|i}^* D_{ll'} = \begin{cases} t/n & l' = 0 \\ 1 - [(t/n)/(q-1)] & l' \neq 0. \end{cases}$$

Therefore, for all λ that satisfy the constraints,

$$\sum_{i=0}^{n-1} \sum_{l=0}^{q-1} \lambda_{l'|i} \sum_{l=0}^{q-1} \lambda_{l|i}^* D_{ll'} = \sum_{l'=1}^{q-1} \sum_{i=0}^{n-1} \lambda_{l'|i} \left(1 - \frac{t/n}{q-1} \right) + \left[\sum_{i=0}^{n-1} \lambda_{0|i} \frac{t}{n} \right]$$

$$= t \left(1 - \frac{t/n}{q-1} \right) + (n-t) \frac{t}{n},$$

Including $\lambda = \lambda^*$. Hence by expanding and cancelling the left side below, we have

$$\sum_i \sum_{l,l'} (\lambda_{l|i} - \lambda_{l|i}^*)(\lambda_{l'|i} - \lambda_{l'|i}^*) D_{ll'} = \sum_i \sum_{l,l'} (\lambda_{l|i} \lambda_{l'|i} - \lambda_{l|i}^* \lambda_{l'|i}^*) D_{ll'}.$$

It suffices to show that the left-hand side of this equation is negative. Hence, define

$$c_{l|i} = (\lambda_{l|i} - \lambda_{l|i}^*),$$

and notice that $\sum_l c_{l|i} = 0$. We need to prove that for each i

$$\sum_{l,l'} (c_{l|i} c_{l'|i}) D_{ll'} \leq 0.$$

But for each i,

$$\sum_{l,l'} c_{l|i} c_{l'|i} D_{ll'} = \sum_{l,l'} c_{l|i} c_{l'|i} - \sum_l c_{l|i}^2$$

$$= 0 - \sum_l c_{l|i}^2 \leq 0.$$

Hence, evaluating $F(\lambda^*)$ completes the proof of the lemma. $\square$

☐ **Theorem 14.4.7 (Elias Bound)** For any t, let

$$T = q^{-(n-k)}(q-1)^t \binom{n}{t}.$$

Every code over $GF(q)$ of rate R and blocklength n has a pair of codewords at distance d satisfying

$$d \leq \frac{T}{T-1} t \left[\frac{q}{q-1} - \frac{1+(q-1)^2}{(q-1)^2} \frac{t}{n} \right],$$

provided $T > 1$.

Proof Choose t in Theorem 14.4.5 such that $\bar{T}_s$ is greater than one. Then for some sphere, T the number of codewords on its surface is greater than one. The average distance between these codewords satisfies

$$d_{av} \leq \frac{T}{T-1} \sum_i \sum_{l,l'} \lambda_{l|i} \lambda_{l'|i} D_{ll'}.$$

Finally, to complete the proof apply lemma 14.4.6 and notice that some pair of codewords must be at least as close as the average. $\square$

☐ **Corollary 14.4.8 (Elias Bound)** For binary codes of rate R, the relative minimum distance asymptotically satisfies

$$\bar{d}(R) \leq 2\rho(1-\rho)$$

for any ρ that satisfies $1 - H_b(\rho) > R$.

Proof Set $q = 2$ and $t/n = \rho$ in Theorem 14.4.7, and write Theorem 14.4.7 as

$$\frac{d^*}{n} \leq \frac{T}{T-1} 2\rho(1-\rho)$$

and

$$T = 2^{n\delta + o(1)},$$

where

$$\delta = H_b(\rho) - 1 + R.$$

By assumption δ is positive, and thus $T/(T-1)$ goes to one as n goes to infinity. The corollary follows. $\square$

14.5 BOUNDS ON MINIMUM DISTANCE FOR CONVOLUTIONAL CODES

The lth minimum distance d_l^* of a convolutional code of blocklength $n = (m+1)n_0$ has been defined as the smallest Hamming distance between any two initial codeword segments that disagree in the initial frame. The minimum distance d^* of the convolutional code is defined as d_{m+1}^* and the free distance is defined as

$$d_\infty = \max_l d_l^*.$$

In this section, we will find Gilbert-type and Elias-type bounds both on d^* and on d_∞.

Clearly, we can take any long segment of length N of a convolutional code to get a block code of length N, and this code cannot be better than the best block code of length N. The need for this section arises because of interest in the behavior of distance with other measures of the code's length, such as blocklength and free length. Of course, if we have several ways to measure code distance, and several ways to measure code length, we can mix these together in various ways and prove a variety of bounds.

The bounds we will derive here can be compared with the bounds for block codes. Conclusions can be misleading, however, because it is not clear which parameter of a convolutional code should be equated to the blocklength of a block code.

For a fixed alphabet size q, define

$$\bar{d}(n, R) = \max_\mathscr{C} d^*(\mathscr{C}),$$

where the maximum is over all convolutional codes of blocklength n and rate R, and $d^*(\mathscr{C})$ is the minimum distance of the code $\mathscr{C}$. The function $\bar{d}(n, R)$ is the largest minimum distance of any convolutional code over $GF(q)$ of rate R and blocklength n. Next, define

$$\bar{d}(R) = \lim_{n \to \infty} \frac{1}{n} \bar{d}(n, R),$$

provided the limit exists. Given the function $\bar{d}(R)$, we can say that for large enough n, the best convolutional code of rate R has a minimum distance d^* approximately equal to $n\bar{d}(R)$. Thus if known, the function $\bar{d}(R)$ would give us a way to judge convolutional codes.

Similar definitions can be made for the free distance. One can get very different functions depending on whether one looks at the ratio of free distance to blocklength or free distance to free length. Define

$$\bar{d}_\infty(n, R) = \max_\mathscr{C} d_\infty(\mathscr{C}),$$

where the maximum is over all convolutional codes of blocklength n and rate R, and $d_\infty(\mathscr{C})$ is the free distance of the code $\mathscr{C}$. The function $\bar{d}_\infty(n, R)$ is the largest free distance of any convolutional code over $GF(q)$ of rate R and blocklength n. Next, define

$$\bar{d}_\infty(R) = \lim_{n \to \infty} \frac{1}{n} \bar{d}_\infty(n, R),$$

provided the limit exists. Again, given the function $\bar{d}_\infty(R)$, we can say that for large enough n, the best convolutional code of rate R and blocklength n has a free distance d_∞ approximately equal to $nd_\infty(R)$.

It is evident that because $d_\infty(\mathscr{C})$ is usually larger than $d^*(\mathscr{C})$, we should expect $\bar{d}_\infty(R)$ to be larger than $\bar{d}(R)$. One might also argue for an alternative definition as follows. Let $\bar{n}_\infty(n, R)$ be the free length of the code that achieves $\bar{d}_\infty(n, R)$. The free length is more closely related to the free distance and the decoder complexity than is the blocklength. Define

$$\hat{d}_\infty(R) = \lim_{n \to \infty} \frac{\bar{d}_\infty(n, R)}{\bar{n}_\infty(n, R)},$$

provided the limit exists. Then given the function $\hat{d}_\infty(R)$, we can say that for large enough free length $\bar{n}$, the best convolutional code of rate R has a free distance approximately equal to $\bar{n}\hat{d}_\infty(R)$.

We will give bounds only on the function $\bar{d}(R)$. The Elias-type bound is easy to obtain by referring to the earlier bound for block codes. We will give the bound only for binary convolutional codes.

□ **Theorem 14.6.1 (Elias Bound)** For binary convolutional codes of rate R, the function $d(R)$ satisfies

$$\bar{d}(R) \leqslant 2\rho(1 - \rho)$$

for any ρ that satisfies $1 - H_b(\rho) > R$.

Proof For each m, truncate the convolutional code of blocklength $n = mn_0$ to get a block code of blocklength n. The rate of the block code is also R because k_0 information symbols are encoded into n_0 codeword symbols. The minimum distance of the convolutional code is not larger than the minimum distance of the best block code. Hence any upper bound on the minimum distance of the block code is also an upper bound on the minimum distance of the convolutional code. The Elias bound is such a bound. □

The Gilbert bound cannot be obtained by referring to the Gilbert bound for block codes. It must be obtained by a direct proof. Notice also that because convolutional codes are linear, the Gilbert bound that follows holds in a stronger sense than the Gilbert bound proved previously for block codes, which only proved the existence of some suitable code, not necessarily linear.

Before we prove the Gilbert bound, we need to prove a lemma. The lemma deals with the initial codeword of the convolutional code; that is, with the first n symbols.

Lemma 14.6.2 An initial codeword that is nonzero in the first frame appears in exactly $q^{(m+1)(n_0-k_0)(k_0-1)}$ distinct systematic (n_0, k_0) convolutional codes with wordlength $(m+1)k_0$.

Proof Because the code is systematic, by giving the initial n codeword symbols, we give the first $(m+1)k_0$ information symbols. The first $(m+1)n_0$ codeword symbols are related to the first $(m+1)k_0$ information symbols by a generator matrix. This matrix is described by $m+1$ matrices $\mathbf{P}_0, \ldots, \mathbf{P}_m$, each of which is a k_0 by (n_0-k_0) matrix. The $m+1$ parity frames $(\mathbf{p}_0, \mathbf{p}_1, \ldots, \mathbf{p}_m)$ are given by the matrix equation:

$$(\mathbf{p}_0, \mathbf{p}_1, \ldots, \mathbf{p}_m) = (\mathbf{i}_0, \mathbf{i}_1, \ldots, \mathbf{i}_m) \begin{bmatrix} \mathbf{P}_0 & \mathbf{P}_1 & \cdots & \mathbf{P}_m \\ \mathbf{0} & \mathbf{P}_0 & \cdots & \mathbf{P}_{m-1} \\ \mathbf{0} & \mathbf{0} & \cdots & \mathbf{P}_{m-2} \\ & & & \vdots \\ & & & \mathbf{P}_0 \end{bmatrix}$$

Thus $\mathbf{i}_0 \mathbf{P}_0 = \mathbf{p}_0$, which imposes $n_0 - k_0$ constraints on the $k_0(n_0 - k_0)$ elements of $\mathbf{P}_0$; this implies that $(k_0 - 1)(n_0 - k_0)$ of the elements can be chosen independently. Hence $\mathbf{P}_0$ can be selected in $q^{(k_0-1)(n_0-k_0)}$ ways and still be consistent with the initial codeword frame. Similarly, $\mathbf{i}_0 \mathbf{P}_1 = \mathbf{p}_1 - \mathbf{i}_0 \mathbf{P}_0$, and $\mathbf{P}_1$ can be selected in $q^{(k_0-1)(n_0-k_0)}$ ways. In turn we see that each $\mathbf{P}_i$ can be selected in this many ways, and thus there are $[q^{(k_0-1)(n_0-k_0)}]^{m+1}$ convolutional codes that have the given initial codeword. $\square$

$\square$**Theorem 14.6.3** Given a rate $R = k_0/n_0$ and a blocklength $n = (m+1)n_0$, let ρ satisfy

$$\sum_{j=1}^{\rho} \binom{n}{j} (q-1)^j < q^{n(1-R)}.$$

Then there exists at least one systematic convolutional code over $GF(q)$ whose minimum distance d^* is larger than ρ.

Proof A convolutional code has a minimum distance greater than ρ if it has no initial codeword of length n and of weight ρ or less for which some information symbol is nonzero in the first frame. In the set of all convolutional codes of blocklength n, we will count the total number of initial codewords that have a weight of ρ or less and are nonzero in the first frame. If this total is less than the number of systematic convolutional codes, then there must be at least one such code with minimum distance greater than ρ.

There are exactly $q^{(m+1)(n_0-k_0)k_0}$ systematic (n_0, k_0) convolutional codes, because it takes $(n_0-k_0)k_0$ generator polynomials of degree of m or less to specify such a code, and each such polynomial may be chosen in q^{m+1} different ways.

There are exactly

$$\sum_{j=1}^{\rho} \binom{n}{j}(q-1)^j$$

nonzero n-tuples of weight ρ or less.

By Lemma 14.6.2, each initial codeword that is nonzero in the first frame can appear in at most $q^{(m+1)(n_0-k_0)(k_0-1)}$ distinct systematic (n_0, k_0) convolutional codes. Hence, if

$$\left[\sum_{j=1}^{\rho} \binom{n}{j}(q-1)^j \right](q^{(m+1)(n_0-k_0)(k_0-1)}) < q^{(m+1)(n_0-k_0)k_0},$$

then there must be at least one code that has a minimum distance greater than ρ. The theorem follows. $\square$

☐ **Corollary 14.6.4 (Gilbert Bound)** For binary convolutional codes,

$$\bar{d}(R) \geqslant H_b^{-1}(1-R).$$

Proof For $q=2$, the theorem asserts that

$$\sum_{j=1}^{\bar{d}(n,R)} \binom{n}{j} \geqslant 2^{n(1-R)}.$$

Hence

$$\frac{1}{n} \log \sum_{j=1}^{\bar{d}(n,R)} \binom{n}{j} \geqslant 1-R.$$

The corollary follows by using Theorem 14.4.1 and taking the limit. $\square$

PROBLEMS

14.1. Consider a $(31, 27)$ Reed-Solomon code.
   a. How many codewords have a weight of 5?
   b. How many error patterns have a weight of 3?
   c. What fraction of error patterns of weight 3 are undetected?
   d. Choose a word at random (equiprobable). What is the probability that it will be decoded?
14.2. Use the MacWilliams identity and Table 5.7 to compute the weight-distribution vector of the dual of the $(24, 12)$ extended Golay code. (In fact, the $(24, 12)$ extended Golay code is its own dual; it is called a *self-dual code*.)
14.3. For a linear block code over $GF(2)$, prove that either no words have odd weight or half of the words have odd weight.

14.4. The simplest two-dimensional binary code with N rows and M columns is a single-error-correcting code that uses a single parity-check on each row and a single parity-check on each column. The minimum distance of the code is 4. Suppose this code is used for error detection on a binary channel with crossover probability q. What is the probability of undetected error? Only the term with the smallest power of q need be included in the calculation.

14.5. A t-error-correcting (n, k) Reed-Solomon code has a minimum distance of $d^* = n - k + 1 = 2t + 1$ and a weight distribution $A_{d*} = \binom{n}{d*}(q - 1)$.
   a. How many error patterns of weight $t + 1$ are there?
   b. By a direct argument, find the number of error patterns of weight $t + 1$ that are incorrectly decoded by a decoder that decodes to the packing radius.
   c. What fraction of error patterns of weight $t + 1$ are incorrectly decoded?
   d. Evaluate the expression of part (c) for $q = 32$, $t = 5$, and for $q = 64$, $t = 6$.

14.6. Evaluate the sum of the weight distribution components $\sum_{l=0}^{n} A_l$.

14.7. A t-error-correcting (n, k) Reed-Solomon code has a minimum distance of $d^* = n - k + 1 = 2t + 1$ and a weight distribution $A_{d*} = \binom{n}{d*}(q - 1)$.
   a. How many burst-error patterns of weight $t + 1$ and length $t + 1$ are there?
   b. Find the number of burst-error patterns of weight $t + 1$ and length $t + 1$ that are incorrectly decoded by a decoder that decodes to the packing radius.
   c. What fraction of burst-error patterns of weight $t + 1$ and length $t + 1$ are incorrectly decoded?
   d. Evaluate the expression of part (c) for $q = 32$, $t = 5$ and for $q = 64$, $t = 6$.

14.8. A Reed-Solomon code over $GF(2^m)$ is used as a multiple-burst-correcting code over $GF(2)$. Discuss the decoding of received words that are found to be outside the packing radius of the code.

14.9. For the binary $(8, 4)$ convolutional code with generator polynomials

$$g_1(x) = x^3 + x + 1 \qquad g_2(x) = x^3 + x^2 + x + 1,$$

find the free distance, the free length, and the number of ones in the input sequence that achieves the path that establishes the free length.

NOTES

The weight distribution of a maximum-distance code was derived independently by Assmus, Mattson, and Turyn (1965); by Forney (1966); and by Kasami, Lin, and Peterson (1966). The MacWilliams identities were derived by her in 1963. The same paper also treated the relationship between the weight distribution and the probability of decoding error. Other treatments may be found in Forney (1966) and in Huntoon and Michelson (1977). The state-diagram method for finding the weight distribution of a convolutional code is from Viterbi (1971).

The lower bound on the minimum distance of block codes was published by Gilbert (1952). Elias never published his upper bound. It first appeared in his classroom lectures in 1960. Better upper bounds are known, but they are far more difficult to prove. The best-known upper bound is from McEliece, Rodemich, Rumsey, and Welch (1977). Recent unpublished work in the Soviet Union shows that the Gilbert bound is not tight in $GF(49)$.

CHAPTER 15

Efficient Signaling for Noisy Channels

A
t the center of a digital communication system, there is usually an analog channel—a channel that is continuous in amplitude and in time. The input signal is an analog waveform, which is either a real-valved or a complex-valved continuous function of time. A digital communication system for such a channel includes a modulator/demodulator (modem) to make the analog channel into a discrete channel for the encoder/decoder (codec).

Error-control codes give the best results if an intelligent interaction exists between the modem design and the codec design. At this level of the design, the subjects of information theory, communication theory, and error-control codes come together. This chapter will briefly touch on some topics from information theory and communication theory in order to provide a broader setting for error-control codes. In this setting, we will more clearly see error-control coding as one of the tools used to design efficient signaling systems for communicating through noisy continuous channels.

Decoding algorithms that use extra information from the demodulator will be developed in this chapter. For a fixed code, these soft-decision decoders generally give better performance than hard-decision decoders, but because they are more complex, they tend to be useful only for smaller codes. An exception is the class of sequential decoders; these decoders readily use soft-decision information even for codes of long constraint length but are subject to buffer-overflow problems.

15.1 THE BANDPASS GAUSSIAN CHANNEL

Over some long signaling interval T, a general waveform channel accepts as input any continuous function $s(t)$ for t running from 0 to T, provided that

$$E_m = \int_0^T s(t)^2 dt$$

is finite. The integral of $s(t)^2$ is called the *message energy*, E_m, for the waveform $s(t)$. If T is allowed to increase without limit, then the *average power*, S, is defined by

$$S = \lim_{T \to \infty} \frac{1}{T} E_m(T),$$

provided that the limit exists, where $E_m(T)$ is the message energy on an interval of length T. If the waveform is chosen randomly from an ensemble of waveforms, one uses other methods of defining power, such as the limit of the expected value of $E_m(T)/T$ over the ensemble of waveforms.

Channels usually have constraints on the allowable waveforms. A bandpass channel is one that passes only those modulated, carrier-based signals known as *bandpass waveforms*. A carrier-based signal is given by

$$s_c(t) = a(t)\cos(2\pi f_0 t + \theta(t))$$

$$= s_R(t)\cos 2\pi f_0 t + s_I(t)\sin 2\pi f_0 t,$$

where $a(t)$ and $\theta(t)$ are real-valued functions called the amplitude and phase modulation, respectively, and $s_R(t)$ and $s_I(t)$ are called the real and imaginary modulation components, respectively. The latter terminology is from the alternative complex description

$$s_c(t) = \text{Re} \left\{ s(t)e^{j2\pi f_0 t} \right\},$$

where $s(t) = s_R(t) + js_I(t)$, which is often more convenient to work with. The complex baseband signal $s(t)$ is only a mathematical artifice; the observed signal $s_c(t)$ is as previously shown. The term f_0, known as the carrier frequency, is a constant and plays no significant role in our problems here, although it is a critical part of the transmitted waveform.

The spectrum of $s(t)$ is given by the Fourier transform

$$S(f) = \int_{-\infty}^{\infty} s(t)e^{-j2\pi ft}dt$$

A bandpass waveform is one whose spectrum is confined to a small interval of the frequency axis around the carrier frequency f_0. The length of this interval is called the *bandwidth*, W, and W is smaller than $2f_0$. In principle, $S(f) = 0$ for $|f - f_0| > W/2$, but in practice one accepts a weaker condition, such as $|S(f)| < \varepsilon$ for $|f - f_0| > W/2$.

After encoding, a codeword or sequence of codewords must be mapped into the modulation signals $(a(t), \theta(t))$ or $(s_R(t), s_I(t))$. This mapping operation is called *modulation*, and its inverse is called *demodulation*. The study of such operations is a major topic of digital communications theory. Historically, the study of error-control codes has been kept separate from the study of digital modulation. In this chapter, however, we will study modulation and demodulation systems where the subjects of error-control codes and digital modulation begin to run together.

A bandpass gaussian channel with input $s(t)$ has output $v(t)$ given by the convolution

$$v(t) = h(t) * (s(t) + n(t)),$$

where $h(t)$ is a bandpass function known as the *impulse response* of the channel, and the *noise signal*, $n(t)$, is a sample function from a gaussian random process.

The case of gaussian noise is the standard that one usually uses in order to judge the quality of a modulation scheme, even though the modem might actually be used with a somewhat different noise process. Even further, the standard gaussian noise process is taken to be white noise. A white noise signal has a one-sided spectral density of N_o watts/hertz.

Digital communication theory teaches that the channel input and output signal need be considered only at discrete, equally spaced time instants, $k\Delta T$, if $2W\Delta T \leqslant 1$. The time-discrete input signal we will study then consists of the samples $s(k\Delta T) = s_R(k\Delta T) + js_I(k\Delta T)$, or in brief, $s_k = s_{Rk} + js_{Ik}$ for $k = 0$, $\pm 1, \pm 2, \ldots$, where s_{Rk} and s_{Ik} are real. The well-known sampling theorem states how to reconstruct $s(t)$ from its samples.

It usually is convenient to pick $h(t)$, possibly by adding special equalization filters to the modulator or demodulator, so that $h(k\Delta T)$ equals zero for k not equal to zero and equals one for k equal to zero. Then the sampled replica of the received signal $v(t)$ is given by the discrete samples

$$v_k = s_k + n_k \qquad k = 0, \pm 1, \pm 2, \ldots,$$
$$= (s_{Rk} + n_{Rk}) + j(s_{Ik} + n_{Ik})$$

where n_k is the sample at time $k\Delta T$ of the noise added by the analog channel. Because the kth output sample depends only on the kth input sample, one says that no intersymbol interference occurs. The n_k are zero-mean complex gaussian random variables when $n(t)$ is a gaussian process. Further, the channel usually can be managed so that the gaussian random variables n_k may be modeled as independent. This is the case that one first studies.

One often designs a digital communication system by choosing a fixed set, called a *signaling constellation* (or a *modulation alphabet*), of 2^m real numbers or complex numbers to represent digital m-bit bytes. Figure 15.1 shows some typical signaling constellations. Shown there are four real modulation alphabets, called M-ary amplitude modulation, and six complex modulation alphabets, called by a variety of names (phase shift keying, quadrature amplitude modulation, amplitude and phase modulation). We will not discuss the design of signal constellations, only their use in conjunction with coding.

Typically, a codeword of length n over $GF(2^m)$ is mapped into a sequence of length n of elements from the modulation alphabet. (Other variations are possible; for example, a modulation alphabet of size $2^{m/2}$ can be used with a code over $GF(2^m)$ by mapping codeword symbols into pairs of letters.) A demodulator that makes a hard decision is a map from the set of real or complex numbers, over which v_k ranges, back into the modulation alphabet, and the codeword symbol follows.

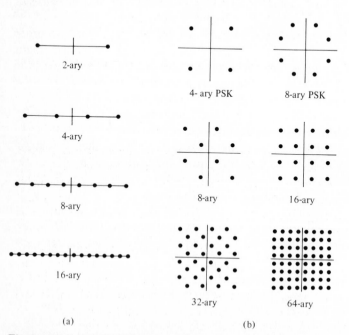

Figure 15.1   Some signal constellations. (a) Real modulation alphabets. (b) Complex modulation alphabets.

15.2 BIT ENERGY AND BIT ERROR RATE

A digital communication system comprises an encoder and a modulator at the transmitter, and a demodulator and a decoder at the receiver. The quality of such a system is judged in part by the probability of bit error, which is also called the *bit error rate* (*BER*). For a fixed digital communication system that transmits digital data through an additive gaussian noise channel, the bit error rate can always be reduced by increasing transmitted power, but it is by the performance at low transmitted power that one judges the quality of a digital communication system. The better of two digital communication systems is the one that can achieve a desired bit error rate with the lower transmitted power.

For a finite-length message of length K information bits and message energy E_m, the bit energy E_b is defined by

$$E_b = \frac{E_m}{K}$$

In general, the bit energy E_b is not an energy that can be found in a single part of the message, nor can it be measured by a meter. It is calculated from the message energy. The definition of E_b is referenced to the number of bits at the input to the encoder/modulator. At the channel input, one may find a message structure in which a larger number of bits are perceived as channel symbols. The extra symbols may be parity symbols for error control or symbols for frame synchronization or channel protocol. These symbols do not represent transmitted information. Only information bits are used in calculating E_b.

For an infinite-length constant-rate message of rate R information bits/second, E_b is defined by

$$E_b = \frac{S}{R},$$

where S is the average power of the message.

In addition to the message energy, the receiver also receives a white noise signal of one-sided spectral density N_o watts/hertz (joules). Clearly, the reception of the signal cannot be affected if both the signal and the noise are doubled. It is only the ratio E_m/N_o or E_b/N_o that affects the bit error rate. Two different signaling schemes are compared by comparing their respective graphs of BER versus required E_b/N_o.

Surprisingly, it is possible to make precise statements about values of E_b/N_o for which good waveforms exist. Our starting point for developing bounds on E_b/N_o is the channel capacity of Shannon. The capacity formula we need is the one for the additive gaussian noise channel. This formula says that any signaling waveform $s(t)$ of power $S = E_b R$ whose spectrum $S(f)$ is constrained to be zero for $|f| > W/2$ can transmit no more than

$$C = W \log_2 \left(1 + \frac{S}{N_o W} \right)$$

bits per second through an additive gaussian noise channel at an arbitrarily low bit error rate. Conversely, there always exists a signaling waveform $s(t)$ that comes arbitrarily close to this rate and bandwidth constraint at any specified and arbitrarily small bit error rate. This celebrated formula, derived in any information-theory textbook, provides a point of reference against which a digital communication system can be judged.

☐ **Theorem 15.2.1** In order to transmit information through white gaussian noise of spectral density N_o, any digital communication system requires an energy per bit satisfying

$$E_b \geqslant N_o \log_e 2 = 0.69 N_o,$$

where E_b is in joules and N_o is in watts/hertz.

Proof Bandwidth W is not constrained in the theorem. Replace S by RE_b in the Shannon capacity formula and let W go to infinity. Then

$$R \leqslant \frac{RE_b}{N_o} \log_2 e,$$

and the theorem follows immediately. ☐

If the ratio E_b/N_o is measured in decibels, then the inequality becomes

$$E_b/N_o \geqslant -1.6 \text{ dB}.$$

The value of $E_b/N_o = -1.6$ dB, therefore, provides a lower limit. Experience shows that it is easy to design waveforms that operate with a small bit error rate if E_b/N_o is about 12 dB or greater. Hence, the province of the waveform designer is between these two numbers, a spread of about 14 dB. This is the regime within which design comparisons are conducted for the gaussian noise channel.

When only a limited bandwidth is available the required energy is greater. Define the spectral bit rate r (measured in bits per second per hertz) by

$$r = \frac{R}{W}.$$

The spectral bit rate r and E_b/N_o are the two most important figures of merit in a digital communication system.

☐ **Theorem 15.2.2** Let r be the spectral bit rate of a digital communication system. Then

$$\frac{E_b}{N_o} \geqslant \frac{2^r - 1}{r}.$$

Further, by appropriate design of the transmission system, for any ε

greater than zero, one can transmit reliably with

$$\frac{E_b}{N_o} \leqslant \frac{2^r - 1}{r} + \varepsilon.$$

Proof The Shannon capacity formula says that for any positive ε', an information rate R can be achieved satisfying

$$R \leqslant W \log_2\left(1 + \frac{R E_b}{W N_o}\right) \leqslant R(1 + \varepsilon').$$

The theorem follows immediately. $\square$

This last corollary tells us that increasing the bit rate per unit bandwidth increases the required energy per bit. This is the basis of the energy/bandwidth trade of digital communication theory, where increasing bandwidth at a fixed information rate can reduce power requirements.

The content of Theorem 15.2.2 is shown in Fig. 15.2. Any communication system can be described by a point lying below this curve, and for any point below the curve one can design a communication system that has as small a bit error rate as one desires. The history of digital communications can be described in part as a series of attempts to move ever closer to this limiting curve with systems that have very low bit error rate. Such systems employ both modem techniques and error-control techniques.

In some digital communication systems, the interface between the modem and the code is not well defined. Extra information is passed by the demodulator, which helps the decoder to improve its performance. Many variations are possible. For example, a binary channel may employ a receiver with a 3-bit output for each bit received. This is called a *soft-decision detector*. An

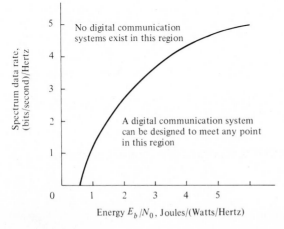

Figure 15.2

all-zero 3-bit pattern denotes that a "sure" zero was received, and an all-one 3-bit pattern denotes that a "sure" one was received. Other 3-bit patterns denote various shades of indecision by the receiver. The decoder can then use these "soft" decisions to improve decoding. We have already seen what amounts to a simpler version of this—the binary erasure channel. The three receiver outputs there can be denoted as 10 (a hard zero), 01 (a hard one), and 00 (an erasure).

Another example of a soft decision is a list decoder for a q-ary channel. The demodulator lists the two or three most likely values of each symbol rather than only the most likely, possibly assigning some likelihood measure to each of them.

Of course for a fixed code, decoders that use soft-decision information can give better performance, and one may choose to use such a decoder for this reason. The issue is never clear-cut, however, First of all, a soft-decision system achieves its potential only if the channel noise statistics are reasonably stationary and reasonably well modeled. If the noise is intermittent, time-varying, or not well known, a hard-decision or hard-decision-with-erasure detector should be preferred. Also, a soft-decision decoder will be more expensive. Within a fixed budget, the blocklength of a code used with a soft-decision decoder will be shorter than that of a code used with a hard-decision decoder. Hence, the soft-decision decoder is not necessarily better. The hard-decision decoder with a longer blocklength may outperform the soft-decision decoder. Sometimes the application can be best satisfied by a soft-decision system. Other times it will be better to use a hard-decision system so that one may then afford to use a more powerful code. Such choices are usually difficult engineering trades. Theory alone cannot make the choice.

15.3 SOFT-DECISION DECODING OF BLOCK CODES

If complexity were not an issue, the probability of decoding error would be minimized by doing the demodulation and the decoding simultaneously. The q^k codewords are mapped into q^k waveforms $s_r(t)$ for $r = 1, \ldots, q^k$ by the modulator. The channel output, $v(t) = s_r(t) + n(t)$ for some r and some noise realization $n(t)$, is represented by its samples $v_l = v(l\Delta T)$ for $l = 1, \ldots, N$. The demodulator and decoder between them must recover the codeword and then the information symbols.

The probability density function of the vector $\mathbf{v}$ given that $s_r(t)$ was transmitted is given by

$$Q(\mathbf{v}|r) = \prod_{l=1}^{N} \frac{1}{\sqrt{2\pi}\sigma} e^{-(v_l - s_{rl})^2/2\sigma^2},$$

provided that the noise samples are independent, identically distributed gaussian random variables of variance σ. Given the received signal $\mathbf{v}$, the maximum-likelihood receiver finds the value of r for which $Q(\mathbf{v}|r)$ is largest and declares that the rth message was the transmitted message.

As we have assumed gaussian noise, however, the maximum-likelihood receiver is identical to the minimum-Euclidean-distance receiver. This receiver finds the value of r for which the Euclidean distance

$$d_E(\mathbf{v}, \mathbf{s}_r) = \sum_{l=1}^{N} (v_l - s_{rl})^2 \qquad r = 1, \ldots, q^k$$

is smallest and declares that the rth message was the transmitted message.

Further, if the energy of $s_r(t)$ is the same for all r, the minimum-Euclidean-distance receiver can be replaced by a correlation receiver. A set of q^k correlation coefficients

$$\rho_r = \sum_{l=1}^{N} v_l^* s_{rl} \qquad r = 1, \ldots, q^k$$

is computed; then codeword $\mathbf{c}_r$ is detected if $\rho_r > \rho_{r'}$ for all $r' \neq r$. The information symbols can then be recovered from $\mathbf{c}_r$. Usually even this receiver is quite impractical because q^k is very large, and one uses a scheme that is more manageable, a scheme of lesser complexity.

Figure 15.3 shows several receiver options. For a fixed modulator and encoder, the topmost option has the smallest symbol error rate and the bottommost option has the largest. From this one might conclude that if

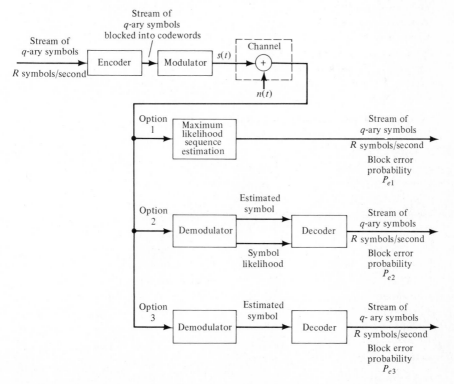

Figure 15.3 Receiver options.

it could be afforded, one would always want to implement the maximum-likelihood receiver. This is generally not the case. More likely, one would spend newly acquired riches on a more powerful code and a more powerful modulation waveform and then decode these with a suboptimal procedure.

In general, the techniques of soft-decision decoding necessitate a design trade between passing more information from the demodulator to the decoder while using a simpler code, and passing less information from the demodulator to the decoder and using a stronger code. At one extreme, the demodulator makes hard decisions; the sequence of real numbers is converted by the demodulator into a sequence of q-ary symbols and the full power of algebraic decoding techniques then can be brought to bear. These decoding algorithms are also available if the demodulator is allowed to make an erasure. At the other extreme, the demodulator makes no decisions at all; it preserves all of the information in the received signal and passes it all on to the decoder.

In a well-designed system, the complexity is balanced between demodulator and decoder. The demodulator makes as strong a decision on the symbol level as it dares, still preserving enough information for the decoder to achieve the desired level of performance. One also has the option of using a nested code. The complexity/performance trades can then be spread across three levels of processing: the demodulator and two levels of decoding. By using a soft-decision decoder on short blocklengths for the inner decoder, and a hard-decision errors-and-erasures decoder to clean up the remaining errors and inner-decoding failures, one can make excellent complexity/performance trades.

The particular soft-decision decoder that we will study here is called the *generalized-minimum-distance (GMD)* algorithm. We will develop this algorithm twice, first for binary codes—where we can develop some geometrical insights—then for codes over any Galois field. In the first case, the demodulator sees a sequence of binary symbols in noise. The ith binary symbol received by the demodulator is described by a real number $\tilde{v}_i \in [-1, 1]$, representing the ith estimated binary symbol and the confidence level. When $\tilde{v}_i$ equals -1, then the ith received bit is a zero with the highest confidence; when $\tilde{v}_i$ equals 1, then the ith received bit is a one with the highest confidence. If we represent $\tilde{v}_i$ in the form of a sign-and-magnitude binary number, then we can think of the sign bit as representing the demodulated value of the ith codeword bit and the remaining bits of $\tilde{v}_i$ as representing the confidence level.

There are two special cases we have already seen. If the demodulator is designed to only set $\tilde{v}_i$ to ± 1, then it is a hard-decision demodulator, and the decoder is an errors-only decoder. If the demodulator is designed to only set $\tilde{v}_i$ to ± 1 or to 0, then it is a hard-decision-with-erasure demodulator, and the decoder is an errors-and-erasures decoder. In this section, we will give a GMD algorithm that allows $\tilde{v}_i$ to be any number between -1 and $+1$. The decoding algorithm can be used with any demodulator rule used to set $\tilde{v}_i$ in the interval $[-1, 1]$.

When a received signal is processed by the demodulator, the output is the received vector

$$\tilde{\mathbf{v}} = (\tilde{v}_0, \dots, \tilde{v}_{n-1}).$$

If the channel made no errors and the demodulator has maximum confidence in every bit, then for codeword $\mathbf{c}_r$, the received vector is equal to -1 in every bit position where $\mathbf{c}_r$ equals zero and is equal to $+1$ in every bit position where $\mathbf{c}_r$ equals one.

Let $\tilde{\mathbf{c}}_r$ be the vector in Euclidean n-space defined by

$$\tilde{\mathbf{c}}_{ri} = \begin{cases} -1 & \text{if } \mathbf{c}_{ri} = 0 \\ +1 & \text{if } \mathbf{c}_{ri} = 1. \end{cases}$$

This is a way of mapping the codewords from $GF(q)^n$ into $\mathbf{R}^n$. We also call $\tilde{\mathbf{c}}_r$ a codeword. The Euclidean distance between received word $\tilde{\mathbf{v}}$ and codeword $\tilde{\mathbf{c}}_r$ is defined as

$$d_E^2(\tilde{\mathbf{v}}, \tilde{\mathbf{c}}_r) = |\tilde{\mathbf{v}} - \tilde{\mathbf{c}}_r|^2 = \sum_{i=0}^{n-1} (\tilde{v}_i - \tilde{c}_{ri})^2.$$

If $\tilde{\mathbf{v}}$ consists only of hard decisions, $\tilde{v}_i = \pm 1$, then the Euclidean distance can be related to the Hamming distance

$$d_E^2(\tilde{\mathbf{v}}, \tilde{\mathbf{c}}_r) = 4d_H(\mathbf{v}, \mathbf{c}_r)$$

where $v_i = 0$ if $\tilde{v}_i = -1$ and $v_i = 1$ if $\tilde{v}_i = 1$. In particular, for any two codewords

$$d_E^2(\tilde{\mathbf{c}}_r, \tilde{\mathbf{c}}_{r'}) = 4d_H(\mathbf{c}_r, \mathbf{c}_{r'}).$$

The minimum Euclidean distance d_E^* of the code and the minimum Hamming distance d^* are related by

$$d_E^{*2} = 4d_H^*.$$

The GMD decoder will be developed using the inner products $\mathbf{v} \cdot \mathbf{c}_r$. First we reinterpret the Euclidean distance of a code in terms of the inner products. We can write   *inner product*

$$d_E^2(\tilde{\mathbf{v}}, \tilde{\mathbf{c}}_r) = |\tilde{\mathbf{v}}|^2 - 2\tilde{\mathbf{v}} \cdot \tilde{\mathbf{c}}_r + |\tilde{\mathbf{c}}_r|^2.$$

For a fixed $\tilde{\mathbf{v}}$, minimizing $d_E(\tilde{\mathbf{v}}, \tilde{\mathbf{c}}_r)$ over r is equivalent to maximizing the inner product $\tilde{\mathbf{v}} \cdot \tilde{\mathbf{c}}_r$ over r because $|\tilde{\mathbf{v}}|^2$ is independent of r, and $|\tilde{\mathbf{c}}_r|^2$ is equal to n for every codeword. Minimizing the Euclidean distance is a more intuitive concept, but maximizing the inner product might be preferred for computations.

An errors-only decoder works with a demodulator that makes only hard decisions. Then $\tilde{v} = \pm 1$, and $d_E^*(\tilde{\mathbf{v}}, \tilde{\mathbf{c}}_r) = 4d_H(\mathbf{v}, \mathbf{c}_r)$. Hence, finding $\tilde{\mathbf{c}}_r$ at minimum Euclidean distance from $\tilde{\mathbf{v}}$ is equivalent to finding $\mathbf{c}_r$ at minimum Hamming distance from $\mathbf{v}$. At most one codeword $\mathbf{c}_r$ will satisfy

$$d_H(\mathbf{v}, \mathbf{c}_r) \leqslant \tfrac{1}{2}(d^* - 1).$$

Hence, at most one codeword $\tilde{\mathbf{c}}_r$ will satisfy

$$d_E^2(\tilde{\mathbf{v}}, \tilde{\mathbf{c}}_r) \leqslant 2(d^* - 1).$$

Finally, because $|\tilde{\mathbf{v}}|^2$ is equal to n for a hard-decision demodulator,

$$d_E^2(\tilde{\mathbf{v}}, \tilde{\mathbf{c}}_r) = 2(n - \tilde{\mathbf{v}} \cdot \tilde{\mathbf{c}}_r),$$

and at most one codeword $\tilde{\mathbf{c}}_r$ will satisfy

$$\tilde{\mathbf{v}} \cdot \tilde{\mathbf{c}}_r \geqslant n - (d^* - 1),$$

where d^* is the minimum Hamming distance of the code. An errors-only decoder is equivalent to finding that unique codeword $\tilde{\mathbf{c}}_r$, if there is one, such that

$$\tilde{\mathbf{v}} \cdot \tilde{\mathbf{c}}_r > n - d^*.$$

Possibly no solution exists, and the decoder will fail to produce a codeword. It is an incomplete decoder but will detect that the error pattern is uncorrectable.

If the demodulator makes hard decisions and erasures, then $\tilde{v}_i = \pm 1$ or 0. By a similar reasoning, an errors-and-erasures decoder is equivalent to finding that unique codeword $\tilde{\mathbf{c}}_r$, if there is one, such that

$$\tilde{\mathbf{v}} \cdot \tilde{\mathbf{c}}_r > n - d^*.$$

Again, this is an incomplete decoder.

The following theorem establishes that the same existence condition holds for soft decisions.

□ **Theorem 15.3.1** There is at most one codeword $\tilde{\mathbf{c}}_r$ in a binary code of blocklength n and minimum Hamming distance d^* such that

$$\tilde{\mathbf{v}} \cdot \tilde{\mathbf{c}}_r > n - d^*$$

whenever the components of $\tilde{\mathbf{v}}$ lie in the interval $[-1, 1]$.

Proof Let $\tilde{\mathbf{c}}_r$ be a codeword that satisfies the above inequality, and let $\tilde{\mathbf{c}}_{r'}$ be any other codeword. Then $\tilde{\mathbf{c}}_{r'}$ differs from $\tilde{\mathbf{c}}_r$ in at least d^* components. Let

$$S = \{i \mid \tilde{c}_{ri} \neq \tilde{c}_{r'i}\}.$$

Then

$$\tilde{\mathbf{v}} \cdot \tilde{\mathbf{c}}_r = \sum_{i \notin S} \tilde{v}_i \tilde{c}_{ri} + \sum_{i \in S} \tilde{v}_i \tilde{c}_{ri} = A_1 + A_2,$$

$$\tilde{\mathbf{v}} \cdot \tilde{\mathbf{c}}_{r'} = \sum_{i \notin S} \tilde{v}_i \tilde{c}_{r'i} + \sum_{i \in S} \tilde{v}_i \tilde{c}_{r'i} = A_1 - A_2.$$

But

$$A_1 = \sum_{i \notin S} \tilde{v}_i \tilde{c}_{ri} \leqslant n - d^*,$$

because it is a sum of at most $n - d^*$ terms, none of which is larger than one. Therefore, because $\tilde{\mathbf{v}} \cdot \tilde{\mathbf{c}}_r > n - d^*$, $A_2 > 0$, and thus $A_1 - A_2 \leqslant n - d^*$, which completes the proof of the theorem. $\square$

As an example, consider the binary $(3, 2)$ code $\mathscr{C} = \{000, 011, 110, 101\}$, which has d^* equal to 2. This example is simple enough to illustrate Theorem 15.3.1 graphically. In Fig. 15.4 we show Euclidean 3-space, which has a cube containing the possible received vectors $\tilde{\mathbf{v}}$. Also shown in the same space are the four codewords. Shaded in one corner is the set of $\tilde{\mathbf{v}}$ that will decode into that corner's codeword according to the rule $\tilde{v}_0 \tilde{c}_{r0} + \tilde{v}_1 \tilde{c}_{r1} + \tilde{v}_2 \tilde{c}_{r2} > 1$. The theorem says that if we establish such a region for each of the four codewords, they will not intersect. A GMD decoder can be built using these four decoding regions. Notice that the four decoding regions do not fill the cube. A tetrahedron will remain in the center, and if $\tilde{\mathbf{v}}$ falls in the tetrahedron, a decoding failure is declared. The decoder is an incomplete decoder with decoding regions in Euclidean space.

A GMD decoder finds the unique codeword satisfying Theorem 15.3.1 if it exists and otherwise declares a decoding failure. Of course it is not practical to find this codeword by computing all 2^k inner products. We will now describe a practical way to find this codeword. The idea is as follows. We already know how to build decoders to correct errors-and-erasures based on hard decisions. We will build an outer processing loop around any available errors-and-erasures decoder. Based on the soft-decision information, it forms a series of trial hard-decision-with-erasure vectors. For each l from 0 to $d^* - 1$, erase the l components for which $|\tilde{v}_i|$ is the smallest. (If for some l, because of ties, these l components are not unique, skip that l.) Set the unerased components to 0 or 1 depending on the sign of $\tilde{v}_i$. In this way a vector $\mathbf{v}^{(l)}$ over $GF(2)$ with erasures is formed. Decode $\mathbf{v}^{(l)}$ using an errors-and-

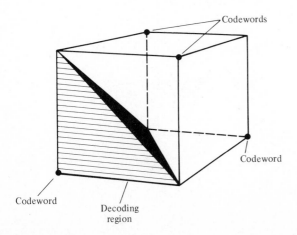

Figure 15.4   GMD decoding region for a (3, 2) binary code.

erasures decoder. If it decodes into codeword $\mathbf{c}_r$, test $\tilde{\mathbf{v}} \cdot \tilde{\mathbf{c}}_r > n - d^*$. If the inequality is satisfied, then $\mathbf{c}_r$ is the GMD-decoded codeword. Otherwise, increase l and repeat unless l exceeds $d^* - 1$, in which case a decoding failure is declared. The GMD algorithm is summarized in Fig. 15.5 for the nonbinary case. Theorem 15.3.2 and Theorem 15.3.4 establish that the GMD algorithm shown in Fig. 15.5 does indeed produce the unique GMD codeword. Notice in the figure that only even l are tested. This suffices because the number of

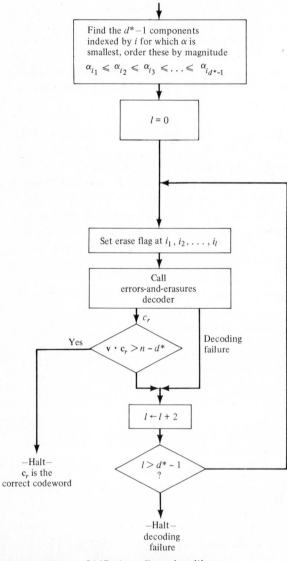

Figure 15.5 GMD decoding algorithm.

errors that can be corrected will change by one if the number of erasures changes by two.

☐ **Theorem 15.3.2**   If $\tilde{\mathbf{v}} \cdot \tilde{\mathbf{c}}_r > n - d^*$, then at least one $\mathbf{v}^{(l)}$ satisfies

$$\mathbf{v}^{(l)} \cdot \mathbf{c}_r > n - d^* \qquad \text{for } l = 0, \ldots, d^* - 1.$$

Proof   This theorem will be proved by proving Theorem 15.3.4, a more general form of the same theorem. ☐

Next we will develop GMD decoders for nonbinary codes. The GMD decoder is about $\frac{1}{2}(d^* - 1)$ times as complex as an errors-and-erasures decoder for the same code. The notion of generalized distance extends naturally to nonbinary signals, just as Hamming distance does. For both notions of distance, the nonbinary problem is treated as a binary problem by distinguishing only whether two symbols are the same or different and ignoring the actual values. The GMD decoder for the nonbinary case is almost unchanged.

Each q-ary symbol received by the demodulator is described by its estimated value v_i, an element of $GF(q)$, and a confidence level α_i, $0 \leqslant \alpha_i \leqslant 1$, measuring the reliability of the estimate. When α_i equals one, the received symbol is v_i with the highest confidence, when α_i equals zero, the received symbol is v_i with the least confidence.

As in the binary case, it does not matter to the decoding algorithm what rule the demodulator uses to set α_i. It may even set α_i always to one, which is a hard-decision demodulator; it may set α_i only to one or zero, which is a hard-decision-with-erasure demodulator; or it may set α_i using a more elaborate confidence measure.

In the binary case we were able to construct a geometrical picture by using the sign of α_i to denote the estimate of the transmitted binary symbol. We do not have this geometrical picture in the $GF(q)$-ary case. To get a product, define for any v',

$$\delta(v, v') = \begin{cases} +1, & v = v' \\ -1, & v \neq v'. \end{cases}$$

Then define

$$\mathbf{v} \cdot \mathbf{c}_r = \sum_{i=0}^{n-1} \alpha_i \delta(v_i, c_{ri}),$$

with which we can prove a $GF(q)$-ary version of Theorem 15.3.1. The notation $\mathbf{v} \cdot \mathbf{c}_r$ is convenient but imprecise, because $\mathbf{v} \cdot \mathbf{c}_r$ also depends on α.

☐ **Theorem 15.3.3**   There is at most one codeword $\mathbf{c}_r$ from a code over $GF(q)$ of length n and minimum distance d^* for which

$$\mathbf{v} \cdot \mathbf{c}_r > n - d^*.$$

Proof The proof is the same as that of Theorem 15.3.1. □

The decoding algorithm is the same as in the binary case. For each l from 0 to $d^* - 1$, erase the components for which α_i is smallest. In this way a vector $\mathbf{v}^{(l)}$ over $GF(q)$ with erasures is formed. Starting with l equal to 0, decode $\mathbf{v}^{(l)}$ using an errors-and-erasures decoder. If it decodes into $\mathbf{c}_r$, test $\mathbf{v} \cdot \mathbf{c}_r > n - d^*$. If it passes, then $\mathbf{c}_r$ is the GMD-decoded codeword. If the test fails, or if the lth decoding fails, increase l and repeat unless l exceeds $d^* - 1$, in which case a decoding failure is declared. This procedure is justified by the following theorem.

□ **Theorem 15.3.4** If $\mathbf{v} \cdot \mathbf{c}_r > n - d^*$ for codeword $\mathbf{c}_r$, then at least one $\mathbf{v}^{(l)}$ satisfies

$$\mathbf{v}^{(l)} \cdot \mathbf{c}_r > n - d^* \qquad \text{for } l = 0, \ldots, d^* - 1.$$

Proof It is sufficient to prove the theorem for l running from 0 to n because the conclusion is clearly not possible for $l \geq d^*$.

Order the α_i by their magnitudes. Let

$$\alpha_{i_1} \leq \alpha_{i_2} \leq \ldots \leq \alpha_{i_n}$$
$$\lambda_0 = \alpha_{i_1},$$
$$\lambda_l = \alpha_{i_{l+1}} - \alpha_{i_l} \quad 1 \leq l \leq n-1,$$

and

$$\lambda_n = 1 - \alpha_{i_n}.$$

Then

$$0 \leq \lambda_l \leq 1$$

and

$$\sum_{l=0}^{n} \lambda_l = 1,$$

and thus the vector λ behaves like a probability distribution. Furthermore,

$$\sum_{l=0}^{l'-1} \lambda_l = \alpha_{i_{l'}},$$

and thus

$$\mathbf{v} = \sum_{l=0}^{n} \lambda_l \mathbf{v}^{(l)}.$$

Suppose that

$$\mathbf{v}^{(l)} \cdot \mathbf{c}_r \leq n - d^* \qquad \text{for all } l.$$

Then

$$\mathbf{v} \cdot \mathbf{c}_r = \sum_{l=0}^{n} \lambda_l \mathbf{v}^{(l)} \cdot \mathbf{c}_r \leqslant (n - d^*) \sum_{l=0}^{n} \lambda_l = n - d^*,$$

in contradiction to the assumption of the theorem. Hence, the theorem is proved. ☐

15.4 SOFT-DECISION DECODING OF CONVOLUTIONAL CODES

The decoding of convolutional codes also can be aided by the use of soft-decision information. The techniques that are available are a soft-decision version of the Viterbi algorithm and soft-decision versions of sequential-decoding algorithms. We shall defer the study of sequential decoding until the next section. In this section, we will study the Viterbi algorithm with a soft-decision demodulator. We will then study the Ungerboeck convolutional codes. These are convolutional codes over the complex field that have large Euclidean free distance and thus are suitable for use on a bandpass channel. These codes are more meaningful for a bandpass channel than are codes designed to have large Hamming free distance.

The Viterbi algorithm finds that path through the trellis that is closest to the received word. The distance of a received word from a path through the trellis is obtained as the sum of the distances branch by branch. Except for the additive structure used in the measure of distance, the nature of the distance is unimportant. Therefore, although the Viterbi algorithm was developed in Section 12.8 using Hamming distance, the same algorithm applies for any definition of distance. It is not even necessary that the distance be a metric.

The Viterbi algorithm is easy to use when the channel noise is stationary and well modeled. Let $Q(v|c)$ be the probability that symbol v is the output of the demodulator given that symbol c is the input to the channel. Even though c may be from a small discrete alphabet, a soft-decision demodulator may have a larger alphabet for v—perhaps a continuous alphabet or an alphabet of m-bit binary numbers. Pick some frame of the received word. It has n_0 components denoted by v_i for $i = 1, \ldots, n_0$. Pick some branch on the trellis. This branch is associated with n_0 codeword components denoted by c_i for $i = 1, \ldots, n_0$. The distance of a codeword frame $\mathbf{c}$ from the corresponding frame of the received word $\mathbf{v}$ is given by the log-likelihood function

$$d(\mathbf{v}, \mathbf{c}) = \sum_{i=1}^{n_0} \log Q(v_i | c_i).$$

This function, called the *branch metric* (or the path metric), has the properties of a distance but it is not a true metric.

A soft-decision Viterbi decoder is the same as a hard-decision Viterbi decoder except that it uses the new path metric in place of Hamming distance. At each iteration, each surviving path to each node is extended in every possible way to a node at the next level, with the branch metrics added to the total accumulated path metrics. The survivor to each new node is kept, and other paths are discarded. Thus the complexity of a Viterbi decoder increases very little when it is revised to accept soft decisions.

When the channel input is a real or complex number and the channel noise is additive, independent, and gaussian, then

$$Q(\mathbf{v} \mid \mathbf{c}) = \prod_{i=1}^{n_0} \left\{ \frac{1}{\sqrt{2\pi}\sigma} \exp\left[-\frac{(c_i - v_i)^2}{2\sigma^2} \right] \right\}.$$

For a gaussian channel maximizing the likelihood function is equivalent to minimizing the Euclidean distance. As the branch metric we use the Euclidean distance

$$d_E(\mathbf{v}, \mathbf{c})^2 = \sum_{i=1}^{n_0} (c_i - v_i)^2.$$

In practice, on many soft-decision channels that are not gaussian, $Q(\mathbf{v}|\mathbf{c})$ is unknown, but Euclidean distance is still used for the branch metric. This is the minimum-Euclidean-distance decoder. It is not the maximum-likelihood decoder, but it is a practical decoder. The Viterbi algorithm looks just the same as the Viterbi algorithm for hard decisions but uses Euclidean distance in place of Hamming distance.

We will consider convolutional codes that are designed for real or complex signaling alphabets with 2^{n_0} points for some n_0. A number of typical signaling alphabets were shown in Fig. 15.1. Each alphabet is a discrete set of points chosen either from the field of real numbers or from the field of complex numbers. A waveform is a sequence of these real or complex numbers.

Each point in a signal constellation will be used to represent one of the 2^{n_0} branch values of an (mn_0, mk_0) binary convolutional code. The constellations of Fig. 15.1 provide for encoded bytes of from 2 bits to 6 bits. The information byte is less than the encoded byte. During each frame, an information byte enters the encoder. Depending on the current state of the encoder, one of the codeword bytes is sent to the channel in the form of a complex number, and the encoder enters a new state.

Let $\mathscr{C}$ be an (mn_0, mk_0) convolutional code over the complex field **C**. The Euclidean distance between two codewords $\mathbf{c}_r$ and $\mathbf{c}_{r'}$ (with complex values c_{ri} and $c_{r'i}$, for $i = 0, \ldots$, respectively) is given by

$$d_E(\mathbf{c}_r, \mathbf{c}_{r'})^2 = \sum_{i=0}^{\infty} |c_{ri} - c_{r'i}|^2.$$

The Euclidean free distance of $\mathscr{C}$, denoted by d_∞, is the minimum over all pairs of codewords in $\mathscr{C}$ of their Euclidean distance. The Euclidean free distance is the right distance by which to measure the code's performance on the gaussian channel. This is because on a gaussian channel the probability of error event asymptotically approaches from above:

$$P_e \geqslant N_d \cdot Q\left(\frac{d_\infty}{2\sigma}\right),$$

where σ is the standard deviation of the noise, Q is the cumulative gaussian distribution, and N_d is the number of codewords at distance d_∞ from the all-zero word. Hence, making d_∞ larger is roughly as good as making σ smaller. This is why the increase in free distance is called the *gain* of the convolutional code.

The Euclidean free distance often is measured in decibels, defined by

$$d_\infty(\text{dB}) = 20 \log_{10} d_\infty.$$

The *asymptotic coding gain* is defined as

$$G = 20 \log_{10} \frac{d_\infty}{d_{\text{ref}}},$$

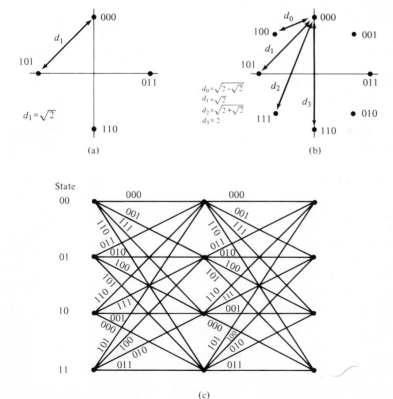

(a)

(b)

(c)

Figure 15.6 A simple coding example. (a) 4-ary PSK constellation for reference-uncoded signaling. (b) 8-ary PSK constellation. (c) Trellis for a (6, 4) convolutional code.

where d_{ref} is the minimum Euclidean distance of an uncoded reference waveform of the same average power.

A simple example is shown in Fig. 15.6. The convolutional code is defined by giving the 8-ary PSK modulation constellation and the trellis for the encoder. This is a (6, 4) code with rate $\frac{2}{3}$. A nonsystematic encoder is shown in Fig. 15.7(a). The code can also be used as a systematic code if the second two bits of each frame are taken as the information bits. Implementing the code systematically, however, requires feedback in the encoder, as shown in Fig. 15.7(b). There are only two information bits per codeword symbol, but the symbol can take on eight different values. By inspection of Fig. 15.7(c), we see that the minimum-weight path is 001 011 000 . . . ; this codeword is at minimum distance from the all-zero codeword. The free distance is $d_0^2 + d_1^2$. In part (a) of the figure is shown the 4-ary PSK constellation for the reference uncoded waveform of the same energy per information bit. The coding gain is $G = 10 \log_{10} (d_0^2 + d_1^2)/d_1^2$, or 1.1 dB, because d_1 is the Euclidean free distance of the uncoded waveform in part (a). This gain is a small improvement and is surprisingly good for such a simple code. The first code shown in Fig. 15.8, however, is a (9, 6) code that yields a 3-dB improvement and is only a little more complicated, and so should be preferred.

A computer program is generally required to find more complex codes, and even then the search needs to be intelligently structured or it will become

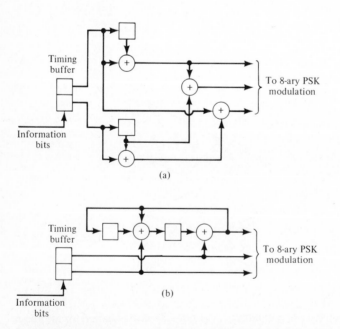

Figure 15.7 Encoders for a (6, 4) convolutional code. (a) Feedforward shift-register encoder. (b) Feedback shift-register encoder.

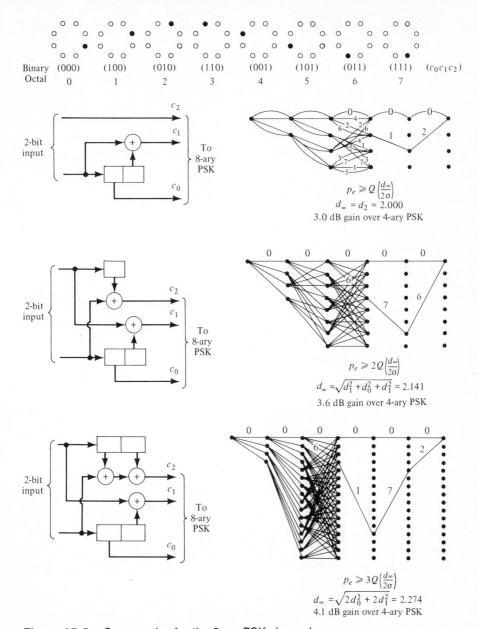

Figure 15.8 Some codes for the 8-ary PSK channel.

impractical. Figure 15.8 shows three codes as examples. In each case the trellis is shown and the path that achieves Euclidean free distance is marked.

Figure 15.9 is a table of Ungerboeck codes of rate $\frac{2}{3}$ for the 8-ary PSK constellation and for the 8-ary AM-PM constellation. The convolutional codes are described by their matrices of parity-check polynomials. Parity-

Codes for the 8-ary PSK Signaling Constellation

Constraint Length	$h_1(x)$	$h_2(x)$	$h_3(x)$	Gain Over Uncoded 4-ary PSK (dB)
2	x^2+1	x	0	~ 3.0
3	x^3+1	x	x^2	3.6
4	x^4+x+1	x^2	x^3+x^2+x	4.1
5	x^5+x^2+1	x^3+x^2+x	$x^4+x^3+x^2$	4.6
6	x^6+x^2+1	$x^4+x^3+x^2+x$	$x^5+x^4+x^3+x^2$	4.8
7	x^7+x+1	x^3+x^2	x^3+x^2+x	5.0
8	x^8+x^2+1	$x^7+x^5+x^3$	$x^6+x^5+x^4+x^3+x^2+x$	5.4
9	x^9+x^2+x+1	$x^6+x^5+x^4+x^2$	$x^7+x^5+x^4$	5.7

Codes for the 8-ary AM-PM Signaling Constellation

Constraint Length	$h_1(x)$	$h_2(x)$	$h_3(x)$	Gain Over Uncoded 4-ary PSK (dB)
2	x^2+1	x	0	~ 2.0
3	x^3+1	x	x^2	3.0
4	x^4+x+1	x^2	x^3+x^2+x	3.8
5	x^5+1	x^2+x	x^3	3.8
6	x^6+1	x^3+x^2+x	$x^5+x^4+x^2$	4.5
7	x^7+x+1	x^3+x^2	x^5+x	5.1
8	x^8+1	$x^5+x^3+x^2+x$	$x^7+x^6+x^5+x^3+x^2$	5.1
9	x^9+1	$x^7+x^6+x^5+x^2+x$	$x^8+x^7+x^3$	5.6

Figure 15.9   A table of Ungerboeck codes.

check polynomials are more convenient than generator polynomials here because the code rate is greater than $\frac{1}{2}$ and because the systematic encoder with feedback is easier to construct starting from the parity-check polynomials.

Any of the Ungerboeck codes in Figure 15.9 can be used as a plug-in replacement for the popular uncoded 4-ary PSK modulator. The information rate is still 2 bits per symbol. There is no change in the symbol rate, and thus the coded system has the same bandwidth as the uncoded system and transmits the same number of bits per symbol. Hence, the user of the system is unaware of the code's presence. The system now can run at a lower signal-to-noise ratio, however; the code with constraint length 9 has a gain of 5.7 dB.

15.5 SEQUENTIAL DECODING

There are two classes of sequential-decoding algorithms in use—the Fano algorithm, which we have already studied for hard-decision channels, and the stack algorithm. These are quite different in structure and in the organization of the hardware. Both can be used on either hard-decision channels or soft-decision channels. The relative merit of the two approaches is a subject of continuing debate. We will begin with a discussion of the stack algorithm.

The class of sequential-decoding algorithms known collectively as the stack algorithm has been developed in order to reduce computational work as compared with the Fano algorithm. The stack algorithm keeps track of the paths it has already searched. This is in contrast to the Fano algorithm, which may search its way out to a node and then back up some distance, only to repeat the search out to the same node. The stack algorithm keeps better records so that it need not repeat unnecessary work. On the other hand, the stack algorithm needs considerably more memory.

The stack algorithm is easy to understand; a simplified flow diagram is shown in Fig. 15.10. The decoder contains a stack of previously searched

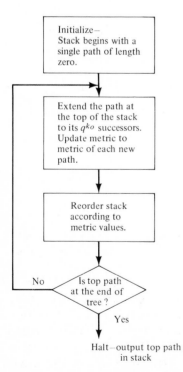

Figure 15.10 Simplified stack algorithm.

paths of various lengths. The stack can be stored as a list in a random-access memory. Each entry in the stack is a path that is recorded in three parts: the path length; the variable-length sequence of information symbols defining the path; and the path metric. Initially, the stack contains only the trivial path of length zero.

The path metric measures the discrepancy between that path and the initial segment of the received word of the same length. The path metric is obtained as the log-likelihood function of that path. We will develop the metric shortly. The first $N + 1$ frames of the received vector can be written as

$$\mathbf{v}^{(N)} = (v_0^1, \ldots, v_0^{n_0}, v_1^1, \ldots, v_1^{n_0}, \ldots, v_N^1, \ldots, v_N^{n_0}).$$

The first $m + 1$ frames of codeword $\mathbf{c}$ can be written as

$$\mathbf{c}^{(m)} = (c_0^1, \ldots, c_0^{n_0}, c_1^1, \ldots, c_1^{n_0}, \ldots, c_m^1, \ldots, c_m^{n_0}).$$

We wish to find the codeword segment that maximizes $\log[\Pr(\mathbf{c}^{(m)}|\mathbf{v}^{(N)})]$. By the definition of the sequential decoder, it must choose the initial codeword segment of length $m + 1$ without looking further out in the tree. But by Bayes' rule,

$$\Pr(\mathbf{c}^{(m)}|\mathbf{v}^{(N)}) = \frac{\Pr(\mathbf{v}^{(N)}|\mathbf{c}^{(m)})\Pr(\mathbf{c}^{(m)})}{\Pr(\mathbf{v}^{(N)})}.$$

By assumption, the codewords are used with equal probability, and thus

$$\Pr(\mathbf{c}^{(m)}) = \frac{1}{q^{(m+1)k_0}}$$

$$= \frac{1}{q^{(m+1)n_0 R}}.$$

The term $\Pr(\mathbf{v}^{(N)}|\mathbf{c}^{(m)})$ can be written as

$$\Pr(\mathbf{v}^{(N)}|\mathbf{c}^{(m)}) = \prod_{i=0}^{m} \prod_{j=1}^{n_0} \Pr(v_i^j|c_i^j) \prod_{i=m+1}^{N} \prod_{j=1}^{n_0} \Pr(v_i^j).$$

The right-hand side is made up of two parts: a product distribution involving the conditional probabilities over the $m + 1$ frames of the codeword, and a product distribution of unconditional probabilities, where the codeword is not yet specified. Dividing the problem into two parts like this is the way in which the definition of sequential decoding imposes itself into the probabilistic description. Now maximize

$$\frac{\Pr(\mathbf{v}^{(N)}|\mathbf{c}^{(m)})\Pr(\mathbf{c}^{(m)})}{\Pr(\mathbf{v}^{(N)})} = \left[\frac{\prod_{i=0}^{m} \prod_{j=1}^{n_0} \Pr(v_i^j|c_i^j)}{\prod_{i=0}^{m} \prod_{j=1}^{n_0} \Pr(v_i^j)} \right] \frac{1}{q^{(m+1)n_0 R}}.$$

The path metric we use for sequential decoding, called the *Fano metric*, is the log function

$$\mu(\mathbf{c}^{(m)}) = \log_q \left[\frac{\Pr(\mathbf{v}^{(N)}|\mathbf{c}^{(m)})\Pr(\mathbf{c}^{(m)})}{\Pr(\mathbf{v}^{(m)})} \right]$$

$$= \sum_{i=0}^{m} \left[\sum_{j=1}^{n_0} \left\{ \log_q \frac{p(v_i^j|c_i^j)}{p(v_i^j)} - R \right\} \right].$$

The inner bracket is the contribution to the Fano metric in the ith frame. Only this term needs to be computed in each frame for each codeword considered. The path metric $\mu(\mathbf{c}^{(m)})$ is obtained by adding the new increment to the Fano metric of the top codeword in the stack on the previous iteration.

Sequential decoding for hard decisions using the Fano algorithm has already been described in Section 12.9, and the same discussion applies to soft-decision channels. The only real difference between the decoders for hard-decision channels and those for soft-decision channels is in the path metric. The appropriate path metric for soft decisions is the Fano metric. The only change needed in the Fano algorithm of Section 12.9 is the new metric. With this change, the Fano decoder of Section 12.9 is suitable for soft-decision channels.

Any sequential decoding algorithm has the properties: that the decoder performs at least one computation at each node it visits; and that branches are examined sequentially so that, at any node, the decoder's choice among previously unexplored branches does not depend on received branches deeper in the tree. This second condition is critical and leads to the peculiar behavior of sequential decoding. Decoders for block codes and syndrome decoders for convolutional codes can use later information to make earlier decisions, and thus their behavior is different.

The number of computations made by any sequential decoder to advance one node deeper into the code tree is a random variable. This is the major characteristic that affects the complexity required to achieve a given level of performance. When there is little noise, the decoder is usually following the correct path using only one computation to advance one node deeper into the code tree. When the noise is severe, however, the decoder may proceed along an incorrect path, and a large number of computations may be required before the decoder finds the correct path. The variability in the number of computations means that a large memory is required to buffer the incoming data. Any finite buffer used with sequential decoding has a nonzero probability of overflowing, an event which must be considered in performance calculations.

PROBLEMS

15.1. Give a simple formula for the Fano metric when the channel is a q-ary symmetric channel and when the channel is a gaussian channel.

15.2. Draw a flowchart of the GMD decoding algorithm for nonbinary codes.

15.3. For the convolutional code with generator matrix

$$G(x) = \begin{bmatrix} x & x^2 & 1 \\ 0 & 1 & x \end{bmatrix},$$

construct a systematic encoder that uses a feedback shift register.

15.4. Use the stack algorithm to decode the case given in Fig. 12.25.

NOTES

Almost since the first codes were discovered, it was realized that soft-decision decoding could be used to improve performance, but good decoders were not really found. The first major attempt to provide an algorithmic soft-decision decoder for block codes was by Forney (1966), who introduced the notion of generalized minimum distance. Chase (1972) gave a slightly different algorithm, which creates an outer loop around an errors-only hard-decision decoder for binary codes. Work by Hartmann and Rudolph (1976) dealt with a soft-decision decoder of a much different type.

In contrast to the case for block codes, soft-decision decoders for convolutional codes were easier to come by and appear more widely in practice. This is because the minimum-distance decoders in use for convolutional codes have less structure than the algebraic decoders in use for block codes such as BCH codes. Hamming distance can be replaced by other measures of the separation between codewords with very little change in the structure of the computations.

Ungerboeck (1977, 1982) designed codes specifically for the soft-decision receiver, in effect combining the modulation design and the code design. The use of the trellis for modulation has also been studied by Anderson and Taylor (1978), but without much connection with coding.

Sequential decoding was introduced by Wozencraft (1957) and further described by Wozencraft and Reiffen (1961). Further developments are from Fano (1963), Zigangirov (1966), and Jelinek (1969). Tutorials by Jelinek (1968) and Forney (1974), and further developments by Chevillat and Costello (1978) and by Haccoun and Ferguson (1975), also advanced the subject.

The lower bounds on the distribution of computation and the illustrative example are from Jacobs and Berlekamp (1967). The complementary upper bound was found by Savage (1966).

References

Textbooks

1. Peterson, W. W., *Error-Correcting Codes*, The M.I.T. Press, Cambridge, Mass., 1961.
2. Peterson, W. W., and E. J. Weldon, Jr., *Error-Correcting Codes*, 2nd ed., The M.I.T. Press, Cambridge, Mass., 1971.
3. Berlekamp, E. R., *Algebraic Coding Theory*, McGraw-Hill, New York, 1968.
4. Forney, G. D., *Concatenated Codes*, The M.I.T. Press, Cambridge, Mass., 1967.
5. Gallager, R. G., *Information Theory and Reliable Communication*, Chapter 6, McGraw-Hill, New York, 1968.
6. Lin, S., *Introduction to Error-Correction Codes*, Prentice-Hall, Englewood Cliffs, N.J., 1970.
7. Lucky, R. W., J. Salz, and E. J. Weldon, Jr., *Principles of Data Communication*, Chapters 11 and 12, McGraw-Hill, New York, 1968.
8. Blake, I. F., and R. C. Mullin, *The Mathematical Theory of Coding*, Academic Press, New York, 1975.
9. Van Lint, J. H., *Coding Theory*, Springer-Verlag, New York, 1973.
10. MacWilliams, F. J., and N. J. A. Sloane, *The Theory of Error-Correcting Codes*, North-Holland, New York, 1977.

11. McEliece, R. J., *The Theory of Information and Coding*, Addison-Wesley, Reading, Mass., 1977.
12. Sloane, N. J. A., *A Short Course on Error-Correcting Codes*, Springer-Verlag, New York, 1975.
13. Wiggert, D., *Error-Control Coding and Applications*, Artech House, Dedham, Mass., 1979.
14. Clark, G. C., and J. Bibb Cain, *Error-Correction Coding for Digital Communications*, Plenum Press, New York, 1981.
15. Pless, V., *Introduction to the Theory of Error-Correcting Codes*, Wiley-Interscience, New York, 1982.

Collections of Papers

1. Blake, I. F., *Algebraic Coding Theory*, Dowden, Hutchinson, and Ross, Stroudsburg, Pa., 1972.
2. Berlekamp, E. R., *Key Papers in the Development of Coding Theory*, *IEEE Press*, New York, 1974.

Chapter 1

1. Shannon, C. E., A Mathematical Theory of Communication, *Bell Syst. Tech. J.* 27 (1948): 379–423 (Part I), 623–656 (Part II) reprinted in book form with postscript by W. Weaver, Univ. of Illinois Press, Urbana, 1949.
2. Hamming, R. W., Error Detecting and Error Correcting Codes, *Bell Syst. Tech. J.* 29 (1950): 147–160.
3. Bose, R. C., and D. K. Ray-Chaudhuri, On a Class of Error-Correcting Binary Group Codes, *Inf. Contr.* 3 (1960): 68–79.
4. Hocquenghem, A., Codes Correcteurs D'erreurs, *Chiffres* 2 (1959): 147–156.
5. Reed, I. S., and G. Solomon, Polynomial Codes Over Certain Finite Fields, *J. Soc. Indust. Appl. Math.* 8 (1960): 300–304.

Chapter 2

1. Birkhoff, G., and S. Mac Lane, *A Survey of Modern Algebra*, rev. ed., Macmillan, New York, 1953.
2. Van der Waerden, B. L., *Modern Algebra* (2 vols.), trans. by F. Blum and T. J. Benac, Frederick Ungar, New York, 1950 and 1953.
3. Thrall, R. M., and L. Tornheim, *Vector Spaces and Matrices*, Wiley, New York, 1957.
4. Fraleigh, J. B., *A First Course in Abstract Algebra*, 2nd ed., Addison-Wesley, Reading, Mass., 1976.
5. Strang, G., *Linear Algebra and Its Applications*, 2nd ed., Academic Press, New York, 1980.
6. Baumslag, B., and B. Chandler, *Theory and Problems of Group Theory*, Schaum's Outline Series, McGraw-Hill, New York, 1968.

Chapter 3

1. Hamming, R. S., Error Detecting and Error Correcting Codes, *Bell Syst. Tech. J.* 29 (1950): 147–160.
2. Golay, M. J. E., Notes on Digital Coding, *Proc. IRE.* 37 (1949): 657.
3. Slepian, D., A Class of Binary Signalling Alphabets, *Bell Syst. Tech. J.* 35 (1956): 203–234.

4. Slepian, D., Some Further Study of Group Codes, *Bell Syst. Tech. J.* 39 (1960): 1219–1252.
5. Kiyasu, Z., *Research and Development Data No. 4*, Electrical Communications Laboratory, Nippon Tele. Corp., Tokyo, 1953.
6. Singleton, R. C., Maximum Distance q-nary Codes, *IEEE Trans. Inf. Theor.* IT-10 (1964): 116–118.
7. Golay, M. J. E., Notes on the Penny-Weighing Problem, Lossless Symbol Coding with Nonprimes, etc., *IRE Trans. Inf. Theor.* IT-4 (1958): 103–109.
8. Cocke, J., Lossless Symbol Coding with Nonprimes, *IRE Trans. Inf. Theor.* IT-5 (1959): 33–34.
9. Tietäväinen, A., A Short Proof for the Nonexistence of Unknown Perfect Codes over $GF(q)$, $q > 2$, *Annales Acad. Scient. Fennicae*, Ser. A, No. 580 (1974): 1–6.
10. Van Lint, J. H., A Survey of Perfect Codes, *Rocky Mountain J. Math.* 5(1975): 199–224.
11. Vasilýev, Y. L., On Nongroup Close-Packed Codes, *Problemi Cybernetica* 8 (1962): 337–339.
12. Schönheim, J., On Linear and Nonlinear Single-Error-Correcting q-nary Perfect Codes, *Inf. and Contr.* 12 (1968): 23–26.
13. Muller, D. E., Application of Boolean Algebra to Switching Circuit Design and to Error Detection, *IRE Trans. Electr. Comp.* EC-3 (1954): 6–12.
14. Reed, I. S., A Class of Multiple-Error-Correcting Codes and the Decoding Scheme, *IRE Trans. Inf. Theor.* IT-4 (1954): 38–49.

Chapter 4

1. Birkhoff, G., and S. Mac Lane, *A Survey of Modern Algebra*, rev. ed., Macmillan, New York, 1953.
2. Van der Waerden, B. L., *Modern Algebra* (2 vols.), trans. by F. Blum and T. J. Benac, Frederick Unger, New York, 1950 and 1953.
3. Berlekamp, E. R., *Algebraic Coding Theory*, McGraw-Hill, New York, 1968.
4. Fraleigh, J. B., *A First Course in Abstract Algebra*, 2nd ed., Addison-Wesley, Reading, Mass., 1976.

Chapter 5

1. Prange, E., *Cyclic Error-Correcting Codes in Two Symbols*, AFCRC-TN-57-103, Air Force Cambridge Research Center, Cambridge, Mass., (Sept.) 1957.
2. Prange, E., *Some Cyclic Error-Correcting Codes with Simple Decoding Algorithms*, AFCRC-TN-58-156, Air Force Cambridge Research Center, Bedford, Mass., (April) 1958.
3. Peterson, W. W., Encoding and Error-Correction Procedures for the Bose-Chaudhuri Codes, *IRE Trans. Inf. Theor.* IT-6 (1960): 459–470.
4. Kasami, T., Systematic Codes Using Binary Shift Register Sequences, *J. Inf. Process. Soc. Japan* 1 (1960): 198–200.
5. Abramson, N., A Note on Single Error-Correcting Binary Codes, *IRE Trans. Inf. Theor.* IT-6 (1960): 502–503.
6. Elspas, B., A Note on P-nary Adjacent-Error-Correcting Codes, *IRE Trans. Inf. Theor.* IT-6 (1960): 13–15.
7. Abramson, N. A., Class of Systematic Codes for Non-Independent Errors, *IRE Trans. Inf. Theor.* IT-5 (1959): 150–157.

8. Kasami, T., Optimum Shortened Cyclic Codes for Burst-Error Correction, *IEEE Trans. Inf. Theor.* IT-9 (1963): 105–109.
9. Peterson, W. W., and E. J. Weldon, Jr., *Error Correcting Codes*, 2nd ed., The M.I.T. Press, Cambridge, Mass., 1971.
10. Fire, P., *A Class of Multiple-Error Correcting Binary Codes for Non-Independent Errors*, Sylvania Report RSL-E-2, Sylvania Reconnaissance Systems Lab., Mountain View, Calif., 1959.
11. Golay, M. J. E., Notes on Digital Coding, *Proc. IRE* 37 (1949): 657.
12. McEliece, R. J., *The Theory of Information and Coding*, Addison-Wesley, Reading, Mass., 1977.
13. Assmus, E. F., Jr., and H. F. Mattson, Jr., Coding and Combinatorics, *SIAM Rev.* 16 (1974): 349–388.

Chapter 6

1. Peterson, W. W., Encoding and Error-Correction Procedures for the Bose-Chaudhuri Codes, *IRE Trans. Inf. Theor.* IT-6 (1960): 459–470.
2. Chien, R. T., Cyclic Decoding Procedures for Bose-Chaudhuri-Hocquenghem Codes, *IEEE Trans. Inf. Theor.* IT-10 (1964): 357–363.
3. Peterson, W. W., *Error Correcting Codes*, The M.I.T. Press, Cambridge, Mass., and Wiley, New York, 1961.
4. Meggitt, J. E., Error-Correcting Codes for Correcting Bursts of Errors, *IBM J. Res. Develop.* 4 (1960): 329–334.
5. Meggitt, J. E., Error-Correcting Codes and Their Implementation, *IRE Trans. Inf. Theor.* IT-7 (1961): 232–244.
6. Kasami, T., A Decoding Procedure for Multiple-Error-Correcting Cyclic Codes, *IEEE Trans. Inf. Theor.* IT-10 (1964): 134–139.
7. MacWilliams, F. J., Permutation Decoding of Systematic Codes, *Bell Syst. Tech. J.* 43 (1964): 485–505.
8. Mitchell, M. E., *Error-Trap Decoding of Cyclic Codes*, G. E. Report No. 62MCD3, General Electric Military Communications Department, Oklahoma City, Okla., 1962.
9. Rudolph, L., and M. E. Mitchell, Implementation of Decoders for Cyclic Codes *IEEE Trans. Inf. Theor.* IT-10 (1964): 259–260.

Chapter 7

1. Hochquenghem, A., Codes Correcteurs D'erreurs, *Chiffres* 2 (1959): 147–156.
2. Bose, R. C., and D. K. Ray-Chaudhuri, On a Class of Error-Correcting Binary Group Codes, *Inf. and Contr.* 3 (1960): 68–79.
3. Reed, I. S., and G. Solomon, Polynomial Codes over Certain Finite Fields, *J. Soc. Indust. Appl. Math.* 8 (1960): 300–304.
4. Kasami, T., and N. Tokura, Some Remarks on BCH Bounds and Minimum Weights of Binary Primitive BCH Codes, *IEEE Trans. Inf. Theor.* IT-15 (1969): 408–412.
5. Chen, C. L., Computer Results on the Minimum Distance of Some Binary Cyclic Codes, *IEEE Trans. Inf. Theor.* IT-16 (1960): 359–360.
6. Peterson, W. W., Encoding and Error-Correction Procedures for the Bose-Chaudhuri Codes, *IEEE Trans. Inf. Theor.* IT-6 (1960): 459–470.
7. Gorenstein, D. C., and N. Zierler, A Class of Error-Correcting Codes in p^m Symbols, *J. Soc. Indust. Appl. Math.* 9 (1961): 207–214.

8. Chien, R. T., Cyclic Decoding Procedures for Bose-Chaudhuri-Hocquenghem Codes, *IEEE Trans. Inf. Theor.* IT-10 (1964): 357–363.
9. Forney, G. D., Jr., On Decoding BCH Codes, *IEEE Trans. Inf. Theor.* IT-11 (1965): 549–557.
10. Berlekamp, E. R., *Algebraic Coding Theory*, McGraw-Hill, New York, 1968.
11. Massey, J. L., Shift-Register Synthesis and BCH Decoding, *IEEE Trans. Inf. Theor.* IT-15 (1969): 122–127.
12. Burton, H. O., Inversionless Decoding of Binary BCH Codes, *IEEE Trans. Inf. Theor.* IT-17 (1971): 464–466.
13. Sugiyama, Y., M. Kasahara, S. Hirasawa, and T. Namekawa, A Method for Solving Key Equation for Decoding Goppa Codes, *Inf. and Contr.* 27 (1975): 87–99.
14. Welch, L. R., and R. A. Scholtz, Continued Fractions and Berlekamp's Algorithm, *IEEE Trans. Inf. Theor.* IT-25 (1979): 19–27.
15. Mandelbaum, D. M., Decoding Beyond the Designed Distance for Certain Algebraic Codes, *Inf. and Contr.* (1977): 209–228.

Chapter 8

1. Reed, I. S., and G. Solomon, Polynomial Codes Over Certain Finite Fields, *J. SIAM* 8 (1960): 300–304.
2. Mattson, H. F., and G. Solomon, A New Treatment of Bose-Chaudhuri Codes, *J. Soc. Indust. Appl. Math.* 9 (1961): 654–699.
3. Mandelbaum, D. M., Construction of Error-Correcting Codes by Interpolation, *IEEE Trans. Inf. Theor.* IT-25 (1979): 27–35.
4. Pollard, J. M., The Fast Fourier Transform in a Finite Field, *Math. Computat.* 25 (1971): 365–374.
5. Gore, W. C., Transmitting Binary Symbols with Reed-Solomon Codes, *Proc. Princeton Conf. Inf. Sci. Syst.* 495–497, Princeton, N.J., 1973.
6. Chien, R. T., and D. M. Choy, Algebraic Generalization of BCH-Goppa-Helgert Codes, *IEEE Trans. Inf. Theor.* IT-21 (1975): 70–79.
7. Lempel, A., and S. Winograd, A New Approach to Error-Correcting Codes, *IEEE Trans. Inf. Theor.* IT-23 (1977): 503–508.
8. Chien, R. T., A New Proof of the BCH Bound, *IEEE Trans. Inf. Theor.* IT-18 (1972): 541.
9. Wolf, J. K., Adding Two Information Symbols to Certain Nonbinary BCH Codes and Some Applications, *Bell Syst. Tech. J.* 48 (1969): 2405–2424.
10. Andryanov, V. I., and V. N. Saskovets, Decoding Codes, *Akad. Nauk. Ukr. SSR Kibernetika* part 1 (1966).
11. Sloane, N. J. A., S. M. Reddy, and C. L. Chen, New Binary Codes, *IEEE Trans. Inf. Theor.* IT-18 (1972): 503–510.
12. Kasahara, M., Y. Sugiyama, S. Hirasawa, and T. Namekawa, A New Class of Binary Codes Constructed on the Basis of BCH Codes, *IEEE Trans. Inf. Theor.* IT-21 (1975): 582–585.
13. Blahut, R. E., On Extended BCH Codes, *Proc. 18th Allerton Conf. Commun., Contr. Comput.*, 50–59, Univ. of Illinois, Monticello, Ill., 1980.
14. Helgert, H. H., Alternant Codes, *Inf. and Contr.*, 26 (1974): 369–381.
15. Goppa, V. C., A New Class of Linear Error-Correcting Codes, *Probl. Peredach. Inf.* 6 (1970): 24–30.
16. Delsarte, P., On Subfield Subcodes of Modified Reed-Solomon Codes, *IEEE Trans. Inf. Theor.* IT-21 (1975): 575–576.

17. Preparata, F. P., A Class of Optimum Nonlinear Double-Error-Correcting Codes, *Inf. and Contr.* 13 (1968): 378–400.

18. Nordstrom, A. W., and J. P. Robinson, An Optimum Linear Code, *Inf. and Contr.* 11 (1967): 613–616.

19. Nadler, M., A 32-Point *n* Equals 12, *d* Equals 5 Code, *IRE Trans. Inf. Theor.* IT-8 (1962): 58.

20. Green, M. W., Two Heuristic Techniques for Block Code Construction, *IEEE Trans. Inf. Theor.* IT-12 (1966): 273.

21. Kerdock, A. M., A Class of Low-Rate Nonlinear Codes, *Inf. and Contr.* 20 (1972): 182–187.

22. Goethals, J.-M., Nonlinear Codes Defined by Quadratic Forms Over *GF*(2), *Inf. and Contr.* 10 (1976): 43–74.

Chapter 9

1. Reed, I. S., and G. Solomon, Polynomial Codes Over Certain Finite Fields, *J. Soc. Indust. Appl. Math.* 8 (1960): 300–304.

2. Mandelbaum, D., On Decoding of Reed-Solomon Codes, *IEEE Trans. Inf. Theor.* IT-17 (1971): 707–712.

3. Paschburg, R. H., *Software Implementation of Error-Correcting Codes*, MS thesis, Univ. of Illinois, Urbana, Ill., 1974.

4. Gore, W. C., Transmitting Binary Symbols with Reed-Solomon Codes, *Proc. Princeton Conf. Inf. Sci. Syst.* 495–497, Princeton, N.J., 1973.

5. Michelson, A., A Fast Transform in Some Galois Fields and an Application to Decoding Reed-Solomon Codes, *IEEE Abstr. of Papers—IEEE Internat. Symp. Inf. Theor.*, Ronneby, Sweden, 1976.

6. Blahut, R. E., Transform Techniques for Error-Control Codes, *IBM J. Res. Develop.* 23 (1979): 299–315.

7. Blahut, R. E., Algebraic Decoding in the Frequency Domain, in *Algebraic Coding Theory and Practice*, ed. by G. Longo, Springer-Verlag, New York, 1979.

8. Blahut, R. E., On Extended BCH Codes, *Proc. 18th Allerton Conf. Circ. Syst. Theor.*, 50–59, Univ. of Illinois, Monticello, Ill., 1980.

9. Mandelbaum, D., Decoding Beyond the Designed Distance for Certain Algebraic Codes, *Inf. and Contr.* 35 (1977): 209–228.

10. Elias, P., Error-Free Coding, *IRE Trans. Inf. Theor.* IT-4 (1954): 29–37.

11. Blum, R. A., and A. D. Weiss, *Further Results in Error-Correcting Codes*, SM thesis, M.I.T., Cambridge, Mass., 1960.

12. Forney, G. D., Jr., On Decoding BCH Codes, *IEEE Trans. Inf. Theor.* IT-11 (1965): 549–557.

13. Wolf, J. K., Adding Two Information Symbols to Certain Nonbinary BCH Codes and Some Applications, *Bell Syst. Tech. J.* 48 (1969): 2405–2424.

14. Kasahara, M., Y. Sugiyama, S. Hirasawa, and T. Namekawa, A New Class of Binary Codes Constructed on the Basis of BCH Codes, *IEEE Trans. Inf. Theor.* IT-21 (1975): 582–585.

15. Patterson, N. J., The Algebraic Decoding of Goppa Codes, *IEEE Trans. Inf. Theor.* IT-21 (1975): 203–207.

16. Helgert, H. J., Decoding of Alternant Codes, *IEEE Trans. Inf. Theor.* IT-23 (1977): 513–514.

17. Delsarte, P. On Subfield-Subcodes of Modified Reed-Solomon Codes, *IEEE Trans. Inf. Theor.* IT-21 (1975): 575–576.

18. Berlekamp, E. R., *Algebraic Coding Theory*, McGraw-Hill, New York, 1968.
19. Hartmann, C. R. P., Decoding Beyond the BCH Bound, *IEEE Trans. Inf. Theor.* IT-18 (1972): 441–444.
20. Vanderhorst, J., and T. Berger, Complete Decoding of Triple-Error-Correcting Binary BCH Codes, *IEEE Trans. Inf. Theor.* IT-22 (1976): 138–147.
21. Bluestein, L. I., Linear Filtering Approach to the Computation of Discrete Fourier Transforms, *IEEE Trans. Audio Electroacoust.* AU-18 (1970): 451–455.
22. Rader, C. M., Discrete Fourier Transforms When the Number of Data Samples is Prime, *Proc. IEEE* 56 (1968): 1107–1108.
23. Goertzel, G., An Algorithm for the Evaluation of Finite Trigonometric Series, *Amer. Math. Mon.* 65 (1968): 34–35.
24. Oppenheim, A. V., and R. W. Schafer, *Digital Signal Processing*, Prentice-Hall, Englewood Cliffs, N.J., 1975.
25. Rabiner, L. R., and B. Gold, *Theory and Application of Digital Signal Processing*, Prentice-Hall, Englewood Cliffs, N.J., 1975.
26. Sarwate, D. V., Semi-Fast Fourier Transforms Over $GF(2^m)$, *IEEE Trans. Comput.* C-27 (1978): 283–284.

Chapter 10

1. Elias, P., Error-Free Coding, *IRE Trans. Inf. Theor.* IT-4 (1954): 29–37.
2. Burton, H. O., and E. J. Weldon, Jr., Cyclic Product Codes, *IEEE Trans. Inf. Theor.* IT-11 (1965): 433–439.
3. Lin, S., and E. J. Weldon, Jr., Further Results on Cyclic Product Codes, *IEEE Trans. Inf. Theor.* IT-16 (1970): 452–459.
4. Reddy, S. M., and J. P. Robinson, Random-Error and Burst Correction by Iterated Codes, *IEEE Trans. Inf. Theor.* IT-18 (1972): 182–185.
5. Weldon, E. J., Jr., Decoding Binary Block Codes on Q-ary Output Channels, *IEEE Trans. Inf. Theor.* IT-17 (1971): 713–718.
6. Blahut, R. E., Transform Techniques for Error-Control Codes, *IBM J. Res. Develop.* 23 (1979): 299–315.
7. Chien, R. T., and S. W. Ng, Dual Product Codes for Correction of Multiple Low-Density Burst Errors, *IEEE Trans. Inf. Theor.* IT-19 (1973): 672–678.

Chapter 11

1. Cooley, J. W. and J. W. Tukey, An Algorithm for the Machine Computation of Complex Fourier Series, *Math. Comp.* 19 (1965): 297–301.
2. Good, I. J., The Interaction Algorithm and Practical Fourier Analysis, *J. Roy. Statist. Soc.* 20 (1958): 361–375; addendum, 22 (1960): 372–375.
3. Thomas, L. H., Using a Computer to Solve Problems in Physics, in *Applications of Digital Computers*, Ginn, Boston, 1963.
4. Justesen, J., On the Complexity of Decoding Reed-Solomon Codes, *IEEE Trans. Inf. Theor.* IT-22 (1976): 237–238.
5. Sarwate, D. V., On the Complexity of Decoding Goppa Codes, *IEEE Trans. Inf. Theor.* IT-23 (1977): 515–516.
6. Agarwal, R., and J. W. Cooley, Algorithms for Digital Convolution, *IEEE Trans. Acoust. Speech Signal Process.* ASSP-25 (1977): 392–410.
7. Winograd, S., On Computing the Discrete Fourier Transform, *Math. Comp.* 32 (1978): 175–199.

8. Nussbaumer, H. J., *Fast Fourier Transform and Convolution Algorithms*, Springer-Verlag, Berlin, 1981.

9. Miller, R. L., T. K. Truong, and I. S. Reed, Efficient Program for Decoding the (255, 223) Reed-Solomon Code Over $GF(2^8)$ with Both Errors and Erasures, Using Transform Decoding, *IEEE Proc.* 127 (1980): 136–142.

10. Blahut, R. E., Efficient Decoder Algorithms Based on Spectral Techniques, *IEEE Abstr. of Papers—IEEE Internat. Sympos. Inf. Theor.*, Santa Monica, Calif., 1981.

11. Preparata, F. P., and D. V. Sarwate, Computational Complexity of Fourier Transforms over Finite Fields, *Math. Comp.* 31 (1977): 740–751.

Chapter 12

1. Elias, P. Error-Free Coding, *IRE Trans. Inf. Theor.* IT-4 (1954): 29–37.

2. Wozencraft, J. M. Sequential Decoding for Reliable Communication, *1957 Nat. IRE Conv. Rec.* 5 (1957): 11–25.

3. Wyner, A. D., and R. B. Ash, Analysis of Recurrent Codes, *IEEE Trans. Inf. Theor.* IT-9 (1963): 143–156.

4. Massey, J. L., *Threshold Decoding*, The M.I.T. Press, Cambridge, Mass., 1963.

5. Costello, D. J., Jr., A Construction Technique for Random-Error-Correcting Codes, *IEEE Trans. Inf. Theor.* IT-15 (1969): 631–636.

6. Bussgang, J. J., Some Properties of Binary Convolutional Code Generators, *IEEE Trans. Inf. Theor.* IT-11 (1965): 90–100.

7. Odenwalder, J. P., *Optimal Decoding of Convolutional Codes*, Ph.D. dissertation, Univ. of California at Los Angeles, 1970.

8. Bahl, L. R., and F. Jelinek, Rate 1/2 Convolutional Codes with Complementary Generators, *IEEE Trans. Inf. Theor.* IT-17 (1971): 718–727.

9. Larsen, K. J., Short Convolutional Codes with Maximal Free Distance for Rates 1/2, 1/3, and 1/4, *IEEE Trans. Inf. Theor.* IT-19 (1973): 371–372.

10. Paaske, E., Short Binary Convolutional Codes with Maximal Free Distance for Rates 2/3 and 3/4, *IEEE Trans. Inf. Theor.* IT-20 (1974): 683–689.

11. Johannesson, R., Robustly Optimal Rate One-Half Binary Convolutional Codes, *IEEE Trans. Inf. Theor.* IT-21 (1975): 464–468.

12. Massey, J. L., and M. K. Sain, Inverses of Linear Sequential Circuits, *IEEE Trans. Comp.* C-17 (1968): 330–337.

13. Forney, G. D., Jr., Convolutional Codes I: Algebraic Structure, *IEEE Trans. Inf. Theor.* IT-16 (1970): 720–738.

14. Lindner, R., and L. Staiger, *Algebraische Codierungstheorie*, Akademie-Verlag, Berlin, 1977.

15. Fano, R. M., A Heuristic Discussion of Probabilistic Decoding, *IEEE Trans. Inf. Theor.* IT-9 (1963): 64–74.

16. Gallager, R. G., *Information Theory and Reliable Communication*, Wiley, New York, 1968.

17. Viterbi, A. J., Error Bounds for Convolutional Codes and an Asymptotically Optimum Decoding Algorithm, *IEEE Trans. Inf. Theor.* IT-13 (1967): 260–269.

18. Heller, J. A., Short Constraint Length Convolutional Codes, *Jet Propulsion Labs. Space Prog. Sum. 37-54* III (1968): 171–177.

19. Viterbi, A. J., and J. K. Omura, *Principles of Digital Communication and Coding*, McGraw-Hill, 1979.

20. Massey, J. L., Error Bounds for Tree Codes, Trellis Codes and Convolutional Codes with Encoding and Decoding Procedures, in *Coding and Complexity*, G. Longo (Ed.), Springer-Verlag, New York, 1975.

21. Forney, G. D., Jr., Convolutional Codes II: Maximum-Likelihood Decoding and Convolutional Codes III: Sequential Decoding, *Inf. and Contr.* 25 (1974): 222–297.

Chapter 13

1. Massey, J. L., *Threshold Decoding*, The M.I.T. Press, Cambridge, Mass., 1963.
2. Reed, I. S., A Class of Multiple-Error-Correcting Codes and the Decoding Scheme, *IRE Trans. Inf. Theor.* IT-4 (1954): 38–49.
3. Robinson, J. P., and A. J. Bernstein, A Class of Recurrent Codes with Limited Error Propagation, *IEEE Trans. Inf. Theor.* IT-13 (1967): 106–113.
4. Wu, W. W., New Convolutional Codes, *IEEE Trans. Communicat. Theor.*, part I, COM-23 (1975): 942–956; part II, COM-24 (1976): 19–33; part III, COM-24 (1976): 946–955.
5. Rudolph, L. D., *Geometric Configuration and Majority-Logic Decodable Codes*, M.E.E. thesis, Univ. of Oklahoma, Norman, Okla., 1964.
6. Rudolph, L. D., A Class of Majority-Logic Decodable Codes, *IEEE Trans. Inf. Theor.* IT-14 (1967): 305–307.
7. Kasama, T., S. Lin, and W. W. Peterson, New Generalizations of the Reed-Muller Codes—Part I: Primitive Codes, *IEEE Trans. Inf. Theor.* IT-14 (1968): 189–199.
8. Kolesnik, V. D., and E. T. Mironchikov, Cyclic Reed-Muller Codes and Their Decoding, *Prob. Perdachi Inf.* 4 (1968): 15–19.
9. Weldon, E. J., Jr., Euclidean Geometry Cyclic Codes, *Proc. Sympos. Combinatorial Math.*, Univ. of North Carolina, Chapel Hill, N.C., 1967.
10. Weldon, E. J., Jr., New Generalizations of the Reed-Muller Codes—Part II: Non-Primitive Codes, *IEEE Trans. Inf. Theor.* IT-14 (1968): 199–206.
11. Kasami, T., S. Lin, and W. W. Peterson, Polynomial Codes, *IEEE Trans. Inf. Theor.* IT-14 (1968): 807–814.
12. Goethals, J. M., and P. Delsarte, On a Class of Majority-Logic Decodable Cyclic Codes, *IEEE Trans. Inf. Theor.* IT-14 (1968): 182–189.
13. Delsarte, P., J. M. Goethals, and F. J. MacWilliams, On Generalized Reed-Muller Codes and Their Relatives, *Inf. and Contr.* 16 (1970): 402–442.
14. Lin, S., and G. Markowsky, On a Class of One-Step Majority-Logic Decodable Cyclic Codes, *IBM J. Res. Develop.* 24 (1980): 56–63.
15. Goethals, J. M., Threshold Decoding—A Tentative Survey, in *Coding and Complexity*, ed. by G. Longo, Springer-Verlag, New York, 1975.

Chapter 14

1. Assmus, E. F., Jr., H. F. Mattson, Jr., and R. J. Turyn, *Cyclic Codes*, AFCRL-65-332, Air Force Cambridge Research Labs, Bedford, Mass., 1965.
2. Forney, G. D., Jr., *Concatenated Codes*, The M.I.T. Press, Cambridge, Mass., 1966.
3. Kasami, T., S. Lin, and W. W. Peterson, Some Results on Weight Distributions of BCH Codes, *IEEE Trans. Inf. Theor.* IT-12 (1966): 274.
4. MacWilliams, F. J., A Theorem on the Distribution of Weights in a Systematic Code, *Bell Syst. Tech. J.* 42 (1963): 79–94.
5. Huntoon, Z. McC., and A. M. Michelson, On the Computation of the Probability of Post-Decoding Error Events for Block Codes, *IEEE Trans. Inf. Theor.* IT-23 (1977): 399–403.
6. Viterbi, A. J., Convolutional Codes and Their Performance in Communication Systems, *IEEE Trans. Communicat. Tech.* COM-19 (1971): 751–772.

7. Gilbert, E. N., A Comparison of Signalling Alphabets, *Bell Syst. Tech. J.* 31 (1952): 504–522.
8. McEliece, R. J., E. R. Rodemich, H. Rumsey, Jr., and L. R. Welch, New Upper Bounds on the Rate of a Code via the Delsarte-MacWilliams Inequalities, *IEEE Trans. Inf. Theor.* IT-23 (1977): 157–166.
9. Costello, D. J., Free Distance Bounds for Convolutional Codes, *IEEE Trans. Inf. Theor.* IT-20 (1974): 356–365.
10. Savage, J. E., Minimum Distance Estimates of the Performance of Sequential Decoding, *IEEE Trans. Inf. Theor.* IT-15 (1969): 128–140.

Chapter 15
1. Forney, G. D., Jr., Generalized Minimum Distance Decoding, *IEEE Trans. Inf. Theor.* IT-12 (1966): 125–131.
2. Chase, D., A Class of Algorithms for Decoding Block Codes with Channel Measurement Information, *IEEE Trans. Inf. Theor.* IT-18 (1972): 170–182.
3. Hartmann, C. R. P., and L. D. Rudolph, An Optimum Symbol-by-Symbol Decoding Rule for Linear Codes, *IEEE Trans. Inf. Theor.* IT-22 (1976): 514–517.
4. Ungerboeck, G., Trellis Coding with Expanded Channel Signal Sets, *Abstr.—1977 IEEE Internat. Sympos. Inf. Theor.*, Ithaca, New York, 1977.
5. Ungerboeck, G., Channel Coding with Multilevel Phase Signals, *IEEE Trans. Inf. Theor.* IT-28 (1982): 55–67.
6. Anderson, J. B., and D. P. Taylor, A Bandwidth-Efficient Class of Signal-Space Codes, *IEEE Trans. Inf. Theor.* IT-24 (1978): 703–712.
7. Wozencraft, J. M., Sequential Decoding for Reliable Communication, *1957 Nat. IRE Conv. Rec.*, 5, part 2 (1957): 11–25.
8. Wozencraft, J. M., and B. Reiffen, *Sequential Decoding*, The M.I.T. Press, Cambridge, Mass., 1961.
9. Fano, R. M., A Heuristic Discussion of Probablistic Decoding, *IEEE Trans. Inf. Theor.* IT-9 (1963): 64–74.
10. Zigangirov, K., Some Sequential Decoding Procedures, *Problemy Peredachi Inf.* 2 (1966): 13–25.
11. Jelinek, F., A Fast Sequential Decoding Algorithm Using a Stack, *IBM J. Res. Develop.* 13 (1969): 675–685.
12. Forney, G. D., Jr., Convolutional Codes III: Sequential Decoding, *Inform. Contr.* 25 (1974): 267–297.
13. Jelinek, F., *Probabilistic Information Theory*, McGraw-Hill, New York, 1968.
14. Chevillat, P. R., and D. J. Costello, Jr., An Analysis of Sequential Decoding for Specific Time-Invariant Convolutional Codes, *IEEE Trans. Inf. Theor.* IT-24 (1978): 443–451.
15. Haccoun, D., and M. J. Ferguson, Generalized Stack Algorithms for Decoding Convolutional Codes, *IEEE Trans. Inf. Theor.* IT-21 (1975): 638–651.
16. Savage, J. E., Sequential Decoding—The Computation Problem, *Bell Syst. Tech. J.* 45 (1966): 149–175.
17. Jacobs, I. M., and E. R. Berlekamp, A Lower Bound to the Distribution of Computations for Sequential Decoding, *IEEE Trans. Inf. Theor.* IT-13 (1967): 167–174.
18. Jelinek, F., An Upper Bound on Moments of Sequential Decoding Effort, *IEEE Trans. Inf. Theor.* IT-15 (1969): 140–149.

Index